VMware vSphere™ PowerCLI Reference

Automating vSphere Administration

Luc Dekens
Alan Renouf
Glenn Sizemore
Arnim van Lieshout
Jonathan Medd

WILEY

Wiley Publishing, Inc.

Acquisitions Editor: Agatha Kim
Development Editor: Mary Ellen Schutz, Gentle Editing LLC
Technical Editor: Stuart Radnidge
Production Editor: Eric Charbonneau
Copy Editor: Liz Welch
Editorial Manager: Pete Gaughan
Editorial Consultant: Scott Lowe
Production Manager: Tim Tate
Vice President and Executive Group Publisher: Richard Swadley
Vice President and Publisher: Neil Edde
Book Designer: Franz Baumhackl
Compositor: James D. Kramer, Happenstance Type-O-Rama
Proofreader: Rebecca Rider
Indexer: Nancy Guenther
Project Coordinator, Cover: Katie Crocker
Cover Designer: Ryan Sneed
Cover Image: © Thomas Northcut / Getty Images

ISBN: 978-0-470-89079-0 (pbk)
ISBN: 978-1-118-08463-2 (ebk)
ISBN: 978-1-118-08465-6 (ebk)
ISBN: 978-1-118-08464-9 (ebk)

For general information on our other products and services or to obtain technical support, please contact our Customer Care Department within the U.S. at (877) 762-2974, outside the U.S. at (317) 572-3993 or fax (317) 572-4002.

Wiley also publishes its books in a variety of electronic formats. Some content that appears in print may not be available in electronic books.

Library of Congress Cataloging-in-Publication Data is available from the publisher.

10 9 8 7 6 5 4 3 2 1

Dear Reader,

Thank you for choosing *VMware vSphere PowerCLI Reference: Automating vSphere Administration*. This book is part of a family of premium-quality Sybex books, all of which are written by outstanding authors who combine practical experience with a gift for teaching.

Sybex was founded in 1976. More than 30 years later, we're still committed to producing consistently exceptional books. With each of our titles, we're working hard to set a new standard for the industry. From the paper we print on, to the authors we work with, our goal is to bring you the best books available.

I hope you see all that reflected in these pages. I'd be very interested to hear your comments and get your feedback on how we're doing. Feel free to let me know what you think about this or any other Sybex book by sending me an email at nedde@ wiley.com. If you think you've found a technical error in this book, please visit http://sybex.custhelp.com. Customer feedback is critical to our efforts at Sybex.

Best regards,

Neil Edde
Vice President and Publisher
Sybex, an Imprint of Wiley

To my family, friends and colleagues: This took quite a bit of our time away.

Luc

For my perfect wife and children, my inspiration in life

Alan

To my Grandfather: You made me the man I am…

Glenn

To Victor, My Father, Present in Absence and therefore never Past

Arnim

For my family, for putting up with me whilst I worked on this

Jonathan

ACKNOWLEDGMENTS

We'd all like to thank Pete Gaughan, editorial manager; Agatha Kim, acquisitions editor; Eric Charbonneau, production editor; Liz Welch, copyeditor; Nancy Guenther, indexer; Rebecca Rider, proofreader; and Jim Kramer, compositor. Without each of their contributions, this book would never have made it to the presses. In particular, we would like to thank our developmental editor, Mary Ellen Schutz, for making us all literate. Without her attention to detail, we wouldn't have been able to produce the complete manual you're now reading. Finally, we would like to thank Stuart Radnidge, our technical editor. Stu Rad held us all to the highest standards. He left no script unturned and no explanation unchecked. He served as the gatekeeper, ensuring that any code you find herein will run the first time, every time. (You can visit his blog by searching for vinternals from your favorite browser.) While we didn't always see eye to eye, without the professionals at Sybex this book would never have been possible. Thanks, guys, it was a blast.

Thanks to my fellow authors and all the people at Sybex who were involved with this book. And a special thanks to "our Gentle Editor, the little old lady from Wisconsin." She had to organize all this geek talk into the book you're now holding in your hands. I would also like to thank all the people from VMware who produced such a great product—especially the PowerCLI Development Team in Sofia, Bulgaria, and Carter Shanklin, who made this product what it is today. Thanks also to Pablo Roesch, although we aren't developers, we appreciate the drive with which you help us evangelize this wonderful piece of software. And finally, thanks to Jeffrey Snover and the PowerShell Team at Microsoft. Without PowerShell, none of this would have been possible. You shook the automation world!

Luc

I'd like to thank my wonderful wife and children for supporting me throughout this book and my life. To my fellow authors and everyone who has worked on this book: I would like to say thank you for staying with me and allowing me to push the boundaries time and time again. I would also like to thank my father. If he had not dragged me along to my first computer club and bought me the ZX Spectrum, I would not be here today. Thanks to my mother for her ongoing support—I know you will read this even though you don't know what PowerShell is!

Alan

I'd like to thank my wife Kristine for marrying me in the first place. Without her support, I would not have taken on this project. To Luc and Alan: It was an honor working with you both—thank you for including me. I'd also like to thank Roger Williams and Charlie Louk; you both taught me my trade. Without your teachings, I wouldn't be where I am today. To my fellow vExpert, co-worker, and friend: Andrew, you push me every day. Keep it up; I think it's working!

Glenn

I'd like to thank my wife Alexandra for putting up with me and for going to bed alone many nights while I was working on this book. To my oldest son: Thank you for your patience and understanding. Yes, now I finally have time to rebuild your PC. To my middle son: Thank you for your forbearance. We now can jump on the trampoline together 'til we drop. To my newborn son: Thank you for entering my life during the process. You really gave me new inspiration.

I'd also like to thank Luc and Alan for the opportunity to realize a dream, VMware for starting the x86 virtualization revolution, the VMware PowerCLI development team for creating such a great product and finally, to all the other authors of this book: It was great working with you guys.

Arnim

I'd like to thank Alan and Luc for offering me the opportunity to be involved with the book, Alan for the remote use of his test lab, all of the authors of the book for their help and contributions, and finally the guys at Special Operations Software for suggesting in 2007 that I should learn PowerShell.

Jonathan

ABOUT THE AUTHORS

Most projects have to start somewhere as an idea, and this one was no different. Alan and I had discussed the idea of a PowerCLI book. When Sybex contacted us, our idea suddenly became a reality. As probably all first-time authors do, we horribly underestimated the effort that goes into writing a book like the one we had in mind. Luckily we had the good fortune to be able to attract some outstanding co-authors like Glenn, Arnim, and Jonathan. We hope that you, the reader, will enjoy reading this book as much as we did writing it.

Luc Dekens started many moons ago in the mainframe world as a system programmer. While the companies he worked for took Unix and Windows boxes on board, it was a natural evolution for him to expand into those areas. A couple of years ago Luc was impressed by a new scripting tool, Monad, that Microsoft was bringing to market. When the organization Luc works for was expanding their virtualization platform, he stumbled on a product called VI Toolkit. It was ideal for automating many administrative tasks. Luc was admitted to the early beta program and started contributing to the ever-growing PowerCLI community. After attending VMworld 2009 in San Francisco, where he did a session together with Hal Rottenberg, Luc started a blog (`http://lucd.info`). During VMworld 2010 in the US and in Europe, Luc did a session together with Alan Renouf that sold out several times.

Alan Renouf has worked in IT since 1998, starting as a junior desktop support engineer and working in a variety of IT jobs. Currently he works as a vSpecialist for EMC. Alan was named a vExpert in both 2009 and 2010. He presented a PowerCLI session with Luc Dekens at both VMworld San Francisco and Copenhagen (2010). Alan first started scripting in his childhood, copying code from magazines onto a ZX Spectrum and tweaking scripts until they worked. He worked his way through a variety of languages before settling on PowerShell. Alan is the co-host of the Get-Scripting PowerShell podcast at `http://get-scripting.blogspot.com` and the author of a PowerCLI-related blog at `http://virtu-al.net`. You can follow Alan on Twitter at `http://twitter.com/alanrenouf`.

Glenn Sizemore has held just about every position one could hold in IT—everything from cable dog to enterprise architect. He started scripting early in his IT career and had mastered VBScript by the time PowerShell first shipped. As a scripter, he was an early adopter and had conquered PowerShell when the VMware Toolkit for Windows (PowerCLI) first shipped. Curiosity carried Glenn to an internal team-testing virtualization. Three years later, he was attending his third VMworld and had just been awarded the status of VMware vExpert. Along the way, Glenn started a blog, www.Get-Admin.com, to share scripts and automation techniques. Outside of work, Glenn is the proud father of two beautiful children and an avid PowerShell evangelist.

Arnim van Lieshout has been in the IT industry for 12 years, working mainly with operating systems. He holds key industry certifications and recognitions from VMware, Microsoft, and Citrix. For the last 5 years Arnim has been focusing on virtualization and as a virtualization architect he has been helping enterprise customers get the most out of virtualization, especially in server consolidation and business continuity. The last few years, he has been focusing on automating tasks using PowerShell. Arnim is an active member of the VMware Community forums and is a contributor to the VMware Community PowerPack (http://vmcompack.codeplex.com/). In 2010, Arnim was awarded third place in the VMware Script-O-Mania contest and, later that year, he was designated a VMware vExpert. He runs his own blog at www.van-lieshout.com, which is focused on virtualization and utilizing PowerShell in VMware environments. You can follow Arnim on Twitter at http://twitter.com/avlieshout.

Jonathan Medd has been working with Windows Infrastructure products since 1997 and, more recently, virtualization technologies from VMware. In 2007, he discovered Windows PowerShell and now spends a lot of time encouraging IT pros he meets to use PowerShell by talking with them, giving presentations to user groups, and via posts on his blog http://jonathanmedd.net. He also co-hosts the Get-Scripting PowerShell podcast, which provides information on how to learn PowerShell and what's going on in the PowerShell world—you can find this at http://get-scripting.blogspot.com. In April 2010, Jonathan was awarded status as a Microsoft Most Valuable Professional (MVP) for PowerShell. You can follow him on Twitter at http://twitter.com/jonathanmedd.

CONTENTS AT A GLANCE

TABLE OF CONTENTS

Chapter 23   Add a GUI Front-End to Your Automation Scripts   687

FOREWORD

2010 has been an amazing year for virtualization, the year when the number of server applications deployed as virtual machines is greater than the number deployed directly to physical hardware. The implications of this inflection point are deep, leading to significant changes in the hardware, software, and operation of modern data centers.

It's also a time when IT budgets and resources are more squeezed than ever, and the lure of allegedly more efficient cloud computing weighs on everyone's mind. As such, the need for great operational efficiency improvements looms large. In aiming to do even more with less, IT departments often focus substantially improving the application-to-admin ratio. Leading industry analysts estimate that the average ratio is roughly 72:1 in the virtualized world, already substantially higher than the 20:1 ratio in the physical world. This number derives very heavily from the amount of automation that an IT staff can utilize, and virtualization's containerization and standardization of workloads helps unlock more automation than can be found in the physical world. And whether you use commercial or home-grown tools, this automation can be exploited through mature and flexible virtualization APIs and scripting capabilities.

If you find yourself repeating the same administrative task more than 3 times per week, this is the right book for you. The vSphere Automation book provides real world, hands on scenarios written by Alan Renouf and Luc Dekens. Alan and Luc are both vExperts and have worldwide reputations as the leading PowerCLI scripting authorities. The vSphere Automation Book looks at the world from the point of view of someone new to vSphere as well as someone that has been managing the vSphere platform for years.

With this book and the resources available from VMware and its user community, you will enjoy automating the tasks you have always wanted to, ultimately leading to a more stable and efficient data center. And so I wish you happy scripting, and happy virtualization!

Dr. Stephen Alan Herrod
Palo Alto, California
December 2010

FOREWORD

When asked why he robbed banks, Willie Sutton replied, "because there's where the money is." So when I attended the 2010 VMWorld conference and people asked me why a Distinguished Engineer from Microsoft was attending, my reply was similar, "because there's where a big PowerShell community is." I was delighted when I first heard about VMware's PowerCLI and amazed to watch that community adopt PowerShell and become one of the more active centers of PowerShell scripting.

As I investigated this more, two things became clear:

1. To anyone virtualizing their IT operations, automation was the difference between success and failure.

2. It takes the right people with the right approach to transform a group of people into a thriving community.

PowerCLI had a group of people that combined a passion for PowerShell and helping other people with a very pragmatic approach to getting things done. I attended a packed session of Luc Deken's and Alan Renouf's PowerCLI talk and watched as most hands in the room went up when asked the question "how many of you have gotten answers to your questions in the PowerCLI community forums?" A large number of those hands stayed up when the next question was, "how many of you got that answer within a couple of minutes of asking it?"

How can you get better than that? Well you are holding the answer in your hands. Those same community superstars; Alan Renouf, Luc Dekens, Glenn Sizemore, Arnim van Lieshout and Jonathan Medd; have joined forces and produced a book codifying their collective wisdom on how to use PowerShell and PowerCLI to manage your systems. Enjoy!

Jeffrey Snover
Distinguished Engineer and Inventor of PowerShell

INTRODUCTION

This book is about automation; the title should have been a dead giveaway. More specifically, it's about automation of your VMware vSphere environment. And, as you might have guessed from the title of the book, we automate with PowerCLI. When we were asked to write this book, one of the first decisions we made was that it had to be a practical book—a book that showed you, the reader, how to automate all the aspects of your vSphere management tasks with PowerCLI. A quick glance at the table of contents will show you that we tried to cover what we considered the most important of these management tasks. We tried to follow the same order that you, as an administrator, will encounter during the life cycle of your VMware vSphere environment.

As the saying goes, "When you do something more than once, automate it!"

Who Should Read This Book

The book is, of course, primarily targeted at administrators of vSphere environments who want to automate tasks. But the subjects that we discuss in the book cover so many aspects of the management of a VMware vSphere environment that everyone who comes into contact with a VMware vSphere environment will be able to pick up something useful.

In our day-to-day contact with PowerCLI users, we noticed that most of them start with what we like to call the reporting phase. Thanks to the natural look and feel of PowerShell and PowerCLI, it is quite easy for beginners to produce impressive reports about their vSphere environment. That's why we included several chapters on different types of reporting. The somewhat more advanced user will go into the configuration phase. That is the moment when you start changing settings on your virtual guests and in the vSphere servers. There is an extensive number of chapters for this phase in the book.

The ultimate phase you can achieve through the use of PowerCLI is the process automation phase. As an administrator, you are now going to automate complex processes in your vSphere environment. This process can range from automating the deployment of vSphere servers all the way to automating the switch to a disaster recovery center. Again, the book offers several chapters for this phase.

Since PowerCLI runs as a snap-in in PowerShell, you might think that you have to be a Windows administrator to profit from the book. Although that is indeed the targeted audience, there are some automation aspects that are only (or at least easily) accessible through the PowerCLI snap-in. So, even if you are primarily a *nix shop, you can still profit from using PowerCLI for some of your administrative tasks.

What You Will Learn

The book shows you how you can use PowerCLI to automate your administrator tasks—not an alphabetical listing of the 250+ PowerCLI cmdlets, but a practical guide with example scripts that you can use immediately in your environment. The chapters are organized in such a way that each of them reflects a specific type of task. You probably already have done most of these tasks more than once. Now, we will show you how to automate them. In other words, you script them once and run them multiple times.

Several of the scripts we show are quite long, at least for a PowerShell script. Of course, you will not have to type them in. You will be able to download all the scripts from the book's update page on the Sybex website at

www.sybex.com/go/vmwarevspherepowercliref

To run the scripts, you can start up the PowerCLI prompt, enter cmdlets interactively, or provide the name of the PS1 file you want to execute. Most of the scripts do not have the extensive annotations you will find on our blog posts; the book had to be a manageable size. Also, since a book has a limited page size, we often had to break single lines in our scripts over two or more lines on the printed page. The scripts that you download have the original, optimized layout.

What You Need

Software is a dynamic organism, it will have successive versions, releases, and builds. Because a book has to be published at one point in time, we aligned all our scripts and sample code on a specific set of versions. The following list contains the versions of the software we used to develop and test the scripts in this book:

VMware vSphere PowerCLI, version 4.1

VMware vCenter Server, version 4.0

VMware ESX, version 4.0

PowerShell, version 2.0

PowerGUI, version 2.2

PowerWF Studio, version 2.3

OS Platform, Windows XP Pro SP3 or higher

To know which operating systems you can use to run the PowerCLI cmdlets and scripts, you will have to look at the release notes that came with the PowerCLI build you are using.

A number of graphical environments are available that allow you to execute cmdlets and scripts. Programs like PowerGUI, PowerShellPlus, or PowerWF Studio all give you a GGI-based editor from which you can run and debug your scripts.

What Is Covered in This Book

VMware vSphere PowerCLI Reference: Automating vSphere Administration broadly follows the life cycle of your VMware vSphere environment:

Part I: Install, Configure, and Manage the vSphere Environment

Chapter 1 through Chapter 4 show you how to automate the installation and configuration of your VMware vSphere environment. They include a discussion of the vCenter Server, the ESX and ESXi servers, storage, and networking as well as some advanced vSphere features like host profiles and dvSwitches.

Chapter 1: Automating vCenter Server Deployment and Configuration takes you through some common areas automated within vSphere, starting at the beginning of the virtual infrastructure. Not only will we show you how to automate the build, but we'll also provide examples of scripts that will help you export information into a centralized area ready for use in reports or for the import process of another setup.

Chapter 2: Automating vSphere Hypervisor Deployment and Configuration briefly walks you through the various installation methods before taking a deep dive into automating that last 10 percent. In this chapter, we will cover several techniques for streamlining the installation and configuration of vSphere.

Chapter 3: Automating Storage and Networking covers two of the most critical components of a virtual environment. Whether it's deploying a new cluster with new storage and networking, or maintaining and upgrading existing storage and networking, automation can come to the rescue to help you save time and maintain consistency of configuration.

Chapter 4: Using Advanced vSphere Features focuses on automating some of the most advanced features vSphere offers! With the exception of the Distributed Power Management features, an Enterprise Plus license is required to utilize these features.

Part II: Managing the Virtual Machine Life Cycle

Chapter 5 through Chapter 9 tackle all the automation aspects of guests—from creating a virtual machine over linked clones and svMotion all the way to vApps. We will show you how to mass-deploy a number of guests and how to manipulate snapshots.

Chapter 5: Creating Virtual Machines explores the various methods of creating new virtual machines. Then, we will take a deep dive into the vSphere API, where we'll cover more advanced methods and techniques. We will highlight custom attributes and their use, as well as VMware Tools installation.

Chapter 6: Using Templates and Customization Specifications covers creating templates, creating customization specifications, deploying guests, and maintaining templates over the long term. When it comes to deploying virtual machines, the tools provided are templates and customization specifications. Their use is a key part of any administrator's game.

Chapter 7: Configuring Virtual Machine Hardware begins after your environment is all set up and running. Perhaps performance is lacking and you need to throw in an additional vCPU or more memory. Or maybe your disk is running to its maximum capacity and needs to be extended. All of these tasks and other reconfiguration tasks are covered in this chapter.

Chapter 8: Advanced Virtual Machine Features shows you how to interact with the guest operating system using the operating system's native tools and through the PowerCLI methods. You'll learn how to customize the scripts provided by PowerCLI to add support for Windows 7 and Windows 2008 (R2). Next, you explore how to script vMotion and Storage vMotion operations. Finally, we cover creating and maintaining snapshots.

Chapter 9: Using vApps shows you how to import virtual appliances, create your own vApps, maintain vApps, and how to simplify complex applications by providing vSphere valuable metadata about a group of VMs. You'll learn about start order, IP pools, using IP assignments, and modifying vApp product information.

Part III: Securing Your vSphere Environment

In Chapter 10 through Chapter 13, we discuss the security aspects of your VMware vSphere environment. First, we show you how to handle backups and restores. Then, we continue with the automation of your disaster recovery. Patching and hardening of your environment conclude this part.

Chapter 10: Backing Up and Restoring Your Virtual Machines examines one of the most critical areas of any infrastructure—be it virtual or not—backup, the replication of key data to an alternate location in case of data or hardware loss.

Chapter 11: Organize Your Disaster Recovery covers designing your disaster recovery strategy. While the application server is servicing the user interface, the heart of the vCenter Server is stored in the back-end database. Learn how to back up and restore your vCenter Server database when you don't have SQL Server Management Studio available.

Chapter 12: Hardening the vSphere Environment shows how you can use the Hardening Guides to secure your vSphere environment. First, you will see methods to access the parameters mentioned in the Hardening Guides. You'll find a script that allows you to report the current settings. As an option, the same script can also be used to configure these settings as advised in the Hardening Guides.

Chapter 13: Maintain Security in Your vSphere Environment concentrates on host patching. Whatever operating system or application you are responsible for, it is important to keep it up-to-date. ESX(i) is no different in this respect, and VMware provides a management tool known as vCenter Update Manager (VUM) to assist with this process. We'll introduce you to the set of PowerCLI cmdlets available for download that enable automation for VUM.

Part IV: Monitoring and Reporting

Chapter 14 through Chapter 17 show how you can automate all the reporting aspects of your VMware vSphere environment. These chapters discuss how to report on the physical hardware, virtual hardware, and the configuration parameters; how to gather statistical data for performance and capacity planning reports; how to create an audit trail; and how to monitor the environment.

Chapter 14: Reporting the Status of Your vSphere Environment shows you how to report on the most used areas of your virtual environment. When you've learned how to create reports and what to report on, you'll see how to customize reports for your specific needs and how to export them into various formats.

Chapter 15: Using Statistical Data helps you obtain and analyze the built-in statistical data you need to determine how well your vSphere environment is faring over time.

Chapter 16: Monitoring the vSphere Environment helps you determine what you need to monitor and how to employ alarms in the monitoring process. Remember Murphy's Law! To capture these unforeseen events and to react to them as fast as possible, you need to monitor your vSphere environment at all times.

Chapter 17: Auditing the vSphere Environment helps you automatically access the data required for the audit report requests that come your way. Knowing who changed what and when is useful when you are troubleshooting a problem and it is definitely required when an audit team pays you a visit.

Part V: Scripting Tools and Features

In Chapter 18 through Chapter 23, we expand on the automation scripts themselves. We'll show you how you can schedule your scripts, how to use the methods and properties from the SDK in your scripts, and how to use Onyx to help you with the SDK methods and properties. You'll learn how to run your scripts in graphical environments like PowerGUI and vEcoShell, and how to provide your own graphical interface for your scripts. We also introduce PowerWF Studio, a novel way to work with PowerShell and the PowerCLI snap-in.

Chapter 18: Scheduling Automation Scripts examines vCenter Server's scheduling capabilities, helps you schedule your own scripts to run when required, and moves you closer to running a dynamic datacenter. With these scripts at your disposal, you won't have to set your alarm to remind yourself you need to run a script.

Chapter 19: The SDK will show you how you can use the vSphere API. Now why would a book on PowerCLI bother with the vSphere API? The answer is simple. With the help of the vSphere API, your scripts can go that extra mile and perform functions that would otherwise not be available to you.

Chapter 20: The Onyx Project shows you how to use the Onyx Project to improve your understanding of the vSphere API. The Onyx Project was created by the PowerCLI Development Team to help you on your journey through the SDK.

Chapter 21: PowerGUI and vEcoShell examines two GUI automation tools that enable scripts to be presented for execution in graphical form.

Chapter 22: PowerWF Studio shows you a product that takes an original approach to using PowerShell and PowerCLI. PowerWF Studio is a Visual PowerShell development tool that provides an easy way to create powerful automation scripts using a workflow paradigm and a simple drag-and-drop interface.

Chapter 23: Add a GUI Front-End to Your Automation Scripts shows you how to use Windows forms from with PowerShell scripts. You'll learn about PowerShell's ties to .NET and how a .NET subset called WinForms lets you integrate Windows Forms into your scripts.

Online Bonus Content

Appendix A: Basic PowerShell examines some of the basic concepts and sets you on the road to becoming both a PowerShell and PowerCLI expert!

Appendix B: References and Links provides additional resources. Every good book leaves you wanting to know more. Here you'll find some good places to start your search.

How to Contact the Authors

We welcome feedback from you about this book. We've developed a message board for everything related to the book at www.powerclibook.com. Stop by and let us know how we did, check for updates, and join the discussion. If you have specific questions, send us a message at info@powerclibook.com. You can also connect to each of us through our blogs:

Luc Dekens—*LucD notes: My PowerShell Ramblings* at www.lucd.info

Alan Renouf—*VIRTU-AL: Virtually Everything is POSHABLE* at www.virtu-al.net

Glenn Sizemore—*get-admin: Lessons of a Datacenter Administrator* at www.Get-Admin.com

Arnim van Lieshout—*Arnim van Lieshout: About virtualization and more* at www.van-lieshout.com

Jonathan Medd—*Jonathan Medd's Blog: Scripting, PowerShell, VMware, Windows, Active Directory & Exchange. All that kind of stuff...* at www.jonathanmedd.net

Sybex strives to keep you supplied with the latest tools and information you need for your work. Please check the book's update page on the Sybex website at www.sybex .com/go/vmwarevspherepowercliref. Here, we've posted optimized electronic copies of the scripts, batch files, and tools created for this book. We'll post additional content and updates that supplement this book if the need arises.

Install, Configure, and Manage the vSphere Environment

CHAPTER 1

Automating vCenter Server Deployment and Configuration

IN THIS CHAPTER, YOU WILL LEARN TO:

One of the focal points and key use cases of PowerCLI is the automation of tasks that are needed either as part of a disaster recovery (DR) solution or as part of an automated deployment solution that can be used repeatedly—You will be safe in the knowledge that the script will produce a consistent and easy-to-use solution.

This chapter will take you through some common areas automated within vSphere, starting at the beginning of the virtual infrastructure. Not only will we show you how to automate the build, but we'll also provide examples of export scripts that will help you export information into a centralized area, the exported data will then be ready for use in reports or for the import process of another setup.

Prepare the vCenter Installation

As part of the overall virtual infrastructure, one of the first areas you will need to install is the vCenter Server, or Virtual Infrastructure Server. Although this cannot be done directly using PowerCLI cmdlets, you can use the automated nature of PowerCLI and PowerShell to automate the install of vCenter Server.

The key thing to remember while reading this chapter—and indeed the entire book—is that PowerShell reaches past the virtual infrastructure. It can be used to manage most areas of the Windows-based operating system and application set. PowerCLI is purely an addition to PowerShell (known as a snap-in) that allows you to manage the virtual infrastructure.

To automate the installation of vCenter Server and its respective components, including the vSphere Client, Update Manager, Converter, and the corresponding databases, you will need the install media as well as various other items, such as the correct version of the .NET Framework and Windows installed on the server. The components you choose to install will depend on your infrastructure and the type of database you are going to use with your vCenter Server install.

Before you attempt to create an automated installation, be sure that

- ▶ The server meets at least the minimum hardware requirements as specified in the VMware ESX and vCenter Server installation documents provided by VMware.

- ▶ The server is configured with a static IP address.

- ▶ The computer name consists of fewer than 15 characters. (To conform to best practice, ensure that the computer name matches the hostname in the fully qualified domain name [FQDN] of the system.)

▶ The system is joined to a domain, and not a workgroup. While this is not a strict requirement, domain membership ensures that when you're using advanced features like the vCenter Guided Consolidation Service, the vCenter Server will be able to find all domains and systems on the network for the purpose of converting physical systems to virtual machines (VMs).

▶ A supported database is already available, unless you're using the bundled SQL Server 2005 Express Edition.

▶ A valid system data source name (DSN) exists that allows vCenter Server to connect to the created database.

▶ The vCenter Server is able to directly access the hosts it will manage without any network address translation between the server and the hosts.

NO MAGIC WANDS

Notice that all these requirements and recommendations are the same as those you'd check if you were manually installing vCenter Server on a single machine. People often think that scripting introduces some kind of magic or new ways to do things behind the scene. Not so! We use exactly the same methods VMware does for a manual install; it's just automated. If things go wrong, troubleshoot them the same way you would for a standard vCenter Server install that went wrong.

Create an Automated Installation

When installing vCenter Server manually, you first download the media and then run through a series of wizards, ensuring each step within the wizard is correctly configured before completing the installation and waiting for the wizard to install vCenter Server. This process can become cumbersome if the installation needs to be repeated multiple times, and mistakes can be made that could cause key configured items to be incorrect.

Use the script in Listing 1.1 as an example; it shows how you might automate the installation of vCenter Server while ensuring all database components are installed and all connections to the database are created. This example connects to a SQL 2005 database that was set up previously and is ready for install. With all items clearly defined within the script, using a script like this ensures each installation is configured correctly and no mistakes are made.

LISTING 1.1   Sample script for an automated installation of vCenter Server

```
Function New-RegKey ($RegLocation, $RegKey, $RegValue) {
   If (Test-Path $RegLocation) {
   } Else {
      Write "Creating Registry Key $RegLocation"
      Mkdir $RegLocation | Out-Null
   }
   If (Get-ItemProperty $RegLocation $RegKey `
   -ErrorAction SilentlyContinue) {
      Write "Registry Key '$RegKey' already Exists."
   } Else {
      Write "Creating $RegKey with a value of $RegValue"
      New-ItemProperty -Path $RegLocation -Name $RegKey `
      -Value $RegValue `
      | Out-Null
   }
}


#Install VC unattended
$VCMedia = "C:\Temp\InstallMedia"
$LiKey = "XXX-XXX-XXX-XXX"
$Username = "My Name"
$CompanyName = "My Company"
$ODBCName = "vCenter Database"
$DBSrv = "SQL2005DB"
$DBUser = "VMware"
$DBPass = "VCDataba53"


# For SQL 2008 connections ensure the database client is installed
If (-Not (Test-Path 'C:\WINDOWS\system32\sqlncli10.dll')) {
 Write "SQL 2008 Native Client not found.
 Install it & then re-run this script"
 Exit
}


#Create DSN connection
```

```
$DrvPath = "C:\WINDOWS\system32\sqlncli10.dll"
New-Regkey "HKLM:SOFTWARE\ODBC\ODBC.INI\$ODBCName" `
"Driver" $DrvPath
New-RegKey "HKLM:SOFTWARE\ODBC\ODBC.INI\$ODBCName" `
"Description" $ODBCName
New-RegKey "HKLM:SOFTWARE\ODBC\ODBC.INI\$ODBCName" `
"Server" $DBSrv
New-RegKey "HKLM:SOFTWARE\ODBC\ODBC.INI\$ODBCName" `
"LastUser" $DBUser
New-RegKey "HKLM:SOFTWARE\ODBC\ODBC.INI\ODBC Data Sources" `
$ODBCName "SQL Server Native Client 10.0"


# Install vCenter
Write-Host "Installing vCenter"
$exe = "$VCmedia\vpx\VMware-vcserver.exe"
$args = '/q /s /w /L1033 /v" /qr USERNAME=\"$($username)\" '
$args = $agrs + `
'COMPANYNAME=\"$($Companyname)\" LICENSEKEY=\"$($LIKey)\" '
$args = $args + `
'DB_SERVER_TYPE=Custom DB_DSN=\"$($ODBCName)\" '
$args = $args + `
'DB_USERNAME=\"$($DBUser)\" DB_PASSWORD=\"$($DBPass)\" '
$args = $args + 'REBOOT=SUPPRESS'
Start-process $exe $args -Wait


# Initiate the Database Tables
Write-Host "DB tables"
$Exec = "$ENV:PROGRAMFILES\VMware\Infrastructure\VirtualCenter
Server\vpxd.exe"
Start-Process $Exec "-b" -Wait
Start-Service vpxd
```

Additional components, such as the vCenter Client or Update Manager, can easily be added to the previous script. Simply add a few extra lines in the install script, much like the vCenter Client install code that follows:

```
# Install vCenter Client
Write-Host "Installing vCenter Client"
Invoke-Item "$VCMedia\vpx\VMware-viclient.exe /s /w /v /qn `
/L*v %TEMP%\vmvcc.log `
WARNING_LEVEL=0"
```

To add the Host Update Utility component, try this next code:

```
# Install vCenter Client with Host Update Utility
Write-Host "Installing vCenter Client with Host Update Utility"
Invoke-Item "$VCMedia\vpx\VMware-viclient.exe /s /w /v /qn `
/L*v %TEMP%\vmvcc.log `
WARNING_LEVEL=0 `
INSTALL_VIUPDATE=1"
```

VMware supports more automated installation options and parameters, such as installing a linked mode vCenter Server, and maintains an online installation document here:

http://www.vmware.com/pdf/vsp_4_vcserver_cmdline_install.pdf

Set Up Your vCenter Server Folder Structure

Two types of folders are supported in vSphere. From within the Hosts and Clusters view, you are able to create folders at any point under the Datacenter level. These are commonly known as *yellow folders* and can be used throughout the infrastructure to organize the clusters, hosts, and VMs in a logical view.

Blue folders can be seen in the VMs and Templates view. Use these folders to more accurately reflect the layout of your VMs from a logical point of view. For example, you can create folders based on departments (such as Finance, Legal, and Customer Services) or by function (Internet, Active Directory, File Servers, Print Servers, Databases), or any other view that makes sense to your organization. Blue folders could also be used to reflect a security function and used to group the VMs into folders which only certain people can access. Once you create the folder, you can use it to grant access to various vCenter Server permissions.

Creating a Folder Structure from Scratch

You can initially create your folder structure when you create your new VMs; create your templates and move them into the appropriate folder. Another way of creating the folder structure is to plan the layout in a comma-separated variable (CSV) file. This type of plan can easily be created in an Excel document, as shown in Figure 1.1, and then exported to the CSV format needed to create the virtual folder structure.

FIGURE 1.1 Sample CSV layout

	A	B
1	Name	Path
2	Discovered virtual machine	vm\Discovered virtual machine
3	ESX Hosts	vm\ESX Hosts
4	Projects	vm\Projects
5	Templates	vm\Templates
6	Test VMs	vm\Test VMs
7	VDI	vm\VDI
8	vCenter	vm\vCenter
9	Windows 2008 Migration	vm\Projects\Windows 2008 Migration
10	Test	vm\Projects\Test
11	Developers Labs	vm\Projects\Developers Labs
12	Test VMs	vm\VDI\Test VMs

Install, Configure, and Manage the vSphere Environment

PART I

In the example CSV file we created, there are two columns. The first column, Name, is used to define the name of the folder that you wish to create. The second column, Path, is used to show the path to where this folder is to be created in vCenter Server. As seen in Figure 1.1, in the Path column all entries begin with vm\. This folder will not be created but is used by the underlying application programming interface (API). Once you have created the CSV file that contains the layout of your folder structure, a script can easily read your CSV file and create the structure using the code shown in Listing 1.2.

LISTING 1.2 Using a CSV file to create a vCenter file structure

```
function Import-Folders{
<#
.SYNOPSIS
  Imports a csv file of folders into vCenter Server and
  creates them automatically.
.DESCRIPTION
  The function will import folders from CSV file and create
  them in vCenter Server.
.NOTES
  Source:  Automating vSphere Administration
  Authors: Luc Dekens, Arnim van Lieshout, Jonathan Medd,
           Alan Renouf, Glenn Sizemore
.PARAMETER FolderType
  The type of folder to create
.PARAMETER DC
  The Datacenter to create the folder structure
.PARAMETER Filename
  The path of the CSV file to use when importing
```

```
.EXAMPLE 1
  PS> Import-Folders -FolderType "Blue" -DC "DC01" `
      -Filename "C:\BlueFolders.csv"
.EXAMPLE 2
  PS> Import-Folders -FolderType "Yellow" -DC "Datacenter"
  -Filename "C:\YellowFolders.csv"
#>

  param(
  [String]$FolderType,
  [String]$DC,
  [String]$Filename
  )

  process{
    $vmfolder = Import-Csv $filename | `
    Sort-Object -Property Path
   If ($FolderType -eq "Yellow") {
      $type = "host"
    } Else {
      $type = "vm"
    }
    foreach($folder in $VMfolder){
      $key = @()
      $key =  ($folder.Path -split "\\")[-2]
      if ($key -eq "vm") {
       get-datacenter $dc | get-folder $type | `
       New-Folder -Name $folder.Name
      } else {
        Get-Datacenter $dc | get-folder $type | `
        get-folder $key | `
            New-Folder -Name $folder.Name
      }
    }
  }
}

Import-Folders -FolderType "blue" -DC "DC01" `
-Filename "C:\BlueFolders.csv"
```

Exporting a Folder Structure

Both yellow and blue folder views can be exported to a CSV file. You will find this technique useful when you are rebuilding your vCenter Server from scratch or creating a DR replica of the current virtual infrastructure.

The script in Listing 1.3 can be used to export either a blue or a yellow folder structure to a CSV. It can also be used to export the location of the current VMs, ensuring a replicated location when you reimport the structure.

LISTING 1.3   Exporting a vCenter structure to a CSV file

```
Filter Get-FolderPath {
<#
.SYNOPSIS
  Colates the full folder path
.DESCRIPTION
  The function will find the full folder path returning a
  name and path
.NOTES
  Source:  Automating vSphere Administration
  Authors: Luc Dekens, Arnim van Lieshout, Jonathan Medd,
           Alan Renouf, Glenn Sizemore
#>
    $_ | Get-View | % {
        $row = "" | select Name, Path
        $row.Name = $_.Name

        $current = Get-View $_.Parent
        $path = $_.Name
        do {
            $parent = $current
            if($parent.Name -ne "vm"){
             $path = $parent.Name + "\" + $path
            }
            $current = Get-View $current.Parent
        } while ($current.Parent -ne $null)
        $row.Path = $path
        $row
    }
}
```

Install, Configure, and Manage the vSphere Environment

PART I

```
Function Export-Folders {
  <#
.SYNOPSIS
  Creates a csv file of folders in vCenter Server.
.DESCRIPTION
  The function will export folders from vCenter Server
  and add them to a CSV file.
.NOTES
  Source:  Automating vSphere Administration
  Authors: Luc Dekens, Arnim van Lieshout, Jonathan Medd,
           Alan Renouf, Glenn Sizemore
.PARAMETER FolderType
  The type of folder to export
.PARAMETER DC
  The Datacenter where the folders reside
.PARAMETER Filename
  The path of the CSV file to use when exporting
.EXAMPLE 1
  PS> Export-Folders -FolderType "Blue" -DC "DC01" -Filename `
      "C:\BlueFolders.csv"
.EXAMPLE 2
  PS> Export-Folders -FolderType "Yellow" -DC "Datacenter"
  -Filename "C:\YellowFolders.csv"
#>

  param(
  [String]$FolderType,
  [String]$DC,
  [String]$Filename
  )

  Process {
   If ($Foldertype -eq "Yellow") {
      $type = "host"
   } Else {
     $type = "vm"
   }
   $report = @()
   $report = get-datacenter $dc | Get-folder $type | `
```

```
  get-folder | Get-Folderpath
  $Report | foreach {
   if ($type -eq "vm") {
    $_.Path = ($_.Path).Replace($dc + "\","$type\")
   }
  }
  $report | Export-Csv $filename -NoTypeInformation
 }
}


Function Export-VMLocation {
 <#
.SYNOPSIS
 Creates a csv file with the folder location of each VM.
.DESCRIPTION
 The function will export VM locations from vCenter Server
 and add them to a CSV file.
.NOTES
 Source:  Automating vSphere Administration
 Authors: Luc Dekens, Arnim van Lieshout, Jonathan Medd,
          Alan Renouf, Glenn Sizemore
.PARAMETER DC
 The Datacenter where the folders reside
.PARAMETER Filename
 The path of the CSV file to use when exporting
.EXAMPLE 1
 PS> Export-VMLocation -DC "DC01" `
     -Filename "C:\VMLocations.csv"
#>

 param(
 [String]$DC,
 [String]$Filename
 )

 Process {
  $report = @()
  $report = get-datacenter $dc | get-vm | Get-Folderpath
  $report | Export-Csv $filename -NoTypeInformation
```

```
    }
  }

  Export-Folders "Blue" "DC01" "C:\BlueFolders.csv"
  Export-VMLocation "DC01" "C:\VMLocation.csv"
  Export-Folders "Yellow" "DC01" "C:\YellowFolders.csv"
```

Importing a Folder Structure

You can import an existing blue or yellow folder structure into vCenter Server using the `Import-Folders` function previously shown in Listing 1.2. You can also choose if you would like your VMs moved back into their correct blue folders by using the `Import-VMLocation` function, as shown in Listing 1.4.

LISTING 1.4   **Importing VMs to their blue folders**

```
Function Import-VMLocation {
 <#
.SYNOPSIS
  Imports the VMs back into their Blue Folders based on
  the data from a csv file.
.DESCRIPTION
  The function will import VM locations from CSV File
  and add them to their correct Blue Folders.
.NOTES
  Source:  Automating vSphere Administration
  Authors: Luc Dekens, Arnim van Lieshout, Jonathan Medd,
           Alan Renouf, Glenn Sizemore
.PARAMETER DC
  The Datacenter where the folders reside
.PARAMETER Filename
  The path of the CSV file to use when importing
.EXAMPLE 1
  PS> Import-VMLocation -DC "DC01" -Filename "C:\VMLocations.csv"
 #>

  param(
  [String]$DC,
  [String]$Filename
```

```
    )

   Process {
    $Report = @()
    $Report = import-csv $filename | Sort-Object -Property Path
    foreach($vmpath in $Report){
       $key = @()
       $key =  Split-Path $vmpath.Path | split-path -leaf
       Move-VM (get-datacenter $dc `
       | Get-VM $vmpath.Name) `
       -Destination (get-datacenter $dc | Get-folder $key)
    }
   }
  }

  Import-VMLocation "DC01" "C:\VMLocation.csv"
```

Define Users and Their Privileges

The authorization to perform tasks in your virtual infrastructure is controlled by a role-based access control (RBAC) system. A vCenter Server administrator can specify in great detail which users or groups can perform which tasks on which objects. RBAC systems are defined using three key concepts:

Privilege   A privilege is the ability to perform an action or read a property. Examples include powering on a VM or adding a folder.

Role   A role is a collection of privileges. Roles provide a way to add all the individual privileges that are required to perform a number of tasks, such as administer a vSphere host.

Object   An object is an item on which actions can be performed. vCenter Server objects are datacenters, folders, resource pools, clusters, hosts, and VMs.

Granting Privileges

Privileges are found in the vSphere Client. When using the Assign Permissions wizard, you are able to add new permissions. The privileges are listed in Figure 1.2.

FIGURE 1.2   vCenter Server Privileges

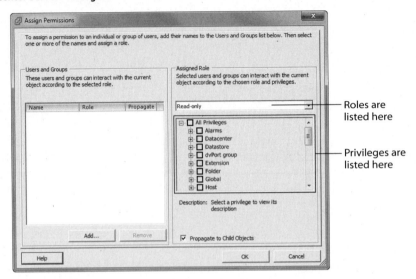

How many privileges are there? Think of any action you have ever performed in the vCenter Client. Think about the actions you have not yet come across or used in your everyday job. Now add them up, and you will have some idea of how many privileges there are in vCenter Server. Luckily, we are able to use PowerCLI to come up with a scientific answer for this question. You can easily list all privileges available to assign to a user through vCenter Server using the Get-VIPrivilege cmdlet.

```
[vSphere PowerCLI] C:\> Get-VIPrivilege | Select Name, Description
```

```
Name                       Description
----                       -----------
Anonymous                  The only privilege held by sessions ...
View                       Visibility without read access to an...
Read                       Grants read access to an entity
Manage custom attributes   Add, remove, and rename custom attri...
Set custom attribute       Set the value of a custom attribute ...
Log event                  Log a user-defined event on an object
Cancel task                Cancel a running task
Licenses                   Manage licenses
Diagnostics                Export diagnostic data
Settings                   Edit global settings
Act as vCenter Server      Act as the vCenter Server
```

```
Capacity planning          Discover and convert physical host t...
Script action             Schedule an external script action
Proxy                     Add or remove endpoints to or from t...
Disable methods           Operations are disabled in vCenter
Enable methods            Operations are enabled in vCenter
Service managers          Access the directory service
Health                    Access the health of vCenter group
...........
```

We purposely truncated the output listing due to the large number of privileges available. You can count the number of privileges available for assigning to your roles and users or groups by using the Measure-Object cmdlet:

```
[vSphere PowerCLI] C:\> Get-VIPrivilege | Measure-Object


Count     : 266
Average   :
Sum       :
Maximum   :
Minimum   :
Property  :
```

You can also use the Get-VIPrivilege cmdlet to show only the privileges available to certain sets of objects like a host:

```
[vSphere PowerCLI] C:\> Get-VIPrivilege -Name *Host*


Name                             Id
----                             --
Host operation                   DVSwitch.HostOp
Add standalone host              Host.Inventory.AddStandaloneHost
Add host to cluster              Host.Inventory.AddHostToCluster
Remove host                      Host.Inventory.
RemoveHostFromClu...
Move cluster or standalone host  Host.Inventory.MoveCluster
Move host                        Host.Inventory.MoveHost
Add host to vCenter              Host.Local.InstallAgent
Host USB device                  VirtualMachine.Config.
HostUSBDevice
Host                             Host
Host profile                     Profile
```

You can view which groups (collections of privileges) are available by using the Get-VIPrivilege cmdlet with the -PrivilegeGroup parameter, as shown here:

```
[vSphere PowerCLI] C:\> Get-VIPrivilege -PrivilegeGroup | `
                        Select Name, Description

Name                              Description
----                              -----------

System                            System
Global                            Global
Folder                            Folder
Datacenter                        Datacenter
Datastore                         Datastore
Network                           Networks
vNetwork Distributed Switch       vNetwork Distributed Switch
dvPort group                      dvPort groups
Host                              Host
Inventory                         Host inventory
Configuration                     Host configuration
Local operations                  Host local operations
CIM                               CIM
Virtual machine                   Virtual machine
Inventory                         Virtual machine inventory
Interaction                       Virtual machine interaction
Configuration                     Virtual machine configuration
State                             Virtual machine state
Provisioning                      Virtual machine provisioning
VRMPolicy                         Virtual Rights Management Policy
Resource                          Resource allocation
Alarms                            Alarms
Tasks                             Tasks
Scheduled task                    Scheduled task
Sessions                          Sessions
Performance                       Performance
Permissions                       Permissions
Extension                         Extensions
vApp                              Privileges related to vApps
Host profile                      Host profile
Storage views                     Storage views
VMware vCenter Update Manager     VMware vCenter Update Manager
```

Manage Baseline	Manage baselines
Upload file	Upload file
Configure	General VMware vCenter Upd...
Manage Patches and Upgrades	Manage virtual machine and...

Creating New Roles

Roles can be found in the vSphere Client whenever you add a new permission. The Assigned Role drop-down box in the Assign Permissions dialog box shown in Figure 1.3 lists your existing roles.

FIGURE 1.3   vCenter Server roles

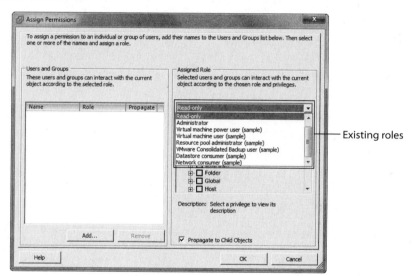

You can see an overview of the predefined roles by using the Get-VIRole cmdlet, as shown here:

```
[vSphere PowerCLI] C:\> Get-VIRole | Select Name, Description
```

```
Name                     Description
----                     -----------
NoAccess                 Used for restricting granted access
Anonymous                Not logged-in user (cannot be granted)
View                     Visibility access (cannot be granted)
ReadOnly                 See details of objects, but not make...
Admin                    Full access rights
```

```
VirtualMachinePowerUser        Provides virtual machine interaction...
VirtualMachineUser             Provides virtual machine interaction...
ResourcePoolAdministrator      Supports delegated resource management
VMwareConsolidatedBackupUser   Used by the Consolidated Backup utility
DatastoreConsumer              Assigned to datastores to allow crea...
NetworkConsumer                Assigned to networks to allow associ...
```

Now that you know that a role is a group of privileges and you've learned to use the Get-VIPrivilege and Get-VIRole cmdlets, we want to introduce you to New-VIRole. You can use the New-VIRole cmdlet with Get-VIPrivilege to define a new role. You can define your own group of privileges, which can later be assigned to your users. An example is shown in Listing 1.5; you can see the results in the vCenter Client, as shown in Figure 1.4.

LISTING 1.5   Creating a new role

```
New-VIRole `
-Name 'New Custom Role' `
-Privilege (Get-VIPrivilege `
-PrivilegeGroup "Interaction","Provisioning")
```

FIGURE 1.4   New roles

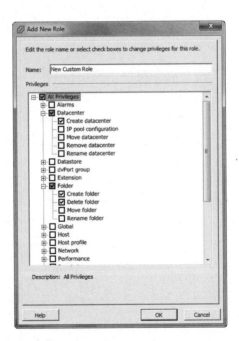

A new role can also be created at a granular level. First choose the privileges you want to use:

```
$Priv = @()
$MyPriv = "Profile", "VCIntegrity.Baseline", `
"VApp.Move", "Profile.Clear"
```

And then add each of them into a custom object:

```
Foreach ($CustPriv in $MyPriv){
    $Priv += Get-VIPrivilege | Where {$_.Id -eq $CustPriv}
}
```

You can then use the custom object to apply your specific permissions to the new role:

```
New-VIRole "New selected Role" -Privilege $Priv
```

Bringing in Users

Now that you have defined your roles, you can start using them. Until now, you have only been working with roles and privileges. Once you define what you want your user to be able to do, you need to add users and grant them access to the roles. You can then enable them to start using the features of the vSphere Client.

A role or privilege can be assigned to any of the objects within a vCenter Server. Each of the objects can be defined by different roles or privileges. Together, objects, roles, and privileges make up a *permission set*. Permission sets can be inherited; inheritance ensures that each object underneath a datacenter, cluster, resource pool, or folder gives the users the correct access privileges.

So it comes as no great surprise that, when adding a permission through PowerCLI, you must consider three areas:

Role   The role which you will assign to the user

Principal   The user or group to which you wish to assign permissions

Entity   The object, folder, cluster, datacenter, or resource pool for which you would like to grant permissions to the user

In the code that follows, we grant a user (MyDomain\User01) access to New Custom Role at the datacenter level:

```
New-VIPermission -Role 'New Custom Role' `
-Principal 'MYDOMAIN\User01' `
-Entity (Get-Datacenter)
```

After you've set up and tested individual permissions, you can export them to a readable, importable format. This eases multiple installations and the transfer of permissions to further vCenter Servers, and ensures consistency as well. We'll show you how next.

Exporting Permissions

The script in Listing 1.6 exports all relevant information into a CSV file, which can later be used to import them back into the same or a different vCenter Server. Exporting the permissions can be a great way to satisfy a security audit or ensure the relevant departments or users have the correct permissions.

LISTING 1.6   **Exporting permissions**

```
Function Export-PermissionsToCSV {
 <#
.SYNOPSIS
  Exports all Permissions to CSV file
.DESCRIPTION
  The function will export all permissions to a CSV
  based file for later import
.NOTES
  Source:  Automating vSphere Administration
  Authors: Luc Dekens, Arnim van Lieshout, Jonathan Medd,
           Alan Renouf, Glenn Sizemore
.PARAMETER Filename
  The path of the CSV file to be created
.EXAMPLE 1
  PS> Export-PermissionsToCSV -Filename "C:\Temp\Permissions.csv"
 #>


  param(
  [String]$Filename
  )


  Process {
  $folderperms = get-datacenter | Get-Folder | Get-VIPermission
  $vmperms = Get-Datacenter | get-vm | Get-VIPermission


  $permissions = get-datacenter | Get-VIpermission
```

```
$report = @()
    foreach($perm in $permissions){
        $row = "" | select EntityId, Name, Role, `
        Principal, IsGroup, Propagate
        $row.EntityId = $perm.EntityId
        $Foldername = (Get-View -id $perm.EntityId).Name
        $row.Name = $foldername
        $row.Principal = $perm.Principal
        $row.Role = $perm.Role
        $row.IsGroup = $perm.IsGroup
        $row.Propagate = $perm.Propagate
        $report += $row
    }


foreach($perm in $folderperms){
        $row = "" | select EntityId, Name, Role, `
        Principal, IsGroup, Propagate
        $row.EntityId = $perm.EntityId
        $Foldername = (Get-View -id $perm.EntityId).Name
        $row.Name = $foldername
        $row.Principal = $perm.Principal
        $row.Role = $perm.Role
        $row.IsGroup = $perm.IsGroup
        $row.Propagate = $perm.Propagate
        $report += $row
    }


foreach($perm in $vmperms){
        $row = "" | select EntityId, Name, Role, `
        Principal, IsGroup, Propagate
        $row.EntityId = $perm.EntityId
        $Foldername = (Get-View -id $perm.EntityId).Name
        $row.Name = $foldername
        $row.Principal = $perm.Principal
        $row.Role = $perm.Role
        $row.IsGroup = $perm.IsGroup
        $row.Propagate = $perm.Propagate
        $report += $row
    }
```

```
    $report | export-csv $Filename -NoTypeInformation
  }
}


Export-PermissionsToCSV -Filename "C:\Temp\Permissions.csv"
```

Importing Permissions

It is equally important to be able to import the permissions back into your vCenter
Server. You can use the script in Listing 1.7.

LISTING 1.7   Importing permissions

```
function Import-Permissions {
<#
.SYNOPSIS
  Imports all Permissions from CSV file
.DESCRIPTION
  The function will import all permissions from a CSV
  file and apply them to the vCenter Server objects.
.NOTES
  Source:  Automating vSphere Administration
  Authors: Luc Dekens, Arnim van Lieshout, Jonathan Medd,
           Alan Renouf, Glenn Sizemore
.PARAMETER DC
  The Datacenter to import the permissions into
.PARAMETER Filename
  The path of the CSV file to be imported
.EXAMPLE 1
  PS> Import-Permissions -DC "DC01" `
      -Filename "C:\Temp\Permissions.csv"
#>


param(
[String]$DC,
[String]$Filename
)


process {
```

```
$permissions = @()
$permissions = Import-Csv $Filename
foreach ($perm in $permissions) {
 $entity = ""
 $entity = New-Object VMware.Vim.ManagedObjectReference
 $object = Get-Inventory -Name $perm.Name
 if($object.Count){
  $object = $object | where {$_.Id -eq $perm.EntityId}
 }
 if($object){
  switch -wildcard ($perm.EntityId)
  {
   Folder* {
    $entity.type = "Folder"
    $entity.value = $object.Id.Trimstart("Folder-")
   }
   VirtualMachine* {
    $entity.Type = "VirtualMachine"
    $entity.value = $object.Id.Trimstart("VirtualMachine-")
   }
   ClusterComputeResource* {
    $entity.Type = "ClusterComputeResource"
    $entity.value = `
    $object.Id.Trimstart("ClusterComputeResource-")
   }
   Datacenter* {
    $entity.Type = "Datacenter"
    $entity.value = $object.Id.Trimstart("Datacenter-")
   }
  }
  $setperm = New-Object VMware.Vim.Permission
  $setperm.principal = $perm.Principal
  if ($perm.isgroup -eq "True") {
   $setperm.group = $true
  } else {
   $setperm.group = $false
  }
  $setperm.roleId = (Get-virole $perm.Role).id
  if ($perm.propagate -eq "True") {
   $setperm.propagate = $true
```

```
  } else {
   $setperm.propagate = $false
  }
  $doactual = Get-View -Id `
  'AuthorizationManager-AuthorizationManager'
  Write-Host "Setting Permissions on `
  $($perm.Name) for $($perm.principal)"
  $doactual.SetEntityPermissions($entity, $setperm)
 }
 }
 }
}


Import-Permissions -DC "DC01" -Filename "C:\Temp\Permissions.csv"
```

Configure Datacenters and Clusters

vCenter Server has a hierarchical management structure similar to that of Microsoft Active Directory. Three main containers can be added to vCenter Server:

► Datacenters

► Clusters

► Folders

Datacenters   A datacenter is a logical container within vCenter Server used to store clusters, folders, and VMs; these are often named for the physical location where the hosts reside, such as "Boston" or "South West Datacenter."

Clusters   A cluster is defined as a group of like-configured computers that act in a fully redundant setup to ensure availability of applications and operating systems. A vCenter Server cluster is no different. Clusters are used in vCenter Server for three main functions: high availability, load balancing, and high-performance computing. A cluster is made up of two or more physical servers that provide resources for the hosts that are assigned to that cluster.

Folders   A folder is a logical way to define how VMs or other vCenter Server objects are organized. Folders are often used to organize VMs into department owners or server functions.

Creating Datacenters

Datacenters are generally created as part of the initial setup process. The setup can be automated by using the following code, which will create a datacenter called Boston and store it in a variable. The `Datacenter` object held within the variable can then be referred to later in the code as you create clusters or folders:

```
$BostonDC = New-Datacenter -Name Boston
```

Creating Clusters

Clusters are more complex than datacenters; there are many configurable items available for a new cluster. Consider the options the vSphere Client gives us: the normal cluster options as well as configuration options for VMware High Availability (HA), VMware Distributed Resource Scheduler (DRS), VMware Enhanced VMotion Compatibility (EVC), and VMware Distributed Power Management (DPM).

To create a new cluster in the Boston datacenter you created earlier, you can use the following code:

```
$ProductionCluster = New-Cluster -Location $BostonDC `
-Name "Production"
```

This code line gives you the basic settings. The sections that follow discuss the additional cluster settings available to you.

Configuring High Availability

When configured in a cluster, VMWare HA gives you many advantages, including the following:

- ▶ Proactive monitoring of all vSphere hosts and VMs
- ▶ Automatic detection of vSphere host failure
- ▶ Rapid restart of VMs affected by host failure
- ▶ Optimal placement of VMs after server failure

Much like the configuration of a cluster through the vSphere client, you can configure HA within a cluster either as part of the initial cluster setup or you can alter an existing cluster object. For example, to configure a new cluster named `Production` with HA enabled and an HA failover level of 1 physical host failure and the HA Restart Priority as Medium, you would use the code in Listing 1.8.

LISTING 1.8   Enabling HA with a failover host level and Restart Priority on a new cluster

```
$ProductionCluster = New-Cluster `
-Location $BostonDC `
-Name "Production" `
-HAEnabled -HAAdmissionControlEnabled `
-HAFailoverLevel 1 `
-HARestartPriority "Medium"
```

To complete this same action on an existing cluster, you first need to retrieve the cluster as an object and then push it down the pipeline into the Set-Cluster cmdlet, as shown in Listing 1.9.

LISTING 1.9   Enabling HA with a failover host level and restart priority on an existing cluster

```
Get-Cluster `
-Location $BostonDC `
-Name "Production" | `
Set-Cluster -HAEnabled $true `
-HAAdmissionControlEnabled $true `
-HAFailoverLevel 1 `
-HARestartPriority "Medium"
```

Configuring Distributed Resource Scheduler

VMware DRS is a configuration made at the cluster level of the vCenter Server environment that balances VM workloads with available host resources. With VMware DRS, you are able to define the rules for allocation of physical resources among the VMs. DRS can be configured for manual or automatic control. If the workload on one or more VMs drastically changes, DRS redistributes the VMs among the physical servers to ensure the resources are available where needed. Much like HA, DRS can be configured as part of the initial cluster setup or as an alteration to an existing cluster object. For example, to configure a new Production cluster with DRS enabled and a DRS automation level of FullyAutomated with DRSMode set to FullyAutomated, you would use the code in Listing 1.10.

LISTING 1.10   Configuring DRS on a new cluster

```
$ProductionCluster = New-Cluster "Production" `
-DrsEnabled `
-DrsAutomationLevel "FullyAutomated" `
-DrsMode "FullyAutomated"
```

To complete this same action on an existing cluster, you would again need to retrieve the cluster object and push the object through the pipe into the `Set-Cluster` cmdlet, as shown in Listing 1.11.

LISTING 1.11 Configuring DRS on an existing cluster

```
Get-Cluster -Location $BostonDC `
-Name "Production" | Set-Cluster `
-DrsEnabled $true `
-DrsAutomationLevel "FullyAutomated" `
-DrsMode "FullyAutomated"
```

Configuring Enhanced vMotion Compatibility

EVC allows you to add multiple hosts with different CPU architectures to your cluster. EVC will, for example, allow you to add older hosts with Intel processors to a cluster that includes hosts with newer Intel processors. It does this by setting a mask on the VMs and ensuring the instruction sets are the same for both sets of hosts. Unfortunately, at this point in time VMware does not include either a PowerCLI cmdlet or a method to enable this feature programmatically. Therefore, configuring EVC is outside the scope of this book.

Configuring Distributed Power Management

DPM provides cost savings by dynamically consolidating VMs onto fewer hosts during periods of low usage. Once the VMs are consolidated onto fewer hosts, the remaining hosts that are no longer hosting any VMs are powered off to save power. Once utilization starts to increase, the vSphere Server will power these hosts back on as needed.

While there are currently no options to enable DPM through the native cmdlets that are provided with PowerCLI, you can address the API and create your own function to enable DPM. For more information about using the SDK/API or Project Onyx, read Chapter 19, "Onyx and the SDK."

Listing 1.12 shows how you can enable DPM on a cluster.

LISTING 1.12 Configuring DPM on a cluster

```
Function Set-DPM {
 <#
.SYNOPSIS
  Enables Distributed Power Management on a cluster
```

Install, Configure, and Manage the vSphere Environment

PART I

```
.DESCRIPTION
  This function will allow you to configure
  DPM on an existing vCenter Server cluster
.NOTES
  Source:  Automating vSphere Administration
  Authors: Luc Dekens, Arnim van Lieshout, Jonathan Medd,
           Alan Renouf, Glenn Sizemore
.PARAMETER Cluster
  The cluster on which to set DPM configuration
.PARAMETER Behavior
  DPM Behavior, this can be set to "off", "manual"
  or "Automated", by default it is "off"
.EXAMPLE 1
  PS> Set-DPM -Cluster "Cluster01" -Behavior "Automated"
#>

param(
  [String]$Cluster,
  [String]$Behavior
  )

  Process {
   switch ($Behavior) {
         "Off" {
            $DPMBehavior = "Automated"
            $Enabled = $false
         }
         "Automated" {
            $DPMBehavior = "Automated"
            $Enabled = $true
         }
         "Manual" {
            $DPMBehavior = "Manual"
            $Enabled = $true
         }
         default {
            $DPMBehavior = "Automated"
            $Enabled = $false
         }
      }
```

```
    $clus = Get-Cluster $Cluster | Get-View
    $spec = New-Object vmware.Vim.ClusterConfigSpecEx
    $spec.dpmConfig = New-Object VMware.Vim.ClusterDpmConfigInfo
    $spec.DpmConfig.DefaultDpmBehavior = $DPMBehavior
    $spec.DpmConfig.Enabled = $Enabled
    $clus.ReconfigureComputeResource_Task($spec, $true)
  }
}


Set-DPM -Cluster "Cluster01" -Behavior "Automated"
```

Licensing

Licensing is one of the first areas that will be critical to setting up a new host. Without a valid license, you can manage and use your host-to-host VMs for only 60 days.

You may be surprised to learn that there are no cmdlets to help with licensing ESX hosts or even viewing the current license details. However, the licensing information is available through the `Get-View` cmdlet, and you can manipulate the SDK to perform the actions necessary to both view license information and set the license key for your hosts. You can write functions to help you deal with these cmdlets and make them a little friendlier than the SDK code.

Viewing License Information

To make things easier, you can use the functions we'll show you next to list all license keys registered on the vCenter Server and also to set a license key on a host. The `Get-LicenseKey` function in Listing 1.13 lists all existing license keys.

LISTING 1.13   Retrieving license key information from vCenter Server

```
Function Get-LicenseKey {
 <#
.SYNOPSIS
  Retrieves License Key information
.DESCRIPTION
  This function will list all license keys added to
  vCenter Server
```

```
.NOTES
  Source:  Automating vSphere Administration
  Authors: Luc Dekens, Arnim van Lieshout, Jonathan Medd,
           Alan Renouf, Glenn Sizemore
.EXAMPLE 1
  PS> Get-LicenseKey
#>

  Process {
   $servInst = Get-View ServiceInstance
   $licMgr = Get-View `
   (Get-View ServiceInstance).Content.licenseManager
   $licMgr.Licenses
  }
}

Get-LicenseKey
```

Each of the existing license keys will be returned in an output listing like this:

```
LicenseKey        : 00000-00000-00000-00000-00000
EditionKey        : eval
Name              : Product Evaluation
Total             : 0
Used              : 0
CostUnit          :
Properties        :
Labels            :
DynamicType       :
DynamicProperty   :


LicenseKey        : AAAAA-BBBBB-CCCCC-DDDDD-EEEEE
EditionKey        : esxEnterprisePlus
Name              : vSphere 4 Enterprise Plus
Total             : 0
Used              : 2
CostUnit          : cpuPackage:12core
Properties        : {ProductName, ProductVersion, feature...}
Labels            :
DynamicType       :
```

```
DynamicProperty :

LicenseKey         : AAAAA-BBBBB-CCCCC-DDDDD-EEEEE
EditionKey         : vc
Name               : vCenter Server 4 Standard
Total              : 0
Used               : 1
CostUnit           : server
Properties         : {ProductName, ProductVersion, feature...}
Labels             :
DynamicType        :
DynamicProperty    :
```

Licensing a Host

Once you have a list of the keys, you can use that information to license the ESX hosts attached to the vCenter Server. Listing 1.14 shows how you set the license key for a specific host.

LISTING 1.14   Adding a license key to a host

```
Function Set-LicenseKey {
 <#
.SYNOPSIS
  Sets a License Key for a host
.DESCRIPTION
  This function will set a license key for a host
  which is attached to a vCenter Server
.NOTES
  Source:  Automating vSphere Administration
  Authors: Luc Dekens, Arnim van Lieshout, Jonathan Medd,
           Alan Renouf, Glenn Sizemore
.PARAMETER LicKey
  The License Key
.PARAMETER VMHost
  The vSphere host to add the license key to
.PARAMETER Name
  The friendly name to give the license key
.EXAMPLE 1
  PS> Set-LicenseKey -LicKey "AAAAA-BBBBB-CCCCC-DDDDD-EEEEE" `
```

```
                            -VMHost "esxhost01.mydomain.com" `
                            -Name $null
            #>

            param(
               [String]$VMHost,
               [String]$LicKey,
               [String]$Name
               )

            Process {
             $vmhostId = (Get-VMHost $VMHost | Get-View).Config.Host.Value
             $servInst = Get-View ServiceInstance
             $licMgr = Get-View $servInst.Content.licenseManager
             $licAssignMgr = Get-View $licMgr.licenseAssignmentManager

             $license = New-Object VMware.Vim.LicenseManagerLicenseInfo
             $license.LicenseKey = $LicKey
             $licAssignMgr.UpdateAssignedLicense(`
             $VMHostId, $license.LicenseKey, $Name)
              }
            }

            Set-LicenseKey -LicKey "AAAAA-BBBBB-CCCCC-DDDDD-EEEEE" `
            -VMHost "esxhost01.mydomain.com" `
            -Name $null
```

Automating vSphere Hypervisor Deployment and Configuration

IN THIS CHAPTER, YOU WILL LEARN TO:

There was a time when automating an installation and configuration of the vSphere Hypervisor was quite difficult. Fortunately, VMware has worked hard to simplify the overall process. Today ninety percent of the installation is automated out of the box. In this chapter we will briefly walk through the various installation methods before taking a deep dive into automating that last 10 percent. We will cover several techniques for streamlining the installation and configuration of vSphere.

Prepare for an Installation

You can choose from several methods to install vSphere. The medium is the starting point from which you work backward. Once you have selected a medium, you then select a level of automation and workflow.

The Installation Medium

The installation medium has more to do with the size of your vSphere environment than anything else. Each level carries with it a series of trade-offs. We'll cover each medium available, highlighting the advantages and disadvantages of each in addition to identifying a target environment size.

CD/DVD   Old faithful, the CD/DVD, has been around since the dawn of ESX, and it continues on with vSphere. This is the most basic medium as it offers no updating facility. CD/DVD should only be used in small environments with fewer than three hosts.

Thumb Drive/USB Key   The heir apparent to the optical drive, USB keys are the preferred installation medium for small/medium environments, generally those with fewer than 10 hosts. They have the inherent ability to be updated easily, and are significantly faster than optical drives. Because they can be easily updated, they are also an excellent source for vSphere Kickstart-based installations.

PXE   The king of all installs, Pre-boot eXecution Environment (PXE) is the fastest possible installation. It is also the easiest to maintain. The only real downside is the infrastructure required to perform a PXE-based installation. While not extreme, it is still a bit much for small/medium environments. However, we consider PXE a minimum requirement for any environment with more than 10 hosts.

Gathering Required Software

We're going to make the giant assumption that, since you're reading a PowerCLI book, your management station is a Windows PC. Therefore, the following requirements apply:

CD/DVD   For a CD/DVD installation, you will need an ISO Image editing tool such as MagicISO, available for download from www.magiciso.com/download.htm.

Thumb Drive/USB Key   For a thumb drive/USB key installation, you'll need UNetbootin, available from http://unetbootin.sourceforge.net/.

PXE   There are many ways to skin this cat. That said, we recommend you use what you're comfortable with. If you have no comfort zone, we recommend Carl Thijssen Ultimate Deployment Appliance (UDA), available from www.rtfm-ed.co.uk/vmware-content/ultimate-da/.

Automate an Installation

Automating a vSphere installation can mean many different things. At its core, it means you have a zero-touch installation. As you learned earlier, this can be accomplished regardless of the media you choose. You will, however, outgrow this minimal automation solution very quickly, as it doesn't help solve the bigger problem of host configuration. To resolve that issue, you must first answer one simple, multiple-choice question.

I am more comfortable using:

    A. BusyBox/Python

    B. PowerCLI

    C. Host profiles

    D. All of the above

If you chose option A, you will try to do as much as possible with the first boot and postinstall sections within Kickstart—but you will find you cannot do everything. The advantage of option A is that there are no external requirements. This is a great solution for small environments. If you have the time and skill set to configure a vSphere host via BusyBox/Python, it is possible to automate just about every aspect of vSphere.

TIP   While this looks and feels very similar to a traditional Linux Kickstart, it's not! Do not assume that because something works in Linux Kickstart that it will work with vSphere.

If you chose option B, you will want to configure the bare minimum via Kickstart. Most likely, you'll configure the Management VMknic and partition assignment. That said, it is exponentially easier to perform some actions, like password and license assignment, from Kickstart.

If you chose option C, you undoubtedly have Enterprise+ licensing and want to use this advanced feature. Unfortunately, there are some things that you cannot do using host profiles (see Chapter 4, "Using Advanced vSphere Features," for more information). Host profiles do offer a compelling capability—compliance. Anything that *can* be done via host profiles *should* be done via host profiles, as they will ensure that your hosts continue to be configured correctly.

If you haven't figured it out already, option D is the best answer. You should use a combination of all three, assuming you have sufficient licensing to utilize host profiles. There are some aspects of vSphere configuration that are just easier to do while loading the host. Some matters are best left to host profiles. PowerCLI is the glue in all this that will bridge these two disparate worlds. If host profiles are off the table, take the path of least resistance and use both Kickstart and PowerCLI.

Customizing an Installation with Kickstart

As of vSphere 4.1, VMware supports a scripted installation mode: Kickstart. Kickstart is a configuration file that the installer reads in and then uses to perform a silent installation. If you like writing Kickstart configuration files, see the VMware vSphere Installation and vCenter Setup Guide for a detailed explanation of the available options. For the rest of us, one of the authors wrote a tool to assist in the basic creation of these files. (You can download the tool, vKickstartomatic, from www.sybex.com/go/vmwarevspherepowercliref.)

vKickstartomatic breaks out all the options available in a vSphere Kickstart and presents them in an easy-to-digest Windows GUI. So, let's create a Kickstart using this new tool. As always, you'll start with a requirement. For this exercise, you'll need to create a Kickstart that will install vSphere 4.1 to the specifications listed in Table 2.1.

TABLE 2.1   vSphere Kickstart specifications for a sample vKickstartomatic installation

Requirement	Specification
Root Password	P33k@Boo!
License Key	xxxxx-xxxxx-xxxxx-xxxxx-xxxxx
Partition	First Available
VM Datastore	Create a second datastore.
Install from	USB
Hostname	vSphere01.vSphere.local
VLAN	30
IP	10.1.1.15
NetMask	255.255.255.0
Gateway	10.1.1.1
DNS	10.1.1.5, 10.1.1.6

Install, Configure, and Manage the vSphere Environment

PART I

Figure 2.1 shows the General tab from the vKickstartomatic tool.

FIGURE 2.1   vKickstartomatic—General

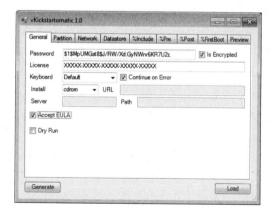

The General tab has only two mandatory parameters. In order for the installation to be successful, you must accept the EULA and enter a root password.

Now, let's move on to the partition configuration. In past versions of ESX, partition creation was a major portion of the Kickstart process. As of vSphere, this is now handled via the Autopart command, represented in the Auto Partitioning section of the Partition tab, shown in Figure 2.2.

ENCRYPTING THE ROOT PASSWORD IN VKICKSTARTOMATIC

If you chose to encrypt the root password—and you should—you'll need to download a copy of OpenSSL:

`www.slproweb.com/products/Win32OpenSSL.html`

Once OpenSSL is installed, you can generate a password hash with one command, as shown here:

FIGURE 2.2   vKickstartomatic—Partition tab

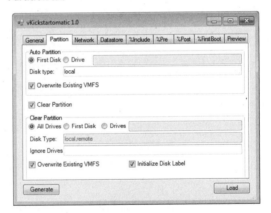

You'll notice that we decided to clear the disk prior to running auto partitioning. Generally, this is not needed as `Autopart` overwrites any existing partitions. However, if the server is being repurposed, you should clear out any remnants of the old system using `Clearpart`. If you're simply reloading vSphere, use `Clearpart` with caution because it is possible to delete any existing VM datastores presented to the host. To avoid this, you can specify a specific drive or driver to either use or ignore. This is the trickiest part of the whole deployment process; take your time and test everything before you run in production. If unsure, you can always look for specific device IDs, either through the vSphere Client (as shown in Figure 2.3) or by using PowerCLI (Listing 2.1). For this application, we're interested in the identifier, as this is how vSphere will address the device at installation.

FIGURE 2.3   vSphere Client disk identifier

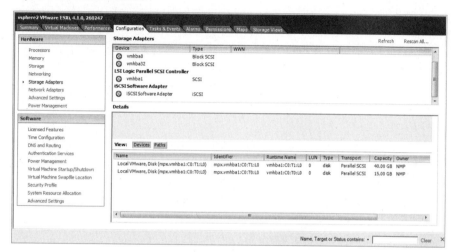

If you obtain the information via PowerCLI, you can get a list of every disk used in an existing datastore for a given host.

LISTING 2.1   Getting the disk identifier

```
Get-VMhost 'ESX01'|
    Get-Datastore |
    Select-Object -ExpandProperty ExtensionData |
    Select-Object -ExpandProperty Info |
    Select-Object -ExpandProperty Vmfs |
    Select-Object -ExpandProperty Extent |
    Select-Object -ExpandProperty DiskName
```

With partitioning taken care of, you can turn your attention to the network configuration. According to the requirements specification for this exercise (Table 2.1), you need to configure a static network. As you can see in Figure 2.4, network configuration using vKickstartomatic is self-explanatory. If you choose to use DHCP, you need only configure a VLAN and target device/MAC address.

FIGURE 2.4 vKickstartomatic—Network tab

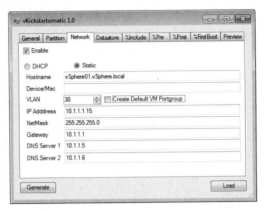

The `Part` command is a remnant of the old ESX Kickstart. Previously, it was used to partition everything. In vSphere, its only purpose is to create a new VMFS datastore. Per our requirement, you want to create a new datastore. Do so by selecting the Datastore tab and clicking the Add Datastore button shown in Figure 2.5 to launch the wizard shown in Figure 2.6.

FIGURE 2.5 vKickstartomatic—Datastore tab

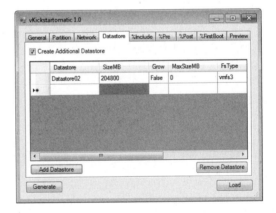

In the Add Datastore wizard, enter a name and the datastore size. You can specify that this partition can grow and then give a maximum datastore size, but doing so is outside the scope of our requirements. As for drive selection, vKickstartomatic doesn't have as many options as `Autopart/Clearpart`. Here, you can either select First Disk and provide a selection order, or provide a specific drive ID. Since you already found the disk identifier back in Figure 2.3, you'll use the drive.

FIGURE 2.6   vKickstartomatic—Add Datastore wizard

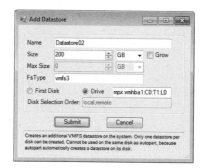

Once you click Submit, your new datastore is added to the Datastore tab. Here you can make any final modifications. At this point, you have met all the requirements listed in Table 2.1 and can generate your Kickstart file by clicking the Generate button. At any point in the process, you can preview changes by selecting the Preview tab, shown in Figure 2.7.

FIGURE 2.7   vKickstartomatic—Preview tab

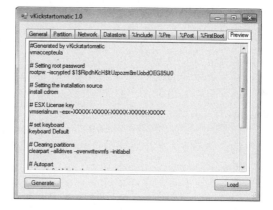

Postinstallation Configuration

As we indicated earlier, you have several options for postinstallation configuration. They all fall into one of two categories: online or stand-alone. An example of a stand-alone installation is the traditional monolithic Kickstart.

A stand-alone installation should only be used in scenarios where the network connectivity cannot be assumed. In such an install, all the postconfiguration tasks must be handled via the Kickstart postinstall and the first boot scripts. This is neither easy nor recommended. For instance, if you needed to configure your network offline because you were utilizing a port-channeled network connection, this could only be done during a postinstall as the network connections will not function properly until fully configured.

As shown in Figure 2.8, we've configured such a network on the %Post tab of vKickstartomatic.

FIGURE 2.8   **vKickstartomatic—%Post tab**

An online installation is the preferred method for configuring vSphere. Host profiles fall into this category because they require network access to function. It is possible to perform online postinstallation configuration as either a semi-automated or fully automated task. For instance, you could manually run a PowerCLI/vCLI script to configure a fresh vSphere host. This approach is still far better than the completely manual process. For example, Listing 2.2 takes a fresh vSphere host and performs the following configuration tasks:

1. Adds the host to vCenter

2. Locks the ESX(i) host down

3. Creates an iSCSI VMkernel port on vSwitch0

   ▶ VLAN: 55

   ▶ IP: 10.10.55.3

   ▶ Mask: 255.255.255.0

4. Configures iSCSI storage

- ▶ Enables the Software iSCSI HBA

- ▶ Renames the host iSCSI IQN

- ▶ Configures CHAP authentication

- ▶ Adds the iSCSI target

LISTING 2.2   Postinstallation configuration from a manually run script

```
# Add our host to vCenter, and immediately enable lockdown mode!
$VMhost = Add-VMHost -Name vSphere03.vSphere.local `
    -User root `
    -Password pa22word `
    -Location (Get-Datacenter) `
    -Force |
    Set-VMHostLockdown -Enable
# Add iSCSI VMkernel vNIC
$vSwitch = Get-VirtualSwitch -VMHost $VMHost -Name 'vSwitch0'
# we have to first create a portgroup to bind our vNIC to.
$vPG = New-VirtualPortGroup -Name iSCSI `
    -VirtualSwitch $vSwitch `
    -VLanId 55
# Create our new vNIC in the iSCSI PG we just created
$vNIC = New-VMHostNetworkAdapter -VMHost $VMHost `
    -PortGroup iSCSI `
    -VirtualSwitch $vSwitch `
    -IP 10.10.55.3 `
    -SubnetMask 255.255.255.0

# Enable the software iSCSI adapter if not already enabled.
$VMHostStorage = Get-VMHostStorage -VMHost $VMhost |
    Set-VMHostStorage -SoftwareIScsiEnabled $True

#sleep while iSCSI starts up
Start-Sleep -Seconds 30

# By default vSphere will set the Target Node name to
# iqn.1998-01.com.vmware:<HostName>-<random number> the
```

```
# following cmd will remove everything after the hostname, set
# Chap auth, and add a send Target.
#
# Example iqn.1998-01.com.vmware:esx01-165435 becomes
# iqn.1998-01.com.vmware:esx01
#
# Note that if your hostname has dashes in it, you'll
# need to change the regex below.
$pattern = "iqn.1998-01.com.vmware\:\w*"
Get-VMHostHba -VMHost $VMHost -Type IScsi |
    Where-Object{ $_.IScsiName -match $pattern}|
    Set-VMHostHba -IScsiName $Matches[0]) |
    Set-VMHostHba -ChapName 'vmware' `
        -ChapPassword 'password' `
        -ChapType "Required" |
    New-IScsiHbaTarget -Address '192.168.1.1' -Port "3260" |
        Out-Null
```

The advantage of a script like the one in Listing 2.2 is that it is efficient and repeatable. You can reload vSphere03 with reckless abandon, knowing it will be a quick and simple process to get your host back to hosting virtual machines. You'll notice that we used a custom PowerCLI function to enable Lockdown mode on the vSphere host. Set-VMHostLockdown, featured in Listing 2.3, can be used to automate vSphere host Lockdown mode en masse.

 TIP   We can't stress enough how important Lockdown mode is! When you manage your hosting environment via vCenter/PowerCLI, you lose nothing by enabling Lockdown, but you eliminate a significant portion of your attack surface by removing physical access from the list of potential attack vectors. You can always use PowerCLI to unlock a given host when you need access to Technical Support mode (TSM). In our opinion, not running a host in Lockdown mode is akin to not running a firewall.

LISTING 2.3   Using the Set-VMHostLockdown **Function**

```
Function Set-VMHostLockdown
{
  <#
  .SYNOPSIS
    Enable or Disable VMhost lockdown mode
```

```
.DESCRIPTION
  Enable or Disable VMhost lockdown mode
.PARAMETER VMHost
  VMHost to modify lockdown mode on.
.PARAMETER Enable
  Enable VMHost lockdown mode.
.PARAMETER Disable
  Disable VMHost lockdown mode.
.EXAMPLE
  Get-VMHost ESX01 | Set-VMHostLockdown -Enable
.EXAMPLE
  Set-VMHostLockdown -VMHost (Get-VMHost ESX08) -Disable
#>
[CmdletBinding(SupportsShouldProcess=$true)]
param(
  [Parameter(
    Mandatory=$true
  , ValueFromPipeline=$true
  , HelpMessage="VMHost"
  ,   ParameterSetName='Enable'
  )]
  [Parameter(
    Mandatory=$true
  , ValueFromPipeline=$true
  , HelpMessage="VMHost"
  ,   ParameterSetName='Disable'
  )]
  [VMware.VimAutomation.ViCore.Impl.V1.Inventory.VMHostImpl]
  $VMHost

,
  [Parameter(
    ParameterSetName='Enable'
  )]
  [switch]
  $Enable

,
  [Parameter(
    ParameterSetName='Disable'
  )]
```

```
    [switch]
    $Disable
)
Begin
{
  $SI = Get-View ServiceInstance -Verbose:$false
  $scheduledTaskManager = `
    Get-View $SI.Content.ScheduledTaskManager `
  -Verbose:$false
  $OnceTaskScheduler = `
    New-Object -TypeName VMware.Vim.OnceTaskScheduler
  $OnceTaskScheduler.runat = (get-date).addYears(5)
  $ScheduledTaskSpec = `
    New-Object -TypeName VMware.Vim.ScheduledTaskSpec
  $ScheduledTaskSpec.Enabled = $true
  $ScheduledTaskSpec.Name = "PowerCLI $(Get-Random)"
  $ScheduledTaskSpec.Scheduler = $OnceTaskScheduler
  $tasks = @()
}
Process
{
  $VMhosts = $null
  Switch ($PSCmdlet.ParameterSetName)
  {
    "Enable"
    {
      $msg = "Enable lockdown mode on $($VMHost.Name)"
      $ScheduledTaskSpec.Description = $msg
      $ScheduledTaskSpec.Action = New-Object `
        -TypeName VMware.Vim.MethodAction `
        -Property @{name="DisableAdmin"}
      $scheduledTaskSpec.Name = "PowerCLI $(Get-Random)"
      $VMHosts = $VMHost |
        Where-Object {!$_.ExtensionData.Config.AdminDisabled}
    }
    "Disable"
    {
      $msg = "Disable lockdown mode on $($VMHost.Name)"
      $ScheduledTaskSpec.Description = $msg
```

```
        $scheduledTaskSpec.Name = "PowerCLI $(Get-Random)"
        $ScheduledTaskSpec.Action = New-Object `
          -TypeName VMware.Vim.MethodAction `
          -Property @{name="EnableAdmin"}
        $VMHosts = $VMHost |
          Where-Object {$_.ExtensionData.Config.AdminDisabled}
      }
    }
  IF ($VMhosts)
  {
    Foreach ($VMHost in $VMhosts)
    {
      if ($PSCmdlet.ShouldProcess($VMHost.name,$msg))
      {
       $TaskMoRef=$scheduledTaskManager.CreateScheduledTask( `
          $vmhost.ExtensionData.MoRef, $ScheduledTaskSpec)
        $ScheduledTask = Get-View $TaskMoRef -Verbose:$false
        $ScheduledTask.RunScheduledTask()
        $i = 0
        while ($ScheduledTask.Info.ActiveTask -ne $null -or `
          $i -ge 100)
        {
          $ScheduledTask.UpdateViewData('Info.ActiveTask')
          $i++
          Start-Sleep -Milliseconds 200
        }
        $tasks += $ScheduledTask
        Write-Output $VMhost
      }
    }
  }
}
End
{
  Foreach ($task in $tasks)
  {
    $task.RemoveScheduledTask()
  }
}
}
```

As powerful as Listing 2.2 is, it can be expanded. By simply adding a couple of parameters and wrapping your work in a PowerCLI script, you can make your one-off solution an enterprise-wide solution. In Listing 2.4, we expanded on our original example. This additional layer of abstraction enables some powerful use cases. For instance, if you loaded a number of hosts, you could then configure them all at once.

```
[vSphere PowerCLI] C:\> 1..50 | ForEach-Object {
    ConfigureVMHost `
        -VMHostName ("vSphere{0:00}.vSphere.local" -f $_) `
        -User root `
        -password pa22word `
        -IPAddress 10.10.1.$_
}
```

HOW MUCH IS TOO MUCH?

You might find yourself wondering, "How much abstraction is too much?" This is a personal preference, but here's our advice: it's okay to statically configure a global setting for your environment. You'll find PowerCLI code is very easy to maintain. The goal is to make your code flexible from the CLI. You don't want to have to modify the script every time you run it, so use parameters for things that change. A script you might show at a user group is *not* the same as the scripts you'll run at work. Honestly, we only show our very best work to others. The majority of your PowerCLI scripts will be somewhere in the middle, but that's okay; you're a virtualization administrator, not a professional scripter! Your goal is to enable the environment and not to write perfect PowerCLI code.

LISTING 2.4   Parameterized vSphere host configuration function

```
Function ConfigureVMHost
{
    Param(
        [String]$VMHostName
    ,   [string]$User
    ,   [string]$password
    ,   [string]$IPAddress
    ,   [object]$Location = (Get-Datacenter| Select -First 1)
    )
    # Add our host to vCenter, and immediately enable
```

```
# lockdown mode!
$VMhost = Add-VMHost -Name $VMHostName `
    -User $user `
    -Password $Password `
    -Location $Location `
    -Force |
    Set-VMHostLockdown -Enable
# Add iSCSI VMkernel vNIC
$vSwitch = Get-VirtualSwitch -VMHost $VMHost `
    -Name 'vSwitch0'
# we have to first create a portgroup to bind our vNIC to.
$vPG = New-VirtualPortGroup -Name iSCSI `
    -VirtualSwitch $vSwitch `
    -VLanId 55
# Create our new vNIC in the iSCSI PG we just created
$vNIC = New-VMHostNetworkAdapter -VMHost $VMHost `
    -PortGroup iSCSI `
    -VirtualSwitch $vSwitch `
    -IP $IPAddress `
    -SubnetMask 255.255.255.0

# Enable the software ISCSI adapter if not already enabled.
$VMHostStorage = Get-VMHostStorage -VMHost $VMhost |
    Set-VMHostStorage -SoftwareIScsiEnabled $True

#sleep while iSCSI starts up
Start-Sleep -Seconds 30

# By default vSphere will set the Target Node name to
# iqn.1998-01.com.vmware:<HostName>-<random number> This
# script will remove everything after the hostname, set Chap
# auth, and add a send Target.
#
# Example iqn.1998-01.com.vmware:esx01-165435 becomes
# iqn.1998-01.com.vmware:esx01
#
# Note that if your hostname has dashes in it, you'll
# need to change the regex below.
```

```
$pattern = "iqn.1998-01.com.vmware\:\w*"
Get-VMHostHba -VMHost $VMHost -Type IScsi |
    Where-Object { $_.IScsiName -match $pattern} |
    Set-VMHostHba -IScsiName $Matches[0]|
    Set-VMHostHba -ChapName 'vmware' `
        -ChapPassword 'password' `
        -ChapType "Required" |
    New-IScsiHbaTarget -Address '192.168.1.1' -Port "3260"|
        Out-Null

}
```

Working with Host Profiles

At this point, you have a fairly high level of automation in play. To bring it to the next level, you need to introduce host profiles. Most settings within host profiles have three possible settings:

▶ User Specified Setting Will Be Applied

▶ Prompt User If No Default Is Provided

▶ Use The Following When Applying

As shown in Figure 2.9, your selection within the host profile will determine how you script against them. If you select User Specified Setting Will Be Applied, you will always have to supply the setting. If you choose Prompt User If No Default Is Provided, you should test whether a value is necessary before providing one. Finally, if you choose to use a static or dynamic value—that is, a static IP or DHCP—you don't have to provide a value. The interdependency mesh that is host profiles has led to a lot of confusion on the topic. We'll go over several techniques to show how to handle each scenario before we circle back around and use host profiles in a vSphere host configuration script.

FIGURE 2.9   Host profile selection

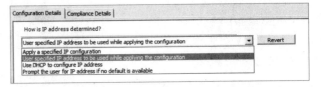

Regardless of how your settings are applied, automating host profiles is a three-step process:

1. Attach a profile.

2. Apply the profile and test only for dependencies.

3. Apply the profile.

For example, to attach the host profile named PROD01 to a vSphere host named vSphere03, run the following command:

```
$HostProfile = Get-VMHostProfile -Name PROD01
$VMHost = Get-VMHost vSphere03*
Apply-VMHostProfile -Entity $VMHost `
    -Profile $HostProfile `
    -AssociateOnly
```

At this point, the PROD01 host profile is attached to vSphere03. Now you need to test apply your profile against the host. If the profile has additional information that needs to be answered before the profile can be applied, the Apply-VMHostProfile will return a hash table of said setting. Therefore, after placing the host in Maintenance mode you could capture the output of this action in a variable for use later:

```
$AdditionalConfiguration = Apply-VMHostProfile `
    -Entity $VMHost `
    -ApplyOnly
```

In our case, it's a hash table of IP settings:

```
[vSphere PowerCLI] C:\> $AdditionalConfiguration |
    Select-Object Name
Name
----
network.hostPortGroup["key-vim-profile-host-HostPortgroup➡
Profile-iSCSI"].ipConfig.IpAddressPolicy.address
network.hostPortGroup["key-vim-profile-host-HostPortgroup➡
Profile-vMotion"].ipConfig.IpAddressPolicy.subnetmask
network.hostPortGroup["key-vim-profile-host-HostPortgroup➡
Profile-vMotion"].ipConfig.IpAddressPolicy.address
network.hostPortGroup["key-vim-profile-host-HostPortgroup➡
Profile-iSCSI"].ipConfig.IpAddressPolicy.subnetmask
```

Before you can apply your profile, you must provide values for these settings. You can accomplish this by addressing each entry in the hash table and setting a simple string value:

```
$AdditionalConfiguration['network.hostPortGroup[➥
"key-vim-profile-host-HostPortgroupProfile-iSCSI"].ipConfig.➥
IpAddressPolicy.address'] = '10.10.10.1'
$AdditionalConfiguration['network.hostPortGroup[➥
"key-vim-profile-host-HostPortgroupProfile-iSCSI"].ipConfig.➥
IpAddressPolicy.subnetmask'] = '255.255.255.0'
$AdditionalConfiguration['network.hostPortGroup[➥
"key-vim-profile-host-HostPortgroupProfile-vMotion"].ipConfig.➥
IpAddressPolicy.address'] = '10.10.10.1'
$AdditionalConfiguration['network.hostPortGroup[➥
"key-vim-profile-host-HostPortgroupProfile-vMotion"].ipConfig. ➥
IpAddressPolicy.subnetmask'] = '255.255.255.0'
```

Only the PowerCLI team knows why it chose to expose such long and unruly key names. Normally, PowerCLI cuts off such long strings, so be sure to pipe to `Select-Object` to get the full key name. You can verify your variables by looking at your `$AdditionalConfiguration` variable once more:

```
[vSphere PowerCLI] C:\> $AdditionalConfiguration

Name                            Value
----                            -----
network.hostPortGroup["key-...  10.10.10.3
network.hostPortGroup["key-...  255.255.255.0
network.hostPortGroup["key-...  10.10.11.3
network.hostPortGroup["key-...  255.255.255.0
```

At this point, you are ready to apply the profile. To accomplish this, omit any optional switches and provide the variable parameter with your additional settings. We will take advantage of the PowerShell pipeline and drop our host in and out of Maintenance mode—all in one command:

```
[vSphere PowerCLI] C:\> Set-VMHost -VMHost $VMHost `
    -State 'Maintenance' |
    Apply-VMHostProfile -Variable $AdditionalConfiguration |
    Set-VMHost -State 'Connected'
```

Once you've satisfied all the requirements, host profiles are quite easy to automate. The tricky part is determining what needs to be configured prior to applying the profile. Sadly, you can't simply just apply everything all the time; PowerCLI will issue an error if you apply a setting the host profile didn't expect. Therefore, to automate host profiles you're forced to either write rather intelligent code or use simplified profiles. For example, Listing 2.5 would safely automate the following tasks:

1. Associate the PROD01 host profile to vSphere03.

2. If needed, apply these additional configuration items:

   ▸ iSCSI vNIC IP: 10.10.10.40

   ▸ iSCSI vNIC MASK: 255.255.255.0

   ▸ vMotion vNIC IP: 10.10.11.40

   ▸ vMotion vNIC MASK: 255.255.255.0

3. Apply the profile.

4. Test for profile compliance.

LISTING 2.5   Applying a host profile to one vSphere host

```
# Get our target Profiles
$HostProfile = Get-VMHostProfile -Name 'PRO*'
# Get our target VMHost
$VMHost = Get-VMHost 192*
# Associate our host profile with the target host
Apply-VMHostProfile -Entity $VMHost -Profile $HostProfile `
    -AssociateOnly | Out-Null
#test.apply the host profile
$AdditionConfiguration = Apply-VMHostProfile -Entity $VMHost `
    -ApplyOnly

# process any required values filling in known values, and
# prompting for anything unexpected.
$Var = @{}
switch ($AdditionConfiguration.GetEnumerator())
{
    {$_.name -like '*iSCSI*.address' }     {
        $var += @{$_.Name = '10.10.10.40'}
    }
```

```
        {$_.name -like '*iSCSI*.subnetmask'}   {
            $var += @{$_.Name = '255.255.255.0'}
        }
        {$_.name -like '*vMotion*.address'}     {
            $var += @{$_.Name = '10.10.11.40'}
        }
        {$_.name -like '*vMotion*.subnetmask'} {
            $var += @{$_.Name = '255.255.255.0'}
        }
        default {
            $value=Read-Host "Please provide a value for $($_.Name)"
            $var += @{ $_.Name = $value}
        }
    }
}
# 1. Place our host in maintenance mode
# 2. Apply our profile
# 3. Exit maintenance mode
# 4. Test for profile compliance
Set-VMHost -VMHost $VMHost -State 'Maintenance' |
    Apply-VMHostProfile -Variable $var |
    Set-VMHost -State 'Connected'|
    Test-VMHostProfileCompliance
```

Now that you have a fully automated host profile implementation, you can step it
up to the next level. Let's wrap everything you've learned thus far into a master
configuration script. Listing 2.6 is a complete vSphere host provisioning script that
will take a new host and perform the following configuration tasks:

1. Add the host to vCenter Server.

2. Lock down the ESX(i) host.

3. Add the host to the designated cluster.

4. Apply that cluster's host profile.

5. Configure iSCSI storage:

- ▸ Enable the Software iSCSI HBA.

- ▸ Rename the host iSCSI IQN.

- ▸ Configure CHAP authentication.

> ► Add the iSCSI target.

> ► Rescan all HBA for storage.

LISTING 2.6   Complete vSphere host configuration function

```
Function ConfigureVMHost
{
    <#
    .SYNOPSIS
        Get-Admin standard vSphere Post configuration script
        Should only be run against a fresh host.
    .DESCRIPTION
        Get-Admin standard vSphere Post configuration script
        Should only be run against a fresh host.
    .PARAMETER IPAddress
        IPAddress of the host to configure
    .PARAMETER Cluster
        Name of the cluster to add our host to
    .PARAMETER User
        User to log in as default is root
    .PARAMETER Password
        Password to log in with if needed
    .EXAMPLE
        ConfigureVMHost -IPAddress 10.10.1.40 `
            -Cluster DC04_PROD_06
    #>
    [cmdletbinding()]
    Param(
        [Parameter(
            Mandatory=$true
        ,   ValueFromPipelineByPropertyname=$true
        )]
        [String]
        $IPAddress

        ,

        [Parameter(
            Mandatory=$true
        ,   ValueFromPipelineByPropertyName=$True
        )]
```

```
    [String]
    $Cluster
,
    [Parameter(
        ValueFromPipelineByPropertyName=$True
    )]
    [string]
    $User = 'root'
,
    [Parameter(
        ValueFromPipelineByPropertyName=$True
    )]
    [string]
    $password
)
# while static enough to not be parameterized we'll still
# define our advanced iSCSI configuration up front thereby
# simplifying any future modifications.
$ChapName = 'vmware'
$ChapPassword ='password'
$ChapType ='Required'
$IScsiHbaTargetAddress ='10.10.11.200','10.10.11.201'
$IScsiHbaTargetPort = '3260'


# we'll use the last octet of the IPAddress as the ID for
# the host.
$ESXID = $IPaddress.split(".")[3]
# Get the actual cluster object for our targeted cluster.
$ClusterImpl = Get-Cluster -Name $Cluster
# Get the parent folder our cluster resides in.
$Folder = `
    Get-VIObjectByVIView $ClusterImpl.ExtensionData.Parent
Write-Verbose "Adding $($IPAddress) to vCenter"
# Add our host to vCenter, and immediately enable
# lockdown mode!
$VMHost = Add-VMHost -Name $IPAddress `
    -User $user `
    -Password $Password `
    -Location $Folder `
```

```
    -Force `
    -EA 'STOP' |
    Set-VMHostLockdown -Enable

# Enter Maintenance mode
$VMHost = Set-VMHost -State 'Maintenance' -VMHost $VMHost |
    Move-VMHost -Destination $Cluster

#$VMHost = Get-VMHost -Name $IPAddress

# Get the Host profile attached to that cluster
$Hostprofile = Get-VMHostProfile -Entity $Cluster

# attach profile to our new host
Apply-VMHostProfile -Entity $VMHost `
    -Profile $HostProfile `
    -AssociateOnly `
    -Confirm:$false |
        Out-Null

# Apply our host profile to gather any required values
$AdditionConfiguration = `
    Apply-VMHostProfile -Entity $VMHost `
    -Profile $HostProfile `
    -ApplyOnly `
    -Confirm:$false
# If we have a hashtable then there are additional config
# items that need to be defined.  Loop through and attempt
# to fill them in, prompting if we come across something
# we're not prepared for.
if ($AdditionConfiguration.gettype().name -eq 'Hashtable')
{
    #Create a new hashtable to hold our information
    $Var = @{}
    # Loop through the collection
    switch ($AdditionConfiguration.GetEnumerator())
    {
        {$_.name -like '*iSCSI*.address' }        {
            $var +=@{$_.Name = $('10.10.10.{0}' -f $ESXID)}}
```

```
                    {$_.name -like '*iSCSI*.subnetmask'}            {
                        $var += @{$_.Name = '255.255.255.0'}}
                    {$_.name -like '*vMotion*.address'}             {
                        $var +=@{$_.Name = $('10.10.11.{0}' -f $ESXID)}}
                    {$_.name -like '*vMotion*.subnetmask'}      {
                        $var += @{$_.Name = '255.255.255.0'}}
                    Default {
                        $value = Read-Host `
                            "Please provide a value for $($_.Name)"
                        $var += @{ $_.Name = $value}
                    }
                }
                # Apply our profile with the additional config info
                $VMHost = Apply-VMHostProfile -Entity $VMHost `
                    -Confirm:$false `
                    -Variable $var
        }
        Else
        {
            # Apply our profile.
            $VMHost = Apply-VMHostProfile -Entity $VMHost `
                -Confirm:$false
        }
        # update vCenter with our new Profile compliance status
        Test-VMHostProfileCompliance -VMHost $VMHost | out-null

        # Enable the software ISCSI adapter if not already enabled.
        $VMHostStorage = Get-VMHostStorage -VMHost $VMhost |
            Set-VMHostStorage -SoftwareIScsiEnabled $True

        #sleep while iSCSI starts up
        Start-Sleep -Seconds 30

        # By default vSphere will set the Target Node name to
        # iqn.1998-01.com.vmware:<HostName>-<random number> This
        # script will remove everything after the hostname, set Chap
        # auth, and add a send Target.
        #
```

```
# Note that if your hostname has dashes in it, you'll
# need to change the regex below.
$pattern = "iqn.1998-01.com.vmware\:\w*"
$HBA = Get-VMHostHba -VMHost $VMHost -Type 'IScsi' |
    Where { $_.IScsiName -match $pattern }
If ($HBA.IScsiName -ne $Matches[0])
{
    $HBA = Set-VMHostHba -IScsiHba $HBA `
        -IScsiName $Matches[0]
}
Set-VMHostHba -IScsiHba $HBA `
    -ChapName $ChapName `
    -ChapPassword $ChapPassword `
    -ChapType $ChapType |
    New-IScsiHbaTarget -Address $IScsiHbaTargetAddress `
        -Port $IScsiHbaTargetPort | Out-Null
}
```

Working Without Access to Host Profiles

That's all well and good, but what if you don't have access to host profiles? Well, you're going to need a bigger script, most of which will be filled with pieces of code from all over this book. You'll have a little storage, network, authentication, licensing, and so on. But wanting to be as complete as possible, we'll highlight a few additional cmdlets that you'll find useful.

NTP   When you're configuring NTP, you should know that the `Add-VmHostNtp Server` cmdlet will do much more than add an NTP server. It can also enable and start the NTP service in case it is stopped:

```
Add-VmHostNtpServer -NtpServer time.nist.gov `
    -VMHost vSphere02.getadmin.local
```

Syslog   Syslog can be configured only on classic ESX/vSphere. If you're running any of the console's hypervisors (ESXi), use the `Set-VMHostSysLogServer` cmdlet to set up Syslog on vSphere:

```
Set-VMHostSysLogServer -SysLogServer splunk01 `
    -SysLogServerPort 507 `
    -VMHost vSphere02.getadmin.local
```

Root Password   You can change the root password by using the `Set-VMHostAccount` cmdlet. Unfortunately, you will have to connect directly to the host to do so.

```
Connect-VIServer -Server vSphere02.getadmin.local `
    -User root `
    -Password ""
Set-VMHostAccount -UserAccount root `
    -Password P33k@B00!
```

SNMP   You will most likely configure SNMP (the old faithful of the monitoring world) at some point. PowerCLI can assist in the gambit of configuration tasks. Unfortunately, this is also a cmdlet that requires that you be connected directly to the vSphere host.

Enabling SNMP

```
Get-VMHostSnmp | Set-VMHostSnmp -Enabled $true
```

Configuring Communities

```
Set-VMHostSnmp -ReadOnlyCommunity 'vSpherero' `
    -HostSnmp (Get-VMHostSnmp)
```

Adding a Target

```
Set-VMHostSnmp -TargetHost "192.168.1.44Ð `
    -TargetCommunity 'vSpherero' `
    -AddTarget
```

Advanced Options   To optimize your infrastructure, you will eventually have to set an option or two—a task easily performed via the `Set-VMHostAdvanced Configuration` cmdlet. To enable vMotion, you run the following:

```
Set-VMHostAdvancedConfiguration `
    -VMHost vSphere02.getadmin.local `
    -Name Migrate.Enabled `
    -Value 1
```

You could configure a set of options all at once by passing a hash table to the `Set-VMHostAdvancedConfiguration` cmdlet. For instance, to tune vSphere to run NFS on an EMC Celerra, you run the following:

```
Set-VMHostAdvancedConfiguration -VMHost $vmhost -NameValue @{
    'NFS.SendBufferSize'=64
    'NFS.ReceiveBufferSize'=64
    'NFS.MaxVolumes'=32
```

```
        'Net.TcpipHeapMax'=120
        'Net.TcpipHeapSize'=30
        'NFS.HeartbeatFrequency'=12
        'NFS.HeartbeatDelta'=12
        'NFS.HeartbeatMaxFailures'=10
    }
```

Using the cmdlets we've highlighted, and the automation workflow from earlier in the chapter, you can create a zero-touch installation for any environment. Now that you have both a zero-touch vSphere installation via Kickstart and a fully automated host configuration script, it's time to glue these together and deliver on the promise of a fully automated host provisioning life cycle. To accomplish this task, we adapted a technique originally documented by Lance Berc. The general workflow looks like this:

1. Kickstart your vSphere host, configuring at a minimum the management network.

2. As part of the first boot process, execute a small Python script that will "touch" a midwife host.

3. The midwife will be listening with a simple PowerCLI script, and will execute our host configuration script when notified.

The PowerCLI script features a custom PowerCLI function, shown in Listing 2.7.

LISTING 2.7   The Trace-Port **Function**

```
Function Trace-Port
{
    <#
    .SYNOPSIS
        Listen on a given port/ip address for a standard socket
        connection. return any text passed along said connection.
    .DESCRIPTION
        Listen on a given port/ip address for a standard socket
        connection. return any text passed along said connection.
    .PARAMETER IPAddress
        IP Address to establish the socket Tcp Listener
    .PARAMETER Port
        Tcp Port to establish listener on
    .EXAMPLE
        Trace-Port -IPAddress 192.168.1.15 -port 8080
```

```
.NOTES
    Adapted from Maish Saidel-Keesing
    http://technodrone.blogspot.com
#>
[cmdletbinding()]
param (
    [Parameter(Mandatory=$true
    ,   Position=0
    ,   HelpMessage="Address to listen for the connection"
    )]
    [string]
    $IPAddress

    ,

    [Parameter()]
    [int]
    $Port=3333
)
End
{
    [byte[]]$bytes = 0..255|%{0}
    $ip = [net.ipaddress]::Parse($IPAddress)
    $listener = new-object System.Net.Sockets.TcpListener( `
        $ip,$Port)
    $listener.start()
    write-debug "Waiting for a connection on port $port..."
    $client = $listener.AcceptTcpClient()
    $RemoteEndPoint = $client.Client.RemoteEndPoint
    $stream = $client.GetStream()
    $raw = while (($i = `
        $stream.Read($bytes, 0, $bytes.Length)) -ne 0)
    {
        $bytes[0..($i-1)]|%{$_}
    }
    $client.Close()
    $listener.Stop()
    write-debug "Connection closed."
```

```
New-Object PSObject -Property @{
    'Source' = $RemoteEndPoint.split(':')[0]
    'Data'   = [string]::Join("",[char[]]$raw)
}
    }
}
```

Now that you have all the tools in place, it's time to put it all together. First, place your Python script into vKickstartomatic, as shown in Figure 2.10. The IP Address in the connect method should be the IP address of your midwife server.

FIGURE 2.10   vKickstartomatic—%FirstBoot tab

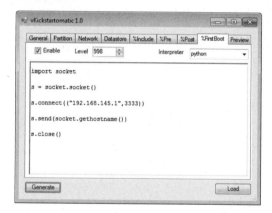

Now, run the following on your midwife server and Kickstart your host. In about 20 minutes, you'll have a new host ready to host virtual machines!

```
Trace-Port -IPAddress 192.168.145.1 -Port 3333 |
    Foreach-Object {
        ConfigureVMHost -IPAddress $_.Source `
            -Cluster prod01 `
            -User root `
            -password pa22word
    }
```

There you have it. You have reduced the incredibly complicated task of provisioning a vSphere host to a single line of PowerCLI code, all the while maintaining small chunks of code that can be easily updated as your environment grows.

CHAPTER 3

Automating Storage and Networking

IN THIS CHAPTER, YOU WILL LEARN TO:

Storage and networking are two of the most critical components of a virtual environment. You need storage to be able to provision virtual machines (VMs) and you need networking to connect these VMs to one another and sometimes to the outside world. Whether you're deploying a new cluster with new storage and networking, or maintaining and upgrading existing storage and networking, automation can come to your rescue to help you save time and maintain consistency of configuration.

Set Up the Storage

From what you have learned in Chapter 1, "Automating vCenter Server Deployment and Configuration," and Chapter 2, "Automating ESX/ESX(i) Server Deployment and Configuration," you will now have your vCenter Server set up and your ESX(i) hosts configured and added to the server. To run VMs on hosts, however, you need connected storage to store the files that make up a VM. In this section, you will learn to automate storage.

Setting Up Different Types of Storage

vSphere hosts can use four types of storage to host VMs: local SCSI disk, Fibre Channel or iSCSI storage area networks (SANs), and Network File System (NFS) storage.

Local Storage Local storage is the easiest type to get up and running. Simply slot the drives into the local ESX(i) host and configure local hardware RAID arrays. The storage will then be available to the host. However, advanced virtualization features, such as vMotion or High Availability (HA), will not be available because they require shared storage among multiple ESX(i) hosts.

Fibre Channel SAN Fibre Channel storage is connected to the ESX(i) host via host bus adapters (HBAs) inside the ESX(i) host and fiber cables via a switch to the storage fabric.

iSCSI SAN iSCSI storage is connected to the ESX(i) host either via a hardware HBA inside the ESX(i) host or via a built-in software iSCSI adapter to ESX(i). The software adapter is typically allocated dedicated standard network adapters to carry the storage traffic over the IP network. The ESX(i) software iSCSI adapter can be configured with PowerCLI. Chapter 2 covered iSCSI SAN configuration in detail, so we'll just gloss over it here.

NFS Storage Finally, NFS storage can be connected to the ESX(i) host via the built-in NFS client to ESXi. Both iSCSI and NFS storage require a VMkernel port group; we'll cover the automation of this port group in the section "Adding VMkernel Port Groups" later in this chapter.

It is possible to view the available HBAs inside a host via the `Get-VMHostHba` cmdlet. The following example shows the available HBAs inside an ESX(i) host with a local Serial Advanced Technology Attachment (SATA) controller, a Fibre Channel HBA, and a software iSCSI adapter:

```
Get-VMHost virtuesx02* | Get-VMHostHba
```

```
Device      Type          Model                         Status
------      ----          -----                         ------
vmhba0      Block         31xESB/632xESB/3100 Chipset... Unknown
vmhba2      FibreChannel  LPe12000 8Gb Fibre Channel ... Unknown
vmhba3      FibreChannel  LPe12000 8Gb Fibre Channel ... Unknown
vmhba32     Block         31xESB/632xESB/3100 Chipset... Unknown
vmhba36     IScsi         iSCSI Software Adapter         Online
```

Configuring an iSCSI Target

Neither local SCSI nor Fibre Channel requires any automation configuration from PowerCLI at the adapter level, but you can automate the configuration of the iSCSI connection. First, let's look at iSCSI. If you don't have a hardware iSCSI HBA and are planning to use the built-in software iSCSI adapter, you must first enable it; it is disabled by default. To enable this adapter for all hosts in `Cluster01`, use the following code:

```
Get-Cluster Cluster01 | Get-VMHost | Get-VMHostStorage |
Set-VMHostStorage -SoftwareIScsiEnabled:$true
```

Your next task is to create an iSCSI target for the adapter on each host using the `New-IScsiHbaTarget` cmdlet. This cmdlet has many parameters, but the only required one is the address of the iSCSI target. If your organization requires the Challenge Handshake Authentication Protocol (CHAP), you will need to set specific parameters from the eight CHAP related parameters available. You might also have to change the network port from the default of 3260 and, if you use a static target, give that target a name.

In the following example, you will create a dynamic iSCSI target with an IP address of 172.25.2.10 and configure CHAP settings for Type, Name, and Password. Note that for each host returned in the cluster, you use the `Get-VMHostHba` cmdlet with the `Type` parameter and `iSCSI` value to ensure that you configure the iSCSI adapter:

```
Get-Cluster Cluster01 | Get-VMHost | Foreach {$_ |
Get-VMHostHba -Type iSCSI | New-IScsiHbaTarget -Address
172.25.2.10 -ChapType Preferred -ChapName Administrator01
-ChapPassword Password01}
```

Rescanning for New Storage

Whatever the type of SCSI storage in use, a common administration task is the need to rescan the storage adapter when new storage has been provisioned. You do this either by hot-adding local disks or by providing a new logical unit number (LUN) from a Fibre Channel or iSCSI SAN. The ESX(i) host cannot see the newly available storage until a rescan task has been initiated on the adapter.

Prior to vSphere 4, rescanning was an onerous task in the vSphere Client. It involved navigating to the Configuration menu for the host and then to the Storage Adapters section, and clicking the Rescan task. For a cluster with a number of hosts, this process could take a long time and was very tedious. In vSphere 4, VMware added the Rescan For Datastores menu item, which becomes available whenever you right-click a Cluster, Folder, or Datacenter object in the vSphere Client. This functionality is also available from the Get-VMHostStorage PowerCLI cmdlet. It is particularly useful for versions of ESX(i) prior to 4 or for rescanning for multiple specific clusters.

For example, the following code rescans for new storage for clusters 01 and 02:

```
Get-Cluster | Where-Object {$_.name -eq 'Cluster01' -or $_.name
-eq 'Cluster02'} | Get-VMHost | Get-VMHostStorage -RescanAllHba
```

Adding Datastores

Now that you have either filled your servers with some local disk drives, connected them to a Fibre Channel or iSCSI SAN, or set up an NFS server, you need to create some datastores that you can store your virtual machines on. To do this, use the New-Datastore PowerCLI cmdlet. (The New-Datastore cmdlet can be used to create datastores for any of the supported types of storage.)

The key to getting it right with this cmdlet is to understand the types of path that you must provide to New-Datastore. Paths vary based on the type of storage. The Get-ScsiLun cmdlet can prove useful in helping you identify the correct path for each type.

Local Storage

Let's look at creating a new datastore on local storage. By using the Get-ScsiLun cmdlet, you can identify the LUN provided by the local SCSI controller. In this example, we used the fact that we have a Dell ESX(i) host with a PERC 6/i integrated RAID controller to identify the LUN it provides:

```
$LocalLun = Get-VMHost VIRTUESX2* | Get-ScsiLun -LunType disk |
Where {$_.Model -match "PERC 6/i"}
```

To create the datastore on the LUN, you need to provide what is known as the *canonical name* to the `New-Datastore` cmdlet. The `$LocalLun` variable includes the `CanonicalName` property, which you can easily retrieve. It will look something like this:

```
$LocalLun.CanonicalName
naa.60022180a9de3f001114e40d06df11de
```

You can now create the datastore using the `New-Datastore` cmdlet:

```
New-Datastore -Vmfs -VMHost VIRTUESX2* -Name LocalStorage
-Path $LocalLun.CanonicalName
```

NAME THAT LUN

The Network Address Authority (NAA) identifier just seen is an industry standard method of generating a unique number to identify a LUN. This value remains the same when accessed by any ESX(i) host. In terms of the object returned by the `Get-SCSILun` cmdlet, it is referred to as the `CanonicalName` property—which was the more commonly used term when identifying LUNs in ESX 3.

SAN Storage

For Fibre Channel or iSCSI SAN storage, you can use the `Get-ScsiLun` cmdlet to identify LUNs made available from a particular vendor. For instance if you have storage from the Vendor NetApp, the `Vendor` property is helpfully tagged as `Netapp`:

```
$iSCSILuns = Get-VMHost VIRTUESX2* | Get-ScsiLun -LunType disk |
Where {$_.Vendor -match "Netapp"}
```

Typically with SAN-based datastores, you will most likely be dealing with multiple datastores and consequently may also want to specify `BlockSize` if some are large. Let's say you need to add 10 new iSCSI datastores with a block size of 2 MB and a naming convention for datastores in the format iSCSI_01, iSCSI_02, and so on. For these datastores, we will start with iSCSI_10:

```
$DatastoreName = 'iSCSI_'
10..19 | Foreach {New-DataStore -VMHost VIRTUESX2* -Vmfs -Path
$iSCSILuns[$_ - 10].CanonicalName -Name (DatastoreName + $_)
-BlockSizeMB 2}
```

NFS Storage

Again, the key to adding a new NFS datastore is determining the path. After that, it's very simple. Once you have the path, the other requirements are a name for the datastore and the NFS host you want to connect to. Let's add an NFS datastore with the path /mnt/nfs/share1 on the NFS host 172.20.1.10:

```
New-Datastore -Nfs -VMHost VIRTUESX2* -Name NFS_1 -Path
  "/mnt/nfs/share1" -NfsHost 172.20.1.10
```

Multiple Datastores

Of course, using PowerCLI you can automate the creation of datastores. Let's take a look at a couple of examples to show how you can save time and effort.

In the first example, your storage team has created some new LUNs on a Fibre Channel SAN and has supplied you with the necessary details via a CSV file. The CSV file contains the HostID, LunID, and Identifier for each LUN. You agreed earlier that it would be a good idea to include the HostIDs and LunIDs in the vSphere datastore naming convention. The CSV file looks like the one shown in Figure 3.1.

FIGURE 3.1   Fibre Channel LUN details

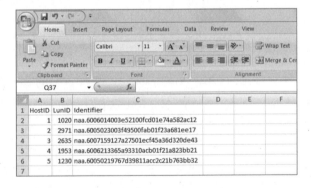

You can use the standard PowerShell cmdlet Import-CSV to access this data source and then feed that data into the New-Datastore cmdlet to create your datastores. You can also use the supplied HostIDs and LunIDs to build the name of the datastore each time, store that in the $Name variable, and use it with the Name parameter of New-Datastore:

```
Import-Csv FibreLuns.csv | Foreach {$Name = 'Fibre_Host' +
  $_.HostID + '_Lun' + $_.LunID; New-Datastore -Vmfs -VMHost
  VIRTUESX2* -Name $Name -Path $_.Identifier}
```

This code would create datastores named

```
Fibre_Host1_Lun1020
Fibre_Host2_Lun2971
Fibre_Host3_Lun2635
Fibre_Host4_Lun1953
Fibre_Host5_Lun1230
```

In this example, we used only five datastores, but you can use exactly the same code to create 50 or 500 datastores; the only item that will need to change is the data source. Similarly, you can take the same approach with NFS datastores to create multiple datastores across different NFS hosts from a data source. For example, take a look at the CSV data supplied by an NFS storage administrator in Figure 3.2.

FIGURE 3.2 NFS storage details

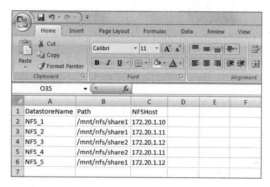

To create these datastores, you can use code similar to the previous example:

```
Import-Csv NFSLuns.csv | Foreach {New-Datastore -NFS -Name
$_.DatastoreName -Path $_.Path -NFSHost $_.NFSHost}
```

You've seen that the process of creating datastores based on information from an accessible data source is straightforward, saves you time, and can be repeated across different types of storage.

Adding Datastores on Free Space Partitions

Say you want to create a Virtual Machine File System (VMFS) datastore on a free partition available on a LUN or local disk. You won't be able to use the `New-Datastore` cmdlet because of a technical limitation associated with this cmdlet.

The `Get-SCSIFreePartition` function shown in Listing 3.1 will help you identify free partitions available to an ESX(i) host.

LISTING 3.1   Retrieving ESX(i) host free partitions

```
function Get-ScsiFreePartition{
    <#
    .SYNOPSIS
        Retrieve ESX(i) Host Free Partitions.
    .DESCRIPTION
        Retrieve ESX(i) Host Free Partitions.
    .NOTES
        Source:  Automating vSphere Administration
        Authors: Luc Dekens, Arnim van Lieshout, Jonathan Medd,
                 Alan Renouf, Glenn Sizemore
    .PARAMETER VMHost
        ESX(i) Host
    .EXAMPLE
        Get-ScsiFreePartition -VMHost Server01
    .EXAMPLE
        $esxName = "esx4i.test.local"
        $esxImpl = Get-VMHost -Name $esxName
        $esxImpl | Get-ScsiFreePartition | ft -AutoSize
    #>
    param (
    [parameter(ValueFromPipeline = $true,Position=1)]
    [ValidateNotNullOrEmpty()]
    [VMware.VimAutomation.ViCore.Impl.V1.Inventory.VMHostImpl]
    $VMHost
    )

    process{
    $esx = $VMHost | Get-View
    $storMgr = Get-View $esx.ConfigManager.DatastoreSystem
    $storSys = Get-View $esx.ConfigManager.StorageSystem

    $lunExt = $storMgr.QueryAvailableDisksForVmfs($null)
    foreach($lun in $lunExt){
    $info = $storMgr.QueryVmfsDatastoreCreateOptions($lun.Device
    Path)
    foreach($dsOpt in $info){
    $info2 = $storSys.ComputeDiskPartitionInfo($lun.DevicePath,
```

```
$dsOpt.Info.Layout)
$info2.Layout.Partition | where {$_.Type -eq "vmfs"} | %{
New-Object PSObject -Property @{
DeviceName = $lun.DeviceName
DeviceSizeMB = $lun.Capacity.block * $lun.Capacity.BlockSize
/ 1MB
Partition = $_.Partition
PartitionSizeMB = ($_.End.block - $_.Start.Block) *
$_.Start.BlockSize / 1MB
FullDisk = &{if($_.Partition -eq 1){$true}else{$false}}
            }
        }
    }
}
}
```

Your sample output will look similar to this:

Device SizeMB	DeviceName	Partition	Partition SizeMB	FullDisk
4096	/vmfs/devices/disks/ mpx.vmhba2:C0:T1:L0	1	4095	True
10240	/vmfs/devices/disks/ mpx.vmhba2:C0:T0:L0	3	8191	False
4096	/vmfs/devices/disks/ mpx.vmhba2:C0:T1:L0	3	2048	False

The New-PartitionDatastore function allows you to create a VMFS datastore on a free partition discovered using the Get-ScsiFreePartition function shown in Listing 3.2.

LISTING 3.2 Creating a VMFS datastore on a free disk partition

```
function New-PartitionDatastore{
    <#
    .SYNOPSIS
        Create a VMFS datastore on a free disk partition.
    .DESCRIPTION
        Create a VMFS datastore on a free disk partition.
```

```
    .NOTES
        Source:  Automating vSphere Administration
        Authors: Luc Dekens, Arnim van Lieshout, Jonathan Medd,
                 Alan Renouf, Glenn Sizemore
    .PARAMETER VMHost
        ESX(i) Host
    .PARAMETER Partition
        Free disk partition from Get-ScsiFreePartition
    .PARAMETER Name
        Name of the new VMFS datastore
    .EXAMPLE
        $esxName = "esx4i.test.local"
        $esxImpl = Get-VMHost -Name $esxName
        $partition = $esxImpl | Get-ScsiFreePartition | Where
        {!$_.FullDisk} | Select -First 1
        $esxImpl | New-PartitionDatastore -Partition $partition
        -Name "MyDS"
#>
param (
[parameter(ValueFromPipeline = $true,Position=1)]
[ValidateNotNullOrEmpty()]
[VMware.VimAutomation.ViCore.Impl.V1.Inventory.VMHostImpl]
$VMHost,
[parameter(Position=2)]
[ValidateNotNullOrEmpty()]
[PSObject]
$Partition,
[parameter(Position=3)]
[ValidateNotNullOrEmpty()]
[String]
$Name
)

process{
    $esx = $VMHost | Get-View
    $storMgr = Get-View $esx.ConfigManager.DatastoreSystem

    $lunExt = $storMgr.QueryAvailableDisksForVmfs($null)
    $device = $lunExt | where {$_.DeviceName -eq
    $Partition.DeviceName}
```

```
$dsOpt = $storMgr.QueryVmfsDatastoreCreateOptions
($Partition.DeviceName) | where
{$_.Info.VmfsExtent.Partition -eq $Partition.Partition}

$spec = $dsOpt.Spec
$spec.Vmfs.VolumeName = $Name
$spec.Extent += $spec.Vmfs.Extent
$dsMoRef = $storMgr.CreateVmfsDatastore($spec)
Get-Datastore (Get-View $dsMoRef).Name
    }
}
```

Executing the `New-PartitionDatastore` function will result in output similar to that of the `New-DataStore` cmdlet:

```
Name             FreeSpaceMB       CapacityMB
----------       -----------       ----------
Datastore12             3296             6372
```

Setting a Multipath Policy

If you are using Fibre Channel SAN, it's a good practice to have multiple HBA connections to the SAN whenever possible. With multiple HBA connections in place, should an active path to your SAN fail, a passive path is then made active so that storage traffic continues and the ESX(i) hosts remain connected to the storage for their VMs. New multipathing features in vSphere 4 make it simple to use Active/Active multipathing instead of Active/Passive. This means that not only do you have resiliency in case of a failed path, you are also able to boost your storage performance by using multiple paths to the storage. The Native Multipathing (NMP) module communicates with the Storage Array Type Plugin (SATP) and the Path Selection Plugin (PSP) to make these multipathing techniques work.

TIP   Contact your storage vendor before continuing further to check support for your storage array and to learn which SATP to use on the ESX(i) host.

Assuming your storage array is supported for multipathing and you have chosen the correct SATP to use, you need to configure the PSP on each LUN where you wish to use multipathing. The PSP is set per LUN and can take three values: `Fixed`, `MostRecentlyUsed`, and `RoundRobin`—for multipathing, use the `RoundRobin` value. You can have a mixture of selections, so it's a good idea to find out what is currently set. To do that, you can use the Get-ScsiLun cmdlet and select the MultipathPolicy property.

```
Get-VMHost VIRTUESX2* | Get-ScsiLun | Select CanonicalName,
MultipathPolicy


CanonicalName                             MultipathPolicy
-------------                             ---------------
mpx.vmhba32:C0:T0:L0                                Fixed
naa.6006016091a934008059cb521a9bca22 MostRecentlyUsed
naa.6006016091a934003a8ef8223a9bca22 MostRecentlyUsed
naa.6006016091a93400185f04866a9bca22 MostRecentlyUsed
```

Typically with Fibre Channel SANs, you will be working with many LUNs, not just three as in the previous example. Even making the change for the PSP to Round Robin via the GUI for three LUNs would soon become tedious, so being able to make this change via PowerCLI can save you a lot of time. By using the -MultipathPolicy parameter of the Set-ScsiLun cmdlet, you can make the change across all your Fibre Channel LUNs in one line of code. You can also use Where-Object to filter out any non–Fibre Channel LUNs, as we did in this example:

```
Get-VMHost VIRTUESX2* | Get-ScsiLun | Where {$_.CanonicalName
 -like 'naa.6006*'} | Set-ScsiLun -MultipathPolicy "RoundRobin"
```

Set Up the Network

Networking is at the heart of vSphere configuration. Now that you have your storage set up, it's time to look at your options for network automation. After the physical network cables have been patched into your ESX(i) hosts, you will need to create vSwitches and port groups in order to make management connections to manage your hosts; VMkernel ports to connect to iSCSI and NFS storage and for vMotion; and virtual machine port groups so that your VMs can communicate with other servers, both in the virtual and physical worlds.

Standard and Distributed Switches

First, you need to create at least one switch. In versions of ESX(i) prior to vSphere 4, you had only one option at this point: the Standard vSwitch. With vSphere 4, you now have the additional option of using a distributed vSwitch. A standard vSwitch extends only to the boundary of an individual host; a distributed vSwitch can extend across that boundary and can be accessed by multiple hosts. This relaxes the requirement that individual standard vSwitches be configured exactly the same across hosts. By definition, a distributed vSwitch appears the same to each host. Toward the end of this chapter, we will demonstrate how to migrate VMs from a standard to a distributed vSwitch. We will cover distributed vSwitches in more depth in Chapter 4, "Using Advanced vSphere Features."

NOTE   Distributed vSwitches require Enterprise Plus licensing for each ESX(i) host you wish to use them with. Not everyone has access to Enterprise Plus licensing.

Let's take a look at configuring standard vSwitches and some of the options you have when working with them. Standard vSwitches must be configured identically across all hosts in a cluster to ensure that technologies like vMotion work correctly. Consequently, PowerCLI is a great choice for this job because you can easily make each vSwitch consistent.

Apart from those switches that VMware refers to as internal (switches that are isolated from the physical network), each switch you create must be assigned to at least one network card. So, before creating your vSwitches, it's a good idea to know what network adapters are present in your host. You can use the Get-VMHostNetworkAdapter to examine this information:

```
Get-VMHost VIRTUESX2* | Get-VMHostNetworkAdapter
```

This code will give you output similar to the following. Hopefully, the information provided will be sufficient for you to identify which network cards should map to each of the vSwitches you have to create.

```
DeviceName Mac                     PortGroupname       vMotionEnabled
---------- ---                     -------------       --------------
vmnic0     00:22:32:fe:c4:25
vmnic1     00:22:32:fe:c4:27
vmnic2     00:2d:43:77:c5:b2
vmnic3     00:2d:43:77:b7:b5
vmnic4     00:2d:43:77:b7:b7
vmnic5     00:2d:43:77:b7:b9
vmk0       00:22:32:fe:c4:25 Management Network False
```

Sometimes further information is required, particularly if you need to liaise with a dedicated network team that manages the physical switches. It is possible to extract Cisco Discovery Protocol information from the ESX(i) host and pass it on to the network team, who can then help you assign the right NICs to the right vSwitches. The Get-HostDetailedNetworkInfo function retrieves this information for an individual host or all hosts in a cluster (Listing 3.3).

LISTING 3.3   Retrieving ESX(i) host networking information

```
function Get-HostDetailedNetworkInfo{
    <#
    .SYNOPSIS
        Retrieve ESX(i) Host Networking Info.
    .DESCRIPTION
        Retrieve ESX(i) Host Networking Info using CDP.
    .NOTES
        Source:  Automating vSphere Administration
        Authors: Luc Dekens, Arnim van Lieshout, Jonathan Medd,
                 Alan Renouf, Glenn Sizemore
    .PARAMETER VMHost
        Name of Host to Query
    .PARAMETER Cluster
        Name of Cluster to Query
    .PARAMETER Filename
        Name of File to Export
    .EXAMPLE
        Get-HostDetailedNetworkInfo -Cluster Cluster01 -Filename
        C:\Scripts\CDP.csv
    #>
    [CmdletBinding()]
    param(
        [String]
        $VMHost

    ,
        [String]
        $Cluster

    ,
        [parameter(Mandatory=$True
        ,    HelpMessage='Name of File to Export'
        )]
        [String]
        $filename

    )


    Write-Host "Gathering VMHost objects"

    if ($Cluster){
```

```
    $vmhosts = Get-Cluster $Cluster | Get-VMHost | Where-Object
    {$_.State -eq "Connected"} | Get-View
    }
else {
    $vmhosts = Get-VMHost $VMHost | Get-View
    }

$MyCol = @()
foreach ($vmwarehost in $vmhosts){
 $ESXHost = $vmwarehost.Name
 Write-Host "Collating information for $ESXHost"
 $networkSystem = Get-View
    $vmwarehost.ConfigManager.NetworkSystem
 foreach($pnic in $networkSystem.NetworkConfig.Pnic){
    $pnicInfo = $networkSystem.QueryNetworkHint($pnic.Device)
    foreach($Hint in $pnicInfo){
        $NetworkInfo = "" | Select-Object Host, PNic, Speed,
         MAC, DeviceID, PortID, Observed, VLAN
        $NetworkInfo.Host = $vmwarehost.Name
        $NetworkInfo.PNic = $Hint.Device
        $NetworkInfo.DeviceID = $Hint.connectedSwitchPort.DevId
        $NetworkInfo.PortID = $Hint.connectedSwitchPort.PortId
        $record = 0
Do{
 If ($Hint.Device -eq
    $vmwarehost.Config.Network.Pnic[$record].Device){
    $NetworkInfo.Speed =
     $vmwarehost.Config.Network.Pnic[$record].LinkSpeed.SpeedMb
    $NetworkInfo.MAC =
     $vmwarehost.Config.Network.Pnic[$record].Mac
        }
        $record ++
    }
 Until ($record -eq ($vmwarehost.Config.Network.Pnic.Length))
        foreach ($obs in $Hint.Subnet){
            $NetworkInfo.Observed += $obs.IpSubnet + " "
            Foreach ($VLAN in $obs.VlanId){
                If ($VLAN -eq $null){
                }
                Else{
```

```
                            $strVLAN = $VLAN.ToString()
                            $NetworkInfo.VLAN += $strVLAN + " "
                        }
                    }
                }
            $MyCol += $NetworkInfo
        }
    }
}
$Mycol | Sort-Object Host,PNic |
 Export-Csv $filename -NoTypeInformation


}
```

Typical output will be as shown in Figure 3.3.

FIGURE 3.3   Host detailed network info

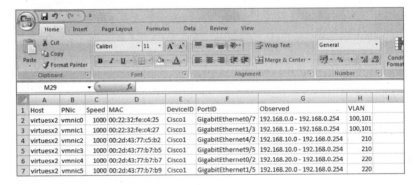

Now that you know which of your physical NICs should be allocated to which
vSwitch, it's time to start creating the switches. By default, an install of ESX(i) creates a virtual machine port group on the same vSwitch as the management NIC.
Since you will want to have NICs dedicated to virtual machine traffic, let's remove
it. Use the `Get-VirtualSwitch` cmdlet to retrieve the default `vSwitch0`, the
`Get-VirtualPortGroup` cmdlet to identify the default VM network port group,
and finally the `Remove-VirtualPortGroup` to remove it:

```
Get-VirtualSwitch -VMHost VIRTUESX2* -Name vSwitch0 |
 Get-VirtualPortGroup -Name "VM Network" |
 Remove-VirtualPortGroup -Confirm:$false
```

Now let's create a new vSwitch to serve virtual machines. In the code that follows, we used the -NumPorts parameter to allocate more ports than the default 64 and assigned the switches to vmnic4 and vmnic5 that we earlier identified as being allocated for this vSwitch:

```
$vSwitch = New-VirtualSwitch -VMHost VIRTUESX2* -Name "vSwitch2"
-NumPorts 256 -Nic vmnic4,vmnic5
```

We stored the result of the command to create the new switch in the $vSwitch variable so that it can be instantly reused in the next command to create a port group for that vSwitch:

```
New-VirtualPortGroup -VirtualSwitch $vSwitch -Name VM220
 -VLanId 220
```

TIP The technique we used for this last example, storing the results of an interactive command, is a good way to save time when you are working in the command shell. Rather than having to repeatedly type commands to work with the same object, you can return that object once and save it in an easily accessible variable for further use.

Adding VMkernel Port Groups

In addition to creating vSwitches and port groups for virtual machines, it is also highly likely that you will need to create VMkernel port groups for use with technologies like vMotion or fault tolerance. As mentioned earlier, VMkernel port groups also are a requirement for iSCSI or NFS storage.

Let's create a VMkernel port group for vMotion; we'll create it as an additional port group for vSwitch0 (you'll see why in the next section when we look at making switches and port groups resilient). In the code that follows, we retrieve vSwitch0 from the variable $vSwitch0. Next, we supply it to the New-VMHostNetwork Adapter to create the port group for vMotion by setting the VMotionEnabled parameter to $true.

```
$vSwitch0 = Get-VirtualSwitch -VMHost VIRTUESX2*
  -Name "vSwitch0"
New-VMHostNetworkAdapter -VMHost VIRTUESX2
  -PortGroup "vMotion"
  -VirtualSwitch $vSwitch0
  -IP 192.168.1.10
  -SubnetMask 255.255.255.0
  -VMotionEnabled:$true
```

Hopefully in your environment, a separate VLAN will be used for vMotion network traffic. To configure the VLAN for the vMotion port group you just created, use the `Set-VirtualPortGroup` cmdlet:

```
$VMotionPG = Get-VirtualPortgroup -VMHost VIRTUESX2*
  -Name vMotion
Set-VirtualPortGroup -VirtualPortGroup $VMotionPG -VLanId 101
```

The process for creating a VMkernel port group for IP-based storage is almost identical. Simply drop the `-VMotionEnabled` parameter from the command used to create the vMotion port group:

```
$vSwitch1 = Get-VirtualSwitch -VMHost VIRTUESX2*
  -Name "vSwitch1"
New-VMHostNetworkAdapter -VMHost VIRTUESX2
  -PortGroup "iSCSI"
  -VirtualSwitch $vSwitch0
  -IP 192.168.20.50
  -SubnetMask 255.255.255.0
```

ESX(i) differs from ESX in that ESX(i) has a VMkernel port group by default; the management network created during installation is a VMkernel port group. While this could be used to connect to iSCSI or NFS storage for testing or low-use purposes, we do not recommend it for production use where dedicated NICs should be used.

Making Your Switches and Port Groups Resilient

In the previous section, you created a vMotion port group. You added it to the existing `vSwitch0`, which already hosts the management network port group and has one NIC assigned, `vmnic0`. Obviously, as a good IT professional you need a plan for those times when things go wrong. So, allocating only one NIC to this configuration is not a very good idea. A better practice for this scenario is to add an additional NIC to the switch for resiliency. Better still, configure `vmnic0` as the active adapter for the management network and standby adapter for the vMotion network, and vice versa for `vmnic1`.

The function `Set-ManagementAndvMotionRedundant` takes input of the host, the names of management and vMotion networks, and the NICs to use, and then sets the first NIC as the active adapter for the management network and standby adapter for the vMotion network, and vice versa for the second NIC (Listing 3.4).

LISTING 3.4   Adding resiliency to the management and vMotion port groups

```
function Set-ManagementAndvMotionResilient{

    <#
    .SYNOPSIS
        Add resiliency to Management and vMotion Port Groups.
    .DESCRIPTION
        Add resiliency to Management and vMotion Port Groups.
    .NOTES
        Source:  Automating vSphere Administration
        Authors: Luc Dekens, Arnim van Lieshout, Jonathan Medd,
                 Alan Renouf, Glenn Sizemore
    .PARAMETER VMHost
        Name of Host to configure
    .PARAMETER Management
        Name of Management Network Port Group
    .PARAMETER vMotion
        Name of vMotion Port Group
    .PARAMETER NIC0
      Name of first NIC to use
    .PARAMETER NIC1
      Name of second NIC to use
    .EXAMPLE
        Set-ManagementAndvMotionResilient -VMhost Server01
        -Management 'Management Network'
        -vMotion vMotion -NIC0 vmnic0 -NIC1 vmnic4
    #>

    [CmdletBinding()]
    Param(
        [parameter(Mandatory=$True
        ,     HelpMessage='Name of Host to configure'
        )]
        [String]
        $VMHost

        [String]
        $Management = 'Management Network'
```

Install, Configure, and
Manage the vSphere
Environment

PART I

```
          ,
              [String]
              $vMotion = 'vMotion'

          ,
              [String]
              $NIC0 = 'vmnic0'

          ,
              [String]
              $NIC1 = 'vmnic1'
          )



    $ManagementNetworkPG = Get-VirtualPortgroup -VMHost $VMHost
     -Name $Management
    $VMotionPG = Get-VirtualPortgroup -VMHost $VMHost -Name $vMotion


    $ManagementNetworkPG | Get-NicTeamingPolicy |
     Set-NicTeamingPolicy -MakeNicActive $NIC0
    $ManagementNetworkPG | Get-NicTeamingPolicy |
     Set-NicTeamingPolicy -MakeNicStandby $NIC1


    $VMotionPG | Get-NicTeamingPolicy | Set-NicTeamingPolicy
     -MakeNicActive $NIC1
    $VMotionPG | Get-NicTeamingPolicy | Set-NicTeamingPolicy
     -MakeNicStandby $NIC0


    }
```

Copying Networking Configuration from Another Host

When working with multiple ESX(i) hosts in a cluster, you must verify that the configuration of vSwitches and port groups is consistent and accurate across all hosts. This ensures that vMotion is possible for all virtual machines across all hosts in the cluster. If port groups are slightly misspelled across hosts, the wrong VLAN ID is entered for one port group, or maybe even a port group is missed, then you are going to have issues.

The larger the environment, the more likely it is that multiple vSwitches and port groups will be required per host. Configuration of these elements through the vSphere Client is laborious, tedious, and liable to lead to costly mistakes. vSphere 4 introduced a new feature, host profiles, to help with this configuration, but again it is only available with Enterprise Plus licensing. So the `Copy-HostNetworking` function enables you to specify source and target ESX(i) hosts. The vSwitches and port groups then are copied from the source host and created on the target host.

During the creation of each vSwitch, you will be prompted for two NICs to add to the vSwitch. This allows for the possibility that the same physical NICs on different hosts are not always patched into the same VLAN, so they can be specified during the running of the function. We have assumed two NICs per vSwitch; you can simply adjust this for your environment if necessary (Listing 3.5).

LISTING 3.5   **Copying switches and port groups from one host to another**

```
function Copy-HostNetworking{

    <#
    .SYNOPSIS
        Copy Switches and Port Groups from one host to another.
    .DESCRIPTION
        Copy Switches and Port Groups from one host to another.
    .NOTES
        Source:  Automating vSphere Administration
        Authors: Luc Dekens, Arnim van Lieshout, Jonathan Medd,
                 Alan Renouf, Glenn Sizemore
    .PARAMETER Source
        Name of Host to copy networking from
    .PARAMETER Target
        Name of Host to copy networking to
    .EXAMPLE
        Copy-HostNetworking -Source Server01 -Target Server02
    #>

    [CmdletBinding()]
    Param(
        [parameter(Mandatory=$True
        ,    HelpMessage='Name of Host to copy networking from'
        )]
        [String]
        $Source

        ,

        [parameter(Mandatory=$True
```

```
        ,       HelpMessage='Name of Host to copy networking to'
    )]
    [String]
    $Target
)


$SourceHost = Get-VMHost $Source
$TargetHost = Get-VMHost $Target

$SourceHost | Get-VirtualSwitch | Where-Object {$_.name -ne
  "vSwitch0"} | Foreach {
If (($TargetHost | Get-VirtualSwitch -Name $_.Name
  -ErrorAction SilentlyContinue) -eq $null){
Write-Host "Creating Virtual Switch $($_.Name)"
$NewSwitch = $TargetHost | New-VirtualSwitch -Name $_.Name
  -NumPorts $_.NumPorts -Mtu $_.Mtu
$vSwitch = $_
[console]::ForegroundColor = "Yellow"
$FirstNIC = Read-Host "Please enter the name of the first
  NIC for $NewSwitch , e.g. vmnic1"
$SecondNIC = Read-Host "Please enter the name of the second
  NIC for $NewSwitch , e.g. vmnic2"
[console]::ResetColor()
$NewSwitch | Set-VirtualSwitch -Nic $FirstNIC,$SecondNIC
}
$_ | Get-VirtualPortGroup | Foreach {
If (($TargetHost | Get-VirtualPortGroup -Name $_.Name
  -ErrorAction SilentlyContinue) -eq $null){
Write-Host "Creating Portgroup $($_.Name)"
$NewPortGroup = $TargetHost | Get-VirtualSwitch -Name
  $vSwitch | New-VirtualPortGroup
    -Name $_.Name -VLanId $_.VLanID
      }
  }
}
}
```

Everything we have done so far has been for a single host. However, it will be very straightforward to build on what you have learned and apply that to multiple hosts.

You've seen how simple it is to extract networking information from a host, or create vSwitches and port groups and apply redundancy to them. All it would take would be a simple `foreach` loop with a list of servers to automate these tasks across multiple hosts.

Typically, a lot of the networking topics we have covered so far are carried out during the build of a host and not altered much during its lifetime. So, why not build up the networking cmdlets and functions into a sequence of tasks and add them to a script for postconfiguration tasks of a newly built host? That way, a lot of time can be saved in the deployment process and consistency of configuration can be guaranteed.

Moving Multiple VMs to a New Port Group

A common admin task is the need to move VMs from one port group to another. Maybe there are behind-the-scenes networking changes that involve a redesign of the network or a change to VLANs. The `Move-ToNewPortGroup` function takes source and target port groups as input, finds each VM in the source port group, and moves them to the new port group (Listing 3.6).

LISTING 3.6   Moving VMs from one port group to another

```
function Move-ToNewPortGroup{

    <#
    .SYNOPSIS
        Move VMs from one Port Group to another.
    .DESCRIPTION
        Move VMs from one Port Group to another.
    .NOTES
        Source:  Automating vSphere Administration
        Authors: Luc Dekens, Arnim van Lieshout, Jonathan Medd,
                 Alan Renouf, Glenn Sizemore
    .PARAMETER Source
        Name of Port Group to move from
    .PARAMETER Target
        Name of Port Group to move to
    .PARAMETER Cluster
        Name of Cluster containing VMs
    .EXAMPLE
        Move-ToNewPortGroup -Source PortGroup01 -Target
```

```
      PortGroup02 -Cluster Cluster01
#>
[CmdletBinding()]
Param(
     [parameter(Mandatory=$True
     ,     HelpMessage='Name of Port Group to move from'
     )]
     [String]
     $Source

     [parameter(Mandatory=$True
     ,     HelpMessage='Name of Port Group to move to'
     )]
     [String]
     $Target

  [String]
     $Cluster
)


$SourceNetwork = $Source
$TargetNetwork = $Target

if ($Cluster){
Get-Cluster $Cluster | Get-VM | Get-NetworkAdapter |
 Where-Object {$_.NetworkName -eq $SourceNetwork } |
 Set-NetworkAdapter -NetworkName $TargetNetwork
 -Confirm:$false
 }
 else {
Get-VM | Get-NetworkAdapter | Where-Object {$_.NetworkName
 -eq $SourceNetwork } | Set-NetworkAdapter -NetworkName
   $TargetNetwork -Confirm:$false
 }
}
```

A similar admin task is to rename a port group. If you carry out this task in the vSphere Client, then any VM with a connection to that port group will appear to be disconnected from the vSwitch. This will have no immediate impact to a running

VM, however upon restart of the VM its NIC would be disconnected; consequently it would not be able to communicate on the network. However, now that the Move -ToNewPortGroup function is available, you can be smart and also use this function to rename a port group, albeit indirectly. All you need to do is create a new port group with the new name for the port group, and then move the VMs from the old to the new port group.

You can also use the Move-ToNewPortGroup function to migrate VMs from a standard vSwitch to a new distributed vSwitch. In fact, it is no different from moving between two standard vSwitches:

```
Move-ToNewPortGroup -Source StandardPortGroup01 -Target
    DistributedPortGroup01 -Cluster Cluster01
```

Install, Configure, and
Manage the vSphere
Environment

PART I

Using Advanced vSphere Features

IN THIS CHAPTER, YOU WILL LEARN TO:

S o far in this book, vSphere 4.1 has proven to be *the* virtualization platform. This chapter focuses on automating some of the most advanced features vSphere offers. With the exception of the Distributed Power Management features, an Enterprise Plus license is required to utilize these features.

Manage vNetwork Distributed Switches

The vNetwork Distributed Switch (vDS) was first introduced in vSphere 4.0. The main feature of the vDS is the central point of management. vDS moves the configuration and control of the network to a top-level vCenter Server object. Because statistics are kept in the vCenter Server database and aren't lost during a vMotion, you have the benefit of greater tracking and analysis. Unfortunately, as of this writing VMware has yet to integrate vDS management into PowerCLI. Fortunately for you, we didn't wait for them! The next section will make use of a custom PowerCLI module, which you can download from www.sybex.com/go/vmwarevspherepowercliref.

If you're accustomed to using a vNetwork Standard Switch (vSS), the vDS can take a little getting used to. The biggest challenge is disassociating the network from the vSphere host. Previously, you would have to connect to each host one at a time. This process could be automated with PowerCLI, but still the level and potential for mistakes made the vSS less than optimal.

Let's take a look at the two processes. To configure a network using a vSS, follow these steps:

1. Create a vSS.

2. Add uplinks to the vSS.

3. Create the port groups.

4. Create the VMkernel ports.

With the new model using the vDS, the configuration now requires the following steps:

1. Create a vDS.

2. Configure the vDS uplink ports.

3. Create the vDS port groups.

4. Create the VMkernel ports.

5. Add the vSphere hosts to the vDS binding your physical NIC (pNIC) to a vDS uplink port.

Wait a second! That's even more steps. How is that easier?

Well, let's compare the steps needed to add a new VM port group to an existing switch using vSS with the steps needed using vDS. For a vSS system, you must complete the following:

1. Get the targeted vSS object.

2. Create a new port group.

3. Repeat steps 1 and 2 for each VMHost.

To add a VM port group to a vDS system, you need only complete two steps:

1. Get the targeted vDS switch.

2. Create the vDS port group.

All that and we removed one measly step? Yes, but the step we removed was the source of many unplanned outages over the years. By making the change once, you allow vCenter Server to ensure the VM port group is configured prior to binding a host. Making the change once ensures that you won't accidentally vMotion a VM to a host with a mistyped VLAN ID. This may sound like a small thing—you could use PowerCLI to automate certain steps and avoid those shortcomings. But take our word for it, this is a huge addition!

Now that we've briefly covered one small advantage a vDS offers, let's build one. First, download the DistributedSwitch PowerCLI module (DistributedSwitch.psm1) from www.sybex.com/go/vmwarevspherepowercliref, copy it to your system, and then load it. Once you load the module, you can take advantage of the custom functions we designed. Use the Import-Module cmdlet to load the module:

```
Import-Module "<Path to file>\DistributedSwitch.psm1"
```

With the DistributedSwitch PowerCLI module loaded, the code in Listing 4.1 will produce a new vDS built to the following specifications:

▶ Datacenter: PROD01

▶ Number of ports: 64

▶ Uplink ports: 4

LISTING 4.1   Creating a new vDS

```
$Datacenter = Get-Datacenter -Name 'PROD01'
New-DistributedSwitch -Name PROD01-vDS01 `
    -Datacenter $Datacenter `
        -NumberOfUplinks 4
```

So far, so good. Next, add a Distributed Virtual Port Group (DVPG) to the vDS you created with Listing 4.1. Listing 4.2 will create the following DVPG:

- Name: dvPG01
- Number of ports: 128
- VLAN: 42

LISTING 4.2　Creating a new DVPG

```
New-DistributedSwitchPortGroup -Name dvPG01 `
    -NumberOfPorts 128 `
    -VLAN 42 `
    -DistributedSwitch 'PROD01-vDS01'
```

You could configure additional information on the vDS and DVPG, but let's skip to the end and reveal the true power here! The code in Listing 4.3 will create a complete vDS that consists of the following:

vDS01

- Atlanta datacenter
- 6 uplinks
- Cisco Discovery Protocol (CDP) enabled, and set to Both
- Administrator: Glenn Sizemore
- Administrator Contact: Glenn.Sizemore@mailinator.com
- Virtual port groups
  - vDS01-VLAN22
    - 256 Ports
    - VLAN: 22
    - Network I/O control enabled
    - Disable Promiscuous mode, Mac Address Changes, and Forged Transmits
  - vDS01-Trunk01
    - 128 Ports
    - VLANs: 7, 19, 25–28
    - Network I/O control enabled

▶ vDS01-10.10.10.0

  ▶ 128 ports

  ▶ Private VLAN 108

  ▶ Uplink ports 1, 4

LISTING 4.3   **Provisioning a complete vDS**

```
#Create and configure our new vDS
$vDS = Get-Datacenter -name 'ATL-PROD'|
    New-DistributedSwitch -Name 'vDS01' `
        -NumberOfUplinks 6 |
        Set-DistributedSwitch -LinkDiscoveryProtocol 'cdp' `
            -LinkDiscoveryOperation 'both' `
            -ContactName 'Glenn Sizemore' `
            -ContactInfo 'Glenn.Sizemore@mailinator.com' `
            -Description 'Atlanta Datacenter Production vSwitch'
# a regular DVPG
$vDS | New-DistributedSwitchPortGroup -Name 'vDS01-VLAN22' `
        -VLAN 22 |
    Set-DistributedSwitchPortGroup -NumberOfPorts 256 `
        -PromiscuousMode $false `
        -MacAddressChanges $False `
        -ForgedTransmits $false `
        -LoadBalancing 'loadbalance_loadbased' `
        -ActiveDVUplinks DVUplink2,DVUplink3,DVUplink5,DVUplink6
# Trunked DVPG
$vDS | New-DistributedSwitchPortGroup -Name 'vDS01-Trunk01' `
        -VLANTrunkRange '7,19,25-28' |
    Set-DistributedSwitchPortGroup -NumberOfPorts 128 `
        -LoadBalancing 'loadbalance_loadbased' `
        -ActiveDVUplinks DVUplink2,DVUplink3,DVUplink5,DVUplink6
# Private VLAN
$vDS | New-DistributedSwitchPrivateVLAN -PrimaryVLanID 108 |
    New-DistributedSwitchPortGroup -Name 'vDS01-10.10.10.0' `
        -PrivateVLAN 108|
    Set-DistributedSwitchPortGroup -NumberOfPorts 128 `
        -ActiveDVUplinks DVUplink1,DVUplink4
```

The only thing left is to assign hosts to the DVUplink ports and you're ready to host VMs. To do this, first test a given host for compatibility. To assist in this task, you can enlist the `Get-DistributedSwitchCandidate` function included in the DistributedSwitch module. For this exercise, we're interested in any VMHost in the Atlanta production datacenter that is capable of being added to our new vDS (Listing 4.4).

LISTING 4.4   **Finding vDS VMHost candidates**

```
[vSphere PowerCLI] C:\> Get-Datacenter -Name 'ATL-PROD' |
    Get-DistributedSwitchCandidate -DistributedSwitch vDS01
```

Name	State	PowerState	Id	CpuUsage Mhz	CpuTotal Mhz
----	-----	----------	--	--------	--------
vsphere01.ge...	Connected	PoweredOn	...-102	42	5338
vsphere02.ge...	Connected	PoweredOn	...-104	77	5338

The code in Listing 4.4 successfully located two vSphere hosts that can be added to our new vDS. Next, identify the pNIC that will bind to the vDS uplinks. To assist with this task and to enable you to programmatically assign the pNIC, use the `Get-VMHostPnic` function in Listing 4.5.

LISTING 4.5   **The `Get-VMHostPnic` function**

```
Function Get-VMHostPnic
{
    [CmdletBinding()]
    Param(
      [Parameter(Mandatory=$true,
          ValueFromPipeline=$true)]
      [VMware.VimAutomation.ViCore.Impl.V1.Inventory.VMHostImpl]
      $VMhost
    , [Parameter()]
      [Switch]
      $UnAssigned
    , [Parameter()]
      [Switch]
      $Assigned
    )
    Begin
    {
        If ($Assigned)        {
```

```
                    $Filter = {$usedPNics[$Pnic.key]}
            }
        ElseIF ($Unassigned){
                $Filter = {-Not $usedPNics[$Pnic.key]}
        }
        Else                  {
                $filter = {$True}
        }
    }
Process
{

    $VMHost | Get-view -Property 'Config.Network'|
    ForEach-Object {
        $UsedPnics = @{}
        Foreach ($Switch in $_.Config.Network.ProxySwitch)
        {
            If ($switch.Pnic)
            {
                Foreach ($Pnic in $switch.Pnic)
                {
                    $UsedPnics.add($Pnic,$switch.DvsName)
                }
            }
        }
        Foreach ($Switch in $_.Config.Network.Vswitch )
        {
            If ($switch.Pnic)
            {
                Foreach ($Pnic in $switch.Pnic)
                {
                    $UsedPnics.add($Pnic,$switch.Name)
                }
            }
        }
        Foreach ($Pnic in $_.Config.Network.Pnic)
        {
            IF (&$Filter)
            {
                New-Object PSObject -Property @{
```

```
                                    Pnic = $Pnic.Device
                                    Switch = $usedPNics[$Pnic.key]
                                    Driver = $Pnic.Driver
                                    VMHost = $VMhost
                                }
                            }
                        }
                    }
                }
            }
```

Using the `Get-VMHostPnic` function, you can quickly obtain pNICs-to-vSS/vDS mappings, as seen here:

```
[vSphere PowerCLI] C:\> Get-VMHostPnic -UnAssigned `
    -VMhost (Get-VMhost vSphere01*)


Name    Switch Driver VMHost
----    ------ ------ ------
vmnic2         e1000  vsphere01.getadmin.local
vmnic3         e1000  vsphere01.getadmin.local
```

Now you're ready to add your hosts. To accomplish this task, use the `Add -DistributedSwitchVMHost` function, shown in Listing 4.6, to add the following:

▶ VMHost: vSphere01

▶ pNIC: vmnic2, vmnic3

▶ vDS: vDS01

LISTING 4.6   Adding a VMHost to a vDS

```
Get-VMhost "vSphere01*" |
    Add-DistributedSwitchVMHost -DistributedSwitch vDS01 `
        -Pnic vmnic2,vmnic3
```

There you have it—from nothing to a vDS ready to host VMs. Now, if you're think-ing, "I bet that could all be combined into one step," you'd be right! Listing 4.7 takes the vDS provisioning to the very end and in one script creates and provisions a vDS.

LISTING 4.7   Fully provisioning the vDS

```
#Create and configure our new vDS
$Datacenter = Get-Datacenter -name 'ATL-PROD'
$vDS = New-DistributedSwitch -Name 'vDS01' `
```

```
    -Datacenter $Datacenter `
    -NumberOfUplinks 6 |
    Set-DistributedSwitch -LinkDiscoveryProtocol 'cdp' `
        -LinkDiscoveryOperation 'both' `
        -ContactName 'Glenn Sizemore' `
        -ContactInfo 'Glenn.Sizemore@mailinator.com' `
        -Description 'Atlanta Datacenter Production vSwitch'
# a regular DVPG
$vDS | New-DistributedSwitchPortGroup -Name 'vDS01-VLAN22' `
    -VLAN 22 |
    Set-DistributedSwitchPortGroup -NumberOfPorts 256 `
        -PromiscuousMode $false `
        -MacAddressChanges $False `
        -ForgedTransmits $false `
        -LoadBalancing 'loadbalance_loadbased' `
        -ActiveDVUplinks DVUplink2,DVUplink3,DVUplink5,DVUplink6
# Trunked DVPG
$vDS | New-DistributedSwitchPortGroup -Name 'vDS01-Trunk01' `
    -VLANTrunkRange '7,19,25-28' |
    Set-DistributedSwitchPortGroup -NumberOfPorts 128 `
        -LoadBalancing 'loadbalance_loadbased' `
        -ActiveDVUplinks DVUplink2,DVUplink3,DVUplink5,DVUplink6
# Private VLAN
$vDS | New-DistributedSwitchPrivateVLAN -PrimaryVLanID 108 |
    New-DistributedSwitchPortGroup -Name 'vDS01-10.10.10.0' `
        -PrivateVLAN 108 |
    Set-DistributedSwitchPortGroup -NumberOfPorts 128 `
        -ActiveDVUplinks DVUplink1,DVUplink4
# add hosts
Get-DistributedSwitchCandidate -DistributedSwitch vDS01 `
        -VIObject $Datacenter |
    ForEach-Object {
        $PNICs = Get-VMHostPnic -VMhost $_ -UnAssigned |
            Select-Object -ExpandProperty Pnic
        IF ($PNICs)
        {
            Add-DistributedSwitchVMHost -VMhost $_ `
                -DistributedSwitch vDS01 `
                -Pnic $PNICs
        }
    }
```

For some reason, VMware decided to provide separate APIs for addition and modification. Therefore, the `Add-DistributedSwitchVMHost` function can only be used on a VMHost that isn't already part of the targeted vDS. If you wish to modify the pNIC mappings after the fact, you'll need to use the `Set-DistributedSwitchVMHost` function, as shown in Listing 4.8.

LISTING 4.8   Modifying an existing vDS-to-VMHost pNIC mapping

```
#Change an existing
Set-DistributedSwitchVMHost -VMhost $vmhost `
    -DistributedSwitch vDS01 `
    -Pnic vmnic0,vmnic2
#Remove all Pnic Mappings
Set-DistributedSwitchVMHost -VMhost $vmhost `
    -DistributedSwitch vDS01 `
    -Pnic ""
```

If you need to remove a host completely, you can do so with the `Remove-DistributedSwitchVMHost` function (Listing 4.9). You can remove a host (in our example, vSphere01) completely from the distributed switch (vDS01). This function is especially handy if you're trying to remove a vSphere host from vCenter Server.

LISTING 4.9   Removing a VMHost from a vDS

```
Remove-DistributedSwitchVMHost -VMhost (Get-VMHost vSphere01*) `
-DistributedSwitch vDS01
```

So, what about VMkernel network adapters in a DVPG? While a little more complicated than their vSS cousins, not only can they be used, but they can also be automated using PowerCLI. In Listing 4.10, we created a new vDS network adapter that meets the following specifications:

- ► vDS: vDS01

- ► DVPG: vMotion

- ► vSphere host: vSphere01.vSphere.local

- ► IP: 192.168.2.40/24

- ► vMotion enabled

LISTING 4.10   Creating network adapters on a DVPG

```
$DVPG = New-DistributedSwitchPortGroup -Name vMotion `
    -VLAN 853 `
    -DistributedSwitch vDS01
$vmhost = Get-VMHost vSphere01*
$vDS = Get-DistributedSwitch -Name 'vDS01'
New-DistributedSwitchNetworkAdapter -VMHost $vmhost -EA Inquire `
    -PortGroup 'vMotion'`
    -DistributedSwitch $vDS `
    -IP '192.168.2.40' `
    -SubnetMask '255.255.255.0' `
    -vmotion
```

As you can see, the process of creating DVPG network adapters is a little more involved. You need quite a few bits of information before anything can be done. The good news is that, once you create them, follow-on management is quite simple. All you need is the network adapter object, as Listing 4.11 shows.

LISTING 4.11   Getting the existing VMHost vDS network adapter

```
Get-DistributedSwitchNetworkAdapter -VMHost $vmhost `
    -PortGroup 'vMotion' `
    -DistributedSwitch 'vDS01'
```

```
Key                    : vmk1
Ip                     : VMware.Vim.HostIpConfig
Mac                    : 00:50:56:7f:85:27
DistributedVirtualPort : VMware.Vim.DistributedVirtualSwitchP…
Portgroup              :
Mtu                    : 1500
TsoEnabled             : True
DynamicType            :
DynamicProperty        :
```

Once you have the network adapter object, you can easily manage any aspect of the VMkernel using the `Set-DistributedSwitchNetworkAdapter` function. In Listing 4.12, we changed an existing network adapter to use DHCP.

LISTING 4.12   Changing the vDS network adapter to use DHCP

```
$NetworkAdapter = Get-DistributedSwitchNetworkAdapter `
    -VMHost $vmhost `
    -PortGroup 'vMotion' `
    -DistributedSwitch 'vDS01'

Set-DistributedSwitchNetworkAdapter -VMHost $vmhost `
    -IPv4DHCP `
    -key $NetworkAdapter.key `
    -NetworkAdapter $NetworkAdapter
```

You will quickly realize the power these functions provide when you have to do something such as enable FT logging on a VMkernel network adapter across an entire cluster. As shown in Listing 4.13, even this task is a snap in PowerCLI.

LISTING 4.13   Enabling FT logging across a cluster

```
Foreach ($VMhost in (Get-Cluster Prod01|Get-VMHost))
{
    Get-DistributedSwitchNetworkAdapter `
        -VMHost $vmhost `
        -PortGroup 'vMotion' `
        -DistributedSwitch 'vDS01' |
        Set-DistributedSwitchNetworkAdapter `
            -FaultToleranceLoggingEnabled $true `
            -VMHost $vmhost
}
```

Removing an existing vDS network adapter is also a snap. Similar to Listing 4.10, where you added a VMkernel network adapter, to remove one you simply provide the following:

- ▶ The VMHost from which to delete the adapter

- ▶ The port group from which to delete the adapter

- ▶ The vDS that the port group resides on

Then, as it did when you created a new network adapter, PowerCLI will find the port in question—only this time it will delete the adapter (Listing 4.14).

LISTING 4.14   Removing an existing vDS network adapter

```
Remove-DistributedSwitchNetworkAdapter
    -VMHost $VMhost
    -PortGroup 'vMotion'
    -DistributedSwitch 'vDS01'
```

We're confident you'll find the vDS to be a key component in your virtual infra-structure, and now you can automate every aspect of that component!

Use Fault Tolerance

VMware Fault Tolerance (FT) was first introduced with vSphere 4.0. FT is an extension of VMware High Availability (HA) that enables guaranteed zero downtime. At a high level, it works by creating a second VM on a compatible vSphere host and replicates every external input to the CPU from the primary VM to the secondary VM. This results in the processors executing the same internal code on a per-instruction basis. Then, if the primary VM dies for any reason, the secondary VM continues executing and picks up where the primary left off. The operating system has no knowledge that it just blinked and awakened on a different physical host. More importantly, your users won't know either. So, how do you enable this uptime pixie dust? In PowerCLI, it's one line (see Listing 4.15).

LISTING 4.15   Enabling FT

```
$VM = Get-VM -Name 'HVMIC'
$VM.ExtensionData.CreateSecondaryVM_Task($Null)
```

Optionally, you could even designate which VMHost the secondary VM is created on by suppling the VMHost's managed object reference, or MoRef (see Listing 4.16).

LISTING 4.16   Specifying where the secondary VM should be created

```
$VMHost = Get-VMHost -Name 'vSphere01*'
$VM = Get-VM -Name 'HVMIC'
$VM.ExtensionData.CreateSecondaryVM_Task($VMHost.Id)
```

As you've seen, it's simple to enable FT and it's just as simple to disable, as Listing 4.17 shows.

LISTING 4.17 Disabling FT

```
$VM = Get-VM -Name 'HVMIC'
$VM.ExtensionData.TurnOffFaultToleranceForVM()
```

You will find that this highly protected state carries with it some baggage. For instance, you can't do anything to a VM while it's protected with FT. You have to follow these steps:

1. Disable FT on the VM.

2. Make the change (virtual hardware, SVMotion, VCB).

3. Enable FT on the VM.

Fortunately, it's relativity easy to wrap the whole change in a PowerCLI script. In Listing 4.18, we changed the RAM allocation on an FT-protected VM.

LISTING 4.18 Modifying FT protected VMs

```
# Get the VM
$VM = Get-VM -Name 'HVMIC'
# Disable FT
$VM.ExtensionData.TurnOffFaultToleranceForVM()
# Add memory
Set-VM -VM $VM -MemoryMB 4096 -Confirm:$false
# Enable FT
$vm.ExtensionData.CreateSecondaryVM_Task($Null)
```

We don't feel FT replaces the need for application-level redundancy. However, when you have to maintain a level of availability with an application that wasn't designed with uptime in mind, FT is an excellent option. If you choose to enable FT in your virtual environment, PowerCLI is the glue that allows you to manage FT-protected VMs at scale.

Configure Storage I/O Control

As of vSphere 4.1, the default storage share allocation is by host. This means that if you have two hosts in a cluster, each host is allocated 50 percent of the available storage array queue. This allocation is done regardless of the actual load on the host. As you can imagine, this allocation results in potential performance issues. Storage

I/O control (SIOC) addresses this potential shortcoming. SIOC enables vSphere to assign shares across physical hosts (see Figure 4.1).

FIGURE 4.1   SOIC enables vSphere to assign shares across physical hosts.

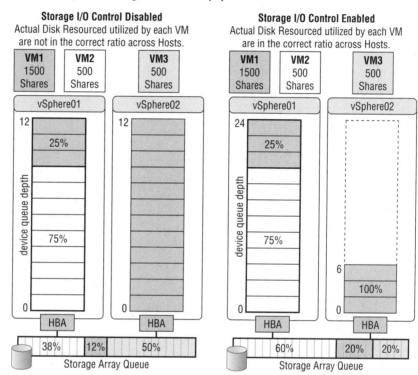

SIOC uses the average latency of all virtual disks across a VMFS datastore to calculate latency. This average is then weighted by the number of input/output operations per second (IOPs). When this weighted latency goes above the configured threshold, SIOC limits throughput to the array by resizing the device queue. Therefore, SIOC only kicks in during times of congestion. Unfortunately, because SIOC uses the device queue to restrict throughput, SIOC is not supported on NFS datastores. So, how can you determine if your environment supports this magic sauce? Listing 4.19 contains a function that reports the status of SIOC for any vSphere host or datastore.

LISTING 4.19   The Get-SIOC function

```
function Get-SIOC
{
  param(
```

```
    [parameter(
      ParameterSetName = "VMHost"
    ,   valuefrompipeline = $true
    ,   position = 0
    ,   HelpMessage = "Enter a host"
    )]
    [VMware.VimAutomation.ViCore.Impl.V1.Inventory.VMHostImpl[]]
    $VMHost
    ,
    [parameter(
      ParameterSetName = "Datastore"
    ,   valuefrompipeline = $true
    ,   position = 0
    ,   HelpMessage = "Enter a datastore"
    )]
    [VMware.VimAutomation.ViCore.Impl.V1.DatastoreManagement.➥
DatastoreImpl[]]
    $Datastore
  )
  process
  {
    switch($PsCmdlet.ParameterSetName)
    {
      "VMHost"
      {
        $si = Get-View 'ServiceInstance'
        $VimService = $si.Client.VimService
        Foreach ($vmh in $VMHost)
        {
          $result =$VimService.QueryIORMConfigOption(`
            [VMWare.Vim.VIConvert]::ToVim41(`
              $si.Content.StorageResourceManager),
            [VMWare.Vim.VIConvert]::ToVim41(`
              $vmh.Extensiondata.MoRef))
          $enabled = $result.enabledOption
          $Threshold = $result.congestionThresholdOption
          New-Object PSObject -Property @{
            'Name' = $vmh.Name
```

```
                        'SIOCSupported' = $enabled.supported
                        'SIOCStateDefault' = $enabled.defaultValue
                        'SIOCThresholdMinimum' = $Threshold.min
                        'SIOCThresholdMaximum' = $Threshold.max
                        'SIOCThresholdDefault' = $Threshold.defaultValue
                    }
                }
            }
            "Datastore"
            {
                Foreach ($ds in $DataStore)
                {
                    $iorm = $ds.Extensiondata.iormConfiguration
                    $cap = $ds.ExtensionData.Capability
                    New-Object PSObject -Property @{
                        'Name' = $Ds.Name
                        'SIOCEnabled' = $iorm.enabled
                        'SIOCThreshold' = `
                            $iorm.congestionThreshold
                        'SIOCSupported' = $cap.StorageIORMSupported
                    }
                }
            }
        }
    }
}
```

Using Get-SIOC, you can quickly determine if you have any hosts that do not support SIOC by running the following command:

```
Get-VMHost | Get-SIOC | Where-Object {-Not $_.SIOCSupported}
```

You could also quickly identify any datastores that support SIOC but don't have it enabled yet:

```
Get-Datastore | Get-Sioc |
    Where-Object {$_.SIOCSupported -And -Not $_.SIOCEnabled}
```

We used the word *yet* as there is no reason to not enable SIOC. Listing 4.20 simplifies the task of enabling SIOC.

LISTING 4.20 The Set-SIOC function

```
Function Set-SIOC
{
  [cmdletBinding(SupportsShouldProcess=$true)]
  param(
    [parameter(
        valuefrompipeline = $true
    ,   valuefrompipelinebypropertyname=$true
    ,   HelpMessage = "Enter a datastore"
    )]
    [VMware.VimAutomation.ViCore.Impl.V1.DatastoreManagement.➡
DatastoreImpl[]]
    $Datastore

  ,
    [parameter(
        valuefrompipelinebypropertyname=$true
    ,   HelpMessage = "Enter a datastore name"
    )]
    [string]
    $Name

  ,
    [parameter(
        valuefrompipeline = $true
    ,   valuefrompipelinebypropertyname=$true
    )]
    [Alias("SIOCEnabled")]
    [bool]
    $Enabled

  ,
    [parameter(
        valuefrompipeline = $true
    ,   valuefrompipelinebypropertyname=$true
    ,   HelpMessage='The latency in ms beyond which the storage➡
array is considered congested'
    )]
    [Alias("SIOCThreshold")]
    [ValidateRange(10,100)]
    [int]
```

```
    $Threshold = 30
)
process
{
    If ($name)
    {
        Try
        {
            $Datastore += Get-Datastore -Name $Name -EA Stop
        }
        Catch
        {
            Write-Warning "$Name not found!"
            continue;
        }
    }
    If ($Enabled)
    {
        $Msg = "Enabling SIOC"
    }
    else
    {
        $Msg = "Disabling SIOC (WHY?!?)"
    }
    $msg = "{0} and setting the threshold t0 {1}" -f `
        $msg,$Threshold
    $si = Get-View ServiceInstance
    $VimService = $si.Client.VimService
    $spec = New-Object VMware.Vim.StorageIORMConfigSpec
    $spec.congestionThreshold = $Threshold
    $spec.enabled = $Enabled
    Foreach ($ds in $Datastore)
    {
        If ($PSCMdlet.Shouldprocess($ds.Name,$msg))
        {
        $taskMoRef = $VimService.ConfigureDatastoreIORM_Task(
            [VMWare.Vim.VIConvert]::ToVim41( `
                $si.Content.StorageResourceManager),
            [VMWare.Vim.VIConvert]::ToVim41( `
```

```
          $ds.Extensiondata.MoRef),
        [VMWare.Vim.VIConvert]::ToVim41($spec))
      $task = Get-View ( `
        [VMWare.Vim.VIConvert]::ToVim($taskMoRef))
      while ("running","queued" -contains $task.Info.State)
      {
        $task.UpdateViewData("Info.State")
      }
      }
    }
  }
}
```

Using `Set-SIOC`, you can easily enable SIOC on every supported datastore in one line of PowerCLI:

```
Get-Datastore |
    Get-SIOC |
    Where-Object {$_.SIOCSupported -And -Not $_.SIOCEnabled} |
    Set-SIOC -Enabled $true
```

As for the congestion threshold, as of this writing VMware recommends that you don't modify that parameter. But if you wanted to do so and wished to determine the supported thresholds of all hosts using a given datastore, you could by running the script in Listing 4.21.

LISTING 4.21 Determining the supported congestion threshold for a datastore

```
$datastore = 'VMdata0'
$SIOC = Get-Datastore $datastore |
    Get-VMHost|
    Get-Sioc
New-Object PSObject -Property @{
    'Min'=($SIOC|Measure-Object -Maximum `
        -Property SIOCThresholdMaximum |
    Select-Object -ExpandProperty Maximum)
    'Max' =($SIOC|Measure-Object -Minimum `
        -Property SIOCThresholdMinimum |
    Select-Object -ExpandProperty Minimum)
}
```

Use Distributed Power Management

Distributed Power Management (DPM) is an extension of the Distributed Resource Scheduler (DRS). DPM focuses on maximizing the power efficiency of your virtual environment. DPM is enabled on a per-cluster basis and achieves power savings by carefully balancing the load across a given cluster. Underutilized hosts are powered off until needed. DPM then carefully monitors the status of the cluster. When it detects an increase in load, it will power on hosts to ensure sufficient capacity to meet the demands of the environment. All in all, DPM is a fantastic technology and should be enabled on all environments.

Unfortunately as of this writing, PowerCLI doesn't offer any cmdlets for managing DPM. We wrote some you can use until VMware offers official support. So, how can you find out if you're running DPM? Listing 4.22 contains a function that gives you the answer.

LISTING 4.22 The `Get-DPM` function

```
Function Get-DPM
{
  [CmdletBinding()]
  param(
  [Parameter(Mandatory=$true
  ,  ValuefrompipelineByPropertyName=$true)]
  [Alias('Name')]
  [String]
  $Cluster
  )
  Process
  {
    $Cluster = Get-view -ViewType 'ClusterComputeResource' `
      -Property 'ConfigurationEx','Name' `
      -Filter @{'Name'=$Cluster}
    if (-Not $Cluster)
    {
      Write-Warning "$Name not found!"
      continue;
    }
    $cluster.ConfigurationEx.DpmConfigInfo |
      Select-Object @{
```

Install, Configure, and Manage the vSphere Environment

PART I

```
            Name='Cluster'
            Expression={$cluster.Name}
        },
        'Enabled',
        'DefaultDpmBehavior',
        'HostPowerActionRate',
        'Option'
    }
}
```

Using the Get-DPM function, you can quickly get the status of DPM running across the environment in one line:

```
[vSphere PowerCLI] C:\> Get-Cluster | Get-DPM
```

Once you've identified the clusters that are not running DPM, you can use the Set-DPM function shown in Listing 4.23 to configure DPM.

LISTING 4.23 The Set-DPM function

```
Function Set-DPM
{
    [CmdletBinding(SupportsShouldProcess=$true)]
    param(
    [Parameter(Mandatory=$true
    ,       ValuefrompipelineByPropertyName=$true)]
    [Alias('Name')]
    [String]
    $Cluster

    ,
    [Parameter(ValuefrompipelineByPropertyName=$true)]
    [bool]
    $Enabled

    ,
    [Parameter(ValuefrompipelineByPropertyName=$true)]
    [ValidateSet("automated","manual")]
    [string]
    $DefaultDpmBehavior

    ,
    [Parameter(ValuefrompipelineByPropertyName=$true)]
    [ValidateRange(1,5)]
    $HostPowerActionRate
```

```
)
Process
{

    $Cluster = Get-view -ViewType ClusterComputeResource `
        -Property 'ConfigurationEx','Name' `
        -Filter @{'Name'=$Cluster}
    if (-Not $Cluster)
    {
        Write-Warning "$Name not found!"
        continue;
    }
    $spec = New-Object VMware.Vim.ClusterConfigSpecEx
    $spec.dpmConfig = $cluster.ConfigurationEx.DpmConfigInfo
    switch ($PSCmdlet.MyInvocation.BoundParameters.keys)
    {
        'Enabled'
        {
            $spec.dpmConfig.enabled = $Enabled
            If ($Enabled)
            {
                $MSG = "Enabling DPM "
            }
            Else
            {
                $MSG = "Disabling DPM "
            }
        }
        'DefaultDpmBehavior'
        {
            $spec.dpmConfig.defaultDpmBehavior = `
                $DefaultDpmBehavior
            $MSG="{0} Setting default behavior: {1} " -f `
                $MSG, $DefaultDpmBehavior
        }
        'HostPowerActionRate'
        {
            $spec.dpmConfig.hostPowerActionRate  = `
                $HostPowerActionRate
            $MSG="{0} Setting power action rate: {1} " -f `
```

```
                        $MSG, $HostPowerActionRate
            }
        }
        If ($PSCmdlet.ShouldProcess($Cluster.Name,$MSG))
        {


            $taskMoRef = `
                $Cluster.ReconfigureComputeResource_Task($spec,
                $true)
            $task = Get-View $taskMoRef
            while("running","queued" -contains $task.Info.State)
            {
                $task.UpdateViewData("Info")
            }
            If ($task.Info.State -eq 'error')
            {
                write-error $task.Info.Error.LocalizedMessage
            }
            Else
            {
                Get-DPM -Cluster $cluster.Name
            }
        }
    }
}
```

Putting it all together, to enable DPM on any cluster where it is currently disabled, you would run:

```
Get-Cluster |
    Get-DPM |
    Where-Object {-Not $_.Enabled} |
    Set-DPM -Enabled $true
```

You can also perform basic administration. For example, you can set the host power action rate to 4 and default DPM behavior to automatic with just one line of PowerCLI:

```
Get-Cluster |
    Get-DPM |
    Where-Object {$_.Enabled} |
    Set-DPM -DefaultDpmBehavior automated -HostPowerActionRate 4
```

HOST POWER ACTION LEVELS

Power action levels define the level at which a power action is recommended. A power action is when vCenter Server either recommends that a host be powered on or powered off. For instance, a power action level 1 setting is the most aggressive for powering hosts on and off. A level 5 is so conservative that it rarely, if ever, powers off a host, and only powers on a host in the event of severe resource imbalance. The double-edged sword that is the power action level is responsible for much confusion. Our advice is to never forget that this setting impacts both actions and you will be all right.

Now that you can automate DPM, get out there and save some energy. In all seriousness, it's understandable to be apprehensive about shutting down vSphere hosts. Our advice is to start conservatively and test DPM in your environment. Slowly, as you gain confidence and start to realize the power savings, you will naturally crank up the automation level. If you're not currently using DPM, start. It is irresponsible to ignore a technology that can save energy! Who knows? Save enough energy and perhaps you can talk your boss into a trip to VMWorld!

Configure Host Profiles

Host profiles are used to ensure compliance across a series of hosts within vCenter Server. This is accomplished by identifying a reference host and creating a host profile. The host profile captures the configuration of that host and saves it into the vCenter Server database. At any time after that, you can test the configuration of a given vSphere host against that profile and report on compliance. If a host has fallen out of compliance, you simply reapply the profile. As of vSphere 4.1, host profiles currently cover the following configuration settings:

- ► Memory reservations
- ► Storage
- ► Networking
- ► Date/time
- ► Firewall
- ► Security
- ► Services

▶ Advanced configuration options

▶ Users

▶ Groups

▶ Authentication

While the list continues to grow, there are some notable items that cannot be configured or monitored via host profiles:

▶ Storage

- ▶ ISCSI HBA and targets

- ▶ LUN multipathing Path Selection Plug-in (PSP) selection

- ▶ Pluggable storage architecture

▶ Network

- ▶ Static IP routes

- ▶ IPv6

- ▶ Selection of physical network adapters based on VLAN

▶ Security

- ▶ Tech Support Mode (TSM) logon banner

Getting started with host profiles is a snap. Simply configure one host to your organization's standards and create a new host profile. In Listing 4.24, we created a host profile for a cluster named `Prod01` based on a vSphere host named `vSphere01`.

LISTING 4.24 Creating a new host profile

```
New-VMHostProfile -Name Prod01 `
    -ReferenceHost (Get-VMHost vSphere01*) `
    -Description "Host profile for cluster Prod01"
```

Once the new profile is created, you can attach it to any vSphere host/cluster in vCenter Server. The code in Listing 4.25 associates the `Prod01` profile to the `Prod01` cluster, and then tests every host in the cluster for compliance.

LISTING 4.25 Associating a host profile and checking for compliance

```
Apply-VMHostProfile -Entity (Get-Cluster prod01) `
```

```
  -Profile (Get-VMHostProfile prod01) `
-AssociateOnly |
    Get-VMHost |
    Test-VMHostProfileCompliance
```

You could even take it a step further and apply your new profile, as shown in Listing 4.26.

NOTE   For more information on automating the application of a host profile, see Chapter 2, "Automating vSphere Hypervisor Deployment and Configuration."

LISTING 4.26   Applying a host profile to any noncompliant host

```
Get-Cluster Prod01 |
Get-VMHost |
Test-VMHostProfileCompliance |
    ForEach-Object {
        $profile = Get-VMHostProfile $_.VMHostProfile
        Set-VMHost -State 'Maintenance' -VMHost $_.VMhost |
            Apply-VMHostProfile -Profile $Profile |
            Set-VMHost -State 'Connected' |
            Test-VMHostProfileCompliance
    }
```

Of course, no environment is static. From time to time, you will need to make changes to hosts under the control of a host profile. As fantastic as vMotion is, it does take quite a bit of time to evacuate a host and a host has to be in Maintenance mode to apply a host profile. Therefore, when you're making changes we highly recommend using the following workflow:

1. Script the change needed to update all affected vSphere hosts in PowerCLI.

2. Update the host profile.

3. Test for compliance.

For example, the script in Listing 4.27 adds a new NFS datastore, updates the host profile, and then scans for compliance.

LISTING 4.27 Making changes on a cluster using host profiles

```
$cluster = Get-Cluster prod01
$VMhostProfile = Get-VMHostProfile -Entity $cluster
# Add the datastore
Get-VMHost -Location $cluster |
    New-Datastore -Name prod01_03 `
        -Nfs `
        -NfsHost 192.168.1.3 `
        -Path /vol/prod01_03
#update host profile
$VMhostProfile = Set-VMHostProfile -Profile $VMhostProfile
Get-VMHost -Location $cluster |
    Test-VMHostProfileCompliance
```

If you are fortunate enough to have the licensing, enjoy host profiles! They are a fantastic tool that truly simplifies the management of any size environment.

Configure Active Directory Integration

One of the most anticipated features released in vSphere 4.1 was the inclusion of an Active Directory (AD) authentication provider. Although AD integration had previously been available in ESX, ESXi had no such ability. This initial offering is not perfect and has some flaws, the most egregious of which is that by default the vSphere hosts look for an ESX Admins group and, if one is found, the host automatically adds it to the administrators group. That aside, local accounts are messy at best and using a directory service has always been best practice. So, how can you add a vSphere host to your AD domain? Out of the box, you cannot. This is one of the features that the PowerCLI team just hasn't gotten to yet. Fear not! We're here for you. Listing 4.28 contains a function that retrieves the current authentication services integration.

LISTING 4.28 The Get-VMHostAuthentication function

```
function Get-VMHostAuthentication
{
    param(
        [parameter(
            ValueFromPipeline = $true
```

```
,   Mandatory = $true)]
    [VMware.VimAutomation.ViCore.Impl.V1.Inventory.VMHostImpl]
    $VMHost
)
process
{
    $confMgr = $VMHost.ExtensionData.ConfigManager
    $filter = New-Object VMware.Vim.PropertyFilterSpec `
        -Property @{
            ObjectSet = New-Object VMware.Vim.ObjectSpec `
                -Property @{
                    Obj=$confMgr.AuthenticationManager
                }
        PropSet = New-Object VMware.Vim.PropertySpec `
            -Property @{
                Type = "HostAuthenticationManager"
                All = $true
            }
    }
    $sc = $VMHost.ExtensionData.Client.ServiceContent
    $collector = Get-View $sc.PropertyCollector
    $content = $collector.RetrieveProperties($filter)
    $stores = $content |
        Select -First 1 -ExpandProperty PropSet |
        Where-Object {$_.Name -eq "info"}
    foreach ($authConfig in $stores.Val.AuthConfig|
        Where-Object {$_.Enabled})
    {
        switch($authConfig.GetType().Name)
        {
            'HostLocalAuthenticationInfo'
            {
                New-Object PSObject -Property @{
                    Name = $VMHost.Name
                    Enabled = $authConfig.Enabled
                    Type = 'Local authentication'
                    Domain = $null
                    Membership = $Null
                    Trust = $null
```

```
                                    }
                                  }
                                'HostActiveDirectoryInfo'{
                                    New-Object PSObject -Property @{
                                        Name = $VMHost.Name
                                        Enabled = $authConfig.Enabled
                                        Type = 'Active Directory'
                                        Domain = $authConfig.JoinedDomain
                                        Membership = `
                                            $authConfig.DomainMembershipStatus
                                        Trust = $authConfig.TrustedDomain
                                    }
                                  }
                              }
                          }
                    }
              }
```

Using the `Get-VMHostAuthentication` function, you can quickly find any hosts that haven't yet been added to AD:

```
Get-VMHost |
        Get-VMHostAuthentication|
        Where {$_.type -eq 'Active Directory' -and -Not
    $_.Enabled}
```

Of course, you'll want a means to add them. For that, we wrote Listing 4.29, which contains the function called `Set-VMHostAuthentication`.

LISTING 4.29   The **Set-VMHostAuthentication** function

```
function Set-VMHostAuthentication
{

    [cmdletbinding(SupportsShouldProcess=$true,
        DefaultParameterSetName='JoinUser')]
    param(
        [parameter(
            ParameterSetName='JoinUser'
        ,   ValueFromPipeline = $true
        ,   Mandatory = $true)]
```

```
            [parameter(
                ParameterSetName='JoinCred'
            ,    ValueFromPipeline = $true
            ,    Mandatory = $true)]
            [parameter(
                ParameterSetName='Remove'
            ,    ValueFromPipeline = $true
            ,    Mandatory = $true)]
    [VMware.VimAutomation.ViCore.Impl.V1.Inventory.VMHostImpl]
        $VMHost
    ,    [parameter(
                ParameterSetName='JoinUser'
            ,    ValueFromPipeline = $true
            ,    Mandatory = $true)]
            [parameter(
                ParameterSetName='JoinCred'
            ,    ValueFromPipeline = $true
            ,    Mandatory = $true)]
            [string]
            $Domain

    ,    [parameter(
                ParameterSetName='JoinUser'
            ,    ValueFromPipelinebyPropertyName = $true
            ,    Mandatory = $true)]
            [string]
            $User

    ,    [parameter(
                ParameterSetName='JoinUser'
            ,    ValueFromPipelinebyPropertyName = $true
            ,    Mandatory = $true)]
            [string]
            $Password

    ,    [parameter(
                ParameterSetName='JoinCred'
            ,    ValueFromPipelinebyPropertyName = $true
            ,    Mandatory = $true)]
```

```
        [System.Management.Automation.PSCredential]
        $Credential

    ,
        [parameter(ParameterSetName='JoinCred')]
        [parameter(ParameterSetName='JoinUser')]
        [switch]
        $Join

    ,
        [parameter(ParameterSetName='Remove'
        ,   Mandatory = $true)]
        [switch]
        $Remove

    ,
        [parameter(ParameterSetName='Remove')]
        [switch]
        $RemovePermission
    )


    process
    {
        $confMgr = $VMHost.ExtensionData.ConfigManager
        $filter = New-Object VMware.Vim.PropertyFilterSpec `
            -Property @{
                ObjectSet = New-Object VMware.Vim.ObjectSpec `
                    -Property @{
                        Obj=$confMgr.AuthenticationManager
                    }
            PropSet = New-Object VMware.Vim.PropertySpec `
                -Property @{
                    Type = "HostAuthenticationManager"
                    All = $true
                }
            }
        $sc = $VMHost.ExtensionData.Client.ServiceContent
        $collector = Get-View $sc.PropertyCollector
        $content = $collector.RetrieveProperties($filter)
        $stores = $content |
            Select-Object -First 1 -ExpandProperty PropSet |
```

```
        Where-Object {$_.Name -eq "supportedStore"}
$result = $stores.Val |
    ? {$_.Type -eq "HostActiveDirectoryAuthentication"}
$hostADAuth = [VMware.Vim.VIConvert]::ToVim41($result)

Switch ($pscmdlet.parameterSetName)
{
    'JoinUser'
    {
        $msg = "Joining $Domain"
        $action = {$VimSvc.JoinDomain_Task($hostADAuth,
            $Domain,$User,$Password)}
    }
    'JoinCred'
    {
        $User,$Pass=$Credential.GetNetworkCredential()|
            Foreach-Object {$_.UserName,$_.Password}
        $msg = "Joining $Domain"
        $action = {$VimSvc.JoinDomain_Task($hostADAuth,
            $Domain,$User,$Pass)}
    }
    'Remove'
    {
        $msg="Removing from Domain"
        if ($RemovePermission) {$r = $True}
        Else {$r = $false}
        $action = {$VimSvc.LeaveCurrentDomain_Task( `
            $hostADAuth,$r)}
    }
}
if ($PSCMdlet.Shouldprocess($VMhost.Name,$msg))
{
    $VimSvc = $VMHost.ExtensionData.Client.VimService
    $taskMoRef = &$action
    $VMHost.ExtensionData.WaitForTask(`
        [VMware.Vim.VIConvert]::ToVim($taskMoRef))
}
    }
}
```

Using the `Set-VMHostAuthentication` function, you can enable AD authentication on a vSphere host like this:

```
Get-VMHost vSphere03* |
    Set-VMHostAuthentication -Domain getadmin.local/vSphere `
        -User gesizem@getadmin.local -Password 'password'
```

vSphere has turned out to be the premier virtualization platform. It offers the most advanced bleeding-edge features, and now you know how to automate some of those features using the world's premier automation engine, PowerCLI!

Managing the Virtual Machine Life Cycle

CHAPTER 5

Creating Virtual Machines

IN THIS CHAPTER, YOU WILL LEARN TO:

S o you've built your vSphere environment. The hosts are loaded, storage is provisioned, and vCenter Server is ready to go. Now it's time to create some virtual machines. In this chapter, we'll start with basic background on the PowerCLI `New-VM` cmdlet. We'll cover the various methods of creating new virtual machines. Then, we'll take a deep dive into the vSphere API, where we'll investigate advanced methods and techniques. We'll highlight custom attributes and their use, as well as explore VMware Tools installation.

Use the New-VM Cmdlet

The `New-VM` cmdlet is used to add, create, clone, or register a new virtual machine (VM). It has grown up over the past four versions of PowerCLI and is quite powerful. It is not, however, complete, and there are still some things that cannot be done natively within PowerCLI. We like to compare using the PowerCLI cmdlets to speaking a foreign language. For the most part, you say all the same things, but you say them in a different order. If the vSphere GUI is your native language, then be prepared to do things out of order.

The `New-VM` cmdlet provides a high-level abstraction over the whole VM creation process. As a result of this abstraction, `New-VM` makes use of some defaults. Unless explicitly told otherwise, the `New-VM` cmdlet will always create a VM with the specifications listed in Table 5.1.

TABLE 5.1   PowerCLI **New-VM** default values

Parameter	Default value
DiskMB	4096
DiskStorageFormat	Thick
GuestId	winXPProGuest
MemoryMB	256
NumCpu	1
Version	7

NOTE   Based on VMware vSphere PowerCLI 4.1 build 264274

When a cmdlet can perform one or more functions, PowerShell groups the parameters for each function into a parameter set. The `New-VM` cmdlet includes four parameter sets, or four separate functions:

- `NewVM`
- `Template`
- `RegisterVm`
- `CloneVm`

Each parameter set is a grouping of parameters that perform a specific function. You cannot mix and match parameters from different parameter sets. For clarity, and because they perform four separate functions, we'll cover each of these parameter sets individually.

So, how does PowerCLI choose which parameter set to use? Each parameter set has at least one unique parameter. The default parameter set is assumed until PowerCLI finds that one unique parameter that differentiates the current application from the configured default. In the case of the `New-VM` cmdlet, the `NewVM` parameter set is assumed until a parameter used elsewhere is found.

Regardless of the parameter set, there are two mandatory parameters: `Name` and `VMHost`. When connected directly to a vSphere host, PowerCLI assumes the `VMHost` parameter. That means that when you are connected directly to a vSphere host, creating a new VM is as easy as `New-VM -Name VM01`.

While this makes for a cool demo, it's not very useful in the real world. Nevertheless, it is useful to understand why that works. PowerCLI inferred both the `VMHost` and the parameter set. It then took the one remaining mandatory parameter, `Name`, and created a new VM using the defaults outlined in Table 5.1. We make this point because PowerCLI and its underlying engine, PowerShell, go to great lengths to "help" you; 99.9 percent of the time the guess is correct, but keep in mind that without explicit instructions from you, PowerCLI will always use those defaults.

Creating a New Virtual Machine

Amazingly, PowerCLI is not often used to create new virtual machines. Somehow, the community at large missed the huge advantage PowerCLI offers in this arena. If your organization makes use of enterprise provisioning systems such as Microsoft's System Center Configuration Manager (SCCM) or HP's Business Service Automation (HP-BSA), you can benefit from automating your new VM creation. Even if you're using a basic OS provisioning tool like Windows Deployment Services, Symantec Ghost, Linux KickStart, or Solaris JumpStart, you still benefit when you ensure that the base virtual hardware is exactly the same every single time!

How can you create a virtual machine? Well, generally the way you solve any problem in PowerCLI is by starting with a statement or question. For example, "I want to create an REHL5 VM with a thin-provisioned 10 GB hard drive, 1 GB of RAM. I want to mount an ISO in datastore0, and the network should be on VLAN 22." From there, you simply parse it out into cmdlets, like those in Listing 5.1.

LISTING 5.1   **Cmdlets to create a New-VM**

```
New-VM -Name REL5_01 `
   -DiskMB 10240 `
   -DiskStorageFormat thin `
   -MemoryMB 1024 `
   -GuestId rhel5Guest `
   -NetworkName vSwitch0_VLAN22 `
   -CD |
   Get-CDDrive |
      Set-CDDrive -IsoPath "[datastore0] /REHL5.2_x86.iso" `
         -StartConnected:$true `
         -Confirm:$False
```

NOTE   PowerShell code should read as a sentence.

The first thing you will notice is that we had to use several cmdlets to perform this task. While the conventional wisdom would be that we could perform all of this with one cmdlet, this is not the case with PowerCLI. This is because every cmdlet is responsible for only one small task or function. Therefore, we have to chain many cmdlets into a pipeline to complete the whole task. For example, the New-VM cmdlet will create only the bare hardware. Everything beyond that—like connecting a CD—must be done after the VM has been created.

You may have noticed the rather cryptic -GuestId. You can find a list of the valid guest IDs in the New-VM help. Unfortunately, the list located in the help is not easy to read. You could always check the vSphere API documentation—visit

www.vmware.com/support/developer/vc-sdk/visdk41pubs/ApiReference/index.html

and check Enumerated Types ➢ VirtualMachineGuestOsIdentifier. But if you like to keep the data in PowerShell where you can manipulate it, use the function in Listing 5.2 to query vCenter Server for supported operating systems and corresponding guest IDs.

LISTING 5.2   Querying vCenter Server for operating systems and guest IDs

```
Function Get-VMGuestId
{
    <#
    .SYNOPSIS
        Query VMHost for a list of the supported Operating
        systems, and their GuestIds.
    .DESCRIPTION
        Query VMHost for a list of the supported Operating
        systems, and their GuestIds.
    .NOTES
        Source:  Automating vSphere Administration
        Authors: Luc Dekens, Arnim van Lieshout, Jonathan Medd,
                 Alan Renouf, Glenn Sizemore
    .PARAMETER VMHost
        VMHost to query for the list of Guest Id's
    .PARAMETER Version
        Virtual Machine Hardware version, if not supplied
        the default for that host will be returned.
        I.E. ESX3.5 = 4, vSphere = 7
    .EXAMPLE
        Get-VMGuestId -VMHost vSphere1
    .EXAMPLE
        Get-VMGuestId -VMHost vSphere1 |
            Where {$_.family -eq 'windowsGuest'}
    #>
    [CmdletBinding()]
    Param(
        [Parameter(Mandatory=$true
        ,   HelpMessage="VMHost object to scan."
        ,   ValueFromPipeline=$true
        )]
        [VMware.VimAutomation.ViCore.Impl.V1.Inventory.VMHostImpl]
```

```
    $VMHost
,
  [int]
  $Version
)
Process
{
    $HostSystem = Get-View -VIObject $VMHost
    $compResource = Get-View -id $HostSystem.Parent
    $EnvironmentBrowser = `
        Get-View -Id $compResource.EnvironmentBrowser
    $VMConfigOptionDescriptors = `
        $EnvironmentBrowser.QueryConfigOptionDescriptor()

    if ($Version)
    {
        $Key = $VMConfigOptionDescriptors |
            Where-Object {$_.key -match "$($Version)$"} |
            Select-Object -ExpandProperty Key
    }
    Else
    {
        $Key = $VMConfigOptionDescriptors |
            Where-Object {$_.DefaultConfigOption} |
            Select-Object -ExpandProperty Key
    }
    $EnvironmentBrowser.QueryConfigOption($Key,
        $HostSystem.MoRef) |
        Select-Object -ExpandProperty GuestOSDescriptor |
        Select-Object @{
                Name='GuestId'
                Expression={$_.Id}
            },
            @{
                Name='GuestFamily'
                Expression={$_.Family}
            },
            @{
                Name='FullName'
```

```
                              Expression={$_.FullName}
                      }
              }
      }
```

When run, the `Get-VMGuestId` function returns a collection of all the supported `Guest` objects. You could then filter said collection down with `Where-Object` and send it to a file, printer, CSV—the world is your oyster at that point. We suggest that you pipe the output to `Out-GridView`. The `Out-GridView` cmdlet was built for situations like this. It enables you to filter, sort, and make sense of large datasets, as shown in Figure 5.1.

FIGURE 5.1   `Get-VMGuestId` piped to `Out-Gridview`

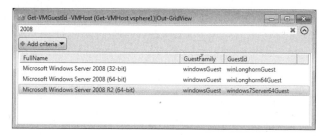

Now, what about a more complex VM—say a SQL Server? Let's create a Windows Server 2008 R2 virtual machine with the following specifications:

- ► 4 vCPUs

- ► 8 GB of RAM

- ► A thin-provisioned 40 GB OS hard drive

- ► 100 GB thick and 10 GB thick hard drive

- ► Two VMXNET3 network adapters on VLAN 22 and VLAN 100

This new VM is to be placed within the SQL resource pool on Cluster PROD01. Listing 5.3 shows how to accomplish this task.

LISTING 5.3   Creating a complex virtual machine

```
$Cluster = Get-Cluster -Name 'PROD01'
$ResourcePool = Get-ResourcePool -Name 'SQL' -Location $Cluster
$VM = New-VM -Name 'SQL01' `
    -NumCpu 4 `
```

```
    -MemoryMB 8096 `
    -DiskStorageFormat 'Thin' `
    -DiskMB 40960 `
    -GuestId 'windows7Server64Guest' `
    -VMHost (Get-VMHost -Location $Cluster|Get-Random) `
    -ResourcePool $ResourcePool
# remove the default e1000 nic that PowerCLI added
$vm | Get-NetworkAdapter | Remove-NetworkAdapter
#Add VMXNET3 Network Adapters
New-NetworkAdapter -NetworkName 'dvSwitch0_VLAN22' `
    -StartConnected `
    -Type 'Vmxnet3' `
    -VM $VM
New-NetworkAdapter -NetworkName 'dvSwitch0_VLAN100' `
    -StartConnected `
    -Type 'Vmxnet3' `
    -VM $VM
#Add additional hard drives
New-HardDisk -CapacityKB (100GB/1KB) -VM $vm
New-HardDisk -CapacityKB (10GB/1KB) -VM $vm
```

Listing 5.3 is slightly more complicated than the previous listing, but it's still easy to comprehend. Sadly, this is about as far as PowerCLI can natively go. If you want to add a paravirtual SCSI controller for your data drives, you must turn to the API.

Cloning a Virtual Machine

There are many reasons to clone a virtual machine. Perhaps the most popular is to create a test instance of a production VM. Clones can serve as a form of backup. We've even seen clones implemented as an inexpensive DR solution. Whatever your reason, PowerCLI can accommodate you.

For example, let's clone that SQL Server we just built. We'll clone it to the Test cluster and name it SQL01_Clone:

```
# Get source VM Object
$SourceVM = Get-VM -Name SQL01
#Get a host within the Test cluster
$VMHost = Get-Cluster Test | Get-VMHost | Get-Random
#Clone SQL01 to SQL01_Clone
$VM = New-VM -Name SQL01_Clone -VM $SourceVM -VMHost $VMHost
```

That's as basic as a clone operation can get; it is both good and bad. On the good side, we have an exact copy of SQL01. On the bad side, we have an exact copy of SQL01. You have to be extra careful with this new virtual machine. Simply powering it on can cause conflicts with the production SQL01 virtual machine. You can overcome this by customizing the clone with an OSCustomization task.

Let's do just that with the SQL virtual machine we just created. SQL01 houses a critical database, and we want to be able to work on an upgrade procedure. To accomplish this task, let's start by cloning SQL01. This time we'll apply an OSCustomization task named SQL_TEST. We'll prepare our virtual machine with Sysprep and change the hostname and IP information all in one shot. To be successful, we also need to change the virtual machine's network to a Dynamic Host Configuration Protocol (DHCP) enabled VLAN.

```
# Get source VM Object
$SourceVM = Get-VM -Name 'SQL01'
#Get a host within the Test cluster
$VMHost = Get-Cluster 'Test' | Get-VMHost | Get-Random
# Get the OS CustomizationSpec
$OSCustomizationSpec = Get-OSCustomizationSpec -Name 'SQL_TEST'
# Clone SQL01 to SQL01_clone
$VM = New-VM -Name 'SQL01_Clone' `
    -VM $SourceVM `
    -VMHost $VMHost `
    -OSCustomizationSpec $OSCustomizationSpec
# Change the Network
Get-NetworkAdapter -VM $VM |
    Set-NetworkAdapter -NetworkName 'dvSwitch0_VLAN100' `
        -Confirm:$false
# PowerOn our clone, triggering the CustomizationSpec
Start-VM -VM $VM
```

Clones when matched with customization specs are limited only by your imagination. They aren't used as heavily as templates, but they can serve the same purpose.

Deploying from a Template

Templates are the preferred means of deploying virtual machines en masse. Using templates is also the easiest of the three. Listing 5.4 deploys a virtual machine using a template.

LISTING 5.4   Deploying a virtual machine from a template

```
# Get source Template
$Template = Get-Template -Name 'REHL5.5'
# Get a host within the development cluster
$VMHost = Get-Cluster 'dev01' | Get-VMHost | Get-Random
# Deploy our new VM
New-VM -Template $Template -Name 'REHL_01' -VMHost $VMHost
```

Given the right template, the code in Listing 5.4 can produce a usable zero touch virtual machine. This would require you to perform all of the preparation ahead of time. Often, templates are paired with customization specs to perform this task postconfiguration. The code in Listing 5.5 deploys a virtual machine with customization specs.

LISTING 5.5   Deploying a VM using a template and customization specs

```
# Get source Template
$Template = Get-Template -Name 'REHL5.5'
# Get a host within the development cluster
$VMHost = Get-Cluster 'dev01' | Get-VMHost | Get-Random
# Get the OS CustomizationSpec
$Spec = Get-OSCustomizationSpec -Name 'REHL5.5'
# Deploy our new VM
New-VM -Template $Template `
    -Name 'REHL_01' `
    -VMHost $VMHost `
    -OSCustomizationSpec $Spec
```

Although the code in Listing 5.5 is complete, it does leave some things to chance. There is nothing keeping you from putting it all together and fully automating the virtual machine deployment. Listing 5.6 shows you how to confirm that your target datastore has sufficient free space before you start the deployment.

LISTING 5.6   Deploying using a template, customization specs, and checks for sufficient free space

```
# Get source Template
$Template = Get-Template -Name 'REHL5.5'
# Get the OS CustomizationSpec
$OSCustomizationSpec = Get-OSCustomizationSpec -Name 'REHL5.5'
# Get a host within the development cluster
$VMHost = Get-Cluster 'dev01' | Get-VMHost | Get-Random
# Determine the capacity requirements of this VM
```

```
$CapacityKB = Get-HardDisk -Template $Template |
    Select-Object -ExpandProperty CapacityKB |
    Measure-Object -Sum |
    Select-Object -ExpandProperty Sum
# Find a datastore with enough room
$Datastore = Get-Datastore -VMHost $VMHost|
    ?{($_.FreeSpaceMB * 1mb) -gt (($CapacityKB * 1kb) * 1.1 )}|
    Select-Object -first 1
# Deploy our Virtual Machine
$VM = New-VM -Name 'REHL_01' `
    -Template $Template `
    -VMHost $VMHost `
    -Datastore $Datastore
    -OSCustomizationSpec $OSCustomizationSpec
```

As you can see, templates can do as much or as little as required. See Chapter 6, "Using Templates and Customization Specifications," for more information on template creation and maintenance.

Registering a Virtual Machine

The fourth and final way to add a new virtual machine to vCenter Server or vSphere is to register an existing virtual machine. To do so, you only need to know the full path to the VM configuration file:

```
New-VM -Name CentOS07 -VMHost $VMHost `
    -VMFilePath '<Full path to the VM configuration File>.vmx'
```

Now, that's all well and good if you know the full path, but how can you find the full path? To assist in these situations, we wrote a simple script you can use to search datastore(s) looking for any file that matches a pattern (Listing 5.7).

LISTING 5.7   Searching a datastore for any file matching a pattern

```
Function Search-Datastore
{
    <#
    .SYNOPSIS
        Search Datastore for anyfile that matched
        the specified pattern.
    .DESCRIPTION
        Search Datastore for anyfile that matched
        the specified pattern.
```

Managing the Virtual
Machine Life Cycle

PART II

```
    .NOTES
        Source:  Automating vSphere Administration
        Authors: Luc Dekens, Arnim van Lieshout, Jonathan Medd,
                 Alan Renouf, Glenn Sizemore
    .PARAMETER Pattern
        Pattern To search for
    .PARAMETER Datastore
        Datastore Object to search
    .EXAMPLE
        Search-DataStore -Pattern *.vmx -Datastore ➥
         (Get-Datastore Datastore1)
    .EXAMPLE
        Get-Datastore | Search-Datastore *.vmdk
    #>
    [CmdletBinding()]
    Param(
        [Parameter(Mandatory=$True
        ,    HelpMessage="Pattern to search for"
        )]
        [String]
        $Pattern

        ,
        [Parameter(Mandatory=$True
        ,   HelpMessage="Datastore Object to search"
        ,   ValueFromPipeline=$True
        ,   ValueFromPipeLineByPropertyName=$True
        )]
        [VMware.VimAutomation.ViCore.Impl.V1.DatastoreManagement.➥
         DatastoreImpl]
        $Datastore
    )
    Process
    {
        $DSObject = Get-View -VIObject $Datastore
        $DSBrowser = Get-View -Id $DSObject.Browser

        $Datacenter = Get-View -Id $DSObject.Parent
        #Walk up the tree until you find the Datacenter
        while($Datacenter.MoRef.Type -ne  "Datacenter"){
            $Datacenter = Get-View $Datacenter.Parent
```

```
        }

        $DSPath  = "[{0}]" -f $DSObject.Name

        $Spec = New-Object VMware.➥
          Vim.HostDatastoreBrowserSearchSpec
        $Spec.MatchPattern = $pattern

        $TaskMoRef = $DSBrowser.SearchDatastoreSubFolders_Task➥
         ($DSPath, $Spec)
        $Task = Get-View -Id $TaskMoRef

        while ("running","queued" -contains $task.Info.State)
        {
            $task.UpdateViewData("Info.State")
        }

        $Task.UpdateViewData("Info.Result")
        $task.Info.Result |
            Where-Object {$_.FolderPath -match ➥
              "\[(?<DS>[^\]]+)\]\s(?<Folder>.+)"} |
            Select-Object -ExpandProperty File |
            Select-Object @{
                Name='Datastore'
                Expression={$DSObject.Name}
            },
            @{
                Name='Path'
                Expression={
                    "[{0}] {1}{2}" -f $Matches.DS, $Matches.Folder,
                    $_.Path
                }
            }
    }
}
```

When used appropriately, Search-Datastore means you only need to know a little about the file you are looking for. For example, say a virtual machine named CentOS07 was accidentally removed from inventory. You could fire up the datastore browser, or you could simply perform a global search.

```
[vSphere PowerCLI] C:\> Get-Datastore |
    Search-Datastore -Pattern CentOS07.vmx


Datastore                      Path
---------                      ----
datastore1                     [datastore1] CentOS07/CentOS07.vmx
```

You could also just wrap it all up into one line, and re-register the virtual machine at the same time:

```
[vSphere PowerCLI] C:\> Get-Datastore |
    Search-Datastore -Pattern CentOS07.vmx |
    ForEach-Object {
        New-VM -Name CentOS07 -VMHost $VMHost `
            -VMFilePath $_.Path
    }


Name                     PowerState Num CPUs Memory (MB)
----                     ---------- -------- -----------
CentOS07                 PoweredOff 1           768
```

You could also re-register any virtual machines that have been removed from inventory but not deleted from disk. This strategy is slightly more complicated, but it still involves just a couple lines of code (Listing 5.8).

LISTING 5.8   **Re-registering virtual machines**

```
# Get every VM registered in vCenter
$RegisteredVMs = Get-VM |
    Select-Object -ExpandProperty ExtensionData |
    Select-Object -ExpandProperty Summary |
    Select-Object -ExpandProperty Config |
    Select-Object -ExpandProperty VmPathName


# Now find every .vmx on every datastore.
# If it's not part of vCenter then add it back in.
Get-Datastore |
    Search-Datastore -Pattern *.vmx|
    Where-Object { $RegisteredVMs -notcontains $_.path } |
    Where-Object {$_.Path -match "(?<Name>\w+).vmx$"} |
    ForEach-Object {
```

```
$VMHost = Get-Datastore -Name $_.Datastore |
    Get-VMHost |
    Get-Random
New-VM -Name $matches.Name `
    -VMHost $VMHost `
    -VMFilePath $_.Path
}
```

As you can see, the New-VM cmdlet is very powerful and for the most part can accommodate all your virtual machine creation needs. We urge you to use the built-in supported cmdlets even if doing so requires more work than using the SDK.

Use the SDK

Sometimes the built-in cmdlets just don't meet your needs. However, those circumstances are disappearing every day. Always check to make sure the PowerCLI team hasn't shipped a new cmdlet before you turn to the API. That said, when all else fails you can always use the API to deploy a new VM.

Let's take our SQL Server from Listing 5.3 and crank up the complexity. We require a Windows Server 2008 R2 virtual machine named SQL09 that meets the following specifications:

- ▶ 2 vCPUs

- ▶ 4 GB of RAM

- ▶ A 40 GB thin-provisioned system drive

- ▶ A second paravirtual SCSI controller with a 5 GB and a 10 GB hard disk

- ▶ 2 VMXNET adapters on VLANs 22 and 100

- ▶ A connection from the CD drive to the Windows ISO to facilitate the OS installation

We also want to enable hot add CPU and memory and set a resource allocation reserving 60 percent of the configured RAM as well as set a high CPU share. We need this VM created in the SQL folder and assigned to the SQL resource pool.

Now that's a big virtual machine with many specific requirements. Although almost all of this could be done with the PowerCLI cmdlets, doing so would not be a trivial task. In this rare case, it is easier to just use the API.

First, create the base configuration specification. Here, you define the basis for your new virtual machine—the name, hardware version, guest ID, vCPU, memory, hot add/remove settings, resource allocation, and the like—basically everything except the actual hardware. Listing 5.9 shows you how.

LISTING 5.9   Defining a new virtual machine

```
# Create a new virtual Machine configuration spec
$config = New-Object VMware.Vim.VirtualMachineConfigSpec
$config.name = "SQL09"
$config.version = "vmx-07"
$config.guestId = "windows7Server64Guest"
# Location for VM home
$config.files = New-Object VMware.Vim.VirtualMachineFileInfo
$config.files.vmPathName = "[datastore1]"
$config.numCPUs = 2
$config.memoryMB = 4096
$config.memoryHotAddEnabled = $true
$config.cpuHotAddEnabled = $true
$config.cpuHotRemoveEnabled = $false


## Resource Allocation
$config.cpuAllocation = `
    New-Object VMware.Vim.ResourceAllocationInfo
$config.cpuAllocation.shares = New-Object VMware.Vim.SharesInfo
$config.cpuAllocation.shares.level = "High"
$config.memoryAllocation = `
    New-Object VMware.Vim.ResourceAllocationInfo
$config.memoryAllocation.reservation = ($config.memoryMB * .6)
```

With the base built, let's now turn our attention to the virtual hardware. Using the New-VM cmdlet involves the concept of a base VM or a bare minimum collection of virtual hardware. This is not the case when working with the API; you must explicitly define any hardware you want added to your target virtual machine.

We'll start with the CD drive. You will notice a flow that will be repeated heavily as you build this new VM. You always start with a VirtualDeviceConfigSpec object. Next, you define what type of operation you will be performing—in this case it's always an add operation. Then you attach your actual hardware device—in this example a virtualCdrom. From there it's a simple matter of defining all the particulars that make up that hardware device. This process can get tricky because it's not always clear what is needed to do what. Just keep in mind that it's a VM; trial and error will be your watchword. Add hardware one piece at a time as you figure it out, and use Onyx to explore adding new hardware (see the sidebar "The Onyx Project").

THE ONYX PROJECT

"What's Onyx?" you say. Well, Onyx is the Microsoft Office macro of the virtualization world. It enables you to perform the action in the comfort of the GUI and capture those mouse clicks as runnable code. While not perfect, Onyx is not a tool to be ignored. And we didn't! Chapter 19, "Onyx and the SDK," will teach you everything you ever wanted to know about this little lifesaver.

```
####### START DEVICE CONFIGURATION ########
## CD Drive
# Create a new device config spec object
$VirtualCdrom = New-Object VMware.Vim.VirtualDeviceConfigSpec
# declare this as an add operation
$VirtualCdrom.operation = "add"
# Add a virtual cdrom to the device config spec
$VirtualCdrom.device = New-Object VMware.Vim.VirtualCdrom
# Create a new device key, a negative number is one that
# should be regenerated.
$VirtualCdrom.device.key = -42
# Connect the new CDRom directly to an ISO on datastore PROD_ISO
$VirtualCdrom.device.backing = `
    New-Object VMware.Vim.VirtualCdromIsoBackingInfo
$VirtualCdrom.device.backing.fileName = `
    "[PROD_ISO] windows2008R2.iso"
# Set CD Connection information
$VirtualCdrom.device.connectable = `
    New-Object VMware.Vim.VirtualDeviceConnectInfo
$VirtualCdrom.device.connectable.startConnected = $true
$VirtualCdrom.device.connectable.allowGuestControl = $true
$VirtualCdrom.device.connectable.connected = $false
# default IDE 1 controller is 201.
```

```
$VirtualCdrom.device.controllerKey = 201
# Slot number for SCSI BUS
$VirtualCdrom.device.unitNumber = 0
# Add CD Drive config spec to VM Build spec.
$config.DeviceChange += $VirtualCdrom
```

Hard disks can be particularly tricky, as you must first define the SCSI controller they will attach to. When doing so, assign a device key; this key will be used to identify the controller later. We recommend assigning a negative number to avoid any potential conflicts. When a negative number is used, vSphere will generate an ID for you at runtime.

```
### SAS Controller
$VirtualLsiLogicSASController = `
    New-Object VMware.Vim.VirtualDeviceConfigSpec
$VirtualLsiLogicSASController.operation = "add"
# Add a virtual LSI SAS Controller to the device config spec
$VirtualLsiLogicSASController.device = `
    New-ObjectVMware.Vim.VirtualLsiLogicSASController
# Create a new device key, a negative number is one that
# should be regenerated.
$VirtualLsiLogicSASController.device.key = -101
# Set the bus location 0 to SCSI 0:x, 1 is SCSI 1:x
$VirtualLsiLogicSASController.device.busNumber = 0
# Set the SCSI BUS Sharing policy
$VirtualLsiLogicSASController.device.sharedBus = "noSharing"
# Add SAS Controller config spec to VM Build spec.
$config.DeviceChange += $VirtualLsiLogicSASController
```

Once you've added your controller, it's time to create and attach a hard disk. This is a straightforward process; again assign a negative device ID. Remember to use the device ID you assigned the SCSI controller for the controllerKey, because this creates that association. You can do a lot of powerful things when adding hard disks this way, such as eager zeroed thick (pre-zero out all of the blocks in the disk) and mounting a snapshot from another virtual machine.

```
### Hard Disk 0
$VirtualDisk = New-Object VMware.Vim.VirtualDeviceConfigSpec
$VirtualDisk.operation = "add"
# declare this to be a new hard disk, aka create the file.
$VirtualDisk.fileOperation = "create"
```

```
# Add a virtual disk to the device config spec
$VirtualDisk.device = New-Object VMware.Vim.VirtualDisk
# Set the device key, a negative number is one that
# should be regenerated
$VirtualDisk.device.key = -1000000
# Set the device backing information, this defines
# what kind of disk we're adding
$VirtualDisk.device.backing = `
    New-Object VMware.Vim.VirtualDiskFlatVer2BackingInfo
# Add a file name here to override <VM Name>.vmdk
$VirtualDisk.device.backing.fileName = ""
# Set the write mode
$VirtualDisk.device.backing.diskMode = "persistent"
# Thin provision the disk
$VirtualDisk.device.backing.thinProvisioned = $true
# Set Hard Disk connection info
$VirtualDisk.device.connectable = `
    New-Object VMware.Vim.VirtualDeviceConnectInfo
$VirtualDisk.device.connectable.startConnected = $true
$VirtualDisk.device.connectable.allowGuestControl = $false
$VirtualDisk.device.connectable.connected = $true
# Assign disk to controller
# (-101 is the key we assigned to the SAS Controller)
$VirtualDisk.device.controllerKey = -101
# Slot number for SCSI BUS, in this case 0 is x:0, 1 is x:1
$VirtualDisk.device.unitNumber = 0
# Hard disk capacity in KB.
$VirtualDisk.device.capacityInKB = 41943040
# Add the HD 0 config spec to VM Build spec.
$config.DeviceChange += $VirtualDisk
```

Here, we chose the paravirtual SCSI controller for the data drives. Don't forget to generate a new device key and increment the busNumber.

```
### ParaVirtual SCSI Controller
$ParaVirtualSCSIController = `
    New-Object VMware.Vim.VirtualDeviceConfigSpec
$ParaVirtualSCSIController.operation = "add"
# Add a ParaVirtual SCSI Controller to the device config spec
$ParaVirtualSCSIController.device = `
```

```
      New-Object VMware.Vim.ParaVirtualSCSIController
# Create a new device key, a negative number is
# one that should be regenerated.
$ParaVirtualSCSIController.device.key = -102
# Set the bus location 0 is SCSI 0:x, 1 is SCSI 1:x
$ParaVirtualSCSIController.device.busNumber = 1
# Set the SCSI BUS Sharing policy
$ParaVirtualSCSIController.device.sharedBus = "noSharing"
# Add ParaVirtual SCSI Controller config spec to VM Build spec.
$config.DeviceChange += $ParaVirtualSCSIController
```

Notice how you can reuse the VirtualDisk object you created earlier. Just change the relevant properties, and add it to the spec!

```
### Hard Disk 1
# modify the VirtualDisk object for the second HD
$VirtualDisk.device.key = -103
$VirtualDisk.device.controllerKey = -102
$VirtualDisk.device.unitNumber = 0
$VirtualDisk.device.capacityInKB = 41943040
$config.DeviceChange += $VirtualDisk


### Hard Disk 2
# modify the VirtualDisk object for the second HD
$VirtualDisk.device.key = -103
$VirtualDisk.device.controllerKey = -102
$VirtualDisk.device.unitNumber = 0
$VirtualDisk.device.capacityInKB = 41943040
$config.DeviceChange += $VirtualDisk
```

Network adapters can be a little troublesome, especially when connecting to a distributed virtual switch (dvSwitch) because you must have the exact port group ID and dvSwitch UID. The good news is that you can easily obtain this information with PowerCLI.

```
### Network Adapter 0
# Find our dv portgroup on the dvSwitch.
$DVPortGroup = Get-View -ViewType network `
    -Filter @{'Name'='dvSwitch0_VLAN100'}
# Use the dvPortGroup to identify the dvSwitch Uuid
$vDS = $DVPortGroup.Config.DistributedVirtualSwitch
```

```
$DVSwitchUID = Get-View $vDS |`
    Select-Object -ExpandProperty Uuid

$VirtualVmxnet3 = New-Object VMware.Vim.VirtualDeviceConfigSpec
$VirtualVmxnet3.operation = "add"
# Add a virtual Vmxnet3 adapter to the device config spec
$VirtualVmxnet3.device = New-Object VMware.Vim.VirtualVmxnet3
$VirtualVmxnet3.device.key = -105
# Set the device backing information, this defines what kind
# of adapter we're adding
$VirtualVmxnet3.device.backing = `
    New-Object VMware.Vim.
VirtualEthernetCardDistributedVirtualPortBackingInfo
# Declare a distributed port group
$VirtualVmxnet3.device.backing.port = `
    New-Object VMware.Vim.DistributedVirtualSwitchPortConnection
# Assign the dvSwitch Uuid
$VirtualVmxnet3.device.backing.port.switchUuid = $DVSwitchUID
# Assign the dvPortGroup key
$VirtualVmxnet3.device.backing.port.portgroupKey = `
    $DVPortGroup.Key
$VirtualVmxnet3.device.connectable = `
    New-Object VMware.Vim.VirtualDeviceConnectInfo
$VirtualVmxnet3.device.connectable.startConnected = $true
$VirtualVmxnet3.device.connectable.allowGuestControl = $true
$VirtualVmxnet3.device.connectable.connected = $true
# Generate MAC
$VirtualVmxnet3.device.addressType = "generated"
# Enable WOL
$VirtualVmxnet3.device.wakeOnLanEnabled = $true
$config.DeviceChange += $VirtualVmxnet3
```

Again, we're reusing an object, this time a network adapter. Just change the relevant properties, and add it back in:

```
### Network Adapter 1
$DVPortGroup = Get-View -ViewType network `
    -Filter @{'Name'='dvSwitch0_VLAN22'}

$vDS = $DVPortGroup.Config.DistributedVirtualSwitch
$DVSwitchUID = Get-View $vDS |
```

```
        Select-Object -ExpandProperty Uuid
# modify the netadapter object for the second NIC
$VirtualVmxnet3.device.key = -106
$VirtualVmxnet3.device.backing.port.switchUuid = $DVSwitchUID
$VirtualVmxnet3.device.backing.port.portgroupKey = `
    $DVPortGroup.Key
$config.DeviceChange += $VirtualVmxnet3
```

At this point, we have finished adding hardware to our new virtual machine. Now we need to define the resource pool our VM will reside in, as well as the folder to create our VM in:

```
# get the MoRef for the SQL Resource pool
$ResourcePool = Get-ResourcePool SQL |
    Select-Object -ExpandProperty ExtensionData|
    Select-Object -ExpandProperty MoRef


# we don't have any additional host parameters
$hostParam = $null


# Get the Managed object for the SQL Folder
$Folder = Get-Folder SQL| Get-View


# Create our VM!
$Folder.CreateVM_Task($config, $ResourcePool, $hostParam)
```

Now that's a big script, but it isn't hard to read. As you can see, every step of the build process follows a common rhythm. It starts with a `VirtualDeviceConfigSpec` object. With this object you define what kind of operation you plan on performing. Then you attach the object type—for instance, a `VirtualVmxnet3`. From there it's just a matter of defining the parameters you care about. We highly recommend you use Onyx heavily for any work like this, because it makes discovery a cinch. You will have to perform significant modifications to the code Onyx outputs, but it's better than starting from scratch.

Perform a Mass Deployment

Shortly after realizing the power space and cooling savings virtualization brings to the table, organizations usually notice the speed of deployment. This discovery isn't all roses, though, as it brings with it the need to pump out virtual machines many times faster than is feasible in the physical world. Fear not! You'll soon learn: with PowerCLI, no project is too big!

Preparing for Mass Deployment

Regardless of whether you are planning to use a third-party provisioning tool such as SCCM, or you have established a gold master image, PowerCLI enables you to effortlessly scale to any size deployment. The real question is how unique is each virtual machine? If you're deploying 1,000 blank Linux virtual machines to load from KickStart, it's one line (see Listing 5.10)!

LISTING 5.10   Mass-deploying blank virtual machines

```
1..1000 |
    Foreach-Object {
        New-VM -Name REL5_($_) `
            -DiskMB 10240 `
            -DiskStorageFormat thin `
            -MemoryMB 1024 `
            -GuestId rhel5Guest `
            -NetworkName vSwitch0_VLAN22 `
            -CD
    }
```

Five hundred Windows desktops deployed from a template? It's just as simple, as you can see in Listing 5.11.

LISTING 5.11   Mass-deploying from a template

```
$template = "WIN_XP_SP3"
$OSCustomizationSpec = Get-OSCustomizationSpec XP
$VMHost = Get-Cluster PROD_01 | Get-VMHost | Get-Random
1..500 |
    Foreach-Object {
        New-VM -Name XP_$_ `
            -Template $template `
            -Host $VMhost `
            -Datastore $datastore `
            -OSCustomizationSpec $OSCustomizationSpec
    }
```

So, what about mass deployments that aren't so cookie cutter? The sky is the limit here, but we're going to focus on using CSVs. First, you need to establish the unique information for each system. In this case, we'll use CPU, memory, hard disk, and network adapter. Simply create a CSV text file; the first row should contain the label of each column, as shown in Figure 5.2.

FIGURE 5.2 `massVM.txt`

To use this information and simplify the deployment process, use a PowerShell cmdlet that will read in the CSV file and create an object (Listing 5.12).

LISTING 5.12 Importing a CSV and creating an object

```
Import-Csv .\massVM.txt |
    Foreach-Object {
        New-VM -Name $_.Name `
            -Host $VMhost `
            -Datastore $datastore `
            -NumCpu $_.CPU `
            -MemoryMB $_.Memory `
            -DiskMB $_.HardDisk `
            -NetworkName $_.NIC
    }
```

Notice how the overall flow doesn't change. Again, you're only limited by your own imagination here. You can incorporate as much or as little as your organization requires.

Running the Deployment Synchronous or Asynchronous

By default, the `New-VM` cmdlet monitors the progress of any provisioning operation, updating a progress bar along the way. While useful, this progress bar can decommission a PowerCLI prompt for minutes or hours depending on the job. It is especially frustrating when you're writing scripts to deploy a large number of VMs. For instance, let's deploy four new virtual machines from a template. We want to balance the load, so we'll manage the datastore placement. Our target environment has two datastores with plenty of free space (see Listing 5.13).

LISTING 5.13 Sychronously deploying four virtual machines

```
$Datastores = Get-Cluster -name 'PROD01'|
        Get-VMHost |
        Get-Datastore
$i=1
While ($i -le 4)
{
    Foreach ($Datastore in $Datastores)
    {
        New-VM -Name "VM0$I" `
            -Host ($Datastore | Get-VMHost | Get-Random) `
            -Datastore $datastore
    }
}
```

At first glance, there appears to be nothing wrong with the script in Listing 5.13, but that pesky progress bar will effectively force our four virtual machines to be deployed serially! To overcome this, you can apply the -RunAsync switch, as shown in Listing 5.14. This switch directs the New-VM cmdlet to return the task object rather than monitor the built progress. You can achieve parity with the synchronous VM deployment by saving these task objects in a variable. You can then pass the objects to the Wait-Task cmdlet.

LISTING 5.14 Asynchronously deploying new virtual machines

```
$Datastores = Get-Cluster -name 'PROD01'|
        Get-VMHost |
        Get-Datastore
$i=1
While ($i -le 4)
{
    Foreach ($Datastore in $Datastores)
    {
        if ($I -le 4)
        {
            [array]$Task += New-VM -Name "VM0$I" `
                -Host ($Datastore | Get-VMHost | Get-Random) `
                -Datastore $datastore `
                -RunAsync
```

```
        }
        $I++
    }
}
Wait-Task -Task $Task
```

You can quickly get to a point where you are maximizing your infrastructure and time by driving vSphere to its full potential. There can be negative effects, however, especially when cloning a VM or deploying from a template. These are fairly high I/O operations, and running too many concurrently can bring a storage array to its knees.

The decision to run your code synchronously or asynchronously has more to do with the code for the VM creation. We recommend that, whenever possible, you run all operations synchronously because this provides a safety blanket. The PowerShell pipeline, with a little help from the PowerCLI team, isolates your actions and limits the potential for mistakes. However, when you find yourself in one of those situations where you need to break out and control the build order yourself, no problem. Just be mindful of the whole process and pay special attention to the execution order at all times.

Postconfiguration and Validating the New Virtual Machines

Thus far, we have been focused solely on the creation of a virtual machine. Now, we are going to shift gears a bit and focus on managing a VM after it has been deployed—particularly, the postbuild configuration. We suggest that you use templates to do the lion's share of this kind of work. The reason is to achieve parity between a virtual machine deployed from PowerCLI and the GUI. As they both use the same sources, they produce identical VMs. Given that, there are some things that cannot be automated via postconfiguration scripts. Sometimes there is a need to use a larger build process—in those circumstances `Invoke-VMScript` is your ace in the hole.

`Invoke-VMScript` uses the VIX API to communicate directly with the VMware Tools service running in the VM. Security folks, fear not: this channel is heavily protected and is not an unattended backdoor. Instead, it's more like a guarded, VIP-only entrance. To use this protected pipeline, you need admin credentials for both the VM host as well as the guest OS. Once authenticated, `Invoke-VMScript` calls the execution engine of your choice and executes the script text passed to it.

Think Secure Shell (SSH) or PowerShell remoting without the need for a network connection! Even if the VM is off the network, you can still programmatically script against the guest OS.

In practice, `Invoke-VMScript` can be used for simple verification of postbuild steps. Say in your organization there is a requirement that the CD drive always be mapped to X. You can invoke a VM script to verify this setting is correct on all your server machines. Listing 5.15 is an excerpt from a postbuild verification script you could use to perform quality assurance on a new VM.

LISTING 5.15 Postbuild verification script

```
$DrvLetter = Invoke-VMScript -VM $VM `
    -GuestCredential $GuestADCredential `
    -HostCredential $HostCredential `
    -ScriptType bat `
    -ScriptText @"
echo list volume > .\list_vol.txt
for /f "usebackq tokens=2,4 skip=6" %%a in (`diskpart /s .\list_
vol.txt`) do (
    if %%b==CD-ROM (
        echo %%a
    )
)
del .\list_vol.txt
"@

IF ($DrvLetter -ne "x")
{
    Write-warning "$VM CD-Drive out of compliance"
}
```

That's not to say you have to script everything out. The PowerCLI team ships a couple of very cool cmdlets that utilize the `Invoke-VMScript` cmdlet to perform basic network configuration.

For instance, with `Get-VMGuestRoute` you can easily extract a virtual machine's IP information. As you can imagine, `Get-VMGuestRoute`/`Set-VMGuestRoute` has a lot of potential, especially for disaster recovery. If you need to rapidly change the default gateway of every VM with `Set-VMGuestRoute`, it is one line of code (see Listing 5.16).

Managing the Virtual
Machine Life Cycle

PART II

LISTING 5.16   Changing the VM's default gateway

```
$GuestCreds = Get-Credential
$HostCreds = Get-Credential
Get-VM |
    Get-VMGuestRoute -GuestCredential $cred `
        -HostCredential $HostCreds |
    Where-Object { $_.Destination -eq "default" `
        -AND $_.Gateway -ne "10.10.10.1"} |
    Set-VMGuestRoute  -Gateway 10.10.10.1 `
        -GuestCredential $cred `
        -HostCredential $HostCreds
```

The PowerCLI team didn't stop there. Perhaps the coolest cmdlet in the toolkit is Set-VMGuestNetworkInterface. Let's pretend you're replicating some SQL Servers to a disaster recovery site but don't have a stretched Ethernet. You can change the IP address of the system in one line of PowerCLI code (see Listing 5.17).

LISTING 5.17   Changing VMs' IP information en masse

```
Get-Cluster SQL_DR |
    Get-VM |
    Get-VMGuestNetworkInterface -GuestCredential $guestCreds `
        -HostCredential $hostcreds |
        Where {$_.ip -match "192.168.145.(?<IP>\d{1,3})"} |
        Set-VMGuestNetworkInterface `
            -Ip 192.168.145.$($Matches.IP) `
            -Netmask 255.255.255.0 `
            -Gateway 192.167.145.2 `
            -GuestCredential $guestCreds `
            -HostCredential $hostcreds
```

YOU MIGHT NEED TO TWEAK

We've experienced mixed results with these cmdlets. It's understandable, considering that behind the scenes the cmdlets are running a bunch of complicated batch scripts. You may need to tweak these scripts to match your environment. As of vSphere 4.1, the enhanced VM guest cmdlets support Windows XP, Windows Server 2003, and Linux Red Hat Enterprise 5. You can extend these cmdlets to support other guest operating systems by modifying or adding custom scripts.

The custom scripts are located in the `Scripts` folder in the PowerCLI installation directory; they are named using the following convention:

```
<CmdletName>_<OS_Identifier>
```

`<CmdletName>` is the name of the cmdlet without a hyphen—for example, `GetVMGuestNetworkInterface`.

`<OS_Identifier>` is the guest family or the guest ID as returned by `Get-Guest`.

We applaud the PowerCLI team for including this extensibility in such a critical cmdlet, but if that seems too complicated to you, there is nothing preventing you from wrapping a bash or DOS script up in `Invoke-VMScript`. (We do later in Listing 5.23.) As we've shown, it is still very much early days for the guest integration cmdlets, but we think you'll find this first attempt very serviceable. It does not take much to build an incredibly powerful solution.

Identify Eye-Catchers for Auditing

During an audit you will be pounded with questions that may have little to do with your day-to-day job as an IT pro. Additionally, your auditors will likely not find any of your jokes funny or care about how optimal your cluster layout is. They will, however, ask you to prove who did what and when, and this is where PowerCLI can provide you with a small win. Enter custom attributes.

Using Custom Attributes

A custom attribute is a name-value pair stored in the vCenter Server database to track extended information on a virtual machine. Its use varies from organization to organization, but in general a custom attribute is used to track configuration items that are deemed important to the Virtual Infrastructure (VI) administrator.

Fortunately, PowerCLI makes reading and writing custom attributes a cinch. For instance, the command to set the `OwnedBy` attribute to `Sales` on the virtual machine `App01` is one line of code:

```
Get-VM App01 | Set-Annotation `
    -CustomAttribute OwnedBy `
    -Value Sales
```

As easy as that is, some administrators will still get lazy and forget to fill out these fields. With that in mind, one of the best uses we've found for custom attributes is to include a mini-report of useful information, such as who created a VM and when. Listing 5.18 is an example.

LISTING 5.18 Custom attributes VM Created by/On

```
Foreach ($VM in Get-VM)
{
    Get-VIEvent -Entity $VM -Types Info |
        Where-Object { $_.Gettype().Name -match "VmBeingDeployedEv
ent|VmCreatedEvent |VmRegisteredEvent|VmClonedEvent"} |
        ForEach-Object {
            Set-Annotation -Entity $VM `
                -CustomAttribute CreatedBy `
                -Value $Event.UserName
            Set-Annotation -Entity $VM `
                -CustomAttribute CreatedOn `
                -Value $Event.CreatedTime
        }
}
```

How about who last modified a virtual machine and when? Listing 5.19 shows you how to get that information.

LISTING 5.19 Create a custom attribute containing VM last modified by, and Created on dates.

```
Foreach ($VM in Get-VM)
{
    Get-VIEvent -Entity $VM -Types info |
        Where {$_.gettype().name -eq "VmReconfiguredEvent"} |
        Sort-Object CreatedTime -Descending |
        Select-Object -First 1 |
        ForEach-Object {
            Set-Annotation -Entity $VM `
                -CustomAttribute LastModifiedBy `
                -Value $_.UserName
            Set-Annotation -Entity $VM `
                -CustomAttribute LastModifiedOn `
                -Value $_.CreatedTime
        }
}
```

Have you spotted the pattern? All you're doing is querying vCenter Server for a particular kind of activity. Then, you can filter through the returned results to find the action of interest. As with most things in PowerCLI, you're limited only by your imagination here.

That's not to say it's perfect. The examples we've provided take a long time to execute in large environments. Therefore, we recommend setting them up in a script that runs at the appropriate interval in a scheduled task. See Chapter 18, "Scheduling Automation Scripts," for more information. If that approach is still not fast enough, you can significantly speed up the process by using the Native API, but in this case we don't recommend it. Just schedule a script to run at 3 a.m.; it will be easier to manage, and you won't even notice the extended execution.

Maintaining Custom Attributes

For all their strengths, there is one glaring weakness with custom attributes: they are stored in the vCenter Server database. If you move a VM between vCenter Server instances or if you accidentally remove a VM from inventory, all those attributes are lost.

You could restore them from a database backup (you have those, right?), but that's like driving in a nail with a semitruck. If only there was another way... Wait, what would survive being removed from inventory? Notes, of course; the answer here is to back up your custom attributes into the Notes field, as shown in Listing 5.20. This works because the notes are saved in the VMX file itself and thus are reimported with the VM.

LISTING 5.20   Backing up custom attributes to notes

```
Function Backup-Annotations
{
    <#
    .SYNOPSIS
       Save a copy of any custom annotations within the
       VM description.
    .DESCRIPTION
       Save a copy of any custom annotations within the
       VM description.
    .NOTES
        Source:  Automating vSphere Administration
        Authors: Luc Dekens, Arnim van Lieshout, Jonathan Medd,
                 Alan Renouf, Glenn Sizemore
```

```
    .PARAMETER VM
        Virtual machine to Backup.
    .EXAMPLE
        Backup-Annotations -VM (Get-VM VM01)
    .EXAMPLE
        Get-VM REHL* | Backup-Annotations
    #>
    [cmdletbinding(SupportsShouldProcess=$true)]
    Param(
        [Parameter(ValueFromPipeline=$True
        ,    Mandatory=$True
        ,    Helpmessage='VMObject to backup'
        )]
        [VMware.VimAutomation.ViCore.Impl.V1.Inventory.➥
VirtualMachineImpl]
        $VM
    )
    Process
    {
        $Skip = $False
        # ignore any previously saved annotations
        IF ($VM.Notes)
        {
            $CleanedNotes = $VM.Notes.split("`n") | %{
                if ($_ -eq '####BEGIN_ANNOTATIONS####')
                {
                    $Skip = $true
                }
                ElseIf ($_ -eq '#####END_ANNOTATIONS#####')
                {
                    $Skip = $False
                }
                Else
                {
                    If (-Not $Skip) {
                        $_
                    }
                }
            }
```

```
            }
            Else
            {
                $CleanedNotes = ""
            }
            $annotations = Get-Annotation -Entity $VM |
                Where-Object {$_.Value} |
                ForEach-Object {"$($_.Name)::$($_.Value)"}

            # Generate our new Notes entry
            $notes = @'
{0}
####BEGIN_ANNOTATIONS####
{1}
#####END_ANNOTATIONS#####
'@ -f $CleanedNotes,($annotations -join "`n")

            # Save our changes
            Set-VM -VM $VM -Description $notes -RunAsync
        }
}
```

`Backup-Annotation` will save any configured custom attributes to the virtual machine's Notes field. See Figure 5.3 for an example.

FIGURE 5.3   Backup-Annotation

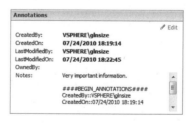

A backup is only as good as its restore, so we've also provided the script (Listing 5.21) to restore those handy attributes.

LISTING 5.21   Restoring custom attributes from notes

```
Function Restore-Annotations
{
```

```
<#
.SYNOPSIS
   Restore the Custom Attributes previously saved in the
   VM description.
.DESCRIPTION
   Restore the Custom Attributes previously saved in the
   VM description.
.NOTES
    Source:  Automating vSphere Administration
    Authors: Luc Dekens, Arnim van Lieshout, Jonathan Medd,
             Alan Renouf, Glenn Sizemore
.PARAMETER VM
    Virtual machine to Restore.
.EXAMPLE
    Restore-Annotations -VM (Get-VM VM01)
.EXAMPLE
    Get-VM REHL* | Restore-Annotations
#>
[cmdletbinding(SupportsShouldProcess=$true)]
Param(
    [Parameter(ValueFromPipeline=$True
    ,     Mandatory=$True
    ,     Helpmessage='VMObject to backup'
    )]
    [VMware.VimAutomation.ViCore.Impl.V1.Inventory.
VirtualMachineImpl]
    $VM
)
Process
{
    $Skip = $true
    IF ($VM.Notes)
    {
        $VM.Notes.split("`n") | %{
            if ($_ -eq '####BEGIN_ANNOTATIONS####')
            {
                $Skip = $False
            }
            ElseIf ($_ -eq '#####END_ANNOTATIONS#####')
            {
```

```
                              $Skip = $True
              }
              Else
              {
                 if($_ -match "(?<Name>[^:]+)::(?<Value>.+)" `
                    -AND -Not $Skip)
                 {
                    Set-Annotation -Entity $VM `
                       -CustomAttribute $Matches.Name `
                       -Value $Matches.Value
                 }
              }
           }
        }
     }
}
```

Although custom attributes can be used within a script, we tend to make the most use of them while in the vSphere Client. There, they can provide information where you need it, when you need it.

TIP   There is no performance overhead associated with custom attributes, but don't get carried away. As with all configuration items, you need to have a reason for capturing any data point. Be mindful of information overload.

Maintain VMware Tools

We consider VMware tools to be mandatory for all virtual machines. The reason for this is simple. As the vSphere administrator, you need to know a handful of things to safely host a VM within a dynamic datacenter. VMware Tools expose that critical information. Without the DNS name, IP, guest OS, and heartbeat information, you may make a decision that impacts a guest adversely. For this reason, you should make VMware Tools a key piece of every service level agreement (SLA) or office level agreement (OLA) you write.

Unfortunately, keeping these tools installed and up-to-date can at times be a full-time job. To help alleviate some of that burden, we've created a few examples to assist your efforts.

Windows Silent Install

Any Windows administrator will tell you that administering Windows remotely is a moving target. With that in mind, we present an example that should work in most environments. It's impossible to address every concern with Group Policy Objects (GPOs), firewalls, and so on. There are a thousand things that could break a remote install. But once you get one working in your environment, they are predictable.

Disclaimer aside, when we need to remotely manage a Windows machine we use two tools: PowerShell and WMI. PowerShell remoting is our primary weapon of choice, but it's not always configured. WMI is still Old Faithful. For this example, we assume WMI is available through the firewall on a Windows Server 2008 R2 virtual machine. Take a look at Listing 5.22.

LISTING 5.22 Windows Silent Install

```
$GuestCred = Get-Credential Administrator
$VM = Get-VM 'Win2k8R2'

# Mount vmware tools media
Mount-Tools -VM $VM

# Find the drive letter of the mounted media
$DrvLetter = Get-WmiObject -Class 'Win32_CDROMDrive' `
    -ComputerName $VM.Name `
    -Credential $GuestCred |
        Where-Object {$_.VolumeName -match "VMware Tools"} |
        Select-Object -ExpandProperty Drive

#Build our cmd line
$cmd = "$($DrvLetter)\setup.exe /S /v`"/qn ➥
REBOOT=ReallySuppress ADDLOCAL=ALL`""
# spawn a new process on the remote VM, and execute setup
$go = Invoke-WMIMethod -path win32_process `
    -Name Create `
    -Credential $GuestCred `
    -ComputerName $VM.Name `
    -ArgumentList $cmd

if ($go.ReturnValue -ne 0)
    {
```

```
    Write-Warning "Installer returned code $($go.ReturnValue)
unmounting media!"
    Dismount-Tools -VM $VM
}
Else
{
    Write-Verbose "Tool installation successfully triggered on
$($VM.Name) media will be ejected upon completion."
}
```

To recap, we mounted the VMware Tools ISO file, connected via WMI, and discovered the drive letter of the VMware Tools ISO file. Finally, we created a process that launches the setup.

Linux Silent Install

Unfortunately, the Linux disclaimer is even worse; needless to say, it will be different depending on the distribution and revision. At a minimum, we assume a SSH Server has been installed and configured to allow remote authentication. This will also vary widely depending on the Linux distribution, but generally you will need a bash script that can independently install VMware Tools. From there, you can use the Invoke-SSH function to remotely execute the script. For example, to install VMware Tools on a Red Hat 5 server, you could use the shell script shown in Listing 5.23.

LISTING 5.23 Linux Silent Install

```
#!/bin/bash

echo -n "Executing preflight checks     "
# make sure we are root
if [ `id -u` -ne 0 ]; then
    echo "You must be root to install tools!"
    exit 1;
fi

# make sure we are in RHEL, CentOS or some reasonable facsimilie
if [ ! -s /etc/redhat-release ]; then
    echo "You must be using RHEL or CentOS for this script to work!"
    exit 1;
fi
```

```
echo "[  OK  ]"
echo -n "Mounting Media              "
# check for the presence of a directory to mount the CD to
if [ ! -d /media/cdrom ]; then
    mkdir -p /media/cdrom
fi

# mount the cdrom, if necessary...this is rudimentary
if [ `mount | grep -c iso9660` -eq 0 ]; then
    mount -o loop /dev/cdrom /media/cdrom
fi

# make sure the cdrom that is mounted is vmware tools
MOUNT=`mount | grep iso9660 | awk '{ print $3 }'`

if [ `ls -l $MOUNT/VMwareTools* | wc -l` -ne 1 ]; then
    # there are no tools here
    echo "No tools found on CD-ROM!"
    exit 1;
fi
echo "[  OK  ]"
echo -n "Installing VMware Tools        "
# extract the installer to a temporary location
tar xzf $MOUNT/VMwareTools*.tar.gz -C /var/tmp

# install the tools, accepting defaults, capture output to a file
(/var/tmp/vmware-tools-distrib/vmware-install.pl --default )>
~/vmware-tools_install.log
# remove the unpackaging directory
rm -rf /var/tmp/vmware-tools-distrib
echo "[  OK  ]"
echo -n "Restarting Network:"
# the vmxnet kernel module may need to be loaded/reloaded...
service network stop
rmmod pcnet32
rmmod vmxnet
modprobe vmxnet
service network start

# or just reboot after tools install
# shutdown -r now
```

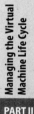

WARNING Linux guests can be particularly tricky as you may need a compiler and kernel sources available on a guest to install VMware Tools.

When you run it, the shell script in Listing 5.23 installs VMware Tools. Now, you need a method to deliver the script. This is where `Invoke-SSH` comes in (Listing 5.24); it is a PowerShell function that wraps `plink.exe` to provide a PowerCLI-friendly SSH interface.

LISTING 5.24 Using the `Invoke-SSH` function

```
Function Invoke-SSH
{
  <#
  .SYNOPSIS
      Execute a command via SSH on a remote system.
  .DESCRIPTION
      Execute a command via SSH on a remote system.
  .NOTES
        Source:  Automating vSphere Administration
        Authors: Luc Dekens, Arnim van Lieshout, Jonathan Medd,
                 Alan Renouf, Glenn Sizemore
  .PARAMETER Computer
    Computer to execute script/command against.
  .PARAMETER Credential
    PSCredential to use for remote authentication
  .PARAMETER Username
    Username to use for remote authentication
  .PARAMETER Password
    Password to use for remote authentication
  .PARAMETER FilePath
    Path to a script to execute on the remote machine
  .PARAMETER ScriptText
    ScriptText to execute on the remote system
  .EXAMPLE
    Invoke-SSH -Credential $Creds `
      -Computer 10.1.1.2 `
      -FilePath .\installtools.sh
  .EXAMPLE
    Invoke-SSH -Credential $Creds `
      -Computer $VM.name `
```

```
        -ScriptText 'rpm -qa' |
          Select-String ssh
#>
[CmdletBinding(DefaultParameterSetName='Command')]
Param(
  [Parameter(Mandatory=$True
  ,    ValueFromPipeline=$True
  ,    ValueFromPipelineByPropertyName=$True
  ,    HelpMessage='ip or hostname of remote computer'
  ,    ParameterSetName='Script'
  )]
  [Parameter(Mandatory=$True
  ,    ValueFromPipeline=$True
  ,    ValueFromPipelineByPropertyName=$True
  ,    HelpMessage='ip or hostname of remote computer'
  ,    ParameterSetName='Command'
  )]
  [string]
  $Computer

  ,
  [Parameter(Mandatory=$False
  ,    ValueFromPipeline=$True
  ,    ParameterSetName='Script'
  )]
  [Parameter(Mandatory=$False
  ,    ValueFromPipeline=$True
  ,    ParameterSetName='Command'
  )]
  [System.Management.Automation.PSCredential]
  $Credential

  ,
  [Parameter(ParameterSetName='Script')]
  [Parameter(ParameterSetName='Command')]
  [string]
  $Username

  ,
  [Parameter(ParameterSetName='Script')]
  [Parameter(ParameterSetName='Command')]
  [AllowEmptyString()]
  [string]
```

```
      $Password
,
    [Parameter(Mandatory=$True
    ,    ParameterSetName='Script'
    ,    ValueFromPipelineByPropertyName=$True
    ,    HelpMessage='Path to shell script'
    )]
    [ValidateScript({Test-Path $_})]
    [alias("PSPath","FullName")]
    [string]
    $FilePath
,
    [Parameter(Mandatory=$True
    ,    ParameterSetName='Command'
    ,    ValueFromRemainingArguments=$True
    ,    HelpMessage='Command to execute'
    )]
    [string]
    $ScriptText
)
Begin
{
  $PLink = "$env:ProgramFiles\PuTTY\plink.exe","plink.exe" |
    Get-Command -EA SilentlyContinue |
    Select-Object -First 1 -ExpandProperty Definition
  If (-Not $PLink)
  {
    throw "PLink could not be found, please install putty!"
    exit 1;
  }

  if ($Credential)
  {
    $Cred = $Credential.GetNetworkCredential()
    $Username = $Cred.UserName
    $Password = $Cred.Password
  }
}
Process
{
```

```
    switch ($PSCmdlet.ParameterSetName)
    {
      "Script"
      {
      & $Plink -l $Username -pw $Password $Computer -m $FilePath
      }
      "Command"
      {
      & $Plink -l $Username -pw $Password $Computer $ScriptText
      }
    }
  }
}
```

Now to bring it all together, you could combine Listing 5.23 and Listing 5.24 to remotely install VMware Tools to a Community Enterprise Operating System (CentOS) 5 server using the code in Listing 5.25.

LISTING 5.25 Remotely installing Linux VMware Tools

```
$VM = Get-VM REHL01
Mount-Tools -VM $VM
Invoke-SSH -Username root `
    -Password 'Pa$$word' `
    -Computer 10.10.10.63 `
    -FilePath .\InstallREHLTools.sh
Dismount-Tools -VM $VM
```

Admittedly, you did most of the heavy lifting in the shell script, but by integrating the installation in PowerCLI, you can plug this solution wherever, whenever you need it. You should be able to use the scripts provided by PowerCLI with minimal modification.

Updating VMware Tools

Prior to PowerCLI 4.0 Update 1, updating VMware Tools programmatically was a big deal. With Update 1, the PowerCLI team shipped an Update-Tools cmdlet with a -NoReboot switch that actually worked! While it is possible to delay the restart of a VM after you update or install VMware Tools, there are some side effects. You may experience excessive CPU usage or intermittent network connectivity.

We don't recommend this approach, but as administrators of several large VI farms, we understand! You can't always reboot a guest, nor can you count on someone else to remember to update VMware Tools. It is very handy to have VMware Tools installed just waiting for the reboot.

In fact, it's so easy we often update smaller Windows environments in one shot (see Listing 5.26).

LISTING 5.26   Installing VMware Tools en masse

```
Get-View -ViewType "VirtualMachine" `
    -Property Guest,name `
    -filter @{
        "Guest.GuestFamily"="windowsGuest";
        "Guest.ToolsStatus"="ToolsOld";
        "Guest.GuestState"="running"
    } |
        Get-VIObjectByVIView |
        Update-Tools -NoReboot
```

Linux virtual machines are a bit trickier. As of PowerCLI 4.1, only Windows machines are supported by the Update-Tools cmdlet. However, you can reuse the remote install script found in Listing 5.23 to perform the update. Additionally, now that VMware Tools are installed on the system, you can use the Invoke-VMScript cmdlet (see Listing 5.27).

LISTING 5.27   Updating VMware Tools for a Linux guest

```
$CMD = Get-Content .\installTools.sh | Out-String
Invoke-VMScript -VM $VM `
    -GuestCredential $guestCreds `
    -HostCredential $hostcreds `
    -ScriptText $cmd
```

WARNING   Be sure you coordinate with the virtual machine owner before triggering a VMware Tools update. Exploiting this connection into the VM is shady at best—and potentially illegal. Be up front and tell the truth; most admins appreciate the help and will work with you.

Using Templates and Customization Specifications

IN THIS CHAPTER, YOU WILL LEARN TO:

C reating new virtual machines (VMs) is a large part of any virtualization administrator's job. With the perceived ease of deployment, we are often asked to meet deployment schedules that aren't possible in the physical world. To meet the demands levied upon us, we have to utilize the full toolkit at our disposal. When it comes to deploying virtual machines, the tools provided are templates and customization specifications. Their use is a key part of any administrator's game. In this chapter, we'll cover creating templates, creating customization specifications, deploying guests, and maintaining templates over the long term.

Use Customization Specifications

A customization specification is a collection of information used to customize a guest operating system. This task can be done in conjunction with a deployment operation or independently on an existing VM as long as the machine in question has the following items installed:

- ▶ VMware Tools
- ▶ 32-bit or 64-bit hardware corresponding to the 32-bit or 64-bit operating system to be installed
- ▶ SCSI disks

Guest customization is accomplished through the use of finalization scripts that are executed through the Virtual Infrastructure eXtension (VIX) API. While this technique works wonderfully, it does require that the finalization script be written for the guest operating system. As of vSphere 4.1, guest customization is supported on all versions of Windows since Windows 2000, as well as most modern RedHat, Debian, Ubuntu, and SUSE Linux distributions. Most Linux distributions based on an officially supported kernel will usually work as well.

TIP   You'll find a complete list of supported operating systems in the vSphere compatibility matrix at `www.vmware.com`.

Creating Customization Specifications

To create a new customization specification from scratch in PowerCLI, you need use only one cmdlet, `New-OSCustomizationSpec`. For instance, to create a new Windows customization specification, you could run the code shown in Listing 6.1.

LISTING 6.1   Creating a new Windows customization specification

```
[vSphere PowerCLI] C:\> New-OSCustomizationSpec -Name 'Win2k8R2' `
    -FullName 'Glenn Sizemore' `
    -OrgName 'Get-Admin' `
    -OSType 'Windows' `
    -ChangeSid `
    -Type 'Persistent' `
    -DnsServer '192.168.145.6', '192.168.145.2' `
    -DnsSuffix 'vSphere.local' `
    -AdminPassword 'Pa22word' `
    -TimeZone 35 `
    -Workgroup 'workgroup' `
    -NamingScheme 'Vm' `
    -LicenseMode 'PerServer' `
    -LicenseMaxConnections 5
```

You can also create a Linux customization specification with the same cmdlet, as you can see in Listing 6.2.

LISTING 6.2   Creating a new Linux customization specification

```
[vSphere PowerCLI] C:\> New-OSCustomizationSpec -Name 'REHL5.5' `
    -OSType 'Linux' `
    -Domain 'vSphere.local' `
    -Type 'Persistent' `
    -DnsServer '192.168.145.6', '192.168.145.2' `
    -DnsSuffix 'vSphere.local' `
    -NamingScheme 'Vm'
```

We doubt you'll create many customization specifications from scratch from PowerCLI. It's one of those activities just meant for the GUI. Honestly, it is much easier to create one from scratch from within the vSphere Client.

Managing Customization Specifications

That's not to say you won't need to automate customization specifications. On the contrary, we highly recommend PowerCLI for all maintenance tasks. For example, if your organization added a new DNS server, adding that server to your existing specifications involves one line of code in PowerCLI.

```
[vSphere PowerCLI] C:\> Get-OSCustomizationSpec |
    Set-OSCustomizationSpec -DnsServer 192.168.1.2, 192.168.1.6
```

PowerCLI is useful for credential management, too. Most organizations require all administrative credentials to be updated quarterly at a minimum. Often, this task is ignored because it is deemed too difficult. Well, in PowerCLI maintaining a password is a snap. Let's update the account used to add machines to the domain. We don't want to update all specs, just the ones that are using this account, so we'll filter those out beforehand:

```
$Credentials = Get-Credential glnsize@vSphere.local
Get-OSCustomizationSpec|
    Where {$_.DomainAdminUsername -eq $Credentials.UserName} |
    Set-OSCustomizationSpec -DomainCredentials $Credentials
```

Maintaining the guest password is a snap as well. You might prefer to either omit the guest password completely or generate a random password for each new guest. If you use a common password for the local administrator account, that password needs to be updated regularly—another complicated and time-consuming task that is simplified with PowerCLI:

```
Get-OSCustomizationSpec |
    Where-Object {$_.OSType -eq 'Windows'}|
    Set-OSCustomizationSpec -AdminPassword 'P33k@B00!'
```

You can also clone an existing customization specification. For example, let's take an existing specification for a Windows 2008 R2 Server and create a new spec that we can use to deploy Server 2008 R2 Core edition web servers. To accomplish this, we're going to add a RunOnce command to the spec to install IIS:

```
Get-OSCustomizationSpec -Name 'Win2k8R2' |
    New-OSCustomizationSpec -Name W2K8R2Core_IIS |
    Set-OSCustomizationSpec -AutoLogonCount 1 `
Get-OSCustomizationSpec -Name 'Win2k8R2' |
    New-OSCustomizationSpec -Name W2K8R2Core_IIS |
    Set-OSCustomizationSpec -AutoLogonCount 1 `
        -GuiRunOnce 'start /w pkgmgr /l:log.etw ➡
/iu:IIS-WebServerRole;WAS-WindowsActivationService;➡
WAS-ProcessModel;WAS-NetFxEnvironment;WAS-ConfigurationAPI'
```

NOTE The GuiRunOnce component within a customization specification has caused much confusion over the years. Remember, when it comes to a Windows machine, Sysprep is doing all the work—VMware is merely automating Sysprep. Therefore, the RunOnce component is the GuiRunOnce from Sysprep. VMware is not using any tools or VIX integration to automate the process. If you're having issues using the RunOnce component, see Microsoft's Sysprep documentation. www.technet.microsoft.com VMware is just the facilitator in this transaction.

Using Customization Specifications

There are two ways to use an OS customization specification:

- ▶ You can apply it to a powered-off VM.

- ▶ You can attach it during a template deployment.

For now, let's stick to using a powered-off machine. Although it's not well known, you can use the Set-VM cmdlet to apply customization specifications to any guest, as long as that guest meets the minimum requirements we described earlier.

The Set-VM cmdlet's -OSCustomizationSpec parameter was intended to be used to apply a customization specification to a cloned VM. However, there is nothing preventing you from employing customization specifications on demand. Let's take an existing VM and migrate both the network and domain at once. We'll use a modified customization specification to perform the migration and readdress the network adapter on the VM (see Listing 6.3).

LISTING 6.3   Employing customization specifications on demand

```
# Save the credential object with permission to join the domain.
$DomainCredentials = Get-Credential glnsize@vSphere.local
# Clone our Spec adding the domain information.
$Spec = Get-OSCustomizationSpec 'Win2k8R2' |
    New-OSCustomizationSpec -Name 'tmp01' -Type NonPersistent |
    Set-OSCustomizationSpec -Domain vSphere.local `
        -DomainCredentials $DomainCredentials
    New-OSCustomizationSpec -Name 'tmp01' -Type NonPersistent |
    Set-OSCustomizationSpec -Domain vSphere.local `
        -DomainCredentials $DomainCredentials
# Update Spec with the new VLAN's IP information
$Spec = Get-OSCustomizationNicMapping -Spec $Spec|
    Set-OSCustomizationNicMapping -IPmode UseStaticIP `
        -IpAddress '10.1.5.42' `
        -SubnetMask '255.255.255.0' `
        -DefaultGateway '10.1.5.1' `
        -Dns '192.168.145.6','192.168.145.2'
$Spec = Get-OSCustomizationSpec 'tmp01'
# Get our VM
$VM = Get-VM -Name w2k8core
# Shut down guest to make change.
Shutdown-VMGuest -VM $VM -Confirm:$false | out-null
```

Managing the Virtual Machine Life Cycle

PART II

```
# Wait while guest shuts down
While ($vm.ExtensionData.Runtime.PowerState -ne 'poweredOff')
{
    Start-Sleep -Seconds 1
    $vm.ExtensionData.UpdateViewData('Runtime.PowerState')
}
# Change network settings
Get-VM w2k8core |
    Get-NetworkAdapter |
    Set-NetworkAdapter -NetworkName 'dvSwitch0_VLAN100' `
        -Confirm:$false |
    out-null
# Apply customization Spec to apply new network settings
Get-VM 'w2k8core'|
    Set-VM -OSCustomizationSpec $Spec -Confirm:$false|
    Start-VM
```

Customization specifications are a tool just like any other component of vSphere. With PowerCLI, you can apply that tool to whatever, wherever you see fit!

Use Templates

A template is a VM that has been placed in a protected, read-only state to be used as a master copy for subsequent virtual machine creation and provisioning tasks. You cannot modify any component of the VM once you've placed it in this state without first converting the template back into a virtual machine. There are many reasons to use templates, but they all boil down to one big plus: templates reduce the number of steps and the time needed to deploy a new virtual machine.

Creating Templates

Now that you know what a template is, you also know that all you need to create a new template is a source VM. Once you've prepared the source VM, you can choose from two ways to create a template:

▶ Convert this gold master VM into a template.

▶ Clone the master to a new template.

The decision of which to use is simple. Do you need the gold master VM for something else? If the answer is yes, then clone the source VM to a template. If the answer is no, then save yourself time and storage input/output operations per second (IOPs) by converting the source VM to a template.

For example, let's say your web team just finished loading a brand-new Linux server and wants you to use it as the source for an upcoming deployment. If you don't need the server for anything else, you can simply convert it to a template using the `Set-VM` cmdlet, as we've done in Listing 6.4.

LISTING 6.4   **Converting a VM to a template**

```
Get-VM WEBXX | Set-VM -ToTemplate
```

Now, if for some reason you need that source VM for another task but you want to use it as a template, you can create a new template by cloning the source to a template, as you can see in Listing 6.5.

LISTING 6.5   **Cloning a VM to a template**

```
$VM = Get-VM WEB07
$Folder = Get-Folder WEB
New-Template -Name 'W2k8R2' -VM $VM -Location $Folder
```

N O T E   Prior to Virtual Center 2.5 update 2, you had to power off the virtual machine to clone to template. Every version since then simply takes a snapshot and clones from that snapshot if the VM is powered on. Although this approach works, it may not result in a usable template, so proceed with caution.

That's all there is to it from a vCenter Server/PowerCLI point of view. The truth about templates is that they are only as good as the source VM—which means all the hard work is done up front in the guest.

Deploying Guests from Templates

Now that you have your templates prestaged, let's deploy some guests. Deploying from a template is a clone operation and, as you learned in Chapter 5, "Creating Virtual Machines," this is accomplished via the `New-VM` cmdlet. The short script in Listing 6.6 deploys a web server from the Windows 2008 R2 template we created in Listing 6.5.

LISTING 6.6   Deploying a guest from a template

```
$Template = Get-Template -Name 'W2K8R2'
$VMHost = Get-VMHost -Name 'vSphere1'
New-VM -Template $Template -Name 'WEB001' -VMHost $VMHost
```

A straight deploy operation is a simple task, but the problem is that everything must be prepared prior to the creation of the template because you're not leveraging any of the integration components. Technically, there is nothing wrong with this approach. We've worked with mature Windows/Linux shops that had their own deployment processes nailed down. They weren't interested in any assistance from VMware. If you're fortunate enough to work in such an environment, keep doing what you do. For the rest of us, there are customization specifications.

As of vSphere 4.1/PowerCLI 4.1, OS customization specifications have matured. Today they are production ready and capable of performing most tasks. To illustrate, we'll go through a series of deployments, gradually cranking up the complexity. We'll start off with a standard Windows Server and assign a static IP address via the customization specification (see Listing 6.7).

LISTING 6.7   Assigning a static IP address to a Windows Server using a customization specification

```
# Update Spec with our desired IP information
Get-OSCustomizationSpec -Name 'Win2k8R2' |
    Get-OSCustomizationNicMapping |
    Set-OSCustomizationNicMapping -IPmode UseStaticIP `
        -IpAddress '192.168.145.78' `
        -SubnetMask '255.255.255.0' `
        -DefaultGateway '192.168.145.2' `
        -Dns '192.168.145.6','192.168.145.2'
# Get updated Spec Object
$Spec = Get-OSCustomizationSpec -Name 'Win2k8R2'
# Get Template to deploy from
$Template = Get-Template -Name 'W2K8R2'
# Get VMHost to deploy new VM on
$VMHost = Get-VMHost -Name 'vSphere1'
# Deploy VM
New-VM -Name 'WEB001' `
    -VMHost $VMHost `
    -Template $Template `
    -OSCustomizationSpec $Spec |
    Start-VM
```

The workflow here is somewhat backward, but it makes sense once you understand what is going on beneath the covers. First, you have to modify your customization specification with the desired IP address. Here is where it gets a little crazy: when you do this, you're updating the actual customization specification—you're not working with an object in memory. Once you retrieve the now modified customization object from vCenter Server along with your template and VMHost, you can simply call the New-VM cmdlet to deploy the new virtual machine.

You'll notice in Listing 6.7 that we piped the New-VM object to Start-VM. You want to do this because that customization information isn't in the guest yet—and won't be until that VM is powered on the first time. Once your new virtual machine is powered on for the first time, vCenter waits for tools to report in. After the VMware Tools report in for the first time, vCenter Server copies a customized Sysprep to the guest VM via VIX integration and then calls a series of finalization scripts that perform the guest customization.

While completely functional, both of our previous examples had one critical flaw: they modified the customization specification back on vCenter Server. This behavior is especially troublesome if, like us, you like to use the Prompt The User For IP Address If No Default Is Available setting within the customization specification. To work around this, you can use nonpersistent OS customization specifications. The process looks identical to the process in Listing 6.7 with one exception: before making any modifications, clone your customization specification to a nonpersistent specification. This step enables you to modify the specification without affecting the copy stored on vCenter Server. In Listing 6.8, we've deployed another Windows Server performing the same customization as before, but this time we're leaving the master copy on vCenter Server unaffected.

LISTING 6.8   Cloning a customization specification to a nonpersistent specification

```
# Clone our Spec
$Spec = Get-OSCustomizationSpec 'Win2k8R2' |
    New-OSCustomizationSpec -Name 'tmp01' -Type NonPersistent
# Update Spec with our desired IP information
Get-OSCustomizationNicMapping -Spec $Spec|
    Set-OSCustomizationNicMapping -IPmode UseStaticIP `
        -IpAddress '192.168.145.42' `
        -SubnetMask '255.255.255.0' `
        -DefaultGateway '192.168.145.2' `
        -Dns '192.168.145.6','192.168.145.2'
# Get updated Spec Object
$Spec = Get-OSCustomizationSpec -Name 'tmp01'
```

```
# Get Template to deploy from
$Template = Get-Template -Name 'W2K8R2'
# Get VMHost to deploy new VM on
$VMHost = Get-VMHost -Name 'vSphere1'
# Deploy VM
New-VM -Name 'WEB001' `
    -VMHost $VMHost `
    -Template $Template `
    -OSCustomizationSpec $Spec |
    Start-VM
```

WARNING   When you clone a nonpersistent customization specification, it is stored in the memory of that PowerCLI session. Other PowerCLI sessions have no knowledge or access to the cloned customization specification. However, within the session where the customization is created, you have to manage it like it was a persistent specification—meaning you cannot have two specs with the same name.

Thus far, all of our examples have had only a single network adapter. What about a machine with multiple network adapters? Well, as it turns out, the process is almost exactly the same. The only difference is that you have to specifically call out each adapter. To set the configuration, you first have to know each network adapter (Nic) position within the customization specification Nic mapping. To get the `Nic` positions, run the `Get-OSCustomizationNicMapping` cmdlet for the spec you're modifying and examine the output:

```
[PowerCLI] C:\> Get-OSCustomizationSpec -name 'W2K8R2Core_IIS' |
>> Get-OSCustomizationNicMapping
>>

SpecId              Position IPMode       IPAddress     DefaultGateway
------              -------- ------       ---------     --------------
W2K8R2Core_IIS             1 PromptUser                 192.168.145.2
W2K8R2Core_IIS             2 UseStaticIP  10.10.10.11
```

Once you know the positions, you can programmatically configure each NIC (Listing 6.9).

LISTING 6.9   Using customization specifications with multiple network adapters

```
# Clone our Spec
$Spec = Get-OSCustomizationSpec 'W2K8R2Core_IIS' |
```

```
    New-OSCustomizationSpec -Name 'tmp_two_nics' `
        -Type NonPersistent
# Get every Nic in our spec
Foreach ($NIC in (Get-OSCustomizationNicMapping -Spec $Spec))
{

    # Set the appropriate NIC settings
    Switch ($NIC.Position)
    {
      1 {
          Set-OSCustomizationNicMapping -IPmode UseStaticIP `
              -OSCustomizationNicMapping $NIC `
              -IpAddress '192.168.145.42' `
              -SubnetMask '255.255.255.0' `
              -DefaultGateway '192.168.145.2' `
              -Dns '192.168.145.6','192.168.145.2'
      }
      2 {
          Set-OSCustomizationNicMapping -IpAddress 10.10.10.42
              -OSCustomizationNicMapping $NIC `
      }
    }
}
# Get the updated Spec Object
$Spec = Get-OSCustomizationSpec -Name 'tmp_two_nics'
# Get Template to deploy from
$Template = Get-Template -Name 'W2K8R2_Core'
# Get VMHost to deploy new VM on
$VMHost = Get-VMHost -Name 'vSphere1'
# Deploy VM
New-VM -Name 'WEB001' `
    -VMHost $VMHost `
    -Template $Template `
    -OSCustomizationSpec $Spec |
    Start-VM
```

Notice how only the customization NIC mapping changed. One of the truly powerful features of PowerCLI is that you don't have to learn a new task each time; instead, you build on your existing knowledge.

So far, we have deployed only Windows guests. Let's shift gears and deploy a Ubuntu 10 server from a template, as shown in Listing 6.10.

LISTING 6.10 Deploying a Linux guest from a template

```
$Template = Get-Template -Name ' Ubuntu10'
$VMHost = Get-VMHost -Name 'vSphere1'
New-VM -Template $Template -Name 'WEB001' -VMHost $VMHost
```

Wait! That looks very similar to the Windows guest we deployed in Listing 6.6. The only difference is the VM name and the template. So now let's add a customization spec and configure the guest postdeployment (see Listing 6.11).

LISTING 6.11 Using a customization spec to configure a Linux guest postdeployment

```
# Clone our Spec
$Spec = Get-OSCustomizationSpec Ubuntu10' |
    New-OSCustomizationSpec -Name 'tmp01' -Type NonPersistent
# Update Spec with our desired IP information
Get-OSCustomizationNicMapping -Spec $Spec|
    Set-OSCustomizationNicMapping -IPmode UseStaticIP `
        -IpAddress '192.168.145.42' `
        -SubnetMask '255.255.255.0' `
        -DefaultGateway '192.168.145.2'
# Get updated Spec Object
$Spec = Get-OSCustomizationSpec -Name 'tmp01'
# Get Template to deploy from
$Template = Get-Template -Name Ubuntu10'
# Get VMHost to deploy new VM on
$VMHost = Get-VMHost -Name 'vSphere1'
# Deploy VM
New-VM -Name 'WEB001' `
    -VMHost $VMHost `
    -Template $Template `
    -OSCustomizationSpec $Spec |
    Start-VM
```

Again, this code looks almost identical to the code from Listing 6.8. That's one of PowerCLI's greatest strengths: behind the scenes, VMware has built an amazing abstraction layer in guest customizations. PowerCLI then takes that abstraction layer and abstracts it again. This means that it is either incredibly easy or incredibly difficult to perform guest customization. Either the guest is supported and it's a snap, or it's not and you have to roll your own. Fear not! If you're not afraid of a little scripting, you can always roll your own guest customizations with `Invoke-VMScript`.

Maintaining Templates

Templates are an incredibly powerful tool—one you wouldn't want to live without. It is, however, important that you keep them up-to-date. It's a level-of-effort deal; it's easier to maintain one template than it is to patch or update a number of VMs postdeployment. Some companies choose to update their templates only quarterly and rely on their management tools to fill that gap. We feel this is foolish: regardless of how good your enterprise toolkit is, why waste cycles on a fresh guest deployment when it is easier to just maintain the source template? Whatever your decisions, just remember: PowerCLI is here to assist in any way you see fit. With that in mind, we'll go over a few common issues, but first we'll solve a universal pain point with templates.

No matter what you're doing, the first step is always to convert your template into a VM and the last step is to convert back to a template. You might or might not need to power on the VM in the middle of the process. You will find that you constantly have to account for the power state of the VM during any update. To assist in this trivial task, you can use `Wait-VMGuest` (see Listing 6.12).

LISTING 6.12 The **Wait-VMGuest** function

```
Function Wait-VMGuest
{

    <#
    .SYNOPSIS
        Wait while the VM performs a power operation.
    .DESCRIPTION
        Wait while the VM performs a power operation.
        Useful when working with VMGuests.  Uses VMware
        tools to denote a startup, and power off.
.NOTES
    Source:  Automating vSphere Administration
    Authors: Luc Dekens, Arnim van Lieshout, Jonathan Medd,
            Alan Renouf, Glenn Sizemore
```

```
.PARAMETER VM
        VM object to wait on
    .PARAMETER VMGuest
        VMGuest object to wait on
    .PARAMETER Operation
        Type of power Operation to wait on
        valid values are: 'Startup', and 'Shutdown'
    .EXAMPLE
        Get-VM VM01 |
            Start-VM |
            Wait-VM -Operation 'Startup'|
            Update-Tools
    .EXAMPLE
        Get-VM VM01 |
            Shutdown-VMGuest |
            Wait-VM -Operation 'Shutdown'|
            Set-vm -NumCpu 2 |
            start-VM
#>    [cmdletbinding(DefaultParameterSetName='VM')]
Param(
    [parameter(Position=0
    ,    ParameterSetName='VM'
    )]
    [parameter(Position=0
    ,    ParameterSetName='Guest'
    )]
    [ValidateSet("Startup","Shutdown")]
    [string]
    $Operation

    ,
    [parameter(Mandatory=$True
    ,    ValueFromPipeline=$True
    ,    HelpMessage='Virtual Machine object to wait on'
    ,    ParameterSetName='VM'
    )]
    [VMware.VimAutomation.ViCore.Impl.V1.Inventory.➡
     VirtualMachineImpl]
    $VM

    ,
```

```
    [parameter(Mandatory=$True
    ,     ValueFromPipeline=$True
    ,     HelpMessage='The VM Guest object to wait on'
    ,     ParameterSetName='Guest'
    )]
    [VMware.VimAutomation.ViCore.Impl.V1.VM.Guest.VMGuestImpl]
    $VMGuest

)
Process {
    IF ($PSCmdlet.ParameterSetName -eq 'Guest') {
        $VM = $VMGuest.VM
    }
    Switch ($Operation)
    {
        "Startup"
        {
            while ($vm.ExtensionData.Guest.ToolsRunningStatus `
              -eq "guestToolsNotRunning")
            {
                Start-Sleep -Seconds 1
                $vm.ExtensionData.UpdateViewData("Guest")
            }
            # return a fresh VMObject
            Write-Output (Get-VM $VM)
            break;
        }
        "Shutdown"
        {
            # wait for the VM to be shut down
            while ($VM.ExtensionData.Runtime.PowerState `
              -ne "poweredOff")
            {
                Start-Sleep -Seconds 1
                $vm.ExtensionData.UpdateViewData( `
                    "Runtime.PowerState")
            }
            # return a fresh VMObject
            Write-Output (Get-VM $VM)
```

```
            break;
        }
    }
  }
}
```

`Wait-VMGuest` simplifies your code by pausing the pipeline while the target VM either shuts down or starts up. You will use this function extensively in the next two sections. Take note of the way it streamlines the code. Can you imagine having to put the pipeline into a loop every time you power-cycle a VM? You'd break the streaming nature of PowerShell. The `Wait-VMGuest` function enables the pipeline to stream while still waiting where needed.

WHAT'S WRONG WITH *START-VM/STOP-VM*?

You might be thinking, "Why create a new function? Why not just use `Start-VM` or `Stop-VM` with `-RunAsync` and pipe that into `Wait-Task`?"

The `Wait-VMGuest` function was designed for situations where you need the VM to be either all the way up and tools started or all the way down and powered off before you release the pipeline. While automating a situation like this, one of the authors started with `Start-VM`/ `Shutdown-VMGuest` and was shocked to discover they only waited for the task to clear vCenter Server.

Upgrading Hardware

Although this doesn't come up very often, if you had a vast collection of templates in VirtualCenter 2.5, the vSphere upgrade would have caused a lot of undo work. Fortunately, this is one of those tasks that lends itself to automation. In Listing 6.13 we'll update the `W2K8R2` template to hardware version 7.

LISTING 6.13   Update VM hardware version

```
$VM = Get-Template 'W2K8R2' | Set-Template -ToVM
$vm.ExtensionData.UpgradeVM("vmx-07")
Set-VM -VM $VM -ToTemplate
```

As tasks go, this one is easy. You get your template object and convert it into a VM. Then, call the `UpgradeVM` method on the virtual machine object to perform the upgrade. Finally, convert the object back into a template. There is one problem, though: VMware requires that a current version of the VMware Tools be installed prior to upgrading a VM's hardware version—which means you must either force the upgrade (which is dangerous) or handle the tools upgrade as well (which is complicated). Ultimately the choice is yours, but you could force the upgrade using code like that shown in Listing 6.14.

LISTING 6.14   Forcing a VM hardware upgrade

```
$VM = Get-Template 'vm01' | Set-Template -ToVM
$taskMoRef = $vm.ExtensionData.UpgradeVM_Task("vmx-07")
$task = Get-View $taskMoRef
while ($task.Info.State -eq 'running')
{
    $task.UpdateViewData("Info.State")
    $Question = Get-VMQuestion -VM $VM
    if ($Question)
    {
        Answer-VMQuestion -VMQuestion $Question `
            -DefaultOption `
            -Confirm:$false
    }
}
Set-VM -VM $VM -ToTemplate -Confirm:$false
```

There are scenarios where you would want to force an upgrade. For example, if the template didn't have an operating system or the VMware Tools weren't installed in the template, you would have to force the upgrade. This situation would be an edge case, in our opinion. Best practice is to always have VMware Tools installed, and a template will almost always have an operating system.

So how can you safely automate an upgrade when the operating system or VMware Tools are missing? Before we get into the actual code, let's talk about what a safe virtual hardware upgrade entails. First, you have to convert the template back into a VM to make it writable. Then, you need to upgrade the VMware Tools. Once you've upgraded, you must power off the VM. Then, you can upgrade the hardware version. For good measure, you should power the template back on and take a look to see how it all went.

Now, let's break that process down into code (see Listing 6.15).

LISTING 6.15   Safely upgrading the VM hardware

```
# get our template, convert it to a VM, and power said VM on.
$VM = Get-Template 'vm01' |
    Set-Template -ToVM |
```

```
    Start-VM |
    Wait-VMGuest Startup
# kick off a tools update and wait for it to finish.
Update-Tools -VM $VM
#Shut down our VM
Shutdown-VMGuest -VM $VM -Confirm:$false |
    Wait-VMGuest Shutdown |
    Out-Null
# Perform the hardware upgrade
$vm.ExtensionData.UpgradeVM("vmx-07")
# Power on our VM
Start-VM -VM $VM
# Log in and make sure the upgrade went okay.
# Power our VM back down
$VM = Shutdown-VMGuest -VM $VM -Confirm:$false |
    Wait-VMGuest Shutdown
# Convert back to template
Set-VM -VM $VM -ToTemplate -Confirm:$false
```

Very straightforward! If you had enough templates to justify the investment, you could automate the complete upgrade lifecycle, like we do with Update-Template Hardware in Listing 6.16. This script handles the complete upgrade life cycle. Additionally, it performs checks before making any modification to ensure you're only affecting templates that require an update.

LISTING 6.16   `Update-TemplateHardware`

```
Function Update-TemplateHardware
{

<#
    .SYNOPSIS
        Update Template to latest hardware version
    .DESCRIPTION
        Update Template to latest hardware version.  Requires
        the Update-Tools cmdlet so any template not supported
        will not work.
    .NOTES
        Source:  Automating vSphere Administration
        Authors: Luc Dekens, Arnim van Lieshout, Jonathan Medd,
                 Alan Renouf, Glenn Sizemore
```

```
.PARAMETER Template
    Template to Update
.PARAMETER Version
    Desired Hardware version default vmx-07
.EXAMPLE
    Update-TemplateHardware -Template (Get-Template WINXP)
.EXAMPLE
    Get-Template | Update-TemplateHardware
#>
[CmdletBinding()]
param(
    [parameter(Mandatory=$True
    ,      ValueFromPipeline=$True
    ,      HelpMessage='Template object to upgrade'
    )]
    [VMware.VimAutomation.ViCore.Impl.V1.Inventory.➥
    TemplateImpl]
    $Template

    ,

    [parameter()]
    [ValidatePattern("vmx-\d\d")]
    [string]
    $Version="vmx-07"
)
Process
{
    # Convert our template back to a VM, and PowerOn.
    $VM = Set-Template -Template $Template -ToVM

     #check VM Hardware version
    IF ($vm.ExtensionData.Config.Version -ne $Version)
    {
        write-host "VM Hardware version out of date!" `
            -ForegroundColor 'RED'
        $VM = Start-VM -VM $VM | Wait-VMGuest Startup

        # Check VMware tools version if tools are out of
        # date upgrade them.
        If ($vm.ExtensionData.Guest.ToolsStatus -ne "ToolsOk")
```

```
    {
        Write-Host 'VMware tools are out of date!' `
                -ForegroundColor 'RED'
        #Kick off a tools update
        Try
        {
            Update-Tools -VM $VM
        }
        Catch
        {
            Write-Warning $_.exception.message
            break;
        }
        Write-Host "Updating Tools..." -NoNewline
        #Wait for the update to finish
        while ($vm.ExtensionData.Guest.ToolsStatus `
         -ne "ToolsOk")
        {
            Start-Sleep -Seconds 1
            Write-Host "." -NoNewline
            $vm.ExtensionData.UpdateViewData("Guest")
        }
        write-host "DONE" -ForegroundColor 'Green'
        Write-Host "Tools upgrade complete"
        Write-Host "Starting hardware Upgrade"
    }
    Else
    {
        Write-Host "ToolsOK Starting hardware Upgrade" `
            -ForegroundColor 'Green'
    }

# Shut the VM back down
Write-Host "Shut down guest"
$VM = Shutdown-VMGuest -VM $VM -Confirm:$false |
    Wait-VMGuest Shutdown
$vm.ExtensionData.UpgradeVM("vmx-07")
Write-Host "VM Hardware updated..."
Write-Host "Starting VM please log in and verify"
```

```
                        $VM = Start-VM -VM $VM
            }
            Else
            {
                write-host "VM Hardware is up to date." `
                    -ForegroundColor 'Green'
                $VM = Set-VM -VM $VM -ToTemplate -Confirm:$false
            }
        }
    }
```

Patching

Once you have a well-established template, you shouldn't need to make many modifications. You will, however, want to keep the template up-to-date. There are several techniques available for this purpose. The first (and most obvious) is to use the VMware Update Manager (VUM). Because VUM is vertically integrated into the vSphere stack, this application is virtualization aware and can leverage that knowledge quite nicely. VUM is covered in greater detail in Chapter 13, "Maintaining Security in Your vSphere Environment." But suffice it to say, if you choose to go the VUM route, updating templates is a highly automated task, as you can see in Listing 6.17.

LISTING 6.17 Patching templates en masse via VUM

```
$tasks = @()
ForEach ($Template in Get-Template)
{
    # Scan template for compliance
    Scan-Inventory -Entity $Template -UpdateType 'VmPatch'
    #Get any baselines attached to template that are not compliant
    $NonCompliant = Get-Compliance -Entity $Template|
        Where-Object {$_.status -ne "Compliant"} |
        Select-Object -ExpandProperty Baseline
    #Remediate any non-compliant baselines
    $Tasks += Remediate-Inventory -Entity $Template `
        -Baseline $nonCompliant `
        -GuestCreateSnapshot $true `
        -GuestKeepSnapshotHours 48 `
        -GuestSnapshotName 'Updates' `
```

```
        -RunAsync `
        -confirm:$false
}
# Wait while remediation tasks run
Wait-Task -Task $Tasks
```

While VUM is completely functional, it is not very mature; few organizations leverage this technology for VMs. To make matters worse, it appears that VMware is dropping guest patching from VUM completely, which has led to poor VUM adoption. Many IT organizations choose to patch their guest operating systems using the native tools for that OS. For example, a Windows shop will leverage Windows Server Update Services (WSUS) or System Center Configuration Manager (SCCM) to patch their Windows VMs. A RedHat shop might use Puppet in conjunction with a satellite server. Smaller organizations might even use a unified patch platform like Shavlik.

N O T E   At the end of the day, VUM's biggest weakness is that it cannot patch a physical host. Therefore, even if an organization decided to try to leverage the advantages VUM offers, they would still have to maintain a separate infrastructure for their physical hosts. This core weakness has resulted in VMware announcing they intend to drop guest patching from the next release of VUM.

Whatever your process, PowerCLI is here to help. By integrating your existing patch management infrastructure with your virtual infrastructure, you can maintain the best of both worlds. For instance, if your organization manually updates all servers, then more than likely you will manually update your templates as well. You can still use PowerCLI to automate the conversions and power operations, but you will have to log in and manually install any pending patches (see Listing 6.18).

LISTING 6.18   Automating the template patch life cycle

```
Get-Template 'w2k8R2' |
    Set-Template -ToVM |
    Start-VM |
    Wait-VMGuest Startup |
    # here you would log in and patch the guest
    Wait-VMGuest Shutdown |
    Set-VM -ToTemplate -Confirm:$false
```

As you saw in the preceding script, we used PowerCLI to convert our template into a VM. We then started the VM and waited while the guest was updated. PowerCLI then detected the power-off, used that as a cue that we were finished with the update, and converted the VM back into a template. This approach has the benefit of organizing the patch process, making it repeatable across any number of VMs, while not requiring a completely automated solution.

You could take this process a step further and automate the whole patch life cycle, as we'll do here in Listing 6.19. This time we'll take a snapshot beforehand. We'll also make sure any needed updates are waiting for the administrator when they log in by triggering update detection within the guest. Finally, we'll clone our updated guest to a new template, thereby fulfilling any failback requirements from our change management processes.

LISTING 6.19   Automating the template patch life cycle

```
$HostCredential = Get-Credential
$GuestCredential = Get-Credential
$DTG = get-date -Format s
#Convert template back into VM
$VM = Get-Template 'w2k8R2' |
    Set-Template -ToVM
#Take a snapshot before we alter our template
$Snapshot = New-Snapshot -VM $VM `
    -Name Updates_$DTG `
    -Description "scheduled updates $DTG"
#Power on the VM, and wait for tools to report in
$VM = Start-VM -VM $VM | Wait-VMGuest 'Startup'
#kick off the windows update detection agent within the guest
Invoke-VMScript -VM $VM `
    -GuestCredential $GuestCredential `
    -HostCredential $HostCredential `
    -ScriptType 'bat' `
        -ScriptType 'bat' `
    -ScriptText '%windir%\system32\wuauclt.exe /reportnow ➡
    /detectnow'
#wait for the VM to be powered off
$VM = Wait-VMGuest -VM $VM -Operation 'Shutdown'
# Create a new template for testing
$Template = New-Template -VM $VM -Name ("{0}_{1}" -f $VM.Name,
$DTG)
```

The next logical step would be to fully automate the installation of patches. You can do that: using a combination of `Invoke-VMScript` and some guest scripting, you can create a hands-free update process. The decision of whether or not you need to depends on your organization.

TIP   When automating your system, keep in mind that there are barriers. You can take automation too far, making it too complex or too delicate. Ultimately, you need to assess whether or not you will see any operational savings from such an investment. We strongly encourage you to use the techniques we described to ensure that, at least from vCenter Server, you remove the potential for mistakes by automating the template life cycle.

Configuring Virtual Machine Hardware

IN THIS CHAPTER, YOU WILL LEARN TO:

After your environment is all set up and running, there comes a time when a virtual machine needs to be reconfigured. Perhaps performance is lacking and you need to throw in an additional vCPU or more memory. Or maybe your disk is running to its maximum capacity and needs to be extended. All of these tasks and some other reconfiguration tasks are covered in this chapter.

Add, Configure, and Remove Virtual Hardware

This section will focus on changing virtual machine (VM) hardware configurations like memory, vCPU, network adapters, and virtual disks.

Changing Virtual Memory

So, you configured your VM initially with 1,024 MB of RAM and you noticed that performance is lacking due to memory resource exhaustion. Let's have a look at how you can change the amount of memory on your VM. To do so, you'll use the Set-VM cmdlet. This cmdlet accepts a -MemoryMB parameter, which allows you to define a new memory size:

```
Set-VM VM001 -MemoryMB 2048 -Confirm:$false
```

Remember that for this line of code to work, your VM must be powered off or support memory hot plug. If your VM doesn't support memory hot plug and you can only shut down your VM during maintenance hours, you might want to schedule an upgrade process.

The small script in Listing 7.1 automates the complete process. The VM is first gracefully shut down, and after upgrading the memory, the VM is powered on again. You can schedule this script to run during maintenance hours overnight, and let the script do the configuration while you get a good night's sleep.

LISTING 7.1   Changing virtual machine memory offline

```
Get-VM VM001 | Shutdown-VMGuest -Confirm:$false
While ((Get-VM VM001).PowerState -eq "PoweredOn"){
  Sleep -Seconds 2
}
Get-VM VM001 | Set-VM -MemoryMB 2048 -Confirm:$false
Get-VM VM001 | Start-VM -Confirm:$false
```

Changing Memory Resources

To guarantee memory entitlement, you can configure a memory reservation for a VM. Memory reservation guarantees that the reserved memory will always be backed up by machine memory, even during times of memory contention. This is something you want to do to ensure some level of performance on a VM. Memory reservations also determine the size of the VM's swap file on the ESX host, as the swap file's size is equal to the VM's configured memory minus its reservation. For VMs with a large amount of memory, a large swap file is created by default, because, by default, no reservation is set. To prevent these massive swap files from eating up precious (and expensive) storage, reservations sometimes are set on VMs with a large memory footprint.

On the other hand, when you want to cap a VM, to prevent it from using too much machine memory, you can limit a VM. This will force any memory above the limit to be provisioned from the VM's swap file on the host. Memory provisioned from the swap file doesn't perform very well in most environments. One exception might be swap files deployed on solid state drives (SSDs). Memory limits are something that you want to use sparingly and only when absolutely necessary. In a highly secured demilitarized zone (DMZ) environment, for instance, you might want to put a memory limit on a VM to prevent a possible denial-of-service (DoS) attack by hogging the VM's memory when that VM is compromised at the cost of some performance.

If you want to change memory resource configurations like limits, reservations, and shares, the Get-VMResourceConfiguration and Set-VMResource Configuration cmdlets are your friends.

To set a memory reservation, use the –MemReservationMB parameter. The value of this parameter ranges from 0 to the value of the memory limit or the amount of configured memory if no limit is set. To set a memory limit, use the –MemLimitMB parameter. The value for this parameter ranges from the value of the memory reservation to the amount of configured memory. Figure 7.1 is a graphical representation of these parameters' ranges.

To set the memory reservation to 1,024 MB and the memory limit to 1,792 MB on your virtual machine, use the following:

```
Get-VM VM001 | Get-VMResourceConfiguration | `
    Set-VMResourceConfiguration -MemReservationMB 1024 `
    -MemLimitMB 1792
```

Managing the Virtual
Machine Life Cycle

PART II

FIGURE 7.1 Memory reservation and limit ranges

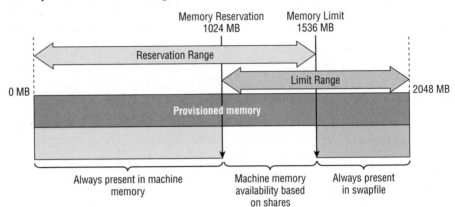

To reset the memory limit on your VM (set it to Unlimited), use the following:

```
Get-VM VM001 | Get-VMResourceConfiguration | `
    Set-VMResourceConfiguration -MemLimitMB $null
```

The third mechanism to configure memory resources is shares. Shares come into play when there's memory contention on a host. In that case, shares determine the VM's entitlement to machine memory for the amount of memory between the reservation and the limit. (See Figure 7.1.) To change the number of memory shares, use the -MemSharesLevel parameter. Possible enumeration values are Custom, High, Low, and Normal. Because this parameter accepts an enumerator value, you can also specify an index value from 0 to 3, where an index value of 0 means Custom, 1 means High, 2 means Low, and 3 means Normal. In Table 7.1, you'll find an overview of the available memory shares levels. If you want to fine-tune the memory shares beyond the factory presets (High, Low, and Normal), you can set the shares level to Custom and specify the number of shares with the -NumMemShares parameter.

TABLE 7.1 Memory shares

Shares level	Shares/MB	Index
Custom	1 – 1,000,000	0
High	20	1
Low	5	2
Normal	10	3

To set the memory share level to a custom value of 1,500, use the following:

```
Get-VM VM001 | Get-VMResourceConfiguration | `
    Set-VMResourceConfiguration -MemSharesLevel "Custom" `
    -NumMemShares 1500
```

When you specify the –NumMemShares parameter, you can omit setting the share level to Custom because it will be set to Custom automatically.

Changing the Number of vCPUs

After upgrading your VM with additional memory, you might notice that CPU utilization is increasing rapidly since the application on this VM went into production. To make sure that performance stays at an acceptable level, you can add an additional CPU to the VM. (Be sure to confirm with the application vendor that the application is multithreaded and can benefit from an extra CPU.) You can change the number of vCPUs in your VM; you need to use the Set-VM cmdlet again as you did to change the amount of memory. This time, however, you have to use the –NumCpu parameter to specify the new number of vCPUs. To add a vCPU to a VM named VM001, use the following:

```
Set-VM VM001 –NumCpu 2 –Confirm:$false
```

Again, remember that your VM needs to support CPU hot plug or be powered off. In Listing 7.2 you'll find a function based on the idea of the code in Listing 7.1 that automates the process of changing the number of vCPUs or amount of memory when your VM doesn't support hot plug.

LISTING 7.2   Changing VM memory and vCPU offline

```
function Set-VMOffline {
<#
.SYNOPSIS
  Changes the vCPU and memory configuration of the
  virtual machine Offline
.DESCRIPTION
  This function changes the vCPU and memory configuration of
  the virtual machine Offline
.NOTES
  Source:   Automating vSphere Administration
  Authors: Luc Dekens, Arnim van Lieshout, Jonathan Medd,
           Alan Renouf, Glenn Sizemore
```

Managing the Virtual Machine Life Cycle

PART II

```
.PARAMETER VM
  Specify the virtual machine
.PARAMETER MemoryMB
  Specify the memory size in MB
.PARAMETER NumCpu
  Specify the number of virtual CPUs
.PARAMETER TimeOut
  Specify the number of seconds to wait for the vm to shut down
  gracefully. Default timeout is 300 seconds
.PARAMETER Force
  Switch parameter to forcibly shutdown the virtual machine
  after timeout
.EXAMPLE
  PS> Get-VM VM001 | Set-VMOffline -memoryMB 4096 -numCpu 2 `
      -timeOut 60
#>

  Param (
    [parameter(valuefrompipeline = $true, mandatory = $true,
    HelpMessage = "Enter a vm entity")]
      [VMware.VimAutomation.ViCore.Impl.V1.Inventory.➥
VirtualMachineImpl]$VM,
    [int64]$memoryMB,
    [int32]$numCpu,
    [Int32]$timeOut = 300,
    [switch]$force)

  Process {
    if ($memoryMB -or $numCpu) {
      if ((Get-VM $vm).PowerState -eq "PoweredOn") {
        $powerState = "On"
        Shutdown-VMGuest $vm -Confirm:$false | Out-Null
      }
      $startTime = Get-Date
      While (((Get-VM $vm).PowerState -eq "PoweredOn") -and
        (((Get-Date) - $startTime).totalseconds -lt $timeOut)){
        Sleep -Seconds 2
      }
      if ((Get-VM $vm).PowerState -eq "PoweredOff" -or $force) {
```

```
if ((Get-VM $vm).PowerState -eq "PoweredOn") {
  Write-Warning "The shutdown guest operation timed out"
  Write-Warning "Forcing shutdown"
  Stop-VM $VM -Confirm:$false | Out-Null
}
if ($memoryMB -and $numCpu) {
  Set-VM $vm -MemoryMB $MemoryMB -NumCpu $numCpu `
    -Confirm:$false | Out-Null
}
elseif ($memoryMB) {
  Set-VM $vm -MemoryMB $MemoryMB -Confirm:$false | `
      Out-Null
}
elseif ($numCpu) {
  Set-VM $vm -NumCpu $numCpu -Confirm:$false | Out-Null
}
else {
  Write-Error `
      "No value for -memoryMB or -numCpu supplied"
}
if ($powerState -eq "On") {
  Start-VM $vm | Out-Null
}
}
else {
  Write-Error "The shutdown guest operation timed out"
}
}
else {
  Write-Error "No value for -memoryMB or -numCpu supplied"
}
}
}
```

Changing vCPU Resources

As with memory resources, you can influence the CPU resource entitlement of a VM by configuring reservations, limits, and shares. Reservations and limits are specified in megahertz (MHz). When you want to guarantee a minimal level of performance for an important production application, you can reserve a certain amount of MHz to that VM. The amount of MHz from the reservation will always be available to that application. On the other hand, you might want to prevent that badly behaving legacy application from hogging valuable CPU resources by configuring a CPU limit. You change vCPU reservations, limits, and shares by using the same `Get-VMResourceConfiguration` and `Set-VMResourceConfiguration` cmdlets as described in the section "Changing Memory Resources." To set a vCPU reservation, you use the `-CpuReservationMhz` parameter. To set a vCPU limit, use the `-CpuLimitMhz` parameter.

Use the following to set a vCPU reservation of 4,000 MHz on a VM named VM001:

```
Get-VM VM001 | Get-VMResourceConfiguration | `
    Set-VMResourceConfiguration -CpuReservationMhz 4000
```

To change the number of vCPU shares, use the `-CpuSharesLevel` parameter. Possible enumeration values are Custom, High, Low, and Normal. Because this parameter accepts an enumerator value, you can also specify an index value from 0 to 3, where index value 0 means Custom, 1 means High, 2 means Low, and 3 means Normal. In Table 7.2 you'll find an overview of the available CPU shares levels. If you want to fine-tune the shares level beyond the factory presets (High, Low, and Normal), you can set the shares level to Custom and specify the number of shares with the `-NumCpuShares` parameter.

TABLE 7.2   CPU shares

Shares level	Shares/vCPU	Index
Custom	1–1,000,000	0
High	2,000	1
Low	500	2
Normal	1,000	3

To set a vCPU share level to High, use the following:

```
Get-VM VM001 | Get-VMResourceConfiguration | `
    Set-VMResourceConfiguration -CpuSharesLevel "High"
```

Resource limits, both CPU and memory, are real performance killers. Memory limits cause the affected VM to start ballooning and swapping in almost all cases. You'll learn how to report the VMs that have CPU and memory limits configured in Chapter 14, "Reporting the Status of Your vSphere Environment." In Listing 14.1, you'll find the code for such a report.

Now that you've tuned your application's CPU and memory entitlement, let's explore how to change the VM's networking hardware.

Adding or Removing a Network Adapter

Design requirements for production environments often dictate that backup traffic must be separated from normal data traffic. Therefore, you need to add an additional network adapter to your VM. You can add a network adapter to your VM by using the New-NetworkAdapter cmdlet. This cmdlet has two mandatory parameters:

▶ The -VM parameter specifies the virtual machine(s) to modify.

▶ The -NetworkName parameter specifies the name of the network to which the network adapter will be connected.

Remember that the network name is case sensitive! By default the newly created network adapter isn't connected to the network, so you might want to specify the -StartConnected switch as well. You can also specify the adapter type using the -Type parameter. Valid types are e1000, Flexible, Vmxnet, EnhancedVmxnet, and Vmxnet3. If this parameter isn't specified, the type will be set to the recommended type by VMware for the guest OS you set.

NOTE Adding (or removing) a network adapter to a powered-on virtual machine is only supported on virtual hardware version 7 or later. If you still have virtual machines running hardware version 4, they must be powered off first. And just in case you're wondering what happened to versions 5 and 6—well, version 5 was skipped for version alignment and version 6 was introduced with VMware Workstation 6.0, and after version 4. The next version compatible with ESX is version 7.

Now, let's create a second network adapter for VM001 and connect that network adapter to a port group named BACKUPVLAN10:

```
[vSphere PowerCLI] C:\Scripts> New-NetworkAdapter -VM VM001 `
    -NetworkName BACKUPVLAN10 -StartConnected

Name              Type      NetworkName    MacAddress

----              ----      -----------    ----------

Network adapter 2  e1000     BACKUPVLAN10   00:50:56:92:00:02
```

Managing the Virtual Machine Life Cycle

PART II

Sometimes an application can have a license that is based on the Media Access Control (MAC) address of the server's network card. In that case, we recommend that you assign a static MAC address to your VM. Using a static MAC address prevents the MAC address from being changed during the application's life cycle. Whatever the reason for adding a static MAC address to your VM, you can specify a static MAC address using the -MacAddress parameter. Remember that the specified MAC address must be in the valid VMware range for static MAC addresses of 00:50:56:00:00:00–00:50:56 :3F:FF:FF. Use the following to create a new network adapter with a static MAC address:

```
New-NetworkAdapter -VM VM001 -NetworkName BACKUPVLAN10 `
    -MacAddress 00:50:56:03:15:10
```

Once you've created a new network adapter, you can change its settings using the Set-NetworkAdapter cmdlet. Perhaps you need to change the MAC address to the static MAC address used to create the production license for your application. Use the code that follows; just substitute your static address for the one we used in the -MacAddress parameter:

```
Get-VM VM001 | Get-NetworkAdapter | Set-NetworkAdapter `
    -MacAddress 00:50:56:03:15:10 -Confirm:$false
```

As a security best practice, it's recommended that all unused hardware be removed from your systems. (You can learn more about hardening your VM in Chapter 12, "Hardening the vSphere Environment.") Suppose your backup application has been upgraded and is now capable of leveraging the VMware Backup APIs to create full-image backups. The extra network adapter connected to the backup network will no longer be used, so you need to remove the network adapter. Removing an adapter is done using the Remove-NetworkAdapter cmdlet. This cmdlet accepts only one parameter: -NetworkAdapter. The parameter specifies the NetworkAdapter object to be removed. You can retrieve the NetworkAdapter object using the Get-NetworkAdapter cmdlet.

Now, let's remove the network adapter that is connected to the BACKUPVLAN10 network from virtual machine VM001. Remember, removing a network adapter from a powered-on virtual machine is supported only on virtual hardware version 7 or later. Be sure to power off the VM before running this code if you are working with an earlier virtual hardware version:

```
Get-VM VM001 | Get-NetworkAdapter | ?{$_.NetworkName -eq `
    "BACKUPVLAN10"} | Remove-NetworkAdapter -Confirm:$false
```

Assigning a Network

After a network adapter is created, there's not much that can be changed. But there may come a time when you need to move your VM to another network. You can accomplish this by using the `Set-NetworkAdapter` cmdlet and using its `-Network Name` parameter. Let's say you need to move your virtual machine VM001 from VM_VLAN101 to VM_VLAN202:

```
Get-VM VM001 | Get-NetworkAdapter | ?{$_.NetworkName -eq `
    "VM_VLAN101"} | Set-NetworkAdapter -NetworkName VM_VLAN202 `
    -Confirm:$false
```

That's really simple, isn't it? Well, switching networks probably also means that you need to assign a different IP address, subnet mask, and/or gateway. But that wasn't changed in the code that moved the VM from VM_VLAN101 to VM_VLAN202, so the virtual machine probably won't have network connectivity anymore. To change the virtual machine's IP address, you can use the `Set-VMGuestNetworkInterface` cmdlet, but there are some restrictions:

- ▶ VMware Tools are required.
- ▶ The cmdlet currently only supports Windows XP, Windows Server 2003, and Linux RedHat Enterprise 5.
- ▶ The cmdlet requires PowerShell to run in 32-bit mode.

The `Set-VMGuestNetworkInterface` cmdlet sends a batch script to the virtual machine that executes inside the VM in the context of the specified guest user. The batch script is located in the `Scripts` folder in the PowerCLI installation directory. In this folder you'll find other custom scripts. The script names have the following format:

```
<CmdletName>_<OS_Identifier>
```

`<CmdletName>` is the name of the cmdlet without a hyphen—for example, `SetVMGuestNetworkInterface`.

`<OS_Identifier>` is the guest family or the guest ID as returned by `Get-VMGuest`.

You can add new scripts to the folder or modify the existing scripts to support other guest operating systems, if necessary. To see an example of modifying such a script, read Chapter 8, "Advanced Virtual Machine Features."

Managing the Virtual
Machine Life Cycle

PART II

In Listing 7.3, you'll find an example of changing a guest's IP address using the `Set-VMGuestNetworkInterface` cmdlet.

LISTING 7.3   Changing the guest's IP address

```
$hostCred = `
    $Host.UI.PromptForCredential("Please enter host credentials",
    "Enter ESX host credentials", "root", "")
$guestCred = `
    $Host.UI.PromptForCredential("Please enter guest credentials",
    "Enter Guest credentials", "", "")
$srcIP = "192.168.1.1"
$destIP = "192.168.2.2"
$destMask = "255.255.255.0"
$destGateway = "192.168.2.254"
Get-VM VM001 | Get-VMGuestNetworkInterface `
    -HostCredential $hostCred -GuestCredential $guestCred | `
    ?{$_.IP -eq $srcIP} | Set-VMGuestNetworkInterface `
    -HostCredential $hostCred -GuestCredential $guestCred `
    -Ip $destIP -Netmask $destMask -Gateway $destGateway
```

Adding a Virtual Disk

No matter how much disk storage you present to your end users, they will fill it up and demand more. As a best practice, always try to right-size your disks from the start and determine a reasonable amount of free space. Remember that you can always extend your disks or add an additional disk when needed.

When designing a virtual Microsoft SQL Server, we always configure every SQL server instance with three separate disks. One disk is used as the base disk on which to install the SQL Server instance and receives a drive letter. The other two are configured as mount points on this base disk: one for data files and one for logging. (Preferably, the disks are deployed from separate datastores.) Whenever a new SQL Server instance needs to be installed, additional disks will be added to the SQL Server.

You can add a new hard disk to a VM with the `New-HardDisk` cmdlet. The `-CapacityKB` parameter allows you to specify the size of the new virtual disk.

TIP Notice that the parameter value is in kilobytes (KB), but you probably want to enter the new disk size in megabytes (MB) or gigabytes (GB). PowerShell comes to the rescue again. It has built-in constants—KB, MB, GB, TB (terabyte), and even PB (petabyte)—for converting values. When you need to convert a disk or memory size value to kilobytes, just divide the value by 1 KB. (Note that in the code there's no space between the value and the constant.)

```
[vSphere PowerCLI] C:\Scripts> 10GB/1KB

10485760
```

You can specify the virtual machine to which the new virtual disk will be added by using the -VM parameter, or you can pass the virtual machine object (retrieved using the Get-VM cmdlet) on the pipeline, as demonstrated in the next example. Let's create a new virtual disk with a size of 10 GB and assign it to VM001:

```
[vSphere PowerCLI] C:\Scripts> Get-VM VM001 | New-HardDisk `
    -CapacityKB (10GB/1KB)


CapacityKB Persistence                              Filename
---------- -----------                              --------
10485760   Persistent              [Datastore1] VM001/VM001_1.vmdk
```

In case of a SQL Server, you want to present the disk for storing the data files from a different datastore than the disk for storing the log files. If you want to specify a different datastore than the default (the datastore where the virtual machine's configuration file [VMX] is stored), use the -Datastore parameter:

```
[vSphere PowerCLI] C:\Scripts> New-HardDisk -VM VM001 `
    -CapacityKB (10GB/1KB) -Datastore Datastore2


CapacityKB Persistence                              Filename
---------- -----------                              --------
10485760   Persistent              [Datastore2] VM001/VM001.vmdk
```

When you set up a new hard disk, you can also specify how changes are written to the disk. Table 7.3 lists the options available to you.

TABLE 7.3   Virtual disk modes

Mode	Description
`Persistent`	The default mode and the only one that allows snapshots. Changes are immediately and permanently written to the disk.
`IndependentPersistent`	The disk is not affected by snapshots. Changes are immediately and permanently written to the disk.
`IndependentNonPersistent`	Changes to this disk are discarded when you power off the VM or revert to a snapshot.

Use the `-Persistence` parameter to make the disk `Persistent`, `Independent Persistent`, or `IndependentNonPersistent`. You can also specify that the new disk be deployed using thin provisioning with the `-ThinProvisioned` switch:

```
Get-VM VM001 | New-HardDisk -CapacityKB (10GB/1KB) `
    -Persistence IndependentPersistent -ThinProvisioned
```

Besides creating new virtual disks, the `New-HardDisk` cmdlet can be used to attach an existing virtual disk. The path to this disk must be specified using the `-DiskPath` parameter:

```
New-HardDisk -VM VM001 -DiskPath `
    "[Datastore2] OtherVM/OtherVM.vmdk"
```

What about adding a raw device mapping (RDM)? No problem. All you need to do is specify the disk type using the `-DiskType` parameter and pass the disk's location (or console device name) to the `-DeviceName` parameter. Valid disk types for RDM disks are `rawVirtual` or `rawPhysical`. The disk's location can be retrieved using the `Get-ScsiLun` cmdlet. Here's the code and a typical return:

```
[vSphere PowerCLI] C:\Scripts> Get-VMHost ESX01 | `
    Get-ScsiLun -LunType disk | Select ConsoleDeviceName

ConsoleDeviceName
-----------------
/vmfs/devices/disks/naa.6006048c8d27a37983d99994cfddcea5
/vmfs/devices/disks/naa.6006048c877401f6aaa26f591bf602d6
/vmfs/devices/disks/mpx.vmhba1:C0:T0:L0
```

Let's assume that the disk with identifier naa.6006048c8d27a37983d99994cfdd cea5 is the RDM disk you want to add. Specify it like this:

```
[vSphere PowerCLI] C:\Scripts> New-HardDisk -VM VM001 `
    -DiskType rawVirtual -DeviceName `
    /vmfs/devices/disks/naa.6006048c8d27a37983d99994cfddcea5
```

```
CapacityKB  Persistence                                 Filename
----------  -----------                                 --------
52428800    Persistent          [Datastore1] VM001/VM001_1.vmdk
```

Removing a Virtual Disk

Sometimes it may be necessary to remove a disk from a VM. In the case of a SQL Server, when a SQL Server instance is removed from the server, it's a best practice to remove the disks associated with it from the VM. You remove a virtual disk by using the `Remove-HardDisk` cmdlet. This cmdlet accepts only one parameter: `-HardDisk`. The `-HardDisk` parameter specifies the hard disk(s) to be removed.

WARNING   If you do not specify a particular hard disk(s) or a particular drive type, all hard disks will be removed from the VM.

To remove all hard disks from a VM named VM001:

```
Get-VM VM001 | Get-HardDisk | Remove-HardDisk -Confirm:$false
```

This may not be very useful. You probably want to be more specific in which hard disks you want to remove. To remove all RDM disks from your virtual machine, use the following:

```
Get-HardDisk -VM VM001 -DiskType rawVirtual,rawPhysical | `
     Remove-HardDisk -Confirm:$false
```

If you want to remove just one specific disk, you need to filter out that disk using a unique property like `Name`, `Id`, or `Filename`. Let's only remove the virtual disk labeled Hard disk 2 from virtual machine VM001:

```
Get-HardDisk -VM VM001 | ?{$_.Name -eq "Hard disk 2"} | `
     Remove-HardDisk -Confirm:$false
```

The hardest part of removing a virtual hard disk can be finding the *right* virtual hard disk. If you have a virtual machine that uses only 2 virtual disks, you're pretty sure which one you need to remove. But what if you have a virtual machine running multiple Microsoft SQL Server instances that happens to have 26 disks?

To make things worse, your Windows administrator probably said, "Remove the K: drive" or "Remove Windows disk 21."

Do you still know which virtual disk to remove? The same problem arises when extending disks, but let's focus on removing disks first. You'll learn how to extend a virtual disk in the next section.

In Listing 7.4 you'll find a function to assist you in identifying the right virtual disk to remove. The `Get-VMDiskMapping` function can be used on both hardware level 4 and hardware level 7. Using mixed SCSI adapter types is not supported on hardware level 4, however.

LISTING 7.4   **Determining which virtual disk corresponds to which Windows disk**

```
function Get-VMDiskMapping {
<#
.SYNOPSIS
  Creates a report to match Windows disk numbers and their
  virtual disk counterparts.
.DESCRIPTION
  This function creates an overview of the virtual machine's
  virtual disks and their Windows counterparts.
.NOTES
  Source:  Automating vSphere Administration
  Authors: Luc Dekens, Arnim van Lieshout, Jonathan Medd,
           Alan Renouf, Glenn Sizemore
.PARAMETER VM
  Specify the virtual machine to report on.
.PARAMETER HostCredential
  Specify a PSCredential object containing the credentials you
  want to use for authenticating with the host.
.PARAMETER GuestCredential
  Specify a PSCredential object containing the credentials you
  want to use for authenticating with the VM guest OS.
.EXAMPLE
  PS> Get-VM VM001 | Get-VMDiskMapping
.EXAMPLE
  PS> Get-VM VM001 | Get-VMDiskMapping -hostCredential `
          $hostCred -guestCredential $guestCred | Out-GridView
#>

  Param (
   [parameter(valuefrompipeline = $true, mandatory = $true,
   HelpMessage = "Enter a vm entity")]
     [VMware.VimAutomation.ViCore.Impl.V1.Inventory.➥
```

```
VirtualMachineImpl]$VM,
   [Parameter(Mandatory = $true,
   HelpMessage = "Enter a PSCredential object for the host")]
    [System.Management.Automation.PSCredential]$hostCredential,
   [Parameter(Mandatory = $true,
   HelpMessage = "Enter a PSCredential object for the guest")]
    [System.Management.Automation.PSCredential]$guestCredential)


  $diskInfo= @()
#Create vbs scriptfile
  $FileName = [System.IO.Path]::GetTempFileName()
'Set objReg = GetObject("winmgmts:{impersonationLevel=➡
impersonate}!\\.\root\default:StdRegProv")' > $filename
'Set objWMI = GetObject("winmgmts:{impersonationLevel=➡
impersonate}!\\.\root\cimv2")' >> $filename
'Set colPCISlotNumber = CreateObject("Scripting.Dictionary")'➡
 >> $filename
'objReg.EnumKey &H80000002,"SYSTEM\CurrentControlSet\Enum\➡
PCI", colHardwareId' >> $filename
'For Each HardwareId In colHardwareId' >> $filename
'  objReg.EnumKey &H80000002,"SYSTEM\CurrentControlSet\Enum\➡
PCI\" & HardwareId, colControllerId' >> $filename
'  For Each ControllerId In colControllerId' >> $filename
'     objReg.GetDWORDValue &H80000002,"SYSTEM\➡
CurrentControlSet\Enum\PCI\" & HardwareId & "\" & ➡
ControllerId, "UINumber", dwUINumber' >> $filename
'     colPCISlotNumber.Add "PCI\" & UCase(HardwareId) & "\" & ➡
UCase(ControllerId), dwUINumber' >> $filename
'  Next' >> $filename
'Next' >> $filename
'Set colDiskDrive = objWMI.ExecQuery("Select * from Win32_➡
DiskDrive")' >> $filename
'Set colSCSIControllerDevice = objWMI.ExecQuery("Select * ➡
from Win32_SCSIControllerDevice")' >> $filename
'WScript.Echo "DiskPNPDeviceId,Index,SCSIPort,SCSITargetId,➡
Size,CtrlPNPDeviceId,CtrlPCIslotNumber"' >> $filename
'For Each Disk in colDiskDrive' >> $filename
'  For Each item in colSCSIControllerDevice' >> $filename
```

```
'     If Replace(Split(item.Dependent,chr(34))(1),"\\","\") = ➥
Disk.PNPDeviceId Then' >> $filename
'       CtrlPNPDeviceId = UCase(Replace(Split(item.Antecedent,➥
chr(34))(1),"\\","\"))' >> $filename
'       Exit For' >> $filename
'     End If' >> $filename
'   Next' >> $filename
'   WScript.Echo Disk.PNPDeviceId & "," & Disk.Index & "," & ➥
Disk.SCSIPort & "," & Disk.SCSITargetId & "," & Disk.Size & ➥
"," & CtrlPNPDeviceId & "," & colPCISlotNumber.Item(➥
CtrlPNPDeviceId)' >> $filename
'Next' >> $filename
#Determine location to copy script to
  $temp = Invoke-VMScript "echo %temp%" -vm $VM `
      -HostCredential $hostCredential -GuestCredential `
      $guestCredential -ScriptType "bat"
  $destFileName = $temp.Trim("`r`n") + "\guestScsiInfo.vbs"
  Copy-VMGuestFile -Source $FileName -Destination `
      $destFileName -VM $VM -LocalToGuest -HostCredential `
      $hostCredential -GuestCredential $guestCredential
  Remove-Item $FileName
#Get Windows disk info
  $error.Clear()
  $Out = Invoke-VMScript `
      "cscript /nologo $destFileName && del $destFileName" `
      -vm $VM -HostCredential $hostCredential `
      -GuestCredential $guestCredential -ScriptType "bat"
  if (!$error -and $out) {
#Export plaintext Windows disk info to temporary file and
#import it again using the Import-Csv CmdLet
      $FileName = [System.IO.Path]::GetTempFileName()
      $Out > $FileName
      $WinDisks = Import-Csv $FileName
      Remove-Item $FileName
#Determine SCSIPort offset
      $portOffset = ($WinDisks | ?{$_.SCSIPort} | `
          Measure-Object -Property SCSIPort -Minimum).Minimum
#All entries that don't match any known pciSlotNumber are
#attached to scsi0. Change these entries to the pciSlotnumber
```

```
#of scsi0
    $scsi0pciSlotNumber = `
        ($VM.Extensiondata.Config.ExtraConfig | ?{$_.key -like `
        "scsi0.pciSlotNumber"}).value
    $scsiPciSlotNumbers= @()
    $VM.Extensiondata.Config.ExtraConfig | ?{$_.key -like `
        "scsi?.pciSlotNumber"} | %{$scsiPciSlotNumbers += `
        $_.value}
    $WinDisks | %{if ($scsiPciSlotNumbers -notcontains `
        $_.CtrlPCISlotNumber) {$_.CtrlPCISlotNumber = `
        ($VM.ExtensionData.Config.Extraconfig | ?{$_.key -like `
        "scsi0.pciSlotNumber"}).value}}
#Create DiskMapping table
    foreach ($VirtualSCSIController in `
        ($VM.Extensiondata.Config.Hardware.Device | `
        where {$_.DeviceInfo.Label -match "SCSI Controller"})) {
        foreach ($VirtualDiskDevice in `
            ($VM.Extensiondata.Config.Hardware.Device | `
            where {$_.ControllerKey -eq `
            $VirtualSCSIController.Key})) {
        $VirtualDisk = "" | Select VMSCSIController, `
            VMDiskName, SCSI_Id, VMDiskFile, VMDiskSizeGB, `
            RawDeviceName, LunUuid, WindowsDisk, `
            WindowsDiskSizeGB
        $VirtualDisk.VMSCSIController = `
            $VirtualSCSIController.DeviceInfo.Label
        $VirtualDisk.VMDiskName = `
            $VirtualDiskDevice.DeviceInfo.Label
        $VirtualDisk.SCSI_Id = `
            "$($VirtualSCSIController.BusNumber) : ➥
$($VirtualDiskDevice.UnitNumber)"
        $VirtualDisk.VMDiskFile = `
            $VirtualDiskDevice.Backing.FileName
        $VirtualDisk.VMDiskSizeGB = `
            $VirtualDiskDevice.CapacityInKB * 1KB / 1GB
        $VirtualDisk.RawDeviceName = `
            $VirtualDiskDevice.Backing.DeviceName
        $VirtualDisk.LunUuid = `
            $VirtualDiskDevice.Backing.LunUuid
```

```
#Match disks
        if  ($vm.version -lt "v7") {
#For hardware v4 match disks based on controller's SCSIPort and
#disk's SCSITargetId.
#Not supported with mixed scsi adapter types.
        $DiskMatch = $WinDisks | `
            ?{($_.SCSIPort - $portOffset) -eq `
            $VirtualSCSIController.BusNumber -and `
            $_.SCSITargetID -eq $VirtualDiskDevice.UnitNumber}
        }
        else {
#For hardware v7 match disks based on controller's pciSlotNumber
#and disk's SCSITargetId
        $DiskMatch = $WinDisks | ?{$_.CtrlPCISlotNumber -eq `
            ($VM.Extensiondata.Config.Extraconfig | `
            ?{$_.key -match "scsi$($VirtualSCSIController.➡
BusNumber).pcislotnumber"}).value -and $_.SCSITargetID -eq `
            $VirtualDiskDevice.UnitNumber}
        }
        if ($DiskMatch){
            $VirtualDisk.WindowsDisk = "Disk $($DiskMatch.Index)"
            $VirtualDisk.WindowsDiskSizeGB = $DiskMatch.Size / 1GB
        }
        else {Write-Warning "No matching Windows disk found ➡
for SCSI id $($virtualDisk.SCSI_Id)"}
        $diskInfo += $virtualDisk
        }
    }
    $diskInfo
 }
 else {Write-Error "Error Retrieving Windows disk info from ➡
guest"}
}
```

The output of the Get-VMDiskMapping function from Listing 7.4 is best viewed in table format using the Format-Table cmdlet, or even better, using the Out-GridView cmdlet. Figure 7.2 shows a sample output.

```
$map = Get-VM VM001 | Get-VMDiskMapping
$map | Out-GridView
```

FIGURE 7.2 Get-VMDiskMapping sample output

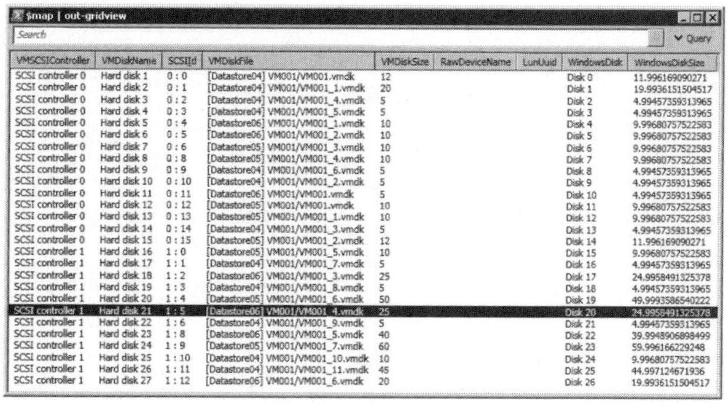

VMSCSIController	VMDiskName	SCSIId	VMDiskFile	VMDiskSize	RawDeviceName	LunUuid	WindowsDisk	WindowsDiskSize
SCSI controller 0	Hard disk 1	0 : 0	[Datastore04] VM001/VM001.vmdk	12			Disk 0	11.996169090271
SCSI controller 0	Hard disk 2	0 : 1	[Datastore04] VM001/VM001_1.vmdk	20			Disk 1	19.9936151504517
SCSI controller 0	Hard disk 3	0 : 2	[Datastore04] VM001/VM001_4.vmdk	5			Disk 2	4.99457359313965
SCSI controller 0	Hard disk 4	0 : 3	[Datastore04] VM001/VM001_5.vmdk	5			Disk 3	4.99457359313965
SCSI controller 0	Hard disk 5	0 : 4	[Datastore06] VM001/VM001_1.vmdk	10			Disk 4	9.99680757522583
SCSI controller 0	Hard disk 6	0 : 5	[Datastore06] VM001/VM001_2.vmdk	10			Disk 5	9.99680757522583
SCSI controller 0	Hard disk 7	0 : 6	[Datastore05] VM001/VM001_3.vmdk	10			Disk 6	9.99680757522583
SCSI controller 0	Hard disk 8	0 : 8	[Datastore05] VM001/VM001_4.vmdk	10			Disk 7	9.99680757522583
SCSI controller 0	Hard disk 9	0 : 9	[Datastore04] VM001/VM001_6.vmdk	5			Disk 8	4.99457359313965
SCSI controller 0	Hard disk 10	0 : 10	[Datastore04] VM001/VM001_2.vmdk	5			Disk 9	4.99457359313965
SCSI controller 0	Hard disk 11	0 : 11	[Datastore06] VM001/VM001.vmdk	5			Disk 10	4.99457359313965
SCSI controller 0	Hard disk 12	0 : 12	[Datastore05] VM001/VM001.vmdk	10			Disk 11	9.99680757522583
SCSI controller 0	Hard disk 13	0 : 13	[Datastore05] VM001/VM001_1.vmdk	10			Disk 12	9.99680757522583
SCSI controller 0	Hard disk 14	0 : 14	[Datastore04] VM001/VM001_3.vmdk	5			Disk 13	4.99457359313965
SCSI controller 0	Hard disk 15	0 : 15	[Datastore05] VM001/VM001_2.vmdk	12			Disk 14	11.996169090271
SCSI controller 1	Hard disk 16	1 : 0	[Datastore05] VM001/VM001_5.vmdk	10			Disk 15	9.99680757522583
SCSI controller 1	Hard disk 17	1 : 1	[Datastore04] VM001/VM001_7.vmdk	5			Disk 16	4.99457359313965
SCSI controller 1	Hard disk 18	1 : 2	[Datastore06] VM001/VM001_3.vmdk	25			Disk 17	24.9958491325378
SCSI controller 1	Hard disk 19	1 : 3	[Datastore04] VM001/VM001_8.vmdk	5			Disk 18	4.99457359313965
SCSI controller 1	Hard disk 20	1 : 4	[Datastore05] VM001/VM001_6.vmdk	50			Disk 19	49.9993586540222
SCSI controller 1	Hard disk 21	1 : 5	[Datastore06] VM001/VM001_4.vmdk	25			Disk 20	24.9958491325378
SCSI controller 1	Hard disk 22	1 : 6	[Datastore04] VM001/VM001_9.vmdk	5			Disk 21	4.99457359313965
SCSI controller 1	Hard disk 23	1 : 8	[Datastore06] VM001/VM001_5.vmdk	40			Disk 22	39.9948906898499
SCSI controller 1	Hard disk 24	1 : 9	[Datastore05] VM001/VM001_7.vmdk	60			Disk 23	59.99616622924 8
SCSI controller 1	Hard disk 25	1 : 10	[Datastore04] VM001/VM001_10.vmdk	10			Disk 24	9.99680757522583
SCSI controller 1	Hard disk 26	1 : 11	[Datastore04] VM001/VM001_11.vmdk	45			Disk 25	44.997124671936
SCSI controller 1	Hard disk 27	1 : 12	[Datastore06] VM001/VM001_6.vmdk	20			Disk 26	19.9936151504517

Notice that the `Remove-HardDisk` cmdlet only removes the specified hard disk from the virtual machine. It doesn't delete the actual virtual disk file from the datastore. Unfortunately, there's no standard parameter or PowerCLI cmdlet available that enables you to delete the actual virtual disks from the datastore. If you want to delete the virtual disks from the datastore as well, you have to turn to the API methods. Listing 7.5 shows a function that removes the virtual disk from the VM and deletes the actual files from the disk. Just use this `Delete-HardDisk` function instead of `Remove-HardDisk` if you want to delete the actual files as well.

LISTING 7.5 Deleting virtual hard disks from the datastore

```
function Delete-HardDisk {
<#
.SYNOPSIS
  deletes the specified virtual hard disks
.DESCRIPTION
  Removes the specified virtual hard disks from the virtual
  machine and deletes the files from the datastore
.NOTES
  Source:  Automating vSphere Administration
  Authors: Luc Dekens, Arnim van Lieshout, Jonathan Medd,
           Alan Renouf, Glenn Sizemore
.PARAMETER HardDisk
  Specify the hard disks you want to remove
.EXAMPLE
  PS> Get-HardDisk -VM $vm | Delete-HardDisk
.EXAMPLE
  PS> Get-VM VM001 | Get-HardDisk | `
```

```
         ?{$_.Name -eq "Hard disk 2"} | Delete-HardDisk
#>

    Param (
      [parameter(valuefrompipeline = $true, mandatory = $true,
      HelpMessage = "Enter a hard disk entity")]
        [VMware.VimAutomation.ViCore.Types.V1.➦
VirtualDevice.HardDisk]$hardDisk)

    process {
        $spec = New-Object VMware.Vim.VirtualMachineConfigSpec
        $spec.deviceChange = `
            New-Object VMware.Vim.VirtualDeviceConfigSpec[] (1)
        $spec.deviceChange[0] = `
            New-Object VMware.Vim.VirtualDeviceConfigSpec
        $spec.deviceChange[0].operation = "remove"
        $spec.deviceChange[0].fileOperation = "destroy"
        $spec.deviceChange[0].device = `
            New-Object VMware.Vim.VirtualDisk
        $spec.deviceChange[0].device.key = `
            $hardDisk.ExtensionData.Key

        $vm = Get-View -Id $hardDisk.ParentID
        $vm.ReconfigVM_Task($spec)
    }
}
```

Extending a Virtual Disk

When you run out of disk space on a disk, you can extend that disk using the
Set-HardDisk cmdlet. You can use the -CapacityKB parameter to specify
the new size of the virtual disk. Let's extend virtual disk Hard disk 2 of virtual
machine VM001 to 10 GB:

```
Get-VM VM001 | Get-HardDisk | ?{$_.Name -eq "Hard disk 2"} |
    Set-HardDisk -CapacityKB (10GB/1KB)
```

As you can see, extending the virtual disk is straightforward and easy to achieve. But
extending the virtual disk is only half the work. You've probably extended the virtual disk because the guest's partition was reaching its capacity. So, you'll also want

to extend the guest's partition to use the newly added capacity. But don't worry; the `Set-HardDisk` cmdlet also supports extending the guest's partition.

To extend the guest's partition, the `Set-HardDisk` cmdlet calls the `Invoke-VMScript` cmdlet in the background and uses a script that runs inside the VM in the context of the specified guest user to extend the guest's partition. These scripts are located in the `Scripts` folder in the PowerCLI installation directory. To specify the guest's partition, use the `-Partition` parameter. If you don't specify a particular partition using this parameter, the last partition on the hard disk is expanded. If you want to specify a Windows partition, specify the drive letter without the colon. There are some restrictions, however:

- ▶ To expand a partition that isn't the last partition on a multipartitioned disk in Windows, the disk must be dynamic.

- ▶ On Linux, only the last partition can be expanded when the disk is multipartitioned and Logical Volume Manager (LVM) is not supported.

Extending the guest's partition is currently only supported on Windows XP, Windows Server 2003, and Linux RedHat Enterprise 5. To extend this functionality to Windows 2008 (R2) and Windows 7, take a look at Chapter 8.

Now, let's extend the guest's Windows partition on the previously extended Hard disk 2 on virtual machine VM001. You can do so by calling the `Set-HardDisk` cmdlet again with a `-CapacityKB` size equal to the virtual disk. You can also specify a greater size, but this will increase the virtual disk as well.

```
Get-VM VM001 | Get-HardDisk | ?{$_.Name -eq "Hard disk 2"} | `
    Set-HardDisk -CapacityKB (10GB/1KB) -HostCredential `
    $hostCredential -GuestCredential $guestCredential
```

When the partition you want to expand is the system disk, other restrictions apply:

- ▶ On Linux, system disks cannot be expanded.

- ▶ On Windows (all editions before Windows 2008 and Windows 7), you'll need a helper virtual machine to expand the system partition.

On Windows, this helper virtual machine can be specified using the `-HelperVM` parameter. When a helper virtual machine is used, all VMs associated with the disk and the helper virtual machine must be powered off before expanding the disk. When you resize more than one disk using a helper virtual machine, the disks are resized one at a time, causing the helper machine to power on and off for each virtual disk. This process might slow down the cmdlet's performance.

Now let's extend a system partition to 20 GB. On our hypothetical virtual machine VM001, the system partition happens to be Hard disk 1. Let's use VM002 as the helper virtual machine. Let's also make sure that both VM001 and VM002 are powered off before extending the disk. Notice that the guest logon credentials used in Listing 7.6 are the guest logon credentials for the helper virtual machine.

LISTING 7.6   **Automated system partition expansion**

```
Get-VM VM001,VM002 | Shutdown-VMGuest -Confirm:$false

While ((Get-VM VM001).PowerState -eq "PoweredOn"){
  Sleep -Seconds 2
}
While ((Get-VM VM002).PowerState -eq "PoweredOn"){
  Sleep -Seconds 2
}

Get-VM VM001 | Get-HardDisk | ?{$_.Name -eq "Hard disk 1"} | `
    Set-HardDisk -CapacityKB (20GB/1KB) -HostCredential `
    $hostCredential -GuestCredential $guestCredential `
    -HelperVM (Get-VM VM002)

Get-VM VM001,VM002 | Start-VM -Confirm:$false
```

Sit back, relax, and enjoy the show. This is really cool stuff!

NOTE   Expanding system volumes is only supported by Microsoft on Windows Server 2008 and Windows 7 or later operating systems.

All the steps involved in expanding the system partition using a helper virtual machine (normally done by hand) are now fully automated. The following tasks are performed automatically for you:

- ▶ Extend the virtual disk in VM001.
- ▶ Add the virtual disk to the helper virtual machine VM002.
- ▶ Power on the helper virtual machine VM002.
- ▶ Expand the partition on the helper virtual machine VM002.

- ▶ Remove the virtual disk from the helper virtual machine VM002.

- ▶ Shut down the helper virtual machine VM002.

Changing Other Hardware

When you need to install software from a CD or ISO image, you'll need to add a CD drive to your VM if it doesn't have one already. A new CD drive can be added to your virtual machine using the New-CDDrive cmdlet. You can connect the CD drive to an ISO image file:

```
Get-VM VM001 | New-CDDrive -IsoPath `
    "[Datastore01] ISO/gparted-live.iso" -StartConnected
```

or direct to the host's CD drive.

```
Get-VM VM001 | New-CDDrive -HostDevice `
    "/vmfs/devices/cdrom/mpx.vmhba32:C0:T0:L0"
```

For security purposes, you should remove all virtual hardware from your VM that is not used. For example, VMs rarely contain a floppy drive anymore, as it's very unlikely that you'll ever need one nowadays. But there might be a time you do need a floppy drive for a legacy application. You can connect a floppy drive using the New-FloppyDrive cmdlet. To connect an ISO image file to our VM001, use the following:

```
Get-VM VM001 | New-FloppyDrive -FloppyImagePath `
    "[Datastore01] ISO/floppy.flp"
```

When you still happen to have an antique piece of hardware that contains a floppy drive as an ESX host, you can connect the host's floppy drive to your VM using the following code:

```
Get-VM VM001 | New-FloppyDrive -HostDevice "/dev/fd0" `
    -StartConnected
```

A new floppy image can be created using the -NewFloppyImagePath parameter and specifying a datastore path to the new floppy image:

```
Get-VM VM001 | New-FloppyDrive -NewFloppyImagePath `
    "[Datastore01] ISO/myNewFloppy.flp"
```

Beginning with vSphere 4, you can add VMDirectPath I/O pass-through devices, also referred to as PCI pass-through devices. The other type of pass-through device

Managing the Virtual Machine Life Cycle

PART II

available is the SCSI pass-through device. You can connect up to two pass-through devices to your virtual machine using the `Add-PassthroughDevice` cmdlet. Remember that before you can connect a PCI pass-through device to your virtual machine, the device must be enabled for pass-through on the ESX host first:

```
$deviceList = Get-VMHost ESX01 | Get-PassthroughDevice
Get-VM VM001 | Add-PassthroughDevice `
    -PassthroughDevice $deviceList[0]
```

If you want to connect other virtual hardware to your virtual machine, such as serial ports, parallel ports, USB devices, and the like, you have to turn to the API methods. Here, Onyx is your best friend. (Not familiar with Onyx? Don't worry. We'll tell you more about Onyx in Chapter 20, "The Onyx Project.") Just configure the hardware one piece at a time using the VI Client and examine the output that Onyx generates for you. For example, to add a USB controller to your VM use the code contained in Listing 7.7.

LISTING 7.7   Adding a USB controller to a VM

```
$spec = New-Object VMware.Vim.VirtualMachineConfigSpec

$deviceCfg = New-Object VMware.Vim.VirtualDeviceConfigSpec
$deviceCfg.operation = "add"
$deviceCfg.device = New-Object VMware.Vim.VirtualUSBController
$deviceCfg.device.key = -1
$deviceCfg.device.connectable = `
New-Object VMware.Vim.VirtualDeviceConnectInfo
$deviceCfg.device.connectable.startConnected = $true
$deviceCfg.device.connectable.allowGuestControl = $false
$deviceCfg.device.connectable.connected = $true
$deviceCfg.device.controllerKey = 100
$deviceCfg.device.busNumber = -1
$deviceCfg.device.autoConnectDevices = $true

$spec.deviceChange += $deviceCfg

$vm = Get-VM VM001 | Get-View
$vm.ReconfigVM_Task($spec)
```

Notice that your script always starts with a `VirtualDeviceConfigSpec` object; it is the required object of the `ReconfigVM_Task` method. Then, you define what type of operation you will be performing. The possible enumeration values are add, remove, or edit. The .device property contains the actual hardware device object. The New-Object line in Listing 7.7 created the VirtualUSBController. From there, it was a simple matter to define all the particulars that make up that hardware device.

Optimize Storage Usage with Thin Provisioning

When you create a virtual disk and don't specify the disk type, the disk type is thick by default. A thick virtual disk preallocates all the space during the creation of the disk. You can also create a thin virtual disk. A thin virtual disk does not preallocate the space. The blocks of a thin virtual disk are allocated on demand when first written to. A thin-provisioned disk is created using the -ThinProvisioned switch on the New-HardDisk cmdlet:

```
Get-VM VM001 | New-HardDisk -CapacityKB (10GB/1KB) `
    -ThinProvisioned
```

In a VMware environment, every VM needs to have its own boot and data volumes. The initial size of the boot volume is dictated by the size of the operating system and applications. The size of the data volume is dictated by the size of the existing application data. Typically, there's also an amount of free space added to each partition to accommodate future patches, service packs, upgrades, and application data growth. Traditionally data volumes are designed to take into account additional data for the upcoming year or even years, because disks used to be fixed in an era when servers were installed on direct attached disks. Nowadays, servers store their files on storage arrays, which are more flexible in size, and presented disks (or logical units) can easily be extended.

But still, servers are many, many times designed the old-school way. This leads to lots of free unutilized space on your expensive storage arrays. Using thin provisioning, you can reclaim this wasted space and increase your storage capacity utilization. This boost in capacity utilization (typically 20–30 percent) also saves an equal percentage of your annual storage costs, because the same servers and applications are stored on less space.

Unused space can be reclaimed by converting the virtual disk to thin. You can accomplish this by using vMotion or by converting the disk in place.

Managing the Virtual Machine Life Cycle

PART II

Converting a Virtual Disk Using Storage vMotion

Converting a thick virtual disk to a thin-provisioned virtual disk, or vice versa, can be accomplished by moving the disk to another datastore using storage vMotion. Because storage vMotion creates a new copy of your hard disk on the destination volume, you're allowed to specify a different disk type for the copy on the destination volume. You do so by using the `Set-HardDisk` cmdlet and specifying the new datastore with the `-Datastore` parameter and the new disk type with the `-DiskType` parameter. The following code uses vMotion to move all virtual disks on virtual machine VM001 to datastore Datastore02 and converts them to thin disks on the fly:

```
Get-VM VM001 | Get-HardDisk | Set-HardDisk `
    -Datastore Datastore02 -StorageFormat thin
```

If you don't want to convert all disks on a VM but just one specific disk, you'll need to filter that disk out using the `Where-Object` cmdlet or its alias, `?`. The following code uses vMotion to move only Hard disk 2 on virtual machine VM001 and converts it to thin on the fly:

```
Get-VM VM001 | Get-HardDisk | ?{$_.name -eq "Hard disk 2"} | `
    Set-HardDisk -Datastore Datastore02 -StorageFormat thin
```

Converting a Virtual Disk in Place

If you don't have another datastore available, you cannot use storage vMotion. The only other way of converting a virtual disk is to copy the virtual disk and then reconfigure the virtual machine to use the new copy. There are some drawbacks to this method, however:

▶ Because you're actually replacing the virtual disk with a cloned copy, the virtual machine must be powered off.

▶ You need to have enough additional free space on your datastore to store the copy of the virtual disk.

▶ For the `Copy-HardDisk` cmdlet to work, you need to be connected directly to an ESX host.

In Listing 7.8 you'll find a function that creates a thin-provisioned cloned copy of your thick virtual disk.

LISTING 7.8   Converting thick to thin in place using a disk copy

```
function Set-ThinDisk {
<#
.SYNOPSIS
  Converts a thick hard disk to a thin provisioned
  hard disk in place
.DESCRIPTION
  Makes a thin provisioned copy of a thick hard disk on the same
  datastore and configures the virtual machine to use the thin
  provisioned copy
.NOTES
  Source:  Automating vSphere Administration
  Authors: Luc Dekens, Arnim van Lieshout, Jonathan Medd,
           Alan Renouf, Glenn Sizemore
.PARAMETER HardDisk
  Specify the hard disks you want to convert
.PARAMETER credential
  A PSCredential object used to authenticate the VMHost server
.PARAMETER user
  The user account used to authenticate the VMHost server
.PARAMETER password
  The password for the account specified by the -User parameter
.PARAMETER replace
  Optional parameter to delete the original thick file
.EXAMPLE
  PS> Get-VM VM001 | Get-HardDisk | Set-ThinDisk -Credentials `
        $hostCred
.EXAMPLE
  PS> $hd = Get-VM VM001 | Get-HardDisk | `
        ?{$_.Name -eq "Hard disk 2"}
  PS> Set-ThinDisk -hardDisk $hd -user "root" -password `
        "password" -replace
#>
  Param (
    [parameter(valuefrompipeline = $true, mandatory = $true,
    HelpMessage = "Enter a hard disk entity")]
```

```
          [VMware.VimAutomation.ViCore.Types.V1.VirtualDevice.➥
   HardDisk]$hardDisk,
      [Parameter(Mandatory = $true, ParameterSetName = "cred",
      HelpMessage = "Enter a PSCredential object")]
        [System.Management.Automation.PSCredential]$credential,
      [Parameter(ParameterSetName = "user")]
      [ValidateNotNullOrEmpty()]
        [string]$user = "root",
      [Parameter(Mandatory = $true, ParameterSetName = "user",
      HelpMessage = "Enter the root account password")]
        [string]$password,
        [switch]$replace)

   process {
      if ($hardDisk.Parent.PowerState -eq "PoweredOff") {
        if ($hardDisk.StorageFormat -ne "Thin") {
          if ($credential) {
            $esxHost = Connect-VIServer `
                -Server $hardDisk.Parent.host.name `
                -Credential $credential -NotDefault
          }
          else {
            $esxHost = Connect-VIServer -Server `
                $hardDisk.Parent.host.name -User $user `
                -Password $password -NotDefault
          }
          $thinFile = $hardDisk.Filename.Replace("/","/thin_")
          $datastore = `
              $hardDisk.Filename.split('[')[1].split(']')[0]
          $esxHardDisk = Get-HardDisk -server $esxHost `
              -Datastore $datastore `
              -DatastorePath $hardDisk.Filename
          Copy-HardDisk -HardDisk $esxHardDisk `
              -DestinationPath $thinFile `
              -DestinationStorageFormat "thin" | Out-Null
          Disconnect-VIServer $esxHost -Confirm:$false

          $spec = New-Object VMware.Vim.VirtualMachineConfigSpec
          $spec.deviceChange = New-Object `
```

```
            VMware.Vim.VirtualDeviceConfigSpec[] (2)
        $spec.deviceChange[0] = New-Object `
            VMware.Vim.VirtualDeviceConfigSpec
        $spec.deviceChange[0].operation = "remove"
        if ($replace) {
          $spec.deviceChange[0].fileOperation = "destroy"
        }
        $spec.deviceChange[0].device = $hardDisk.ExtensionData

        $spec.deviceChange[1] = New-Object `
            VMware.Vim.VirtualDeviceConfigSpec
        $spec.deviceChange[1].operation = "add"
        $spec.deviceChange[1].device = New-Object `
            VMware.Vim.VirtualDisk
        $spec.deviceChange[1].device.key = -100
        $spec.deviceChange[1].device.backing = New-Object `
            VMware.Vim.VirtualDiskFlatVer2BackingInfo
        $spec.deviceChange[1].device.backing.fileName = `
            $thinFile
        $spec.deviceChange[1].device.backing.diskMode = `
            "persistent"
        $spec.deviceChange[1].device.backing.thinProvisioned = `
            $true
        $spec.deviceChange[1].device.controllerKey = `
            $hardDisk.ExtensionData.ControllerKey
        $spec.deviceChange[1].device.unitNumber = `
            $hardDisk.ExtensionData.UnitNumber

        $vm = Get-View -Id $hardDisk.ParentID
        $vm.ReconfigVM_Task($spec) | Out-Null
      }
      else {
        Write-Error "Virtual disk already thin provisioned"
      }
    }
    else {
      Write-Error "Virtual machine must be powered off"
    }
  }
}
```

CHAPTER 8

Advanced Virtual Machine Features

IN THIS CHAPTER, YOU WILL LEARN TO:

This chapter covers advanced virtual machine features. First, you'll learn how to interact with the guest operating system using the operating system's native tools and through the PowerCLI methods. You'll learn how to customize the scripts provided by PowerCLI to add support for Windows 7 and Windows 2008 (R2). Then, you'll explore scripting vMotion and Storage vMotion operations. Last but not least, you'll learn how to create and maintain snapshots.

Interact with the Guest OS

From time to time, you might want to interact with a guest operating system (OS). Perhaps you want to know the letter of the CD-ROM drive in a Windows guest and be able to report all virtual machines (VMs) where the drive letter isn't set to your company's default. Maybe you need to know if a specific Microsoft hotfix is installed on your system. Any number of guest OS–specific items might need your attention. Several options are available when you need to interact with the VM's guest OS. You can use the OS native tools like Windows Management Instrumentation (WMI), Secure Shell (SSH), or PowerShell remoting to interact with the guest, but these techniques might fail due to company system policies or firewall rules. In that case, these options aren't useful. Fear not—VMware PowerCLI contains some cmdlets to help you out in this case. You're going to explore this PowerCLI magic in the next paragraphs, but first we're going to explore the guest's native tools. Table 8.1 explains some pros and cons of various methods available when you need to interact with the guest OS.

USING NATIVE TOOLS

Guest native methods rely on an active network connection between the PowerCLI management station and the guest. You should be aware of the fact that these native protocols might be blocked by a company's or the guest's built-in firewall. To enable these methods to work behind firewalls, you must configure an exception rule in the firewall, which could interfere with company policies and possibly introduce additional security vulnerabilities. These methods also require specific guest OS services to be running; those are often disabled in standard server builds due to company policies.

Obviously the PowerCLI method is the only method that doesn't require a network connection from the PowerCLI management station to the guest and therefore is a uniform method that can be used in almost all cases. The only exception is when you happen to have an unsupported guest OS running that cannot run the VMware Tools package.

TABLE 8.1 Comparing guest OS methods of interactions

Method	Pros	Cons
Linux SSH	Can run anything that can be started from a command line	Returns plain text. Requires a network connection to the guest. A special SSH wrapper function is needed.
WMI	Returns actual PowerShell objects Specifically built to manage system information	Difficult to learn. Requires a network connection to the guest.
PowerShell remoting	Returns actual PowerShell objects	Relatively new. Requires remote systems to be properly configured. Requires a network connection to the guest.
PowerCLI `Invoke-VMScript`	Doesn't require a network connection to the guest Can run anything that can be started from a command line	Returns plain text. VMware Tools need to be installed in the guest.

If you need to interact with the VM's guest OS, the native tools available depend on the installed guest OS. This book focuses on the two most used types of guest operating systems:

- Linux systems
- Windows systems

Using Linux Native Tools

When you need to interact with Linux systems, Secure Shell (SSH) is the protocol of choice. Because you're reading a book about PowerCLI, you're probably running your scripts from a Windows system. The SSH protocol isn't a native Windows protocol, so you need to install PuTTY (available for download from www.chiark .greenend.org.uk/~sgtatham/putty/). PuTTY is a Windows SSH client. The PuTTY package also includes `Plink.exe` (PuTTY Link), a command-line connection tool, which can be called from within PowerShell. After installing PuTTY, you can use the `Invoke-SSH` function from Listing 5.24 in Chapter 5, "Creating Virtual Machines," to send commands or scripts using SSH to remote systems.

With PuTTY in place, you're ready to go. Let's look at an example of interacting with the Linux guest OS using the SSH protocol. To prevent a system from running out of disk space, it's a common practice to monitor its partitions. If you have VMware Tools installed in the guest OS, you can retrieve guest OS partition information from the virtual machine object:

```
[vSphere PowerCLI] C:\Scripts> $vm = Get-VM VM001 | Get-View
[vSphere PowerCLI] C:\Scripts> $vm.Guest.Disk | ft -AutoSize

DiskPath   Capacity   FreeSpace
--------   --------   ---------
/          1300103168 434094080
/local       32490496  27873280
/boot       103512064  91149312
/tmp       2113028096 2076278784
```

You can also retrieve this information from the guest itself using SSH. To get partition information from a Linux guest you need to use the shell command `df`. As mentioned earlier, you can use the `Invoke-SSH` function from Listing 5.24 in Chapter 5.

```
[vSphere PowerCLI] C:\Scripts> Invoke-SSH -Credential $cred `
    -Computer VM005 -ScriptText 'df'

Filesystem            1K-blocks     Used Available Use% Mounted
/dev/mapper/udavg-systemlv
                        1269632   845716    358380  71% /
/dev/mapper/udavg-locallv
                          31729     4509     25582  15% /local
/dev/sda1                101086    12073     83794  13% /boot
tmpfs                    257720        0    257720   0% /dev/shm
/dev/sdb1               2063504    35888   1922796   2% /tmp
```

Notice that the output is similar to the information retrieved through VMware Tools. However, the output is returned as text (not as a PowerShell object this time), so it's going to be a bit harder to extract data. If you are interested in displaying just a subset of the text returned, you can use the `Select-String` cmdlet, which is similar to the `grep` command in Unix. Let's display only information for the boot volume:

```
[vSphere PowerCLI] C:\Scripts> Invoke-SSH -Credential $cred `
    -Computer VM005 -ScriptText 'df' | Select-String '/boot'

/dev/sda1                101086    12073     83794  13% /boot
```

The ability to report shell command output is nice, but in the real world, you probably want to know if the amount of free space is still above the threshold. To accomplish this, you need to extract the text values and store them in a variable. You can use the string's SubString() method to cut the information you need out of the string and then analyze it and get a useful report, as shown in Listing 8.1.

LISTING 8.1   **Converting text to objects using substrings**

```
$output = Invoke-SSH -Credential $cred -Computer VM005 `
    -ScriptText 'df' | Select-String '/boot'

#Create object
$obj = "" | Select FileSystem,Size,Used,Available,Usage,Mount
$obj.FileSystem = $output.ToString().SubString(0,9)
$obj.Size = $output.ToString().SubString(24,6)
$obj.Used = $output.ToString().SubString(35,5)
$obj.Available = $output.ToString().SubString(45,5)
$obj.Usage = $output.ToString().SubString(52,2)
$obj.Mount = $output.ToString().SubString(56)

If ([int]$obj.Available -lt 50MB/1KB) {
  Write-Warning "Alert: Free space on volume /boot is low"
}
```

If you use the code from Listing 8.1 in your environment without modification, you probably won't get the output you were expecting. This is because this method isn't very flexible. If the offset of the columns in the output changes, it will render the script unusable. To make the code from Listing 8.1 work in your environment, you need to adjust the numbers of the SubString() method according to your environment. The first number represents the index number of the starting character, and the second number represents the number of characters to select. SubString(24,6) would mean: start at character 25 and select 6 characters. Remember that the index starts at 0.

A much more flexible solution is to make use of regular expressions (regex). Building a good regex is a complex task, and a regex deep-dive is beyond the scope of this book. But let's take a look at some basics. In Table 8.2, you'll find an explanation of some basic regex characters.

Now let's use the information from Table 8.2 to create a regex and extract the /boot partition's free disk space. In Listing 8.2, you'll find an example of using regex to extract data from the text output.

TABLE 8.2   Regular expressions reference sheet

Character	Definition	Example
. (dot)	Matches any character.	"pos." matches pos1 or posh but not pos12.
+	Preceding item must match one or more times.	"pos.+" matches posh or poshable but not pos.
*	Preceding item must match zero or more times.	"pos*" matches pos and posss but not posh.
()	Creates a substring or group.	"(po)(sh)" matches posh and creates two groups: po and sh.
[]	Matches one of any characters enclosed.	"po[os]h" matches posh and pooh.
\s	A single whitespace character.	"po\ssh" matches po sh but not posh.
\S	A single non-whitespace character.	"po\Sh" matches posh and po$h but not po sh.
\w	A single word character (alphanumeric, numeric, and underscore).	"po\wh" matches posh or po5h but not po$h.
\d	A single numeric character.	"po\dh" matches po5h but not posh.

LISTING 8.2   Converting text to objects using regex

```
$output = Invoke-SSH -Credential $cred -Computer VM005 `
    -ScriptText 'df -P' | Select-String '/boot'
$regex = [regex]"(\S+)\s+(\d+)\s+(\d+)\s+(\d+)\s+(\d+)%\s+(\S+)"
$matches = $regex.Match($output)

#Create object
$obj = "" | Select FileSystem,Size,Used,Available,Usage,Mount
$obj.FileSystem = $matches.Groups[1].value
$obj.Size = $matches.Groups[2].value
$obj.Used = $matches.Groups[3].value
$obj.Available = $matches.Groups[4].value
$obj.Usage = $matches.Groups[5].value
$obj.Mount = $matches.Groups[6].value

If ([int]$obj.Available -lt 50MB/1KB) {
  Write-Warning "Alert: Free space on volume /boot is low"
}
```

Notice that the Groups property is an array of substrings with matches between the parentheses. To test the amount of free space, first cast the string value from the regex into an integer value by specifying [int] in front of the variable, as shown in the if statement.

When the output is in columns where each column is separated by one or more spaces and the value itself doesn't contain a space, you can use an easier approach. First, remove the duplicate whitespaces with a simple regex and then use the string's Split() method to separate the columns, as we did in Listing 8.3. The regex "\s+" matches one or more spaces.

LISTING 8.3 Converting text to objects using a simple regex and Split()

```
$output = Invoke-SSH -Credential $cred -Computer VM005 `
    -ScriptText 'df -P'
$Partitions = @()

#skip the first header line
$output[1..($output.Length - 1)] | %{

  #Remove duplicate whitespaces
  $columns = [regex]::Replace($_,"\s+"," ").Split()

  #Create object
  $obj = "" | Select FileSystem,Size,Used,Available,Usage,Mount
  $obj.FileSystem = $columns[0]
  $obj.Size = $columns[1]
  $obj.Used = $columns[2]
  $obj.Available = $columns[3]
  $obj.Usage = $columns[4]
  $obj.Mount = $columns[5]
  $Partitions += $obj
}
$Partitions | ft -AutoSize
```

Using Windows Native Tools

There are two main ways to interact with the Windows guest OS: Windows Management Instrumentation (WMI) and PowerShell remoting. WMI allows scripting languages like VBScript or Windows PowerShell to manage Microsoft Windows systems, both locally and remotely. WMI is preinstalled in Windows 2000 and newer OSs. PowerShell remoting is Microsoft's new way of interacting with remote systems and comes with PowerShell 2.0. One drawback to both methods is that they require a network connection not be blocked by a company firewall and that the applicable services are configured and running on the remote system. WMI is an interface designed to manage system information using WMI Query Language (WQL), whereas PowerShell remoting is more like a remote shell.

WMI

WMI is the Microsoft implementation of Web-Based Enterprise Management (WBEM), which is an industry initiative to develop a standard technology for accessing management information in an enterprise environment. WMI is very powerful but also hard to understand. Many times, finding the right information requires a lot of digging in the enormous collection of WMI classes. An in-depth study of WMI is beyond the scope of this book. A good starting point for learning WMI is the Microsoft MSDN Library. You can access the library from `http://msdn.microsoft.com/en-us/library/aa394582(v=VS.85).aspx`.

 NOTE   To use WMI, you must be running the Windows Management Instrumentation service. For remote systems, make sure that there's no firewall blocking WMI traffic between your PowerCLI session and the remote system.

In PowerShell, WMI information is retrieved using the `Get-WMIObject` cmdlet. To retrieve information from a remote system, you need to provide the `-Computer` parameter. If you do not specify a machine, the information from your local machine is retrieved. The `-Computer` parameter value can be a fully qualified domain name, a NetBIOS name, or an IP address. You also need to specify the class from which you want to retrieve information from using the `-Class` parameter. This parameter name is optional, however, and may be left out. The next two statements are identical and retrieve a list of services installed on your local system:

```
Get-WmiObject -Class Win32_Service
Get-WmiObject Win32_Service
```

Let's use the `Get-WmiObject` cmdlet to retrieve the drive letter for the CD-ROM drive on a virtual machine named VM001. Information about CD-ROM drives is contained within the `Win32_CDROMDrive` class.

```
[vSphere PowerCLI] C:\Scripts> Get-WmiObject Win32_CDROMDrive `
    -ComputerName VM001 | Format-List


Caption      : NECVMWar VMware IDE CDR00
Drive        : Z:
```

```
Manufacturer : (Standard CD-ROM drives)
VolumeName    :
```

WMI can also be queried using WQL, which is a SQL-like language. WQL queries can be run using the -Query parameter. Let's retrieve the CD-ROM information again, this time using a WQL query:

```
[vSphere PowerCLI] C:\Scripts> Get-WmiObject -Query `
    "Select * From Win32_CDROMDrive" `
    -ComputerName VM001 | Format-List


Caption      : NECVMWar VMware IDE CDR00
Drive        : Z:
Manufacturer : (Standard CD-ROM drives)
VolumeName   :
```

Although you would prefer not to have any local accounts from a management and security perspective, you might still be running some legacy programs that require a local user account. Also, when you are scripting against a multidomain environment, it might come in handy to have a universal local account for running scripts so that you don't have to keep track of specific domain information for each system. Let's retrieve information about the local user accounts from a guest named VM001 using WMI:

```
[vSphere PowerCLI] C:\Scripts> Get-WmiObject Win32_UserAccount `
    -Filter "LocalAccount = True" -ComputerName VM001


AccountType : 512
Caption     : VM001\Scheduler
Domain      : VM001
SID         : S-1-5-21-2765119509-1257391904-1903784409-1005
FullName    : Scheduler
Name        : Scheduler


AccountType : 512
Caption     : VM001\Guest
Domain      : VM001
SID         : S-1-5-21-2765119509-1257391904-1903784409-501
FullName    :
Name        : Guest


AccountType : 512
Caption     : VM001\Administrator
```

```
Domain        : VM001
SID           : S-1-5-21-2765119509-1257391904-1903784409-500
FullName      :
Name          : Administrator


AccountType : 512
Caption       : VM001\Scripting
Domain        : VM001
SID           : S-1-5-21-2765119509-1257391904-1903784409-1006
FullName      : Scripting
Name          : Scripting
```

TIP   Notice that the -Filter parameter was used in the previous example to show only user accounts where the LocalAccount property is set to True. Omitting the -Filter "LocalAccount = True" parameter on a domain member would retrieve *all* user accounts on the system, including *all* domain accounts. This could take a considerable amount of time in a large domain environment!

Notice that the Administrator account was returned. We recommend that, as a security best practice, you rename the local Administrator accounts on your Windows servers. Doing so helps prevent malicious attackers from guessing the Administrator password. Because the Administrator account is vital to your system, the account cannot be locked out and attackers can continue to guess until they get it right. Simply renaming the Administrator account makes this kind of attack much harder. Here's how to use WMI to do just that:

```
[vSphere PowerCLI] C:\Scripts> Get-WmiObject `
    -Query "Select * From Win32_UserAccount
    Where LocalAccount = True And
    Name = 'Administrator'" -ComputerName VM001 | %{
    $_.Rename("GoodForNothing")}


__GENUS          : 2
__CLASS          : __PARAMETERS
__SUPERCLASS     :
__DYNASTY        : __PARAMETERS
__RELPATH        :
__PROPERTY_COUNT : 1
__DERIVATION     : {}
__SERVER         :
```

```
__NAMESPACE      :
__PATH           :
ReturnValue      : 0
```

A `ReturnValue` of 0 means that the rename operation was successful.

In the real world, you want to perform this task for all your Windows servers. Let's take this one step further and expand the code so that all your Windows servers are checked and changed if necessary. The code to perform this task is contained in Listing 8.4.

LISTING 8.4   **Finding and renaming the local Administrator account using WMI**

```
Function Rename-LocalUser {
<#
.SYNOPSIS
  Renames a local user account using WMI
.DESCRIPTION
  This function renames a local user account using WMI on
  the (remote) computer specified by the Computer parameter
.NOTES
  Source:  Automating vSphere Administration
  Authors: Luc Dekens, Arnim van Lieshout, Jonathan Medd,
           Alan Renouf, Glenn Sizemore
.PARAMETER userName
  The name of the local user account to rename
.PARAMETER newUserName
  The new name of the local user account
.PARAMETER computer
  The name of the computer to rename the local user account on.
  To run the operation on the local computer
  use 'localhost' or '.' as computer name
.EXAMPLE
  PS> Rename-LocalUser "Administrator" "GoodForNothing" "."
#>

  param(
    [parameter(mandatory = $true, position=1,
      HelpMessage = "Enter a local user account name")]
    [String]$userName,
    [parameter(mandatory = $true, position=2,
      HelpMessage = "Enter a new user name")]
```

```
        [String]$newUserName,
        [parameter(mandatory = $true, position=3,
          HelpMessage = "Enter a computer name")]
        [String]$Computer)

    $user = Get-WmiObject -Query "Select * From Win32_UserAccount
        Where LocalAccount = True And
        Name = '$userName'" -ComputerName $computer

    If ($user) {
      Write-Host -ForegroundColor Yellow `
          "User $userName found on $computer"
      $result = $user | %{$_.Rename("$newUserName")}
      If ($result.ReturnValue -eq 0) {
        Write-Host -ForegroundColor Yellow `
            "User $userName successfully renamed to $newUserName"
      }
      else {
        Write-Host -ForegroundColor Red `
            "Rename operation failed.
Errorcode $($result.ReturnValue)"
      }
    }
}

$winServers = Get-VM | Where {$_.PowerState -eq "PoweredOn" `
    -and $_.ExtensionData.Config.GuestId -like "win*"}
ForEach ($vm in $winServers) {
  Rename-LocalUser "Administrator" "GoodForNothing" $vm.Name
}
```

The uses for WMI are almost endless. We'll explore more WMI magic a little later in the "Using PowerCLI Methods" section, but first let's have a look at the other Windows native method, PowerShell remoting.

PowerShell Remoting

PowerShell remoting is Microsoft's new way of managing remote systems and will become increasingly important over time. Microsoft is strategically moving PowerShell more and more to the forefront. Consider the management of Microsoft Exchange 2010; it totally relies on PowerShell.

PowerShell remoting requires that PowerShell v2.0 and Windows Remote Management (WinRM) be installed and running. Windows 7 and Windows 2008 R2 come with WinRM preinstalled.

For Windows Vista, Windows XP, Windows 2003, and Windows 2008, you need to install the service. For these operating systems, WinRM is available together with PowerShell 2.0 in the Windows Management Framework and is available for download from the Microsoft website at http://support.microsoft.com/kb/968929.

To check if WinRM is already installed on your system, you could check for the existence of a Windows Remote Management service in the Services Microsoft Management Console (MMC), but because this book is about PowerCLI, we'll use the PowerShell Get-Service cmdlet:

```
[vSphere PowerCLI] C:\Scripts> Get-Service WinRm


Status    Name            DisplayName
------    ----            -----------
Running   WinRM           Windows Remote Management (WS-Manag...
```

To enable PowerShell remote sessions on a Windows system, PowerShell remoting must be enabled. This procedure is only necessary on systems that need to receive remote sessions (receiver systems). On the sender system, no additional procedure is necessary to take advantage of the PowerShell remoting possibilities. (Sender systems actually run the remote session scripts.) To enable PowerShell remoting, use the Enable-PSRemoting cmdlet. This cmdlet will configure your system, including:

▶ Starting or restarting (if already started) the WinRM service.

▶ Setting the WinRM service type to start automatically.

▶ Creating a listener to accept requests on any IP address.

▶ Enabling a firewall exception for WS-Management traffic (for HTTP only).

```
[vSphere PowerCLI] C:\Scripts> Enable-PSRemoting


WinRM Quick Configuration
Running command "Set-WSManQuickConfig" to enable this machine
for remote management through WinRM service.
 This includes:
    1. Starting or restarting (if already started) the WinRM
       service
    2. Setting the WinRM service type to auto start
```

3. Creating a listener to accept requests on any IP address

4. Enabling firewall exception for WS-Management traffic (for http only).

Do you want to continue?
[Y] Yes [A] Yes to All [N] No [L] No to All [S] Suspend
    [?] Help (default is "Y"): y
WinRM already is set up to receive requests on this machine.
WinRM has been updated for remote management.
Created a WinRM listener on HTTP://* to accept WS-Man requests to any IP on this machine.
WinRM firewall exception enabled.

POWERSHELL REMOTING IN A DOMAIN ENVIRONMENT

When you are using Windows 7 or Windows 2008 R2, PowerShell remoting is preinstalled. When dealing with these systems in a domain environment, you'll find it much easier to control PowerShell remoting through Group Policies. You can find more information on enabling Group Policies at

www.jonathanmedd.net/2010/03/enabling-powershell-2-0-remoting-in-an-enterprise.html

Now that the system is ready to receive remote PowerShell sessions, let's give it a try. Remember that the user performing remote script execution must be a member of the Administrators group on the remote computer to be able to run commands.

There are two varieties of PowerShell remoting: temporary sessions and persistent sessions. Temporary sessions are sessions that are opened to run a command and immediately closed when that command is finished. This kind of session is usually created when you specify the –ComputerName parameter on a cmdlet. Let's use the Invoke-Command cmdlet to create a temporary session and retrieve WMI information from the remote guest:

```
[vSphere PowerCLI] C:\Scripts> Invoke-Command `
    -ComputerName VM001 -ScriptBlock {
        Get-WmiObject Win32_CDROMDrive} | Format-List


Caption      : NECVMWar VMware IDE CDR00
Drive        : Z:
```

```
Manufacturer : (Standard CD-ROM drives)
VolumeName    :
PSComputerName : VM001
```

Notice that we used the `Get-WmiObject` cmdlet, but we used it without specifying the `-ComputerName` parameter so that the WMI query will run locally on the remote machine.

You can also start an interactive session using the `Enter-PSSession` cmdlet:

```
[vSphere PowerCLI] C:\Scripts> Enter-PSSession VM001
[VM001]: PS C:\>
```

Notice that the command prompt changed to `[VM001]: PS C:\>` to indicate that you are now working on remote computer VM001. When you're finished, exit the interactive session by issuing the `Exit-PSSession` cmdlet.

Let's take it one step further and use this new PowerShell remoting technology in a script. In Listing 8.5, you'll find a script that reports the status of a service using PowerShell remoting. The optional switches allow the start or restart of a service.

LISTING 8.5   **Reporting the status of a service using PowerShell remoting**

```
Function Check-Service {
<#
.SYNOPSIS
  Checks the state of a service using PowerShell remoting
.DESCRIPTION
  This function checks the state of a service using
  PowerShell remoting. The optional restart switch can be used
  to restart a service if it is stopped.
.NOTES
  Source:  Automating vSphere Administration
  Authors: Luc Dekens, Arnim van Lieshout, Jonathan Medd,
           Alan Renouf, Glenn Sizemore
.PARAMETER Computer
  One or more computer names to check the service on
.PARAMETER Service
  One or more service names to check
.PARAMETER Start
  Optional parameter to start a stopped service
.PARAMETER Restart
  Optional parameter to restart a service
```

```
.EXAMPLE
  PS> Check-Service -Computer VM001 -Service wuauserv
#>

  Param(
    [parameter(mandatory = $true,
    HelpMessage = "Enter a computer name")]
    [string]$Computer,
    [parameter(mandatory = $true,
    HelpMessage = "Enter a service name")]
    [string]$Service,
    [switch]$Start,
    [switch]$Restart)

  $report=@()
#establish a persistent connection
  $session = New-PSSession $Computer
  $remoteService = Invoke-Command -Session $session `
      -ScriptBlock {
    param($ServiceName)
    $localService = Get-Service $ServiceName
    $localService
  } -ArgumentList $Service
  If ($Start -and $remoteService.Status -eq "Stopped") {
    Invoke-Command -Session $session -ScriptBlock {
        $localService.Start()
    }
    $remoteService | Add-Member -MemberType NoteProperty `
      -Name Started -Value $True
  }
  If ($Restart) {
    Invoke-Command -Session $session -ScriptBlock {
      $localService.stop()
      $localService.WaitForStatus("Stopped")
      $localService.start()
    }
    $remoteService | Add-Member -MemberType NoteProperty `
        -Name Restarted -Value $True
  }
```

```
  $report += $remoteService
#close persistent connection
  Remove-PSSession $session
  $report
}
```

Because setting up a session each time you run a remote command slows down performance, you can create a persistent session using the New-PSSession cmdlet, as we did in Listing 8.5. A persistent session can then be specified using the -Session parameter. To close the persistent session, use the Remove-PSSession cmdlet.

As an example, let's make sure that a remote server named VM001 is still receiving Windows updates by reporting the status of the wuauserv service using the function from Listing 8.5. Here's the output.

```
[vSphere PowerCLI] C:\Scripts> Check-Service VM001 wuauserv


Status    Name        DisplayName            PSComputerName
------    ----        -----------            --------------
Running   wuauserv    Automatic Updates      VM001
```

T I P   If you want to know more about PowerShell remoting, the PowerShell about_remote **help file is a good starting point:**

```
[vSphere PowerCLI] C:\Scripts> Help about_remote
```

The drawback to the OS native methods is that a network connection is always required. But what about VMs behind a firewall or in completely isolated networks? Luckily, there is a PowerCLI method available. Let's take a look.

Using PowerCLI Methods

PowerCLI enables you to run scripts inside your VM using the Invoke-VMScript cmdlet. The only requirement is that you must have VMware Tools installed on the VM you're querying. This way, you can interact with the guest OS without worrying about firewalls or services that need to be running, as you must when you employ guest OS native methods. There's also no need to install PuTTY for interacting with Linux OSs. This is a uniform way of interacting with the guest OS no matter what, as long as VMware Tools is installed. Using the Invoke-VMScript cmdlet, you can run PowerShell or batch scripts on Windows machines and Bash scripts on Linux machines. To run PowerShell scripts, PowerShell needs to be installed on the guest.

Because batch and Bash scripts are supported, you can, in fact, run anything that can be started through a batch or Bash script, like your old pre-PowerShell Visual Basic Scripting Edition (VBScript) scripts in Windows, for example, or maybe even Perl scripts in your Linux guests. To accomplish this, you can copy the VBScript or Perl file to the guest using the `Copy-VMGuestFile` cmdlet or make the script file accessible over the network by placing it on a file share.

```
Copy-VMGuestFile -Source C:\Scripts\myScript.vbs `
    -Destination C:\Temp\ -VM VM001 -LocalToGuest `
    -HostCredential $hostCred -GuestCredential $guestCred

$script = 'cscript C:\Temp\myScript.vbs'

Invoke-VMScript -ScriptText $script -VM VM001 `
    -HostCredential $hostCred -GuestCredential $guestCred `
    -ScriptType Bat
```

> **NOTE**   You can find an example of using `Invoke-VMScript` to run a VBScript in a Windows VM in Listing 7.4 in Chapter 7, "Configuring Virtual Machine Hardware."

Notice that the output returned by the `Invoke-VMScript` cmdlet is plain text. Still, remember the methods to convert text to objects from a previous section about using Linux Native OS Tools? Good! These methods can also be used here.

On Linux systems, you can run Bash scripts. Let's retrieve the partition information for the Linux VM again, but this time use the `Invoke-VMScript` cmdlet:

```
$output = Invoke-VMScript 'df -P' -VM VM005 `
    -HostCredential $HostCred -GuestCredential $GuestCred `
    -ScriptType "bash"
```

The `$output` variable, containing the output text, can be processed using the techniques you learned earlier in Listing 8.1, Listing 8.2, and Listing 8.3.

Another method of converting text to PowerShell objects that we've found to be very useful is making sure that the information returned from the guest is in comma-separated values (CSV) format. You can then forward this output to a temporary file and import that file again using the `Import-Csv` cmdlet.

Let's go back to using WMI for a while. Microsoft also provides a command-line interface to WMI called Windows Management Instrumentation Command Line (WMIC).

This utility supports a /format parameter to present WMI information in CSV format. For example, have a look at that CD-ROM drive again on VM001:

```
C:\> wmic path Win32_CDROMDrive get Caption, Drive,➥
Manufacturer /format:csv


Node,Caption,Drive,Manufacturer
VM001,NECVMWar VMware IDE CDR00,Z:,(Standard CD-ROM drives)
```

Notice that a get parameter was used to retrieve only the specified properties. To retrieve all properties, provide the get parameter without any properties. Let's use this knowledge with the Invoke-VMScript cmdlet:

```
$script = "wmic path Win32_CDROMDrive get /format:csv"
$textOutput = Invoke-VMScript $script -vm VM001 `
    -HostCredential $HostCred -GuestCredential $GuestCred `
    -ScriptType "bat"
```

Now, we have the CSV-formatted output as plain text stored in the $textOutput variable. Let's export the text output to a temporary file and import it again using the Import-Csv cmdlet:

```
$fileName = [System.IO.Path]::GetTempFileName()
$textOutput.Trim() > $fileName
$cdrom = Import-Csv $FileName
Remove-Item $fileName
```

Notice that we used the .Trim() method to strip off the nasty empty line returned by wmic at the start of the output; without it, the CSV output would be invalid. CSV headers must start at the first line in a CSV file. The $cdrom variable now contains all the information we were looking for in a nice PowerShell object-oriented way:

```
[vSphere PowerCLI] C:\Scripts> $cdrom
Node                    : WIN-V47IN52HGDT
Availability            : 3
Capabilities            : {3;7}
CapabilityDescriptions  : {Random Access; Supports Removable...}
Caption                 : NECVMWar VMware IDE CDR00 ATA Device
CompressionMethod       : Unknown
ConfigManagerErrorCode  : 0
ConfigManagerUserConfig : FALSE
CreationClassName       : Win32_CDROMDrive
DefaultBlockSize        :
Description             : CD-ROM Drive
```

```
...
Output truncated, you get the picture.
```

In addition to the `Invoke-VMScript` cmdlet, other PowerCLI cmdlets interact with the guest OS. These include:

- `Get-VMGuestRoute`
- `New-VMGuestRoute`
- `Remove-VMGuestRoute`
- `Get-VMGuestNetworkInterface`
- `Set-VMGuestNetworkInterface`
- `Set-HardDisk`

These cmdlets send batch scripts using the `Invoke-VMScript` cmdlet to the guest OS, which executes in the context of the specified guest user. In Chapter 5 and Chapter 7, you'll find several examples of using these cmdlets.

The batch scripts are located in the `Scripts` folder in the PowerCLI installation directory. These batch scripts have the following format:

```
<CmdletName>_<OS_Identifier>
```

where `<OS_Identifier>` is the guest family or the guest ID as returned by `Get-VMGuest` and `<CmdletName>` is the name of the cmdlet without a hyphen—for example, `SetVMGuestNetworkInterface`.

Whenever you use one of these cmdlets, the cmdlet will look for a file that is specifically named with the VM's guest ID. If none is found, the file named for the specific guest family is used. For instance, when you run the `Set-HardDisk` cmdlet against Windows 2008, the cmdlet searches for a file called `GuestDiskExpansion_WinLongHornGuest.bat` first. If that file is found, it will be run inside the guest OS. If the file can't be found, the cmdlet looks for a more general guest family file named `GuestDiskExpansion_WindowsGuest.bat`.

TIP To find the guest ID of your operating system, simply look in the help file for the `Set-VM` cmdlet. All possible guest IDs are listed under the `GuestID` parameter section. If you need to know the Guest ID for a specific VM, query the `.ExtensionData.Guest` `.GuestId` property of that VM. Another option is to use the `Get-VMGuestId` function from Listing 5.2 (in Chapter 5) to query your host for a list of supported operating systems and their `GuestIds`. Unfortunately, these cmdlets support only a handful of operating systems and Windows 7 or Windows 2008 (R2) aren't supported yet.

Now, let's put an end to the Windows 7/Windows 2008 (R2) limitation for the `Set-HardDisk` cmdlet and extend its functionality to support Windows 7 and Windows 2008 (R2). When you try to extend the hard disk on any of these operating systems using the `Set-HardDisk` cmdlet, you'll get an error like this one:

```
Set-HardDisk : 06-11-2010 6:41:09 PM    Set-HardDisk
    Execution of the  script in guest OS on VM 'Arnim1' failed:
'Specified disk "SCSI:0:0" was not found
...
Error Message truncated
```

Go to the `Scripts` folder in the PowerCLI installation directory and find a file named `GuestDiskExpansion_WindowsGuest.bat`. We'll spare you the details of this batch script, but the script calls `DiskPart.exe` to extend the partitions. The version of the DiskPart utility that ships with Windows 7 and Windows 2008 (R2) produces a slightly different output than earlier versions. In fact, it displays one line less and therefore the line showing the actual Windows 7 or Windows 2008 (R2) disk is skipped by the general script, resulting in the error that SCSI disk 0:0 was not found. Let's update the batch file so that it works with the 64-bit version of Windows 2008. Copy the file and rename it **GuestDiskExpansion_winLonghorn64Guest.bat**. Remember that a script for a specific operating system must be named using its guest ID. In Table 8.3 you'll find the possible guest IDs for the different versions of Windows 7 and Windows 2008.

TABLE 8.3   Windows 7 and Windows 2008 guest IDs

Operating system	Guest ID
Windows 7	Windows7Guest
Windows 7 (64-bit)	Windows7_64Guest
Windows Server 2008	WinLonghornGuest
Windows Server 2008 (64-bit)	WinLonghorn64Guest
Windows Server 2008 R2 (64-bit)	Windows7Server64Guest

Now open the file in a text editor and find lines 64, 74, and 121. They all start with `for /F "tokens=` as listed in the code that follows:

```
 64:for /F "tokens=2 skip=8" %%A in ...
 74:for /F "tokens=1,2 skip=9 delims=:" %%M in ...
121:for /F "tokens=1,2,3 skip=9" %%X in ...
```

The `skip` parameter is used to specify the number of lines that will be skipped before processing the output. Because in Windows 7 and Windows 2008 the DiskPart utility displays one line less, all you need to do is decrease the `skip=` value by 1. So, `skip=8` becomes `skip=7`, and so on. After decreasing these values, save the file and you're done.

The complete modified batch file can be downloaded from `www.sybex.com/go/vmwarevspherepowercliref`. Create a copy for each operating system in Table 8.3 to make sure the `Set-HardDisk` cmdlet works for all available versions.

Use vMotion and Storage vMotion

vMotion is a feature of VMware vCenter Server and allows the live migration of virtual machines between ESX hosts with zero downtime. Storage vMotion, on the other hand, allows the live migration of virtual machine disk files across datastores with zero downtime. Remember that shared storage is required if you wish to use either of these vMotion technologies.

When you need to perform maintenance on an ESX host, you can use vMotion to evacuate all VMs off the ESX host with zero downtime. Maintenance might include a memory upgrade of your ESX host, a degraded memory module replacement, or even the complete replacement of the server. You might use a storage vMotion for any of several reasons:

▶ The datastore is running out of free disk space and you want to free up space by moving a VM to another datastore.

▶ You want to convert your virtual hard disk(s) format to thin provisioned, or vice versa.

▶ You need to move your VMs to another storage box.

▶ You need to move your VM to a datastore formatted with a different block size.

Whatever your reason, vMotion and Storage vMotion are your friends.

Examining vMotion Requirements

To utilize vMotion, the hosts and the VMs that are involved must meet the following requirements:

▶ A Gigabit Ethernet network must be available between the hosts.

▶ A VMkernel port must be defined and enabled for vMotion on each host.

- ▶ Virtual switches on both hosts must be configured identically. If you are using vNetwork distributed switches (vDSs), both hosts must participate in the same vDS.

- ▶ All port groups to which the VM is attached must exist on both hosts. You can use the script in Listing 14.7 from Chapter 14, "Reporting the Status of Your vSphere Environment," to determine port group inconsistencies between ESX(i) hosts if you're using standard switches.

- ▶ The processors in both hosts must be compatible.

- ▶ The VM must not be connected to any device that is physically available to only one host. This includes CD/DVD drives, floppy drives, serial or parallel ports, and disk storage. One of the most common reasons for a failing vMotion are connected CD-ROMs or floppy drives.

- ▶ The VM must not be connected to an internal-only virtual switch.

- ▶ The VM must not have CPU Affinity set.

Moving a Virtual Machine

Moving a virtual machine using vMotion can be accomplished by using the `Move-VM` cmdlet. This cmdlet is able to move your VM to another ESX host using a standard vMotion or to move your VM's files to another datastore using a Storage vMotion. Storage vMotion is only available in the Enterprise and Enterprise Plus editions.

vMotion technology is also used by a vCenter Server feature called the Distributed Resource Scheduler (DRS), which evenly distributes workloads across the ESX hosts in a cluster. If the automation level of DRS is set to Fully Automated, all VMs will be moved to a different host whenever the host is put in Maintenance mode. DRS is only available in the Enterprise and Enterprise Plus editions.

```
Get-VMHost -Name ESX01 | Set-VMHost -State Maintenance
```

If DRS isn't set to Fully Automated on the cluster, DRS won't do anything when a host is put into Maintenance mode. If individual virtual machine automation levels are configured, DRS will not migrate VMs that aren't set to Fully Automated. In that case, or when you don't have an Enterprise or Enterprise Plus edition, you can use the script in Listing 8.6 to employ vMotion to manually evacuate VMs from the ESX host.

Managing the Virtual Machine Life Cycle

PART II

LISTING 8.6   Evacuating VMs from the ESX host

```
Function Evacuate-VMHost {
<#
.SYNOPSIS
  Puts host into maintenance mode and moves all VMs on the host
  to other members in the same cluster
.DESCRIPTION
  This function puts a host in maintenance mode and moves all
  VMs from the VMHost randomly to other hosts in the cluster.
  If -TargetHost is specified, all VMs are moved to this
  TargetHost instead of random cluster members.
.NOTES
  Source:  Automating vSphere Administration
  Authors: Luc Dekens, Arnim van Lieshout, Jonathan Medd,
           Alan Renouf, Glenn Sizemore
.PARAMETER VMHost
  The source host to put into maintenance mode
.PARAMETER TargetHost
  Optional target host
.EXAMPLE
  PS> Evacuate-VMHost -VMHost ESX01
.EXAMPLE
  PS> Evacuate-VMHost -VMHost ESX01 -TargetHost ESX02
#>

  Param(
      [parameter(mandatory = $true, position=1,
    HelpMessage = "Enter a source server")]
    [PSObject]$VMHost,
    [PSObject]$TargetHost)

  if ("String","VMHostImpl" -notcontains `
      $VMHost.GetType().Name) {
    throw "No valid type for -VMHost specified"
  }
  if ($TargetHost -and "String","VMHostImpl" -notcontains `
      $TargetHost.GetType().Name) {
    throw "No valid type for -TargetHost specified"
  }

  $sourceHost = Get-VMHost $VMHost
```

```
    if ($TargetHost) {
      $TargetHost = Get-VMHost $TargetHost
      if (!$TargetHost) {
        throw "-TargetHost cannot be found"
      }
    }
    else {
      $cluster = Get-Cluster -VMHost $sourceHost
      if (!$cluster) {
        throw "No cluster found"
      }
      $clusterHosts = $cluster | Get-VMHost | ?{$_.Name -ne `
          $sourceHost.Name -and $_.State -eq "Connected"}
      if (!$clusterHosts) {
        throw "No valid cluster members found"
      }
    }

#Evacuate all VMs from host
  foreach ($vm in ($sourceHost | Get-VM)) {
    if ($TargetHost) {
      $vmDestination = $TargetHost
    }
    else {
      $vmDestination = $clusterHosts | Get-Random
    }
    Move-VM -VM $vm -Destination $vmDestination `
        -RunAsync:$true -Confirm:$false | Out-Null
  }

#Put host into maintenance mode
  $sourceHost | Set-VMHost -State "Maintenance" `
      -RunAsync:$true | Out-Null
}
```

The Move-VM cmdlet can also be used to perform a storage vMotion. To perform a storage vMotion using Move-VM, you need to specify the target datastore using the -Datastore parameter. Remember that when you perform a storage vMotion on ESX 3.5, a snapshot is created under the hood and extra disk space is needed. When your datastore has already run out of free space, don't try to perform a storage vMotion, as that will only make things worse. In that case, the best way to free up disk space is to power down one or more VMs that you wish to Storage vMotion. This frees up extra space if the VMs you powered down happen to have their swap files stored on the affected datastore. When the VMs are powered down, move these powered-down VMs to another datastore. Storage vMotion on vSphere uses the new Changed Block Tracking (CBT) feature and won't create snapshots and require extra space.

```
Get-VM VM001 | Move-VM –Datastore Datastore02
```

Notice that using the `Move-VM` cmdlet moves the complete VM. If you need to move only a specific hard disk, use the `Set-HardDisk` cmdlet. This is useful when you want to use separate datastores for the data and log disks on an SQL Server:

```
$hd = Get-VM VM001 | Get-HardDisk | ?{$_.Name -eq "Hard disk 2"}
$hd | Set-HardDisk -Datastore Datastore02
```

Not all moves can be accomplished with PowerCLI cmdlets. For example, if you want to move the VM's configuration file only, then you're out of luck using the PowerCLI cmdlets. You need to use the SDK in this case. We used the SDK approach in Listing 8.7 to build a function to move the registered content from one datastore to another. The function gets all VMs with a relation to the source datastore and migrates only the files that are actually stored on the source datastore to the destination datastore. This function is useful when you need to migrate your datastores to another storage array or to datastores using a different block size.

LISTING 8.7   **Moving all VMs from one datastore to another**

```
Function Move-Datastore {
<#
.SYNOPSIS
  Moves all registered .vmx and .vmdk files to another datastore
.DESCRIPTION
  This function moves all registered vms from the source
  datastore to the target datastore
.NOTES
  Source:  Automating vSphere Administration
  Authors: Luc Dekens, Arnim van Lieshout, Jonathan Medd,
           Alan Renouf, Glenn Sizemore
.PARAMETER SourceDatastore
  The source datastore name or object
```

```
.PARAMETER TargetDatastore
  The target datastore name or object
.EXAMPLE
  PS> Move-Datastore -SourceDatastore "Datastore01" `
      -TargetDatastore "Datastore02"
.EXAMPLE
  PS> Move-Datastore "Datastore01" "Datastore02"
#>

  param(
    [parameter(mandatory = $true, position=1,
    HelpMessage = "Enter a source datastore")]
    [PSObject]$SourceDatastore,
    [parameter(mandatory = $true, position=2,
    HelpMessage = "Enter a target datastore")]
    [PSObject]$TargetDatastore)

  if ("String","DatastoreImpl" -notcontains `
      $SourceDatastore.GetType().Name) {
    throw "No valid type for -SourceDatastore specified"
  }
  if ("String","DatastoreImpl" -notcontains `
      $TargetDatastore.GetType().Name) {
    throw "No valid type for -TargetDatastore specified"
  }

  $SourceDatastore = Get-Datastore $SourceDatastore
  $TargetDatastore = Get-Datastore $TargetDatastore
  foreach($vm in ($SourceDatastore | Get-VM)) {
    $configFile = $vm.ExtensionData.Config.Files.VmPathName
    $configDatastoreName = $configFile.Trim('[').Split(']')[0]
    if ($configDatastoreName -eq $SourceDatastore.Name) {
      $configDatastoreName = $TargetDatastore.Name
    }
    $spec = New-Object VMware.Vim.VirtualMachineRelocateSpec
    $dsView = Get-Datastore $configDatastoreName | Get-View
    $spec.Datastore = $dsView.MoRef
    foreach ($disk in $vm.HardDisks) {
```

```
        $diskDatastoreName= $disk.FileName.Trim('[').Split(']')[0]
        if ($diskDatastoreName -eq $SourceDatastore.Name) {
          $diskDatastoreName = $TargetDatastore.Name
        }
        $objDisk = New-Object VMware.Vim.➥
VirtualMachineRelocateSpecDiskLocator
        $objDisk.DiskID = $disk.Id.Split('/')[1]
        $dsView = Get-Datastore $diskDatastoreName | Get-View
        $objDisk.DataStore = $dsView.MoRef
        $spec.Disk += $objDisk
      }
    $vm.ExtensionData.RelocateVM_Task($spec, "defaultPriority")
  }
}
```

Use and Manage Snapshots

vSphere allows the administrator to create snapshots of virtual machines. This creates a point-in-time "backup" of the VM. Notice that backup is mentioned within quotation marks, as a snapshot is not equivalent to a regular VM backup. Learn more about VM backup solutions in Chapter 10, "Backing Up and Restoring Your Virtual Machines." The snapshot saves a copy of the complete state of the virtual machine at the time it is taken (although saving the memory state is optional), allowing you to quickly revert back to that state when necessary, without the need for restoring backups. A lot of administrators think about redo files or delta files whenever a snapshot is mentioned. Those thoughts cause confusion when you need to permanently delete the snapshot in order to record the changes that were made since the snapshot was taken. A snapshot is much more than a delta VMDK file. So just forget about all the details that vSphere uses under the hood; it's all about virtual machine states. (Maybe it should be named vState instead of snapshot.)

A snapshot is a safety net. We recommend you create one whenever you need to modify the virtual machine's configuration, be it at the VM's hardware level or a modification of the guest operating system. Snapshots are often created before installing new software, patching the operating system, or making changes to the operating system's configuration (like Windows Registry changes). If something goes wrong, you can revert back to a known good state. When the change is successfully tested, you can delete the snapshot.

Creating and Removing Snapshots

Creating a snapshot is any easy task in the vSphere client—just a few clicks and the virtual machine has a known good state to revert back to if an issue occurs. But what if you wanted to create a scheduled snapshot or create snapshots for a number of virtual machines—remember the golden rule of scripting: "If you repeat it more than once, script it!"

Snapshots are created using the `New-Snapshot` cmdlet. To preserve the VM's memory state, specify the `-Memory` parameter, but keep in mind that this increases the size of the snapshot state file (VMSN) with the size of the VM's configured memory for a running virtual machine. Be sure that you preserve some free disk space on your datastores to store snapshot files.

RESERVING FREE SPACE

Determining the amount of free space to reserve for snapshots really depends on the dynamics of your environment. Questions you could ask yourself are:

- ▶ How often are snapshots taken?
- ▶ Are there multiple snapshots active per VM?
- ▶ How many snapshots (or VMs) are on my datastore?
- ▶ How much data is changed on my VMs when snapshots are active?
- ▶ Are my snapshots well managed?

Always remember that a snapshot cannot grow larger than its base disk plus some overhead depending on the size of the virtual disk. Commonly an amount equal to 20 percent of each datastore is reserved as free space. This takes into account snapshots and leaves enough room for future growth of existing VMDK files—although we've seen well-managed environments get away with as little as 10 percent or even less.

The following line of code shows you how to easily create a snapshot for a single machine:

```
Get-VM VM001 | New-Snapshot -Name "Before Patch" `
    -Description "Installation of patches from 5th Nov." `
    -Memory
```

A single cmdlet can create a snapshot, but what about multiple VMs? In a vSphere client, you would need to go to each VM individually and create the snapshot, retyping the information for each one. Imagine how long this could take with hundreds of VMs! You can easily create a snapshot for multiple VMs in PowerCLI using the same code but specifying multiple VMs as follows:

```
Get-VM Win* | New-Snapshot -Name "Before Patch" `
    -Description "Installation of patches from 5th Nov." `
    -Memory
```

To make sure that a guest file system is in a consistent state before you create a snapshot, use the -Quiesce parameter. This is particularly useful if you want to make a backup or clone of a running virtual machine and want to make sure the clone starts without a corrupted file system. To use this option, VMware Tools need to be installed on the VM, as they are used to quiesce the guest's file system.

```
Get-VM VM001 | New-Snapshot -Name "Daily Backup" `
    -Description "Daily snapshot for VM backup" -Quiesce
```

When you are certain that your change to the virtual machine is successful, you can remove the snapshot using the Remove-Snapshot cmdlet:

```
Get-Snapshot -VM VM001 -Name "Before Patch" | Remove-Snapshot
```

Or for multiple VMs, you can adjust the code slightly as follows:

```
Get-VM Win* | Get-Snapshot -Name "Before Patch" | `
 Remove-Snapshot
```

Whenever something goes wrong during your change to the VM, you can revert back to the snapshot. Reverting to a snapshot is done using the Set-VM cmdlet:

```
$snap = Get-Snapshot -VM VM001 -Name "Before Patch"
Set-VM -VM VM001 -Snapshot $snap -Confirm:$false
```

Now that you know how to create and remove snapshots, let's find a way to maintain your snapshots in your environment.

Maintaining Snapshots

The ability to create a snapshot is very useful, but make sure that you manage your snapshots. Monitor them regularly to detect snapshots that are getting old and/or large. If you fail to do so, your datastores might run out of free space and might get you into troubles. To learn how to generate a report for your snapshots, have a look at Chapter 14, "Reporting the Status of Your vSphere Environment."

To keep track of snapshots from within the vSphere client, you would need to go to each VM to check its snapshots and see how many snapshots have been created. But what if you wanted to check how much space was being used on your datastores by the snapshots? Other than going through each folder on each datastore, there is no easy way from within the vSphere client. PowerCLI, however, makes this very easy. With the following code, you can list all snapshots belonging to your VMs and include information about the size of the snapshots and the date they were created:

```
Get-VM | Get-Snapshot | Select VM, Name, SizeMB, Created
```

With some extra work, you can narrow your search. Listing 8.8 shows a function we created that lists only the VMs that are more than 2 weeks old and provides information about the person who created them.

LISTING 8.8 Listing snapshots over 2 weeks old (including creator)

```
function Get-SnapshotTree{
  param($tree, $target)
  $found = $null
  foreach($elem in $tree){
    if($elem.Snapshot.Value -eq $target.Value){
      $found = $elem
      continue
    }
  }
  if($found -eq $null -and $elem.ChildSnapshotList -ne $null){
    $found = Get-SnapshotTree $elem.ChildSnapshotList $target
  }
  return $found
}


function Get-SnapshotExtra ($snap){
  $guestName = $snap.VM #The name of the guest
  $tasknumber = 999 #Windowsize of the Task collector
  $taskMgr = Get-View TaskManager

#Create hash table. Each entry is a create snapshot task
  $report = @{}

  $filter = New-Object VMware.Vim.TaskFilterSpec
```

```
$filter.Time = New-Object VMware.Vim.TaskFilterSpecByTime
$filter.Time.beginTime = (($snap.Created).AddDays(-5))
$filter.Time.timeType = "startedTime"

$collectionImpl = `
    Get-View ($taskMgr.CreateCollectorForTasks($filter))

$dummy = $collectionImpl.RewindCollector
$collection = $collectionImpl.ReadNextTasks($tasknumber)
while($collection -ne $null){
  $collection | where {$_.DescriptionId -eq `
      "VirtualMachine.createSnapshot" -and $_.State -eq `
      "success" -and $_.EntityName -eq $guestName} | %{
    $row = New-Object PsObject
    $row | Add-Member -MemberType NoteProperty -Name User `
        -Value $_.Reason.UserName
    $vm = Get-View $_.Entity
    if($vm -ne $null){
      $snapshot = Get-SnapshotTree `
          $vm.Snapshot.RootSnapshotList $_.Result
      if($snapshot -ne $null){
        $key = $_.EntityName + "&" + `
            $snapshot.CreateTime.ToString()
        $report[$key] = $row
      }
    }
  }
  $collection = $collectionImpl.ReadNextTasks($tasknumber)
}
$collectionImpl.DestroyCollector()

# Get the guest's snapshots and add the user
$snapshotsExtra = $snap | % {
  $key = $_.vm.Name + "&" + ($_.Created.ToString())
  if($report.ContainsKey($key)){
    $_ | Add-Member -MemberType NoteProperty -Name Creator `
        -Value $report[$key].User
  }
  $_
```

```
    }
    $snapshotsExtra
}

$Today = Get-Date
$2WeeksAgo = $Today.AddDays(-14)
Get-VM | Get-Snapshot | Where {$_.Created -lt $2WeeksAgo} | %{
    Get-SnapshotExtra $_ | Select VM, Name, Created, Creator
}
```

While reporting snapshots that are older than a set number of days is a nice way to create an overview, it still requires your intervention. If the creation of snapshots is not under your control, you might end up chasing the person who created the snapshot to verify that it can be safely deleted. Why not take the maintenance of your snapshots to another level and have the creator automatically notified whenever a snapshot is getting too old? Take a look at the script in Listing 8.9. It gets the user ID of the snapshot's creator, searches for the corresponding email address in Active Directory, and sends an email with the snapshot's details. This script is based on Alan Renouf's SnapReminder script.

 N O T E The script in Listing 8.9 only works when your users have their email address configured in Active Directory (AD). The Get-ADUserObject function is used to retrieve a user object from the AD. Notice that the samAccountName parameter is just a String value to specify the user account, like Get-ADUserObject "vinternals" or something like that. The script needs to run under a domain user account. When you're not logged in to the domain, you have no access to query the AD.

LISTING 8.9   Sending email to the snapshot creator

```
Function Get-ADUserObject {
<#
.SYNOPSIS
  Retrieves a user object from Active Directory
.DESCRIPTION
  This function retrieves a user object from Active Directory
  specified by the -UserName variable
.NOTES
  Source:  Automating vSphere Administration
  Authors: Luc Dekens, Arnim van Lieshout, Jonathan Medd,
           Alan Renouf, Glenn Sizemore
```

```
.PARAMETER UserName
  The SAM account name of the user object to retrieve
.EXAMPLE
  PS> Get-ADUserObject "administrator"
#>

  Param ([parameter(valuefrompipeline = $true, mandatory=$true,
    HelpMessage = "Enter a user SAM accountname")]
    [string]$userName)

  $ds = New-Object system.DirectoryServices.DirectorySearcher
  $ds.searchRoot = [ADSI]""
  $ds.searchScope = "subtree"
  $ds.filter = "(&(objectClass=user)(samAccountName=$userName))"
  $result = $ds.findOne()
  if ($result) {
    return $result.GetDirectoryEntry()
  }
}

Function Get-SnapshotCreator {
<#
.SYNOPSIS
  Retrieves the user who created the snapshot
.DESCRIPTION
  This function retrieves the user who created the snapshot
  specified by the -Snapshot parameter
.NOTES
  Source:  Automating vSphere Administration
  Authors: Luc Dekens, Arnim van Lieshout, Jonathan Medd,
           Alan Renouf, Glenn Sizemore
.PARAMETER Snapshot
  The snapshot to return the creator of
.EXAMPLE
  PS> Get-SnapshotCreator $mySnapshot
.EXAMPLE
  PS> $mySnapshot | Get-SnapshotCreator
#>

  Param ([parameter(valuefrompipeline = $true, mandatory=$true,
```

```
        HelpMessage = "Enter a snapshot entity")]
    [VMware.VimAutomation.ViCore.Impl.V1.VM.SnapshotImpl]$snapshot)

    $taskNumber = 100
    $taskMgr = Get-View TaskManager

    $filter = New-Object VMware.Vim.TaskFilterSpec
    $filter.Time = New-Object VMware.Vim.TaskFilterSpecByTime
    $filter.Time.beginTime = (($snapshot.Created).AddDays(-1))
    $filter.Time.endTime = ($snapshot.Created)
    $filter.Time.timeType = "startedTime"
    $filter.Entity = New-Object VMware.Vim.TaskFilterSpecByEntity
    $filter.Entity.Entity = $snapshot.extensiondata.vm
    $filter.state = New-Object VMware.Vim.TaskInfoState
    $filter.state = "success"

    $taskCollector = Get-View `
        ($taskMgr.CreateCollectorForTasks($filter))

    $taskCollector.RewindCollector | Out-Null
    $taskCollection = $taskCollector.ReadNextTasks($taskNumber)
    $matches=@()
    while ($taskCollection) {
      $matches += $taskCollection | Where {$_.DescriptionId -eq `
          "VirtualMachine.createSnapshot" `
          -and $_.Result.ToString() -eq $snapshot.Id}
      $taskCollection = $taskCollector.ReadNextTasks($taskNumber)
    }
    $taskCollector.DestroyCollector()
    $matches | %{$_.Reason.UserName}
}

#Use variables below to define your settings
$smtpServer = "mySMTP.myDomain.local"
$mailFrom = "Admin@myDomain.local"
$mailSubject = "Snapshot too old"
$snapshotAge = (Get-Date).AddDays(-14)

Get-VM | Get-Snapshot | Where {$_.Created -lt $snapshotAge} | %{
  $creator = $_ | Get-SnapshotCreator
```

Managing the Virtual
Machine Life Cycle

PART II

```
    $samAccountName = $creator.split('\') | Select -Last 1
    $adUser = $samAccountName | Get-ADUserObject

    $mailMessage = @"
Dear $($adUser.givenName),
`
It appears that you've created a snapshot that is older than
the maximum allowed number of days.
Please delete the snapshot.
`
Snapshot details:
`
Name: $($_.Name)
VM: $($_.VM.Name)
Description: $($_.Description)
Created on: $($_.Created)
Days old: $(((Get-date)-$_.Created).days)
Size: $($_.SizeMB)MB
`

`
Regards,
Your VMware Administrator
"@

    Send-MailMessage -SmtpServer $smtpServer -From $mailFrom `
        -To $($adUser.Mail) -Subject $mailSubject `
        -Body $mailMessage
}
```

Don't forget to change the $smtpServer, $mailFrom, $mailSubject, and $snapshotAge variables to reflect your needs before use. Make sure that you run this script regularly (preferably on a daily basis) using the Windows scheduler.

Restricting the Creation of Snapshots

You might want to restrict the creation of snapshots in your environment. As discussed earlier, if multiple snapshots are taken or if they are left on the virtual machines for a long time, they can cause performance or disk space issues.

HERE-STRINGS

Notice the way the email message ($mailMessage) was created in Listing 8.9. We used something called a here-string. A here-string is a special string used to hold multiline literal text. A here-string starts with an open delimiter (@" or @') and ends with a close delimiter ("@ or '@), each on a line by itself. All characters between the open and close delimiters are considered to be the string text. Using a here-string preserves any special characters like line breaks, double and single quotation marks, blank spaces, and so forth in the string's body.

```
[vSphere PowerCLI] C:\Scripts> $x = @"
This is a "Here-String" defined in
Windows PowerShell.
Special characters like $, @, # , ", ', (, )
are allowed and don't break anything.
Pretty cool, huh?
"@
[vSphere PowerCLI] C:\Scripts> $x
This is a "Here-String" defined in
Windows PowerShell.
Special characters like $, @, # , ", ', (, )
are allowed and don't break anything.
Pretty cool, huh?
```

When a here-string is declared with double quotes, it allows variables and expressions to be evaluated:

```
[vSphere PowerCLI] C:\Scripts> $x = @"
Today's date and time is: $(Get-Date)
"@
[vSphere PowerCLI] C:\Scripts> $x
Today's date and time is: 10/22/2010 14:47:45
```

If it is declared with single quotes, no variables are evaluated; they are considered plain text.

```
[vSphere PowerCLI] C:\Scripts> $x = @'
Today's date and time is: $(Get-Date)
'@
[vSphere PowerCLI] C:\Scripts> $x
Today's date is $(Get-Date)
```

Until recently there has been no publicly known way to restrict the creation of snapshots on VMs (other than to change the security permissions to remove the ability from user accounts). This is now possible thanks to an undocumented configuration setting that you can make to the VM advanced configuration or VMX file, as shown in Figure 8.1.

FIGURE 8.1   **Example VM advanced configuration**

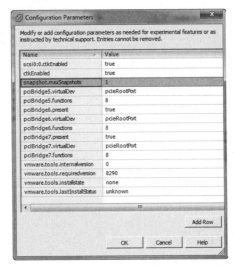

This setting was exposed by William Lam of www.virtuallyghetto.com and can be used to not only restrict the use of snapshots but also set a numeric value on the number of snapshots that can be created per virtual machine.

To do this on multiple virtual machines, the obvious answer is to script it. The code for disabling the creation of snapshots on multiple VMs is shown in Listing 8.10.

LISTING 8.10   **Restricting the creation of snapshots**

```
function Set-VMAdvancedConfiguration{
<#
.SYNOPSIS
  Sets an advanced configuration setting (VMX Setting) for a VM
  or multiple VMs
.DESCRIPTION
  The function will set a VMX setting for a VM
  or multiple VMs
.NOTES
  Source:  Automating vSphere Administration
```

```
      Authors: Luc Dekens, Arnim van Lieshout, Jonathan Medd,
               Alan Renouf, Glenn Sizemore
.PARAMETER VM
   A virtual machine or multiple virtual machines
.PARAMETER Key
   The Key to use for the advanced configuration
.PARAMETER Value
   The value of the key
.EXAMPLE 1
   PS> Set-VMAdvancedConfiguration -key log.rotatesize `
           -value 10000
#>

   param(
      [Parameter(Mandatory=$true,ValueFromPipeline=$true)]
        $vm,
      [Parameter(Mandatory=$true)]
        [String]$key,
      [Parameter(Mandatory=$true)]
        [String]$value)


   process{
     $vmConfigSpec = `
         new-object VMware.Vim.VirtualMachineConfigSpec
     $vmConfigSpec.ExtraConfig += `
         new-object VMware.Vim.OptionValue
     $vmConfigSpec.ExtraConfig[0].key = $key
     $vmConfigSpec.ExtraConfig[0].value = $value

     foreach ($singlevm in $vm) {
       $VMview = $singlevm | get-view
       $Task = $VMview.ReconfigVM_Task($vmConfigSpec)
       Write "Set Advanced configuration for $($singleVM.Name):➥
$key = $value"
     }
   }
}


Get-VM APP* | Set-VMAdvancedConfiguration `
    -key snapshot.maxSnapshots -value 0
```

Using vApps

IN THIS CHAPTER, YOU WILL LEARN TO:

As vSphere has developed, the term *vApp* has come to mean many different things. Some refer to any virtualized workload as a virtual application, or vApp, whereas others use vApp to refer to a VM that has been exported to an Open Virtualization Format (OVF) template. With the release of vSphere 4.1, VMware extended the vApp concept to a next level. A vApp is now a virtual container similar to a resource pool. A vApp can contain one or more VMs and is managed as a single logical unit. The modern vApp can be powered on or off and even cloned like a standard VM. vApps allow you to simplify complex applications by providing vSphere with valuable metadata about a group of VMs. For instance, you can capture the startup/shutdown sequence for a web farm. Then, from within vSphere, you simply power on or off the vApp and vSphere handles the rest. In this chapter you will learn to import virtual appliances, create and manage vApps, and automate some of the more advanced vCenter features surrounding vApps.

Import Virtual Appliances

In 2006, VMware opened the Virtual Appliance Marketplace. The idea was that third-party developers could provide whole VMs preconfigured, thereby eliminating complex installers and simplifying the deployment of new applications. The Marketplace has proven to be a little hit or miss, but the concept itself has been a smash hit. Virtual appliances have become mainstream, and virtually all software/hardware companies offer them. The installation of a vApp is simple. You simply download the zip file containing the Open Virtualization File (OVF) and Virtual Machine Disk (VMDK) files and then import the appliance. But before we get into that, let's look take a closer look at the OVF.

The OVF file contains all the metadata for a given appliance. You could fire up your favorite XML reader and have a look, but we knew you would want that data in PowerCLI. So, we wrote `Get-OvfDetails` (Listing 9.1), a function that uses the vSphere parser to allow you to explore the properties of an OVF template. This information will come in handy later in the chapter. (The downloadable version of this code also includes help. You can access the code at www.sybex.com/go/vmwarevspherepowercliref.)

LISTING 9.1 The `Get-OvfDetails` function

```
Function Get-OvfDetails
{
    Param(
        [Parameter(ValueFromPipeline=$true
```

```
,       ValueFromPipelineByPropertyName=$True)]
    [ValidateScript({Test-Path $_})]
    [ValidatePattern('.ovf$')]
    [Alias("PSPath")]
    [string]
    $Path
)
Begin
{
    $pdp = New-Object VMware.Vim.OvfParseDescriptorParams
    $pdp.locale = ""
    $pdp.deploymentOption = ""
}
Process
{
    $OvfM = Get-View -Id 'OvfManager-OvfManager'
    $OvfM.ParseDescriptor( `
        (Get-Content $path|Out-String),$pdp)
}
}
```

You can then leverage the metadata to programmatically make decisions when deploying a new appliance. Listing 9.2 adds the vSphere Management Assistant (vMA) to vCenter Server and selects the destination datastore, automatically, based on your vSphere host selection.

LISTING 9.2 Importing the vMA OVF into vCenter Server

```
$VMHost = Get-VMHost "vSphere03*"
$PathtoOvf = ".\vMA-4.1.0.0-268837.ovf"

# Parse OVF
$OVF = Get-OvfDetails -Path $PathtoOvf
# Convert to MB
$Size = $ovf.ApproximateFlatDeploymentSize/1mb
# find appropriate datastore
$DS = Get-Datastore -VMHost $VMHost|
    Where-Object {$_.FreeSpaceMB -gt $Size} |
    Sort-Object FreeSpaceMB -Descending |
    Select-Object -First 1
```

```
#Import our vApp
Import-VApp -Source $PathtoOvf `
    -Name 'vMA4.1' `
    -VMHost $VMHost `
    -Datastore $DS
```

Virtual appliances can simplify the deployment of a new VM. vApps bring that simplicity at a scale that was previously only available to the largest hosting providers.

Create Your Own vApps

vApps are a resource pool at their base, so when you're creating a new vApp resource, guarantees are where it all starts. There are three ways to create a new vApp in your environment:

▶ Create a new vApp.

▶ Clone an existing vApp.

▶ Import a vApp from an OVF.

Therefore, to create a new vApp that meets the specifications listed next, we wrote the "Creating a New vApp" script (Listing 9.3):

▶ Name: App01

▶ Location: Cluster Prod01

▶ Reserve 4 GHz CPU

▶ Reserve 3 GB of RAM

LISTING 9.3   Creating a new vApp

```
New-VApp -Name App01 `
    -Location (get-cluster prod01) `
    -CpuExpandableReservation $true `
    -CpuReservationMhz 4000 `
    -MemExpandableReservation $true `
    -MemReservationMB (3gb/1mb)
```

You can also clone an existing vApp with the New-vApp cmdlet. As shown in Listing 9.4, we cloned a vApp named App01 to a new vApp named App02. Be aware that when you clone a vApp, the clone includes any child VMs or vApps.

LISTING 9.4   Cloning an existing vApp

```
New-VApp -Name App02 `
    -Location (get-cluster prod01) `
    -vApp (Get-VApp App01) `
    -Datastore vmdata0
```

The third way to create a vApp is to import one from an OVF. This is most often used as either an inexpensive vApp backup or to copy vApps between vCenter Servers. Before you can import a vApp, you must export an existing vApp. For that, PowerCLI gives us the Export-VApp cmdlet. Like cloning, exporting a vApp results in the VMs being exported as well. This is very useful as it enables you to move a complete system using one logical container. You will not lose anything in the move because settings such as the startup order, IP allocation, and resource allocation are all encompassed in the exported OVF.

So, how do you export an OVF? Easy! Simply provide an existing vApp object and the name of the OVF package to be created, as we did in Listing 9.5.

LISTING 9.5   Exporting an existing vApp

```
Export-VApp -VApp (Get-VApp App02) `
    -Name "app02_$(Get-Date -Format MM_dd_yyyy)"
```

Once the vApp is exported, importing is very similar to importing a virtual appliance. The difference is that when you import an OVF, the whole vApp is re-created along with its children vApps and VMs. To reimport the vApp named App02 that we exported in Listing 9.5, you simply point the Import-vApp cmdlet to the OVF file, VMHost, and a datastore (Listing 9.6).

LISTING 9.6   Importing a vApp from OVF

```
Import-VApp -Source .\app02_10_29_2010.ovf `
    -Name 'App02' `
    -VMHost 'vShere01*' `
    -Datastore ISCSI_03
```

 N O T E   If App02 already exists on your system, the import will be unsuccessful.

Although vApps were originally a version 1 offering, VMware has done a good job with them. They are on par with VMs when it comes to deployment options, with one notable exception. As of this writing, when you deploy a vApp you cannot target a specific hard drive or VM to a datastore. This leads to a two-step process when you wish to spread the I/O load of a vApp. You must first deploy to a datastore large enough to hold the entire vApp and then, after it's been deployed, you can SVMotion individual hard disks and VMs to different datastores.

Maintain vApps

Now that you've created a new vApp, the fun really starts. First, you'll need to add some VMs to your new vApp. (We've done just that in Listing 9.7).

LISTING 9.7   **Adding VMs to an existing vApp**

```
Get-VM vMA4.1, SQL01, VUM01|
    Move-VM -Destination (Get-VApp -Name 'App01')
```

Setting the Start Order

Now you'll want to set the startup order for your vApp—even if every VM powers on and shuts down at the same time. Doing so enables any administrator to safely perform a power operation on the vApp. Unfortunately PowerCLI doesn't currently contain any cmdlets for managing the startup order, so we wrote our own. Before you can modify the startup order settings, you need to get the current values. To accomplish that task, we wrote `Get-vAppStartOrder` (Listing 9.8).

LISTING 9.8   **The `Get-vAppStartOrder` function**

```
Function Get-vAppStartOrder
{
  [cmdletbinding()]
  Param(
    [Parameter(ValueFromPipeline=$True)]
    [VMware.VimAutomation.ViCore.Impl.V1.Inventory.➥
VirtualMachineImpl]
    $VM
    ,
    [Parameter(ValueFromPipeline=$True)]
    [VMware.VimAutomation.ViCore.Impl.V1.Inventory.VAppImpl]
    $vApp
  )
```

```
Process
{
  if ($VM)
  {
    Try
    {
      $vApp =Get-VIObjectByVIView $vm.ExtensionData.ParentVApp
    }
    catch
    {
      Write-Warning "$($VM.name) doesn't belong to a vApp."
      continue;
    }
  }
  Elseif (-Not $vApp)
  {
    Write-Warning 'vApp was not specified'
    break;
  }
  $vApp.ExtensionData.VAppConfig.EntityConfig |
    Where-Object {$_.Key -match $VM.ID} |
    Select-Object @{
      name='VM'
      Expression={Get-VIObjectByVIView $_.Key}
    },
    @{
      name='vApp'
      Expression={$vApp.name}
    },
    'StartOrder','StartDelay',
    'WaitingForGuest','StartAction',
    'StopDelay','StopAction',
    @{
      name='DestroyWithParent'
      Expression={IF ($_.DestroyWithParent -eq $null){
          $False
        }
        else
        {
```

```
            $_.DestroyWithParent
         }
       }
     }
   }
 }
```

Using the `Get-vAppStartOrder` function, you can query a vApp for its current settings. As shown in Listing 9.8, we get the current start order settings for the vApp created in Listing 9.9.

LISTING 9.9   **Getting the start order settings for vApp01**

```
[vSphere PowerCLI] C:\> Get-VApp app01 | Get-vAppStartOrder

VM                  : vMA4.1
vApp                : App01
StartOrder          : 1
StartDelay          : 120
WaitingForGuest     : False
StartAction         : powerOn
StopDelay           : 120
StopAction          : powerOff
DestroyWithParent   : False

VM                  : SQL01
vApp                : App01
StartOrder          : 2
StartDelay          : 120
WaitingForGuest     : False
StartAction         : powerOn
StopDelay           : 120
StopAction          : powerOff
DestroyWithParent   : False

VM                  : VUM01
vApp                : App01
StartOrder          : 3
StartDelay          : 120
WaitingForGuest     : False
```

```
StartAction       : powerOn
StopDelay         : 120
StopAction        : powerOff
DestroyWithParent : False
```

By default a vApp powers on and off based on the order in which the VMs were added. This will likely not be the order you want, so you're going to need a means to adjust these settings. For that, we wrote the Set-vAppStartOrder function (Listing 9.10).

LISTING 9.10 The **Set-vAppStartOrder** function

Managing the Virtual Machine Life Cycle

PART II

```
Function Set-vAppStartOrder
{
  [CmdletBinding(SupportsShouldProcess=$true,
    DefaultParameterSetName='ByVM')]
  Param(
    [Parameter(Mandatory=$true
    ,   ValueFromPipelineByPropertyName=$true
    ,   ValueFromPipeline=$True
    ,   ParameterSetName='ByVM'
    )]
    [VMware.VimAutomation.ViCore.Impl.V1.Inventory.➥
VirtualMachineImpl]
    $VM

    ,
    [Parameter(ValueFromPipeline=$True
    ,   ParameterSetName='ByvApp'
    )]
    [VMware.VimAutomation.ViCore.Impl.V1.Inventory.VAppImpl]
    $vApp

    ,
    [Parameter(ValueFromPipelineByPropertyName=$true
    ,   ParameterSetName='ByvApp'
    )]
    [Parameter(ValueFromPipelineByPropertyName=$true
    ,   ParameterSetName='ByVM'
    )]
    [int]
    $StartOrder
```

```
'
[Parameter(ValueFromPipelineByPropertyName=$true
,   ParameterSetName='ByvApp'
)]
[Parameter(ValueFromPipelineByPropertyName=$true
,   ParameterSetName='ByVM'
)]
[int]
$StartDelay

'
[Parameter(ValueFromPipelineByPropertyName=$true
,   ParameterSetName='ByVM'
)]
[bool]
$WaitingForGuest

'
[Parameter(ValueFromPipelineByPropertyName=$true
,   ParameterSetName='ByvApp'
)]
[Parameter(ValueFromPipelineByPropertyName=$true
,   ParameterSetName='ByVM'
)]
[ValidateSet("none","powerOn")]
[string]
$StartAction

'
[Parameter(ValueFromPipelineByPropertyName=$true
,   ParameterSetName='ByvApp'
)]
[Parameter(ValueFromPipelineByPropertyName=$true
,   ParameterSetName='ByVM'
)]
[int]
$StopDelay

'
[Parameter(ValueFromPipelineByPropertyName=$true
,   ParameterSetName='ByvApp'
)]
[Parameter(ValueFromPipelineByPropertyName=$true
```

```
,    ParameterSetName='ByVM'
)]
[ValidateSet('none','powerOff','guestShutdown','suspend')]
[string]
$StopAction
,
[Parameter(ValueFromPipelineByPropertyName=$true
,    ParameterSetName='ByvApp'
)]
[bool]
$DestroyWithParent
)
process
{

  Try
  {
    $vApp = Get-VIObjectByVIView $vm.ExtensionData.ParentVApp
  }
  catch
  {
    Write-Warning "$($VM.name) doesn't belong to a vApp."
    continue;
  }
  $EntityConfig = $vApp.ExtensionData.VAppConfig.EntityConfig

  $spec = New-Object VMware.Vim.VAppConfigSpec
  $spec.entityConfig = `
    Foreach ($Conf in ($EntityConfig.GetEnumerator()))
    {
      If ($Conf.Key.ToString() -eq $VM.ID.tostring())
      {
        $msg = "Setting $($VM.Name) start order to:"
        Switch ($PSCmdlet.MyInvocation.BoundParameters.keys)
        {
          'StartOrder'
          {
            $msg = "{0} StartOrder:{1}" -f $msg,
              $StartOrder
```

```
              $Conf.StartOrder = $StartOrder
        }
        'StartDelay'
        {
          $msg = "{0} StartDelay:{1}" -f $msg,
            $StartDelay
          $Conf.StartDelay = $StartDelay
        }
        'WaitingForGuest'
        {
          $msg = "{0} WaitingForGuest:{1}" -f $msg,
            $WaitingForGuest
          $Conf.WaitingForGuest = $WaitingForGuest
        }
        'StartAction'
        {
          $msg = "{0} StartAction:{1}" -f $msg,
            $StartAction
          $Conf.StartAction = $StartAction
        }
        'StopDelay'
        {
          $msg = "{0} StopDelay:{1}" -f $msg,
            $StopDelay
          $Conf.StopDelay = $StopDelay
        }
        'StopAction'
        {
          $msg = "{0} StopAction:{1}" -f $msg,
            $StopAction
          $Conf.StopAction = $StopAction
        }
        'DestroyWithParent'
        {
          $msg = "{0} DestroyWithParent:{1}" -f $msg,
            $DestroyWithParent
          $Conf.DestroyWithParent = $DestroyWithParent
        }
    }
```

```
      }
      $conf
   }
If ($pscmdlet.shouldprocess($vApp.Name, $msg))
{
   $vApp.ExtensionData.UpdateVAppConfig($spec)
}
   }
}
```

Using this new function, you can correct the startup order for the vApp. Listing 9.11 sets the startup order to the following specification:

Startup Group 1

► vMA4.1

   ► Startup Action: PowerOn

   ► Startup Delay: 0

   ► Shutdown Action: Shutdown Guest

► SQL01

   ► Startup Action: PowerOn

   ► Startup Delay: 120 sec or VMware Tools

   ► Shutdown Action: Shutdown Guest

   ► Shutdown Delay: 120 sec

Startup Group 2

► VUM01

   ► Startup Action: PowerOn

   ► Startup Delay: 0

   ► Shutdown Action: Shutdown Guest

LISTING 9.11   Setting the start order for the VMs in App01

```
Get-Vm 'vMA4.1' | Set-vAppStartOrder -StartOrder 1 `
   -StartAction 'powerOn' `
```

```
    -StartDelay 0 `
    -StopAction 'guestShutdown'

Get-Vm 'SQL01' | Set-vAppStartOrder -StartOrder 1 `
    -StartAction 'powerOn' `
    -StartDelay 120 `
    -WaitingForGuest $true `
    -StopAction 'guestShutdown' `
    -StopDelay 120

Get-Vm 'VUM01' | Set-vAppStartOrder -StartOrder 2 `
    -StartDelay 0 `
    -StartAction 'powerOn' `
    -StopAction 'guestShutdown'
```

Using IP Pools

Of course, power management is only part of vApps. To ease deployment of application, vApps can also supply the IP information for the VM(s) within a vApp. This is accomplished by passing the request to an external DHCP server, or vCenter Server can issue an IP from an IP pool. You can obtain a list of IP pools by running the Get-IpPool function (Listing 9.12).

LISTING 9.12 The Get-IpPool function

```
Function Get-IPPool
{
    [cmdletbinding()]
    Param(
        [Parameter(ValueFromPipeline=$True
        ,   ValueFromPipelineByPropertyName=$True)]
        [VMware.VimAutomation.ViCore.Impl.V1.Inventory.➡
DatacenterImpl[]]
        $Datacenter = (Get-Datacenter)

        ,
        [Parameter(ValueFromPipeline=$True
        ,   ValueFromPipelineByPropertyName=$True)]
        [String]
        $Name = "*"
    )
```

```
Process
{
    Foreach ($dc in $Datacenter)
    {
        $IPPoolManager = Get-View `
            -Id 'IpPoolManager-IpPoolManager'
        $IPPoolManager.QueryIpPools($dc.ID) |
            Where-Object {$_.Name -like $name}| %{
            New-Object PSObject -Property @{
                'Name' = $_.Name
                'DnsDomain' = $_.DNSDomain
                'DNSSearchPath' = $_.DNSSearchPath
                'HostPrefix' = $_.HostPrefix
                'HttpProxy' = $_.HttpProxy
                'NetworkAssociation' = $_.NetworkAssociation
                'IPv4SubnetAddress' = `
                    $_.ipv4Config.SubnetAddress
                'IPv4Netmask'=$_.ipv4Config.netmask
                'IPv4Gateway'=$_.ipv4Config.Gateway
                'IPv4Range'=$_.ipv4Config.Range
                'IPv4DNS'=$_.ipv4Config.DNS
                'IPv4DHCP'=$_.ipv4Config.DhcpServerAvailable
                'IPv4IpPoolEnabled' = `
                    $_.ipv4Config.IpPoolEnabled
                'IPv6SubnetAddress' = `
                    $_.ipv6Config.SubnetAddress
                'IPv6Netmask'=$_.ipv6Config.netmask
                'IPv6Gateway'=$_.ipv6Config.Gateway
                'IPv6Range'=$_.ipv6Config.Range
                'IPv6DNS'=$_.ipv6Config.DNS
                'IPv6DHCP'=$_.ipv6Config.DhcpServerAvailable
                'IPv6IpPoolEnabled' = `
                    $_.ipv6Config.IpPoolEnabled
                'Datacenter'=$dc
            }
        }
    }
}
```

Managing the Virtual
Machine Life Cycle

PART II

Of course if you don't have any IP pools, you must first create a new IP pool within vCenter Server. The code in Listing 9.13 enables you to do so via PowerCLI.

LISTING 9.13   The `New-IpPool` function

```
Function New-IpPool
{
    [cmdletbinding()]
    Param(
        [Parameter(Mandatory=$True
        ,    ValueFromPipeline=$True
        ,    ValueFromPipelineByPropertyName=$True)]
        [VMware.VimAutomation.ViCore.Impl.V1.Inventory.➥
DatacenterImpl]
        $Datacenter
    ,   [Parameter(Mandatory=$true
        ,    ValueFromPipelineByPropertyName=$True)]
        [String]
        $Name
    ,   [Parameter(ValueFromPipelineByPropertyName=$True)]
        [String]
        $DnsDomain = ""
    ,   [Parameter(ValueFromPipelineByPropertyName=$True)]
        [String[]]
        $DNSSearchPath = ""
    ,   [Parameter(ValueFromPipelineByPropertyName=$True)]
        [String]
        $HostPrefix = ""
    ,   [Parameter(ValueFromPipelineByPropertyName=$True)]
        [String]
        $HttpProxy = ""
    ,   [Parameter(ValueFromPipeline=$True
        ,    ValueFromPipelineByPropertyName=$True)]
        [VMware.Vim.IpPoolAssociation[]]
        $NetworkAssociation
    ,   [Parameter(ValueFromPipelineByPropertyName=$True)]
        [String]
        $IPv4SubnetAddress = ''
    ,   [Parameter(ValueFromPipelineByPropertyName=$True)]
        [String]
```

```
        $IPv4Netmask = '255.255.255.0'
    ,   [Parameter(ValueFromPipelineByPropertyName=$True)]
        [String]
        $IPv4Gateway = ''
    ,   [Parameter(ValueFromPipelineByPropertyName=$True)]
        [String]
        $IPv4Range
    ,   [Parameter(ValueFromPipelineByPropertyName=$True)]
        [String[]]
        $IPv4DNS = @("")
    ,   [Parameter(ValueFromPipelineByPropertyName=$True)]
        [bool]
        $IPv4DHCP = $false
    ,   [Parameter(ValueFromPipelineByPropertyName=$True)]
        [bool]
        $IPv4IpPoolEnabled = $false
    ,   [Parameter(ValueFromPipelineByPropertyName=$True)]
        [String]
        $IPv6SubnetAddress = ''
    ,   [Parameter(ValueFromPipelineByPropertyName=$True)]
        [String]
        $IPv6Netmask = "ffff:ffff:ffff:ffff:ffff:ffff::"
    ,   [Parameter(ValueFromPipelineByPropertyName=$True)]
        [String]
        $IPv6Gateway = ""
    ,   [Parameter(ValueFromPipelineByPropertyName=$True)]
        [String]
        $IPv6Range
    ,   [Parameter(ValueFromPipelineByPropertyName=$True)]
        [String[]]
        $IPv6DNS = @()
    ,   [Parameter(ValueFromPipelineByPropertyName=$True)]
        [bool]
        $IPv6DHCP = $false
    ,   [Parameter(ValueFromPipelineByPropertyName=$True)]
        [bool]
        $IPv6IpPoolEnabled = $false
    )
Process
```

```
{
    $pool = New-Object VMware.Vim.IpPool
    $pool.name = $Name
    $pool.ipv4Config = `
        New-Object VMware.Vim.IpPoolIpPoolConfigInfo
    $pool.ipv4Config.subnetAddress = $IPv4SubnetAddress
    $pool.ipv4Config.netmask = $IPv4Netmask
    $pool.ipv4Config.gateway = $IPv4Gateway
    $pool.ipv4Config.dns = $IPv4DNS
    $pool.ipv4Config.dhcpServerAvailable = $IPv4DHCP
    $pool.ipv4Config.ipPoolEnabled = $IPv4IpPoolEnabled
    $pool.ipv6Config = `
        New-Object VMware.Vim.IpPoolIpPoolConfigInfo
    IF ($IPv4Range)
    {
        $pool.ipv4Config.range = $IPv4Range
    }
    $pool.ipv6Config.subnetAddress = $IPv6SubnetAddress
    $pool.ipv6Config.netmask = $IPv6Netmask
    $pool.ipv6Config.gateway = $IPv6Gateway
    $pool.ipv6Config.dns = $IPv6DNS
    $pool.ipv6Config.dhcpServerAvailable = $IPv6DHCP
    $pool.ipv6Config.ipPoolEnabled = $IPv6IpPoolEnabled
    IF ($IPv6Range)
    {
        $pool.ipv6Config.range = $IPv6Range
    }
    $pool.dnsDomain = $DnsDomain
    $pool.dnsSearchPath = $DNSSearchPath
    $pool.hostPrefix = $HostPrefix
    $pool.httpProxy = $HttpProxy
    if ($NetworkAssociation)
    {
        $pool.NetworkAssociation = $NetworkAssociation
    }
    $IpPoolManager = Get-View 'IpPoolManager-IpPoolManager'
    $IpPoolManager.CreateIpPool($DataCenter.id, $pool) |
        Out-Null
    if ($?)
```

```
        {
            Get-IPPool -Datacenter $DataCenter -Name $Name
        }
    }
}
```

Using the `New-IpPool` function, you can create a new IP pool to be allocated to your vApp. For instance, the code in Listing 9.14 creates such a pool.

LISTING 9.14 Creating a new IP pool

```
Get-Datacenter 'ATL-PROD'|
    New-IPPool -Name '10.10.10.0' `
    -IPv4SubnetAddress '10.10.10.0' `
    -IPv4Gateway '10.10.10.1' `
    -IPv4Netmask '255.255.255.0' `
    -IPv4Range '10.10.10.11#244' `
    -IPv4DNS '10.10.10.5','10.10.10.6' `
    -DnsDomain 'getadmin.local' `
    -DNSSearchPath 'lab.getadmin.local','getadmin.local' `
    -IPv4IpPoolEnabled $true
```

Now that you've created a new IP pool, you'll need to associate a virtual network and associate that network with your new IP pool. To assist in this task, we wrote the `Get-Network` function (Listing 9.15). This function retrieves the objects you'll need to perform the network association.

LISTING 9.15 The `Get-Network` function

```
Function Get-Network
{
    [cmdletbinding(DefaultParameterSetName='name')]
    Param(
        [Parameter(ParameterSetName='name'
        ,   ValueFromPipeline=$True
        ,   ValueFromPipelineByPropertyName=$True)]
        [String]
        $Name = "*"
    ,   [Parameter(ParameterSetName='MoRef'
        ,   ValueFromPipeline=$True
        ,   ValueFromPipelineByPropertyName=$True)]
        [VMware.Vim.ManagedObjectReference]
```

```
            $Network
        )
        Process
        {
            IF ($pscmdlet.parametersetname -eq 'name')
            {
                $net = Get-View -ViewType network |
                    Where-Object {$_.name -like $Name}
            }
            Else
            {
                $net = Get-View -Id $Network
            }
            If ($net)
            {
                Foreach ($N in $net)
                {
                    New-Object VMware.Vim.IpPoolAssociation `
                        -Property @{
                            Network=$N.MoRef
                            NetworkName=$N.Name
                        }
                }
            }
        }
    }
}
```

Using the Get-Network function, you can get the networks you need to configure IP pools on. Listing 9.16 shows just how we did that.

LISTING 9.16   Getting networks that need to be configured

```
[vSphere PowerCLI] C:\> Get-VApp app01|
    Get-VM|
    Get-NetworkAdapter|
    Select-Object -ExpandProperty NetworkName -Unique |
    Get-Network

Network                                      NetworkName
-------                                      -----------
DistributedVirtualPortgroup-dvportgroup-109  vDS01-10.10.10.0
```

In this case, only one network needs to be configured. For that task we wrote another function—Set-IpPool, shown in Listing 9.17.

LISTING 9.17   The **Set-IpPool** function

```
Function Set-IPPool
{
    [cmdletbinding()]
    Param(
        [Parameter(Mandatory=$True
        ,    ValueFromPipeline=$True
        ,    ValueFromPipelineByPropertyName=$True)]
        [VMware.VimAutomation.ViCore.Impl.V1.Inventory.➥
DatacenterImpl]
        $Datacenter
    ,    [Parameter(Mandatory=$true
        ,    ValueFromPipelineByPropertyName=$True)]
        [String]
        $Name
    ,    [Parameter(ValueFromPipelineByPropertyName=$True)]
        [String]
        $NewName
    ,    [Parameter(ValueFromPipelineByPropertyName=$True)]
        [String]
        $DnsDomain
    ,    [Parameter(ValueFromPipelineByPropertyName=$True)]
        [String[]]
        $DNSSearchPath
    ,    [Parameter(ValueFromPipelineByPropertyName=$True)]
        [String]
        $HostPrefix
    ,    [Parameter(ValueFromPipelineByPropertyName=$True)]
        [String]
        $HttpProxy
    ,    [Parameter(ValueFromPipeline=$True
        ,    ValueFromPipelineByPropertyName=$True)]
        [VMware.Vim.IpPoolAssociation[]]
        $NetworkAssociation
    ,    [Parameter(ValueFromPipelineByPropertyName=$True)]
        [String]
```

```
        $IPv4SubnetAddress
    ,   [Parameter(ValueFromPipelineByPropertyName=$True)]
        [String]
        $IPv4Netmask
    ,   [Parameter(ValueFromPipelineByPropertyName=$True)]
        [String]
        $IPv4Gateway
    ,   [Parameter(ValueFromPipelineByPropertyName=$True)]
        [String]
        $IPv4Range
    ,   [Parameter(ValueFromPipelineByPropertyName=$True)]
        [String[]]
        $IPv4DNS
    ,   [Parameter(ValueFromPipelineByPropertyName=$True)]
        [bool]
        $IPv4DHCP
    ,   [Parameter(ValueFromPipelineByPropertyName=$True)]
        [bool]
        $IPv4IpPoolEnabled
    ,   [Parameter(ValueFromPipelineByPropertyName=$True)]
        [String]
        $IPv6SubnetAddress
    ,   [Parameter(ValueFromPipelineByPropertyName=$True)]
        [String]
        $IPv6Netmask
    ,   [Parameter(ValueFromPipelineByPropertyName=$True)]
        [String]
        $IPv6Gateway
    ,   [Parameter(ValueFromPipelineByPropertyName=$True)]
        [String]
        $IPv6Range
    ,   [Parameter(ValueFromPipelineByPropertyName=$True)]
        [String[]]
        $IPv6DNS
    ,   [Parameter(ValueFromPipelineByPropertyName=$True)]
        [bool]
        $IPv6DHCP
    ,   [Parameter(ValueFromPipelineByPropertyName=$True)]
        [bool]
        $IPv6IpPoolEnabled
```

```
)
Process
{
    $IPPoolManager = Get-View 'IpPoolManager-IpPoolManager'
    $pool = $IPPoolManager.QueryIpPools($Datacenter.ID)|
        Where-Object {$_.Name -eq $Name}
    Switch ($PSCmdlet.MyInvocation.BoundParameters.keys)
    {
        'NewName' {
            $pool.name = $Name
        }
        'IPv4SubnetAddress' {
            $pool.ipv4Config.subnetAddress=$IPv4SubnetAddress
        }
        'IPv4Netmask' {
            $pool.ipv4Config.netmask = $IPv4Netmask
        }
        'IPv4Gateway' {
            $pool.ipv4Config.gateway = $IPv4Gateway
        }
        'IPv4DNS' {
            $pool.ipv4Config.dns = $IPv4DNS
        }
        'IPv4DHCP' {
            $pool.ipv4Config.dhcpServerAvailable = $IPv4DHCP
        }
        'IPv4IpPoolEnabled' {
            $pool.ipv4Config.ipPoolEnabled=$IPv4IpPoolEnabled
        }
        'IPv4Range' {
            $pool.ipv4Config.range = $IPv4Range
        }
        'IPv6SubnetAddress' {
            $pool.ipv6Config.subnetAddress=$IPv6SubnetAddress
        }
        'IPv6Netmask' {
            $pool.ipv6Config.netmask = $IPv6Netmask
        }
        'IPv6Gateway' {
            $pool.ipv6Config.gateway = $IPv6Gateway
```

```
            }
            'IPv6DNS' {
                $pool.ipv6Config.dns = $IPv6DNS
            }
            'IPv6DHCP' {
                $pool.ipv6Config.dhcpServerAvailable = $IPv6DHCP
            }
            'IPv6IpPoolEnabled' {
                $pool.ipv6Config.ipPoolEnabled=$IPv6IpPoolEnabled
            }
            'IPv6Range' {
                $pool.ipv6Config.range = $IPv6Range
            }
            'DnsDomain' {
                $pool.dnsDomain = $DnsDomain
            }
            'DNSSearchPath' {
                $pool.dnsSearchPath = $DNSSearchPath
            }
            'HostPrefix' {
                $pool.hostPrefix = $HostPrefix
            }
            'HttpProxy' {
                $pool.httpProxy = $HttpProxy
            }
            'NetworkAssociation' {
                $pool.NetworkAssociation = $NetworkAssociation
            }
        }
        $IpPoolManager = Get-View 'IpPoolManager-IpPoolManager'
        $IpPoolManager.UpdateIpPool($DataCenter.id, $pool) |
            Out-Null
        if ($?)
        {
            Get-IPPool -Datacenter $DataCenter -Name $Name
        }

    }
}
```

Now, you're ready to associate your new IP pool with the virtual network the VM(s) are using. Listing 9.18 accomplishes just that in one line of PowerCLI!

LISTING 9.18   Associating the IP pool to a virtual network

```
Get-VApp app01| Get-VM | Get-NetworkAdapter |
    Select-Object -ExpandProperty NetworkName -Unique |
    Get-Network |
        Set-IPPool -Name '10.10.10.0' `
            -Datacenter (Get-Datacenter 'ATL-PROD')
```

Using IP Assignment

With your IP pool established, you're now ready to configure your vApp to provision IP addresses. By default, a new vApp does not have any IP protocols or allocation methods enabled, and its IP allocation policy is set to `fixedPolicy`. That means that, out of the box, vApp IP allocation is disabled. Enabling IP assignment is a two-step process.

1. Enable the IP allocation/protocol.

2. Set the IP allocation/protocol.

Since you'll find yourself working with existing vApps more often than creating new ones, we created a function to get the current IP assignment settings. You'll find it in Listing 9.19.

LISTING 9.19   The **Get-vAppIPAssignment** function

```
Function Get-vAppIPAssignment
{
    [cmdletbinding()]
    Param(
        [Parameter(ValueFromPipeline=$True)]
        [VMware.VimAutomation.ViCore.Impl.V1.Inventory.VAppImpl]
        $vApp
    )
    Process
    {
        $vapp.ExtensionData.VAppConfig.IpAssignment | %{
            New-Object PSObject -Property @{
                'vApp'=$vApp
```

```
            'IpProtocol'=$_.IpProtocol
            'IpAllocationPolicy'=$_.IpAllocationPolicy
            'SupportedIpAllocation'= `
                $_.SupportedAllocationScheme
            'SupportedIpProtocol'=$_.SupportedIpProtocol
        }
    }
}
}
```

Using this function, you can easily obtain the current settings for any given vApp. You can see that, out of the box, a new vApp is configured to use static IP assignment.

```
[vSphere PowerCLI] C:\> Get-VApp App01| Get-vAppIPAssignment


IpProtocol            : IPv4
SupportedIpAllocation :
vApp                  : App01
IpAllocationPolicy    : fixedPolicy
SupportedIpProtocol   :
```

Therefore to enable this powerful feature, you must enable IP assignment and specify which protocols will be used. This is broken up into a two-step process in the vSphere client, but the Set-vAppIPAssignment function (Listing 9.20) enables you to configure IP assignment in one line of PowerCLI.

LISTING 9.20 The **Set-vAppIPAssignment** function

```
Function Set-vAppIPAssignment
{
    [cmdletbinding(SupportsShouldProcess=$True)]
    Param(
        [Parameter(ValueFromPipeline=$True)]
        [VMware.VimAutomation.ViCore.Impl.V1.Inventory.VAppImpl]
        $vApp
    ,   [Parameter(ValueFromPipelineByPropertyName=$True)]
        [ValidateSet('IPv4','IPv6')]
        [string]
        $IpProtocol
    ,   [Parameter(ValueFromPipelineByPropertyName=$True)]
        [ValidateSet('dhcpPolicy',
                'transientPolicy',
```

```
                             'fixedPolicy')]
        [string]
        $IpAllocationPolicy
    ,   [Parameter(ValueFromPipelineByPropertyName=$True)]
        [ValidateSet('ovfenv','dhcp')]
        [string[]]
        $SupportedIpAllocation
    ,   [Parameter(ValueFromPipelineByPropertyName=$True)]
        [ValidateSet('IPv4','IPv6')]
        [string[]]
        $SupportedIpProtocol
    )
    Process
    {
        $spec = New-Object VMware.Vim.VAppConfigSpec
        $spec.ipAssignment = `
            $vApp.ExtensionData.VAppConfig.IpAssignment
        $msg = "Modifing $($vApp.Name)"
        Switch ($PSCmdlet.MyInvocation.BoundParameters.keys)
        {
            'IpProtocol'
            {
                $msg = "{0} IP protocol:{1}" -f $msg,
                    $IpProtocol
                $spec.ipAssignment.ipProtocol = $IpProtocol
            }
            'IpAllocationPolicy'
            {
                $msg = "{0} IP allocation policy:{1}" -f $msg,
                    $IpAllocationPolicy
                $spec.ipAssignment.ipAllocationPolicy = `
                    $IpAllocationPolicy
            }
            'SupportedIpAllocation'
            {
                $msg="{0} supported allocation policy:{1}" -f `
                    $msg, $($SupportedIpAllocation -join ',')
                $spec.ipAssignment.supportedAllocationScheme= `
                    $SupportedIpAllocation
            }
```

```
                'SupportedIpProtocol'
                {
                    $msg = "{0} supported IP protocol:{1}" -f $msg,
                        $($SupportedIpProtocol -join ',')
                    $spec.ipAssignment.supportedIpProtocol = `
                        $SupportedIpProtocol
                }
            }
            if ($PSCmdlet.ShouldProcess($vApp.Name,$msg))
            {
                $vApp.ExtensionData.UpdateVAppConfig($spec)
                if ($?)
                {
                    Get-vAppIPAssignment -vApp $vApp
                }
            }
        }
    }
```

Using the `Set-vAppIPAssignment` function, you can see that we enabled both
DHCP and IP pools for IPv4 and IPv6. Then, we set the vApp to obtain its IP from
the IP pool using a temporary IPv4 address.

```
[vSphere PowerCLI] C:\> Get-VApp App01 | Set-vAppIPAssignment `
    -SupportedIpAllocation ovfenv,DHCP `
    -SupportedIpProtocol ipv4,ipv6 `
    -IpProtocol ipv4 `
    -IpAllocationPolicy transientPolicy


IpProtocol            : IPv4
SupportedIpAllocation : {ovfenv, dhcp}
vApp                  : App01
IpAllocationPolicy    : transientPolicy
SupportedIpProtocol   : {IPv4, IPv6}
```

Modifying vApp Product Information

Digging deeper into vApps, you can find additional metadata in the form of product
information. To get the product information of an existing vApp, we created the
`Get-vAppProductInfo` function (Listing 9.21).

LISTING 9.21 The `Get-vAppProductInfo` function

```
Function Get-vAppProductInfo
{
    [cmdletbinding()]
    Param(
        [Parameter(ValueFromPipeline=$True
        ,    ValueFromPipelineByPropertyName=$True)]
        [VMware.VimAutomation.ViCore.Impl.V1.Inventory.VAppImpl]
        $vApp
    )
    Process
    {
        $vApp.ExtensionData.VAppConfig.Product |
            Select-Object -Property @{
                    Name='vApp'
                    Expression={$vApp}
                },'Name','Vendor','Version','FullVersion',
                'VendorUrl','ProductUrl','AppUrl'
    }
}
```

Of course, if you're dealing with a brand-new vApp, the Product information will likely be blank. We wrote the `Set-vAppProductInfo` function (Listing 9.22) to supply that information. Note that the `Get-vAppProductInfo` function (Listing 9.21) must be loaded into your PowerCLI session before you use the `Set-vAppProductInfo` function.

LISTING 9.22 The `Set-vAppProductInfo` function

```
Function Set-vAppProductInfo
{
    [cmdletbinding()]
    Param(
        [Parameter(ValueFromPipeline=$True
        ,    ValueFromPipelineByPropertyName=$True)]
        [VMware.VimAutomation.ViCore.Impl.V1.Inventory.VAppImpl]
        $vApp
    ,    [Parameter(ValueFromPipelineByPropertyName=$True)]
        [string]
        $Name
```

```
        ,   [Parameter(ValueFromPipelineByPropertyName=$True)]
            [string]
            $Vendor
        ,   [Parameter(ValueFromPipelineByPropertyName=$True)]
            [string]
            $Version
        ,   [Parameter(ValueFromPipelineByPropertyName=$True)]
            [string]
            $FullVersion
        ,   [Parameter(ValueFromPipelineByPropertyName=$True)]
            [string]
            $VendorUrl
        ,   [Parameter(ValueFromPipelineByPropertyName=$True)]
            [string]
            $ProductUrl
        ,   [Parameter(ValueFromPipelineByPropertyName=$True)]
            [string]
            $AppUrl
        )
    Process
    {
        $spec = New-Object VMware.Vim.VAppConfigSpec
        $spec.product = `
            New-Object VMware.Vim.VAppProductSpec[] (1)
        $spec.product[0]= New-Object VMware.Vim.VAppProductSpec
        $spec.product[0].operation = "edit"
        $spec.product[0].info = `
            New-Object VMware.Vim.VAppProductInfo
        $spec.product[0].info.key = `
            $vApp.ExtensionData.VAppConfig.Property|
            Select -ExpandProperty Key -First 1
        $msg = "Modifying Advanced Properties "
        Switch ($PSCmdlet.MyInvocation.BoundParameters.keys)
        {
            'Name'
            {
                $spec.product[0].info.Name = $name
                $msg = "{0} Name:{1}" -f $msg,$Name
            }
```

```
'Vendor'
{

    $spec.product[0].info.Vendor = $Vendor
    $msg = "{0} Vendor:{1}" -f $msg,$Vendor
}
'Version'
{
    $spec.product[0].info.Version = $Version
    $msg = "{0} Version:{1}" -f $msg,$Version
}
'FullVersion'
{
    $spec.product[0].info.FullVersion = $Fullversion
    $msg = "{0} Full version:{1}" -f $msg,
        $Fullversion
}
'VendorUrl'
{
    $spec.product[0].info.VendorUrl = $vendorURL
    $msg = "{0} vendor URL:{1}" -f $msg,$vendorURL
}
'ProductUrl'
{
    $spec.product[0].info.ProductUrl = $productUrl
    $msg = "{0} product Url:{1}" -f $msg,
        $productUrl
}
'AppUrl'
{
    $spec.product[0].info.AppUrl = $AppUrl
    $msg = "{0} App Url:{1}" -f $msg,$AppUrl
}
}

if ($PSCmdlet.ShouldProcess($vApp.Name,$msg))
{
    $vApp.ExtensionData.UpdateVAppConfig($spec)
    if ($?)
```

Managing the Virtual
Machine Life Cycle

PART II

```
                {
                     Get- vAppProductInfo -vApp $vApp
                }
            }
        }
    }
```

vApps are the future of VM deployments. It will take a couple years for third-party developers to wrap their heads around this paradigm shift, but when they do your life will get a lot easier! In the meantime, feel free to roll your own vApps, if for nothing more than to control the startup and shutdown order of a complex virtual application. Either way, you now have the tools not only to implement vApps in your environment, but also to do so in a repeatable way via PowerCLI.

PART **III**

Securing Your vSphere Environment

Backing Up and Restoring Your Virtual Machines

IN THIS CHAPTER, YOU WILL LEARN TO:

One of the most critical areas of any infrastructure—whether it is virtual or not—is backup, the replication of key data to an alternate location in case of data or hardware loss. Most organizations have a full backup strategy with complex replication scenarios and standby hardware on separate sites in case a disaster strikes. Other aspects of backup protect the system administrator and the users of the virtual infrastructure and its VMs from more day-to-day data loss or operating system corruption. This chapter will show you how you can use PowerCLI in both of these areas to help back up your VMs and also how you can use PowerShell-enabled products from vendors to automate your backup tasks.

Work with Snapshots

Using VMware snapshots can be a great way to enable a quick and easy method to return to a particular point in time without needing to restore backups. A snapshot captures the state of a virtual machine and its configuration. Snapshots are a powerful tool for the VMware administrator as, once created, they act as a safety net ensuring any changes to the VM can be reverted if necessary. They are a restore point and should be created prior to installing new software, patching operating systems, or even making configuration changes. If you are unfamiliar with creating, maintaining, and restricting the creation of snapshots, see Chapter 8, "Advanced Virtual Machine Features."

WARNING   Because of the way in which snapshots are created, they are a great mechanism for a quick backout plan, but be warned: Do not leave them in place for a long time, as they could cause issues with space on datastores or reduced speed and performance when multiple snapshots are created on the same VM. Remember to keep track of them and remove snapshots that are no longer needed. You also might find it useful to restrict the creation of snapshots in your environment. You'll find scripts to assist you with these tasks in Chapter 8.

Create Do-It-Yourself Backups

Many organizations employ complex, commercially available products for creating backups. But what if you wanted to perform your own backups? Perhaps you want to copy your VM offsite to another datacenter—set, ready, and waiting to protect you in the event of disaster. Perhaps you just want to make a copy of the VM or VMs on a scheduled basis to ensure that your data has a backup.

With the code in Listing 10.1, you can make a backup copy of your VMs to an alternate datastore. The script creates a snapshot of the VM and then, from this snapshot, it clones the information to create a new VM on an alternate datastore. The script can be used to back up one or more VMs. As written, the log currently outputs to screen, but you can just as easily write to a log file or email the details as they are completed.

LISTING 10.1 DIY backups

```
Function Write-Log ($text) {
 $LogTime = (Get-Date).DateTime
 Write-Host "$($LogTime): $Text"
}


function Backup-VM{
 <#
 .SYNOPSIS
 Imports a csv file of folders into vCenter Server and
 creates them automatically.
 .DESCRIPTION
 The function will import folders from CSV file and create
 them in vCenter Server.
 .NOTES
  Source:  Automating vSphere Administration
  Authors: Luc Dekens, Arnim van Lieshout, Jonathan Medd,
           Alan Renouf, Glenn Sizemore
  Original: Adjusted from simonlong.co.uk
  Note: This script is not meant for use
  with RDM or independent disks.
 .PARAMETER FolderType
 The type of folder to create
 .PARAMETER DC
 The Datacenter to create the folder structure
 .PARAMETER Filename
 The path of the CSV file to use when importing
 .EXAMPLE 1
 PS> Import-Folders -FolderType "Blue" `
 -DC "DC01" -Filename "C:\BlueFolders.csv"
 .EXAMPLE 2
 PS> Import-Folders -FolderType "Yellow" -DC "Datacenter"
 -Filename "C:\YellowFolders.csv"
 #>
```

```
param(
 $VM,
 $Datastore
)

process{
#Set Date format for clone names
$date = Get-Date -Format "yyyyMMdd"

#Set Date format for emails
$time = (Get-Date -f "HH:MM")

foreach ($CurrentVM in $VM) {

 Write-Log "$($CurrentVM.Name) Backing up"
 Write-Log "$($CurrentVM.Name) Creating Snapshot"
 # Create new snapshot for clone
 $cloneSnap = $CurrentVM | New-Snapshot `
 -Name "Snapshot created on $Date by backup script"

 # Get managed object view
 $vmView = $CurrentVM | Get-View

 # Get folder managed object reference
 $cloneFolder = $vmView.parent

 $CloneVM = "$CurrentVM-$date"

 Write-Log "$($CurrentVM.Name)
Cloning from snapshot to $CloneVM"
 # Build clone specification
 $cloneSpec = new-object Vmware.Vim.VirtualMachineCloneSpec
 $cloneSpec.Snapshot = $vmView.Snapshot.CurrentSnapshot

 # Make linked disk specification
 $cloneSpec.Location = `
 new-object Vmware.Vim.VirtualMachineRelocateSpec
 $cloneSpec.Location.Datastore = ($Datastore | Get-View).MoRef
 $cloneSpec.Location.Transform =  [Vmware.Vim.VirtualMachineReloc
ateTransformation]::flat
```

```
# Create clone
$CreateClone = `
$vmView.CloneVM( $cloneFolder, $CloneVM, $cloneSpec )

Write-Log "$($CurrentVM.Name) Clone created"

Write-Log "$($CurrentVM.Name) Removing Snapshot"
# Remove Snapshot created for clone
Get-Snapshot -VM (Get-VM -Name $CurrentVM) `
-Name $cloneSnap | Remove-Snapshot -confirm:$False
Write-Log "$($CurrentVM.Name) Backup completed"
 }
 }
}


Backup-VM -VM (Get-VM DOMAIN01) `
 -Datastore (Get-Datastore "VBlock Storage #1")
```

While this script will perform the backup to the datastore provided, there are a few things you must keep in mind:

> ▶ The amount of disk space needed for the backup will be exactly the same as the current virtual machine's disks.

> ▶ No de-duplication methods were applied to this backup. Third-party software could have made use of de-duplication, in which case the amount of data being stored would be significantly reduced.

> ▶ The backup file will be a complete copy of the virtual machine, which means if you were to power it on you would have an exact replica on the network, conflicting IP addresses, SID, and all!

> ▶ The script will not work if the VM has raw device mappings (RDM) or independent disks.

In the next section, you will learn how to change these en masse to help you double-check that your backups have completed successfully and that you have a working VM.

Restore Your VMs from a DIY Backup

Having backed up your virtual machines using a do-it-yourself (DIY) script, you obviously will want to restore them. At other times, you will want to use this technique to automate a move to an isolated network so that you can verify that a virtual machine boots correctly into a working state. This is a great way to ensure the data you are backing up is the data you need and not a corrupted VM.

As you know, we named the backup VMs we created earlier in this chapter with a naming convention that added the prefix BAK- to the VM name. (We defined the prefix addition in the code in Listing 10.1.) Now, you can easily specify these backed up VMs and perform various recovery actions on them. Here's how.

To ensure that the backup VMs will not conflict with the original VMs, you can use the following script and change the network to a preconfigured isolated network:

```
Get-VM BAK-* | Get-NetworkAdapter | `
Set-NetworkAdapter -NetworkName "Isolated Network"
```

This simple code allows you to be safe in the knowledge that the virtual machines are now in an isolated network—away from our production network. While in the isolated network, they can be powered on and checked for a confirmed, good restore; are used to restore individual files; or even be used to replicate a live environment for testing purposes.

Change Block Tracking

One of the feature enhancements introduced in vSphere 4 is the ability to enable Changed Block Tracking (CBT). CBT is often described in the same way as differential backups. Initially, you copy all data from source to target. This first copy (often called a seed) is a full copy of the data. With CBT enabled, when you go to copy the data the next time you copy only data that have been changed since the last backup. ESX will track the block changes that have taken place since a given point in time. Before this feature was available on vSphere, both host CPU and memory resources had to be used as backup software and compared the versions of data and established the areas that had changed needed to be backed up. Now that this feature has been implemented, ESX will track the block changes that have taken place since a given point in time. ESX tracks the changes by keeping a log of all blocks that have been changed. It does not keep a copy of the changed blocks themselves. Overall this makes the backup of your virtual machines much quicker. ESX is now able to examine the log and tell your backup application exactly what has changed since the last backup, thereby reducing the amount of data being transferred.

Before CBT can be used, the following must be completed:

▶ Your ESX hosts will need to be on ESX 4 at least.

▶ Your VMs will need to be updated to hardware version 7.

▶ VMs must have the latest VMware Tools installed.

REMEMBER TO CHECK

Not all backup applications support CBT. If you wish to take advantage of the resource savings made available with CBT, make sure that your backup application fully supports both CBT and ESX 4.

Checking CBT Status

As mentioned earlier, before CBT can be used, each VM must have been upgraded to hardware version 7 and CBT must have been enabled. You can check both of these requirements using the script in Listing 10.2.

LISTING 10.2 CBT pre-requests

```
New-VIProperty -Name ToolsVersion -ObjectType VirtualMachine `
 -ValueFromExtensionProperty 'config.tools.ToolsVersion' `
 -Force

New-VIProperty -Name CBTEnabled -ObjectType VirtualMachine `
 -ValueFromExtensionProperty 'Config.ChangeTrackingEnabled' `
 -Force

Get-VM VM01 | Select Name, Version, ToolsVersion, CBTEnabled
```

Enabling/Disabling CBT

Currently, no native cmdlet exists to enable or disable CBT for your VMs. But we've got your back. We wrote an advanced function (Listing 10.3) that you can use to enable or disable CBT on either a single VM or multiple VMs.

LISTING 10.3 Enabling and disabling CBT

```
function Set-CBT{
<#
.SYNOPSIS
 Enables and disables CBT for a VM or multiple VMs
```

```
.DESCRIPTION
  The function will enable and disable CBT for a VM
  or multiple VMs
.NOTES
  Authors:  Luc Dekens & Alan Renouf
.PARAMETER VM
  A virtual machine or multiple virtual machines
.PARAMETER Enabled
  Specify if CBT shoud be enabled with $true
  or disabled with $false

.EXAMPLE 1
  PS> Set-CBT -VM (Get-VM VM01) -Enabled $true
.EXAMPLE 2
  PS> Set-CBT -VM (Get-VM VM*) -Enabled $false
#>

 param(
  $VM,
  [String]$Enabled
 )

 process{
  $VM | Foreach {
   $vmView = $_ | Get-View
   $vmConfigSpec = New-Object VMware.Vim.VirtualMachineConfigSpec
   if ($Enabled -eq $true) {
    Write-Host "Enabling CBT for $($_.Name)"
    $vmConfigSpec.changeTrackingEnabled = $true
   } Else {
    Write-Host "Disabling CBT for $($_.Name)"
    $vmConfigSpec.changeTrackingEnabled = $false
   }
   $vmView.ReconfigVM($vmConfigSpec)
  }
  New-VIProperty -Name CBTEnabled -ObjectType VirtualMachine `
  -ValueFromExtensionProperty 'Config.ChangeTrackingEnabled' `
  -Force
  Get-VM $VM | Select Name, CBTEnabled
```

```
    }
    }
```

```
Set-CBT -VM (Get-VM PRINT*) -Enabled $false
```

Use Site Recovery Manager

One area that also fits nicely into this chapter is disaster recovery. Anyone who has been using VMware products for a long period of time already knows how virtual machines have enabled a new era of mobility when it comes to the movement of servers and applications. This has been further enhanced by a product from VMware called Site Recovery Manager (SRM).

SRM is a great product that works with storage vendors to ensure the replication of key data is mirrored to a disaster recovery (DR) site or set of equipment. SRM allows companies to ensure that if there is a major issue (and the datacenter is left in a "big smoking hole"), protected VMs can be recovered on a DR site with little or no loss to data within the virtual machines. The fast recovery times enable the business to be back up and running in a short period of time.

You can use your automation skills with SRM in two ways: make the process easier to manage or improve the out-of-the-box application to add further functionality. The first way is to connect to the SRM server and build your own set of PowerShell functions. This makes those PowerShell features available in the SRM software. The second is to add a new step in the SRM recovery plan to enable you to call PowerCLI to add custom features to the SRM recovery plan. Both of these techniques will be discussed in the following sections.

Automating SRM Using PowerShell Functions

Luckily PowerShell makes it easy to connect to common programmable interfaces. With PowerShell, you can make a connection to the SRM application via a Web Services Description Language (WSDL) file hosted on the SRM server. These web services are easily accessed using PowerShell and the built in `New-WebService Proxy` cmdlet. Once connected, you can automate the current features of SRM using PowerShell. To make the automation easier, we have included some functions that you can download as part of the code file hosted here: www.sybex.com/go/vmware vspherepowercliref. These functions will enable you to automate some of the most common processes in SRM. Table 10.1 provides an overview of the functions included within the downloaded code file.

TABLE 10.1 SRM functions

Name	Description
Connect-SRMServer	Connects to an SRM server using the custom WSDL file
Disconnect-SRMServer	Disconnects from a connected SRM server
Get-SRMRecoveryPlan	Retrieves a list of all SRM plans
Invoke-SRMRecoveryPlan	Invokes a recovery plan
Test-SRMRecoveryPlan	Tests a recovery plan
Suspend-SRMRecoveryPlan	Suspends a recovery plan
Exit-SRMRecoveryPlan	Exits a recovery plan
Resume-SRMRecoveryPlan	Resumes a suspended recovery plan
Get-SRMPlanStatus	Gets the status of a recovery plan
Approve-SRMPlanPrompt	Approves a prompt during a plan
Get-SRMPlanFinalResponse	Retrieves the final plan response

WARNING Because of a feature in the srm.wsdl file which comes pre-installed with SRM Version 4.1.0, you will need to copy a custom `srm1.wsdl` file to the `%program files%\VMware\VMware vCenter Site Recovery Manager\www` folder. (You can download this custom file from `www.sybex.com/go/vmwarevspherepowercliref`.) Remember to check with VMware when using the customized WSDL files as support will need to be verified.

Customizing Recovery Plans

Recovery plans are a key part of SRM. These plans detail the steps to be followed when the big red button is pushed, enforcing the failover of key virtual machines to the DR site. Normally rigid steps included in recovery plans are created automatically by SRM as you add and remove virtual machines from the plan. With this said, however, you can add custom steps to the plan that allow you to run batch files. Guess what? From within the batch files, you can call PowerCLI to add some new customized magic to the recovery plan!

With this technique, you can bring the functionality of PowerCLI to your recovery plans. Here are a few examples of where you might want to use this capability:

▶ Import the limits and reservations of the virtual machines that failed over to the recovery site.

▶ Change the CPU or memory allocation once the virtual machines have been failed over to the recovery site. Often recovery hardware is less powerful than the failed machine.

▶ Perform data updates on configuration management databases or guest customization.

Use the following steps to add a customized script into an SRM recovery plan:

1. From within the vCenter Client, click the Home button and then click the Site Recovery icon in the Solutions and Applications area, as shown in Figure 10.1.

FIGURE 10.1   Click the Site Recovery icon on the Home screen

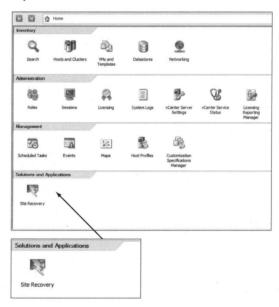

2. Expand Recovery Plans and select a recovery plan from the list of existing plans.

3. Click the Recovery Steps tab and then select the step titled "Message: Test recovery complete. Please…" New recovery steps are added before the selected step. For this exercise, you will add your custom scripts after the recovery of the virtual machines.

4. Click the Add Command Step button, as shown in Figure 10.2.

5. When the Edit Command Step dialog box opens, type the full command needed to run your batch file in CMD mode, as shown in Figure 10.3.

6. Once completed, the customized step will be displayed as shown in Figure 10.4.

Securing Your vSphere Environment

PART III

FIGURE 10.2   Click the Add Command Step button.

FIGURE 10.3   Batch file command

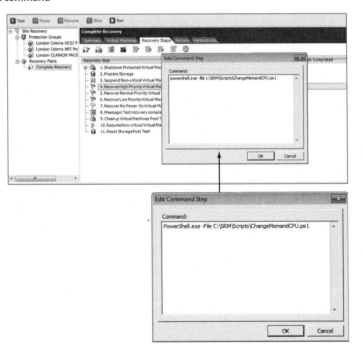

FIGURE 10.4   Custom step

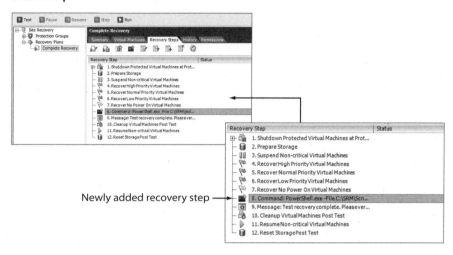

Newly added recovery step ⟶

Provide PowerShell Support for Corporate Backup Applications

There are obvious reasons to use a corporate backup application. These dedicated applications have great features that enable better data compression, de-duplicate, and provide scheduling advantages. Packages have often been purchased as part of a strategic corporate backup plan and are used for both physical and virtual environments, backing up to multiple locations, and verifying the consistency of data.

Recently, backup vendors have been adding PowerShell to their packages. (By now you should realize that PowerShell is a great and easy way to add automation to any product. It makes sense that backup software vendors have come to that realization, too.)

Think about how long it would take you to

▶ Add multiple backup jobs for multiple servers.

▶ Change the backup schedule for multiple servers.

▶ Extract information for multiple servers.

▶ Remove a backup job for multiple servers.

If you have a corporate backup application, we suggest that you check it now to see what you can achieve by using PowerShell. The remaining sections of this chapter present two such applications and discuss the kind of things you can achieve with PowerShell in a commercial backup environment.

Quest

Quest has a PowerShell-enabled backup product called vRanger. vRanger has a variety of backup methods and a good compression algorithm to ensure the size of backups and the time it takes to back them up is greatly reduced. vRanger has its own Active Block Mapping feature, which reads only active blocks from the image, similar to VMware's CBT, as discussed earlier in this chapter. With vRanger, you can back up and restore VMs at the same time. Leveraging distributed processing avoids impact on host operations and sends VM data through a single, central server.

vRanger also has great vCenter Server integration, allowing it to see which VMs have been protected, when backup jobs are completed, and which VMs still need backup protection. You can configure new backup jobs that are automatically refreshed to stay current with new VMs as they are added to the virtual environment.

Quest was one of the first vendors to include PowerShell cmdlets to allow you to manage every aspect of vRanger, ensuring automation at all levels of the virtual infrastructure. Quest has not only added 62 cmdlets, but has also created a PowerPack and added additional nodes to the VMware PowerPack, which integrates vRanger into PowerShell at a whole new level. In Figure 10.5, you see a list of VMs and a set of vRanger actions you can do alongside your daily virtualization management. Quest's approach is to include and consider data protection as something administrators require alongside daily checks and balances of their environment.

In Figure 10.6, notice the depth of vRanger-specific capabilities and, most importantly, a list of best practices shown in the lower-left corner.

Table 10.2 shows how extensive the Quest cmdlets can be and gives you an idea of the areas that could be controlled with PowerShell as of this writing.

FIGURE 10.5   vRanger actions

VM listing

vRanger actions

FIGURE 10.6   vRanger capabilities

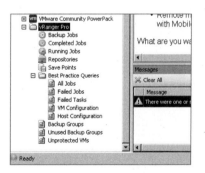

TABLE 10.2   Quest cmdlets available in PowerShell

Name	Description
`Add-BackupGroupEntity`	Adds a backup group.
`Add-BackupJobTemplate`	Adds a backup job template. The user also has the option of running the job immediately after the template is created.
`Add-CifsRepository`	Adds a Common Internet File System (CIFS) repository to vRanger.
`Add-FtpRepository`	Adds an FTP repository to vRanger.
`Add-NfsRepository`	Adds a network file share repository to vRanger.
`Add-ReplicationJobTemplate`	Adds a replication job template. The user also has the option of running the job immediately after the template is created.
`Add-RestorefromManifestJobTemplate`	Adds a restore job template from a manifest file. The user also has the option of running the job immediately after the template is created.
`Add-RestoreJobTemplate`	Adds a restore job template. The user also has the option of running the job immediately after the template is created.
`Add-S3Repository`	Adds an Amazon S3 repository to vRanger.
`Add-SftpRepository`	Adds an SFTP repository to vRanger.
`Add-VirtualAppforLinuxFLR`	Adds a virtual appliance to perform Linux FLR.
`Get-Addressbook`	Gets a list of email addresses from the address book.
`Get-BackupGroupEntity`	Returns backup group entities.
`Get-CatalogSearchData`	Gets a list of search results from the catalog database for the matched search string.
`Get-CatalogStatus`	Gets the active status of the catalog for a list of savepoints.
`Get-Configoption`	Returns the config option values for a specified type.
`Get-Connection`	Gets configured connections to hosts or vCenters in vRanger.
`Get-Datastore`	Returns all datastores associated with the host.
`Get-InventoryEntity`	Returns inventory entities.
`Get-Job`	Returns vRanger jobs. Since the number of jobs returned by this cmdlet is potentially large, use as many cmdlet parameters as you possibly can to achieve better performance.

(continues)

TABLE 10.2   *(continued)*

Name	Description
Get-JobTemplate	Returns scheduled jobs (job templates).
Get-LinuxVolumes	Returns Linux volumes.
Get-Network	Returns all networks associated with the host.
Get-Repository	Gets the repositories configured in vRanger.
Get-RepositoryJob	Returns jobs associated with the repository.
Get-RepositorySavePoint	Returns a list of savepoints in the repository created during the specified time period.
Get-SavepointDisk	Returns the VM disks that the savepoint contains.
Get-SavePointFileSize	Returns the size of the savepoint in bytes.
Get-SavePointManifest	Returns the size of the savepoint in bytes.
Get-VmDisk	Returns a list of VmDisks for the VM list in the same order of the input.
Get-VMDKVolume	Returns all volumes on a certain VM disk.
Move-ToolsToVA	
New-BackupFlag	Creates a new BackupFlag object for later use.
New-BackupGroupMember	Adds members to backup group.
New-DailySchedule	Returns a Schedule object. The schedule provides a template daily schedule that can be further customized before use.
New-EmailAddress	Adds new email address to address book.
New-IntervalSchedule	Returns an interval schedule.
New-MonthlySchedule	Returns a Schedule object. The schedule provides a template monthly schedule that can be further customized before use.
New-ReplicationFlag	Creates a new ReplicationFlag object for later use.
New-RestoreFlag	Creates restore flags for later use.
New-SMTPServer	Add a new SMTP server.
New-SpaceSavingType	Creates SpaceSavingTechnologyType for later use.
New-WeeklySchedule	Returns a Schedule object. The schedule provides a template weekly schedule that can be further customized before use.

Securing Your vSphere Environment

PART III

(continues)

TABLE 10.2   *(continued)*

Name	Description
New-YearlySchedule	Returns a `Schedule` object. The schedule provides a template yearly schedule that can be further customized before use.
Remove-AllMount	Removes all previously mounted paths.
Remove-BackupGroupEntity	Removes a backup group.
Remove-BackupGroupMember	Removes member from backup Group.
Remove-Catalog	Deletes the catalog data from the database for a list of savepoints.
Remove-JobTemplate	Removes a `JobTemplate`.
Remove-LinuxVolume	
Remove-Repository	Removes a repository along with all the savepoints in it.
Remove-SavePoint	Removes savepoints.
Run-JobsNow	Runs jobs specified by their template IDs.
Set-Cataloging	Enables/disables global cataloging.
Set-CBTonVM	Enables/disables CBT for VMs.
Set-LinuxVolume	
Set-MountPath	Sets mount path for a volume.
Set-Resources	Sets value for vRanger resources.
Update-BackupJobTemplate	Updates a backup job template. The user also has the option of running the job immediately after the template is updated.
Update-ReplicationJobTemplate	Updates a replication job template. The user also has the option of running the job immediately after the template is updated.
Update-RestoreJobTemplate	Updates a restore job template. The user also has the option of running the job immediately after the template is updated.

Veeam

Veeam is a vendor best known for their backup and replication software for virtual machines. By leveraging the virtual environment and Veeam vPower technology, Veeam always seems to be on the forefront of backup technologies, introducing new and innovative ways to not only back up the virtual environment but also restore.

They have several methods that ensure each of the backups created can be 100 percent guaranteed to restore. With Veeam you can instantly recover a VM directly from a backup file, restore individual objects (email messages, database records, files, etc.) from any virtualized application or file system, verify the recoverability of every backup, and provide near-continuous data protection for any application.

Veeam was also one of the first vendors to add PowerShell support to their application. As of this writing, they have 75 cmdlets that can be used to manage this application. Table 10.3 contains a list of the cmdlets and a brief synopsis of each.

TABLE 10.3   PowerShell cmdlets supported in Veeam

Name	Synopsis
Add-VBRBackupJob	Creates a backup job.
Add-VBRCopyJob	Creates a copy job.
Add-VBRESX	Adds an ESX host to Veeam Backup & Replication.
Add-VBRESXi	Adds an ESXi server to Veeam Backup & Replication.
Add-VBRJobObject	Adds VMs or VM containers to the existing job.
Add-VBRLinux	Adds a Linux host to Veeam Backup & Replication.
Add-VBRReplicaJob	Creates a replica job.
Add-VBRvCenter	Adds vCenter Server to Veeam Backup & Replication.
Add-VSBApplicationGroup	Creates an application group.
Add-VSBJob	Creates a SureBackup job.
Add-VSBVirtualLab	Creates a virtual lab.
Connect-VSBVirtualLab	Connects an existing virtual lab to the Veeam Backup & Replication server.
Copy-VBRJob	Copies an existing backup job.
Export-VBRBackup	Exports the selected backup to some directory on the disk.
Export-VBRJob	Exports existing backup jobs.
Export-VBRServer	Exports the names of Veeam Backup & Replication servers.
Find-VBRDatastore	Returns all datastores connected to the specified ESX/ESXi server.
Find-VBRObject	Returns all VMs and VM containers on the specified ESX/ESXi server.
Find-VBRResourcePool	Returns all resource pools on the specified ESX/ESXi server.

(continues)

Securing Your vSphere Environment

PART III

TABLE 10.3   (continued)

Name	Synopsis
Find-VSBVirtualLab	Returns all virtual labs created on the specified ESX/ESXi server.
Get-VBRBackup	Returns all backups.
Get-VBRBackupSession	Returns all backup sessions.
Get-VBRFilesInRestorePoint	Returns all files for the selected restore point.
Get-VBRInstantRecovery	Returns an instant VM recovery session.
Get-VBRJob	Returns all created jobs.
Get-VBRJobObject	Returns a specified job.
Get-VBRJobObjectVssOprions	Returns a list of VSS settings set for specific VMs or VM containers in the job.
Get-VBRJobOptions	Returns a list of job settings for a created job.
Get-VBRJobScheduleOptions	Returns a list of job scheduling options for a created job.
Get-VBRJobVSSOptions	Returns a list of VSS settings for a job.
Get-VBRLocalhost	Returns an object of the current Veeam Backup & Replication server.
Get-VBRReplica	Returns objects of all replication jobs.
Get-VBRRestorePoint	Returns objects of all restore points for the specified backup job.
Get-VBRRestoreSession	Returns objects of all restore sessions that were performed.
Get-VBRServer	Returns objects of all servers connected to Veeam Backup & Replication.
Get-VSBApplicationGroup	Gets objects of all application groups.
Get-VSBJob	Gets objects of all SureBackup jobs.
Get-VSBJobOptions	Returns a list of job settings for the specified SureBackup job.
Get-VSBJobScheduleOptions	Returns a list of job scheduling options for the specified SureBackup job.
Get-VSBSession	Returns all SureBackup sessions.
Get-VSBTaskSession	
Get-VSBVirtualLab	Gets objects of all virtual labs.
Import-VBRBackup	Imports a created backup to Veeam Backup & Replication.
Import-VBRJob	Imports backup jobs to Veeam Backup & Replication from an external file.
Import-VBRServer	Imports a list of servers connected to Veeam Backup & Replication from an external file.

(continues)

TABLE 10.3   *(continued)*

Name	Synopsis
Remove-VBRBackup	Removes the specified backup.
Remove-VBRBackupSession	Removes the specified session.
Remove-VBRJob	Removes the specified job.
Remove-VBRJobObject	Removes VMs or VM containers from the specified job.
Remove-VBRReplica	Removes a replica from Veeam Backup & Replication.
Remove-VBRRestoreSession	Removes the specified restore session.
Remove-VBRServer	Removes a server from Veeam Backup & Replication.
Remove-VSBApplicationGroup	Removes the specified application group.
Remove-VSBJob	Removes the specified SureBackup job.
Remove-VSBSession	Removes the specified SureBackup job session.
Remove-VSBVirtualLab	Removes the specified virtual lab.
Set-VBRJobObject	Changes the list of VMs and VM containers in the specified job.
Set-VBRJobObjectVssOprions	Changes VSS settings for the created job.
Set-VBRJobOptions	Changes settings of the specified job.
Set-VBRJobScheduleOptions	Changes scheduling settings of the specified job.
Set-VBRJobVssOptions	Changes VSS settings of the specified job.
Set-VSBJobOptions	Changes settings of the specified SureBackup job.
Set-VSBJobScheduleOptions	Changes scheduling settings of the specified SureBackup job.
Start-VBRInstantRecovery	Performs instant recovery of a VM.
Start-VBRJob	Starts a created job.
Start-VBRReplicaFailover	Fails over a corrupted VM to its successfully created replica (restore point).
Start-VBRRestoreVM	Performs restore of the entire VM.
Start-VBRRestoreVMFiles	Starts the file-level-restore process for VMs running Windows.
Start-VBRWindowsFileRestore	Restores VM files (VMX, VMDK, etc.).
Start-VSBJob	Starts the created SureBackup job.
Stop-VBRInstantRecovery	Stops the initiated instant VM recovery process.
Stop-VBRJob	Stops the initiated job.
Stop-VBRReplicaFailover	Undoes the replica failover.
Stop-VBRWindowsFileRestore	Stops the initiated guest file recovery process for VMs running Windows.
Stop-VSBJob	Stops the initiated SureBackup job.

CHAPTER 11

Organize Your Disaster Recovery

IN THIS CHAPTER, YOU WILL LEARN TO:

When it comes to designing your disaster recovery strategy, there are several aspects you should take into account. The vCenter Server installation consists of two parts: an application server and a backend database. While the application server is servicing the user interface, the heart of the vCenter Server is stored in the backend database. In this chapter, you'll learn how to back up and restore your vCenter Server database when you don't have SQL Server Management Studio available. We'll explore methods to export and import specific items of your vCenter Server inventory. These exports can be used to create a replica for testing or disaster recovery purposes even if your destination vCenter Server database is hosted on another database platform.

Back Up Your vCenter Server

Once upon a time, there was a system administrator. Every day, he verified his backup logs. He always checked with the people responsible for changing the backup tapes at the branch offices. Had the backup run? Had they changed the tapes properly? He never experienced a problem with restoring files that had been erased by some miscreant. He thought everything was taken care of until the phone rang. A fire had broken out in the server room of a branch office; the file server was lost. "A problem, but not a serious one," the system administrator thought as he left to set up a replacement server.

After the server was set up, he contacted the person who had so diligently run the backup and changed the tapes, day in and day out.

"Where are the backup tapes?" asked the administrator.

"I keep them on top of the file server, why?"

Is your backup secured? This example, based on a true story, is particularly gruesome, but it illustrates that a good backup system is more than just the technology alone.

Some see backup as a necessary evil and do only a simple file backup of the vCenter Server. You should always remember that the backup is the first step to being able to restore your infrastructure; make sure that you know what elements you'll need for your environment.

To restore your vCenter Server, you'll need the following:

▶ The installation media for the version of vCenter Server you are restoring.

▶ The database server backup files.

- ▶ The SSL certificate files. For Windows 2003, you'll find these files in `%ALLUSERSPROFILE%\Application Data\VMware\VMware VirtualCenter\SSL` and for Windows 2008 in `C:\ProgramData\VMware\VMware VirtualCenter\SSL`.

- ▶ The vCenter Server config file: `vpxd.cfg`

If you still have ESX3.*x* hosts running in your infrastructure, you also need the backup copy of your VMware Infrastructure 3 license file from the license server running on your vCenter Server. Let's take a look at the processes for creating the backup files you'll need.

Backing Up Your vCenter Server Database

The heart of your vCenter Server is stored in its backend database. This database is an essential part of your backup strategy, and a simple file backup of your vCenter Server is insufficient. Let's see how to properly backup the vCenter Server database.

As a best practice, schedule your database backup of the vCenter Server database according to your database management system's vendor recommendations. For a Microsoft SQL database, that involves using SQL Server Management Studio to schedule backups. For Oracle,you'll be using the Oracle Recovery Manager (RMAN). However, if you have a small environment or test setup, you probably have Microsoft SQL Express 2005 installed; it came along with the vCenter Server installation. One of the limitations of Microsoft SQL Express 2005 is that you can't schedule jobs, and therefore you can't schedule a backup (as you can with SQL Server Management Studio or RMAN). Luckily,you have PowerShell to help you.

SCRIPT REQUIREMENTS

To use the PowerShell functions included with this chapter, you need to have the SQL Server Native Client and the Microsoft SQL Server 2005 Management Objects Collection packages installed. These packages are installed as part of the SQL installation on your vCenter Server. If you want to run the scripts from another system, you can download the packages from the Microsoft download site:

`www.microsoft.com/downloads/`

When running the SQL scripts on a 64-bit operating system, make sure that you start PowerCLI in 32-bit mode or the SQL scripts won't work.

Securing Your vSphere Environment

PART III

Although this chapter focuses on SQL Server Express 2005, you can use the steps and functions outlined here for any SQL Server 2005 or 2008 edition installation. However, we recommend using SQL Server Management Studio to schedule maintenance tasks (including backups) for non-Express installations.

> **WARNING**   Make sure that you don't interfere with an active backup schedule on your database! If you're not sure whether a backup schedule is active on your database, consult your database administrator before continuing with the PowerShell backup and restore functions in this chapter.

Creating a Full Database Backup

To interact with Microsoft SQL Server in your scripts, you need to load the SQL Server Management Objects (SMO) in your scripts first. To load SQL Server SMO assemblies, use this command:

```
[System.Reflection.Assembly]::LoadWithPartialName( `
    "Microsoft.SqlServer.Smo") | Out-Null
```

For SQL Server 2008, you need to load an extra assembly. To load this assembly, called `Microsoft.SqlServer.SmoExtended`, use this command:

```
[System.Reflection.Assembly]::LoadWithPartialName( `
    "Microsoft.SqlServer.SmoExtended") | Out-Null
```

Next, create a new instance of the SQL Server object and the backup object. Then, define the properties you need to perform the actual backup. The first property is the `Database` property, which defines the name of the database you want to backup. The default name of a vCenter Server database is VIM_VCDB.

```
$serverObject = `
    New-Object "Microsoft.SqlServer.Management.Smo.Server" `
    "LOCALHOST\SQLEXP_VIM"

$backupObject = `
    New-Object "Microsoft.SqlServer.Management.Smo.Backup"

$backupObject.Database  = "VIM_VCDB"
```

Now, add the backup file to the devices collection and define the backup type. The backup type is defined in the `Action` property. To perform a full database backup, you need to set the `Action` property to `Database`.

```
$backupObject.Devices.AddDevice("YourBackupFile.bak", "File")
$backupObject.Action = 'Database'
```

To perform the actual backup, you just have to call the `SqlBackup()` method of the backup object:

```
$backupObject.SqlBackup($serverObject)
```

Putting all the code snippets together, you can create a script that makes a full backup of your vCenter Server database, as shown in Listing 11.1.

LISTING 11.1   **Creating a full database backup**

```
# Load SQLServer SMO assemblies
[System.Reflection.Assembly]::LoadWithPartialName( `
    "Microsoft.SqlServer.Smo") | Out-Null

# Create SQL Server object
$serverObject = `
    New-Object "Microsoft.SqlServer.Management.Smo.Server" `
    "LOCALHOST\SQLEXP_VIM"

# Create Backup object
$backupObject = `
    New-Object "Microsoft.SqlServer.Management.Smo.Backup"

# Define the database to back up
$backupObject.Database = "VIM_VCDB"

# Add the backup file to the devices collection
$backupObject.Devices.AddDevice( `
    "D:\Backup\VIM_VCDB_FULL.bak", "File")

# Define the backup type to generate a FULL backup
$backupObject.Action = 'Database'

# Start the backup
$backupObject.SqlBackup($serverObject)
```

Creating a Differential Backup

You can also create a differential backup. Differential backups are particularly useful if you have a large database with minimal changes. A differential backup stores only the changes since the last full backup of your database. This approach decreases the backup window, but that decrease comes at a cost. If you are using differential backups and need to restore your database, you have to restore the last full backup, followed by the last differential backup. Differential backups can only be performed on databases that are not in "Simple" recovery mode. By default, the vCenter Server installation installs the database in Simple recovery mode.

To create a differential backup, specify the `Incremental` property and assign it the value 1:

```
# Define the backup type to generate a DIFF backup
$backupObject.Incremental = 1
```

Creating a Log Backup

The third type of backup you can make is a log backup. With log backups you can recover the database to a specific point in time. Log backups generally use fewer resources than database backups, and as a result, you can create them more often. Note that you can only perform log backups on databases that are not in Simple recovery mode. To perform a backup of your database transactional log files, change the `Action` property to `Log`:

```
# Define the backup type to generate a Log backup
$backupObject.Action = 'Log'
```

Putting It All Together

Now let's use everything you've learned about database backups so far and combine it in a function. We created such a function, called `Backup-MsSqlDatabase`, in Listing 11.2. This function accepts the server instance, the database, the backup type, and the backup file as arguments. If no databases are specified, all databases on the server instance are backed up. This function can easily be scheduled using the Windows Task Manager to back up your database on a regular basis. Besides the vCenter Server database, make sure you back up the system databases (master, model, and msdb) too, as they contain vital system information.

LISTING 11.2 Backing up `MsSqlDatabase`

```
function Backup-MsSqlDatabase {
<#
.SYNOPSIS
  Back up a Microsoft SQL database
.DESCRIPTION
  This function backs up a Microsoft SQL database using
  SQL Server Management Objects (SMO)
.NOTES
  Source:  Automating vSphere Administration
  Authors: Luc Dekens, Arnim van Lieshout, Jonathan Medd,
           Alan Renouf, Glenn Sizemore
.PARAMETER instance
  The SQL Server instance to back up. e.g. VC01\SQLEXP_VIM
.PARAMETER database
  An array of databases to back up.
  If omitted, all databases on the server instance are backed up
.PARAMETER backupType
  The backup type. Valid options are Full,Diff,Log
.PARAMETER path
  The path where the backup files will be written.
  If omitted, the default server backup location will be used
.EXAMPLE
  PS> Backup-MsSqlDatabase -Instance vc01\sqlexp_vim `
          -Database vim_vcdb -Backuptype full -Path c:\sqlbackup
#>

  Param (
    [parameter(mandatory = $true,
    HelpMessage = "Enter an MSSQL instance")]
      [String]$Instance,
      [string[]]$Database,
    [parameter(mandatory = $true,
    HelpMessage = "Enter the backup type (Full,Diff,Log)")]
      [string]$BackupType ,
    [parameter(mandatory = $true,
    HelpMessage = "Enter the backup path")]
      [string]$Path)
```

Securing Your vSphere
Environment

PART III

```
# Load SQLServer SMO assemblies
  [System.Reflection.Assembly]::LoadWithPartialName( `
      "Microsoft.SqlServer.Smo") | Out-Null
# For SQL Server 2008, you also need to load
# Microsoft.SqlServer.SmoExtended
  [System.Reflection.Assembly]::LoadWithPartialName( `
      "Microsoft.SqlServer.SmoExtended") | Out-Null

# Create backup directory
  if (-not (Test-Path $path)){
    New-Item $path -type directory | out-null
  }

# Create objects
  $serverObject = `
      New-Object "Microsoft.SqlServer.Management.Smo.Server" `
      "$instance"

  $timeStamp = Get-Date -format yyyyMMddHHmmss
  if (-not $database) {
    foreach ($db in $serverObject.databases) {
# Exclude tempdb
      if ($db.Name -ne "tempdb") {$database += $db.name}
    }
  }

# process databases
  foreach ($db in $database) {
    $backupObject = `
        New-Object "Microsoft.SqlServer.Management.Smo.Backup"
# evaluate backup type
    Switch ($backupType) {
      "Full" {
        $backupObject.Action = 'Database'
        $extension=".BAK"
        $message="Full Backup of "
      }
      "Diff" {
```

```
        $backupObject.Incremental = 1
        $extension=".DIFF"
        $message="Differential Backup of "
    }
    "Log" {
        $backupObject.Action = 'Log'
        $extension=".LOG"
        $message="Transactional Log Backup of "
    }
    default {
        Write-Host -foregroundcolor Red `
            'Invalid Backup Type specified!'
        return
    }
}


$backupObject.BackupSetName = $db + " Backup"
$backupObject.BackupSetDescription = $message + $db
$backupObject.Devices.AddDevice($path + "\" + $db + "_" + `
    $timeStamp + $extension, "File")
$backupObject.Database = $db
$backupObject.SqlBackup($serverObject)

Write-Host $message$db finished
    }
}
```

Backing Up Your vCenter Server Configuration

Although the heart of the vCenter Server is inside the database, there are several other files that you need to back up:

▶ SSL certificates

▶ Config file

▶ License files

If you installed vCenter Server on Windows 2003, the SSL certificate files are stored under %ALLUSERSPROFILE%\Application Data\VMware\VMware VirtualCenter\SSL on your vCenter Server. If you installed vCenter Server on a

Windows 2008 server, the SSL certificate files are stored under `C:\ProgramData\VMware\VMware VirtualCenter\SSL`. These certificate files are used to authenticate your ESX hosts. If you lose these files, vCenter Server won't be able to decrypt the ESX host passwords. This leads to all ESX hosts showing up as disconnected. When that happens, you won't be able to manage your ESX hosts until you reauthenticate every host by reconnecting them after the restore.

If you made changes to the `vpxd.cfg` file, you can include this file in your backup too. This file is stored under `%ALLUSERSPROFILE%\Application Data\VMware\VMware VirtualCenter` on your vCenter Server.

If you still have ESX3.*x* hosts in your infrastructure, you also need to backup your license files from the license server.

Use the `Copy-Item` cmdlet to copy these files to a backup location. You can use the `Backup-VcConfig` function we created in Listing 11.3 to perform the backup of these configuration files.

LISTING 11.3 Backing up vCenter config files

```
function Backup-VcConfig {
<#
.SYNOPSIS
  Back up a vCenter Server's configuration files
.DESCRIPTION
  This function backs up the configuration data from
  a vCenter Server.
.NOTES
  Source:  Automating vSphere Administration
  Authors: Luc Dekens, Arnim van Lieshout, Jonathan Medd,
           Alan Renouf, Glenn Sizemore
.PARAMETER vCenter
  The vCenter Servername by which it will be reachable
  over the network.
.PARAMETER destination
  The destination path where the backup files will be stored
.PARAMETER vi3license
  Optional parameter to specify to back up the VI3 license file
  if you happen to still have ESX 3.x hosts in your environment
.PARAMETER ssl
  Optional parameter to specify to back up the ssl certificate
```

```
.PARAMETER config
  Optional parameter to specify to back up the vCenter
  config file
.EXAMPLE
  PS> Backup-VcConfig -vCenter VC01 -destination c:\temp
#>
  Param (
    [parameter(mandatory = $true,
    HelpMessage = "Enter your vCenter Server")]
      [String]$vCenter,
    [parameter(mandatory = $true,
    HelpMessage = "Enter a destination path")]
      [string]$destination,
    [switch]$vi3License, [switch]$ssl, [switch]$config)


# Define default paths
# Modify these paths to match your installation.
#
# Default paths for Windows2003
# $sslPath="\\$vCenter\C$\Documents and Settings\All Users\"+
#     "Application Data\VMware\VMware VirtualCenter\SSL"
# $configPath="\\$vCenter\C$\Documents and Settings\All Users\"+
#     "Application Data\VMware\VMware VirtualCenter\vpxd.cfg"
#
# Default paths for Windows2008
# $sslPath="\\$vCenter\C$\ProgramData\VMware\"+
#     "VMware VirtualCenter\SSL"
# $configPath="\\$vCenter\C$\ProgramData\VMware\"+
#     "VMware VirtualCenter\vpxd.cfg"

  $sslPath="\\$vCenter\C$\ProgramData\VMware\"+
      "VMware VirtualCenter\SSL"
  $configPath="\\$vCenter\C$\ProgramData\VMware\"+
      "VMware VirtualCenter\vpxd.cfg"
  $licensePath="\\$vCenter\C$\Program Files (x86)\VMware\"+
      "VMware License Server\Licenses"

  $sourceFiles=@()
  if ($vi3License) {$sourceFiles += $licensePath}
```

```
    if ($ssl) {$sourceFiles += $sslPath}
    if ($config) {$sourceFiles += $configPath}
    if ($vi3License,$ssl,$config -notcontains $true) {
      $sourceFiles = $SSLPath,$configPath
    }

# Create backup directory
    if (-not (Test-Path $destination)){
      New-Item $destination -type directory |  out-null
    }

# Create backup
    Copy-Item -Path $sourceFiles -Destination $destination `
        -Recurse -Force
}
```

Restore Your vCenter Server

When it comes to restoring your vCenter Server environment, there are several possibilities depending on your original setup. If you used an external database, recover your database first. Follow your database vendor's guidelines. After your database is online, follow the steps as outlined in the next section to install and recover your vCenter Server environment.

If you used the Microsoft SQL Express 2005 installation that came with your vCenter Server installation, you can't restore the database until you've gone through the vCenter Server installation. Just proceed with the steps outlined in the next section and restore the database afterwards.

The Restore Sequence

First, restore your SSL certificates to the %ALLUSERSPROFILE%\Application Data\VMware\VMware VirtualCenter\SSL folder before installing vCenter Server.

```
$vCenter="myvCenter"
$sslPath="\\$vCenter\C$\Documents and Settings\All Users\" +
    "Application Data\VMware\VMware VirtualCenter\SSL"

# Create SSL directory if not exists
if (-not (Test-Path $sslPath)) {
```

```
    New-Item $sslPath -type directory | out-null
}
Copy-Item -Path C:\Backup\SSL -Destination $sslPath `
    -Recurse -Force
```

Install your vCenter Server as you normally would. If you're using an external database, point the installer to the existing database during the setup process and make sure that you choose not to reinitialize the database. You can make use of the unattended deployment of your vCenter Server as discussed in Chapter 1, "Automating vCenter Server Deployment and Configuration." If you chose to install the Microsoft SQL Express 2005 database engine, you'll need to restore the database after the vCenter Server installation has finished. We'll explain that process in detail in the next section.

If you modified your vpxd.cfg file, restore that file now, and then restart your vCenter Server service. To restart a service, use the Restart-Service cmdlet:

```
$vCenter = "myvCenter"
$configPath = "\\$vCenter\C$\Documents and Settings\All Users\"+
    "Application Data\VMware\VMware VirtualCenter\vpxd.cfg"
Copy-Item -Path C:\Backup\vpxd.cfg -Destination $configPath `
    -Force
Restart-Service vpxd
```

After the installation is finished, vCenter should start up and your ESX hosts should show up as connected without problems. If your ESX hosts show up as disconnected, there's a problem with the SSL certificates. Most frequently, this happens when you forget to copy the SSL files prior to installing vCenter Server. In this case, you need to reauthenticate every host by reconnecting them.

Restoring Your vCenter Server Database

Before restoring your database, you need to stop the vCenter Server service using the Stop-Service cmdlet. Because the vCenter Server service has dependent services, you must provide the -Force parameter:

```
Stop-Service vpxd -Force
```

To restore the database, use the SQL Server Management Objects again. The restore is similar to the backup except that you have to create an instance of the restore object instead:

```
$restoreObject = `
    New-Object "Microsoft.SqlServer.Management.Smo.Restore"
```

Just like the backup object, the restore object has some properties that you'll need to define. First, provide the restore type you want to perform. In this case, you'll want to restore the database and overwrite it if the database already exists:

```
$restoreObject.ReplaceDatabase = $true
$restoreObject.Action = "Database"
```

Now, you need to add the backup file to the devices collection:

```
$restoreObject.Devices.AddDevice("YourBackupFile.bak", "File")
```

The last property you'll need defines the database that you want to restore. It can be retrieved from the backup file:

```
$restoreInfo = $restoreObject.ReadBackupHeader($serverObject)
$restoreObject.Database = $restoreInfo.Rows[0]["DatabaseName"]
```

To perform the actual restore, you just need to call the `SqlRestore()` method of the restore object:

```
$restoreObject.SqlRestore($serverObject)
```

After the restore is finished, you can start vCenter Server again using the `Start -Service` cmdlet:

```
Start-Service vpxd
```

All these restore steps are put together in the `Restore-MsSqlDatabase` function in Listing 11.4, which can assist you in the restore process.

LISTING 11.4   Restoring `MsSqlDatabase`

```
function Restore-MsSqlDatabase {
<#
.SYNOPSIS
  Restore a Microsoft SQL database
.DESCRIPTION
  This function restores a Microsoft SQL database using
  SQL Server Management Objects (SMO)
.NOTES
  Source:  Automating vSphere Administration
  Authors: Luc Dekens, Arnim van Lieshout, Jonathan Medd,
           Alan Renouf, Glenn Sizemore
```

```
.PARAMETER instance
  The SQL Server instance to restore the database
  to. e.g. VC01\SQLEXP_VIM
.PARAMETER backupFile
  The backup file to restore
.PARAMETER NoRecovery
  Optional switch to prevent transaction recovery.
.EXAMPLE
  PS> Restore-MsSqlDatabase -instance vc01\sqlexp_vim `
      -backupFile c:\sqlbackup\VIM_VCDB_20100729233423.BAK
#>

  Param (
    [parameter(mandatory = $true,
    HelpMessage = "Enter an MSSQL instance")]
      [String]$instance,
    [parameter(mandatory = $true,
    HelpMessage = "Enter the backup file")]
      [string]$backupFile,
    [switch]$NoRecovery)


# Load SQLServer SMO assemblies
  [System.Reflection.Assembly]::LoadWithPartialName( `
    "Microsoft.SqlServer.Smo") | Out-Null
# For SQL Server 2008, you'll also need to load
# Microsoft.SqlServer.SmoExtended
  [System.Reflection.Assembly]::LoadWithPartialName( `
    "Microsoft.SqlServer.SmoExtended") | Out-Null


# Test backupFile
  if (-not (Test-Path $backupfile)){
    Write-Host backup file: $backupFile not found!
    Return
  }


# Create objects
  $serverObject = `
      New-Object "Microsoft.SqlServer.Management.Smo.Server" `
```

```
        "$instance"
    $restoreObject = `
        New-Object "Microsoft.SqlServer.Management.Smo.Restore"

    if ($NoRecovery) {
      $restoreObject.NoRecovery = $true
    }
    else {
      $restoreObject.NoRecovery = $false
    }
    $restoreObject.ReplaceDatabase = $true
    $restoreObject.Action = "Database"
    $restoreObject.Devices.AddDevice($backupFile, "File")

#determine database to restore
    $restoreInfo = $restoreObject.ReadBackupHeader($serverObject)
    $restoreObject.Database = $restoreInfo.Rows[0]["DatabaseName"]

#restore database
    $restoreObject.SqlRestore($serverObject)

    Write-Host Restore of $restoreObject.Database finished
}
```

Reconnecting ESX Hosts

When you restore your vCenter Server without a backup of the original SSL certificate, vCenter Server won't be able to decrypt the ESX host passwords. All ESX hosts
will show up as disconnected. In this case, you'll have to reauthenticate every host
by reconnecting them. When replacing the vCenter Server certificates, you must
also reconnect all ESX hosts to update the ESX host passwords.

You can reconnect an ESX host using the Set-VMHost cmdlet. This cmdlet is used
to change the configuration of the host. Set the -State parameter to Connected to
reconnect a disconnected host. To disconnect a host, set the -State parameter to
Disconnected.

```
    Set-VMHost esx01 -State Connected
```

You should understand that if the SSL certificates aren't valid, the Set-VMHost
cmdlet doesn't let you reconnect the server and the following error is thrown:
"Cannot complete login due to an incorrect user name or password."

When you have to deal with invalid SSL certificates and you're solely working with PowerCLI cmdlets, your only option is removing and adding the host back again using the `Remove-VMHost` and `Add-VMHost` cmdlets. There's a drawback to this approach. Removing an ESX host will remove all of the host's configuration, including resource pools, VM folders, and the like. This is something you definitely don't want to happen in a production environment or during a restore operation.

The good news is that there is one other option. It relies on the vSphere API objects that are retrieved using the `Get-View` cmdlet:

```
$vmHostView = Get-View -ViewType HostSystem `
    -Filter @{"Name" = "esx01"}
```

The `VMware.Vim.HostSystem` object contains a `ReconnectHost_Task()` method. If you view the method's definition, you will see that the `ReconnectHost_Task()` method accepts a `VMware.Vim.HostConnectSpec` object as input. This object lets you specify the username and password to authenticate the ESX host, as shown next:

```
$objHostConnectSpec = New-Object VMware.Vim.HostConnectSpec
$objHostConnectSpec.userName = $user
$objHostConnectSpec.password = $password
```

To reconnect the ESX host, you just need to call the `ReconnectHost_Task()` method using the `$objHostConnectSpec` variable you just defined:

```
$vmHostView.ReconnectHost_Task($objHostConnectSpec)
```

To assist you in reconnecting an ESX host, you can use the `Connect-VMHost` function we created in Listing 11.5. This function accepts a `VMHost` object from the pipeline or through the `-VMHost` parameter. Because each ESX host needs to be reauthenticated, you need to specify the `-User` and `-Password` parameters. The optional `-Reconnect` switch forces an ESX host to disconnect first, which is ideal for testing purposes.

LISTING 11.5 Reconnecting ESX hosts

```
function Connect-VMHost {
<#
.SYNOPSIS
  Connect a disconnected ESX host
.DESCRIPTION
  This function (re)connects a disconnected ESX host.
```

```
  .NOTES
    Source:  Automating vSphere Administration
    Authors: Luc Dekens, Arnim van Lieshout, Jonathan Medd,
             Alan Renouf, Glenn Sizemore
  .PARAMETER vmHost
    The VMHost object to connect
  .PARAMETER credential
    A PSCredential object used to authenticate the VMHost server
  .PARAMETER user
    The user account used to authenticate the VMHost server
  .PARAMETER password
    The password for the account specified by the -User parameter
  .PARAMETER reconnect
    An optional switch parameter to force a disconnect first
  .EXAMPLE
    PS> Connect-VMHost -VMHost MyESX -User root -Password password
  .EXAMPLE
    PS> Get-VMHost myESX | Connect-VMHost -User root -Password `
        password -Reconnect
  .EXAMPLE
    PS> Get-VMHost myESX | Connect-VMHost `
        -Credential (Get-Credential)
  #>

  Param (
    [Parameter(ValueFromPipeline = $true, Position = 0,
    Mandatory = $true,
    HelpMessage = "Enter an ESX(i) host entity")]
      [VMware.VimAutomation.ViCore.Impl.V1.Inventory.➥
VMHostImpl]$vmHost,
    [Parameter(Mandatory = $true, ParameterSetName = "cred",
    HelpMessage = "Enter a PSCredential object")]
      [System.Management.Automation.PSCredential]$credential,
    [Parameter(ParameterSetName = "user")]
    [ValidateNotNullOrEmpty()]
      [string]$user = "root",
    [Parameter(Mandatory = $true, ParameterSetName = "user",
    HelpMessage = "Enter the root account password")]
      [string]$password,
```

```
        [switch]$reconnect)


    Process {
      if($vmHost) {
        $vmHostView = $vmHost | Get-View
      }
      else {
        $vmHostView = $_ | Get-View
      }


# Create a new HostConnectSpec object
      $objHostConnectSpec = New-Object VMware.Vim.HostConnectSpec
      if ($credential) {
        $objHostConnectSpec.userName =
          $credential.GetNetworkCredential().UserName
        $objHostConnectSpec.password =
          $credential.GetNetworkCredential().Password
      }
      else {
        $objHostConnectSpec.userName = $user
        $objHostConnectSpec.password = $password
      }


# if Reconnect switch is specified disconnect host first
      if ($reconnect) {
        Write-Host "Disconnecting $($vmHost.Name) " -NoNewline
        $taskMoRef = $vmHostView.DisconnectHost_Task()
        $task = Get-View $taskMoRef
        while ("running","queued" -contains $task.Info.State){
          Write-Host "." -NoNewline
          Sleep 2
          $task.UpdateViewData("Info.State")
        }
        Write-Host "Done"
        $task.UpdateViewData("Info.Result")
        $task.Info.State
      }
```

Securing Your vSphere Environment

PART III

```
# Connect host
    Write-Host "Connecting $($vmHost.Name) " -NoNewline
    $taskMoRef = `
        $vmHostView.ReconnectHost_Task($objHostConnectSpec)
    $task = Get-View $taskMoRef
    while ("running","queued" -contains $task.Info.State){
      Write-Host "." -NoNewline
      Sleep 2
      $task.UpdateViewData("Info.State")
    }
    Write-Host "Done"
    $task.UpdateViewData("Info.Result")
    $task.Info.State
  }
}
```

Export vCenter Server Inventory Items

An alternate approach to backing up your complete vCenter Server database is exporting the specific database objects that are of importance in your environment. Using this approach, you can restore your inventory (or maybe just a part of your inventory) to a separate database for testing purposes or create a disaster recovery (DR) replica of your inventory on another vCenter Server. Using this approach, you can even restore your vCenter Server environment to a vCenter Server that is using a different database platform for the backend database.

We once encountered an environment where, due to a database move, the SQL agent rollup jobs weren't available. The person moving the database was unaware of the existence of any SQL agent rollup jobs. As a result, the real-time performance statistics weren't consolidated. By the time someone noticed that there was something wrong with the performance charts, the database had grown very, very large. Performance was degrading, and statistics were being deleted from the database. Using a SQL script provided by VMware would have required vCenter Server to be offline for a number of days. Restoring the database from backup was not an option either, since it was a very dynamic environment. The backup was several weeks out-of-date. A restore would result in the loss of many, many changes.

In the end, we used the functions discussed next to re-create the database overnight at the cost of losing all the performance data. But, since the performance statistics were corrupted, we were more than willing to pay that price. It beat having the vCenter Server down for several days. After the rebuild process was done, these functions were still being used to replicate some parts (like roles, permissions, and folders) to a DR environment on a regular basis.

Although this sounds great, the structure of the vCenter Server inventory is complex and contains many different object types and configuration items that are linked to each other one way or the other. To show you how to export all possible objects in your inventory would make this chapter probably 100 pages or more, so we'll stick to the most common objects to give you an idea of the possibilities.

Folders

Let's start at the top of the inventory, the root folder, and retrieve the complete folder structure of your environment. The folder structure is the logical layout of your environment, and because folders function as containers for other objects, they are an essential part of your environment. The root folder object is the only object that's always present in your inventory. You can retrieve all the folders in your inventory using the `Get-Folder` cmdlet. To retrieve the root folder only, use the `-NoRecursion` parameter.

```
[vSphere PowerCLI] C:\Scripts> Get-Folder -NoRecursion


Name                            Id
----                            --
Datacenters                     Folder-group-d1
```

As you can see, the root folder is always called `Datacenters`. This is because at this level the only objects you can create (other than subfolders) are datacenter objects. To retrieve the subfolders, you use the root folder object and pass it along the pipeline to the `Get-folder` cmdlet again:

```
[vSphere PowerCLI] C:\Scripts> Get-Folder -NoRecursion | `
Get-Folder -NoRecursion


Name                            Id
----                            --
EMEA                            Folder-group-d2058
US                              Folder-group-d2059
```

You can continue this recursive process for every child folder over and over again to retrieve the full folder structure. This is illustrated in the `Get-FolderStructure` function we created in Listing 11.6.

LISTING 11.6 Retrieving the folder structure

```
function Get-FolderStructure {
<#
.SYNOPSIS
  Retrieve folder structure
.DESCRIPTION
  This function retrieves the folder structure beneath
  the given container
.NOTES
  Source:  Automating vSphere Administration
  Authors: Luc Dekens, Arnim van Lieshout, Jonathan Medd,
           Alan Renouf, Glenn Sizemore
.EXAMPLE
  PS> Get-Datacenter DC01 | Get-FolderStructure
#>

  process {
    $folder = "" | select Name,Children
    $folder.Name = $_.Name
    $folder.Children = @($_ | Get-Folder -NoRecursion | `
      Get-FolderStructure)
    $folder
  }
}
```

You only need to feed this function a folder- or datacenter object, and it will return the full folder structure beneath it. Let's try this and store the root folder's structure in a hash table called $folderStructure:

```
$folderStructure=@{}
Get-Folder -NoRecursion | Get-FolderStructure | `
%{$folderStructure[$_.name] = $_.Children}
```

Because you supplied the root folder as an input object, you only retrieved the datacenter folders, but not the folders beneath the datacenters. Now, use the same function to retrieve the folder structure beneath each datacenter in your inventory. To retrieve the datacenters, use the Get-Datacenter cmdlet. First, have a look at the root folders directly beneath the datacenter:

```
[vSphere PowerCLI] C:\Scripts> Get-Datacenter DC01 | `
    Get-Folder -NoRecursion
```

```
Name                      Id
----                      --
vm                        Folder-group-v2081
host                      Folder-group-h2082
datastore                 Folder-group-s2083
```

Notice that the three folders returned aren't visible in your inventory. These are special root folders, just like the datacenter root folder. Virtual machines go in the vm root folder. Subfolders are represented as blue folders inside your inventory. The host folder contains your clusters and hosts and its subfolders are represented as yellow folders inside your inventory. The datastore folder is for datastores.

Now, let's use the Get-FolderStructure function again to retrieve the folder structure beneath the datacenter and store it in the $folderStructure hash table:

```
Get-Datacenter | Get-FolderStructure | %{
  $folderStructure[$_.name] = $_.Children
}
```

All folder structures are now captured into the $folderStructure hash table. You now only need to export this hash table to a file. The most appropriate format for storing objects is XML. Therefore, use the Export-Clixml cmdlet to export the $folderStructure object to an XML file:

```
$folderStructure | Export-Clixml C:\Export\Folders.xml
```

Datacenters

The datacenter is a container in your inventory, just like a folder. It can contain folders, clusters, and hosts. Although in most cases there will be only one or two datacenter objects in the inventory and re-creating them by hand is quick and painless, using a PowerCLI script to export them enables you to automate the complete rebuild process without user intervention. To retrieve the datacenters, use the Get-Datacenter cmdlet again:

```
[vSphere PowerCLI] C:\Scripts> Get-Datacenter

Name                              Id
----                              --
DC01                              Datacenter-datacenter-2080
DC02                              Datacenter-datacenter-2
```

Securing Your vSphere Environment

PART III

Like datacenters, all inventory objects have a specific location in your inventory. When you want to re-create any object later, you can specify the object's inventory location using the –Location parameter. To retrieve the object's full path you can use something similar to the Get-FolderStructure function in Listing 11.6, except that you need to work your way up to the root folder this time. In Listing 11.7 you'll find a function to retrieve the path called Get-VIPath.

LISTING 11.7 Retrieving the object path

```
function Get-VIPath {
<#
.SYNOPSIS
  Retrieve the full path of an inventory object
.DESCRIPTION
  This function retrieves the full path of the given
  inventory object
.NOTES
  Source:  Automating vSphere Administration
  Authors: Luc Dekens, Arnim van Lieshout, Jonathan Medd,
           Alan Renouf, Glenn Sizemore
.PARAMETER inputObject
  The inventory object to retrieve the full path from
.PARAMETER childPath
  Optional parameter used by the function when calling itself
  recursively
.EXAMPLE
  PS> Get-Datacenter DC01 | Get-VIPath
#>

  param (
    [parameter(valuefrompipeline = $true, mandatory = $true,
    HelpMessage = "Enter an inventory object entity")]
      $inputObject,
    [parameter(mandatory = $false,
    HelpMessage = "Enter a path object")] $childPath)

  process {
    if($inputObject.parent) {
      $parent = Get-View $inputObject.parent
      if ($parent.gettype().name -eq "Datacenter") {
        $childPath
```

```
    } else {
      $path = "" | select Name,Child
      $path.Name = $parent.Name
      $path.Child = $childPath
      $parent | Get-VIPath -Child $path
    }
  }
  else {
    $childPath
  }
 }
}
```

You can use the Get-VIPath function to retrieve the datacenter's path and add a VIPath property to the datacenter object using the Add-Member cmdlet. Let's put this in a small ForEach loop and store the datacenters in an array. When all is processed, simply export the array using the Export-Clixml cmdlet.

```
$datacenters = @()
ForEach ($dc in Get-Datacenter) {
  $dc | Add-Member -MemberType Noteproperty -Name VIPath `
      -Value ($dc | Get-View | Get-VIPath)
  $datacenters += $dc
}
$datacenters | Export-Clixml "C:\Export\Datacenters.xml"
```

Clusters

Clusters function as a pool of resources and are the home location of your ESX hosts, which in turn provide the resources to the clusters' root resource pool. If you need to re-add your ESX hosts in your environment, you need to have the clusters in place. Exporting them makes for an easy, fully automated restore. Clusters are retrieved using the Get-Cluster cmdlet.

```
[vSphere PowerCLI] C:\Scripts> Get-Cluster
```

Name	HAEnabled	HAFailover Level	DrsEnabled	DrsAutomationLevel
CL01	True	1	False	FullyAutomated
CL02	True	1	True	FullyAutomated
CL03	False	1	False	FullyAutomated

In addition to all the cluster properties, you'll need to know to which datacenter the cluster belongs so that you can re-create the cluster in the right datacenter. To accomplish this, iterate through the datacenters first and then retrieve the clusters. The datacenter can then be added to the cluster object as a new property using the `Add-Member` cmdlet. You can also use the `Get-VIPath` function from Listing 11.7 again to retrieve the cluster's path.

```
$clusters = @()
ForEach ($dc in Get-Datacenter) {
  ForEach ($cluster in ($dc | Get-Cluster)) {
    $cluster | Add-Member -MemberType Noteproperty `
        -Name Datacenter -Value $dc.name
    $cluster | Add-Member -MemberType Noteproperty `
        -Name VIPath -Value ($cluster | Get-View | Get-VIPath)
    $clusters += $cluster
  }
}
$clusters | Export-Clixml "C:\Export\Clusters.xml"
```

Roles

Roles are a collection of privileges and provide a way to aggregate all the individual privileges required to perform a specific task in your infrastructure. When assigning permissions, you assign a role to a specific user or group. If you've created custom roles, you probably don't want to re-create them by hand in case of disaster. Exporting them also makes it possible to import these custom roles into another vCenter installation. You could, for example, create and test new custom roles in a test environment and when you're done, export them to a file and import them in the production environment. Roles are retrieved using the `Get-VIRole` cmdlet.

```
[vSphere PowerCLI] C:\Scripts> Get-VIRole
```

Name	IsSystem
NoAccess	True
Anonymous	True
View	True
ReadOnly	True
Admin	True
VirtualMachineAdminist...	False
DatacenterAdministrator	False

```
VirtualMachinePowerUser    False
VirtualMachineUser         False
...
```

Because you don't want to export the default system roles, you'll need to filter these out before exporting them to a file:

```
Get-VIRole | Where-Object {-not $_.IsSystem} | `
    Export-Clixml "C:\Export\Roles.xml"
```

Permissions

After defining roles, the next step in setting up your security is assigning permissions to users and groups. In case of disaster, it's always nice to be able to restore permissions to a recent state. You can quickly restore access to the vCenter Server without making everyone an administrator (temporarily) until you sort out the permissions. To retrieve permissions, you can use the `Get-VIPermission` cmdlet:

```
[vSphere PowerCLI] C:\Scripts> Get-VIPermission

EntityId          Role      Principal         IsGroup Propagate
--------          ----      ---------         ------- ---------
Folder-group-d1   ReadOnly  VIReport          False   True
Folder-group-d1   Admin     Administrators    True    True
```

Because you can put permissions on a lot of different object types, you'll want to know what object type the permission is granted to. Therefore, you'll need to retrieve the SDK object using the `EntityId` property and use the `GetType()` method to retrieve the object type:

```
(Get-View $permission.EntityID).GetType().Name
```

You can simply add the object type to the permission object using the `Add-Member` cmdlet:

```
$permissions=@()
ForEach ($permission in Get-VIPermission) {
  $permission | Add-Member -MemberType Noteproperty `
      -Name EntityType `
      -Value (Get-View $permission.EntityID).gettype().Name
  $permissions += $permission
}
$permissions | Export-Clixml "C:\Export\Permissions.xml"
```

VM Locations

Just like datacenters and clusters, your virtual machines have a specific location. This is represented in your infrastructure by the blue folders. The blue folders are perfect candidates for assigning permissions, so be sure to export every VM's locations. If you don't, users might not be able to access the VMs if they're not restored to the correct location. To export each VM's location, use the `Get-VIPath` function from Listing 11.7. In addition to the location, you must know which datacenter the VM belongs to. Use the `Add-Member` cmdlet to add both properties to the VM object you're retrieving using the `Get-VM` cmdlet. When all VM objects are retrieved, you can then simply export them to an XML file.

```
$vmLocations = @()
foreach ($vm in Get-VM) {
   $vm | Add-Member -MemberType Noteproperty -Name Datacenter `
       -Value $($vm | Get-Datacenter).Name
   $vm | Add-Member -MemberType Noteproperty -Name VIPath `
       -Value ($vm | Get-View | Get-VIPath)
   $vmLocations += $vm
}
$vmLocations | Export-Clixml "C:\Export\VMLocations.xml"
```

Hosts

The hosts in your inventory can be either part of a cluster or a stand-alone hosts. You want to make sure that you can import the hosts to their original locations. Failing to do so might put the host's resources in the wrong cluster and might impact the resources available to your VMs. If you have a stand-alone host, you are interested in the location of that host in your inventory. Here again the `Get-VIPath` function from Listing 11.7 can be helpful. If the host is part of a cluster you'll only need to know the cluster name.

```
$vmHosts = @()
foreach ($vmHost in Get-VMHost) {
   $vmHost | Add-Member -MemberType Noteproperty -Name `
       Datacenter -Value $(Get-Datacenter -VMHost $vmHost).Name
   $vmHost | Add-Member -MemberType Noteproperty -Name Cluster `
       -Value $($vmHost | Get-Cluster).Name
   if (-not $vmHost.Cluster) {
     $vmHost | Add-Member -MemberType Noteproperty -Name VIPath `
```

```
            -Value ($vmHost | Get-View | Get-VIPath)
    }
    $vmHosts += $vmHost
  }
  $vmHosts | Export-Clixml "C:\Export\VMHosts.xml"
```

Import vCenter Server Inventory Items

In the previous section, you learned how you can export inventory items to an XML file. In this section you'll learn how you can use these files to rebuild your inventory. Let's start with an empty inventory. As you'll recall from the "Export vCenter Server Inventory Items" section, an empty inventory only contains the root folder named Datacenters.

Folders and Datacenters

The first items you need to restore are your folders and datacenters beneath the root folder. Three steps are involved in the restore process:

1. Import the datacenter folders.

2. Import the datacenter objects.

3. Import the VM and host folders.

To import the XML files, use the Import-Clixml cmdlet:

```
$folderStructure = Import-Clixml "C:\Export\Folders.xml"
```

If you followed the process we outlined in the last section, you exported the folders using nested objects, so you'll need a special helper filter to re-create the folders recursively. (A filter is nothing more than a function with only a process script block.) The filter first checks if the folder exists. If the folder doesn't exist, it creates that folder and passes the child property to the filter recursively. Folders are created using the New-Folder cmdlet, as shown in Listing 11.8.

LISTING 11.8 Creating a folder structure

```
filter New-FolderStructure {
  param($parent)
  if (-not($folder = Get-Folder $_.name -Location $parent `
      -ErrorAction:SilentlyContinue)) {
```

```
      $folder = New-Folder $_.name -Location $parent
    }
    $_.children | New-FolderStructure($folder)
}
```

Datacenter Folders

Let's start by creating the datacenter folders. Because the $folderStructure variable is a hash table, you can simply retrieve the datacenter folders item using its name, Datacenters:

```
[vSphere PowerCLI] C:\Scripts> $folderStructure["Datacenters"]
```

```
Name                              Children
----                              --------
EMEA                              {@{Name=BE; Children=…
US                                {}
```

Now just use the pipeline to pass the objects to the New-FolderStructure filter and pass the root folder as the parent object:

```
$folderStructure["Datacenters"] | `
    New-FolderStructure(Get-Folder -NoRecursion)
```

Datacenter Objects

With the datacenter folders in place, you can now create the datacenters. Because the datacenter is the root of the vm and host folders, you'll have to create the datacenters before you can continue creating folders. Datacenters are created using the New-Datacenter cmdlet.

Again you'll need a special helper filter, Get-VILocation (Listing 11.9), to retrieve the location of the datacenters that you've exported using the Get-VIPath function to the VIPath property in the export section.

LISTING 11.9 Retrieving locations

```
filter Get-VILocation {
  param($parent)
  if ($_.child) {
    $_.child | Get-VILocation(Get-Folder -Location $parent `
        $_.Name)
  } else {
```

```
    Get-Folder -Location $parent $_.Name
  }
}
```

The `Get-VILocation` filter retrieves the parent folder (location) of the object using the nested objects stored in the `VIPath` property. You need to use this filter in the `-Location` parameter of the `New-Datacenter` cmdlet:

```
ForEach ($dc in Import-Clixml "C:\Export\Datacenters.xml") {
  New-Datacenter -Location ($dc.VIPath | Get-VILocation) `
    -Name $dc.Name
  }
```

VM and Host Folders

Creating the vm and host folders is similar to creating the datacenter folders, except that you need to provide the datacenter object as the parent object. Use the `GetEnumerator()` method to put all the hash table items on the pipeline. This, however, will also put the datacenter folders on the pipeline and you already imported them, so you need to filter them out:

```
$folderStructure.GetEnumerator() | %{
  If ($_.Name -ne "Datacenters") {
    $_.Value | New-FolderStructure(Get-Datacenter $_.Name)
  }
}
```

Clusters

You create clusters by using the `New-Cluster` cmdlet. Because this cmdlet only accepts DRS parameters when the `-DrsEnabled` parameter is set to true, you'll need to make this a multistep action in case one of your clusters has DRS (temporarily) disabled. First, you'll need to create the clusters and set the `-DrsEnabled` parameter to `$true`. After the cluster is created, you'll use the `Set-Cluster` cmdlet to set DRS and HA according to the exported settings. The `Set-Cluster` cmdlet is used to change cluster settings.

```
ForEach ($cluster in Import-Clixml "C:\Export\Clusters.xml") {
  $newCluster = New-Cluster -Location ($cluster.VIPath | `
    Get-VILocation(Get-Datacenter $cluster.Datacenter)) `
    -Name $cluster.Name
  Set-Cluster -Cluster $newCluster -DrsEnabled:$True `
```

Securing Your vSphere Environment

PART III

```
            -VMSwapfilePolicy $cluster.VMSwapfilePolicy `
            -DrsAutomationLevel $cluster.DrsAutomationLevel `
            -DrsMode $cluster.DrsMode `
            -HAAdmissionControlEnabled `
                $cluster.HAAdmissionControlEnabled `
            -HAFailoverLevel $cluster.HAFailoverLevel `
            -HAIsolationResponse $cluster.HAIsolationResponse `
            -HARestartPriority $cluster.HARestartPriority `
            -Confirm:$false
        Set-Cluster -Cluster $newCluster `
            -DrsEnabled $cluster.DrsEnabled `
            -HAEnabled $cluster.HAEnabled -Confirm:$false

    }
```

Hosts

Now that your clusters are created, you can add your hosts. Hosts can be added using the Add-VMHost cmdlet. To add a host, you must also provide a user account with sufficient permissions to logon to that specific host. Usually, this is the root account. You can specify the username and password as a string using the -User and -Password parameters, or you can ask for credentials at runtime using the Get-Credential cmdlet:

```
Get-Credential root
```

The drawback to using the Get-Credential cmdlet is that you can't specify the caption and a message in the log-in dialog box, shown in Figure 11.1.

FIGURE 11.1   Default Credential Request dialog box

As an alternative, you can use the PromptForCredential() method of the $host object, which lets you specify the window caption, message, and default username that appear in the message box. The method's syntax is `$Host.UI.PromptFor Credential($Caption,$Message,$UserName,$Domain)`. The `$Domain` parameter is not visible in the dialog box but will be prepended to the username in the credential object that's returned in the form of `"$Domain\$UserName"`. Figure 11.2 shows a custom credential dialog box.

```
$hostCredential = $Host.UI.PromptForCredential( `
    "Please enter host credentials", `
    "Enter ESX host credentials", "root", "")
```

FIGURE 11.2   Custom credential dialog box

If the host isn't part of a cluster, the host's location can be retrieved using the `Get-VILocation` filter from Listing 11.9:

```
ForEach ($vmhost in Import-Clixml "C:\Export\VMHosts.xml") {
  if ($vmhost.Cluster) {
    Add-VMHost $vmhost.Name `
        -Location (Get-Cluster $vmhost.Cluster `
        -Location (Get-Datacenter $vmhost.Datacenter)) `
        -Credential $hostCredential -Force
  }
  else {
    Add-VMHost $vmhost.Name -Location ($vmhost.VIPath | `
        Get-VILocation(Get-Datacenter $vmhost.Datacenter)) `
        -Credential $hostCredential -Force
  }
}
```

VM Locations

If the VMs are still registered on your ESX hosts, adding the hosts also imported the registered VMs. The VMs are all imported into the default `Discovered virtual machine` folder, and luckily you've exported each VM's location. To move a VM to a folder, you'll have to use the `Move-VM` cmdlet. You can easily retrieve the original location using the `Get-VILocation` function from Listing 11.9 again:

```
ForEach ($vm in Import-Clixml "C:\Export\VMLocations.xml") {
   $dc = Get-Datacenter $vm.Datacenter
   Move-VM ($dc | Get-VM $vm.Name) -Destination ($vm.VIPath | `
      Get-VILocation($dc))
}
```

Roles

New roles are created using the `New-VIRole` cmdlet. Before restoring your roles, you should remove all existing roles, including the default sample roles that came with your vCenter Server installation. Otherwise, you'll receive errors when trying to import a role that already exists. System roles can't be deleted, so filter them out first:

```
Get-VIRole | Where-Object {-not $_.IsSystem} | `
   Remove-VIRole -Confirm:$false
```

When restoring a role, you'll need to specify which privileges are attached to the role. These privileges have to be specified as privilege objects. When exporting roles, however, the privileges are returned as strings. So before adding privileges to the new role, you'll need to find a way to convert the string values to privilege objects. This can be achieved by retrieving all privileges first using the `Get-VIPrivilege` cmdlet and then matching the privilege IDs against the `privilegelist` property of the role you want to import. Let's import the roles:

```
ForEach ($role in Import-Clixml "C:\Export\Roles.xml") {
   $privileges = Get-VIPrivilege -PrivilegeItem
   New-VIRole -Name $role.Name -Privilege ($privileges | `
      ? {$role.PrivilegeList -contains $_.id})
}
```

Permissions

Now that the roles are in place, you can start to restore the permissions throughout your inventory. New permissions can be assigned using the `New-VIPermission` cmdlet. Because you can assign permissions to all kinds of objects in your inventory, you'll first need to determine what object type you want to restore permissions to in order to use the right cmdlet to retrieve that object. If the object is a folder, you'll need to use the `Get-Folder` cmdlet. If the object is a datacenter, you'll need to use the `Get-Datacenter` cmdlet, and so forth.

However, this can be more easily achieved using the `Get-View` cmdlet and making use of the full SDK objects, because this cmdlet allows you to specify the entity type and hence can be used to retrieve all kinds of objects. When using the `Get-View` cmdlet, you must specify a filter to indicate the objects you want to return. For example, to retrieve a VM called VM001, you would use the following:

```
Get-View -ViewType "VirtualMachine" -Filter @{"Name" = "VM001"}
```

One important thing to know is that `Get-View` filters are regular expressions. Regular expressions can contain metacharacters that serve special uses. Because these characters can also be part of the object's name, you'll have to escape them using the \ character. We've created a small helper function for this in Listing 11.10.

LISTING 11.10   Escaping regular expression metacharacters

```
filter Escape-MetaCharacters {
  ForEach($MetaChar in '^','$','{','}','[',']','(',')','.', `
     '*','+','?','|','<','>','-','&') `
     {$_=$_.replace($MetaChar,"\$($Metachar)")}
  }
  $_
}
```

To assign permissions using the SDK, use the `AuthorizationManager` and its `SetEntityPermissions()` method. This method accepts a `ManagedObjectReference` to an inventory object and a `VMware.Vim .Permission` object:

```
ForEach ($permission in Import-Clixml `
    "C:\Export\Permissions.xml") {
  $entityView = Get-View -ViewType $permission.EntityType `
     -Filter @{"Name" = $($permission.Entity.Name | `
     Escape-MetaCharacters)}
  $newVIPermission = New-Object VMware.Vim.Permission
  $newVIPermission.principal = $permission.Principal
  $newVIPermission.group = $permission.IsGroup
  $newVIPermission.propagate = $permission.Propagate
  $newVIPermission.roleId = $(Get-VIRole $permission.Role).id
  $authMgr = Get-View AuthorizationManager
  $authMgr.SetEntityPermissions($entityView.MoRef, `
     $newVIPermission)
}
```

Recover Virtual Machines

If you've lost your ESX host and have to reinstall or restore it, you've also lost all VM registrations. So, you'll need to register your VMs first before you can restore your VMs to their original location. To register a VM, you'll need the exact path of its VMX file. You could browse your datastores using the vSphere Client and register every VMX file found one at a time, or you can use PowerCLI to do this daunting task for you.

Browsing the datastores from the PowerCLI console is very easy, because PowerCLI includes a datastore provider. To view all installed providers, use the Get-PSProvider cmdlet, and to view all mapped drives, use the Get-PSDrive cmdlet.

```
[vSphere PowerCLI] C:\Scripts> Get-PSDrive


Name        Used (GB)     Free (GB) Provider       Root
----        ---------     --------- --------       ----
A                                   FileSystem     A:\
Alias                               Alias
C           10,89         1,09      FileSystem     C:\
...
vi                                  VimInventory   \LastConnected
                                                   VCenterServer
vis                                 VimInventory   \
vmstore                             VimDatastore   \LastConnected
                                                   VCenterServer
vmstores                            VimDatastore   \
...
```

Notice the vmstore drive. You can use this drive to browse the datastores just like you'd browse your local hard drive. So, just use the Get-ChildItem cmdlet, its alias dir, or even ls if you prefer the Unix style:

```
[vSphere PowerCLI] C:\Scripts> dir vmstore:


Name                        Type                    Id
----                        ----                    --
DC01                        Datacenter              Datacenter-d...


[vSphere PowerCLI] C:\Scripts> Get-ChildItem vmstore:DC01
```

Name	FreeSpaceMB	CapacityMB
----	-----------	----------
ESXTST01_Local_01	419497	476672
ESX02_Local_Datastore	143127	151296
VSAPROD1_NotReplicated	65626	99840

To find all VMX files, you just have to provide the -Include *.vmx and -Recurse parameters. To register the found VMX files, you'll use the New-VM cmdlet.

```
Get-ChildItem vmstore: -include *.vmx -recurse | %{
   New-VM -VMHost (Get-Datastore $_.Datastore | Get-VMHost | `
      Get-Random) -VMFilePath $_.DatastoreFullPath
}
```

To assist in the registration process, you can use the Register-VMX function, which is shown in Listing 11.11. This function provides much more flexibility as you can search for one or more datastores, a host, a cluster, or a datacenter. Also, it speeds things up by using SDK objects instead of the datastore provider, which is more than welcome in a larger environment.

LISTING 11.11   Searching datastores for VMX files

```
function Register-VMX {
<#
.SYNOPSIS
  Find and register virtual machines
.DESCRIPTION
  This function searches datastores for vmx or vmtx files and
  then registers the virtual machines. You can search on one or
  more datastores, a host, a cluster or a datacenter
.NOTES
  Source:  Automating vSphere Administration
  Authors: Luc Dekens, Arnim van Lieshout, Jonathan Medd,
           Alan Renouf, Glenn Sizemore
.PARAMETER entityNames
  An array of entity names. Only clusters, datacenters or
  ESX hosts are allowed.
  Wildcards are supported. (mutually exclusive with -dsNames)
.PARAMETER dsNames
  An array of datastore names. Wildcards are supported.
  (mutually exclusive with -entityNames)
```

```
.PARAMETER ignore
  An array of folder names that shouldn't be checked.
  No wildcards allowed!
.PARAMETER template
  when set, the function searches for templates (.vmtx)
  otherwise it will search for guests (.vmx)
.PARAMETER checkNFS
  When set, the NFS datastores are included in the search
.PARAMETER whatif
  When set, the function will only list output to the console
  and not register the found vmx files
.EXAMPLE
  PS> Register-VMX -entityName "MyDatacenter"
.EXAMPLE
  PS> Register-VMX -dsNames "datastore1","datastore2" `
        -template:$true
.EXAMPLE
  PS> Register-VMX -dsNames "datastore3" -ignore "SomeFolder" `
         -checkNFS:$true
.EXAMPLE
  PS> Register-VMX -entityName "MyCluster" -whatif:$true
#>
  param(
     [Parameter(Mandatory = $true,
     ParameterSetName = "entityNames",
     HelpMessage = "Enter cluster, datacenter or ESX host name")]
       [string[]]$entityNames,
     [Parameter(Mandatory = $true, ParameterSetName = "dsNames",
     HelpMessage = "Enter one or more datastore names")]
       [String[]]$dsNames,
     [switch]$template, [string[]]$ignore,
     [switch]$checkNFS, [switch]$whatif)

   if($dsNames) {
     $datastores = Get-Datastore -Name $dsNames | where {
       $_.Type -eq "VMFS" -or $checkNFS} | Select -Unique
   }
   else {
     $datastores=@()
     foreach($entity in Get-Inventory -Name $entityNames) {
```

```
switch(($entity | Get-View).GetType().Name){
    "ClusterComputeResource" {
        $datastores += Get-Cluster -Name $entity | `
            Get-VMHost | Get-Datastore | where {
            $_.Type -eq "VMFS" -or $checkNFS} | Select -Unique
    }
    "Datacenter" {
        $datastores += Get-Datacenter -Name $entity |
        Get-Datastore | where {
            $_.Type -eq "VMFS" -or $checkNFS} | Select -Unique
    }
    "HostSystem" {
        $datastores += Get-VMHost -Name $entity |
        Get-Datastore | where {
            $_.Type -eq "VMFS" -or $checkNFS} | Select -Unique
    }
    Default {
        Write-Host -foregroundcolor Red `
            "Invalid entity type [$_] specified!"
        Return
    }
    }
    }
}
if($template){
    $pattern = "*.vmtx"
}
else {
    $pattern = "*.vmx"
}
if ($datastores) {
    $datastores = $datastores | Select -Unique | Sort-Object `
        -Property Name
    foreach($datastore in $datastores){
        Write-Host "Checking " -NoNewline
        Write-Host -ForegroundColor red -BackgroundColor yellow `
            $datastore.Name
        $dsView = $datastore | Get-View
        $dsBrowser = Get-View $dsView.Browser
        $dc = Get-View $dsView.Parent
```

```
while($dc.MoRef.Type -ne "Datacenter"){
  $dc = Get-View $dc.Parent
}
$targetFolder = Get-View $dc.VmFolder
$esxHost = Get-View ($dsView.host | Get-Random).key
$pool = Get-View (Get-View $esxHost.Parent).ResourcePool

$registeredVMs = @()
foreach($vm in $dsView.Vm){
  $vmView = Get-View $vm
  $registeredVMs += $vmView.Config.Files.VmPathName
}
$datastorepath = "[" + $dsView.Name + "]"

$searchspec = `
    New-Object VMware.Vim.HostDatastoreBrowserSearchSpec
$searchspec.MatchPattern = $pattern

$taskMoRef = $dsBrowser.SearchDatastoreSubFolders_Task( `
  $datastorePath, $searchSpec)

$task = Get-View $taskMoRef
while ("running","queued" -contains $task.Info.State){
  $task.UpdateViewData("Info.State")
}
$task.UpdateViewData("Info.Result")
foreach ($folder in $task.Info.Result){
  if($folder.file -ne $null){
    if($folder.FolderPath[-1] -ne "/"){
      $folder.FolderPath += "/"
    }
    $vmx = $folder.FolderPath + $folder.File[0].Path
    $skip = $false
    if($ignore){
      $folder.FolderPath.Split("]")[1].Trim(" /"). `
          Split("/") | `
          %{$skip = $skip -or ($ignore -contains $_)}
    }
    if($skip) {
      Write-Host -ForegroundColor red "`t" $vmx "Ignored!"
```

```
          }
        else {
          $exists = $false
          foreach($registeredVM in $registeredVMs){
            if($vmx -eq $registeredVM){
              $exists = $true
            }
          }
          if ($exists){
            Write-Host -ForegroundColor red `
              "`t" $vmx "Skipped! Already registered"
          }
          else {
            if($template){
              $params = @($vmx,$null,$true,$null,
                $esxHost.MoRef)
            }
            else{
              $params = @($vmx,$null,$false,$pool.MoRef,$null)
            }
            if(!$whatif){
              $taskMoRef = $targetFolder.GetType().GetMethod(
                "RegisterVM_Task").Invoke(
                $targetFolder, $params)
              Write-Host -ForegroundColor green `
                "`t" $vmx "registered"
            }
            else{
              Write-Host -ForegroundColor green `
                "`t" $vmx "registered" -NoNewline
              Write-Host -ForegroundColor blue `
                -BackgroundColor white " ==> What If"
            }
          }
        }
      }
    }
  Write-Host "Done"
  }
 }
}
```

Securing Your vSphere Environment

PART III

Hardening the vSphere Environment

IN THIS CHAPTER, YOU WILL LEARN TO:

Hardening a system involves closing the potential security holes. Examples of security holes include unnecessary software and user accounts, unused services, unused network ports, and the mixing of management traffic with client traffic over a port group. Hardening a system improves the security of that system by diminishing the number of potential vectors of attack. Nowadays you can't risk running a nonsecure system, unless you run a completely isolated system or you simply don't care if the system becomes compromised. And don't forget that there are many legal requirements that oblige you to secure your systems.

If you would have to harden your vSphere environment from scratch, you would be facing a tremendous task. Luckily, VMware published a vSphere 4.0 Security Hardening Guide (`www.vmware.com/resources/techresources/10109`), that lists most, if not all, of the potential holes. The Hardening Guide not only lists the potential holes, but it also shows you what action you should take to close the hole.

Use the Hardening Guide

The vSphere 4.0 Security Hardening Guide consists of a considerable number of guidelines. The document uses a straightforward classification scheme. The guidelines are organized around five areas:

- ▶ Virtual Machines

- ▶ ESX(i) Hosts

- ▶ Virtual Networking or vNetwork

- ▶ vCenter Server

- ▶ Console Operating System (COS)

These areas are also reflected in the name of the guidelines. For example, a guideline for virtual machines that describes a configuration parameter has a code starting with VMX. A guideline that handles an aspect of hosts system logging is identified with a name that starts with HLG.

Each guideline has one or more of the three recommendation levels:

- ▶ Enterprise covers most enterprise production systems.

- ▶ Demilitarized Zone (DMZ) was originally intended for Internet-facing systems but is also used for systems that require above-Enterprise grade security.

- ▶ Specialized Security Limited Functionality (SSLF) is intended for specialized environments.

Higher recommendation levels typically include all recommendations from the levels below.

For each guideline, the document describes a method to remediate the potential threat. These methods can be one or more of the following items:

- ▶ Parameter settings (what to set or unset)

- ▶ Component configuration (installing and/or configuring components)

- ▶ Operational pattern (a way to operate or interact with the system)

It's obvious that it is not equally feasible to automate each of these types of remediation. An operational procedure, for example, will be harder to automate than a parameter setting.

Work with the Guidelines

Several of the Guidelines contain a specific parameter that needs to be set or unset to close the security hole. Other parts of the Guidelines contain operational advice. These won't be discussed in this chapter, but know that they exist and are equally important to follow. Guideline VMP01 is an example of operational advice; it tells you to run antivirus and antispyware in the OS that runs in the guests. Sound advice, but hard to automate. The next sections show examples of how you can automate the types of guidelines that contain explicit instructions on what to verify and configure.

Virtual Machines

The guidelines in this group most of the time refer to settings in the VMX file, the configuration file, of a virtual machine. Let's take the Guideline VMX01 as an example. (Table 12.1 provides details.) This guideline states, in the parameter setting section, that the `diskWiper` and `diskShrinker` options should be disabled.

To implement the guideline, you need the following entries in the VMX file of each virtual machine:

```
isolation.tools.diskWiper.disable=TRUE
isolation.tools.diskShrink.disable=TRUE
```

The script in Listing 12.1 changes the settings in the VMX file by using the `ReconfigVM` method to push the entries to the VMX file.

Securing Your vSphere Environment

PART III

TABLE 12.1   Guideline VMX01

Parameter element	Description
Code	VMX01
Name	Prevent virtual disk shrinking.
Description	Shrinking a virtual disk reclaims unused space in it. If there is empty space in the disk, this process reduces the amount of space the virtual disk occupies on the host drive. Normal users and processes—that is, users and processes without root or administrator privileges—within virtual machines have the capability to invoke this procedure. However, if this is done repeatedly, the virtual disk can become unavailable while this shrinking is being performed, effectively causing a denial of service. In most datacenter environments, disk shrinking is not done, so you should disable this feature by setting the parameters listed in the Parameter setting section of this guideline.
Threat	Repeated disk shrinking can make a virtual disk unavailable. Capability is available to nonadministrative users in the guest.
Recommendation level	Enterprise
Parameter setting	`isolation.tools.diskWiper.disable=TRUE` `isolation.tools.diskShrink.disable=TRUE`
Effect on functionality	

Source: VMware vSphere™ 4.0 Security Hardening Guide, copyright © 2011 VMware, Inc. All rights reserved. This product is protected by U.S. and international copyright and intellectual property laws. VMware products are covered by one or more patents listed at http://www.vmware.com/go/patents.

LISTING 12.1   Implementing Guideline VMX01

```
# Set up the VirtualMachineConfigSpec object
$vmConfigSpec = New-Object VMware.Vim.VirtualMachineConfigSpec
$option1 = New-Object VMware.Vim.optionvalue
$option1.Key = "isolation.tools.diskShrink.disable"
$option1.Value = "TRUE"
$vmConfigSpec.ExtraConfig += $option1

$option2 = New-Object VMware.Vim.optionvalue
$option2.Key = "isolation.tools.diskWiper.disable"
$option2.Value = "TRUE"
$vmConfigSpec.ExtraConfig += $option2

# Loop through all Virtual Machines
Get-VM | %{
  $_.Extensiondata.ReconfigVM($vmConfigSpec)
}
```

Notice that you need to restart the virtual machine to activate these new settings—a reboot of the guest OS is not sufficient!

Part of maintaining a hardened system is regularly checking the actual settings in the system. An ideal script would be one where you can combine the remediation and reporting steps in one script. The script in Listing 12.2 is one way of doing this. In that script, we used a hash table (also referred to as a dictionary or an associative array) to store all the entries we retrieve for a guest. This allows us to use the ContainsKey method on the hash table to check whether a specific key is present in the guest's VMX file.

LISTING 12.2   Reporting and Remediating Guideline VMX01

```
function Assert-VMX01{
  param(
  [parameter(valuefrompipeline = $true)]
  [ValidateNotNullOrEmpty()]
  [PSObject]$Entity,
  [switch]$Report = $true,
  [switch]$Remediate = $false
  )

  begin{
    $keys = "isolation.tools.diskShrink.disable",
            "isolation.tools.diskWiper.disable"
    $values = "TRUE",
              "TRUE"

    if($Remediate){
# Set up the VirtualMachineConfigSpec object
      $vmConfigSpec = `
        New-Object VMware.Vim.VirtualMachineConfigSpec

      0..($keys.Count - 1) | %{
        $option = New-Object VMware.Vim.optionvalue
        $option.Key = $keys[$_]
        $option.Value = $values[$_]
        $vmConfigSpec.ExtraConfig += $option
      }
    }
  }

  process{
```

Securing Your vSphere Environment

PART III

```
      if($Entity.GetType().Name -eq "String"){
        $object = Get-VM -Name $Entity
      }
      else{
        $object = $Entity
      }
      if($Remediate){
        $object.Extensiondata.ReconfigVM($vmConfigSpec)
      }
      if($Report){
        $vmxEntries = @{}
        $object.ExtensionData.Config.ExtraConfig | %{
          $vmxEntries[$_.Key] = $_.Value
        }
        $compliant = $true
        0..($keys.Count - 1) | %{
          $key = $keys[$_]
          if($vmxEntries.ContainsKey($key)){
            $compliant = $compliant -and `
              ($vmxEntries[$key] -eq $values[$_])
          }
          else{
            $compliant = $false
          }
        }
        New-Object PSObject -Property @{
          Name = $object.Name
          Compliant = $compliant
        }
      }
    }
  }
}
```

With this script you can now do your reporting like this:

```
PS C:\> Get-VM | Assert-VMX01 -Report | ft -AutoSize

Name Compliant
---- ---------
PC1       True
Srv1     False
```

And at the same time, you can use the script to remediate a selected number of guests:

```
PS C:\Scripts> Get-VM | Assert-VMX01 -Remediate
PS C:\Scripts> Get-VM | Assert-VMX01 -Report | ft -AutoSize

Name Compliant
---- ---------

PC1      True
Srv1     True
```

Besides these VMX entry-based guidelines, there are also some guidelines for virtual machines that do not involve adding or changing entries in the VMX file. A good example is Guideline VMX22. (Table 12.2 provides details.) This guideline states that for guests located in the DMZ, you should not use independent-nonpersistent disks.

TABLE 12.2   Guideline VMX22

Parameter element	Description
Code	VMX22
Name	Avoid using independent-nonpersistent disks.
Description	The security issue with nonpersistent disk mode is that successful attackers, with a simple shutdown or reboot, might undo or remove any traces that they were ever on the machine.
	To safeguard against this risk, you should set production virtual machines to use either persistent disk mode or nonpersistent disk mode; additionally, make sure that activity within the virtual machine is logged remotely on a separate server, such as a syslog server or equivalent Windows-based event collector.
Threat	Without a persistent record of activity on a virtual machine, administrators might never know whether they have been attacked or hacked.
Recommendation level	DMZ
Parameter setting	If remote logging of events and activity is not configured for the guest, scsiX:Y.mode should be either:
	a. Not present
	b. Not set to independent nonpersistent
Effect on functionality	Won't be able to make use of nonpersistent mode, which allows rollback to a known state when rebooting the virtual machine.

Securing Your vSphere Environment

PART III

There are two ways of checking for independent-nonpersistent disks. The first method is to look in the VMX files for entries with the format scsi*X:Y*, where *X* is the SCSI bus number and *Y* is the SCSI device ID. If there are entries like that, you should check that the entry doesn't say `independent-nonpersistent`.

The other method is to use the `VirtualDevice` objects that are present for a specific guest and examine the `DiskMode` property. The script in Listing 12.3 shows how to do that.

LISTING 12.3 Finding independent-nonpersistent vDisks for VMX022

```
foreach($vm in Get-VM){
  $vm.Extensiondata.Config.Hardware.Device | `
  where {$_.DeviceInfo.Label -like "Hard disk*"} | `
  Select @{N="VMname";E={$vm.Name}},
    @{N="HD";E={$_.DeviceInfo.Label}},
    @{N="Mode";E={$_.Backing.DiskMode}}
}
```

This small script produces output similar to this:

```
VMname      HD             Mode

------      --             ----

Srv1        Hard disk 1    persistent
Srv1        Hard disk 2    independent-persistent
Srv2        Hard disk 1    independent_nonpersistent
```

It shows that the virtual disk called Hard disk 1 on a guest called Srv2 represents a security risk according to Guideline VMX022. As a side note, Hard disk 2 on Srv1 is an RDM-based virtual disk. The guideline advises to change the disk mode from `independent-nonpersistent` to `independent-persistent`.

You could try to make the change through the scsi*X:Y* entry in the VMX file, but that will not work. The reason is documented in the VMware vSphere API Reference Documentation under the `extraConfig` property in the `VirtualMachineConfig Spec` object. It says there: "Configuration keys that would conflict with parameters that are explicitly configurable through other fields in the ConfigSpec object are silently ignored." Instead, use the `-Persistence` parameter on the `Set-Hard Disk` cmdlet. The script could look something like the one in Listing 12.4.

LISTING 12.4 Changing independent-nonpersistent vDisks for VMX022

```
$tgtMode = "IndependentPersistent"
```

```
foreach($vm in Get-VM){
  foreach($hd in (Get-HardDisk -VM $vm | `
    where{$_.Persistence -eq "IndependentNonPersistent"})){
    if(Get-Snapshot -VM $vm){
      Write-Host $vm.Name "has snapshot(s). Can't convert" `
        $hd.Name "to" $tgtMode
    }
    else{
      Set-HardDisk -HardDisk $hd -Persistence $tgtMode `
        -Confirm:$false
    }
  }
}
```

T I P   Notice that the script tests for the presence of one or more snapshots on the guest. The reason is that the mode change will not work if there is a snapshot present. Instead of removing the snapshot automatically, our script displays a message. It's up to the administrator to take further action.

ESX(i) Hosts

Now, the VMX file approach won't work for ESX(i) hosts; you don't have a VMX file. The configuration properties for a host are more complex than those of a virtual machine. But you can still automate all the guidelines except the operational advice.

Let's take as a first example Guideline HST01. (Table 12.3 provides the details.) This guideline discusses CHAP authentication for iSCSI traffic.

Note that iSCSI and CHAP were already discussed in broad terms in Chapter 2, "Automating vSphere Hypervisor Deployment and Configuration," and Chapter 3, "Automating Storage and Networking." To better understand CHAP authentication, you need to know that you can define CHAP authentication on three levels (see Figure 12.1):

> ▶ Per iSCSI host bus adapter (HBA)

> ▶ Per dynamic or send target (the Dynamic Discovery tab)

> ▶ Per static or discovered target (the Static Discovery tab)

The send targets and the static targets can inherit the CHAP settings from their parent HBA.

Securing Your vSphere Environment

PART III

TABLE 12.3   Guideline HST01

Parameter element	Description
Code	HST01
Name	Ensure bidirectional CHAP authentication is enabled for iSCSI traffic.
Description	vSphere allows for the use of bidirectional authentication of both the iSCSI target and host. Choosing not to enforce more stringent authentication can make sense if you create a dedicated network or VLAN to service all your iSCSI devices. If the iSCSI facility is isolated from general network traffic, it is less vulnerable to exploitation.
Threat	By not authenticating both the iSCSI target and host, there is a potential for a man-in-the-middle attack in which an attacker might impersonate either side of the connection to steal data. Bidirectional authentication can mitigate this risk.
Recommendation level	DMZ
Parameter setting	Configuration —> Storage Adapters —> iSCSI Initiator Properties —> CHAP —> CHAP (Target Authenticates Host) and Mutual CHAP (Host Authenticates Target), both set to Use CHAP and each with a Name and Secret configured.
Effect on functionality	

Source: VMware vSphere™ 4.0 Security Hardening Guide, copyright © 2011 VMware, Inc. All rights reserved. This product is protected by U.S. and international copyright and intellectual property laws. VMware products are covered by one or more patents listed at http://www.vmware.com/go/patents.

TIP   The scripts in the following sections that discuss iSCSI-related guidelines will not return anything if they can't find any iSCSI adapters on your server!

To check the configuration of the CHAP authentication on the HBAs, you can use something like the script in Listing 12.5.

LISTING 12.5   Checking HBA CHAP authentication for HST01

```
Get-VMHost | `
Get-VMHostHba -Type ISCSI | `
where {$_.AuthenticationProperties.ChapType -ne "Required"} | `
Select Device,
   @{N="CHAPType";E={$_.AuthenticationProperties.ChapType}}
```

FIGURE 12.1   CHAP settings inheritance

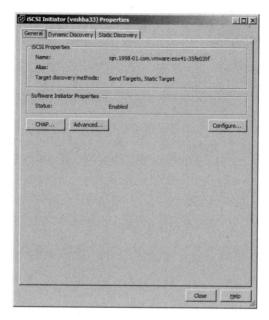

When you run the script in Listing 12.5, it will produce output that looks something like this:

```
Device              CHAPType

------              --------

vmhba33             Prohibited
```

In this example, you can see that CHAP is not configured.

Sometimes, you might find it necessary to configure different CHAP settings for different send targets. You can use the Get-IScsiHbaTarget cmdlet to check the CHAP settings for each send or static target, as we did in Listing 12.6.

LISTING 12.6   Checking target CHAP authentication for HST01

```
Get-VMHost | `
Get-VMHostHba -Type ISCSI | `
Get-IScsiHbaTarget | `
where {$_.AuthenticationProperties.ChapType -ne "Required"} | `
Select Name,Type,IScsiHbaName,
  @{N="CHAPType";E={$_.AuthenticationProperties.ChapType}}
```

The script in Listing 12.6 produced a listing like this:

```
Name                         Type IScsiHbaName
----                         ---- -----------
192.168.111.1:3260    Send iqn.1998-01.com.vmware:esx41-35fe03...

192.168.111.1:3260   Static iqn.1998-01.com.vmware:esx41-35fe03...
```

Unfortunately, as we worked with this automation, we found a few problems with the Get-IScsiHbaTarget cmdlet in the PowerCLI build we used for this book (VMware vSphere PowerCLI, version 4.1). To bypass these problems and as an example of how you can use the vSphere object properties from your scripts, we provide the Get-IScsiHbaTargets function in Listing 12.7, which emulates the Get-IScsiHbaTarget cmdlet. The function also shows you if the CHAP setting is enabled for each target and if it was inherited from the CHAP settings of the parent.

LISTING 12.7 Get-IScsiHbaTargets **function**

```
function Get-IScsiHbaTargets{
<#
.SYNOPSIS
  Returns the iScsi targets
.DESCRIPTION
  The function returns all the iScsi targets of the
  requested Type for one or more iScsi HBAs
.PARAMETER IScsiHba
  The iScsi HBA(s) for which you want to retrieve the
  targets
.PARAMETER Type
  The type of iScsi HBA targets you want to retrieve.
  The valid values are Send and Static
.NOTES
  Source:  Automating vSphere Administration
  Authors: Luc Dekens, Arnim van Lieshout, Jonathan Medd,
           Alan Renouf, Glenn Sizemore.PARAMETER SqlServer
.EXAMPLE
  PS> Get-IScsiHbaTargets -IScsiHba $hba -Type Static
.EXAMPLE
  PS> Get-VMHost MyESX | `
  >> Get-VMHostHba -Type IScsi | `
  >> Get-IScsiHbaTargets
```

```
#>

  param(
  [Parameter(Position=1,ValueFromPipeline=$true)]
  [VMware.VimAutomation.ViCore.Types.V1.Host.Storage.IScsiHba[]]
  ${IScsiHba},
  [ValidateNotNullOrEmpty()]
  [VMware.VimAutomation.ViCore.Types.V1.Host.Storage.~CA
    IScsiHbaTargetType[]]
  ${Type}
  )


  begin{}


  process{
    foreach($hba in $IScsiHba){
      if(!$Type -or $Type -contains "Send"){
        foreach($target in
  $hba.Extensiondata.ConfiguredSendTarget){
          $target | Select Address,Port,
          @{N="IScsiHbaKey";E={$hba.Key}},
          @{N="CHAPType";E={
        $temp =
$target.AuthenticationProperties.ChapAuthenticationType
      $temp.Replace("chap","Chap:")}},
          @{N="CHAPEnabled";E={
         $target.AuthenticationProperties.ChapAuthEnabled}},
          @{N="CHAPInherited";E={
        $target.AuthenticationProperties.ChapInherited}},
          @{N="mutualCHAPType";E={
        $temp =
$target.AuthenticationProperties.MutualChapAuthenticationType
      $temp.Replace("chap","Chap:")}},
          @{N="mutualCHAPInherited";E={
        $temp =
    $target.AuthenticationProperties.MutualChapInherited}},
          @{N="Type";E={"Send"}},
          @{N="Uid";E={$hba.Uid + "/IScsiHbaTarget=" + `
        $target.Address + ":" + $target.Port + ":Send/"}},
```

Securing Your vSphere Environment

PART III

```
                @{N="Name";E={$target.Address + ":" + $target.Port}},
                @{N="IScsiHbaName";E={$hba.IScsiName}}
              }
            }
          if(!$Type -or $Type -contains "Static"){
            foreach($static in
            $hba.Extensiondata.ConfiguredStaticTarget){
              $static | Select IScsiName,Address,Port,
              @{N="IScsiHbaKey";E={$hba.Key}},
              @{N="CHAPType";E={
          $temp =
        $static.AuthenticationProperties.ChapAuthenticationType
                $temp.Replace("chap","Chap:")}},
              @{N="CHAPEnabled";E={
            $static.AuthenticationProperties.ChapAuthEnabled}},
              @{N="CHAPInherited";E={
            $static.AuthenticationProperties.ChapInherited}},
                @{N="mutualCHAPType";E={
            $temp =
        $static.AuthenticationProperties.MutualChapAuthenticationType
            $temp.Replace("chap","Chap:")}},
                @{N="mutualCHAPInherited";E={
            $static.AuthenticationProperties.MutualChapInherited}},
                @{N="Type";E={"Static"}},
                @{N="Uid";E={$hba.Uid + "/IScsiHbaTarget=" + `
              $static.Address + ":" + $static.Port + ":Static/"}},
                @{N="Name";E={$static.Address + ":" + $static.Port}},
                @{N="IScsiHbaName";E={$hba.IScsiName}}
              }
            }
          }
        }
      }
```

With this function, you could produce output similar to the one the `Get-IScsiHba` `Target` cmdlet produces, but with the distinction that the script also displays the CHAP information for each target:

```
PS C:\ > Get-VMHost esx41.test.local | `
>> Get-VMHostHba -Type IScsi | `
```

```
>> Get-IScsiHbaTargets -Type Send
>>

Address              : 192.168.111.1
Port                 : 3260
IScsiHbaKey          : key-vim.host.InternetScsiHba-vmhba33
CHAPType             : Chap:Required
CHAPEnabled          : True
CHAPInherited        : True
mutualCHAPType       : Chap:Prohibited
mutualCHAPInherited  : True
Type                 : Send
Uid                  : /VIServer=@vsphere:443/VMHost=HostSys…
Name                 : 192.168.111.1:3260
IScsiHbaName         : iqn.1998-01.com.vmware:esx41-35fe039f
```

Based on this output, it is now easy to report all the targets that do not have CHAP configured. You could do, for example, something like this:

```
PS C:\ > Get-VMHost esx41.test.local | `
>> Get-VMHostHba -Type IScsi | `
>> Get-IScsiHbaTargets -Type Static
>> where {$_.CHAPType -ne "Chap:Required" -or `
>> $_.mutualCHAPType -ne "Chap:Required"} | `
>> Select IScsiName

IScsiName
---------
iqn.2008-08.com.starwindsoftware:walhalla.local.test-disk1
iqn.2008-08.com.starwindsoftware:walhalla.local.test-disk3
```

Once you know which HBAs or targets have missing CHAP settings, you can start the remediation process. The Set-VMHostHba cmdlet allows you to define the CHAP settings for an HBA and the Set-IScsiHbaTarget cmdlet allows you to define the CHAP settings for the send and/or static targets, as we did in Listing 12.8.

TIP A CHAP secret has to be between 12 and 16 characters long.

LISTING 12.8   Setting up HBA CHAP authentication for HST01

```
foreach($esx in Get-VMHost){
  $iHBA = Get-VMHostHba -VMHost $esx -Type ISCSI | `
  where {$_.AuthenticationProperties.ChapType -ne "Required"}

  if($iHBA){
    $iHBA | Set-VMHostHba `
      -ChapType "Required" -ChapName "targetname" `
        -ChapPassword "secret123456" `
      -MutualChapEnabled:$true -MutualChapName "mutualname" `
        -MutualChapPassword "secret654321"
    Get-VMHostStorage -VMHost $esx -RescanAllHba
  }
}
```

To set up CHAP on targets, you have to change the previous code snippet slightly and add the `Set-IScsiHbaTarget` cmdlet to the pipeline, as we've done in Listing 12.9.

LISTING 12.9   Setting up target CHAP authentication for HST01

```
foreach($esx in Get-VMHost){
  $iTgt = Get-VMHostHba -VMHost $esx -Type ISCSI | `
  Get-IScsiHbaTarget -Type Send | `
  where {$_.AuthenticationProperties.ChapType -ne "Required"}

  if($iTgt){
    $iTgt | Set-IScsiHbaTarget `
    -ChapType "Required" -ChapName "targetname" `
    -ChapPassword "secret123456" `
      -MutualChapEnabled:$true -MutualChapName "mutualname" `
    -MutualChapPassword "secret654321"
    Get-VMHostStorage -VMHost $esx -RescanAllHba
  }
}
```

Some of the ESX(i) guidelines are host specific—in other words, the guideline is only applicable to a specific type of host. As an example, we take Guideline HCM03, which advises you to disable Web Access for ESX hosts that are located in a DMZ. (See Table 12.4 for details.)

T I P   It is always advisable to run a rescan of all the HBAs after you make changes to the CHAP settings. That way, you are sure the system is aware of the changes you made. In both Listing 12.8 and Listing 12.9, this was accomplished with the `Get-VMHostStorage` **cmdlet.**

TABLE 12.4   Guideline HCM03

Parameter element	Description
Code	HCM03
Name	Disable vSphere Web Access (ESX only).
Description	vSphere Web Access provides a means for users to view virtual machines on a single ESX host and perform simple operations such as power-on and suspend. It also provides a way to obtain console access to virtual machines. All of this is governed by the user's permissions on the local ESX host.
	In most cases, users should manage virtual machines through vCenter Server, using either the vSphere Client or the vCenter vSphere Web Access.
	Note: ESXi does not have vSphere Web Access; this guideline is not relevant for ESXi.
Threat	This is a web interface and therefore has some of the general risks associated with all web interfaces.
Recommendation level	DMZ
Parameter setting	In the vSphere Client, select the host, click the Configuration tab, and select the Security Profile item. Click Properties; then in the list of services, ensure that the vSphere Web Access check box is deselected.
Effect on functionality	vSphere Web Access will no longer be available.

Source: VMware vSphere™ 4.0 Security Hardening Guide, copyright © 2011 VMware, Inc. All rights reserved. This product is protected by U.S. and international copyright and intellectual property laws. VMware products are covered by one or more patents listed at `http://www.vmware.com/go/patents`.

To report on this guideline, you can use the `Get-VMHostFirewallException` cmdlet as follows. Notice how the script in Listing 12.10 uses the `Where-Object` cmdlet to let only the ESX hosts pass.

LISTING 12.10   Checking vSphere Web Access for HCM03

```
foreach($esx in (Get-VMHost | `
where {$_.Extensiondata.Config.Product.ProductLineId -eq "esx"})){
  Get-VMHostFirewallException -VMHost $esx `
    -Name "vSphere Web Access" | `
  Select @{N="Hostname";E={$esx.Name}},Name,Enabled
}
```

Securing Your vSphere Environment

PART III

The script in Listing 12.11 uses the same logic and disables the Firewall rule for Web Access with the `Set-VMHostFirewallException` cmdlet.

LISTING 12.11 Disable vSphere Web Access for HCM03

```
Get-VMHost | `
  where {$_.Extensiondata.Config.Product.ProductLineId -eq `
    "esx"} | `
  Get-VMHostFirewallException -Name "vSphere Web Access"} | `
  Set-VMHostFirewallException -Enabled:$false
```

Another interesting guideline in the hosts section is HCM04. (See Table 12.5 for details.) This guideline advises you to make sure that all sessions are encrypted.

TABLE 12.5 Guideline HCM04

Parameter element	Description
Code	HCM04
Name	Ensure that ESX is configured to encrypt all sessions.
Description	Sessions with the ESX server should be encrypted because transmitting data in plain text can be viewed as it travels through the network.
Threat	The use of unencrypted client sessions leaves communications between the different components of vSphere open to man-in-the-middle attacks.
Recommendation level	Enterprise
Parameter setting	`<httpPort>` and `<accessMode>` XML settings in the `proxy.xml` file.
Effect on functionality	In the `proxy.xml` file, ensure that for all the different entries `<httpPort>` `-1</httpPort>` is set and that the `<accessMode> </accessMode>` parameters are not set to `http`. They can be set to either `httpsWith Redirect` or `httpsOnly`.

This guideline asks you to make changes to the `proxy.xml` file that lives on the ESX(i) host. Unfortunately, there is no public API to interact with the `proxy.xml` file, but you can get the job done with some external tools. On an ESX server you can access the XML file with the help of the `pscp.exe` utility that is part of the PuTTY Suite (see `www.chiark.greenend.org.uk/~sgtatham/putty/`). The `pscp.exe` utility functions in the same way as the `scp` command from *nix environments. It allows you to copy a file from a server to your local machine in a secure way. You can also access the `proxy.xml` file, in read-only mode, via `https://<hostname>/host/proxy.xml`, but that method will not allow you to upload the changed proxy.xml file. This is a nice method to quickly check the contents of the proxy.xml file, though.

TIP When you use any of the PuTTY tools against a host, that host's key must be stored in the registry on your client. To fix that problem, you should run one of the PuTTY tools at least once on the client. Otherwise, the scripted call of the pscp.exe tool will not work!

On an ESXi server, you can use the Get-VMHostFirmware cmdlet to retrieve the proxy.xml file. The only problem here is that the cmdlet produces a TGZ file (a gzipped tar file) from which you have to extract the proxy.xml file. To handle the TGZ files, the script in Listing 12.12 uses the tar and gzip commands from the GnuWin32 project (see http://gnuwin32.sourceforge.net).

TIP All these external tools will need to be present on the client from which you call the functions from Listing 12.12.

In Listing 12.12, you find the functions that are needed to retrieve and store the proxy.xml file, both for ESX and ESXi servers.

LISTING 12.12 Retrieving and saving the proxy.xml file

```
# Update the following paths to reflect
# your local installation
$PuTTY = "C:\PuTTY"
$GnuWin = "C:\Program Files (x86)\GnuWin32\bin"

$pscp = $PuTTY + "\pscp.exe"
$GnuGzip = $GnuWin + "\gzip.exe"
$GnuTar = $GnuWin + "\tar.exe"

# Executes a command without opening a Command box
function Invoke-CmdHidden{
  param(
  [string]$Executable,
  [string]$Parameters,
  [string]$WorkDirectory
  )

  process{
```

```
        $startInfo = New-Object System.Diagnostics.ProcessStartInfo
        $startInfo.CreateNoWindow = $true
        $startInfo.WindowStyle = "hidden"
        $startInfo.UseShellExecute = $false
        $startInfo.FileName = $Executable
        $startInfo.Arguments = $Parameters
        $startInfo.WorkingDirectory = $WorkDirectory
        $process = [System.Diagnostics.Process]::Start($startInfo)
        if(!$process.HasExited){$process.WaitForExit()}
    }
}

# Retrieve a file through pscp
function Get-FileScp{
  param(
  [string]$Hostname,
  [string]$SourcePath,
  [string]$Destination,
  [System.Management.Automation.PSCredential]$Credential
  )

  process{
    $txt = $Credential.GetNetworkCredential()
    $user = $txt.UserName
    $pswd = $txt.Password
    $PscpParams = "-batch -pw " + $pswd + " " + `
      $user + "@" + $Hostname + ":" + $SourcePath + " ."
    Invoke-CmdHidden -Executable $pscp `
      -Parameters $PscpParams -WorkDirectory $Destination
  }
}

# Deflate a .tgz file
function Expand-Tgz{
  param(
  [string]$TgzName
  )

  process{
    $TgzFileName = Split-Path $TgzName -Leaf
    $TarFileName = $TgzFileName.Replace('.tgz','.tar')
```

```
    $Directory = Split-Path $TgzName


    $GnuTgzParams = "-d " + '"' + $TgzFileName + '"'
    $GnuTarParams = "xf " + '"' + $TarFileName + '"'

# Expand the GZIP file
    Invoke-CmdHidden -Executable $GnuGzip `
        -Parameters $GnuTgzParams -WorkDirectory $Directory
# Create the .tgz file
    Invoke-CmdHidden -Executable $GnuTar `
        -Parameters $GnuTarParams -WorkDirectory $Directory
  }
}


# Create a .tgz file from 1 or more files
function Compress-Tgz{
  param(
  [string]$TgzName,
  [string[]]$Files
  )


  process{
    $TarName = $TgzName.Replace('.tgz','.tar')
    $TgzFileName = Split-Path $TgzName -Leaf
    $TarFileName = Split-Path $TarName -Leaf
    $Directory = Split-Path $TgzName

    if (Test-Path $TgzName) {
      Remove-Item -Path $TgzName -Force
    }
    if (Test-Path $TarName) {
      Remove-Item -Path $TarName -Force
    }
    $GnuTgzParams = "-1 " + '"' + $TarFileName + '"'

# Create the .tar file
    $FirstFile = $true
    $Files | %{
      if($FirstFile){
        $GnuTarParams = "-cvvf " + '"' + `
          $TarFileName + '"' + " " + '"' + $_ + '"'
```

```
          }
          else{
            $GnuTarParams = "-rvvf " + '"' + `
              $TarFileName + '"' + " " + '"' + $_ + '"'
          }
          Invoke-CmdHidden -Executable $GnuTar `
            -Parameters $GnuTarParams `
            -WorkDirectory $Directory
          $FirstFile = $false
        }
  # Create the .tgz file
      Invoke-CmdHidden -Executable $GnuGzip `
        -Parameters $GnuTgzParams -WorkDirectory $Directory
      Get-ChildItem -Path $Directory -Filter "*.tar.gz" | `
        Rename-Item -NewName $TgzFileName
      if (Test-Path $TarName) {
        Remove-Item -Path $TarName -Force
      }
    }
  }


# Retrieve the proxy.xml file
function Get-ProxyXml{
  param(
  [Parameter(Position=1,ValueFromPipeline=$true)]
  [Alias('Host')]
  [ValidateNotNull()]
  [VMware.VimAutomation.ViCore.Types.V1.Inventory.VMHost]
  ${VMHost},
  [System.Management.Automation.PSCredential]$Credential
  )
  process{
    $workFolder = $env:temp + "\" + $VMHost.Name
    if (Test-Path $workFolder) {
      Remove-Item -Path $workFolder -Force -Recurse
    }
    New-Item -Path ($env:temp + "\" + $VMHost.Name) `
      -ItemType directory -Confirm:$false | Out-Null

    $esxType = `
      $VMHost.Extensiondata.Config.Product.ProductLineId
```

```
        if($esxType -eq "embeddedEsx"){
          $bundle = Set-VMHostFirmware -VMHost $VMHost `
            -DestinationPath $workFolder -BackupConfiguration
          Copy-Item -LiteralPath $bundle.Data.FullName `
            -Destination `
                $bundle.Data.FullName.Replace(".tgz",".copy.tgz")
          Expand-Tgz -TgzName $bundle.Data.FullName

          $stateTgz = $workFolder + "\state.tgz"
          Expand-Tgz -TgzName $stateTgz

          $localTgz = $workFolder + "\local.tgz"
          Expand-Tgz -TgzName $localTgz
          $proxyLocation = `
                $workFolder + "\etc\vmware\hostd\proxy.xml"
        }
        else{
          $proxyXml = Get-FileScp -HostName $VMHost.Name `
            -SourcePath "/etc/vmware/hostd/proxy.xml" `
            -Destination $workFolder `
            -Credential $Credential
          $proxyLocation = $workFolder + "\proxy.xml"
        }

        $proxyXml = New-Object XML
        $proxyXml.Load($proxyLocation)
        $proxyXml
    }
}


# Save the proxy.xml file
function Set-ProxyXml{
  param(
  [Alias('Host')]
  [ValidateNotNull()]
  [VMware.VimAutomation.ViCore.Types.V1.Inventory.VMHost]
  ${VMHost},
  [System.Xml.XmlDocument]$InputObject,
  [System.Management.Automation.PSCredential]$Credential
  )
```

Securing Your vSphere
Environment

PART III

```
    process{
      $esxType = `
          $VMHost.Extensiondata.Config.Product.ProductLineId
      if($esxType -eq "embeddedEsx"){
        $workFolder = $env:temp + "\" + $VMHost.Name
        $InputObject.Save($workFolder + `
            "\etc\vmware\hostd\proxy.xml")

        $localTgz = $workFolder + "\local.tgz"
        Compress-Tgz -TgzName $localTgz -Files ("etc")

        $stateTgz = $workFolder + "\state.tgz"
        Compress-Tgz -TgzName $stateTgz -Files ("local.tgz")

        $bundleName = (Get-ChildItem -Path $workFolder `
          -Filter "configBundle*tgz").FullName.Replace(".copy","")
        Compress-Tgz -TgzName $bundleName `
          -Files ("state.tgz","Manifest.txt")

        Set-VMHostFirmware -Restore -SourcePath $bundleName `
          -VMHost $VMHost `
          -HostCredential $Credential -Confirm:$true
        Remove-Item -Path $workFolder -Force -Recurse
      }
      else{
        Set-FileScp -HostName $VMHost.Name `
          -SourcePath "/etc/vmware/hostd/proxy.xml" `
          -Destination $workFolder `
          -Credential $Credential
      }
    }
}
```

The script in Listing 12.13 shows how you can now report, with the help of the functions from Listing 12.12, on the settings in the proxy.xml file for both types of servers.

LISTING 12.13 Reporting session encryption settings for HCM04

```
$credentials = Get-Credential

foreach($esx in Get-VMHost){
```

```
$proxy = Get-ProxyXml -VMHost $esx -Credential $credentials
$proxy.ConfigRoot.EndpointList.e | `
    Select @{N="Host";E={$esx.Name}},accessMode,Port
}
```

TIP   As we mentioned earlier, you have read-only access to the `proxy.xml` file through `https://<hostname>/host/proxy.xml`. To produce a report where you only need to read the `proxy.xml` file, you can automate the HTTPS access with the help of the `system .net.webclient` class.

And if you want to automate the remediation for this guideline, you can use something like the script in Listing 12.14. Note that your ESXi server needs to be in Maintenance mode for changing the `proxy.xml` file. The ESXi server will automatically reboot after the upload is finished.

WARNING   Watch out when applying the script in Listing 12.14 to an ESXi host! Once the script has run you will not be able to use the `Set-VMHostFirmware` cmdlet anymore.

LISTING 12.14   Configuring encrypted sessions for HCM04

```
$credentials = Get-Credential

foreach($esx in Get-VMHost){
  $proxy = Get-ProxyXml -VMHost $esx -Credential $credentials
  $proxy.ConfigRoot.EndpointList.e | %{
    $_.accessMode = "httpsOnly"
    if($_.Port){
      $_.Port = [string]-1
    }
  }
  Set-ProxyXml -VMHost $esx -InputObject $proxy `
    -Credential $credentials
}
```

Since the ESXi servers run without a COS, there are specific guidelines for working with this type of hypervisor. In some rare situations, you will need to log on directly to the ESXi server through the Direct Console User Interface (DCUI). And since this is consequently a critical component, there are guidelines that allow you to limit the risk coming from the DCUI connections. Guideline HCN01 states that only authorized users should have access to use the DCUI. This access control is managed through a local group called localadmin.

TABLE 12.6   Guideline HCN01

Parameter element	Description
Code	HCN01
Name	Ensure that only authorized users have access to the DCUI.
Description	Users who are members of the local group called localadmin have the ability to log in to the DCUI. Only those who are authorized should be members of this group.
Risk or control	Anyone with credentials to access the DCUI can reconfigure the host or reboot and turn it off.
Recommendation level	Enterprise
Parameters or Objects Configuration	Check the users in the local group named localadmin and ensure that only authorized users are present.
Test	Unauthorized users should not be able to enter credentials and log into the DCUI.

Source: VMware vSphere™ 4.0 Security Hardening Guide, copyright © 2011 VMware, Inc. All rights reserved. This product is protected by U.S. and international copyright and intellectual property laws. VMware products are covered by one or more patents listed at http://www.vmware.com/go/patents.

The script in Listing 12.15 shows how you can check or list the members of this group.

LISTING 12.15   Reporting access rights to DCUI for HCN01

```
Get-VMHostAccount -Group | `
  where {$_.Id -eq "localadmin"} | `
  Select -ExpandProperty Users
```

To close down this potential security risk, you can change the members of the localadmin group. The script in Listing 12.16 shows one way of doing this. The accounts that need to be removed are specified in a variable.

LISTING 12.16   Configuring access rights to DCUI for HCN01

```
$removeUsers = "user1","user2"
Get-VMHostAccount -Group | `
  where {$_.Id -eq "localadmin"} | `
  Set-VMHostAccount -UnassignUsers $removeUsers
```

In Guideline HCN02, you are advised to use the Lockdown mode on all the ESXi servers to restrict root access. This way, you force all changes to the ESXi host to be made through the DCUI. In the PowerCLI build available as of this writing, there were no cmdlets that allowed you to manipulate lockdown mode.

TABLE 12.7   Guideline HCN02

Parameter element	Description
Code	HCN02
Name	Enable lockdown mode to restrict root access.
Description	Lockdown mode can be enabled after an ESXi host is added to vCenter Server. Enabling lockdown mode disables all remote root access to ESXi 4.0 machines. Any subsequent local changes to the host must be made: • Using the DCUI • In a vSphere Client session or using vCLI commands to vCenter Server • In a vSphere Client session or using vCLI commands direct to the ESXi 4.0 system
Threat	Security best practices dictate that the root password should be known to as few individuals as possible. The root account should not be used if any alternative is possible. It is an anonymous account, and activity by the root user cannot be definitively associated with a specific individual.
Recommendation level	Enterprise
Parameter setting	To do this manually, in the vSphere Client, click the Configuration tab for the host, and in the Security Profile setting, click the Lockdown Mode check box. This can also be done using PowerCLI or with an API client. Lockdown mode can also be enabled and disabled from the DCUI.
Effect on Functionality	Enabling lockdown prevents all API-based access by the root account to the ESXi host. This includes vSphere Client, vCLI, PowerCLI, and any API-based client. Nonroot accounts are not affected.

Source: VMware vSphere™ 4.0 Security Hardening Guide, copyright © 2011 VMware, Inc. All rights reserved. This product is protected by U.S. and international copyright and intellectual property laws. VMware products are covered by one or more patents listed at http://www.vmware.com/go/patents.

To check the status of the Lockdown mode, you can use the simple script found in Listing 12.17. It uses the `Extensiondata` property to access the `HostSystem` object.

LISTING 12.17   Checking Lockdown mode for HCN02

```
Get-VMHost | Select Name,
   @{N="Lockdown";E={$_.Extensiondata.Config.adminDisabled}}
```

With the script in Listing 12.18, you can set all ESXi servers in Lockdown mode.

LISTING 12.18   Configuring Lockdown mode for HCN02

```
Get-VMHost | `
```

```
where {$_.Extensiondata.Config.Product.ProductLineId -eq `
   "embeddedEsx"} | %{
   $_.ExtensionData.EnterLockdownMode()
}
```

vNetwork

In the vNetwork chapter of the Hardening Guide, there are several guidelines that specify how specific port groups should be isolated. The level of the isolation depends on the level, Enterprise or SSLF, for which the recommendation needs to be applied. Most of these guidelines can be checked and configured by similar scripts. Let's take Guideline NAR01 as a sample. This guideline specifies that the management traffic should be on an isolated network. We've included the details in Table 12.8.

TABLE 12.8   **Guideline NAR01**

Parameter element	Description
Code	NAR01
Name	Ensure that vSphere management traffic is on a restricted network.
Description	The vSphere management network provides access to the vSphere management interface on each component. Any remote attack would most likely begin with gaining entry to this network. The vSphere management interfaces include: • Service console interface on ESX • Management VMkernel interface on ESXi
Risk or control	Services running on the management interface provide an opportunity for an attacker to gain privileged access to the systems.
Recommendation level	Enterprise
Parameters or objects configuration	The vSphere management port group should be in a dedicated VLAN on a common vSwitch. The vSwitch can be shared with production (virtual machine) traffic, as long as the vSphere management port group's VLAN is not used by production virtual machines.
Test	

Note: Guideline NAR01 also includes a recommendation for SSLF.

Source: VMware vSphere™ 4.0 Security Hardening Guide, copyright © 2011 VMware, Inc. All rights reserved. This product is protected by U.S. and international copyright and intellectual property laws. VMware products are covered by one or more patents listed at http://www.vmware.com/go/patents.

For each port group that is used for management traffic, the script in Listing 12.19 displays the VLANid and the number of portgroups that exist on the vSwitch.

LISTING 12.19 Display Management portgroups

```
function Assert-NAR01{
  param(
  [VMware.VimAutomation.ViCore.Impl.V1.Inventory.VMHostImpl]
  $VMHost
  )

  if($VMHost.Extensiondata.Config.Product.ProductLineId `
    -eq "esx"){
    $nics = Get-VMHostNetworkAdapter -Console -VMHost $VMHost
  }
  else{
    $nics = Get-VMHostNetworkAdapter -VMKernel -VMHost $VMHost
  }

  foreach($vmk in $nics){
    if($vmk.Extensiondata.Spec.DistributedVirtualPort){
      Get-VirtualPortGroup -Name $vmk.PortGroupName `
        -Distributed | Select @{N="Server";E={$esx.Name}},
        @{N="PgName";E={$vmk.PortGroupName}},
        VLanId,@{N="vSwitch";E={$_.VirtualSwitch.Name}},
        @{N="Pg-on-vSwitch";E={(Get-VirtualPortGroup `
          -VirtualSwitch (Get-VirtualSwitch `
          -Name $_.VirtualSwitch.Name -VMHost $VMHost)).Count}}
    }
    else{
      Get-VirtualPortGroup -Name $vmk.PortGroupName `
        -VMHost $esx | Select @{N="Server";E={$esx.Name}},
      @{N="PgName";E={$vmk.PortGroupName}},
      VLanId,@{N="vSwitch";E={$_.VirtualSwitchName}},
      @{N="Pg-on-vSwitch";E={(Get-VirtualPortGroup `
        -VirtualSwitch (Get-VirtualSwitch `
        -Name $_.VirtualSwitchName -VMHost $VMHost)).Count}}
    }
  }
}
```

The script produces output that looks like this:

```
PS C:\ > Assert-NAR01 -VMHost $esx


Server          PgName           VLanId vSwitch  Pg-on-vSwitch
------          ------           ------ -------  -------------
esx41.test.local Service Console    900 vSwitch0             2
esx41.test.local dvPg1                  dvSw1                3
```

Notice that the script reports not only on port groups that are on regular virtual switches, but also on port groups that exist on distributed virtual switches. From this report, you can see immediately that the dvPg1 has no VLANid defined and that both management port groups are not on a dedicated virtual switch. As you can probably understand, it is difficult to provide a generic remediation script for this kind of guideline since the network architecture is too specific for each environment.

In the vNetwork chapter there is another set of guidelines, labeled NCNxx, that define specific policy settings. As an example, we take Guideline NCN03, which specifies that MAC address changes should be rejected on all virtual switches (see Table 12.9).

TABLE 12.9   Guideline NCN03

Parameter element	Description
Code	NCN03
Name	Ensure that the MAC Address Change policy is set to reject.
Description	To protect against MAC impersonation, this option should be set to reject, ensuring that the virtual switch does not honor requests to change the effective MAC address to anything other than the initial MAC address.
Threat	If the virtual machine operating system changes the MAC address, it can send frames with an impersonated source MAC address at any time. This allows it to stage malicious attacks on the devices in a network by impersonating a network adaptor authorized by the receiving network.
Recommendation level	Enterprise
Parameter setting	MAC address changes set to reject (accept by default) on all vSwitches.
Effect on functionality	This will prevent virtual machines from changing their effective MAC address. It will affect applications that require this functionality. An example of an application like this is Microsoft Clustering, which requires systems to effectively share a MAC address. This will also affect how a Layer 2 bridge will operate. vShield Zones will not operate properly if MAC Address Change is set to reject. This will also affect applications that require a specific MAC address for licensing. An exception should be made for the port groups that these applications are connected to.

The script in Listing 12.20 checks to see whether MAC address changes are allowed and displays the results for all virtual switches on a specific ESX(i) server.

LISTING 12.20 Displaying the MAC Address Change policy

```
function Assert-NCN03{
  param(
  [VMware.VimAutomation.ViCore.Impl.V1.Inventory.VMHostImpl]
  $VMHost
  )
  process{
    foreach($sw in Get-VirtualSwitch -VMHost $VMHost){
      $swType = $sw.Extensiondata.GetType().Name
      $ext = $sw.Extensiondata
      if($swType -eq "HostVirtualSwitch"){
        $sw | Select @{N="VMHost";E={$VMHost.Name}},
        Name,
        @{N="MAC Change Allowed";
      E={$ext.Spec.Policy.Security.MacChanges}}
      }
      else{
        $sw | Select @{N="VMHost";E={$VMHost.Name}},
        Name,
        @{N="MAC Change Allowed";E={`
$ext.Config.DefaultPortConfig.SecurityPolicy.MacChanges.Value}}
      }
    }
  }
}
```

When you run this script, the output you see will look something like this:

```
PS C:\ > Assert-NCN03 -VMHost $esx


VMHost              Name      MAC Change Allowed
------              ----      ------------------
esx41.test.local dvSw1                     True
esx41.test.local dvSw2                     True
esx41.test.local vSwitch0                  True
esx41.test.local vSwitch1                  True
```

To remediate for this guideline, you need to take into account that there will be regular virtual switches and distributed virtual switches. The script in Listing 12.21 handles both types.

Securing Your vSphere Environment

PART III

TIP   Some remarks on the script in Listing 12.21:

▶ The `UpdateVirtualSwitch` method that is used to reconfigure a regular virtual switch requires that all properties be populated. The script takes the easy solution and copies these properties from the `$sw` variable.

▶ The `ReconfigureDvs` method, and in fact all distributed virtual switch–related methods, use the `configVersion` property as a kind of locking mechanism. This prevents two different scripts from making changes to the configuration at the same time.

▶ The script was not tested on the Nexus v1000 distributed virtual switch. Run at your own risk!

LISTING 12.21   Setting the MAC Address Change policy to `reject`

```
function Remediate-NCN03{
  param(
  [VMware.VimAutomation.ViCore.Impl.V1.Inventory.VMHostImpl]
  $VMHost
  )
  process{
    $netSys = Get-View `
      $VMhost.ExtensionData.ConfigManager.NetworkSystem
    foreach($sw in Get-VirtualSwitch -VMHost $vmhost){
      $swType = $sw.Extensiondata.GetType().Name
      $ext = $sw.ExtensionData
      if($swType -eq "HostVirtualSwitch"){
        $spec = New-Object VMware.Vim.HostVirtualSwitchSpec
        $spec.Bridge = $ext.Spec.Bridge
        $spec.Mtu = $ext.SPec.Mtu
        $spec.numPorts = $sw.NumPorts
        $spec.Policy = $ext.Spec.Policy
        $spec.Policy.Security.macChanges = $false
        $netSys.UpdateVirtualSwitch($sw.Name,$spec)
      }
      else{
        $dvSw = Get-View $sw.Id
        $spec = New-Object VMware.Vim.DVSConfigSpec
        $spec.configVersion = $dvSw.Config.ConfigVersion
        $spec.defaultPortConfig = `
```

```
        New-Object VMware.Vim.VMwareDVSPortSetting
      $spec.defaultPortConfig.securityPolicy = `
        New-Object VMware.Vim.DVSSecurityPolicy
      $spec.defaultPortConfig.securityPolicy.macChanges = `
        New-Object VMware.Vim.BoolPolicy
      $spec.defaultPortConfig.securityPolicy.macChanges.value'
        = $false
      $dvSw.ReconfigureDvs($spec)
    }
  }
  }
}
```

You call the script as follows:

```
PS C:\ > Remediate-NCN03 -VMHost $esx
```

It is probably obvious that you can use the same scripts that we just used for Guideline NCN03 to report on and remediate the other NCN*xx* guidelines. In fact, you can combine most of the NCN*xx* guidelines in one `Assert` and one `Remediate` script.

vCenter Server

Since the vCenter Server runs most of the time on a Windows-based OS, most of the guidelines in this chapter have to do with common best practices for a Windows OS. These guidelines are outside the scope of this book.

COS

The guidelines for the COS will become obsolete with the next ESX version. All hypervisors will be of the ESXi type, which means no more COS. But since it will take some time before every site is converted to ESXi only, let's look at some of the guidelines for the COS.

Several of the COS Guidelines have to do with the firewall configuration on an ESX server. With the `Get-VMHostFirewallDefaultPolicy` and the `Set-VMHost FirewallDefaultPolicy` cmdlets, PowerCLI gives you the tools to check and configure the firewall according to the guidelines. As an example, let's take Guideline CON01; it states that the ESX firewall should be configured to High Security. Table 12.10 provides the details.

Securing Your vSphere
Environment

PART III

TABLE 12.10   Guideline CON01

Parameter element	Description
Code	CON01
Name	Ensure that the ESX firewall is configured to High Security.
Description	ESX Server includes a built-in firewall between the service console and the network. A high-security setting disables all outbound traffic and allows only selected inbound traffic.
Risk or control	Prevention of network-based exploits.
Recommendation level	Enterprise

Parameters or Objects Configuration	The following commands configure high security on the firewall:
	`esxcfg-firewall — blockIncoming`
	`esxcfg-firewall — blockOutgoing`

Test	Ensure that outbound connections are blocked and only selected inbound connections are allowed.

To check the current configuration, you can do the following:

```
PS C:\ > Get-VMHostFirewallDefaultPolicy -VMHost $esx

VMHostId               IncomingEnabled OutgoingEnabled
--------               --------------- ---------------
HostSystem-host-2... False            False
```

And to configure the Firewall policy (as advised by Guideline CON01), you could do something like this:

```
PS C:\ > $fw = Get-VMHostFirewallDefaultPolicy -VMHost $esx
PS C:\ > Set-VMHostFirewallDefaultPolicy -Policy $fw `
>> -AllowIncoming $false -AllowOutgoing $false
VMHostId               IncomingEnabled OutgoingEnabled
--------               --------------- ---------------
HostSystem-host-2... False            False
```

If you need to allow exceptions to the default Firewall rule (although the Hardening Guide advises you not to), you can use the `Get-VMHostFirewallException` and `Set-VMHostFirewallException` cmdlets.

Bring It All Together

In this chapter, we looked at a selection of the security hardening guidelines. For several of these guidelines, we provided scripts to detect whether a security hole was present. We provided a command or script for you to use to close the security hole. Instead of running these detection and remediation scripts separately for each of the guidelines, it would be a lot more practical if you could do all this with just one script. That is of course perfectly possible with PowerShell and PowerCLI.

The only problem here is that we would need a lot more pages to describe a general-purpose script. Let us know on the book's web page (see www.powerclibook.com/) if there is interest for such a script and we will try to oblige.

Enjoy making your vSphere environment more secure with the help of PowerCLI.

Securing Your vSphere Environment

PART III

Maintain Security in Your vSphere Environment

IN THIS CHAPTER, YOU WILL LEARN TO:

Whatever operating system or application the administrator is responsible for, it is always highly important to keep it up-to-date by applying software updates from the vendor. ESX(i) is no different in this respect, and VMware provides a management tool known as vCenter Update Manager (VUM) to assist with this process. The tool can be used to manage hosts, guests, and virtual appliances. A separate set of PowerCLI cmdlets is available for download that enables automation for VUM. VMware announced that the release of VUM 4.1 will be the last to feature Windows and Linux guest operating system patching, so we will concentrate on host patching in this chapter.

Install the vCenter Update Manager PowerCLI Snap-in

Before you can use the VUM PowerCLI Snap-in, you must first download and install it. It is probably obvious from the name that the vCenter Update Manager product requires vCenter Server to operate. A separate tool known as the VMware Host Update Utility can be used to update ESX(i) hosts in systems without vCenter Server. However, this tool does not lend itself to automation and so will not be covered in this book.

As of this writing, two versions of the vCenter Update Manager PowerCLI Snap-in are available: 4.0 Update 1 and 4.1. In general, the system requirements are very similar; they differ in the following aspects:

Update Manager Releases

▶ Update Manager PowerCLI 4.0 Update 1 works only with the corresponding Update Manager 4.0 Update 1 (and later releases of the 4.0 release, such as 4.0 Update 2).

▶ Update Manager PowerCLI 4.0 Update 1 does not work with versions of Update Manager prior to 4.0 Update 1, such as Update Manager 4.0 GA or Update Manager 1.0 (which accompanied the vCenter 2.5 product).

▶ Update Manager PowerCLI 4.1 works only with vCenter Update Manager 4.1; it does not work with any version of Update Manager prior to this version.

PowerCLI Releases

▶ Update Manager PowerCLI 4.0 Update 1 requires VMware vSphere PowerCLI 4.0 Update 1.

▶ Update Manager PowerCLI 4.1 requires VMware vSphere PowerCLI 4.1.

Supported Platforms

▶ Update Manager PowerCLI 4.0 Update 1 is supported on the following 32-bit and 64-bit versions of Windows:

   ▶ Windows Server 2008

   ▶ Windows Server 2003 SP2

   ▶ Windows Vista

   ▶ Windows XP SP2

▶ Update Manager PowerCLI 4.1 adds support for the following 32-bit and 64-bit version of Windows:

   ▶ Windows 7

Common Requirements

Both versions of Update Manager PowerCLI require:

▶ .NET 2.0 SP1

▶ Windows PowerShell 1.0 or higher

Once all the requirements have been met and the Update Manager PowerCLI cmdlets have been installed, make them available to your existing PowerShell session with the following line:

```
Add-PSSnapin VMware.VumAutomation
```

To save the effort of having to do this every time, consider adding the same line into your PowerShell profile. The PowerShell profile is a script file that is executed each time a PowerShell session is opened. Consequently, it is useful to add items to your profile that you frequently need, such as third-party snap-ins like PowerCLI, or functions you have created yourself.

By default, the PowerShell profile .ps1 file does not exist; you can create one with the following:

```
New-Item -Path $profile -Type file -force
```

To edit the profile file, which will start out as blank, you can open it in Notepad:

```
notepad $profile
```

Now add snap-ins, functions, or other items into the file; save and close it; and then the next time you open a PowerShell session, everything in the profile file will execute.

Work with Baselines

Once vCenter Update Manager has been installed and configured, and the patch repository has been populated with the available patches, the first step when working with VUM is to create a set of baselines. *Baselines* determine the set of patches to be applied to a host or guest machine. We will consider two types of baselines: static and dynamic. The essential difference between the two is that static baselines are not updated when new patches are downloaded to the patch repository, whereas dynamic baselines are updated when newly downloaded patches fall into the criteria specified when the dynamic baseline was created.

Creating a Baseline

Included in the set of Update Manager cmdlets is the `New-PatchBaseline` cmdlet, which you can use in conjunction with the `Get-Patch` cmdlet to create all the baselines needed in your organization.

First, let's retrieve a set of patches to add to a new static baseline. This baseline will contain patches for host machines from VMware for ESX(i) that have been released since November 1, 2009.

```
$patches = Get-Patch -TargetType Host -Vendor VMware* -Product
 Embedded* -After 1.11.2009


$patches


Name                    Release Date  Severity  Vendor Id
----                    ------------  --------  ---------
Firmware update f...    19/11/2009    0..Critical  ESXi400-200911201-UG
Tools update for ...    19/11/2009    0..Critical  ESXi400-200911202-UG
VI Client update ...    19/11/2009    0..Critical  ESXi400-200911203-UG
Updates Firmware        05/01/2010    0..Critical  ESXi400-200912401-BG
Updates VMware Tools    05/01/2010    0..Critical  ESXi400-200912402-BG
Updates Firmware        03/03/2010    0..Critical  ESXi400-201002401-BG
Updates VMware Tools    03/03/2010    0..Critical  ESXi400-201002402-BG
Updates Firmware        01/04/2010    0..Critical  ESXi400-201003401-BG
Updates Firmware        27/05/2010    0..HostSec.  ESXi400-201005401-SG
```

```
Updates VMware Tools 27/05/2010 0..Critical ESXi400-201005402-BG
Firmware update f... 10/06/2010 0..Critical ESXi400-201006201-UG
Tools update for ... 10/06/2010 0..Critical ESXi400-201006202-UG
VI Client update ... 10/06/2010 0..Critical ESXi400-201006203-UG
VMware ESXi 4.0 U... 19/11/2009 0..Critical ESXi400-Update01
VMware ESXi 4.0 U... 10/06/2010 0..Critical ESXi400-Update02
```

Now that you have your required patches stored in the $patches variable, these patches can be provided as part of a new static baseline created with New-Patch Baseline:

```
New-PatchBaseline -Static -TargetType Host
 -Name 'ESXi - Current (Static)'
 -Description 'ESXi patches since 1.11.2009 - 10.06.2010'
 -IncludePatch $patches
```

In a similar vein, you could create a new dynamic baseline, which essentially starts out the same as the static one. This baseline would be for host machines from VMware for ESX(i) that have been released since November 1, 2009.

```
New-PatchBaseline -Dynamic
 -TargetType Host
 -Name 'ESXi - Current (Dynamic)'
 -Description 'ESXi patches up to the current date'
 -SearchPatchVendor VMware*
 -SearchPatchProduct Embedded*
 -SearchPatchStartDate 1.11.2009
```

While on October 6, 2010 these two baselines would contain the same patches, three months down the line the static baseline would still contain the same list of patches but the dynamic baseline would have been updated with any new patches that met the search criteria and would have been downloaded into the Update Manager repository. The patching approach taken by your organization will naturally lend itself to either or both of these types of baselines.

Baselines are not just for hosts. You can create baselines for virtual machines (VMs) in much the same manner. This time specify the TargetType as VM and specify criteria for the patches you require. The following command creates a new virtual machine dynamic baseline for Windows 7 patches from Microsoft:

```
New-PatchBaseline -Dynamic
 -TargetType VM
```

```
-Name 'Windows 7 - Current (Dynamic)'
-Description 'Windows 7 patches up to the current date'
-SearchPatchVendor Microsoft
-SearchPatchProduct 'Windows 7*'
```

The download schedule for new patches is typically once a day. Should you need to initiate a one-off download outside of this schedule, a `Download-Patch` cmdlet is available. Simply executing this command instigates a Download Patch Definitions task, as shown in Figure 13.1.

FIGURE 13.1   Download Patch Definitions task

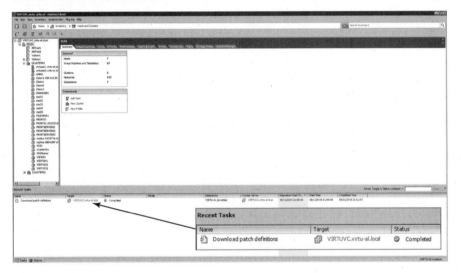

Executing `Download-Patch` generates a task object, which consequently can be managed with any of the PowerCLI `*-Task` cmdlets. For instance, running `Get-Task` returns details of the `Download-Patch` task:

```
Get-Task
```

```
Name                   State    % Complete Start Time   Finish Time
----                   -----    ---------- ----------   -----------
Download patch defi. Success       100 10:04:10 PM  10:04:21 PM
```

So far, this process wouldn't have saved the system administrator much effort and the purpose of this book is automation, saving time, and generally making the administrator's life easier. So it's useful to see how these initial learning points can be extended to larger automation possibilities. Consider the scenario where a system administrator now needs to create multiple baselines, not just one. For simplicity's sake, baselines have been detailed into a CSV file. Table 13.1 and Table 13.2 list the contents of a typical baseline.

TABLE 13.1   Baseline target details

Name	Description	Target type
ESXi - Current (Dynamic)	ESXi patches up to the current date	Host
ESX - Current (Dynamic)	ESX patches up to the current date	Host
Windows 7 - Current (Dynamic)	Windows 7 patches up to the current date	VM
Acrobat Read - Current (Dynamic)	Acrobat Reader patches up to the current date	VM
Mozilla Thunderbird- Current (Dynamic)	Mozilla Thunderbird patches up to the current date	VM

TABLE 13.2   Baseline patch details

Name	Search patch vendor	Search patch product	Search patch start date
ESXi - Current (Dynamic)	VMware*	embeddedesx 4.0.0	1.11.2009
ESX - Current (Dynamic)	VMware*	ESX 4.0.0	1.11.2009
Windows 7 - Current (Dynamic)	Microsoft	Windows 7*	22.10.2009
Acrobat Read - Current (Dynamic)	Adobe	Acrobat Reader*	1.1.2006
Mozilla Thunderbird- Current (Dynamic)	Mozilla*	Thunderbird*	1.1.2008

The asterisks in the 'Search patch vendor' column make it easier to search for all of the possible options for a vendor that has multiple categories in VUM.

By using the standard PowerShell cmdlet `Import-Csv` to read the data from the CSV file, the objects created can be piped into the `New-PatchBaseline` cmdlet to create all of the baselines simultaneously.

```
Import-Csv Baselines.csv
  | foreach {New-PatchBaseline -Dynamic
  -TargetType $_.TargetType
  -Name $_.Name
  -Description $_.Description
```

```
          -SearchPatchVendor $_.SearchPatchVendor
          -SearchPatchProduct $_.SearchPatchProduct
          -SearchPatchStartDate $_.SearchPatchStartDate}
```

This example only has five baselines, but it would be exactly the same code for twenty or fifty baselines. In addition, it is quite likely that with multiple vCenter Servers the same baselines would need to be created in each one, so running this one line command against each of the vCenter Servers would further extend the automation.

Before moving on to examine updating baselines, it is worth noting that in addition to the patch baselines, upgrade baselines are also available. These can involve either a host being upgraded from, say, ESX 3.5 to ESX 4.0, or the built-in upgrade baselines for VM Tools or Hardware Version. It's worth noting that the cmdlet `Get-Baseline` returns both upgrade baselines, such as those just mentioned, and any patch update baselines created already. The cmdlet `Get-PatchBaseline`, however, only returns patch update baselines and will not return upgrade baselines. For instance, the next command returns the built-in VM upgrade baselines:

```
Get-Baseline -TargetType VM -BaselineType Upgrade | Format-Table
  Name,Description
```

```
Name                                Description
----                                -----------
VMware Tools Upgrade to Match Host  A predefined baseline for
                                    upgrading to the latest
                                    VMware Tools version
                                    supported by the host
VM Hardware Upgrade to Match Host   A predefined baseline for
                                    upgrading to the latest VM
                                    hardware version supported by
                                    the host
```

Updating a Baseline

Once you've created baselines, either static or dynamic, you can manipulate them and keep them up-to-date for any new requirements with the `Set-PatchBaseline` cmdlet.

Let's take an example where the static baseline created earlier in the chapter for hosts contains a patch (ESXi400-200911201-UG) that causes issues in your organization. You now need to update your baseline to exclude this patch.

First, retrieve a new set of patches minus the one causing the issue:

```
$updatedpatches = Get-Patch -TargetType Host
 -Vendor VMware*
 -Product Embedded*
 -After 1.11.2009
 | Where {$_.IdByVendor -ne 'ESXi400-200911201-UG'}
```

You can now update the static baseline to remove this patch from the list of patches to be deployed by applying the updated set of patches to it:

```
Get-PatchBaseline -Name 'ESXi - Current (Static)'
 | Set-PatchBaseline -IncludePatch $updatedpatches
```

The number of patches now present in this baseline is 14, one less than the previous 15:

```
((Get-PatchBaseline
 -Name 'ESXi - Current (Static)').CurrentPatches).count
```

Other properties or search criteria used to create baselines can also be modified using the `Set-PatchBaseline` cmdlet.

Attaching and Detaching Baselines

Now you have learned how to automate the creation of baselines, but they are not much use until they are attached to a host or VM. To be able to scan a host or VM to discover what patches are required and subsequently deploy them, you must first have one or more baselines attached. You can attach a baseline directly to a host or VM or allow the baseline to be inherited from a parent object such as a cluster or datacenter.

The `Attach-Baseline` cmdlet is used to connect a baseline with a vCenter Server object. Although it is possible to attach a baseline directly to all hosts in a cluster, it is easier to attach the baseline at the cluster level and let the hosts inherit it. This means that any new hosts in the cluster will automatically inherit the correct baseline as well.

The code we'll show you next retrieves all the hosts in a cluster named `Cluster01` and attaches baselines named `ESXi - Current (Dynamic)` and `ESX - Current (Dynamic)` to each one.

```
Get-Cluster Cluster01 | Get-VMHost | Attach-Baseline -Baseline
 (Get-PatchBaseline ESX*)
```

Securing Your vSphere Environment

PART III

To attach at a cluster level, simply return the cluster object and attach the baseline to that object:

```
Get-Cluster Cluster01 | Attach-Baseline -Baseline
  (Get-PatchBaseline ESX*)
```

When a baseline is no longer required, use the `Detach-Baseline` cmdlet:

```
Get-Cluster Cluster01 | Detach-Baseline -Baseline
  (Get-PatchBaseline ESX*)
```

Work with Upgrades and Patches

Now that you have patch baselines created and attached, either directly to hosts or indirectly via cluster and datacenter objects, it's time to look at how to deploy those patches to hosts.

Scanning a Host

To determine which patches a host needs to have installed, it first must be scanned against an attached baseline(s). The `Scan-Inventory` cmdlet can accept pipeline input from the typical `Get-VMHost` or `Get-Cluster` cmdlets or, in fact, from the `Get-Inventory` cmdlet.

As with the VUM GUI, you have the option to specify the type of scan to carry out: host patch, host upgrade, VM patch, or VM upgrade. In the next example, we scanned all the hosts in `Cluster01` for patch updates of previously attached baselines:

```
Get-Cluster Cluster01 | Scan-Inventory -UpdateType HostPatch
```

The obvious first question that springs to mind after a scan completes is whether the hosts or VMs in question are compliant against the attached baselines. The `Get-Compliance` cmdlet can be used to retrieve this information. It returns results for any attached baseline. The next example retrieves compliance data for each of the hosts in `Cluster01`. Note that we use the `-Detailed` parameter to find out the exact number of patches required. Later in this chapter, we will use this cmdlet again to produce a more extensive compliance report.

```
Get-Cluster Cluster01 | Get-Compliance -Detailed
```

Entity	Baseline	Status	CompliantPatches	NotCompliantPatches	UnknownPatches	NotApplicablePatches
virtuesx1	Critical Host.	Compl...	0	0	0	61
virtuesx1	Non-Critical .	Compl...	0	0	0	82
virtuesx1	ESXi - Curren.	Compl...	4	5	0	15
virtuesx2	Critical Host.	Compl...	0	0	0	61
virtuesx2	Non-Critical .	Compl...	0	0	0	82
virtuesx2	ESXi - Curren.	Compl...	4	5	0	15

Staging Patches to a Host

Once you have determined which patches a host requires, the next steps involve getting those patches down to the host and installing them. You can accomplish this using either a one- or a two-step process. The process known in VUM as Remediate places a host in Maintenance mode, copies the patches to the host, and installs them (rebooting the host if necessary)—all in one task. An alternative method first stages the patches to a host (copies the patch files onto the host) and then installs them via a Remediate task at a later time and date. This method is useful when the system administrator has a limited maintenance window to carry out all the necessary patching. By staging the patches in advance, you save time working on each host and make greater use of the maintenance window.

Use the `Stage-Patch` cmdlet for this task. The following one-liner copies all the patches in the `ESXi 4.0 U2 - Current` baseline to all the hosts in `Cluster01`:

```
Get-Cluster Cluster01 | Stage-Patch -Baseline
  (Get-Baseline 'ESXi 4.0 U2 - Current')
```

Although this can be a useful approach, you must watch one thing—available disk space on the host. You must have enough free space to hold all the staged patches. With the classic ESX product in particular, the total size of the required patches for a host can start to mount up, especially if a long period of time is left between patching cycles. Staged patches are stored in `/tmp/updatecache`. The default size of the `/tmp` folder when installing ESX 4.0 is 1 GB.

In Chapter 5, "Creating Virtual Machines," you were introduced to the `Invoke-SHH` function (you'll find the listing in the "Linux Silent Install" section). The `Invoke-SSH` function enables you to execute commands in the ESX Service Console from

PowerShell. You can use this function to check for available free space in the /tmp folder. First, use the Get-Credential PowerShell cmdlet to store credentials for connecting to the ESX host and save them in the $creds variable. Next, supply these credentials to the Invoke-SSH function along with the name of the ESX host and the command you wish to execute. In this case, you should use the Linux command df to show available disk space:

```
$creds = Get-Credential
Invoke-SSH -Credential $Creds -Computer virtuesx02
  -scripttext 'df'
```

The expected output would be along the lines of this:

```
Filesystem 1Kblocks      Used Available Use% Mounted on
/dev/sde5    5044156 2032844   2755080  43% /
/dev/sde2    2016044   94344   1819288   5% /var/log
/dev/sda1     248895   72104    163941  31% /boot
/dev/sda2    5162828 1986400   2914168  41% /esx3-install
/dev/sda1     248895   72104    163941  31% /esx3-install/boot
/dev/sda6    2063504  197920   1760764  11% /esx3-install/tmp
/dev/sda5    2063504   74172   1884512   4% /esx3-install/var/log
```

Remediating a Host

Once a host has been scanned against one or more patch baselines (and possibly had patches staged to it), it's time to remediate that host against the required baselines. Use the Remediate-Inventory cmdlet for this task. It is possible to remediate an individual host, as well as submit a task to remediate the entire cluster, datacenter, or folder. The task first places each host in Maintenance mode, evacuating VMs in the process; copies the patches to the host; installs them; and finally reboots the host if the patches require it.

To remediate all the hosts in Cluster01 against the baseline ESXi 4.0 U2 - Current, execute the following command:

```
Get-Cluster Cluster01 | Remediate-Inventory -Baseline
  (Get-Baseline 'ESXi 4.0 U2 - Current')
```

There are some additional advanced parameters for the Remediate-Inventory task. First, the host-specific parameters include the following:

▶ HostRetryDelaySeconds

▶ HostNumberof Retries

▶ `HostFailureAction`

▶ `HostDisableMediaDevices`

These are essentially the options presented when you step through the wizard in the GUI (Figure 13.2).

FIGURE 13.2   Remediate failure options

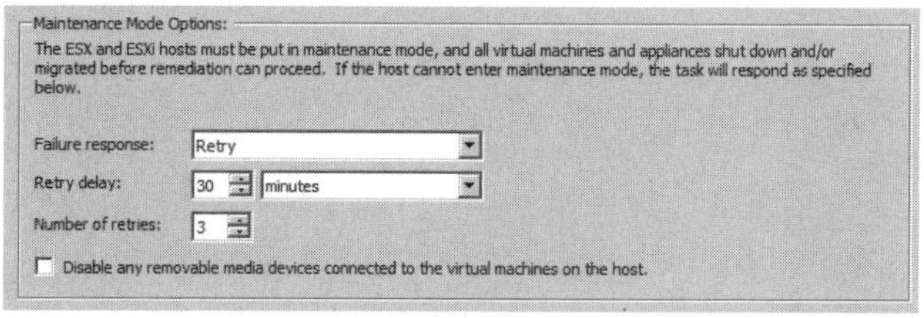

There are also some advanced cluster parameters:

▶ `ClusterDisableDistributedPowerManagement`

▶ `ClusterDisableHighAvailability`

▶ `ClusterDisableFaultTolerance`

When initiating a `Remediate-Inventory` against a cluster object, these additional parameters allow the disabling of DPM, HA, or FT, which has the potential to make for smoother patching depending on requirements in your environment.

As mentioned earlier in the chapter, you can use the patching cmdlets against VMs as well as hosts. `Scan-Inventory` works the same way. `Stage-Patch` is only available for host systems. `Remediate-Inventory` is similar to patching hosts, but instead of the advanced parameters for hosts, it has some guest-specific parameters. The guest-specific advanced parameters are optional and can be used if you decide you wish to take a snapshot of the VM prior to patching:

▶ `GuestCreateSnapshot`

▶ `GuestKeepSnapshotHours`

▶ `GuestTakeMemoryDump`

▶ `GuestSnapshotName`

▶ `GuestSnapshotDescription`

These are the options available to you when you step through the VM Remediation wizard in the vSphere client (Figure 13.3).

Securing Your vSphere Environment

PART III

FIGURE 13.3   VM rollback options

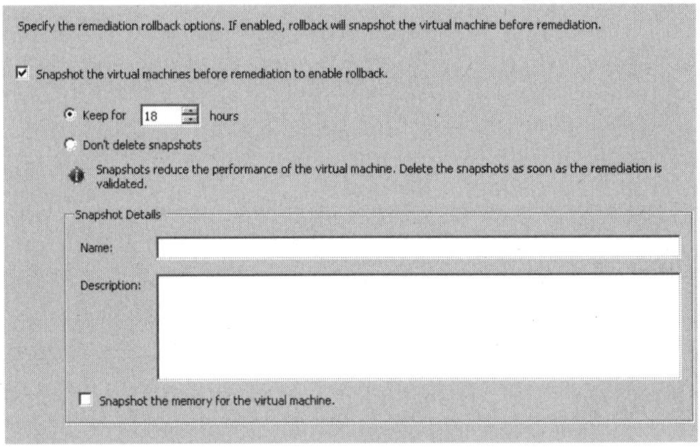

Including Patching as Part of Host Deployment

So far, we have only discussed patching existing ESX(i) hosts, typically in clusters, which already exist and can be updated during maintenance windows. However, how about giving consideration to deployment of new hosts and ensuring that they go into service at the same patch level as existing hosts?

Your method of deployment might normally involve constantly updating build images on DVD or USB media or other deployment scenarios such as the ESX Deployment Appliance (EDA) or the Ultimate Deployment Appliance (UDA). Perhaps it would be better to include patching to a known baseline as part of a postbuild configuration script. That task would be a simple case of putting together a few of the cmdlets you used in the configuration script we created earlier in the chapter.

When you use a baseline in VUM, the current patch level can be easily maintained and new hosts can be remediated against that baseline. We are then further heading to the goal of this book, which is enabling you to automate and save as much time as possible on administration tasks.

For example, add the following code to the end of a host configuration script and the host will always be deployed at the latest patch level:

```
$NewVMHost = Get-VMHost NewHostName
$Baseline = Get-PatchBaseline 'ESXi 4.0 U2 - Current'
$NewVMHost | Attach-Baseline -Baseline $Baseline
$NewVMHost | Scan-Inventory -UpdateType HostPatch
$NewVMHost | Remediate-Inventory -Baseline $Baseline
```

Countering the Self-Aware Update Manager

Many organizations deploying virtualization solutions based on VMware products install both vCenter Server and VUM inside virtual machines; in fact, VMware now considers this a best practice deployment. With vSphere 4.0, it was discovered that when a remediation task was submitted to a cluster that contained a VM with vCenter Server or VUM installed, an error would be generated. When VUM detected a VM within the cluster that was running one of these two products, it skipped that VM. In previous versions of vCenter Server, this was not an issue—the entire cluster could be automatically patched via a remediation task. But now, the vCenter Update Manager had become self-aware!

A log entry now indicates that the VM in question needs to be migrated to another host before the remediation task can proceed. Unfortunately, that means that the management VMs must be manually migrated, potentially to another cluster. Only then can the cluster be remediated fully (and automatically) without problems.

To counter this issue, the `Update-vCenterCluster` function (Listing 13.1) determines which VMs contain vCenter Server and VUM and then works through the hosts in the cluster, patching each one against the specified baseline. When it reaches a host that contains either of the management VMs, it migrates the VM to another host in the cluster before initiating the remediation task for that host. Consequently, self-awareness does not cause the task to fail.

LISTING 13.1   Updating a vCenter cluster

```
function Update-vCenterCluster {

    <#
    .SYNOPSIS
        Patch a cluster that contains vCenter or VUM VMs.
    .DESCRIPTION
        Patch a cluster that contains vCenter or VUM VMs.
    .NOTES
     Source:  Automating vSphere Administration
     Authors: Luc Dekens, Arnim van Lieshout, Jonathan Medd,
              Alan Renouf, Glenn Sizemore
    .PARAMETER ClusterName
        Name of cluster to patch
    .PARAMETER BaselineName
        Name of baseline to use for patching
```

```
.EXAMPLE
    Update-vCenterCluster -ClusterName Cluster01
     -BaselineName 'ESXi 4.0 U2 - Current'
#>

[CmdletBinding()]
Param(
    [parameter(Mandatory=$True
    ,    HelpMessage='Name of cluster to patch'
    )]
    [String]
    $ClusterName
    ,
    [parameter(Mandatory=$True
    ,    HelpMessage='Name of baseline to use for patching'
    )]
    [String]
    $BaselineName
)



$baseline = Get-Baseline -Name $BaselineName

# Find VUM server
$extMgr = Get-View ExtensionManager
$vumExt = $extMgr.ExtensionList | where {$_.Key -eq
 "com.vmware.vcIntegrity"}
$vumURL = ($vumExt.Server | where {$_.Type -eq "SOAP"}).Url
$vumSrv = ($vumUrl.Split("/")[2]).Split(":")[0]
$vumSrvShort = $vumSrv.Split(".")[0]
$vumVM = Get-VM -Name $vumSrvShort

# Find VC server
$vcSrvShort = $extMgr.Client.ServiceUrl.Split("/")[2].Split
 (".")[0]
$vcVM = Get-VM -Name $vcSrvShort

# Patch the cluster nodes
$hostTab = @{}
```

```
Get-Cluster -Name $ClusterName | Get-VMHost | %{
    $hostTab[$_.Name] = $_
}

$hostTab.Values | %{
    $vm = $null
    if($_.Name -eq $vumVM.Host.Name){
        $vm = $vumVM
    }
    if($_.Name -eq $vcVM.Host.Name){
        $vm = $vcVM
    }
    if($vm){
        $oldNode = $_
        $newNode = $hostTab.Keys | where
        {$_ -ne $oldNode.Name} | Select -First 1
        $vumVM = $vumVM | Move-VM -Destination $newNode
         -Confirm:$false
    }
    Remediate-Inventory -Entity $_ -Baseline $baseline
}

}
```

Report the Security Status

So far in this chapter, we have looked at creating and updating baselines, scanning, and patching systems. Naturally, it's useful both before and after patching cycles to find out the compliance status of the systems within the organization that you are responsible for. Knowing the security status is essential not only for planning patching work, but for providing those reports that management are always looking to get.

Understanding Datacenter Compliance

The VUM set of cmdlets includes Get-Compliance, which allows you to report on host and VM compliance against their attached baselines. You can run this cmdlet against a top-level datacenter object and generate a report for all hosts and VMs and their compliance status against any attached baseline.

TIP If you run the cmdlet against a top-level datacenter object, it will take a long time to run—particularly if the count of objects within the datacenter is in the hundreds or thousands.

Execute the following code to generate a compliance report for all hosts and VMs in Datacenter01.

```
Get-Compliance -Entity (Get-Datacenter 'Datacenter01')
```

`Get-Compliance` returns a compliance status result for each attached baseline. So if multiple baselines are attached, there will be multiple rows of data for that host or virtual machine. Sample output would be along the lines of the output shown next:

```
Entity     Baseline                              Status
------     --------                              ------
VM01       VMware Tools Upgrade to Match Host    Compliant
VM01       VM Hardware Upgrade to Match Host     NotCompliant
VM01       Windows 2003 - Current                NotCompliant
VM02       VMware Tools Upgrade to Match Host    Compliant
VM02       VM Hardware Upgrade to Match Host     NotCompliant
VM02       Windows 2003 - Current                NotCompliant
VM03       VMware Tools Upgrade to Match Host    Compliant
VM03       VM Hardware Upgrade to Match Host     NotCompliant
VM03       Windows 2003 - Current                Compliant
VM04       VMware Tools Upgrade to Match Host    Incompatible
VM04       VM Hardware Upgrade to Match Host     Incompatible
VM04       Windows 2003 - Current                Compliant
esx04      ESXi 4.0 U2 - Current                 NotCompliant
esx03      ESXi 4.0 U2 - Current                 Compliant
esx02      vSphere 4 Host Upgrade                Compliant
```

This, of course, was output to the PowerShell console. Most likely, you are required to produce a more typical report format such as CSV or XML. To do so, select the properties required for your report and use one of the standard PowerShell cmdlets, like `Export-CSV`, to generate the final report, as we did:

```
Get-Compliance -Entity (Get-Datacenter 'Datacenter01')
| Select-Object Entity,Baseline,Status
| Export-CSV ComplianceStatus.csv -NoTypeInformation -UseCulture
```

Notice, however, that if you select the same three properties (in this case, `Entity`, `Baseline`, and `Status`) with both `Get-Compliance` and `Select-Object` and then use the `Export-CSV` cmdlet to generate a report, the report will look like the one shown in Figure 13.4—not quite what you expected.

FIGURE 13.4   Compliance report with incorrect baseline column

	A	B	C
1	Entity	Baseline	Status
2	VM01	VMware.VumAutomation.Types.PatchBaselineImpl	Compliant
3	esx04	VMware.VumAutomation.Types.PatchBaselineImpl	NotCompliant
4	esx03	VMware.VumAutomation.Types.PatchBaselineImpl	Compliant
5	esx02	VMware.VumAutomation.Types.HostUpgradeBaselineImpl	Compliant

For a new user to PowerCLI / PowerShell, this can be quite confusing. The expectation would be that, by selecting properties that you saw in the console, the required information should output to a report exactly the same. What happened is that the cmdlet developers specified as part of the PowerCLI package how to format the console output of each cmdlet. Every PowerShell cmdlet, or pipeline concatenation of cmdlets, is processed under the hood and, as a final step, piped to `Out-Default`. For instance:

```
Get-Compliance -Entity (Get-Datacenter 'Datacenter01')
```

returns exactly the same output in the console as

```
Get-Compliance -Entity (Get-Datacenter 'Datacenter01') |
  Out-Default
```

Consequently, the `Out-Default` cmdlet determines how to format the output of the previous cmdlet in the pipeline to the console.

To do this, `Out-Default` looks to see if there is a registered view for the output type; registered views define which properties to display by default and how to format them. These are defined in a `ps1xml` file supplied by the cmdlet developers as part of the installation of the VUM PowerCLI Snap-in. For instance, the `ps1xml` file for the PowerCLI VUM cmdlets is `C:\Program Files\VMware\Infrastructure\vSphere PowerCLI\VMware.VumAutomation.Format.ps1xml`. You can examine it to see how the output to the console has been defined.

 WARNING   Do not attempt to alter `ps1xml` files, even if you decide that the default output to the console for a particular cmdlet is not to your liking! These files are digitally signed. Altering them yourself will render them useless and a replacement file or reinstall of the VUM PowerCLI cmdlets will be required.

Securing Your vSphere Environment

PART III

All is not lost for our report, though; we must simply work a bit harder and use what are known as calculated properties to get the desired output for the Baseline column in the CSV file. When using `Select-Object`, you can create your own property by using this syntax:

```
Select-Object @[Name='PropertyName';Expression={Scriptblock}}
```

(`Name` and `Expression` can be shortened to `N` and `E`, respectively). So in the next example, we created our own `Baseline` property using the `-ExpandProperty` parameter of the `Select-Object` cmdlet to expand the `Baseline` object and then pick the `Name` property:

```
Get-Compliance -Entity (Get-Datacenter 'Datacenter01')
| Select-Object Entity,
@{N='Baseline';E={($_ | Select-Object -ExpandProperty
  Baseline).Name}},Status
  | Export-CSV ComplianceStatus.csv -NoTypeInformation
    -UseCulture
```

Now, the CSV report (Figure 13.5) looks more like we expected!

FIGURE 13.5   Compliance report with all correct columns

	A	B	C
1	Entity	Baseline	Status
2	VM01	Windows 2003 - Current	Compliant
3	esx04	ESXi 4.0 U2 - Current	NotCompliant
4	esx03	ESXi 4.0 U2 - Current	Compliant
5	esx02	vSphere 4 Host Upgrade	Compliant

Implementing Specific Baseline Compliance

So far, we have looked at the big picture—patching compliance at the datacenter level. In addition, you will encounter requirements to create more granular reports and look at individual clusters, hosts, or VMs. `Get-Compliance` can accept any of these types of objects as an entity, including from the pipeline, so it's very simple to find the required information. You can also use the `-Baseline` parameter to narrow the search further and report on specific baselines.

Examining the compliance status of all hosts in `Cluster01` for the patch baseline `ESXi 4.0 U2 - Current` is a straightforward task. Retrieve the hosts with the usual PowerCLI cmdlets and pipe the results into `Get-Compliance` with a specified baseline:

```
Get-Cluster 'Cluster01' | Get-VMHost | Get-Compliance -Baseline
  (Get-PatchBaseline 'ESXi 4.0 U2 - Current')
```

The typical output would look like this:

```
Entity      Baseline              Status
------      --------              ------
esx01       ESXi 4.0 U2 - Current Compliant
esx02       ESXi 4.0 U2 - Current NotCompliant
esx03       ESXi 4.0 U2 - Current Compliant
esx04       ESXi 4.0 U2 - Current Compliant
esx05       ESXi 4.0 U2 - Current NotCompliant
esx06       ESXi 4.0 U2 - Current Compliant
```

The same principle can be applied to VMs. Let's examine the compliance status of all the VMs in Cluster01 for the baseline VMware Tools Upgrade to Match Host.

```
Get-Cluster 'Cluster01' | Get-VM | Get-Compliance -Baseline
  (Get-Baseline 'VMware Tools Upgrade to Match Host')
```

The typical output would look like this:

```
Entity      Baseline                              Status
------      --------                              ------
VM01        VMware Tools Upgrade to Match Host     Compliant
VM02        VMware Tools Upgrade to Match Host     Compliant
VM03        VMware Tools Upgrade to Match Host     NotCompliant
```

Both of these sets of cmdlets will return basic compliance status: Compliant, NotCompliant, Unknown, or Incompatible. Again, this information is useful for a high-level view. But what if more detail is required? Fortunately, the PowerCLI developers have given the Get-Compliance cmdlet the -Detailed parameter. Let's look at these same two examples again, but this time with the addition of the -Detailed parameter. We'll start with the compliance check of hosts in Cluster01. This time, the number of required patches is displayed:

```
Get-Cluster 'Cluster01' | Get-VMHost | Get-Compliance -Baseline
  (Get-PatchBaseline 'ESXi 4.0 U2 - Current') -Detailed
```

Entity	Baseline	Status	Compli antPat ches	NotCom pliant Patches	Unknow nPaches	NotAppli cablePat ches
esx01	ESXi 4.0 U2 -...	Compl...	4	0	0	0
esx02	ESXi 4.0 U2 -...	NotCo...	0	4	0	0

```
esx03  ESXi 4.0 U2 -... Compl... 4        0        0        0
esx04  ESXi 4.0 U2 -... Compl... 4        0        0        0
esx05  ESXi 4.0 U2 -... NotCo... 0        4      . 0        0
esx06  ESXi 4.0 U2 -... Compl... 4        0        0        0
```

Let's do a similar check for the VMs in `Cluster01`. This time the `VMToolsStatus` is displayed as well:

```
Get-Cluster 'Cluster01' | Get-VM | Get-Compliance -Baseline
  (Get-Baseline 'VMware Tools Upgrade to Match Host') -Detailed
```

```
Entity    Baseline              Status          VMToolsStatus
------    --------              ------          -------------
VM01      VMware Tools Upgrade  Compliant       GuestTools
          to Match Host                         Current
VM02      VMware Tools Upgrade  Compliant       GuestTools
          to Match Host                         Current
VM03      VMware Tools Upgrade  NotCompliant    GuestTools
          to Match Host                         NeedUpgrade
```

Implementing Required Patches

When planning maintenance windows and the work to be carried out, teams are often required to provide detailed information about the patches they are planning to install in advance. While the VUM GUI can provide detailed information about the patches, there is no way to export the data into a common report type. Of course you can use the VUM PowerCLI cmdlets to help you get this information; the `Get-Compliance` cmdlet is especially useful.

Let's take an example where you need to prepare a list of patches to apply to ESX 4.0 servers during the next patching window. Via the vSphere Client, you can see access information, but there is no way to extract it for a distributable report.

To retrieve this same information using the `Get-Compliance` cmdlet, retrieve compliance data from a host that has had the baseline in question attached and scanned against. In particular, look at the `NotCompliantPatches`. Then, select the properties you wish to export for the report, including a calculated property named `Product`, and export the results to a CSV file.

```
(Get-Compliance -Entity esx01 -Detailed).NotCompliantPatches
  | Select-Object Name,IDByVendor,Description,@{N='Product';
```

```
     E={$_.product | Select-Object -expandproperty Version}},
     ReleaseDate
   | Export-Csv patches.csv -NoTypeInformation -UseCulture
```

The information produced in our result is listed in Table 13.3 and Table 13.4.

TABLE 13.3   Noncompliant patch descriptions

Name	Description
Updates the ESX 4.0 Service Console glibc components	This bulletin updates the Service Console glibc components of VMware ESX 4.0 to improve host stability, and may provide minor enhancements to functionality. For a detailed list of changes associated with this bulletin, please see KB article…
VMware ESX 4.0 Complete Update 1	This bulletin includes all software updates required to install VMware ESX 4.0 Update 1 on a host. A host will not be considered running Update 1 until it is compliant with this bulletin. For a detailed list of changes associated with this bulletin,…
Updates vmx, vmkernel, etc.	This patch contains the following fixes: * Fixes an issue that will circumvent the need to wait for VMFS operations to complete, thereby reducing occurrence of virtual machines lockup. * On ESX 4.0 hosts connected through vSphere Client and…
Updates OpenSSL	This patch has the following security fix: Service console package for OpenSSL is updated to version openssl097a-0.9.7a-9.el5_2.1. The functions inside OpenSSL incorrectly check the result after calling the EVP_VerifyFinal function, which allows a…
Updates NSS and NSPR	This patch has the following security fixes: Service console packages for NSS and NSPR are updated to version nss-3.12.3.99.3-1.2157 and nspr-4.7.6-1.2213 respectively. This patch fixes several security issues in the service console packages for Network…
Updates DHCP	This patch contains a fix for a security vulnerability in the ISC third-party DHCP client. This vulnerability allows for code execution in the client by a remote DHCP server through a specially crafted subnet-mask option. The Common Vulnerabilities and…
Updates vmkernel64,vmx,hostd, etc.	Some of the issues fixed by this patch are: - On some systems under heavy networking and processor load (large number of virtual machines), it is observed that some NIC drivers will try to randomly attempt to reset the device and fail. - ESX hosts do…
Updates initscripts	This patch fixes an issue where pressing Ctrl+ Alt + Delete on service console causes ESX 4.0 hosts to reboot. See http://kb.vmware.com/kb/1017459 for more details…
Updates glib2	The service console package for GLib2 is updated to version glib2-2.12.3-4.el5_3.1. This GLib update fixes an issue where the functions inside GLib incorrectly allows multiple integer overflows leading to heap-based buffer overflows in GLib's Base64…

Securing Your vSphere Environment

PART III

(continues)

TABLE 13.3   (continued)

Name	Description
Updates megaraid-sas	This patch fixes an issue where some applications do not receive events even after registering for Asynchronous Event Notifications (AEN). This issue occurs when multiple applications register for AENs. See http://kb.vmware.com/kb/1017461 for more details…
Updates newt	The service console package for Newt library is updated to version newt-0.52.2-12.el5_4.1. This security update of Newt library fixes an issue where an attacker might cause a denial of service or possibly execute arbitrary code with the privileges of a us…
Updates nfs-utils	The service console package for nfs-utils is updated to version nfs-utils-1.0.9-42.el5. This security update of nfs-utils fixes an issue which might permit a remote attacker to bypass an intended access restriction. The Common Vulnerabilities and Exposure…
Updates Enic driver	In situations where Pass Thru Switching (PTS) is in effect, if virtual machines are powered up, there is a risk that the network interface might not come up. In PTS mode, when the network interface is brought up, PTS figures the MTU from the network.

TABLE 13.4   Noncompliant patch details

Name	IdByVendor	Product	Release date
Updates the ESX 4.0 Service Console glibc components	ESX400-200912101-UG	4.0.0	12/9/2009 8:00
VMware ESX 4.0 Complete Update 1	ESX400-Update01a	4.0.0	12/9/2009 8:00
Updates vmx, vmkernel, etc.	ESX400-200912401-BG	4.0.0	1/5/2010 8:00
Updates OpenSSL	ESX400-200912402-SG	4.0.0	1/5/2010 8:00
Updates NSS and NSPR	ESX400-200912403-SG	4.0.0	1/5/2010 8:00
Updates DHCP	ESX400-200912404-SG	4.0.0	1/5/2010 8:00
Updates vmkernel64,vmx,hostd, etc.	ESX400-201002401-BG	4.0.0	3/3/2010 8:00
Updates initscripts	ESX400-201002402-BG	4.0.0	3/3/2010 8:00
Updates glib2	ESX400-201002404-SG	4.0.0	3/3/2010 8:00
Updates megaraid-sas	ESX400-201002405-BG	4.0.0	3/3/2010 8:00
Updates newt	ESX400-201002406-SG	4.0.0	3/3/2010 8:00
Updates nfs-utils	ESX400-201002407-SG	4.0.0	3/3/2010 8:00
Updates Enic driver	ESX400-201002408-BG	4.0.0	3/3/2010 8:00

Monitoring and Reporting

Reporting the Status of Your vSphere Environment

IN THIS CHAPTER, YOU WILL LEARN TO:

Probably the most common use case for PowerCLI is reporting. In this chapter, you'll learn how to report on the most used areas of your virtual environment. Once you know how to create reports and what to report on, you'll see how to customize reports for your specific needs and how to export those reports into various formats.

Determine What to Report

Reporting is all about retrieving and formatting information from your environment, so you're going to use the Get-<noun> cmdlets a lot. After the information is retrieved, you'll export the information to a report and store it in a format for later reference.

Although there are many areas in your virtual infrastructure for which you'll want to create reports, this chapter focuses on three main areas:

► Virtual machines

► Hosts

► Clusters

VCHECK

One of the most comprehensive reports available today is the vCheck report created by Alan Renouf. vCheck Version 5.0 contains 44 different checks and is highly customizable to your specific needs. Although the report can be displayed directly to your screen, it is designed to run as a scheduled task before you get in the office to present you with an email with key information about your infrastructure in a nice, easily readable format. The report can be downloaded from Alan's site at www.virtu-al.net/featured-scripts/vcheck/.

The vCheck report is also available as a node in the VMware Community PowerPack available from Alan's site at www.virtu-al.net/featured-scripts/vmware-powerpack/.

See Chapter 21, "PowerGUI and vEcoShell," to learn more about using vEcoShell and the VMware Community PowerPack.

Virtual Machines

Virtual machine (VM) information is retrieved using the Get-VM cmdlet. The cmdlet in its simplest form returns all VMs in your infrastructure:

```
[vSphere PowerCLI] C:\Scripts> Get-VM
```

```
Name                    PowerState Num CPUs Memory (MB)
----                    ---------- -------- -----------
VM001                   PoweredOn  1        1024
VM002                   PoweredOff 1        1024
VM003                   PoweredOn  2        2048
```

You can specify a VM name via the -Name parameter to be more specific in your request. If you prefer, you can omit the -Name parameter name and use wildcards. By default, only the default properties defined in the types.ps1xml file, located in the PowerShell installation directory, are displayed. To view all properties, you can use the Format-List cmdlet on the pipeline. The Format-List cmdlet formats the output of a command as a list of properties in which each property is displayed on a separate line. You can specify which properties are displayed using the -property parameter. Specifying the parameter name is optional and therefore the parameter name may be omitted. Since wildcards are allowed, just specify an asterisk (*) to display all properties.

```
[vSphere PowerCLI] C:\Scripts> Get-VM VM001 | Format-List *

PowerState              : PoweredOn
Version                 : v7
Description             :
Notes                   :
Guest                   : VMware.VimAutomation.ViCore.Impl.V1.➥
                          VM.Guest.VMGuestImpl
NumCpu                  : 1
MemoryMB                : 1024
HardDisks               : {Hard disk 1}
NetworkAdapters         : {Network adapter 1}
UsbDevices              : {}
CDDrives                : {CD/DVD Drive 1}
FloppyDrives            : {Floppy drive 1}
Host                    : esx001.mydomain.local
HostId                  : HostSystem-host-2177
VMHostId                : HostSystem-host-2177
VMHost                  : esx001.mydomain.local
VApp                    :
FolderId                : Folder-group-v874
Folder                  : Discovered virtual machine
ResourcePoolId          : ResourcePool-resgroup-163
ResourcePool            : Resources
PersistentId            : 503dc141-f749-110e-727b-57cfa46a38fa
```

```
UsedSpaceGB                 : 12.17572
ProvisionedSpaceGB          : 23.00673
DatastoreIdList             : {Datastore-datastore-2181}
HARestartPriority           : ClusterRestartPriority
HAIsolationResponse         : AsSpecifiedByCluster
DrsAutomationLevel          : AsSpecifiedByCluster
VMSwapfilePolicy            : Inherit
VMResourceConfiguration     : VMware.VimAutomation.ViCore.Impl.V1.➥
                              VM.VMResourceConfigurationImpl
CustomFields                : {}
ExtensionData               : VMware.Vim.VirtualMachine
Id                          : VirtualMachine-vm-2192
Name                        : VM001
Uid                         : /VIServer=@vc01:443/VirtualMachine=
                              VirtualMachine-vm-2192/
```

Simply displaying all VMs isn't very useful in the real world. Let's take it one step further and look at ways to generate a more meaningful report. What about finding out which VMs are powered off?

```
[vSphere PowerCLI] C:\Scripts> Get-VM | ?{$_.PowerState -eq
    "PoweredOff"}


Name                  PowerState Num CPUs Memory (MB)
----                  ---------- -------- -----------
VM002                 PoweredOff 1           1024
```

Or what about reporting on each VM's VMware Tools version?

```
[vSphere PowerCLI] C:\Scripts> Get-VM | Get-View |
    Select-Object Name, @{Name="ToolsVersion";
    Expression={$_.config.tools.toolsVersion}}


Name                                       ToolsVersion
----                                       ------------
VM001                                      7302
VM002                                      8192
VM003                                      7303
```

Notice how the Select-Object cmdlet is used to filter the specified properties. In fact, when you use the Select-Object cmdlet, a new object is created with the specified properties and the property values are copied from the input object. Besides selecting an existing property like the Name property, you can also use the

Select-Object cmdlet to create a calculated property like a ToolsVersion property. The ToolsVersion property is created by specifying a hash table for the property. Valid keys inside the hash table are Name and Expression, where the Name key specifies the property name and the Expression key specifies its value. Instead of typing the full key names, you can also type just **N** for Name or **E** for Expression:

```
[vSphere PowerCLI] C:\Scripts> Get-VM | Get-View |
    Select-Object Name, @{N="ToolsVersion";
    E={$_.config.tools.toolsVersion}}
```

HASH TABLES

Hash tables, also known as associative arrays, are two-dimensional arrays that contain key-value pairs. A hash table is created using key-value pairs enclosed in curly brackets ({}). Multiple key-value pairs are separated by the semicolon (;) character.

```
[vSphere PowerCLI] C:\Scripts> $vm = @{Name = "VM001";
    IP = "192.168.1.1"; PowerState = "PoweredOn"}
[vSphere PowerCLI] C:\Scripts> $vm

Name                             Value
----                             -----
Name                             VM001
PowerState                       PoweredOn
IP                               10.10.10.1
```

To access a key's value, you can either use the dot notation or use square brackets, like in arrays:

```
[vSphere PowerCLI] C:\Scripts> $vm.PowerState

PoweredOn

[vSphere PowerCLI] C:\Scripts> $vm["PowerState"]

PoweredOn
```

Note that, when using square brackets, the key names must be enclosed in quotation marks. You don't have to do this if you use the dot notation.

Let's make it a bit more complicated and generate a report that lists each VM and its associated host, cluster, and datastores. Again, you're going to use the Select -Object cmdlet and calculated properties.

```
[vSphere PowerCLI] C:\Scripts> Get-VM | Select-Object Name,
    Host, @{N="Cluster";E={$_ | Get-Cluster}},
    @{N="Datastore";E={$_ | Get-Datastore}}
```

Name	Host	Cluster	Datastore
VM001	esx001.mydomain.local	CL02	{Datatore_01, Datastore_02}
VM002	esx002.mydomain.local	CL02	Datatore_01
VM003	esx003.mydomain.local	CL01	Datatore_04

Resource Limits

Now that you're getting familiar with it, let's have a look at some more examples. Do you know if any of your VMs in your infrastructure have resource limits or reservations set? You can retrieve this information by using the Get-VMResource Configuration cmdlet:

```
[vSphere PowerCLI] C:\Scripts> Get-VM |
    Get-VMResourceConfiguration | Select VM, cpuReservationMhz,
    cpuLimitMhz, memReservationMB, memLimitMB | Format-Table
```

VM	CpuReservation Mhz	CpuLimit Mhz	MemReservation MB	MemLimit MB
VM001	0	-1	0	-1
VM002	0	-1	0	-1
VM003	0	-1	0	1024
VM004	0	40284	0	512

The output will include all VMs in the report. In a real-world scenario, you're probably only interested in the VMs that are nondefault and have a reservation or limit set. In Listing 14.1 you'll find a script that filters out the default VMs and puts the nondefault VMs into an array called $report.

LISTING 14.1 Resource limits and reservations

```
$report=@()
foreach ($vm in Get-VM | Get-VMResourceConfiguration) {
  if (($vm.CpuReservationMhz -ne '0') -or
```

```
    ($vm.CpuLimitMhz -ne '-1') -or
    ($vm.MemReservationMB -ne '0') -or
    ($vm.MemLimitMB -ne '-1')) {
    $Report += $vm
  }
}
$report | Format-Table
```

Snapshots

One of our favorite vSphere features is the ability to take snapshots of a virtual machine, but when unmanaged, snapshots can be catastrophic as well. The problem with snapshots is that they tend to be forgotten once created. For each snapshot you create, vSphere creates a new hard disk underwater, also referred to as delta disk, for every disk that's affected by the snapshot operation. These delta disks keep track of the changes made to their parent disk and therefore grow as more data is modified. When the snapshot is kept for a long time, these delta disks can grow quite large and could eventually occupy all the free space on your datastore. Large delta disks slow down the performance of your VM and when you eventually want to delete the snapshot, it can take hours until all the changes are committed to the parent disks, which in turn can lead to unavailability of your VM. Snapshot information is retrieved using the Get-Snapshot cmdlet. Let's create a simple overview of all snapshots in your infrastructure:

```
[vSphere PowerCLI] C:\Scripts> Get-VM | Get-Snapshot

Name                    Description                 PowerState
----                    -----------                 ----------
Snap001                 Before upgrade              PoweredOff
VM001_Snap01            Installation test 1         PoweredOn
VM003_01                Before patches              PoweredOn
```

There are other interesting properties that aren't shown by default, like the SizeMB and Created properties. The SizeMB property calculates the total size of all related snapshot files on disk. In the real world you would use this property to monitor the size of your snapshot files on disk so that they don't become very large. This way, you can avoid havoc caused by large snapshots. The Created property contains the date and time at which the snapshot is created. As stated before, you don't want your snapshots to live a long life. Best practice is to never let a snapshot get older than a couple of days. Now, let's use the Created property to calculate the age of the snapshot in days so that you can easily spot snapshots that are older than the maximum allowed number of days:

```
[vSphere PowerCLI] C:\Scripts> Get-VM | Get-Snapshot |
    Select VM, Name, Description, @{N="DaysOld";
    E={((Get-Date) - $_.Created).Days}}
```

VM	Name	Description	DaysOld
VM002	Snap001	Before upgrade	1
VM001	VM001_Snap01	Installation test 1	40
VM003	VM003_01	Before patches	20

Now that you know the age of the snapshot in days, you can easily report only the snapshots that are older than, for instance, 7 days:

```
[vSphere PowerCLI] C:\Scripts> Get-VM | Get-Snapshot |
    Select VM, Name, Description, @{N="DaysOld";
    E={((Get-Date) - $_.Created).Days}} | ? {$_.DaysOld -gt 7}
```

VM	Name	Description	DaysOld
VM001	VM001_Snap01	Installation test 1	40
VM003	VM003_01	Before patches	20

Guest Operating Systems

With VMware Tools installed, it is possible to retrieve information from a virtual machine's guest OS. By default, a number of properties are available in the virtual machine object, such as the operating system and IP address, which you can retrieve by using the Get-VMGuest cmdlet:

```
[vSphere PowerCLI] C:\Scripts> Get-VMGuest -VM VM001
```

State	IPAddress	OSFullName
Running	{192.168.1.1}	Microsoft Windows Server 2008 (64-bit)

If other information is needed, you can use the Invoke-VMScript cmdlet to run scripts inside the guest. See Chapter 8, "Advanced Virtual Machine Features" for more information on using the Invoke-VMScript cmdlet. Also available is the

Get-VMGuestNetworkInterface cmdlet that uses the Invoke-VMScript cmdlet under the hood. For more information and examples on using the Get -VMGuestNetworkInterface cmdlet, see Chapter 5, "Creating Virtual Machines" and Chapter 7, "Configuring Virtual Machine Hardware."

Let's look at how the VMGuest object can be used to create a report about the guest's disk usage.

VM Guest Disk Usage

In Listing 14.2 you'll find a function that uses the virtual machine's guest information to report on the guest's disk usage. Using this report, you can easily spot volumes that are running out of disk space and take actions accordingly to avoid a system crash. This report can also be used to spot volumes that are heavily underutilized, and you can replace those disks with smaller ones or convert them to thin-provisioned disks to free up valuable space on your datastores.

LISTING 14.2 `Get-VMGuestDiskUsage`

```
function Get-VMGuestDiskUsage {
<#
.SYNOPSIS
  Gets a vm's guest OS disk usage information
.DESCRIPTION
  This function creates a report with disk usage information
  of the vm's guest OS
.NOTES
  Source:  Automating vSphere Administration
  Authors: Luc Dekens, Arnim van Lieshout, Jonathan Medd,
           Alan Renouf, Glenn Sizemore
.PARAMETER VM
  The VM object to create a report on
.EXAMPLE
  PS> Get-VMGuestDiskUsage -VM (Get-VM WIN*)
.EXAMPLE
  PS> Get-VM | Get-VMGuestDiskUsage
#>

  param(
    [parameter(valuefrompipeline = $true, mandatory = $true,
      HelpMessage = "Enter a vm entity")]
```

```
      [VMware.VimAutomation.ViCore.Impl.V1.Inventory.➥
VirtualMachineImpl]$VM)

  process {
#Hide errors which appear if VMware Tools is not installed
#or VM is PoweredOff
    $ErrorActionPreference = "SilentlyContinue"

  foreach ($disk in $VM.Guest.disks) {
    $objDisk = New-Object System.Object
    $objDisk | Add-Member -MemberType NoteProperty `
      -Name VM -Value $VM.Name
    $objDisk | Add-Member -MemberType NoteProperty `
      -Name Volume -Value $disk.Path
    $objDisk | Add-Member -MemberType NoteProperty `
      -Name CapacityMB -Value `
      ([math]::Round($disk.Capacity / 1MB))
    $objDisk | Add-Member -MemberType NoteProperty -Name `
      FreeSpaceMB -Value ([math]::Round($disk.FreeSpace/1MB))
    $objDisk | Add-Member -MemberType NoteProperty -Name `
      Usage% -Value ("{0:p2}" -f `
      (($disk.Capacity - $disk.FreeSpace ) / $disk.Capacity))
    $objDisk
    }
  }
}
```

Hosts

Host information is retrieved using the Get-VMHost cmdlet:

```
[vSphere PowerCLI] C:\Scripts> Get-VMHost | Format-Table

WARNING: 2 columns do not fit into the display and were removed.

Name            State        PowerState    Id CpuUsage CpuTotal
                                              Mhz      Mhz

----            -----        ----------    -- -------- --------
ESX001.mydom... Connected    PoweredOn  ...3513    1195    22496
ESX002.mydom... Mainten...   PoweredOn  ...4277      33    22496
```

You can specify a hostname via the -Name parameter to be more specific in your request. If you have a virtual machine, datastore, or folder object, you can pass that object on the pipeline to get only the hosts associated with that object:

```
[vSphere PowerCLI] C:\Scripts> Get-VM VM001 | Get-VMHost | FT

WARNING: 2 columns do not fit into the display and were removed.

Name            State        PowerState       Id CpuUsage CpuTotal
                                                      Mhz      Mhz
----            -----        ----------       -- -------- --------
ESX001.mydom... Connected    PoweredOn    ...3513     1195    22496
```

Now, let's look at some more advanced reporting.

Host Bus Adapters

For the sake of documentation, you probably want a report on your host's host bus adapters. This information can be retrieved using a simple one-liner:

```
[vSphere PowerCLI] C:\Scripts> Get-VMHost -Name "ESX001" |
    Get-VMHostHba | Select Pci,Device,Type,Model,Status |
    Format-Table -AutoSize

WARNING: column "Status" does not fit into the display and was
removed.

Pci        Device        Type   Model
---        ------        ----   -----
02:04.0    vmhba0        Block  Smart Array 5i
03:07.0    vmhba1   FibreChannel QLA2300 64-bit Fibre Channel ...
03:08.0    vmhba2   FibreChannel QLA2300 64-bit Fibre Channel ...
00:04.1    vmhba3        Block  AMD 8111 IDE/PATA Controller
00:04.1    vmhba32       Block  AMD 8111 IDE/PATA Controller
```

When you want to know the World Wide Port Numbers (WWPN) of the host's Fibre Channel adapters, you can query the PortWorldWideName property. This property is an integer value, however, and it probably doesn't mean anything to you in this format. WWPNs are commonly denoted in hexadecimal format. You can convert the reported value to hexadecimal using the PowerShell -f format operator:

```
"{0:x}" -f $intVariable
```

To generate the full report, you can use the script in Listing 14.3. This script creates a report of all storage adapters on all hosts in all clusters.

LISTING 14.3   Host bus adapter report

```
$hbaReport = @()
foreach ($cluster in Get-cluster) {
  foreach ($vmHost in @($cluster | Get-vmhost)) {
    foreach ($hba in @($vmHost | Get-VMHostHba)) {
      $objHba = "" | Select ClusterName,HostName,Pci,Device, `
          Type,Model,Status,Wwpn
      $objHba.ClusterName = $cluster.Name
      $objHba.HostName = $vmhost.Name
      $objHba.Pci = $hba.Pci
      $objHba.Device = $hba.Device
      $objHba.Type = $hba.Type
      $objHba.Model = $hba.Model
      $objHba.Status = $hba.Status
      $objHba.Wwpn = "{0:x}" -f $hba.PortWorldWideName
      $hbaReport += $objHba
    }
  }
}

$hbaReport | Export-Csv HbaReport.csv
```

Network Interface Cards

As with the host bus adapter report, you can report the status of your network interface cards. You can retrieve network interface card information by using the Get-VMHostNetworkAdapter cmdlet:

```
[vSphere PowerCLI] C:\Scripts> Get-VMHost -Name "ESX001" |
    Get-VMHostNetworkAdapter | Select DeviceName,Mac,
    BitRatePerSec,FullDuplex


DeviceName Mac                BitRatePerSec FullDuplex
---------- ---                ------------- ----------
vmnic1     00:aa:bb:cc:dd:e1              0      False
vmnic0     00:aa:bb:cc:dd:e0           1000       True
vmnic2     00:aa:bb:cc:dd:e2           1000       True
```

```
vmnic3      00:aa:bb:cc:dd:e3          1000        True
vswif0      00:50:56:cc:dd:ee
vmk0        00:50:56:cc:dd:ef
```

If you want to know the Peripheral Component Interconnect (PCI) information for the network card, you have to query the underlying SDK object; the information isn't available from the objects returned by the Get-VMHostNetworkAdapter cmdlet. This can be done through the .ExtensionData property. Let's generate a full report like the HBA report we created with the script in Listing 14.3. The script in Listing 14.4 creates a report of all network interface cards on all hosts in all clusters.

LISTING 14.4 Network interface cards report

```
$nicReport=@()
foreach ($cluster in Get-cluster) {
  foreach ($vmHost in @($cluster | Get-vmhost)) {
    foreach ($nic in @($VMHost | Get-VMHostNetworkAdapter)) {
      $objNic = "" | Select ClusterName,HostName,Pci, `
          DeviceName,Mac,BitRatePerSec,FullDuplex
      $objNic.ClusterName = $cluster.Name
      $objNic.HostName = $vmHost.Name
      $objNic.Pci = $nic.ExtensionData.Pci
      $objNic.DeviceName = $nic.DeviceName
      $objNic.Mac = $nic.Mac
      $objNic.BitRatePerSec = $nic.BitRatePerSec
      $objNic.FullDuplex = $nic.FullDuplex
      if ($nic.ExtensionData.Pci) {
        $nicReport += $ObjNic
      }
    }
  }
}
$nicReport | Export-Csv NicReport.csv
```

PCI Devices

Besides storage adapters and network cards, there is a lot of other hardware present in your hosts. The function in Listing 14.5 generates a report of all hardware devices present in your host. The function downloads PCI information from http://pci -ids.ucw.cz/ to provide more information on each PCI device found. To use the function, provide one or more VMHost objects through the pipeline or use the -VMHost parameter:

```
Get-VMhost "ESX001" | Get-VMHostPciDevice | Format-Table
```

LISTING 14.5   The **Get-VMHostPciDevice** function

```
function Get-VMHostPciDevice {
<#
.SYNOPSIS
  Returns the ESX(i) host's PCI Devices
.DESCRIPTION
  This function returns the ESX(i) host's PCI devices and the
  associated ESX devices. Pci device information is downloaded
  from http://pci-ids.ucw.cz/
.NOTES
  Source:  Automating vSphere Administration
  Authors: Luc Dekens, Arnim van Lieshout, Jonathan Medd,
           Alan Renouf, Glenn Sizemore
.PARAMETER VMHost
  The ESX(i) host entity for which the PCI devices should be
  returned
.PARAMETER forceDownload
  Switch parameter to force a download of the pci information
.EXAMPLE
  PS> Get-VMHostPciDevice -VMHost (Get-VMHost "esx001")
.EXAMPLE
  PS> Get-VMHost "esx001" | Get-VMHostPciDevice
#>

  Param (
  [parameter(valuefrompipeline = $true, mandatory = $true,
  HelpMessage = "Enter an ESX(i) host entity")]
  [VMware.VimAutomation.ViCore.Impl.V1.Inventory.VMHostImpl] `
      $VMHost,
  [Switch]$forceDownload)

  Begin {
    $urlPci = "http://pci-ids.ucw.cz/v2.2/pci.ids"
    $filename = "pci.ids"
    $pciDevices= @{}
# Download file if not present or if forced download
```

```powershell
    if(!(Test-Path $filename) -or $forceDownload){
      $web = New-Object net.WebClient
      $web.downloadfile($urlPCI,$filename)
    }
# Read file into hash tab
    Get-Content $filename | where {
        $_.Length -ne 0 -and $_[0] -ne "#"} | %{
      if($_[0] -eq "`t"){
        if($_[1] -eq "`t"){
          $subdeviceId = $_.Substring(2,4)
          if(!$pciDevices[$vendorId].deviceTab.ContainsKey( `
            $subdeviceId)){
            $pciDevices[$vendorId].deviceTab[$subdeviceId] =
              $_.Substring(6).TrimStart(" ")
          }
        }
        else{
          $deviceId = "0x" + $_.Substring(1,4)
          if(!$pciDevices[$vendorId].deviceTab.ContainsKey( `
            $deviceId)){
            $pciDevices[$vendorId].deviceTab[$deviceId] =
              $_.Substring(5).TrimStart(" ")
          }
        }
      }
      else{
        $vendorId = "0x" + $_.Substring(0,4)
        if(!$pciDevices.ContainsKey($vendorId)){
          $pciDevices[$vendorId] = New-Object PSObject `
            -ArgumentList @{
            Vendor = $_.Substring(4).TrimStart(" ")
            deviceTab = @{}
          }
        }
      }
    }
# Create PCI class array
    $PciClass = @("Unclassified device",
      "Mass storage controller","Network controller",
      "Display controller","Multimedia controller",
      "Memory controller","Bridge","Communication controller",
```

```
            "Generic system peripheral","Input device controller",
            "Docking station","Processor","Serial bus controller",
            "Wireless controller","Intelligent controller",
            "Satellite communications controller",
            "Encryption controller","Signal processing controller")
        }

    Process {
# Get the host's PCI Devices
        $hostDevices = @()
        foreach ($dev in $VMHost.ExtensionData.Hardware.PciDevice) {
            $strVendorId = "0x" + "{0}" -f
               [Convert]::ToString($dev.VendorId,16).ToUpper(). `
                  PadLeft(4, '0')
            $strDeviceId = "0x" + "{0}" -f
               [Convert]::ToString($dev.DeviceId,16).ToUpper(). `
                  PadLeft(4, '0')
            $objDevice = "" |
               Select Pci, ClassName, VendorName, DeviceName, `
                  EsxDeviceName
            $objDevice.Pci = $dev.Id
            $objDevice.ClassName = $PciClass[[int]($dev.ClassId/256)]
            if($pciDevices.ContainsKey($strVendorId)){
               $objDevice.VendorName = $pciDevices[$strVendorId].Vendor
            }
            else{
               $objDevice.VendorName = $strVendorId
            }
            if($pciDevices[$strVendorId].deviceTab.ContainsKey( `
                 $strDeviceId)){
               $objDevice.DeviceName =
                  $pciDevices[$strVendorId].deviceTab[$strDeviceId]
            }
            else{
               $objDevice.DeviceName = $strDeviceId
            }
            $hostDevices += $objDevice
         }

# Find associated ESX storage devices
         foreach ($hba in $_.ExtensionData.Config.StorageDevice. `
            HostBusAdapter) {
```

```
$hostDevices | ? {$_.Pci -match $hba.Pci} | % {
    $_.EsxDeviceName = "["+$hba.device+"]"}
}

# Find associated ESX network devices
    foreach ($nic in $_.ExtensionData.Config.Network.Pnic) {
        $hostDevices | ? {$_.Pci -match $nic.Pci} | % {
            $_.EsxDeviceName = "["+$nic.device+"]"}
    }
    $hostDevices
  }
}
```

Clusters

You retrieve cluster information by using the Get-Cluster cmdlet:

```
[vSphere PowerCLI] C:\Scripts> Get-Cluster | FT -AutoSize


Name HAEnabled HAFailoverLevel DrsEnabled DrsAutomationLevel
---- --------- --------------- ---------- ------------------
CL01 True      1               False      FullyAutomated
CL05 False     1               False      FullyAutomated
CL02 False     1               True       FullyAutomated
CL03 False     1               False      FullyAutomated
CL04 False     1               False      FullyAutomated
```

The cluster objects returned contain only basic High Availability (HA) and Distributed Resource Scheduler (DRS) information. If you want to know more information, you have to use the underlying SDK object, which is accessible through the .extension data property. If you want to know the number of hosts in a cluster, you can simply count the items in the .extensiondata.host property.

```
[vSphere PowerCLI] C:\Scripts> Get-Cluster | Select Name, `
    @{N="hosts";E={$_.extensiondata.host.count}} | ft -AutoSize


Name #hosts
---- ------
CL01     0
CL05     0
CL02     3
CL03     0
CL04     0
```

Notice the use of the –AutoSize parameter with the Format-Table cmdlet to automatically size the width of the columns according to their content.

Cluster Summary Report

Let's generate a small summary report on the clusters. Things that are interesting to include in this report are the number of hosts, VMs, datastores, networks, and numbers on memory and CPU usage. The function in Listing 14.6 will generate such a report.

LISTING 14.6 Get-ClusterSummary

```
function Get-ClusterSummary {
<#
.SYNOPSIS
  Gets summary information from the cluster
.DESCRIPTION
  This function creates a report with summary information of the
  cluster
.NOTES
  Source:  Automating vSphere Administration
  Authors: Luc Dekens, Arnim van Lieshout, Jonathan Medd,
           Alan Renouf, Glenn Sizemore
.PARAMETER Cluster
  The cluster object to create a report on
.EXAMPLE
  PS> Get-ClusterSummary -Cluster (Get-Cluster CL01)
.EXAMPLE
  PS> Get-Cluster | Get-ClusterSummary
#>

  param(
    [parameter(valuefrompipeline = $true, mandatory = $true,
      HelpMessage = "Enter a cluster entity")]
    [VMware.VimAutomation.ViCore.Impl.V1.Inventory.ClusterImpl] `
        $cluster)

  process {
    $objCluster = "" | Select ClusterName, NumHost, NumVM, `
        NumDatastore, NumNetwork, AssignedCpu, NumCores, `
        vCpuPerCore, TotalCpuGHz, TotalMemGB, AssignedMemGB, `
        MemUsagePct
```

```
$vm = @($cluster | Get-VM)
$objCluster.ClusterName = $cluster.Name
$objCluster.NumHost = `
    $cluster.ExtensionData.Summary.NumHosts
$objCluster.NumVM = $vm.Count
$objCluster.NumDatastore = `
    $cluster.ExtensionData.Datastore.Count
$objCluster.NumNetwork = `
    $cluster.ExtensionData.Network.Count
$objCluster.AssignedCpu = ($vm | Where {
  $_.PowerState -eq "PoweredOn"} |
  Measure-Object -Property NumCpu -Sum).Sum
$objCluster.NumCores = `
    $cluster.ExtensionData.Summary.NumCpuCores
$objCluster.vCpuPerCore = "{0:n2}" -f
  ($objCluster.AssignedCpu / $objCluster.NumCores)
$objCluster.TotalCpuGhz = "{0:n2}" -f
  ($cluster.ExtensionData.Summary.TotalCpu / 1000)
$objCluster.TotalMemGB = "{0:n2}" -f
  ($cluster.ExtensionData.Summary.TotalMemory / 1GB)
$objCluster.AssignedMemGB = "{0:n2}" -f (($vm |
  Where {$_.PowerState -eq "PoweredOn"} |
  Measure-Object -Property MemoryMB -Sum).Sum / 1024)
$objCluster.MemUsagePct = "{0:p2}" -f
  ($objCluster.AssignedMemGB / $objCluster.TotalMemGB)
$objCluster
  }
}
```

Now that you've examined the Get-ClusterSummary function, let's give it a try and have a look at the generated report:

```
[vSphere PowerCLI] C:\Scripts> Get-Cluster CL02 |
    Get-ClusterSummary

ClusterName   : CL02
NumHost       : 3
NumVM         : 48
NumDatastore  : 13
NumNetwork    : 15
AssignedCpu   : 63
NumCores      : 24
```

```
vCpuPerCore   : 2.63
TotalCpuGHz   : 64.08
TotalMemGB    : 135.67
AssignedMemGB : 90.95
MemUsagePct   : 67.04 %
```

Generating this report for just one cluster is nice, but what about your other clusters? The benefit of writing the `Get-ClusterSummary` code as a function is that you can use the code with any cluster object you like. To generate a report for all your clusters, you only have to put them all on the pipeline by just removing the cluster name from the `Get-Cluster` cmdlet:

```
[vSphere PowerCLI] C:\Scripts> Get-Cluster |
    Get-ClusterSummary | Format-Table
```

Cluste rName	Num Host	NumVM	NumDat astore	NumNe twork	Assig nedCpu	NumCo res	vCpuP erCore	Total CpuGHz	Total MemGB
CL01	5	102	14	62	138	64	2.16	151.07	335.99
CL02	3	48	13	15	63	24	2.63	64.08	135.67
CL03	1	16	4	5	16	8	2.00	22.50	40.00
CL04	2	24	3	14	28	16	1.75	44.99	111.99

Notice that the `Format-Table` cmdlet is used here to display the output in a table format. The output shown is also edited to fit onto the page.

Inconsistent Port Groups

If you're using standard switches, it's important that all port groups be consistently defined on all hosts in your cluster. If you fail to do so, you might encounter vMotion errors. The function in Listing 14.7 will help you detect inconsistently named port groups.

LISTING 14.7 `Get-MissingPortGroups`

```
function Get-MissingPortgroups {
<#
.SYNOPSIS
  Gets the inconsistent virtual portgroups in a cluster
.DESCRIPTION
  This function creates a report of the inconsistent portgroups
  in a cluster. It reports which portgroups are missing on which
  host.
```

```
.NOTES
  Source:   Automating vSphere Administration
  Authors: Luc Dekens, Arnim van Lieshout, Jonathan Medd,
           Alan Renouf, Glenn Sizemore
.PARAMETER Cluster
  The cluster object to check
.EXAMPLE
  PS> Get-MissingPortGroups -Cluster (Get-Cluster CL01)
.EXAMPLE
  PS> Get-Cluster | Get-MissingPortGroups
#>

  param(
    [parameter(valuefrompipeline = $true, mandatory = $true,
      HelpMessage = "Enter a cluster entity")]
    [VMware.VimAutomation.ViCore.Impl.V1.Inventory.ClusterImpl] `
        $cluster)

  process{
#create an array with all available portgroups in the cluster
    $clusterHosts = @($cluster | Get-VMHost)
    $refPortGroups = @($clusterHosts | Get-VirtualPortGroup |
      Select-Object -Unique)

#compare the hosts against the reference array
    foreach ($vmHost in $clusterHosts) {
      $difPortGroups = @($vmHost | Get-VirtualPortGroup)
      $differences = @(Compare-Object $refPortGroups `
          $difPortGroups)
      foreach ($item in $differences) {
        $objPG = "" | Select Cluster,HostName,MissingPortGroup
        $objPG.Cluster = $cluster
        $objPG.HostName = $vmHost.Name
        $objPG.MissingPortGroup = $item.InputObject
        $objPG
      }
    }
  }
}
```

Now let's take a look at the report:

```
[vSphere PowerCLI] C:\Scripts> Get-Cluster CL02 |
      Get-MissingPortGroups

Cluster         HostName                      MissingPortGroup
-------         --------                      ----------------
CL02            esx001.mydomain.local         Management Network
CL02            esx003.mydomain.local         Management Network
CL02            esx002.mydomain.local         VLAN020
```

Notice that the hosts esx001 and esx003 are both missing a Management Network port group and that host esx002 doesn't contain the VLAN020 port group.

Customize Your Reports

In this section, you're going to learn about the various customization options available to you to generate reports that match your needs. You start with extending the standard objects and then learn how to create your own. In the last section you're going to explore the different output options for your reports.

Adding Properties to Existing Objects

Many times, the standard objects just aren't good enough and are missing that one property you want to include in your report. Remember the VMware Tools property from the VM report? Or what about adding the number of VMs to the cluster object?

Add-Member

To extend an existing object, you can use the Add-Member cmdlet. This cmdlet is used to add a user-defined property to an instance of a PowerShell object. Remember that Add-Member only adds the property to a specific object instance and not to the object's definition itself. Any new objects created won't have the newly added property. If you want the property to be available in all new instances, you'll need to modify the object's definition in the Types.ps1xml file. This file, which is located in the PowerShell installation directory, is digitally signed to prevent tampering, but you can create your own Types.ps1xml file to further extend the types. Extending object definitions is beyond the scope of this book. If you want to modify the object types, start with looking at the PowerShell built-in `about_Types.ps1xml` help topic.

```
[vSphere PowerCLI] C:\Scripts> Help about_Types.ps1xml
```

Now, let's use the `Add-Member` cmdlet to add a `numVM` property to a cluster object, which holds the number of virtual machines in the cluster:

```
$clusterReport =@()
foreach ($cluster in Get-Cluster) {
  $cluster | Add-Member -MemberType NoteProperty -Name numVM `
      -Value @($cluster | Get-VM).count
  $clusterReport += $cluster
}
$clusterReport | Select Name, numVM
```

New-VIProperty

One of the new features of PowerCLI 4.1 is the `New-VIProperty` cmdlet. This cmdlet lets you add your own properties to a specified PowerCLI object type. Because you are changing the object type (and not just an existing instance like the `Add-Member` cmdlet does), the new property will be available on the next retrieval of the corresponding objects. Let's illustrate this with an example we used earlier. Remember the report on the VM Tools version in the "Virtual Machines" section?

```
Get-VM | Get-View | Select-Object Name, @{Name="ToolsVersion";
    Expression={$_.config.tools.toolsVersion}}
```

Here, you were forced to use the `Get-View` cmdlet to get access to the underlying SDK object to retrieve the Tools version. Using the `New-VIProperty` cmdlet, you can create a new property to hold this information, so you don't need to retrieve the underlying SDK anymore:

```
New-VIProperty -Name toolsVersion -ObjectType VirtualMachine `
    -ValueFromExtensionProperty 'config.tools.toolsVersion'
Get-VM | Select Name, toolsVersion
```

You'll notice that the code using the `New-VIProperty` cmdlet is much faster. This is because you don't have to fetch the complete SDK object using the `Get-View` cmdlet.

Monitoring and Reporting

PART IV

Creating Custom Objects

When you need to gather information from different objects to include in your report, it's much easier to create your own custom object rather than extending an existing object. The best way to create a report is to define a custom object that includes all the properties you need in your report. A custom object can be created using the `New-Object` cmdlet and properties can be defined with the `Add-Member` cmdlet:

```
$myObject = New-Object Object
$myObject | Add-Member -MemberType NoteProperty `
    -Name Vm -Value $null
$myObject | Add-Member -MemberType NoteProperty `
    -Name HostName -Value $null
$myObject | Add-Member -MemberType NoteProperty `
    -Name ClusterName -Value $null
```

CHOOSE THE METHOD THAT SUITS YOUR NEED

As mentioned in the "Virtual Machines" section, you can also create properties using the `Select-Object` cmdlet. Notice that `Select-Object` creates a copy of the source object while `Add-Member` adds a property to the source object itself:

```
$myObject = New-Object Object |
    Select-Object Vm, HostName, ClusterName
```

When you don't need to copy properties from a source object, it doesn't really matter what type of source object you use. In practice, you'll see a lot of people using an empty string as a source object for the `Select-Object` cmdlet, because this is the fastest way to define an object in PowerShell.

```
$myObject = "" | Select-Object Vm, HostName, ClusterName
```

Which method to use is totally up to you. The easiest way to craft your own object is using the `Select-Object` method. Notice, however, that this method will only create `NoteProperty` type properties. A `NoteProperty` can only hold a static value, but most of the time this is all you need. The `Add-Member` method requires much more code, but on the other hand, it enables you to create other property types, like a `ScriptProperty`. A `ScriptProperty` is a property whose value is the output of a script.

If these methods still don't fit your needs, you can even use the `Add-Type` cmdlet to define your own Microsoft .NET class. The default source code language is C#, but you can also use Visual Basic or JScript.

```
Add-Type @'
public class MyClass
{
    public string Vm;
    public string HostName;
    public string ClusterName;
}
'@
$myObject = New-Object MyClass
```

Exporting Output

Now that you've learned to use PowerCLI to create reports, you'll want to export these reports to a file rather than writing it to the console. There are several options available for exporting your report.

Out-GridView

If you want to quickly view your report in a nice interactive table, you can use the `Out-GridView` cmdlet. Remember that this feature requires Microsoft .NET Framework 3.5 with Service Pack 1 to work. Using the interactive table, you can sort your data on any column by clicking the column header. To hide, show, or reorder columns, right-click a column header. You can also apply a search filter or define criteria by unfolding the Query window and adding criteria using the Add button. Figure 14.1 shows a typical `Out-GridView` report.

Output to CSV

You can simply export your report to CSV using the `Export-Csv` cmdlet. This way, the report can be easily imported into a spreadsheet program, like Microsoft Excel:

```
$report | Export-Csv c:\temp\MyReport.csv -NoTypeInformation
```

By default, the first line of the CSV file contains #TYPE followed by the fully qualified name of the type of the .NET Framework object. To omit the type information, use the -NoTypeInformation parameter.

FIGURE 14.1 `Out-GridView` example of the `Get-VMHostPciDevice` function's output

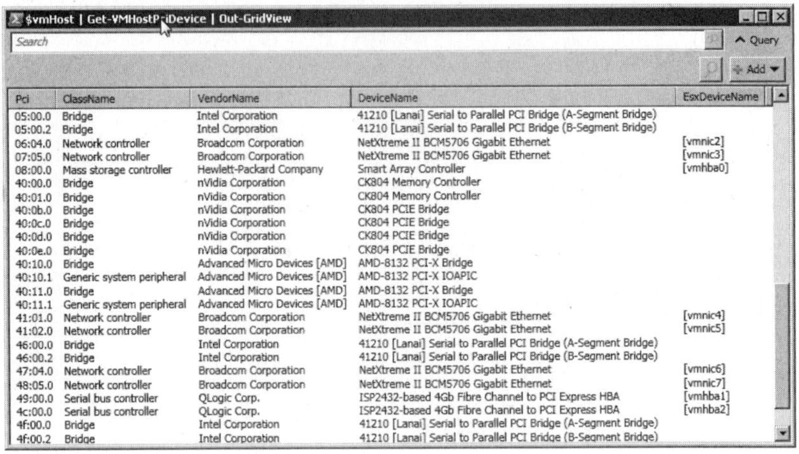

Pci	ClassName	VendorName	DeviceName	EsxDeviceName
05:00.0	Bridge	Intel Corporation	41210 [Lanai] Serial to Parallel PCI Bridge (A-Segment Bridge)	
05:00.2	Bridge	Intel Corporation	41210 [Lanai] Serial to Parallel PCI Bridge (B-Segment Bridge)	
06:04.0	Network controller	Broadcom Corporation	NetXtreme II BCM5706 Gigabit Ethernet	[vmnic2]
07:05.0	Network controller	Broadcom Corporation	NetXtreme II BCM5706 Gigabit Ethernet	[vmnic3]
08:00.0	Mass storage controller	Hewlett-Packard Company	Smart Array Controller	[vmhba0]
40:00.0	Bridge	nVidia Corporation	CK804 Memory Controller	
40:01.0	Bridge	nVidia Corporation	CK804 Memory Controller	
40:0b.0	Bridge	nVidia Corporation	CK804 PCIE Bridge	
40:0c.0	Bridge	nVidia Corporation	CK804 PCIE Bridge	
40:0d.0	Bridge	nVidia Corporation	CK804 PCIE Bridge	
40:0e.0	Bridge	nVidia Corporation	CK804 PCIE Bridge	
40:10.0	Bridge	Advanced Micro Devices [AMD]	AMD-8132 PCI-X Bridge	
40:10.1	Generic system peripheral	Advanced Micro Devices [AMD]	AMD-8132 PCI-X IOAPIC	
40:11.0	Bridge	Advanced Micro Devices [AMD]	AMD-8132 PCI-X Bridge	
40:11.1	Generic system peripheral	Advanced Micro Devices [AMD]	AMD-8132 PCI-X IOAPIC	
41:01.0	Network controller	Broadcom Corporation	NetXtreme II BCM5706 Gigabit Ethernet	[vmnic4]
41:02.0	Network controller	Broadcom Corporation	NetXtreme II BCM5706 Gigabit Ethernet	[vmnic5]
46:00.0	Bridge	Intel Corporation	41210 [Lanai] Serial to Parallel PCI Bridge (A-Segment Bridge)	
46:00.2	Bridge	Intel Corporation	41210 [Lanai] Serial to Parallel PCI Bridge (B-Segment Bridge)	
47:04.0	Network controller	Broadcom Corporation	NetXtreme II BCM5706 Gigabit Ethernet	[vmnic6]
48:05.0	Network controller	Broadcom Corporation	NetXtreme II BCM5706 Gigabit Ethernet	[vmnic7]
49:00.0	Serial bus controller	QLogic Corp.	ISP2432-based 4Gb Fibre Channel to PCI Express HBA	[vmhba1]
4c:00.0	Serial bus controller	QLogic Corp.	ISP2432-based 4Gb Fibre Channel to PCI Express HBA	[vmhba2]
4f:00.0	Bridge	Intel Corporation	41210 [Lanai] Serial to Parallel PCI Bridge (A-Segment Bridge)	
4f:00.2	Bridge	Intel Corporation	41210 [Lanai] Serial to Parallel PCI Bridge (B-Segment Bridge)	

Output to Excel

If you want to export your report to Excel directly, you're out of luck with standard PowerShell. There is no cmdlet available. But don't let that hold you back. Because Microsoft Office is also .NET based, you can create an Excel object using

```
$excelApp = New-Object -ComObject "Excel.Application"
```

In Listing 14.8 you'll find an `Export-Xls` function to assist you in exporting to Excel format. It even lets you insert charts into your Excel worksheets. Now, who said PowerShell wasn't fun?

LISTING 14.8 `Export-Xls`

```
#requires -version 2

function Export-Xls{
  <#
.SYNOPSIS
  Saves Microsoft .NET Framework objects to a worksheet in an
  XLS file
.DESCRIPTION
  The Export-Xls function allows you to save Microsoft .NET
  Framework objects to a named worksheet in an Excel file
  (type XLS). The position of the worksheet can be specified.
```

```
  .NOTES
    Source:  Automating vSphere Administration
    Authors: Luc Dekens, Arnim van Lieshout, Jonathan Medd,
             Alan Renouf, Glenn Sizemore
  .PARAMETER InputObject
    Specifies the objects to be written to the worksheet.
    The parameter accepts objects through the pipeline.
  .PARAMETER Path
    Specifies the path to the XLS file.
  .PARAMETER WorksheetName
    The name for the new worksheet. If not specified the name will
    be "Sheet" followed by the "Ticks" value
  .PARAMETER SheetPosition
    Specifies where the new worksheet will be inserted in the
    series of existing worksheets. You can specify "begin" or
    "end". The default is "begin".
  .PARAMETER ChartType
    Specifies the type of chart you want add to the worksheet.
    All types in the [microsoft.Office.Interop.Excel.XlChartType]
    enumeration are accepted.
  .PARAMETER NoTypeInformation
    Omits the type information from the worksheet. The default is
    to include the "#TYPE" line.
  .PARAMETER AppendWorksheet
    Specifies if the worksheet should keep or remove the existing
    worksheet in the spreadsheet. The default is to append.
  .EXAMPLE
    PS> $data = Get-Process | Select-Object Name, Id, WS
    PS> Export-Xls $data C:\Reports\MyWkb.xls `
            -WorksheetName "WS" -AppendWorksheet:$false
  .EXAMPLE
    PS> $data = Get-Process | Select-Object Name, Id, WS
    PS> Export-Xls $data C:\Reports\MyWkb.xls -SheetPosition "end"
  .EXAMPLE
    PS> $data = Get-Process | Select-Object Name, Id, WS
    PS> Export-Xls $data C:\Reports\MyWkb.xls `
            -WorksheetName "WS" -ChartType "xlColumnClustered"
#>
  param(
```

```
[parameter(ValueFromPipeline = $true,Position=1)]
[ValidateNotNullOrEmpty()]
  $InputObject,
[parameter(Position=2)]
[ValidateNotNullOrEmpty()]
  [string]$Path,
  [string]$WorksheetName = ("Sheet " + (Get-Date).Ticks),
  [string]$SheetPosition = "begin",
  [PSObject]$ChartType,
  [switch]$NoTypeInformation = $true,
  [switch]$AppendWorksheet = $true
)

begin{
  [System.Reflection.Assembly]::LoadWithPartialName( `
      "Microsoft.Office.Interop.Excel")
  if($ChartType){
    [microsoft.Office.Interop.Excel.XlChartType]$ChartType = `
        $ChartType
  }

  function Set-ClipBoard{
    param(
      [string]$text
    )
    process{
      Add-Type -AssemblyName System.Windows.Forms
      $tb = New-Object System.Windows.Forms.TextBox
      $tb.Multiline = $true
      $tb.Text = $text
      $tb.SelectAll()
      $tb.Copy()
    }
  }

  function Add-Array2Clipboard {
    param (
      [PSObject[]]$ConvertObject,
      [switch]$Header
    )
```

```powershell
  process{
    $array = @()

    if ($Header) {
      $line =""
      $ConvertObject | Get-Member -MemberType Property, `
          NoteProperty,CodeProperty | `
          Select -Property Name | %{
        $line += ($_.Name.tostring() + "`t")
      }
      $array += ($line.TrimEnd("`t") + "`r")
    }
    else {
      foreach($row in $ConvertObject){
        $line =""
        $row | Get-Member -MemberType Property, `
            NoteProperty | %{
          $Name = $_.Name
          if(!$Row.$Name){$Row.$Name = ""}
          $line += ([string]$Row.$Name + "`t")
        }
        $array += ($line.TrimEnd("`t") + "`r")
      }
    }
    Set-ClipBoard $array
  }
}


$excelApp = New-Object -ComObject "Excel.Application"
$originalAlerts = $excelApp.DisplayAlerts
$excelApp.DisplayAlerts = $false
if(Test-Path -Path $Path -PathType "Leaf"){
  $workBook = $excelApp.Workbooks.Open($Path)
}
else{
  $workBook = $excelApp.Workbooks.Add()
}
$sheet = $excelApp.Worksheets.Add( `
    $workBook.Worksheets.Item(1))
if(!$AppendWorksheet){
```

```
    $workBook.Sheets | where {$_ -ne $sheet} | %{$_.Delete()}
  }
  $sheet.Name = $WorksheetName
  if($SheetPosition -eq "end"){
    $nrSheets = $workBook.Sheets.Count
    2..($nrSheets) |%{
      $workbook.Sheets.Item($_).Move( `
          $workbook.Sheets.Item($_ - 1))
    }
  }
  $sheet.Activate()
  $array = @()
}

process{
  $array += $InputObject
}

end{
  Add-Array2Clipboard $array -Header:$True
  $selection = $sheet.Range("A1") ·
  $selection.Select() | Out-Null
  $sheet.Paste()
  $Sheet.UsedRange.HorizontalAlignment = `
      [microsoft.Office.Interop.Excel.XlHAlign]::xlHAlignCenter
  Add-Array2Clipboard $array
  $selection = $sheet.Range("A2")
  $selection.Select() | Out-Null
  $sheet.Paste() | Out-Null
  $selection = $sheet.Range("A1")
  $selection.Select() | Out-Null

  $sheet.UsedRange.EntireColumn.AutoFit() | Out-Null
  $workbook.Sheets.Item(1).Select()
  if($ChartType){
    $sheet.Shapes.AddChart($ChartType) | Out-Null
  }
  $workbook.SaveAs($Path)
  $excelApp.DisplayAlerts = $originalAlerts
```

```
    $excelApp.Quit()
    Stop-Process -Name "Excel"
  }
}
```

Output to HTML

While exporting to a CSV file is nice, if you want to do calculations, sorting, or filtering afterward, the format is not always well suited for a readable and distributable report. To create a more portable report, HTML is the preferred format. To create an HTML report, use the `ConvertTo-Html` cmdlet. Let's use the NIC report (Listing 14.4) created in the "Hosts" section and convert it into an HTML page like the one shown in Figure 14.2:

```
$nicReport | ConvertTo-Html > nicreport.html
```

FIGURE 14.2 Simple NIC HTML report

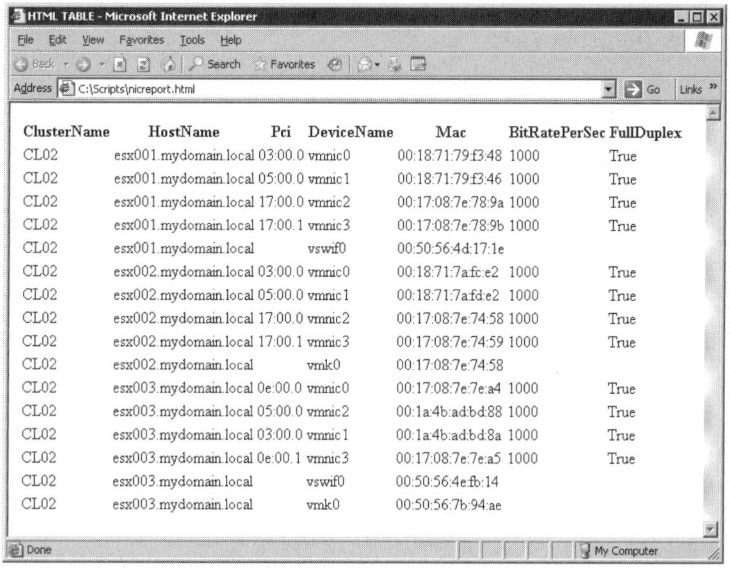

ClusterName	HostName	Pci	DeviceName	Mac	BitRatePerSec	FullDuplex
CL02	esx001.mydomain.local	03:00.0	vmnic0	00:18:71:79:f3:48	1000	True
CL02	esx001.mydomain.local	05:00.0	vmnic1	00:18:71:79:f3:46	1000	True
CL02	esx001.mydomain.local	17:00.0	vmnic2	00:17:08:7e:78:9a	1000	True
CL02	esx001.mydomain.local	17:00.1	vmnic3	00:17:08:7e:78:9b	1000	True
CL02	esx001.mydomain.local		vswif0	00:50:56:4d:17:1e		
CL02	esx002.mydomain.local	03:00.0	vmnic0	00:18:71:7a:fc:e2	1000	True
CL02	esx002.mydomain.local	05:00.0	vmnic1	00:18:71:7a:fd:e2	1000	True
CL02	esx002.mydomain.local	17:00.0	vmnic2	00:17:08:7e:74:58	1000	True
CL02	esx002.mydomain.local	17:00.1	vmnic3	00:17:08:7e:74:59	1000	True
CL02	esx002.mydomain.local		vmk0	00:17:08:7e:74:58		
CL02	esx003.mydomain.local	0e:00.0	vmnic0	00:17:08:7e:7e:a4	1000	True
CL02	esx003.mydomain.local	05:00.0	vmnic2	00:1a:4b:ad:bd:88	1000	True
CL02	esx003.mydomain.local	03:00.0	vmnic1	00:1a:4b:ad:bd:8a	1000	True
CL02	esx003.mydomain.local	0e:00.1	vmnic3	00:17:08:7e:7e:a5	1000	True
CL02	esx003.mydomain.local		vswif0	00:50:56:4e:fb:14		
CL02	esx003.mydomain.local		vmk0	00:50:56:7b:94:ae		

Monitoring and Reporting

PART IV

The HTML report shown in Figure 14.2 is still very basic, but there are ways to go beyond the ordinary. Let's make it a bit fancier. The `ConvertTo-Html` cmdlet accepts several parameters that give you more flexibility in creating HTML output.

The `-Body` parameter is used to specify content that appears directly after the <body> tag and hence before the HTML table. This parameter is useful when you want to specify a header for your report:

```
$header = "<H2>Network Interface Card Report</H2>"
```

The -Head parameter is used to specify the content of the <head> tag. One very important thing that can be defined in the <head> section is style information for the HTML document using the <style> tag. Let's create a custom <head> section and define some fancy HTML styles, like those shown in Figure 14.3:

```
$myStyle = @"
<title>My Fancy Html Nic Report</title>
<style>
body {background-color: coral;}
table {border-collapse: collapse; border-width: 1px;
    border-style: solid; border-color: black;}
tr {padding: 5px;}
th {border-width: 1px; border-style: solid; border-color: black;
    background-color: blue; color: white;}
td {border-width: 1px; border-style: solid; border-color: black;
    background-color: palegreen;}
</style>
"@

$nicReport |
    ConvertTo-Html -Body $header -Head $myStyle > nicreport.html
```

FIGURE 14.3 A Fancy HTML Report

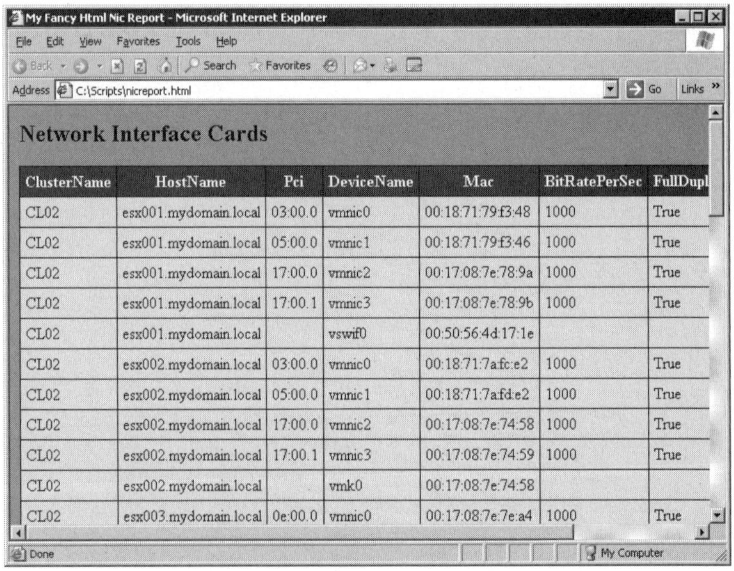

ClusterName	HostName	Pci	DeviceName	Mac	BitRatePerSec	FullDupl
CL02	esx001.mydomain.local	03:00.0	vmnic0	00:18:71:79:f3:48	1000	True
CL02	esx001.mydomain.local	05:00.0	vmnic1	00:18:71:79:f3:46	1000	True
CL02	esx001.mydomain.local	17:00.0	vmnic2	00:17:08:7e:78:9a	1000	True
CL02	esx001.mydomain.local	17:00.1	vmnic3	00:17:08:7e:78:9b	1000	True
CL02	esx001.mydomain.local		vswif0	00:50:56:4d:17:1e		
CL02	esx002.mydomain.local	03:00.0	vmnic0	00:18:71:7a:fc:e2	1000	True
CL02	esx002.mydomain.local	05:00.0	vmnic1	00:18:71:7a:fd:e2	1000	True
CL02	esx002.mydomain.local	17:00.0	vmnic2	00:17:08:7e:74:58	1000	True
CL02	esx002.mydomain.local	17:00.1	vmnic3	00:17:08:7e:74:59	1000	True
CL02	esx002.mydomain.local		vmk0	00:17:08:7e:74:58		
CL02	esx003.mydomain.local	0e:00.0	vmnic0	00:17:08:7e:7e:a4	1000	True

The new report style shown in Figure 14.3 probably isn't the best you've seen, but it's just to give you an idea of the possibilities here. You'll want your reports to use your company's style. In that case, use the -CssUri parameter to include your company's CSS style sheet:

```
$nicReport |
    ConvertTo-Html -CssUri c:\mystylesheet.css > nicreport.html
```

If you don't want to create a full HTML document but rather just an HTML table, use the -Fragment parameter. That way, you can build your own custom HTML report and include multiple objects into the same report. In Listing 14.9, you find an example of how to create your own custom HTML report. This example converts the HBA report from Listing 14.3 and the NIC report from Listing 14.4 into one HTML report. As you can see, the only limitation is your own imagination.

LISTING 14.9 A custom HTML report

```
$html = @"
<!DOCTYPE html PUBLIC "-//W3C//DTD XHTML 1.0 Strict//EN"
  "http://www.w3.org/TR/xhtml1/DTD/xhtml1-strict.dtd">
<html><head>
<title>My Fancy Html Report</title>
<style>
body {background-color: coral;}
table {border-collapse: collapse; border-width: 1px;
    border-style: solid; border-color: black;}
tr {padding: 5px;}
th {border-width: 1px; border-style: solid; border-color: black;
    background-color: blue; color: white;}
td {border-width: 1px; border-style: solid; border-color: black;
    background-color: palegreen;}
</style>
</head><body>
"@

$html += "<h2>Network Interface Cards</h2>"
$html += $nicReport | ConvertTo-Html -Fragment

$html += "<h2>Host Bus Adapters</h2>"
```

```
$html += $hbaReport | ConvertTo-Html -Fragment

$html += @"
</body>
</html>
"@

$html > nicreport.html
```

Sending Email

When you're scheduling reports to run at a regular basis, it is always nice to receive the generated report in your mailbox. From within PowerShell you can send an email using the `Send-MailMessage` cmdlet. You can send a simple mail message that the report is finished, you can include the report as an attachment, or if you've created an HTML report, you can include it in the body of the mail message.

To email a fancy-looking HTML report to your manager

```
Send-MailMessage -SmtpServer "myMailServer@mydomain.local" `
   -From "myServer@mydomain.local" `
   -To "me@mydomain.local","myManager@mydomain.local" `
   -Subject "My management report" `
   -Body $myHtmlReport -BodyAsHtml
```

To email some detailed reports as attachments to yourself

```
Send-MailMessage -SmtpServer "myMailServer@mydomain.local" `
   -From "myServer@mydomain.local" `
   -To "me@mydomain.local" `
   -Subject "My detailed reports" `
   -Body "Please review the attached detailed reports" `
   -Attachments "c:\temp\report1.csv","c:\temp\report2.csv"
```

Using Statistical Data

IN THIS CHAPTER, YOU WILL LEARN TO:

N ow that you have your vSphere environment running like you designed it, you want to know how it is faring over time. For this, you can use the built-in statistical data. When you are using vCenter Server, you will have access to aggregated data from the last year. When you are using stand-alone ESX(i) servers, the data at your disposal is much more limited.

The statistical data will allow you to show:

► If some guests are lacking or overcommitting resources

► How much of the available hardware resources you are using

► If it is time to acquire some additional hardware

Understand Some Basic Concepts

To understand what is available and how you can use it, you need to grasp some basic concepts related to the statistical data.

What Does vCenter Server Add?

When you are using stand-alone ESX(i) servers, you have access to statistical data, but what is offered is limited. You can get *real-time* data, which spans 20-second intervals, and *aggregated* data, which is collected over 5-minute intervals. The data for both intervals is kept on the ESX(i) server. If you add a vCenter Server, you will get more, as shown in Figure 15.1.

The vCenter Server keeps the statistical data in four *historical intervals (HIs)*, also known as *statistical intervals*. The data is transferred from the ESX(i) server into Historical Interval 1 (HI1) on the vCenter Server. The historical intervals HI2, HI3, and HI4 are populated through aggregation. The aggregation process is done through three SQL jobs that are created when you install the vCenter Server and its database, as shown in Figure 15.2.

FIGURE 15.1 vCenter Server gives you access to statistical data.

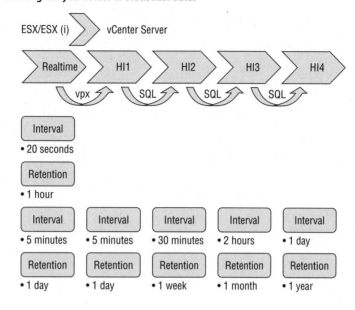

INTERVALS, INTERVALS, INTERVALS

As you work with vSphere and PowerCLI, you find three types of intervals:

▶ Historical intervals are referred to in the vSphere API Reference.

▶ Statistics intervals appear in the vSphere Client and in the PowerCLI References.

▶ Collection intervals are altogether different.

Historical or statistics intervals hold aggregated data; they are the same intervals known by two different names. Collection intervals are, in fact, the intervals into which data is aggregated. Five minutes, 30 minutes, two hours, and one day are the collection intervals available. Collection intervals are linked to historical intervals but express the length of time over which one value was aggregated.

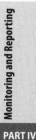

With the function shown in Listing 15.1, you can get a closer look at what the aggregation jobs on the SQL Server that hosts the vCenter database are doing.

FIGURE 15.2 Aggregation jobs

vCenter Server SQL statistical data aggregation jobs

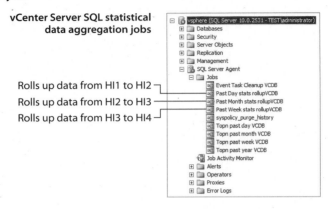

Rolls up data from HI1 to HI2

Rolls up data from HI2 to HI3

Rolls up data from HI3 to HI4

LISTING 15.1   Listing the vCenter Server aggregation jobs

```
function Get-AggregationJobs{
<#
.SYNOPSIS
  Returns the SQL jobs that perform vCenter statistical data
  aggregation
.DESCRIPTION
  The function takes all SQL jobs in the "Stats Rollup" category
  and returns key data for each of the jobs
.NOTES
  Source:   Automating vSphere Administration
  Authors:  Luc Dekens, Arnim Lieshout, Johnathan Medd,
            Alan Renouf, Glenn Sizemore
.PARAMETER SqlServer
  Name of the SQL server where the vSphere database is hosted
.EXAMPLE
  PS> Get-AggregationJobs "serverA"
#>

  param(
    [parameter(mandatory = $true,
      HelpMessage = "Enter the name of the vCenter SQL server")]
    [string]$SqlServer)

  $SMO = 'Microsoft.SqlServer.SMO'
  [System.Reflection.Assembly]::LoadWithPartialName($SMO) | `
    out-null
```

```
$SMOSrv = 'Microsoft.SqlServer.Management.Smo.Server'
$sqlSRv = new-object ($SMOSrv) $sqlServer

$sqlSrv.JobServer.Jobs | `
  where {$_.Category -eq "Stats Rollup"} | %{
  New-Object PSObject -Property @{
    Name = $_.Name
    Description = $_.Description
    LastRun = $_.LastRunDate
    NextRun = $_.NextRunDate
    LastRunResult = $_.LastRunOutcome
    "Schedule(s)" = $_.JobSchedules | %{$_.Name}
  }
 }
}
```

 N O T E   The Get-AggregationJobs function assumes that your Windows account has the necessary rights to open and query the vCenter Server database and that the SQL Management Studio is installed on the machine where you execute the function.

The function produces an output listing similar to this:

```
[vSphere PowerCLI] C:\> Get-AggregationJobs -SqlServer vSphere


Name          : Past Day stats rollupVCDB
LastRun       : 5/16/2010 22:00:01
NextRun       : 1/1/0001 00:00:00
Description   : This job is to roll up 5 min stats and should…
LastRunResult : Succeeded
Schedule(s)   : 30 min schedule


Name          : Past Month stats rollupVCDB
LastRun       : 5/19/2010 17:30:12
NextRun       : 1/1/0001 00:00:00
Description   : This job is to roll up Past Month stats and …
LastRunResult : Succeeded
Schedule(s)   : Daily schedule


Name          : Past Week stats rollupVCDB
LastRun       : 5/16/2010 21:20:00
```

```
NextRun        : 1/1/0001 00:00:00
Description    : This job is to roll up past week stats
                 and should run every 2 hours
LastRunResult  : Succeeded
Schedule(s)    : 2 hour schedule
```

Historical Intervals

An ESX(i) server gathers statistical data over a *20-second interval*. This interval is called the *real-time* interval. On ESX(i) servers, these 20-second intervals are aggregated into 5-minute intervals. Unmanaged ESX(i) servers keep the aggregated data for approximately 1 day.

Managed ESX(i) server(s), those connected to a vCenter Server, send the 5-minute interval data to the vCenter Server. The vCenter Server aggregates the data from these initial 5-minute intervals into longer intervals. These intervals are called *historical intervals*. Historical interval data is stored in the vCenter Server database.

On the vCenter Server you find the following four default historical intervals:

Historical Interval 1 contains data for the 5-minute intervals and this data is kept for 1 day.

Historical Interval 2 contains data for the 30-minute intervals and it is kept for 1 week.

Historical Interval 3 contains data for the 2-hour intervals and it is kept for 1 month.

Historical Interval 4 contains data for the one-day intervals and the data is kept for 1 year.

The settings for the historical intervals can be consulted and configured from the vSphere Client. See Figure 15.3.

FIGURE 15.3 Select settings for collecting vCenter Server statistics.

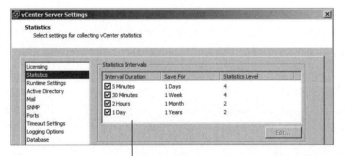

Historical Intervals settings for the statistics

You can, of course, also use PowerCLI to report the historical interval settings:

```
Get-StatInterval
```

This produces a listing similar to the following:

```
[vSphere PowerCLI] C:\> Get-StatInterval

ServerId              : @vsphere@443
Name                  : Past day
SamplingPeriodSecs    : 300
StorageTimeSecs       : 86400
Client                : VMware.VimAutomation.Client20.VimClient


ServerId              : @vsphere@443
Name                  : Past week
SamplingPeriodSecs    : 1800
StorageTimeSecs       : 604800
Client                : VMware.VimAutomation.Client20.VimClient


ServerId              : @vsphere@443
Name                  : Past month
SamplingPeriodSecs    : 7200
StorageTimeSecs       : 2592000
Client                : VMware.VimAutomation.Client20.VimClient


ServerId              : @vsphere@443
Name                  : Past year
SamplingPeriodSecs    : 86400
StorageTimeSecs       : 31536000
Client                : VMware.VimAutomation.Client20.VimClient
```

You can change the parameters for one or more historical intervals. Listing 15.2 shows how you could change, for example, how long the statistical data is kept in the Past year interval. Using this script, the default of 1 year is changed to 2 years.

LISTING 15.2 Changing historical interval parameters

```
$2Years = 2 * 365 * 24 * 60 * 60
Get-StatInterval -Name "Past year" | `
  Set-StatInteval -StorageTimeSecs $2Years -Confirm:$false
```

The length of the retention period has to be specified in seconds! The calculation is in the line where $2Years is created.

Make sure you know what you are doing when changing these intervals. Changing the parameters may have a serious impact on the size of the vCenter Server database. And it could mean that you lose data—data you wanted to keep—the moment the aggregation job on the SQL server fires. Remember, if you shorten the retention period of a HI, the next time the aggregation jobs run they will remove the data that falls outside the new retention period. Also note that you cannot specify just any value for these parameters. The accepted values are restricted. See Table 15.1 for the values that are accepted in vSphere 4.1.

TABLE 15.1 Edit statistics interval

	Interval duration	Save for	Statistics level
Historical Interval 1	1–5 minutes	1–5 days	1–4
Historical Interval 2			1–4
Historical Interval 3			1–4
Historical Interval 4		1–5 years	1–4

A statistics level can never be greater than the level of the previous historical interval.

Statistics Levels

The *statistics level* defines which metrics are available in a specific historical interval. (In the real-time interval, all metrics are available.) The four statistics levels shown in Table 15.2 are available.

TABLE 15.2 Statistic levels

Level	Content
1	Basic metrics. Device metrics excluded. Only average rollups.
2	All metrics except those for devices. Maximum and minimum rollups excluded.
3	All metrics, maximum and minimum rollups excluded.
4	All metrics.

You can change the statistics level through the vSphere Client.

Your first reaction may be to set all the historical intervals to level 4 with the idea "you never have enough input." But reconsider for a minute. Is it really useful to know, for example, what the daily minimum and maximum memory usage was?

If you do not think you have a use case for this data, set the statistics level for the historical interval to level 2. This removes the data for minima and maxima during the aggregation. And most important, it will save space on your vCenter Server database, make the statistic queries faster, and make the aggregation job a bit faster.

> **NOTE**   You will encounter the terms average, minimum, and maximum quite often when dealing with vSphere statistics. But what is actually behind these terms?
>
> In short, the "Realtime" values are averages samples over a 20 second interval on the ESX(i) server. When these values are transferred to the vCenter Server, they are aggregated a first time into a 5-minute interval. The new average is the average value calculated from all the values from the 20-second intervals. The highest and lowest values encountered will become respectively the maximum and minimum values of the 5-minute interval.
>
> Further aggregation of the values to the following Historical Intervals will use the same procedure.

If you are looking to change the statistics levels from PowerCLI, you won't find a parameter on the `Set-StatInterval` cmdlet to do this in the current build. But with the help of the SDK method called `UpdatePerfInterval`, it is quite easy, as shown in Listing 15.3.

LISTING 15.3   Changing the statistics level

```
function Set-StatIntervalLevel{
  <#
.SYNOPSIS
  Change the statistics level of a Historical Interval
.DESCRIPTION
  The function changes the statistics level, specified in $Name,
  to a new level, specified in $Level.
  The new statistics level can not be higher than the statistics
  level of the previous Historical Interval
.NOTES
  Source:    Automating vSphere Administration
  Authors:   Luc Dekens, Arnim Lieshout, Johnathan Medd,
             Alan Renouf, Glenn Sizemore
.PARAMETER Interval
  The Historical Interval for which you want to change the level
.PARAMETER Level
  New statistics level
```

```
 .EXAMPLE
   PS> Set-StatIntervalLevel -Level 3 `
   >> -Interval (Get-StatInterval -Name "Past week")
 .EXAMPLE
   PS> Get-StatInterval -Name "Past day" | `
   >> Set-StatIntervalLevel -Level 4
#>

 param(
 [parameter(valuefrompipeline = $true, mandatory = $true,
 HelpMessage = "Enter the name of the interval")]
 [VMware.VimAutomation.Types.StatInterval]$Interval,
 [parameter(mandatory = $true,
 HelpMessage = `
   "Enter the new level of the Historical Interval")]
 [string]$Level)

 Begin{
   $si = Get-View ServiceInstance
   $perfMgr = Get-View $si.content.perfManager
 }

 Process{
   $intervalSDK = $perfMgr.historicalInterval | `
     where {$_.Name -eq $Interval.Name}
   $intervalSDK.Level = $level
   $perfMgr.UpdatePerfInterval($intervalSDK)
 }

 End{}
}
```

With the Set-StatIntervalLevel function, it is now very easy to change the statistics level from within a script. If you want to automate your vCenter Server setup, use this function (Listing 15.4) to automate the level part of the statistics.

Note that the vCenter Server does not allow a higher statistics level for a historical interval than the statistics level used in the preceding historical interval. For example, you can't specify a statistics level 3 for HI4 when HI3 has a statistics level of 2.

LISTING 15.4 Changing the statistics level of a historical interval

```
[vSphere PowerCLI] C:\> Set-StatIntervalLevel -Interval `
>> (Get-StatInterval -Name "Past month") -Level 3
>>
[vSphere PowerCLI] C:\> Get-StatInterval -Name "Past week" | `
>> Set-StatIntervalLevel -Level 3
>>
```

FIGURE 15.4 Resulting statistics levels

The script from Listing 15.5 changed the statistics level for HI2 and HI3.

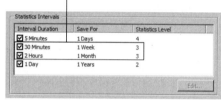

Metrics

Several managed entities provide utilization and other performance metrics. These managed entities are as follows:

- Hosts
- Virtual machines
- Compute resources (the cluster base type)
- Resource pools
- Datastores
- Networks

Each of the performance providers that generate the statistical data has its own set of performance counters. Each performance counter is identified by a unique ID, which you will also find in the statistical data.

The performance counters are organized in groups based on the resources they cover (Table 15.3).

TABLE 15.3 Performance counter groups

Group	Description
Cluster Services	Performance for clusters using DRS and/or HA
CPU	CPU utilization
Disk I/O Counters	IO performance
Storage Utilization Counters	Storage utilization
Management Agent	Consumption of resources by the various management agents
Memory	All memory statistics for guest and host
Network	Network utilization for pNIC,vNIC, and other network devices
Resource Scheduler	CPU-load-history statistics about resource pools and virtual machines
System	Overall system availability
Virtual Machine Operations	Virtual machine power and provisioning operations in a cluster or datacenter

A good source of information for the available metrics is the `PerformanceManager` entry. For each of the groups listed in Table 15.3, you will find a list of the available metrics.

But you can also use PowerCLI to compile a list of metrics yourself. First, it is important to know that there are only metrics for the following entities in your vSphere environment: clusters, hosts, virtual machines, and resource pools. Second, the `Get-StatType` cmdlet returns only the name of the metrics. (See Listing 15.5.)

LISTING 15.5 The *Get-StatType* cmdlet, which returns metric names

```
[vSphere PowerCLI] C:\> Get-StatType -Entity (Get-VMHost | `
>> Select-Object -First 1)
>>
cpu.usage.average
cpu.usage.average
cpu.usage.minimum
cpu.usage.minimum
cpu.usage.maximum
cpu.usage.maximum
cpu.usagemhz.average
cpu.usagemhz.minimum
cpu.usagemhz.maximum
cpu.used.summation
```

```
mem.usage.average
mem.usage.minimum
mem.usage.maximum
mem.granted.average
mem.granted.minimum
mem.granted.maximum
mem.active.average
mem.active.minimum
mem.active.maximum
mem.shared.average
```

With the following code (Listing 15.6), you can capture the metrics in text files. Notice the -Unique parameter on the Sort-Object cmdlet; this ensures there won't be any duplicate entries due to the different instances (as you'll learn later in this chapter) that can be present for a specific metric.

LISTING 15.6 Retrieving the metrics

```
# Cluster metrics
Get-StatType -Entity (Get-Cluster | Select-Object -First 1) | `
Out-File "C:\Cluster-metrics.txt"
# Host metrics
Get-StatType -Entity (Get-VMHost | Select-Object -First 1) | `
Sort-Object -Unique | `
Out-File "C:\Host-metrics.txt"
# Virtual machine metrics
Get-StatType -Entity (Get-VM | Select-Object -First 1) | `
Sort-Object -Unique | `
Out-File "C:\VM-metrics.txt"
# Resource pool metrics
Get-StatType -Entity (Get-ResourcePool | `
Select-Object -First 1) | `
Sort-Object -Unique | `
Out-File "C:\Resource-pool-metrics.txt"
```

While the resulting text files give you a complete list of the available metrics, there is still a lot of the available information that stays hidden. By using an SDK method, you can produce a better and more detailed report of the available metrics. The function in Listing 15.7 uses the SDK methods to return more details about the available metrics for an entity.

Monitoring and Reporting

PART IV

LISTING 15.7 Listing available metrics

```
function Get-StatTypeDetail{
    <#
.SYNOPSIS
  Returns available metrics for an entity
.DESCRIPTION
  The function returns the available metrics for a specific
  entity. Entities can be ESX(i) host, clusters, resource
  pools or virtual machines.
  The function can return the available metrics for all the
  historical intervals together or for the realtime interval
.NOTES
  Source:   Automating vSphere Administration
  Authors:  Luc Dekens, Arnim Lieshout, Johnathan Medd,
            Alan Renouf, Glenn Sizemore
.PARAMETER Entity
  The entity for which the metrics should be returned
.PARAMETER Realtime
  Switch to select the realtime metrics
.EXAMPLE
  PS> Get-StatTypeDetail -Entity (Get-VM "Guest1")
.EXAMPLE
  PS> Get-StatTypeDetail -Entity (Get-VMHost "esx41") -Realtime
.EXAMPLE
  PS> Get-VM "Guest1" | Get-StatTypeDetail
#>

  param(
    [parameter(valuefrompipeline = $true, mandatory = $true,
    HelpMessage = "Enter an entity")]
    ["VMware.VimAutomation.ViCore.Impl.V1.Inventory." +
      "InventoryItemImpl"[]]$Entity,
    [switch]$Realtime)

  Begin{
# Create performance counter hashtables
    $si = Get-View ServiceInstance
    $perfMgr = Get-View $si.Content.perfManager
    $pcTable = New-Object Hashtable
```

```
$keyTable = New-Object Hashtable
foreach($pC in $perfMgr.PerfCounter){
  if($pC.Level -ne 99){
    $pCKey = $pC.GroupInfo.Key + "." + $pC.NameInfo.Key +`
      "." + $pC.RollupType
    if(!$pctable.ContainsKey($pCKey.ToLower())){
      $pctable.Add($pCKey,$pC.Key)
      $keyTable.Add($pC.Key, $pC)
    }
  }
}
}


Process{
  if($Entity){
    $entSDK = $entity | Get-View
  }
  else{
    $entSDK = $_ | Get-View
  }


# Get the metrics
  $entSDK | %{
    $metrics = $perfMgr.QueryAvailablePerfMetric(
                $entSDK.MoRef,
                $null,
                $null,
                $numinterval)
    $metricsNoInstances = $metrics | where {$_.Instance -eq ""}
    $metricslist = @()
    foreach($pmId in $metricsNoInstances){
      $row = "" | select Group, Name, Rollup, Id, Level, Type, Unit
      $pC = $keyTable[$pmId.CounterId]
      $row.Group = $pC.GroupInfo.Key
      $row.Name = $pC.NameInfo.Key
      $row.Rollup = $pC.RollupType
      $row.Id = $pC.Key
      $row.Level = $pC.Level
      $row.Type = $pC.StatsType
      $row.Unit = $pC.UnitInfo.Key
```

```
        $metricslist += $row
    }
  }
}


End{
  $metricslist | Sort-Object -Property Group,Name,Rollup
}
}
```

A run of the Get-StatTypeDetail function returns detailed information about the available metrics for the entity. Note that if you use the -Realtime switch, the entity should be accessible. An ESX(i) host, for example, has to be in the Connected state.

```
[vSphere PowerCLI] C:\> Get-StatTypeDetail `
>>-Entity (Get-VMHost | Select-Object -First 1) -Realtime | `
>>ft -AutoSize -Force
>>
```

Group	Name	Rollup	Id	Level	Type	Unit
clusterServices	cpufairness	latest	121	1	absolute	number
clusterServices	memfairness	latest	122	1	absolute	number
cpu	usage	average	2	1	rate	perc
cpu	usage	maximum	4	4	rate	perc
cpu	usage	minimum	3	4	rate	perc
cpu	usagemhz	average	6	1	rate	megaHz
cpu	usagemhz	maximum	8	4	rate	megaHz
cpu	usagemhz	minimum	7	4	rate	megaHz
disk	maxTotalLat	latest	106	1	absolute	msec
disk	read	average	103	2	rate	kBPS
disk	usage	average	98	1	rate	kBPS
disk	usage	maximum	100	4	rate	kBPS
disk	usage	minimum	99	4	rate	kBPS
disk	write	average	104	2	rate	kBPS
mem	active	average	25	2	absolute	kB
mem	active	maximum	27	4	absolute	kB
mem	active	minimum	26	4	absolute	kB
mem	consumed	average	90	1	absolute	kB

mem	consumed	maximum 92	4	absolute kB
mem	consumed	minimum 91	4	absolute kB
mem	granted	average 21	2	absolute kB
mem	granted	maximum 23	4	absolute kB
mem	granted	minimum 22	4	absolute kB
mem	heap	average 53	2	absolute kB

Instances

Instance is the last concept we want to introduce before we start with the more complex examples. The official definition of an instance comes from the VMware vSphere API Reference Documentation: "An identifier that is derived from configuration names for the device associated with the metric. It identifies the instance of the metric with its source.

Let's try to make this a bit more understandable through an example.

Take the CPU-related metrics for a host. If the host is, for example, equipped with a quad-core CPU, there will be four instances for each CPU-related metric: 0, 1, 2, and 3. In this case, each instance corresponds with the numeric position of the core within the CPU block. And there will be an additional instance, the so-called aggregate, which is the metric averaged over all the other instances.

Each instance gets a unique identifier, which is included in the returned statistical data. The aggregate instance is always represented by a blank identifier.

If you want to list the available instances for a metric on a specific entity, you will have to make use of an SDK method called QueryAvailablePerfMetric, as shown in Listing 15.8.

LISTING 15.8   Listing available instances

```
function Get-StatInstances{
  <#
.SYNOPSIS
  Returns the available instances for a specific metric and entity
.DESCRIPTION
  The function returns all the available instances for a metric on
  an entity. The entity can be an ESX(i) host, a cluster, a
  resource pool or a virtual machine.
.NOTES
  Source:   Automating vSphere Administration
  Authors:  Luc Dekens, Arnim Lieshout, Johnathan Medd,
```

Monitoring and Reporting

PART IV

```
                    Alan Renouf, Glenn Sizemore
      .PARAMETER Entity
        The entity or entities for which the instances should be returned
      .PARAMETER Stat
        The metric or metrics for which the instances should be returned
      .PARAMETER Realtime
        Switch to select the realtime metrics
      .EXAMPLE
        PS> Get-StatInstances -Entity (Get-VM "Guest1") `
        >> -Stat "cpu.usage.average"
      .EXAMPLE
        PS> Get-StatInstances -Entity $esx -Stat "cpu.usage.average" `
        >> -Realtime
      .EXAMPLE
        PS> Get-VMHost MyEsx | Get-StatInstances `
        >> -Stat "disk.devicelatency.average"
      #>

        param(
        [parameter(valuefrompipeline = $true, mandatory = $true,
        HelpMessage = "Enter an entity")]
        [PSObject[]]$Entity,
        [parameter(mandatory=$true,
        HelpMessage = "Enter a metric")]
        [string[]]$Stat,
        [switch]$Realtime)

        begin{
      # Create performance counter hashtables
          $si = Get-View ServiceInstance
          $perfMgr = Get-View $si.content.perfManager
          $pcTable = New-Object Hashtable
          foreach($pC in $perfMgr.PerfCounter){
            if($pC.Level -ne 99){
              $pCKey = ($pC.GroupInfo.Key + "." + $pC.NameInfo.Key +`
                "." + $pC.RollupType)
              $pCKey = $pCKey.ToLower()
              if(!$pctable.ContainsKey($pCKey)){
                $pctable.Add($pcKey,$pC.Key)
```

```
            }
          }
        }
      }

    process{
      if($Entity){
        $entSDK = $entity | Get-View
      }
      else{
        $entSDK = $_ | Get-View
      }

# Handle the Realtime switch
      $numinterval = $null
      if($Realtime){
        $provSum = $perfMgr.QueryPerfProviderSummary($entSDK.MoRef)
        $numinterval = $provSum.refreshRate
      }

# Get the metrics for the entity
      $entSDK | %{
        $metrics += $perfMgr.QueryAvailablePerfMetric($_.MoRef,
                                                       $null,
                                                       $null,
                                                       $numinterval)

# Check is stat is valid
        foreach($st in $stat){
          if(!$pcTable.ContainsKey($st.ToLower())){
            Throw "-Stat parameter $st is invalid."
          }
          else{
            $ids += $pcTable[$st]
          }
          foreach($metric in $metrics){
            if($metric.CounterId -eq $pcTable[$st.ToLower()]){
              New-Object PSObject -Property @{
                StatName = $st
```

```
                    Instance = $metric.Instance
              }
          }
        }
      }
    }
  }

  end{}
}
```

With the `Get-StatInstances` function, you can list the instances that are available for one or more metrics (Listing 15.9).

LISTING 15.9 Listing the available instances for a metric

```
[vSphere PowerCLI] C:\> Get-StatInstances `
>> -Entity (Get-VMHost | Select -First 1) `
>> -Stat cpu.usage.average
>>

Instance                                StatName
--------                                --------
                                        cpu.usage.average
0                                       cpu.usage.average


[vSphere PowerCLI] C:\> Get-VMHost | Select -First 1 | `
>> Get-StatInstances -Stat disk.kernelLatency.average
>>

Instance                                StatName
--------                                --------
eui.0307cf5fa7c2eb72                    disk.kernelLatency.average
eui.840b6fa6de6c389b                    disk.kernelLatency.average
mpx.vmhba0:C0:T0:L0                     disk.kernelLatency.average
```

Gather Statistical Data

When you're comfortable with these basic concepts, you can start working with the statistical data.

The Cmdlets

The PowerCLI snap-in offers several cmdlets for use with performance data. Let's have a quick look:

- ► `Get-StatType` returns the available metrics for a specific object.

- ► `Get-StatInterval` returns the available statistics intervals.

- ► `Get-Stat` returns the statistical data for one or more specific objects.

- ► `Set-StatInterval` changes settings on the specified statistics interval.

- ► `New-StatInterval` is obsolete, unless you're still on Virtual Center 2.x.

- ► `Remove-StatInterval` is obsolete, unless you're still on Virtual Center 2.x.

The most important cmdlet in this list is the `Get-Stat` cmdlet. It gives you access to the statistical data that is stored on your ESX(i) servers and on the vCenter Server(s).

Let's have a look at the important parameters you can use with the `Get-Stat` cmdlet:

`-Entity`   This parameter specifies one or more objects for which you want to retrieve the statistics. You can pass the name of the entity, but be aware that there will be execution time overhead since the cmdlet logic will have to fetch that object for the entity.

`-Stat`   This parameter specifies one or more metrics for which you want to retrieve the statistics. If you want to retrieve more than one metric, specify them as a string array. The names of the metrics are not case sensitive.

`-Start`   This defines the beginning of the time range for which you want to retrieve statistics.

`-Finish`   Specifies the end of the time range for which you want to retrieve statistics.

`-Realtime`   This parameter specifies that you want to retrieve real-time statistics. These come directly from your ESX(i) server(s) and by default use a 20-second interval.

What Is in the Statistical Data?

The `Get-Stat` cmdlet returns the statistical data as one or more `FloatSampleImpl` objects. To have a good grasp of what you can do with the returned data, you should know what is present in the `FloatSampleImpl` object. With the `Get-Member` cmdlet, it is easy to check what properties are available in the object; see Listing 15.10.

LISTING 15.10 Using the `Get-Stat` and `Get-Member` cmdlets to obtain statistical data

```
[vSphere PowerCLI] C:\> Get-Stat -Entity (Get-VMHost | `
>> Select -First 1) -Stat "mem.usage.average" `
>> -MaxSamples 1 | Select-Object *
>>


Value        : 56.35
Timestamp    : 5/15/2010 02:00:00
MetricId     : mem.usage.average
Unit         : %
Description  : Memory usage as percentage of total configured…
Entity       : esx41.test.local
EntityId     : HostSystem-host-3312
IntervalSecs : 86400
Instance     :


[vSphere PowerCLI] C:\> Get-Stat -Entity (Get-VMHost | `
>> Select -First 1) -Stat "mem.usage.average" `
>> -MaxSamples 1 | Get-Member -MemberType Property
>>


   Type: VMware.VimAutomation.ViCore.Impl.V1.Stat.FloatSampleImpl

Name         MemberType Definition
----         ---------- ----------
Description   Property   System.String Description {get;set;}
Entity        Property   VMware.VimAutomation.Types.VIObject E…
EntityId      Property   System.String EntityId {get;}
Instance      Property   System.String Instance {get;set;}
IntervalSecs  Property   System.Int32 IntervalSecs {get;set;}
MetricId      Property   System.String MetricId {get;set;}
Timestamp     Property   System.DateTime Timestamp {get;set;}
Unit          Property   System.String Unit {get;set;}
Value         Property   System.Single Value {get;}
```

Most of these properties are self-explanatory and use a basic type like string, int32, or DateTime. The exception is the Entity property. This property contains the actual automation object—in other words, the object that cmdlets like Get-VM or

`Get-VMHost` would return. This behavior can be useful in your reporting scripts if you need to include certain properties of the entity.

Know Which Metrics to Use

Now that you have everything set up as you want, it's time to start producing some reports. The first problem you will encounter is the selection of the metrics for your reports. Given the huge number of available metrics in vSphere, this book is not going to describe in detail what is available or when to use a specific metric. But the `Get-StatReference` function might help you. The function creates an HTML page containing all the metrics that are available on the vCenter Server where you are connected. Because you can easily re-create this page, you will always have access to the latest list of metrics. Listing 15.11 provides a description of the `Get-StatReference` function.

LISTING 15.11   The `Get-StatReference` function

```
function Get-StatReference{
  <#
.SYNOPSIS
  Creates a HTML reference of all the available metrics
.DESCRIPTION
  The function returns a simple HTML page which contains all the
  available metrics in the environment where you are connected.
.NOTES
  Source:    Automating vSphere Administration
  Authors:   Luc Dekens, Arnim Lieshout, Johnathan Medd,
.EXAMPLE
  PS> Get-StatReference | Out-File "$env:temp\metricRef.html"
#>

  Begin{
# In API 4.0 there is a bug.
# There are 4 duplicate metrics that only differ in the case
# These are excluded with the -notcontains condition
    $badMetrics = "mem.reservedcapacity.average",
      "cpu.reservedcapacity.average",
      "managementAgent.swapin.average",
      "managementAgent.swapout.average"
    $si = Get-View ServiceInstance
```

```
        $perfMgr = Get-View $si.content.perfManager
    }


    Process{
# Create performance counter hashtables
    $metricRef = foreach($pC in $perfMgr.PerfCounter){
        if($pC.Level -ne 99){
            $pCKey = ($pC.GroupInfo.Key + "." + $pC.NameInfo.Key + `
                    "." + $pC.RollupType)
            if($badMetrics -notcontains $pCKey){
                $pCKey = $pCKey.ToLower()
                New-Object PSObject -Property @{
                    Metric = $PCKey
                    Level = $pC.Level
                    Unit = $pC.UnitInfo.Label
                    Description = $pC.NameInfo.Summary
                }
            }
        }
    }


    End{
        $metricRef | Sort-Object -Property Metric | `
            ConvertTo-Html -Property Metric,Level,Unit,Description
    }
}
```

You produce the HTML page as follows:

```
Get-StatReference | Out-File "C:\metricRef2.html"
```

Besides the VMware documentation, there are several sources available where you can learn which metric should be used for what. A good starting point is the Performance Community on VMware Technology Network (VMTN). Appendix B, "Reference and Links," in this book lists several other sources of information.

Techniques

There are several techniques (such as defining the correct time range, selecting the correct intervals, and the like) that you will use regularly when you are working with statistical data. It will be worth your while to spend a bit of time practicing these basic techniques.

Using the Correct Time Range

The -Start and -Finish parameters determine for which time period you want to retrieve the statistics.

TIP   The simplest method is to pass a string, with date and time specified in the correct format.

```
[vSphere PowerCLI] C:\> Get-Stat -Entity (Get-VMHost | `
>> Select -First 1) -Stat "mem.usage.average" `
>> -Start "05/21/2010 17:15:20" -Finish "05/21/2010 17:16"
>>
```

```
MetricId              Timestamp              Value Unit      Instance
---------             ----------             ----- ----      --------
mem.usage.average     5/21/2010 17:16:00     56.35 %
mem.usage.average     5/21/2010 17:15:40     56.35 %
mem.usage.average     5/21/2010 17:15:20     56.35 %
```

The format depends on the regional settings on the station from where you run the Get-Stat cmdlet. You can check which format to use with the Get-Culture cmdlet. The seconds can be left out for the time portion.

```
[vSphere PowerCLI] C:\> (Get-Culture).DateTimeFormat.`
>> ShortDatePattern
>>
M/d/yyyy
[vSphere PowerCLI] C:\> (Get-Culture).DateTimeFormat.`
>> LongTimePattern
>>
HH:mm:ss
```

The next run of the Get-Stat cmdlet was on a system with a customized en-GB setting. Notice how the date portion is entered in a different format:

```
[vSphere PowerCLI] C:\> Get-Stat -Entity (Get-VMHost | `
>> Select -First 1) -Stat "mem.usage.average" `
```

```
>> -Start "21-05-2010 19:15" -Finish "21-05-2010 19:16"


MetricId            Timestamp            Value Unit      Instance
--------            ---------            ----- ----      --------

mem.usage.average   21-05-2010 19:16:00  9,46 %
mem.usage.average   21-05-2010 19:15:40  9,46 %
mem.usage.average   21-05-2010 19:15:20  9,46 %
mem.usage.average   21-05-2010 19:15:00  9,46 %
```

The DateTime *constructor*, which is inherited from the .NET Framework, is handy to create DateTime objects with the use of variables. Notice how you can use specific properties from the DateTime object returned by the Get-Date cmdlet to populate variables.

```
[vSphere PowerCLI] C:\Scripts> $year = (Get-Date).Year
[vSphere PowerCLI] C:\Scripts> $day = 21
[vSphere PowerCLI] C:\Scripts> $hour = 18
[vSphere PowerCLI] C:\Scripts> New-Object  `
>> DateTime($year,5,$day,$hour,30,0)
>>


Friday, May 21, 2010 18:30:00
```

You can use the Get-Date cmdlet with its parameters in a similar way:

```
[vSphere PowerCLI] C:\Scripts> Get-Date  `
>> -Year $year -Day $day -Hour $hour
>>


Friday, May 21, 2010 18:46:00
```

Selecting the Correct Intervals

An often overlooked point is which intervals you need to include in your calculations. Suppose you want to produce a report that covers from 17:50 until 18:00 and that you must use real-time data. Which intervals do you need to include?

To answer this question, you first need to understand the Timestamp property. Does the timestamp give you the time the interval started, stopped, or some value smack in the middle of the interval?

According to the SDK Reference, `Timestamp` represents "the time at which the sample was collected." In other words, `Timestamp` is at the end of the measured interval. So for our example, we don't want the interval with the timestamp 17:50, because that contains the measured data for the interval from 17:49:40 until 17:50:00. The first interval we use will have a timestamp of 17:50:20.

What about the end of the requested interval? It is quite clear that we need to stop with the data that has a `Timestamp` of 18:00:00, because that interval measured data from 17:59:40 until 18:00:00. This is an important concept that we will return to later.

Scripting for Recurring Time Frames

When you're scripting the creation of your statistical reports, you don't want to use hard-coded dates and times. Luckily PowerShell provides multiple methods and properties on the `DateTime` type to allow you to get exactly the time interval you want.

It's handy to know how to get the specifications for the `-Start` and `-Finish` parameters for recurring time frames. Armed with this knowledge, you'll find it easy to roll your own.

Midnight until now

```
$todayMidnight = (Get-Date -Hour 0 -Minute 0 -Second 0)
$Start = $todayMidnight.AddSeconds(1)
$Finish = Get-Date
```

Yesterday

```
$todayMidnight = (Get-Date -Hour 0 -Minute 0 -Second 0)
$Start = $todayMidnight.AddDays(-1).AddSeconds(1)
$Finish = $todayMidnight
```

Day before yesterday

```
$todayMidnight = (Get-Date -Hour 0 -Minute 0 -Second 0)
$Start = $todayMidnight.AddDays(-2).AddSeconds(1)
$Finish = $todayMidnight.AddDays(-1)
```

Previous week

```
$todayMidnight = (Get-Date -Hour 0 -Minute 0 -Second 0)
$endOfWeek = $todayMidnight.`
AddDays(-$todayMidnight.DayOfWeek.value__ +1)
$Start = $endOfWeek.AddDays(-7).AddSeconds(1)
$Finish = $endOfWeek
```

Monitoring and Reporting

PART IV

"x" months back

```
$monthsBack = <number-of-months-back>
$todayMidnight = (Get-Date -Hour 0 -Minute 0 -Second 0)
$11MonthsAgoMidnight = $todayMidnight.AddMonths(-$monthsBack + 1)
$endOfMonth = $11MonthsAgoMidnight.`
AddDays(-$11MonthsAgoMidnight.Day)
$Start = $endOfMonth.AddMonths(-1).AddDays(1).AddSeconds(1)
$Finish = $endOfMonth Grouping your Data
```

Group the Data

When you collect statistical data, an important time-saver is the use of the Group
-Object cmdlet. This cmdlet offers so many features that it should definitely be in
your PowerShell tool belt.

Single Property

The script in Listing 15.12 shows how to use grouping to produce a report for an
individual server. This simple example produces a report that shows the average
CPU usage per core on a specific ESX(i) server over the previous day. In this case, the
Instance property is used for the grouping. The aggregate data is skipped by filtering out that group, characterized by an empty string in the Instance property.

LISTING 15.12 Average transmit rate per pNIC on a single server

```
$esxName = "esx41.test.local"
$metric = "net.transmitted.average"

# Define the time frame
$todayMidnight = (Get-Date -Hour 0 -Minute 0 -Second 0)
$Start = $todayMidnight.AddDays(-1).AddSeconds(1)
$Finish = $todayMidnight

# Get the entity
$esxImpl = Get-VMHost -Name $esxName

# Produce the report

Get-Stat -Entity $esxImpl -Stat $metric -Start $Start `
  -Finish $Finish | Group-Object -Property Instance | `
    where {$_.Name -ne ""} | %{
      New-Object PsObject -Property @{
```

```
    pNIC = $_.Name
    AvgKbps = [Math]::Round(($_.Group | `
      Measure-Object -Property Value -Average).Average, 1)
    TotalKbps = [Math]::Round(($_.Group | `
      Measure-Object -Property Value -Sum).Sum, 1)
  }
}
```

The script produces a simple table that lists the average and total transmit rate per physical NIC for the previous day, like the one shown in the code that follows. This table allows you to see if your load-balancing is performing as expected.

```
TotalKbps pNIC    AvgKbps
--------- ----    -------
      282 vmnic0    5,9
    35338 vmnic1  736,2
        5 vmnic6    0,1
        0 vmnic7      0
```

In this case, vmnic0 and vmnic7 were in a port group without load balancing active.

Multiple Properties

If you want to run the previous example against multiple ESX(i) servers, you have to introduce a second level of grouping: the ESX(i) hostname.

The script in Listing 15.13 produces a table similar to the one in the previous section, but it will also include a column with the ESX(i) hostname.

There are some noteworthy points in this script:

▶ You can use metacharacters in the Get-VMHost cmdlet for the -Name parameter. In this script, the following were used:

    ▶ A choice of specific characters in a position is indicated by square brackets. For example, [01] means that in that position there can be a 0 or a 1.

    ▶ The asterisk at the end of the name string indicates that there can be any character, zero or more times, in that position.

▶ You can pass multiple entities to the Get-Stat cmdlet.

▶ The Group-Object cmdlet uses the Values property to store an array with the specific values that were used for that group. The order of the elements in the Values property corresponds with the order used in the -Property parameter.

Monitoring and Reporting

PART IV

LISTING 15.13   Average transmit rate per pNIC over several servers

```
$esxName = "esx[01][01289]*"
$metric = "net.transmitted.average"

# Define the time frame
$todayMidnight = (Get-Date -Hour 0 -Minute 0 -Second 0)
$Start = $todayMidnight.AddDays(-1).AddSeconds(1)
$Finish = $todayMidnight

# Get the entity
$esxImpl = Get-VMHost -Name $esxName

# Produce the report
Get-Stat -Entity $esxImpl -Stat $metric -Start $Start `
  -Finish $Finish | Group-Object -Property Entity,Instance | `
    where {$_.Values[1] -ne ""} | %{
      New-Object PsObject -Property @{
        ESXname = $_.Values[0]
        pNIC = $_.Values[1]
        AvgKbps = [Math]::Round(($_.Group | `
          Measure-Object -Property Value -Average).Average, 1)
        TotalKbps = [Math]::Round(($_.Group | `
          Measure-Object -Property Value -Sum).Sum, 1)
      }
    }
```

The script in Listing 15.13 produces a simple table (similar to the following) that lists the average and total transmit rate per pNIC for the previous day on each server. This table allows you to see how your load balancing is performing across several servers.

```
TotalKbps ESXname          pNIC    AvgKbps
--------- -------          ----    -------
      282 esx08.test.local vmnic0    5,9
    35338 esx08.test.local vmnic1  736,2
        5 esx08.test.local vmnic6    0,1
        0 esx08.test.local vmnic7      0
      210 esx09.test.local vmnic0    4,4
    13368 esx09.test.local vmnic1  278,5
        0 esx09.test.local vmnic6      0
        1 esx09.test.local vmnic7      0
      175 esx10.test.local vmnic0    3,6
```

```
26463  esx10.test.local  vmnic1    551,3
    0  esx10.test.local  vmnic6        0
    0  esx10.test.local  vmnic7        0
  186  esx11.test.local  vmnic0      3,9
12857  esx11.test.local  vmnic1    267,9
    0  esx11.test.local  vmnic6        0
 4460  esx11.test.local  vmnic7     92,9
  287  esx12.test.local  vmnic0        6
17960  esx12.test.local  vmnic1    374,2
    0  esx12.test.local  vmnic6        0
    1  esx12.test.local  vmnic7        0
```

If you investigate the Values array closely, you will notice that the first element is the complete VMHostImpl object, not just the name property. In this sample script, that didn't make a difference, but if you want to use only the ESX(i) host's name, just replace the line containing the Group-Object cmdlet with this line:

```
$stats | Group-Object -Property {$_.Entity.Name},Instance | `
```

The -Property parameter only accepts statistics level 1 properties—you can't descend to lower-level properties. To use those, you have to fall back on a code block. In that code block, the incoming object is represented by the $_ variable. Your code block has to produce a value that the logic of the Group-Object cmdlet can use to bring the objects in the correct groups. In this case, the code block returns the name of the ESX(i) host. Notice that you can combine such a code block with a level 1 property.

Expressions

As we explained in the previous section, you are not obliged to use actual level 1 properties as a grouping criterion; you can also use a code block, in which you can perform whatever computation you want and return a value to the Group-Object cmdlet.

This feature comes in quite handy when you are working with statistical data. Assume you want a report on the pNICs but you only want to see a line in the report when the transmission rate goes above a certain threshold. That would make it easy to see, for example, at which points in time your pNICs have to deal with a heavier transmission rate.

LISTING 15.14 Extracting potentially problematic transmit rates

```
$esxName = "esx10.test.local"
$metric = "net.transmitted.average"


# Define the time frame
```

Monitoring and Reporting

PART IV

```
$todayMidnight = (Get-Date -Hour 0 -Minute 0 -Second 0)
$Start = $todayMidnight.AddDays(-1).AddSeconds(1)
$Finish = $todayMidnight

# Transmission groups
$codeBlock = {
  if($_.Instance -ne ""){
    if($_.Value -lt 750){"OK"}
    elseif($_.Value -lt 1500){"Investigate"}
    else{"Problem"}
  }
}

# Get the entity
$esxImpl = Get-VMHost -Name $esxName

# Produce the report
Get-Stat -Entity $esxImpl -Stat $metric -Start $Start `
  -Finish $Finish | Group-Object -Property $codeBlock | `
  where {$_.Name -eq "Problem"} | %{
    $_.Group |%{
      New-Object PsObject -Property @{
        ESXname = $_.Entity.Name
        Time = $_.Timestamp
        pNIC = $_.Instance
        TransmittedKbps = $_.Value
      }
    }
  }
```

The script in Listing 15.14 produces an output table similar to the one that follows. Because the script deals with yesterday's data, it falls within Historical Interval 2, which has a reporting interval of 30 minutes. That means that in the 30 minutes before 00:30 there was an average transmission rate on vmnic1 of 11341 Kbps. That could be the backup window!

```
TransmittedKbps ESXname              pNIC    Time
--------------- -------              ----    ----
          11342 esx10.test.local     vmnic1  23-05-2010 00:30:00
           1527 esx10.test.local     vmnic1  23-05-2010 12:30:00
           4123 esx10.test.local     vmnic1  23-05-2010 23:30:00
```

As you saw in the previous section, you pass a code block to the -Properties parameter of the Group-Object cmdlet. This script uses another PowerShell feature where you can store a code block in a variable and use it later to pass as a parameter to a cmdlet. This feature is handy when you have to use, for example, the same set of group selection criteria in multiple reports. A good use for this feature could be grouping your statistical data to show business-hour and non-business-hour activity.

> **TIP** As always, with PowerShell there is more than one way of reaching the desired result. You could use a Where-Object construction instead of the Group-Object cmdlet to get the same result.

Nested Groups

Nested groups allow you to use the groups resulting from the first Group-Object cmdlet as input to a second Group-Object cmdlet. As an example, say you want to get two separate reports on the average transmission rates, one for the backup administrator and one for the vSphere administrator. Now, if you want to report over an interval that is not one of those predefined historical intervals, you will have to do the required calculations in your script. As so often is the case, the Group-Object comes to the rescue, as shown in Listing 15.15.

LISTING 15.15 Extracting potentially problematic transmit rates per time period

```
$esxName = "esx10.test.local"
$metric = "net.transmitted.average"

# Define the time frame
$todayMidnight = (Get-Date -Hour 0 -Minute 0 -Second 0)
$Start = $todayMidnight.AddDays(-1).AddSeconds(1)
$Finish = $todayMidnight

# Transmission groups
$codeBlock1 = {
  if($_.Instance -ne ""){
    if($_.Value -gt 750){"Problem"}
    else{"No problem"}
  }
}

$codeBlock2 = {
  if($_.Timestamp.Hour -le 1 -or $_.Timestamp.Hour -ge 23){
```

```
      "Backup window"
    }
    else{
      "Outside backup window"
    }
  }


  # Get the entity
  $esxImpl = Get-VMHost -Name $esxName

  # Produce the report
  Get-Stat -Entity $esxImpl -Stat $metric -Start $Start `
    -Finish $Finish | Group-Object -Property $codeBlock1 | `
    where {$_.Name -eq "Problem"} | %{
    $_.Group | Group-Object -Property $codeBlock2 | %{
      if($_.Name -eq "Outside backup window"){
        Write-Host "`n==> Report for the vSPhere admin <==`n"
      }
      else{
        Write-Host "`n==> Report for the backup admin <==`n"
      }
      $_.Group | %{
        Write-Host $_.Timestamp $_.Entity.Name $_.Instance $_.Value
      }
    }
  }
```

Since the script was written for demonstration purposes, we did not include any fancy output formatting. As you can see in the output that follows, the second Group-Object cmdlet smoothly allows the script to produce two separate reports based on the time frame:

```
==> Report for the backup admin <==


23-05-2010 23:30:00    esx10.test.local vmnic1 4123
23-05-2010 00:30:00    esx10.test.local vmnic1 11342


==> Report for the vSPhere admin <==


23-05-2010 12:30:00    esx10.test.local vmnic1 1527
```

```
23-05-2010 12:00:00    esx10.test.local vmnic1 819
23-05-2010 09:30:00    esx10.test.local vmnic1 954
23-05-2010 09:00:00    esx10.test.local vmnic1 886
23-05-2010 06:00:00    esx10.test.local vmnic1 1067
```

Interval Manipulation

As we explained earlier in the "Understand Some Basic Concepts" section, there are four statistics intervals and one real-time interval, each with its own interval duration. However, the statistics intervals vCenter Server provides are not always the intervals you want to use in your reports.

There are several ways to produce reports with user-defined intervals. Listing 15.16 shows one of the methods. The script generates a report with the average CPU busy metric over a business day for all of the previous week's business days.

LISTING 15.16   Report with user-defined intervals

```
$esxName = "esx10.test.local"
$metric = "cpu.usage.average"

# Define the time frame
$todayMidnight = (Get-Date -Hour 0 -Minute 0 -Second 0)
$endOfWeek = $todayMidnight.`
  AddDays(-$todayMidnight.DayOfWeek.value__ +1)
$Start = $endOfWeek.AddDays(-7).AddSeconds(1)
$Finish = $endOfWeek
$workingDays = "Monday","Tuesday","Wednesday","Thursday","Friday"
$businessStart = New-Object DateTime(1,1,1,7,30,0)     # 09:00 AM
$businessEnd = New-Object DateTime(1,1,1,17,30,0)      # 05:00 PM

# Group per hour
$codeBlock1 = {
  $_.Timestamp.Day
}

# Aggregate value for Business hours
$codeBlock2 = {
  if($_.Instance -eq "" -and
    $workingDays  -contains $_.Timestamp.DayOfWeek -and
```

```
    $_.Timestamp.TimeOfDay -gt $businessStart.TimeOfDay -and
    $_.Timestamp.TimeOfDay -lt $businessEnd.TimeOfDay){
      $true
    }
    else{
      $false
    }
}


# Get the entity
$esxImpl = Get-VMHost -Name $esxName

# Produce the report
Get-Stat -Entity $esxImpl -Stat $metric -Start $Start `
  -Finish $Finish | `
  Group-Object -Property $codeBlock1,$codeBlock2 | `
  where {$_.Values[1] -eq $true} | %{
      New-Object PsObject -Property @{
        ESXname = ($_.Group | Select-Object -First 1).Entity.Name
        Time = ($_.Group | Select-Object -First 1).Timestamp.Date
        AvgCPU = [Math]::Round(($_.Group | `
          Measure-Object -Property Value -Average).Average, 1)
      }
    }
```

The script produces the following output:

```
AvgCPU ESXname              Time
------ -------              ----
  21,6   esx10.test.local   17-05-2010 00:00:00
  18,1   esx10.test.local   18-05-2010 00:00:00
  20,3   esx10.test.local   19-05-2010 00:00:00
  20,5   esx10.test.local   20-05-2010 00:00:00
  17,7   esx10.test.local   21-05-2010 00:00:00
```

Improving Execution Time

As we've said many times before, with PowerShell there is always more than one way to do something. At times, you'll find that the path you chose was not the optimal path. When you are working with lots of statistical data, the execution time of your script can become a critical factor. The following list shows some ways to improve execution time.

- ► Limit the number of calls to the Get-Stat cmdlet.

    - ► Combine entities.

    - ► Combine metrics.

- ► Combine reporting groups in one call to Group-Object.

- ► Use only metrics that are meaningful for your report.

Offload Statistical Data

As you learned in the "Understand Some Basic Concepts" section, the data for HI4 is kept for one year by default. You can change the retention time to five years, but that will increase the size of your vCenter Server database with a possible performance impact.

If you want to be able to run a statistics report on older data, there is another solution. At regular points in time, collect the oldest statistical data you want to use later and store it in an external file. PowerShell provides the Export-Clixml cmdlet to store PowerShell objects in an external file. Later, you can use the Import-Clixml cmdlet to retrieve the objects and bring them back into your PowerShell session.

The script in Listing 15.17 exports some basic metrics to an external file.

LISTING 15.17 Exporting statistical data

```
$entityNames = "esx[01][01289]*"
$metrics = "cpu.usage.average","mem.usage.average",
  "disk.usage.average","net.usage.average"
$archiveLocation = "C:\Archive"

# Time range - 12 months ago
$monthsBack = 12
$todayMidnight = (Get-Date -Hour 0 -Minute 0 -Second 0)
$xMonthsAgoMidnight = $todayMidnight.AddMonths(-$monthsBack + 1)
$endOfMonth = $xMonthsAgoMidnight.`
  AddDays(-$xMonthsAgoMidnight.Day)
$Start = $endOfMonth.AddMonths(-1).AddDays(1).AddSeconds(1)
```

```
$Finish = $endOfMonth

# All entities
$entities = Get-VMHost -Name $entityNames

$archiveFilename = "Stat-" + $Start.ToShortDateString() + "-" + `
                   $Finish.ToShortDateString() + ".xml"

# Export statistics
Get-Stat -Entity $entities -Stat $metrics -Start $Start `
  -Finish $Finish | Export-Clixml `
  -Path ($archiveLocation + "\" + $archiveFilename)
```

The following script reads the "archive" file back into a PowerShell array. You can work with that imported array just as you would if you had created it with the Get-Stat cmdlet.

```
$archiveFilename = "C:\Archive\Stat-01-01-2010-31-01-2010.xml"
$stats = Import-Clixml -Path $archiveFilename
```

TIP Make sure you use a file-naming schema that clearly defines what kind of data is stored in each file. You could include the entity type, the start and finish dates, the metrics that were used, and similar information.

Monitoring the vSphere Environment

IN THIS CHAPTER, YOU WILL LEARN TO:

n several of the preceding chapters, we have shown you how to automate the deployment and much of the management of your vSphere environment. Thanks to this high level of automation, you avoid a lot of human errors. But even when you have everything running as designed, there can be mishaps. Remember Murphy's Law! To capture these unforeseen events and to react to them as fast as possible, you need to monitor your vSphere environment at all times.

In this chapter, you will determine what you need to monitor and how to employ alarms in the monitoring process.

Determine What to Monitor

The short answer to the "What should I monitor?" question is, of course, "Everything!" The problem with that statement is that you can never foresee everything. Until you realize that certain events are possible causes of problems, you won't be able to monitor them.

Then, how should you tackle this monitoring thing?

We think you have to adopt a commonsense strategy. Take a couple of steps back and look at your vSphere environment. What is actually there? When you take this approach, it becomes clear that there are two major abstract groups present in every vSphere environment: resources and services.

In the resources group, you have elements like servers, storage, and networks. In the services group, you will find elements like hosting platforms, virtual machines, HA, DRS, vMotion, and SVMotion. Each of these two major groups will need to be detailed further to arrive at manageable chunks that you can monitor. Here are some examples of these lower-level elements that you can monitor:

- ► Server availability

- ► CPU usage

- ► Memory usage

- ► Datastore usage

- ► Network connectivity

- ► vMotion and svMotion functionality

It should be obvious that this list is just an example and that your list is in reality much more extensive. It should also be obvious that the list created for Company A will be different from the list compiled for Company B.

Once you have confirmed your requirements and planned out the elements to monitor, your next step is to use vCenter Server alarms to alert yourself or other teams in your organization that an issue has occurred.

Use Alarms

As you might have noticed, vCenter Server comes with a number of built-in alarms. (The list keeps getting longer and better with each release.) On top of that it is quite easy to roll your own. Unfortunately, until now the PowerCLI package hasn't offered anything for working with alarms. In the VI Toolkit for Windows Community Extensions, there are a number of functions that will allow you to work with alarms. But if you want to set up your own functions to work with alarms, you will have to fall back on the methods available in the SDK.

NOTE   Alarms are only available on a vCenter Server.

Alarms, in general, follow a rather simple principle. You start by defining one or more triggers for the alarm. When the alarm fires, the actions associated with the alarm are taken. So, let's take a look at how to get started with alarms.

Designing an Alarm

The `Alarm` managed object—or, in other words, the object that is used to represent an alarm in a vSphere environment—has the properties described in Table 16.1. Figure 16.1 shows how the various elements of an alarm relate to one another. You'll need to understand each of these elements if you intend to design useful alarms for your system.

TABLE 16.1   Alarm managed object properties

Property	Description
Name	The name of the alarm. Be descriptive when you name your alarms.
Description	A description of the alarm.
Enabled	A Boolean value that indicates whether an alarm is enabled.
Setting	Defines how long to wait before an alarm is triggered again and whether the alarm should use a range around the threshold value.
Expression	Defines the conditions that must be met before an alarm is triggered.

(continues)

TABLE 16.1   *(continued)*

Property	Description
Action	Defines what must be done when an alarm is triggered.
ActionFrequency	Defines how often the actions connected to the alarm should be repeated.

FIGURE 16.1   Alarm schematic

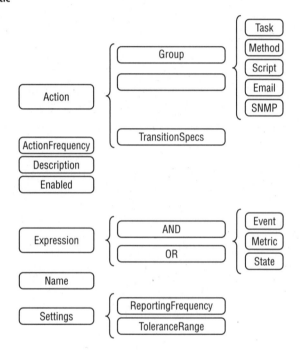

Alarm Actions

The action part of an alarm is where you can define what needs to be done when an alarm is fired. vCenter Server offers the actions described in Table 16.2. Note that you can define multiple actions on a single alarm.

TABLE 16.2   Alarm managed object actions

Action	Description
Create a Task	Create a task that will run on vCenter Server.
Method Action	Execute a method against a particular entity.
Run Script	A script that will run on vCenter Server.
Email	Send an email to one or more recipients. For this action to work, you must have defined an SMTP server in your vCenter Server Settings.

(continues)

TABLE 16.2   *(continued)*

Action	Description
SNMP	Send an SNMP trap. This action requires that the SNMP settings be configured on your vCenter Server.
Group Alarm Action	Not really an action, but a group alarm action allows you to combine a number of the previous actions. You can, for example, have an alarm send an email message and send an SNMP trap. Note that this type of action is not visible in the vSphere Client. When you add actions to an alarm in the vSphere Client, the Group Alarm Action is created for you by the vSphere Client.

Alarm Firing Mechanisms

There are, in the current vSphere environment, three types of firing mechanisms available, as described in Table 16.3.

TABLE 16.3   Alarm managed object firing mechanisms

Firing Mechanism	Description
Event	A specific event in the event stream that will trigger the alarm.
State	The state of a VM or of a host that triggers the alarm.
Metric	When a threshold for a metric is crossed (in both directions), the alarm will fire.

Alarm Expressions

Let's take a quick tour of the three types of alarm expressions and how to provide values to the important properties. For the expression object in an alarm specification, you have two choices: an `AndAlarmExpression` or an `OrAlarmExpression`. Use `AndAlarmExpression` with `AND` operators and `OrAlarmExpression` with `OR` operators. These are, of course, for expressions with multiple conditions. With a single-trigger alarm, there is no associated single trigger alarm expression, so you can use either `AndAlarmExpression` or `OrAlarmExpression` to achieve the same result.

Let's see how you would create expressions for these three different scenarios:

Single-Trigger Expression

```
$expression = New-Object VMware.Vim.AndAlarmExpression
```

AND Operator Expression

```
$expression = New-Object VMware.Vim.AndAlarmExpression
```

OR Operator Expression

```
$expression = New-Object VMware.Vim.OrAlarmExpression
```

Monitoring and Reporting

PART IV

Event Alarms

As you will see in Chapter 17, "Auditing the vSphere Environment," the vSphere environment generates an event for nearly every activity that occurs. Events can range from the creation of a guest, to a failing cluster node, all the way to detection of a guest that doesn't have the VMware Tools installed. Some extensions, like for example, the Update Manager, generate their own events. Any event can be used to trigger an alarm. The moment vCenter Server sees an event of the type you specified, it will trigger the corresponding alarm.

The API Reference documentation describes three types of events; we will use this knowledge in Listing 16.1 to examine requirements for an `EventAlarmExpression`:

- ► Regular

- ► EventEx

- ► ExtendedEvent

We use the term *regular* to group all the events that are not of the `EventEx` or `ExtendedEvent` type. Some samples of such regular events include `Account CreatedEvent`, `ClusterReconfiguredEvent`, and `HostIPChangedEvent`. More than 400 types of events are included in the regular events group.

The `EventEx` and `ExtendedEvent` types contain events that are introduced in vCenter Server by the installation of extensions. The License Manager is such an extension, and it introduces additional events on vCenter Server.

The first step in the creation of event alarms is to determine which specific event to use to define the alarm and which properties you need to provide in the method call to create it. To help you find the data you need to define the alarm event you wish to monitor, we created the `Get-AlarmEventId` function (see Listing 16.1). It produces a list that contains all the information you need to define the alarm trigger. This information is not well documented in the vSphere Reference and by using Listing 16.1 you are able, for example, to export the information into a CSV file for easy examination. The CSV file will contain the correct names for the `EventType` and `EventTypeId` properties you will have to provide when you are setting up the event alarm.

LISTING 16.1   Get-AlarmEventId **function**

```
function Get-AlarmEventId{
    <#
```

```
.SYNOPSIS
 Returns the data needed to define an EventAlarmExpression
.DESCRIPTION
 The function will return the required properties that
 are needed to populate the eventType and eventTypeId
 properties
.NOTES
    Source:  Automating vSphere Administration
    Authors: Luc Dekens, Arnim van Lieshout, Jonathan Medd,
             Alan Renouf, Glenn Sizemore
.EXAMPLE
 PS> Get-AlarmEventId | Export-Csv "C:\Alarm-eventId.csv"
#>

 begin{
   $commonArgs = "changeTag","computeResource",
                 "computeResource.name","datacenter",
                 "datacenter.name","ds","ds.name","dvs",
                 "dvs.name","fullFormattedMessage","host",
                 "host.name","net","net.name","userName","vm",
                 "vm.name"
 }

 process{
   $evtMgr = Get-View EventManager

   $evtMgr.Description.EventInfo |%{
     $row = "" | Select EventType,EventTypeId,Group,Description
      ,Attributes
     $row.Description = $_.Description
     if($_.Key -eq "eventEx"){
       $eventTypeName = $_.FullFormat.Split("|")[0]
       $row.EventType = "EventEx|ExtendedEvent"
       $row.EventTypeId = $_.FullFormat.Split("|")[0]
       $attributes = $evtMgr.RetrieveArgumentDescription
       ($row.EventTypeId)
       if($attributes){
         $specialAttributes = $attributes | `
           where{$commonArgs -notcontains $_.Name} | `
```

```
          %{$_.Name + "(" + $_.Type + ")"}
        if($specialAttributes.Count){
          $row.Attributes =
            [string]::Join(',',$specialAttributes)
        }
        elseif($specialAttributes){
          $row.Attributes = $specialAttributes
        }
      }
      $row.Group = "EventEx"
    }
    elseif($_.Key -eq "ExtendedEvent"){
      $row.EventType = "ExtendedEvent|EventEx"
      $row.EventTypeId = $_.FullFormat.Split("|")[0]
      $attributes =
       $evtMgr.RetrieveArgumentDescription($row.EventTypeId)
      if($attributes){
        $specialAttributes = $attributes | `
          where{$commonArgs -notcontains $_.Name} | `
          %{$_.Name + "(" + $_.Type + ")"}
        if($specialAttributes.Count){
          $row.Attributes =
            [string]::Join(',',$specialAttributes)
        }
        elseif($specialAttributes){
          $row.Attributes = $specialAttributes
        }
      }
      $row.Group = "ExtendedEvent"
    }
    else{
      $eventTypeName = $_.Key
      $row.EventType = $eventTypeName
      $row.EventTypeId = "vim.event." + $_.Key
      $attributes =
       $evtMgr.RetrieveArgumentDescription($row.EventTypeId)
      if($attributes){
        $specialAttributes = $attributes | `
          where{$commonArgs -notcontains $_.Name} | `
```

```
            %{$_.Name + "(" + $_.Type + ")"}
          if($specialAttributes.Count){
            $row.Attributes =
              [string]::Join(',',$specialAttributes)
          }
          elseif($specialAttributes){
            $row.Attributes = $specialAttributes
          }
        }
        $row.Group = "regular"
      }
      $row
    }
  }
}
```

A sample run of the function results in a listing of the EventType and EventTypeId values you'll need in order to define your trigger. Here's a sample output that displays all three types: regular, EventEx, and ExtendedEvent:

```
PS> Get-AlarmEventId | Select-Object -First 3


EventType    : AccountRemovedEvent
EventTypeId  : vim.event.AccountRemovedEvent
Group        : regular
Description  : Account removed
Attributes   : account(string),group(bool)


EventType    : EventEx|ExtendedEvent
EventTypeId  : com.vmware.license.AddLicenseEvent
Group        : EventEx
Description  : Added License
Attributes   : eventTypeId(string),message(string),objectId(st...
  objectName(string),severity(string),licenseKey(string)


EventType    : ExtendedEvent|EventEx
EventTypeId  : com.vmware.vc.HA.ClusterFailoverActionCompleted...
Group        : ExtendedEvent
Description  : HA completed a failover
Attributes   : message(string),eventTypeId(string),managedObje...
```

Monitoring and Reporting

PART IV

Now that you have seen illustrations of the three expression types—regular (the standard set of events that come with vSphere), `EventEx`, and `ExtendedEvent`—and you know what information needs to be supplied to define the event, let's create an example.

First, let's create an `EventEx` type alarm expression that will fire when the network redundancy for the dvPorts is restored. Both properties in the `EventAlarm Expression` object would be populated like this:

```
$expression = New-Object VMware.Vim.EventAlarmExpression
$expression.eventType = "EventEx"
$expression.eventTypeId = `
    "esx.clear.net.dvport.redundancy.restored"
```

According to the vSphere Reference, you can use the values `EventEx` or `Extended Event` for the `eventType` property. Just make sure that the `eventType` property is not empty!

Now, let's look at an example using a regular event. Here we'll monitor the status of file ownership. The `ChangeOwnerOfFileEvent` event will fire when the ownership of a file has changed. To specify this event, you will need to populate the properties as follows:

```
$expression = New-Object VMware.Vim.EventAlarmExpression
$expression.eventType = " ChangeOwnerOfFileEvent"
$expression.eventTypeId = "vim.event.ChangeOwnerOfFileEvent"
```

Notice that we added the prefix `vim.event` before the name of the event. For regular events, the prefix is required when you fill in the `eventTypeId` property. The `Get-AlarmEventId` function from Listing 16.1 does that for you, and in the output produced by the function, you will find the correct string to assign to the `eventTypeId` property.

The `comparisons` property is another important, but optional, property that you can use when creating an event alarm. The operators you can use for these comparisons are documented in the `EventAlarmExpressionComparisonOperator` enumerator that you can find in the SDK Reference. (If you're not familiar with the SDK Reference, don't worry. We'll tell you all about it in Chapter 19, "The SDK.")

Using the `comparisons` property, you can test attributes. But how can you find out which attributes there are? Turns out that there is a method, `RetrieveArgument Description`, that returns all arguments (or attributes) that you can use with an event trigger. Table 16.4 lists the attributes that you can use with any event. The attributes that are marked as having the `moid` types are, in fact, managed object IDs. Not too handy to use in a comparison, but we included them in the table since the `RetrieveArgumentDescription` method will return them!

TABLE 16.4   Common event attributes

Attribute	Type
changeTag	string
computeResource	moid
computeResource.name	string
datacenter	moid
datacenter.name	string
ds	moid
ds.name	string
dvs	moid
dvs.name	string
fullFormattedMessage	string
host	moid
host.name	string
net	moid
net.name	string
username	string
vm	moid
vm.name	string

In addition to the common attributes, some events accept additional attributes. Those are listed under the `Attributes` property in the objects that the `Get-Alarm EventId` function returns. With the `AccountRemovedEvent` event, for example, you can use the account attribute to filter out the alarms for test accounts. The operators you can use for these comparisons are documented in the `EventAlarm ExpressionComparisonOperator` enumerator that you can find in the SDK Reference. The other properties in the `EventAlarmExpression` object are clearly explained in the vSphere API Reference documentation.

State Alarms

State alarms allow you to trigger an alarm based on the state of a virtual machine, a vSphere Server, or a datastore. In vSphere 4.1, the states listed in Table 16.5 can be used to trigger an alarm.

TABLE 16.5   State alarm

Type	statePath	Values
VirtualMachine	runtime.powerState	poweredOff
		poweredOn
		suspended
	summary.quickStats.guestHeartbeatStatus	gray
		green
		red
		yellow
	summary.quickStats.ftLatencyStatus	gray
		green
		red
		yellow
HostSystem	runtime.connectionState	connected
		disconnected
		notResponding
	runtime.powerState	poweredOff
		poweredOn
		standby
		unknown
Datastore	summary.accessible	true
		false

Metric Alarms

An alarm expression based on a metric has some intricacies. The `metricId` you use in the expression can be different on different vCenter Servers. For that reason, the `New-Alarm` function you will see later in this chapter will allow you to specify the metric by its name. That means you can specify `cpu.usage.average` instead of a number.

Alarm Actions

Alarm actions are many and varied. Some are quite simple to work with, such as group, method, task, or SNMP actions. We'll provide an overview of those actions. Others, like script or email actions, are more flexible and complex. We'll cover those in greater detail.

Grouping Actions   The SDK Reference indicates that you can have a single `Alarm TriggeringAction` without a `GroupAlarmAction`. And it is indeed possible to define an alarm with a single action. The problem comes when you try to edit the settings of that alarm from the vSphere Client; the Edit Settings option is grayed out. For that reason we advise you to always specify your actions, even if it is only one action, under a `GroupAlarmAction`. When you want to create an alarm without any action, there is no need for the `GroupAlarmAction` either.

Method Action   Method actions are only available for `HostSystem` and `Virtual Machine` objects. Using a method action, you can call any SDK method that is available on the `HostSystem` or `VirtualMachine` object that fired the alarm.

Task Action   Task actions also are only available for `HostSystem` and `Virtual Machine` objects. You can call any of the tasks that are available on the extensions active on your vCenter Server.

SNMP Action   Simple Network Management Protocol (SNMP) actions are the simplest of all actions. They don't require any parameters. The SNMP trap will be sent to the SNMP communities you defined in your vCenter Server.

Script Action

Script actions take one parameter—the command that you want vCenter Server to execute when an alarm is fired. There can be some issues related to how you achieve this, in particular with the security account used to execute the script and the privileges within vCenter Server that are required. We prefer to take the following approach:

▶ The vCenter Service runs with a domain account. Consequently, the scripts execute through the Security Support Provider Interface (SSPI) and use single sign-on to connect to vCenter Server. Therefore you don't need to specify separate credentials.

▶ The domain account that the vCenter Server runs under holds the required privileges within vCenter's permission model to execute whatever you want to accomplish in the script.

Unlike the code you'll see next, the actual text for the Configuration field is entered in one line, with no carriage returns or linefeeds. (We had to break the text into three lines here; it's too long to fit on the page.) For a 64-bit OS, like Windows 2008, it would look like Listing 16.2.

LISTING 16.2   An example script action

```
C:\Windows\System32\cmd.exe /c powershell.exe -PSConsolefile
C:\Scripts\MyConsole.psc1 -noninteractive -noprofile -file
C:\Scripts\Alarm-action-script.ps1
```

A common method for monitoring processes on a Windows Server is to use the Process Explorer tool from Microsoft's Sysinternals website at http://technet .microsoft.com/en-gb/sysinternals. When you use Process Explorer on your vCenter Server, you can see how vCenter Server runs your alarm script. Process Explorer allows you to see the parameters that are used for each of the spawned processes. Open the properties of the cmd.exe and the powershell.exe processes. Process Explorer also allows you to verify when your alarm script is finished. Just check whether the cmd.exe and powershell.exe processes have disappeared below the vpxd.exe process.

In Listing 16.2, notice the use of the console file on the command line. With this file, you can define the snap-in(s) that need to be loaded into the PowerShell session that will run your script. The use of console files is covered in more detail in Chapter 18, "Scheduling Automation Scripts."

Script actions can take quite a bit of time to completely execute. This depends on the load of your vCenter Server but also on the number of snap-ins you are loading through the console file. So be patient when you want to check the results of your alarm script.

On the command line, you can pass one or more of the predefined variables that vCenter Server provides. Again, you'll enter the information on one line with no carriage returns or line breaks (Listing 16.3).

LISTING 16.3   An example script action with predefined variables

```
C:\Windows\System32\cmd.exe /c powershell.exe
-PSConsolefile C:\Scripts\MyConsole.psc1 -noninteractive
-noprofile -file C:\Scripts\Alarm-action-script.ps1
{alarmName} {targetName}
```

Note that these parameters are case sensitive. That means that, for example, you can't use {targetname}. You can find the complete list of parameters in the vSphere

Basic System Administration Guide (`http://www.vmware.com/pdf/vsphere4/r40/vsp_40_admin_guide.pdf`). The script can access these parameters as regular PowerShell function parameters. In other words, you can use the `$Args` variable or you can define a `param` statement in your script.

Before using your script action in an alarm, it's a good idea to first test it by running it as an individual piece of code. That way, you can guarantee it is going to run successfully as part of the alarm and there will be no issues, such as the local security policy preventing its execution, or problems with permissions in vCenter Server.

If you want to capture the execution of the alarm script, you could consider using the `Start-Transcript` and `Stop-Transcript` cmdlets. But because of a documented PowerShell "feature," there will be no output in your transcript file. A valid bypass for this problem is to pipe all output to the `Out-File` cmdlet. That way, all output from the script is captured in a file. An alarm script that logs the parameters it receives to a file could look something like this:

```
$outFile = C:\Alarm\alarm.log
$Args | Out-File -FilePath $outFile -Append
```

There is an alternative for accessing information about the alarm that triggered your script. vCenter Server spawns your alarm script with a number of environment variables that contain information about the alarm that triggered the script. The following line lists all these environment variables:

```
(Get-Item env:).GetEnumerator() | where {$_.Key -like
"VMWARE_*"}
```

This code produces a list with information like that in Table 16.6.

TABLE 16.6   Environment variables

Name	Value
VMWARE_ALARM_TRIGGERINGSUMMARY	Event: Custom field value changed (116195)
VMWARE_ALARM_TARGET_NAME	PC1
VMWARE_ALARM_EVENT_USERNAME	TEST\administrator
VMWARE_ALARM_DECLARINGSUMMARY	([Event alarm expression: Custom field value
VMWARE_ALARM_EVENT_VM	PC1
VMWARE_ALARM_TARGET_ID	vm-5106
VMWARE_ALARM_EVENT_DVS	
VMWARE_ALARM_EVENT_HOST	esx41.test.local

(continues)

Monitoring and Reporting

PART IV

TABLE 16.6 *(continued)*

Name	Value
VMWARE_ALARM_EVENTDESCRIPTION	Changed custom field CF1 on PC1 in DC1 to abc
VMWARE_ALARM_EVENT_COMPUTER	CLUS1
VMWARE_ALARM_EVENT_DATASTORE	
VMWARE_ALARM_EVENT_DATACENTER	DC1
VMWARE_ALARM_OLDSTATUS	Green
VMWARE_ALARM_NEWSTATUS	Red
VMWARE_ALARM_ALARMVALUE	Event details
VMWARE_ALARM_ID	alarm-1082
VMWARE_ALARM_NAME	Change custom field
VMWARE_ALARM_EVENT_NETWORK	

You can use these environment variables in your script through the environment variable provider. A short example is shown in Listing 16.4.

LISTING 16.4 Environment variable provider example

```
$outFile = "C:\outfile.txt"

$report = @()

$report += ("Time:`t" + (Get-Date).ToShortTimeString())

$report += ("Alarm:`t" + $env:VMWARE_ALARM_NAME)

$report += ("On:`t" + $env:VMWARE_ALARM_TARGET_NAME)

$report += ("User:`t" + $env:VMWARE_ALARM_EVENT_USERNAME)


$report | Out-File -FilePath $outFile
```

This script will produce something like this:

```
Time:  3:21 AM
Alarm:  Change custom field
On:  PC1
User:  TEST\administrator
```

If you are going to use PowerCLI cmdlets in your script, you will need to connect to a vSphere Server. As we said earlier, these alarm scripts are spawned from the vCenter service; just make sure that this service runs with a domain account that has the required privileges. That way, you can connect through SSPI and you don't have to provide credentials.

The environment variables that are available in the alarm script contain a number of ID values. Take, for example, the VMWARE_ALARM_TARGET_ID variable (see Table 16.6). Unfortunately, this is not the kind of ID that can be used in a PowerCLI cmdlet like Get-View. Consequently, it is much better to use the environment variables that end with a name suffix. These contain the name of the vSphere entity that you can use to access (through the PowerCLI cmdlets) the vSphere object in your script. The code in Listing 16.5 shows how to use, for example, the VMWARE_ALARM_TARGET _NAME environment variable to retrieve the virtual machine and datastore.

LISTING 16.5   Accessing vSphere objects in an action script

```
$outFile = "C:\outfile.txt"


Connect-VIServer -Server vSPhere
$vm = Get-VM -Name $env:VMWARE_ALARM_TARGET_NAME
$ds = Get-Datastore -VM $vm


$report = @()
$report += ("Time:`t" + (Get-Date).ToShortTimeString())
$report += ("Alarm:`t" + $env:VMWARE_ALARM_NAME)
$report += ("On:`t" + $env:VMWARE_ALARM_TARGET_NAME)
$report += ("User:`t" + $env:VMWARE_ALARM_EVENT_USERNAME)
$report += ("DS:`t" + $ds.Name)


$report | Out-File -FilePath $outFile
```

We used the Out-File cmdlet to track what the script did. You can use that same log file to track any errors your alarm script produces. The script in Listing 16.6 appends the $error variable to the log file you created in Listing 16.5. Note that for the purpose of illustration, Listing 16.5 generates an error. To force the error, we supplied an incorrect vCenter Server (WrongvSphere).

LISTING 16.6   Appending errors to the alarm script log file

```
$ErrorActionPreference = "SilentlyContinue"
$Error.Clear()


$outFile = "C:\outfile.txt"


Set-PowerCLIConfiguration -DefaultVIServerMode Single `
```

```
    -Confirm:$false
Connect-VIServer -Server WrongvSphere

$report = @()
$report += ("Server:`t" + $defaultVIServer.Name)

$report | Out-File -FilePath $outFile

"==> Errors" | Out-File -FilePath $outFile -Append
$Error | Out-File -FilePath $outFile -Append
```

By choosing `SilentlyContinue` for the `$ErrorActionPreference`, we made sure that the script would continue even when errors were encountered. At the end of the script, we dumped the `$Error` variable via the `Out-File` cmdlet to the external file. Notice that we cleared the `$Error` variable at the beginning of the script to prevent any prior and irrelevant errors from the current PowerShell session being included in the log file. You can, of course, use different files for your regular output and for the dump of the `$Error` variable by changing the value of the `$outfile` variable.

You might wonder why we included the `Set-PowerCLIConfiguration` cmdlet at the beginning of the script. We needed that code line because the first time you connect to a vSphere Server, the `Connect-VIServer` will prompt you to specify whether you want to work in single mode or multimode. To avoid this question, PowerCLI provides this script to set the mode before the `Connect-VIServer` cmdlet.

In the sample, we used a nonexistent vCenter Server name to force an error. The resulting output file looks something like this:

```
Server:
==> Errors
Connect-VIServer : 12/5/2010 1:23:16 PM    Connect-VIServer
    Could not resolve the requested VC server.
At C:\Scripts\Alarm-action-script.ps1:14 char:17
+ Connect-VIServer <<<<  -Server vSPhere2
    + CategoryInfo          : ObjectNotFound: (:)
       [Connect-VIServer], ViServer
    ConnectionException
      + FullyQualifiedErrorId :
```

```
Client20_ConnectivityServiceImpl_Reconnect_Name
ResolutionFailure,VMware.VimAutomation.ViCore.Cmdlets
.Commands.ConnectVIServer
```

The fact that we can now see at least the error messages from our alarm script makes it a lot easier to debug the script.

To conclude this section, the complete alarm script is displayed in Listing 16.7. It uses the technique from Listing 16.5 to retrieve additional information about an environment variable through the use of a PowerCLI cmdlet. This alarm could be used when monitoring virtual machines. When triggered, the alarm script will return the vCenter Server name, the time, the alarm name, the alarm event username, the VM, and the datastore that the VM resides on.

LISTING 16.7 The complete alarm script

```
$ErrorActionPreference = "SilentlyContinue"
$Error.Clear()

$outFile = "C:\outfile.txt"

Set-PowerCLIConfiguration -DefaultVIServerMode Single `
  -Confirm:$false
Connect-VIServer -Server vSphere

$vm = Get-VM -Name $env:VMWARE_ALARM_TARGET_NAME
$ds = Get-Datastore -VM $vm

$report = @()
$report += ("Server:`t" + $defaultVIServer.Name)
$report += ("Time:`t" + (Get-Date).ToShortTimeString())
$report += ("Alarm:`t" + $env:VMWARE_ALARM_NAME)
$report += ("User:`t" + $env:VMWARE_ALARM_EVENT_USERNAME)
$report += ("VM:`t" + $vm.Name)
$report += ("DS:`t" + $ds.Name)

$report | Out-File -FilePath $outFile

if($Errors){
```

```
    "==> Errors" | Out-File -FilePath $outFile -Append
    $Error | Out-File -FilePath $outFile -Append
}
```

The result of this alarm script looks like this:

```
Server:  vSPhere
Time:  2:15 PM
Alarm:   Book: Change custom field
User:  TEST\administrator
VM:  PC1
DS:  DS1
```

Email Action

Provided you have defined an SMTP server on your vCenter Server, the email action will send an email message when an alarm is fired. You can specify the To: field, the Cc: field, the subject, and the body of the email message.

In the Body property, you can use the same environment variables that we showed you in the "Script Action" section. vCenter Server will replace these variables with actual values before it sends the email. The list of the available environment variables can be found in the vSphere Basic System Administration Guide.

The SNMP Action

SNMP is the simplest of all actions. It doesn't require any parameters. The SNMP trap will be send to the SNMP communities you defined in your vCenter Server.

A General Alarm Creation Function

An Alarm object is quite complex, and since it necessitates a large numbers of parameters on a function to create an alarm, we decided to provide several specific functions, each with a manageable number of parameters. The diagram in Figure 16.2 shows which function to use to define the different parts of an alarm specification.

The ultimate function, called New-Alarm.ps1, uses all the objects you created and creates the alarm on your vCenter Server. It is available for download from www.sybex.com/go/vmwarevspherepowercliref.

Listing 16.8 creates an alarm that sends an SNMP trap when one of the hosts has an average CPU usage above 75 percent for longer than 25 seconds. The alarm will be yellow.

FIGURE 16.2 Alarm creation functions

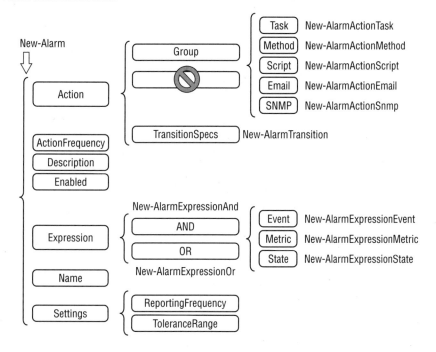

With the help of the `New-Alarm` function you can construct separate building blocks (transition states, actions, expressions). And with the `New-Alarm` function you bring them all together—just like a LEGO project! Let's look at some examples.

> **NOTE** Note that when creating advanced trigger conditions via the command line, the vSphere Client will correctly display that an advanced trigger condition has been set, but viewing it will display an empty dialog box. This can cause confusion as to whether it was successfully created correctly. Hopefully VMware will fix this in a future release of vSphere.

LISTING 16.8 Yellow CPU usage alarm

```
# The transition state for green to yellow
$trans = @()
$trans += New-AlarmTransition -Start "green" -Final "yellow"

# Send a SNMP trap
$action = New-AlarmActionSnmp
```

```
# Combine the transition and the action
$groupactions = @()
$groupactions += New-AlarmTriggerAction -Action $action `
  -Transition $trans

# Fire the alarm on the metric cpu.usage.average
$expression = @()
$expression += New-AlarmExpressionAnd
$expression += New-AlarmExpressionMetric -Metric
 "cpu.usage.average" `
  -Object "HostSystem" -Operator "isAbove" `
  -YellowValue 7000 -YellowInterval 25

# Create the alarm in the vCenter root
Get-Inventory -Name "Datacenters" | `
New-Alarm -Name "Book: host busy" -Description "Host too busy" `
  -Action $groupactions -Expression $expression -Enabled
```

The next alarm, shown in Listing 16.9, sends an email and an SNMP trap when a guest loses its network connectivity. The alarm is enabled for all guests in datacenter DC1.

LISTING 16.9 Guest network connectivity alarm

```
# The transition state
$trans = @()
$trans += New-AlarmTransition -Start "green" -Final "yellow" `
  -Repeat:$true

$groupactions = @()

# Send an SNMP trap
$action = New-AlarmActionSnmp
$groupactions += New-AlarmTriggerAction -Action $action `
  -Transition $trans

# Send an Email
$action = New-AlarmActionEmail -To "lucd@lucd.info" `
  -Subject "Mail subject" -Body "Body text"
$groupactions += New-AlarmTriggerAction -Action $action `
  -Transition $trans
```

```
# Fire the alarm on the vmNetworkFailed event
$expression = @()
$expression += New-AlarmExpressionOr
$expression += New-AlarmExpressionEvent -Event
 "VmNetworkFailedEvent" `
  -Object "VirtualMachine" -Status "red"


# Create the alarm in the vCenter root
$dc = Get-Datacenter -Name "DC1"
New-Alarm -Name "Book: guest lost network" -Description
 "VM network lost" `
  -Entity $dc `
  -Action $groupactions -Expression $expression -Enabled
```

The next example, in Listing 16.10, creates an alarm that will fire when someone changes a custom attribute on a guest. The alarm will run a PowerShell script.

LISTING 16.10 Guest custom attribute change alarm

```
# The transition state
$trans = @()
$trans += New-AlarmTransition -Start "green" -Final "yellow"


$groupactions = @()


# Run a script
$cmd = "C:\Windows\System32\cmd.exe /c powershell.exe" + `
  "-PSConsolefile C:\Scripts\MyConsole.psc1 -noninteractive" + `
  "-noprofile -file C:\Scripts\Custom-changed.ps1"
$action = New-AlarmActionScript -Path $cmd
$groupactions += New-AlarmTriggerAction -Action $action `
-Transition $trans


# Fire the alarm on the metric cpu.usage.average
$expression = @()
$expression += New-AlarmExpressionOr
$expression += New-AlarmExpressionEvent `
  -Event "CustomFieldValueChangedEvent" `
  -Object "VirtualMachine" -Status "yellow"
```

```
# Create the alarm on the datacenter
$dc = Get-Datacenter -Name DC1
New-Alarm -Name "Book: CA changed" `
  -Description "custom attribute changed" `
  -Entity $dc `
  -Action $groupactions -Expression $expression -Enabled
```

The script that is run through the action looks like the code found in Listing 16.11.

LISTING 16.11 Custom-changed.ps1

```
$ErrorActionPreference = "SilentlyContinue"
$Error.Clear()

$errorFile = "C:\error.txt"

$line = "Time:" + (Get-Date).ToShortTimeString()
$line += (",User:" + $env:VMWARE_ALARM_EVENT_USERNAME)
$line += (",On:" + $env:VMWARE_ALARM_TARGET_NAME)
$line += (",Description:" + $env:VMWARE_ALARM_EVENTDESCRIPTION)

$line | Out-File -FilePath "C:\CA-changes.txt" -Append

if($Errors){
  "==> Errors" | Out-File -FilePath $errorFile -Append
  $Error | Out-File -FilePath $errorFile -Append
}
```

Removing Alarms

The Remove-Alarm function (see Listing 16.12) is quite straightforward; it deletes one or more alarms that you pass to the function.

LISTING 16.12 Removing an alarm

```
function Remove-Alarm{
  <#
.SYNOPSIS
  Removes one or more alarms
```

```
.DESCRIPTION
  The function will remove all the alarms whose
  name matches.
.NOTES
    Source:  Automating vSphere Administration
    Authors: Luc Dekens, Arnim van Lieshout, Jonathan Medd,
             Alan Renouf, Glenn Sizemore
.EXAMPLE
  PS> Remove-Alarm -Name "Book: My Alarm"
.EXAMPLE
  PS> Remove-Alarm -Name "Book:*"
#>

  param(
  [string]$Name
  )

  process{
    $alarmMgr = Get-View AlarmManager
    $alarmMgr.GetAlarm($null) | %{
      $alarm = Get-View $_
      if($alarm.Info.Name -like $Name){
        $alarm.RemoveAlarm()
      }
    }
  }
}
```

The Remove-Alarm function is rather simple to use. Use the -Name parameter to specify a specific alarm for removal. The -Name parameter can also be a mask, for example Test*, to remove several alarms whose name starts with Test.

```
Remove-Alarm -Name "Book: obsolete alarm"
Remove-Alarm -Name "Test*"
```

Modifying Alarms

With PowerCLI 4.1.1 a number of alarm-related cmdlets were introduced. Although PowerCLI still doesn't offer all the functionality that you may need, you can make changes to existing alarms with the help of these new cmdlets.

The new cmdlets are called `Set-AlarmDefinition`, `New-AlarmAction`, `New-AlarmActionTrigger`, `Remove-AlarmAction`, and `Remove-Alarm ActionTrigger`.

Moving Alarms

Moving alarms within the same vCenter Server is quite easy, and there are numerous scripts available in the blogosphere; just Google or Bing around a bit. One example of such a script can be found at `http://www.lucd.info/2010/02/20/ alarms-moving-them-around/`.

When you want to move alarm definitions between vCenter Servers that don't "see" each other, you can't use a script that reads the alarm definitions from one vCenter Server and then re-creates these alarms on another vCenter Server. The script in this case will need to store the alarm definitions somewhere where they can be picked up when the script is running on the target vCenter Server. Unfortunately, serializing and deserializing PowerShell objects is not too straightforward. That is why we came up with the following alternative. The `Get-AlarmScript` function takes an object, produced by the `Get-Alarm` function, and will generate PowerShell code that contains all the necessary statements to create the alarm. This PowerShell code can be saved in a PS1 file and can be transferred to your destination vCenter Server. When you execute the code on the destination vCenter Server, the alarm will be created. You can download a copy of the `Get-AlarmScript` from `www.sybex .com/go/vmwarevspherepowercliref`.

A sample run of the script produces:

```
Get-Alarm -Name "Book: test alarm" | Get-AlarmScript |`
Set-Content "C:\myAlarm.ps1"
```

The file `myAlarm.ps1` file will contain a PS1 script that you can execute on another vCenter Server and, provided the entity on which the original alarm was defined is there, the script will create a new alarm identical to the one you started from. The generated script looks something like Listing 16.13.

LISTING 16.13   myAlarm.ps1

```
#requires -version 2
#requires -pssnapin VMware.VimAutomation.Core -version 4.1

$spec = New-Object VMware.Vim.AlarmSpec
```

```
$spec.Name = "Book: Change custom field"
$spec.Description = ""
$spec.ActionFrequency = 0
$spec.Enabled = $True

$action = New-Object VMware.Vim.GroupAlarmAction

$action1 = New-Object VMware.Vim.AlarmTriggeringAction
$action1.Green2yellow = $False
$action1.Red2yellow = $False
$action1.Yellow2green = $False
$action1.Yellow2red = $False
$trans1 = New-Object
 VMware.Vim.AlarmTriggeringActionTransitionSpec
$trans1.StartState = "green"
$trans1.FinalState = "yellow"
$trans1.Repeats = $False

$action1.TransitionSpecs += $trans1

$action.Action += $action1


$spec.Action = $action

$expression = New-Object VMware.Vim.OrAlarmExpression

$expression1 = New-Object VMware.Vim.EventAlarmExpression
$expression1.EventType = CustomFieldValueChangedEvent
$expression1.EventTypeId =
 vim.event.CustomFieldValueChangedEvent
$expression1.ObjectType = VirtualMachine
$expression1.status = yellow

$expression.Expression += $expression1

$spec.Expression = $expression

$setting = New-Object VMware.Vim.AlarmSetting
```

```
$setting.reportingFrequency = 0
$setting.toleranceRange = 0

$spec.Setting = $setting

$entity = Get-Inventory -Name DC1

$alarmMgr = Get-View AlarmManager
$alarmMgr.CreateAlarm($entity.Extensiondata.MoRef,$spec)
```

Auditing the vSphere Environment

IN THIS CHAPTER, YOU WILL LEARN TO:

n your vSphere environment, you want to keep track of who changed what at which time. This information can be useful when you are troubleshooting a problem, and it will definitely come in handy when an audit team pays you a visit.

Luckily, vCenter Server and ESX(i) provide you with all you need to access the data required for most audit report requests that come your way.

On an ESX(i) server, only the last 1,000 events are retained. On a vCenter Server, the duration depends on what you specified in the Database Retention policy for events; the default is to keep all events.

Understand Tasks and Events Data

vCenter Server records every task (and the resulting events) in its database. The tasks and events data contains everything you see in the Tasks & Events tab in your vSphere Client, and more. In all Inventory views, vSphere Client offers two ways of looking at tasks and events. In Tasks view, you can view a list of all the tasks (upper pane), with the related events for each task (lower pane). For example, Figure 17.1 shows a task list of the events related to a particular task.

FIGURE 17.1 Tasks & Events—Tasks view

Tasks

Related Events

You can also view a flat list of all the events, as shown in Figure 17.2. Notice how the start of each task is represented as a separate event.

FIGURE 17.2 Task & Events—Events view

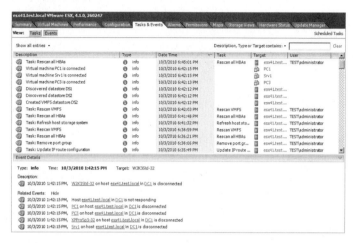

It is important that you understand the difference between these two ways of representing tasks and events. These two concepts will come into play when you report on tasks and events.

There are currently more than 430 event types defined in the vSphere environment. Some extensions, like Converter and Update Manager, add even more events to the list. So, the total count of events in your vSphere environment can be considerably higher. To compile an overview of all the available events in your vSphere environment, use the `Get-VIEventType` function, shown in Listing 17.1.

LISTING 17.1 The `Get-VIEventType` function

```
function Get-VIEventType{
  <#
.SYNOPSIS
  Returns all the available event types in the vSphere environment
  Can be used on against a vCenter and an ESX(i) server
.DESCRIPTION
  The function returns a string array that contains all the
  available eventtypes in the current vSphere environment.
.NOTES
  Source:   Automating vSphere Administration
  Authors:  Luc Dekens, Arnim Lieshout, Johnathan Medd,
```

```
                    Alan Renouf, Glenn Sizemore
         .PARAMETER Category
           Select the eventtype to report on.
           Default values are: info,warning,error,user
         .EXAMPLE
           PS> Get-VIEventType | `
           >> Export-Csv -Path $csvName -NoTypeInformation
         #>
           param(
           [parameter(
           HelpMessage = "Accepted categories: info,warning,error,user")]
           [string[]]$Category = @("info","warning","error","user"))
           begin{
             $si = Get-View ServiceInstance
             $eventMgr = Get-View $si.Content.EventManager
             $oldErrorActionPreference = $ErrorActionPreference
             $ErrorActionPreference = "SilentlyContinue"
           }

           process{
             $eventMgr.Description.EventInfo | `
             where {$Category -contains $_.Category} | %{
               New-Object PSObject -Property @{
                 Name = $_.Key
                 Category = $_.Category
                 Description = $_.Description
                 Hierarchy = &{
                   $obj = New-Object -TypeName ("VMware.Vim." + $_.Key)
                   if($obj){
                     $obj = $obj.GetType()
                     $path = ""
                     do{
                       $path = ($obj.Name + "/") + $path
                       $obj = $obj.BaseType
                     } until($path -like "Event*")
                     $path.TrimEnd("/")
                   }
                   else{
                     "--undocumented--"
```

```
            }
          }
        }
      }
    }

    end{
      $ErrorActionPreference = $oldErrorActionPreference
    }
  }
```

The simplest use of the `Get-VIEventType` function returns all the events known in your vSphere environment. Notice how the `Hierarchy` property shows how each event was derived from the base class `Event`:

```
PS C:\Scripts> Get-VIEventType | fl
```

```
Name        : AccountCreatedEvent
Hierarchy   : Event/HostEvent/AccountCreatedEvent
Description : Account created
Category    : info


Name        : AccountRemovedEvent
Hierarchy   : Event/HostEvent/AccountRemovedEvent
Description : Account removed
Category    : info


Name        : AccountUpdatedEvent
Hierarchy   : Event/HostEvent/AccountUpdatedEvent
Description : Account updated
Category    : info
```

You will also find some undocumented, and hence unsupported, events in the list:

```
Name        : ChangeOwnerOfFileEvent
Hierarchy   : --undocumented--
Description : Change owner of file
Category    : info


Name        : ChangeOwnerOfFileFailedEvent
Hierarchy   : --undocumented--
```

```
Description : Cannot change owner of file name
Category   : error
```

And you will also encounter several of the special event types, `ExtendedEvent` and `EventEx`:

```
Name        : ExtendedEvent
Hierarchy   : Event/GeneralEvent/ExtendedEvent
Description : com.vmware.vcIntegrity.VMToolsNotRunning
Category    : error


Name        : EventEx
Hierarchy   : EventEx
Description : Lost Network Connectivity
Category    : error
```

You'll find it useful to have a list with all the available events handy. With the `Get-VIEventType` function, producing such a list is quite easy:

```
Get-VIEventType | `
Export-Csv "C:\events.csv" -NoTypeInformation -UseCulture
```

Remember that you must use the `-UseCulture` parameter when your regional settings are not en-US. The parameter ensures that the `Export-Csv` cmdlet uses the correct separators between the fields in the CSV file.

The `Get-VIEventType` function also allows you to find all the events that are derived from a specific base class. For example, if you want to list all the events that are derived from the `Alarm` event, you can do this:

```
PS C:\Scripts> Get-VIEventType | `
>> where {$_.Hierarchy -match "/alarmevent/"} | Select Name
>>

Name
----
AlarmActionTriggeredEvent
AlarmCreatedEvent
AlarmEmailCompletedEvent
AlarmEmailFailedEvent
AlarmReconfiguredEvent
AlarmRemovedEvent
```

```
AlarmScriptCompleteEvent
AlarmScriptFailedEvent
AlarmSnmpCompletedEvent
AlarmSnmpFailedEvent
AlarmStatusChangedEvent
```

When you run the function against an ESX(i) server, you will see fewer events being returned. That's because the `ExtendedEvent` and `EventEx` entries are unknown on an ESX(i) server.

You'll use the `Get-VIEventType` function later in this chapter when we produce reports on specific event types.

Report the PowerCLI Way

In the previous section, you discovered that there are numerous types of events a vCenter Server or an ESX(i) server logs. In the following sections you will learn what you can do with these events.

What Does *Get-VIEvent* Return?

The PowerCLI snap-in allows the `Get-VIEvent` cmdlet to gain access to the tasks and events data. The `Get-VIEvent` cmdlet returns the data in the Events view, shown earlier in Figure 17.2. In other words, it produces a flat list of all events, including `TaskEvents`.

When you look at the following output, notice that

- ▶ The events are returned in reverse chronological order. It is a last-in, first-out (LIFO) repository.

- ▶ Tasks are returned as `TaskEvent` objects, not as `TaskInfo` objects.

- ▶ The actual `Task` information is located in the `Info` property of the `TaskEvent` object.

- ▶ The tasks and events are chained together. The chain can be followed through the `ChainId` property.

- ▶ The returned objects contain pointers to the involved `Entity` and its parents.

- ▶ The `DateTime` values in the `CreatedTime` property are in local time.

Here is some sample output:

```
PS C:\Scripts> $esx = Get-VMHost esx4i.test.local
PS C:\Scripts> Get-VIEvent -Entity $esx -MaxSamples 3

Key                  : 75575
ChainId              : 75573
CreatedTime          : 7/4/2010 11:54:14
UserName             : Administrator
Datacenter           : VMware.Vim.DatacenterEventArgument
ComputeResource      : VMware.Vim.ComputeResourceEventArgument
Host                 : VMware.Vim.HostEventArgument
Vm                   :
Ds                   :
Net                  :
Dvs                  :
FullFormattedMessage : Host esx4i.test.local in DC1 has enter…
ChangeTag            :
DynamicType          :
DynamicProperty      :

Key                  : 75574
ChainId              : 75573
CreatedTime          : 7/4/2010 11:54:12
UserName             : Administrator
Datacenter           : VMware.Vim.DatacenterEventArgument
ComputeResource      : VMware.Vim.ComputeResourceEventArgument
Host                 : VMware.Vim.HostEventArgument
Vm                   :
Ds                   :
Net                  :
Dvs                  :
FullFormattedMessage : Host esx4i.test.local in DC1 has start…
ChangeTag            :
DynamicType          :
DynamicProperty      :

Info                 : VMware.Vim.TaskInfo
Key                  : 75573
ChainId              : 75573
CreatedTime          : 7/4/2010 11:54:12
```

```
UserName            : Administrator
Datacenter          : VMware.Vim.DatacenterEventArgument
ComputeResource     : VMware.Vim.ComputeResourceEventArgument
Host                : VMware.Vim.HostEventArgument
Vm                  :
Ds                  :
Net                 :
Dvs                 :
FullFormattedMessage : Task: Enter maintenance mode
ChangeTag           :
DynamicType         :
DynamicProperty     :
```

To have a better view of what is returned, let's have a look at the name of the returned objects themselves:

```
PS C:\> Get-VIEvent -Entity $esx -MaxSamples 3 | `
>> Select @{Name="ObjectName";E={$_.GetType().Name}}
>>


ObjectName
----------
EnteredMaintenanceModeEvent
EnteringMaintenanceModeEvent
TaskEvent
```

Notice how the task is returned in a `TaskEvent` object and how the events resulting from the task are returned in their own proper object types (`EnteringMaintenanceModeEvent` and `EnteredMaintenanceModeEvent`).

Using the *Get-VIEvent* Cmdlet

Since the possibilities you have with the `Get-VIEvent` cmdlet are endless, the following sections present some real-life examples of how you can use the `Get-VIEvent` cmdlet.

How Many Guests Were Created in the Last Month?

How many guests were created in the last 30 days is a straightforward question and probably one that you will hear regularly from your management. From the list of events, it is obvious that we need to look for `VmCreatedEvent` in this case (see Listing 17.2).

LISTING 17.2 Listing guests created in the last 30 days

```
Get-VIEvent -Start (Get-Date).adddays(-30) | `
  where {$_.gettype().Name -eq "VmCreatedEvent"} | `
  select @{N="VMname"; E={$_.Vm.Name}},
    @{N="CreatedTime"; E={$_.CreatedTime}},
    @{N="Host"; E={$_.Host.Name}},
    @{N="User"; E={$_.UserName}}
```

This one-liner produces a list on the console for each guest created during the last 30 days. The report includes which ESX(i) host the guest was created on and which user created the guest.

How Many Guests Were Cloned in the Last Month?

The number of guests cloned in the last 30 days is similar to the previous question, but this time you use VmClonedEvent. Just replace VMCreatedEvent with VMClonedEvent (see Listing 17.3).

LISTING 17.3 Listing guests cloned in the last 30 days

```
Get-VIEvent -Start (Get-Date).adddays(-30) | `
  where {$_.gettype().Name -eq "VmClonedEvent"} | `
  select @{N="VMname"; E={$_.Vm.Name}},
    @{N="CreatedTime"; E={$_.CreatedTime}},
    @{N="Host"; E={$_.Host.Name}},
    @{N="User"; E={$_.UserName}}
```

You can use the same basic script to answer numerous questions—it's just a matter of looking for the right events. And for that, the Get-VIEventType function comes in very handy.

Who Added a vCPU on That Guest?

"Who changed the number of virtual CPUs on that guest?" is another typical question you will encounter in your day-to-day life as an administrator. Again, obtaining the data is quite straightforward. The event we're after is VmReconfiguredEvent. The vSphere API Reference documentation explains that this event type has, under the property configSpec, a VirtualMachineConfigSpec object that will list all the changes that were made.

In this case, we are looking for changes in the number of vCPUs, so we test the numCPUs property (see Listing 17.4).

LISTING 17.4   Listing guests where the number of vCPUs was changed in the last 30 days

```
Get-VIEvent -Start (Get-Date).AddDays(-30) | `
  where {$_.gettype().Name -eq "VmReconfiguredEvent" `
        -and $_.ConfigSpec.NumCPUs -ne 0} | `
  select @{N="VMname"; E={$_.Vm.Name}},
        @{N="CreatedTime"; E={$_.CreatedTime}},
        @{N="Host"; E={$_.Host.Name}},
        @{N="User"; E={$_.UserName}},
        @{N="NumCPUs"; E={$_.ConfigSpec.NumCPUs}}
```

It's clear that this event can be used to track all kinds of configuration changes on guests. The configSpec property will show what exactly was changed.

Who's Manipulating Roles?

The vSphere roles are the basis of your vSphere security. It is important that you know about all changes that have been made to these roles. All the activity on roles produces events. A simple way to find the events that hold this critical information is to use the Get-VIEventType function. In the Hierarchy column, you can look for the RoleEvent qualifier. As you read through the code in Listing 17.5, notice how we avoided the parent RoleEvent by adding a slash to the end of the qualifier.

LISTING 17.5   Finding changes to vCenter Server roles over the last 7 days

```
$tgtEvents = Get-VIEventType | `
  where {$_.Hierarchy -match "/RoleEvent/"} | %{$_.Name}

Get-VIEvent -Start (Get-Date).AddDays(-7) | `
where {$tgtEvents -contains $_.gettype().Name} | `
  select @{N="CreatedTime"; E={$_.CreatedTime}},
        @{N="User"; E={$_.UserName}},
        @{N="Message"; E={$_.FullFormattedMessage}},
        @{N="Privileges"; E={$_.PrivilegeList}}
```

The output generated by the small script in Listing 17.5 shows what manipulations were done on the security roles by which user over the last 7 days. When a role is created or modified, the result shows the privileges involved.

What Permissions Were Changed?

When you do security auditing, you want to see whether any changes have been made to the permissions on your vSphere objects. Again, use the Get-VIEventType function to collect the events in a string array (see Listing 17.6).

Monitoring and Reporting

PART IV

LISTING 17.6 Finding changes to vCenter Server permissions

```
$tgtEvents = Get-VIEventType | `
  where {$_.Hierarchy -match "/PermissionEvent/"} | %{$_.Name}

Get-VIEvent -Start (Get-Date).AddDays(-1) | `
where {$tgtEvents -contains $_.gettype().Name} | `
  select @{N="CreatedTime"; E={$_.CreatedTime}},
         @{N="User"; E={$_.UserName}},
         @{N="Message"; E={$_.FullFormattedMessage}},
         @{N="Role"; E={$_.Role.Name}},
         @{N="Principal"; E={$_.Principal}},
         @{N="Entity"; E={$_.Entity.Name}},
         @{N="Propagate"; E={$_.Propagate}}
```

To find out which properties are available for a specific event, you can look up the event in the VMware vSphere API Reference Documentation (see the sidebar "SDK Documentation" for the URL). Figure 17.3 shows a typical event entry, in this case for the PermissionAddedEvent.

FIGURE 17.3 `PermissionAddedEvent`

Event-specific properties

Inherited properties

SDK DOCUMENTATION

You'll find links to the VMware vSphere Web Services SDK Documentation at

```
www.vmware.com/support/developer/vc-sdk/
```

The vSphere API reference in particular can be found at

```
www.vmware.com/support/developer/vc-sdk/visdk41pubs/
ApiReference/index.html
```

The `PermissionAddedEvent` entry tells you that there are two properties specific to this event: `propagate` and `role`. It also shows that the event inherits several properties from four parent objects.

- ▶ `PermissionEvent`
- ▶ `AuthorizationEvent`
- ▶ `Event`
- ▶ `DynamicData`

TIP When you use events to create auditing reports, it is very important to understand this inheritance process.

Did All My Jobs Complete Successfully?

As you know from other chapters, you can schedule jobs. It can be useful, at times, to verify that all the jobs completed successfully. As it happens, there are several events related to scheduled tasks. For the small script in Listing 17.7, we didn't want all the scheduled task events—just the ones that tell us when a scheduled task is started, when it completed, or when it failed.

LISTING 17.7 Reporting the completion status of all scheduled tasks

```
$tgtEvents = "ScheduledTaskStartedEvent",
             "ScheduledTaskCompletedEvent",
             "ScheduledTaskFailedEvent"

Get-VIEvent -Start (Get-Date).AddDays(-1) | `
```

```
where {$tgtEvents -contains $_.gettype().Name} | `
  select @{N="CreatedTime"; E={$_.CreatedTime}},
         @{N="User"; E={$_.UserName}},
         @{N="Message"; E={$_.FullFormattedMessage}},
         @{N="Entity"; E={$_.Entity.Name}},
         @{N="Task"; E={$_.ScheduledTask.Name}}
```

The script in Listing 17.7 also shows how you can create an array of specific events.

What Has Update Manager Been Doing?

When you looked at the list created by the `Get-VIEventType` function, you probably noticed that there are a whole bunch of events that have the name `ExtendedEvent`. These events are, as the name says, extensions of the classic events we have been working with until now. This type of event has a new property, called `eventTypeId`, that shows why the event was generated. Extended events originate from the several extensions in the vSphere environment. Two of the better-known extensions are *Update Manager* and *Converter*. Extended events can also be created by some of the advanced features of the vSphere environment, like fault tolerance, virtual appliances, guest customization while cloning, and so on.

The script in Listing 17.8 exports all Update Manager–related messages to a CSV file. Notice how the script uses `eventTypeId` to keep only Update Manager–related events.

LISTING 17.8   Reporting on the tasks performed by Update Manager

```
Get-VIEvent -Start (Get-Date).AddDays(-1) | `
  where {$_.EventTypeId -like "com.vmware.vcIntegrity*"} | `
  Sort-Object -Property CreatedTime | %{
    New-Object PSObject -Property @{
      Date = $_.CreatedTime
      User = $_.UserName
      Host = $_.Host.Name
      Message = $_.FullFormattedMessage
    }
} | Export-Csv "C:\Update-Manager-report.csv" `
-NoTypeInformation -UseCulture
```

The result of this script is a CSV file that looks like this:

```
"Host","Message","User","Date"
```

```
"esx42.test.local",➡
"Successfully scanned esx42.test.local for patches",➡
"Administrator","6/15/2010 18:52:42"
,"Successfully downloaded host patch definitions.➡
New patches: 29","Administrator","6/15/2010 19:55:42"
,"Successfully downloaded guest patch definitions.➡
New patches: 30","Administrator","6/15/2010 20:02:07"
"esx42.test.local","Successfully scanned esx42.test.local➡
for patches","Administrator","6/15/2010 20:25:30"
"esx42.test.local","Successfully scanned esx42.test.local➡
for patches","Administrator","6/15/2010 20:27:48"
"esx42.test.local","Start staging of patch on esx42.test.local:➡
ESX400-201006201-UG, ESX400-201006202-UG, ESX400-201006203-UG,➡
ESX400-201006204-UG, ESX400-201006205-UG, ESX400-201006211-UG,➡
ESX400-201006212-UG, ESX400-201006214-UG, ESX400-201006215-UG,➡
ESX400-201006217-UG, ESX400-201006218-UG, ESX400-201006219-UG,➡
ESX400-201006220-UG, ESX400-201006224-UG, ESX400-201006225-UG,➡
ESX400-201006226-UG, ESX400-Update02(*).","Administrator",➡
"6/15/2010 20:27:49"
"esx42.test.local","Stage of patch on➡
esx42.test.local Succeeded.","Administrator","6/15/2010
20:35:58"
"esx42.test.local","Staging succeeded for esx42.test.local",➡
"Administrator","6/15/2010 20:35:58"
"esx42.test.local","Successfully scanned esx42.test.local➡
for patches","Administrator","6/15/2010 20:36:21"
```

> **TIP**   The script from Listing 17.8 will produce no output when Update Manager is not installed in your vSphere environment—there will be no events returned by the `Get-VIEvent` **cmdlet.**

Report the SDK Way

You can also use methods from the SDK APIs to access the Task and Event objects.

The important difference with the `Get-VIEvent` cmdlet is that with the SDK APIs you can choose to use the Tasks view (shown in Figure 17.1 earlier).

Why Use the SDK API?

The primary reason to use SDK APIs is that some features are not yet available in the PowerCLI build. Most of the time, the PowerCLI Development catches up quite quickly in succeeding builds, but there are always some features left that necessitate that you use the SDK APIs.

The second reason to use SDK APIs is speed. Although the succeeding builds of PowerCLI have improved the execution speed considerably, there remains an important difference in some execution times. If you run your scripts against larger vSphere environments, it could be worthwhile to use the SDK APIs.

What Is a Collector?

When you work with the SDK APIs, the Task and Event entries are retrieved through a `HistoryCollector`. The `Collector` allows you to retrieve historical data and new updates. When you create a `Collector`, you have to provide a filter. The filter allows you to specify which kind of records you want to retrieve. You can specify a time range, the entity, the source from where the record originated, and much more.

The `Collector` has two specific derived types: the `TaskHistoryCollector` and the `EventHistoryCollector`. When you work with these `Collector`s, it is important to understand that you will retrieve the historical data through a "scrollable view," a kind of "window" on the stack of historical data. You can specify whether you want your "window" to start with the oldest entries or with the latest entries, and you can specify whether you want to retrieve the historical data in forward or reverse mode.

TIP   When working with `Collector`s you can have only 32 collectors of each type. So, there can only be at most 32 `TaskHistoryCollector`s and 32 `EventHistoryCollector`s.

Fitting Collectors into Your Script

To make it easier to use the SDK `Collector`s, we have created two functions: `Get-VITaskSdk` and `Get-VIEventSdk`. These functions hide some of the complexity of the API methods. As always when using PowerShell, this is only one way you can achieve the same result; numerous other implementations are possible.

The functions also provide some extra functionality that you don't have in the current `Get-VIEvent` implementation. You can, for example, follow the chain of events that were triggered by a specific task.

First, let's look at the functions.

Get-VITaskSDK

The `Get-Task` cmdlet allows you to query tasks only in a specific state. In some situations, it might be useful to be able to query tasks within a specific time frame. You might also want to find tasks that ran against specific entities. Listing 17.9 shows how you can retrieve tasks that ran against a specific entity using `Get-VITaskSDK`.

LISTING 17.9   Retrieving tasks that ran against a specific entity

```
function Get-VITaskSDK{
<#
.SYNOPSIS
  Returns Tasks that comply with the specifications passed
  in the parameters
.DESCRIPTION
  The function will return vSphere tasks, as TaskInfo objects,
  that fit the specifications passed through the parameters.
  A connection to a vCenter is required!
.NOTES
  Source:   Automating vSphere Administration
  Authors:  Luc Dekens, Arnim Lieshout, Johnathan Medd,
            Alan Renouf, Glenn Sizemore
.PARAMETER Entity
  The entity whose tasks shall be returned
.PARAMETER EntityChildren
  A switch that specifies if the tasks for the Entity or for
  the Entity and all its children shall be returned
.PARAMETER Start
  The beginning of the time range in which to look for tasks.
  If not specified, the function will start with the oldest
  available task.
.PARAMETER Finish
  The end of the time range in which to look for tasks.
  If not specified, the function will use the current time
  as the end of the time range.
```

```
.PARAMETER State
  The state of the tasks. Valid values are error, queued,
  running, success
.PARAMETER User
  If specified will only return tasks started by this user.
  If not specified the function will return tasks started by
  any user.
.EXAMPLE 1
  PS> Get-VITaskSDK -Entity (Get-Cluster -Name "MyCluster")
.EXAMPLE 2
  PS> Get-VITaskSDK -State "error"
#>

param(
[parameter(ValueFromPipeline = $true,Position=1)]
$Entity,
[switch]$EntityChildren = $false,
[DateTime]$Start,
[DateTime]$Finish,
$State,
$User
)

process{
  $taskMgr = Get-View TaskManager
  $taskNumber = 100

  if($defaultVIServer.ProductLine -ne "vpx"){
    Write-Error "Error : you need to be connected to a vCenter"
    return
  }

  $taskFilter = New-Object VMware.Vim.TaskFilterSpec

  if($Entity){
    $taskFilter.Entity = `
      New-Object VMware.Vim.TaskFilterSpecByEntity
    $taskFilter.Entity.entity = ($Entity | Get-View).MoRef
    if($EntityChildren){
      $taskFilter.Entity.recursion = "self"
```

```
        }
        else{
          $taskFilter.Entity.recursion = "all"
        }
      }

      if($Start -or $Finish){
        $taskFilter.Time = `
          New-Object VMware.Vim.TaskFilterSpecByTime
        if($Start){
          $taskFilter.Time.beginTime = $Start
        }
        if($Finish){
          $taskFilter.Time.endTime = $Finish
          $taskFilter.Time.timeType = "startedTime"
        }
      }

      $taskCollector = Get-View `
        ($taskMgr.CreateCollectorForTasks($taskFilter))
      $taskCollector.RewindCollector | Out-Null

      $tasks = $taskCollector.ReadNextTasks($taskNumber)
      while($tasks){
        $tasks | % {
          $_
        }
        $tasks = $taskCollector.ReadNextTasks($taskNumber)
      }
      # By default 32 task collectors are allowed.
      # Destroy this task collector.
      $taskCollector.DestroyCollector()
    }
  }
```

Get-VIEventSDK

The Get-VIEvent cmdlet returns all events within a specific time frame. Sometimes, it could be handy to retrieve only events that were produced by a specific entity, eventually including all the entity's children.

The function in Listing 17.10 can be run against a vCenter Server as well as an ESX(i) server. When you run it against an ESX(i) server, it will return the last 1,000 events (or all events since the last reboot of the server if there are less than 1,000 events).

LISTING 17.10 Retrieving events produced by specific entities

```
function Get-VIEventSDK{
<#
.SYNOPSIS
  Returns Events that comply with the specifications passed
  in the parameters
.DESCRIPTION
  The function will return vSphere events, as Event objects,
  that fit the specifications passed through the parameters.
.NOTES
  Source:    Automating vSphere Administration
  Authors:   Luc Dekens, Arnim Lieshout, Johnathan Medd,
             Alan Renouf, Glenn Sizemore
.PARAMETER Entity
  The entity whose events shall be returned
.PARAMETER EntityChildren
  A switch that specifies if the events for the Entity or for
  the Entity and all its children shall be returned
.PARAMETER Start
  The beginning of the time range in which to look for events.
  If not specified, the function will start with the oldest
  available event.
.PARAMETER Finish
  The end of the time range in which to look for events.
  If not specified, the function will use the current time
  as the end of the time range.
.PARAMETER EventChainId
  The function will only return events that have this specific
  EventChainId.
.PARAMETER User
  If specified will only return events for tasks triggered by
  this user. If not specified the function will return events
  independent of the user that started the task.
.EXAMPLE 1
  PS> Get-VIEventSDK -Entity (Get-Cluster -Name "MyCluster")
```

```
.EXAMPLE 1
  PS> Get-VIEventSDK -EventChainId $task.EventChainId
#>

    param(
    [parameter(ValueFromPipeline = $true,Position=1)]
    $Entity,
    [switch]$EntityChildren = $false,
    [DateTime]$Start,
    [DateTime]$Finish,
    [Int]$EventChainId,
    [String]$User
    )

    process{
        $si = Get-View ServiceInstance
        $eventMgr = Get-View $si.Content.EventManager
        $eventNumber = 100

        $eventFilter = New-Object VMware.Vim.EventFilterSpec

        if($Entity){
            $eventFilter.Entity = `
              New-Object VMware.Vim.EventFilterSpecByEntity
            $eventFilter.Entity.entity = `
              ($Entity | Get-View).MoRef
            if($EntityChildren){
                $eventFilter.Entity.recursion = "self"
            }
            else{
                $eventFilter.Entity.recursion = "all"
            }
        }

        if($Start -or $Finish){
            $eventFilter.Time = `
              New-Object VMware.Vim.EventFilterSpecByTime
            if($Start){
                $eventFilter.Time.beginTime = $Start
            }
            if($Finish){
```

```
                    $eventFilter.Time.endTime = $Finish
                    $eventFilter.Time.timeType = "startedTime"
                }
            }

            if($EventChainId){
                $eventFilter.eventChainId = $EventChainId
            }

            $eventCollector = Get-View `
              ($eventMgr.CreateCollectorForEvents($eventFilter))
            $eventCollector.RewindCollector | Out-Null

            $events = $eventCollector.ReadNextEvents($eventNumber)
            while($events){
                $events | % {
                    $_
                }
                $events = `
                  $eventCollector.ReadNextEvents($eventNumber)
            }
            # By default 32 task collectors are allowed.
            # Destroy this task collector.
            $eventCollector.DestroyCollector()
        }
    }
```

The flow of these two functions is quite similar:

1. Create a filter that contains all the specifications you passed via the function's parameters.

2. Create the `Collector`.

3. Use the Collector, in a `while` loop, to retrieve all the objects that fit the specifications. Notice that these methods use a kind of sliding window that scrolls through all the tasks and events.

4. Remove the `Collector`. Remember: there can only be 32 task and 32 event `Collectors` in existence.

5. Exit the function.

Sample Scripts

The sections that follow provide script samples that you can implement to

► Create a tasks and events report

► Report on all vMotions in a cluster

Create a Tasks and Events Report

The script in Listing 17.11 produces an HTML report whose layout resembles the one shown in Figure 17.1. First, we use the Get-VITaskSDK function to retrieve all the Tasks for the last full day. For each Task, we then fetch the related Events with the help of the -EventChainId parameter.

LISTING 17.11 Creating a task and events report

```
$report = @()
$entity = Get-Cluster -Name $clusterName
$start = (Get-Date).AddDays(-1)
$tasks = Get-VITaskSDK -Entity $entity -Start $start

$tasks | %{
  $task = $_
  Get-VIEventSDK -EventChainId $_.EventChainId | %{
    $row = "" | Select TaskName,Target,Status,Start,
      Completed,EventStart,EventMessage
    $row.TaskName = $task.Name
    $row.Target = $task.EntityName
    $row.Status = $task.State
    $row.Start = $task.StartTime
    $row.Completed = $task.CompleteTime
    $row.Eventstart = $_.CreatedTime
    $row.EventMessage = $_.FullFormattedMessage
  }
}
$report | ConvertTo-Html | Out-File "C:\Task-Event-report.html"
```

Each line in the resulting HTML report is a combination of the Task and its resulting Events.

Monitoring and Reporting

PART IV

Report on All vMotions in a Cluster

Before we could create an accurate report of all vMotions in a cluster, we had to resolve a practical problem with the `Export-Csv` cmdlet. The `Export-Csv` cmdlet assumes that all the rows in any array you want to export are of equal length. In other words, all rows have the same number of columns or properties. If you use `Export-Csv` with an array containing rows of varying length, the export will succeed but the resulting report could be missing some columns. The reason is that the cmdlet takes the first row of the array to determine how many columns there are. If the first row in the array is not the longest row, you might miss some properties on the other rows.

We used this knowledge about the first row to bypass that problem. We first sorted the array in descending order by the number of columns in a row.

The script shown in Listing 17.12 uses the `Get-VITaskSDK` and `Get-VIEventSDK` functions.

LISTING 17.12 Generating a report on all vMotions in a cluster

```
$start = (Get-Date).AddDays(-1)
$tgtTaskDescriptions = "VirtualMachine.migrate",
                       "Drm.ExecuteVMotionLRO"

$migrations = @()
$report = @()
# Get the guests for which we want the report
$vmHash = @{}
Get-Datacenter -Name $datacenterName | Get-VM | %{
  $vmHash[$_.Name] = $_.Host
}
$tasks = Get-VITaskSDK -Start $start
$tasks | %{
  $tasks | where `
        {$tgtTaskDescriptions -contains $_.DescriptionId} | % {
    $task = $_
    Get-VIEventSDK -EventChainId $task.EventChainId | %{
      $event = $_
      switch($event.GetType().Name){
        "VmBeingHotMigratedEvent" {
          $migrations += New-Object PSObject -Property @{
            VMname = $task.EntityName
            Source = $event.Host.Name
```

```
                    Destination = $event.DestHost.Name
                    Start = $task.StartTime
                    Finish = $task.CompleteTime
                    Result = $task.State
                    User = $task.Reason.UserName
                    DRS = &{if($task.DescriptionId -like "Drm.*"){
                        $true
                      }
                      else{
                        $false
                      }
                    }
                  }
                }
              Default {}
            }
          }
        }
      }


# Handle the guests that have been vMotioned
$grouped = $migrations | Group-Object -Property VMname
$grouped | Sort-Object -Property Count -Descending | `
  where{$vmHash.ContainsKey($_.Name)} | %{
  $i = 1
  $row = New-Object PSObject
  Add-Member -InputObject $row -Name VM -Value $_.Name `
    -MemberType NoteProperty
  $_.Group | Sort-Object -Property Finish | %{
    # The original location of the guest
    if($i -eq 1){
      Add-Member -InputObject $row -Name ("Time" + $i) `
        -Value $start -MemberType NoteProperty
      Add-Member -InputObject $row -Name ("Host" + $i) `
        -Value $_.Source -MemberType NoteProperty
      $i++
    }
    # All the vMotion destinations
    Add-Member -InputObject $row -Name ("Time" + $i) `
      -Value $_.Finish -MemberType NoteProperty
```

```
        Add-Member -InputObject $row -Name ("Host" + $i) `
          -Value $_.Destination -MemberType NoteProperty
        Add-Member -InputObject $row -Name ("DRS" + $i) `
          -Value $_.DRS -MemberType NoteProperty
        Add-Member -InputObject $row -Name ("User" + $i) `
          -Value $_.User -MemberType NoteProperty
        $i++
      }
      $report += $row
      $vmHash.Remove($_.Name)
    }
    # Add remaining guests to report
    $vmHash.GetEnumerator() | %{
      $row = New-Object PSObject
      Add-Member -InputObject $row -Name VM -Value $_.Name `
        -MemberType NoteProperty
      Add-Member -InputObject $row -Name Time1 -Value $start `
        -MemberType NoteProperty
      Add-Member -InputObject $row -Name Host1 -Value $_.Value `
        -MemberType NoteProperty
      Add-Member -InputObject $row -Name DRS1 -Value $false `
        -MemberType NoteProperty
      $report += $row
    }
    $report | Export-Csv "C:\vMotion-history.csv" `
      -NoTypeInformation -UseCulture
```

Listing 17.12 is a somewhat bigger script, but what we really want to show here is the use of `Get-VITaskSDK` and `Get-VIEventSDK` functions. Also note that use of the `Sort-Object -Property Count -Descending` line to order the results by descending number of columns.

Configure Tasks and Events Retention

As we mentioned in the preceding sections, a default installation of vCenter Server keeps all tasks and events forever in its database. If you can live with having a limited time period for keeping tasks and events available for your audit report, you should specify a retention period (see Figure 17.4).

FIGURE 17.4 Default retention for tasks and events

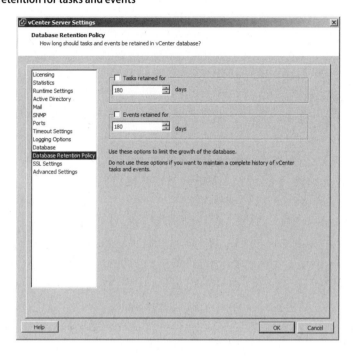

You can specify a retention period via the vSphere Client, but since this book is about automation we'll show you a way to configure the retention status and duration from within a script. With the help of the Get-VpxOption (Listing 17.13) and the Set-VpxOption (Listing 17.14) functions, you can set up functions to achieve this.

First, let's take a closer look at the two general functions that will allow retrieval and manipulation of all vCenter's Advanced options.

LISTING 17.13 Get-VpxOption

```
function Get-VpxOption{
<#
.SYNOPSIS
  Fetches the values for one or more vCenter Advanced Options
.DESCRIPTION
  The function returns the settings for a vCenter Advanced
  Option. If the function is called without a specific key,
  all options are returned.
  This function requires a connection to a vCenter
```

```
    .NOTES
      Source:    Automating vSphere Administration
      Authors:   Luc Dekens, Arnim Lieshout, Johnathan Medd,
                 Alan Renouf, Glenn Sizemore
    .PARAMETER Key
      The key(s) of the requested option(s).
      When $null the function returns all options.
    .EXAMPLE
      PS> Get-VpxOption -Key "mail.smtp.server"
    #>

    param(
    [parameter(HelpMessage =
      'The key(s) of (an) Advanced Option(s) or $null')]
    [string[]]$Key = $null)

        $optTab = @{}
    $si = Get-View ServiceInstance
    $optMgr = Get-View $si.Content.setting
    $optMgr.SupportedOption | %{
      $optTab[$_.Key] = New-Object PSObject -Property @{
        Label = $_.Label
        Default = $_.OptionType.DefaultValue
        Min = $_.OptionType.Min
        Max = $_.OptionType.Max
        ReadOnly = $_.OptionType.ValueIsReadOnly
        Summary = $_.Summary
      }
    }
    $optMgr.Setting | where{$optTab.ContainsKey($_.Key)} | `
            where{!$Key -or $Key -contains $_.Key} | %{
      $row = "" | `
        Select Key,Value,DeFault,Label,Summary,Min,Max,ReadOnly
      $row.Key = $_.Key
      $row.Value = $_.Value
      $row.Default = $optTab[$_.Key].Default
      $row.Label = $optTab[$_.Key].Label
      $row.Summary = $optTab[$_.Key].Summary
```

```
        $row.Min = $optTab[$_.Key].Min
        $row.Max = $optTab[$_.Key].Max
        $row.ReadOnly = $optTab[$_.Key].ReadOnly
        $row
    }
}
```

LISTING 17.14 Set-VpxOption

```
function Set-VpxOption{
<#
.SYNOPSIS
  Sets new values for vCenter Advanced Options
.DESCRIPTION
  The function sets new values for one or more vCenter Advanced
  Options. If multiple keys are passed, an equal amount of values
  must be passed
  This function requires a connection to a vCenter
.NOTES
  Authors:  Luc Dekens
.PARAMETER Key
  The keys of the options that will get new values.
.PARAMETER Value
  The new valuex of the options.
.EXAMPLE
  PS> Set-VpxOption -Key "mail.smtp.server" `
  >> -Value "mail.test.local"
#>

  param(
  [parameter(mandatory=$true,
  HelpMessage = "The keys of the Advanced Options")]
  [string[]]$Key,
  [parameter(mandatory=$true,
  HelpMessage = "The new values of the Advanced Options")]
  [PSObject[]]$Value
  )

  $si = Get-View ServiceInstance
```

```
    $optMgr = Get-View $si.Content.setting
    $changedValue = @()
    $i = 0
    $Key | %{
      $changedValue += New-Object VMware.Vim.OptionValue `
        -Property @{
        Key = $Key[$i]
        Value = $Value[$i]
      }
      $i++
    }
    $optMgr.UpdateOptions($changedValue)
}
```

With the help of the Get-VpxOption (Listing 17.13) and the Set-VpxOption (Listing 17.14) functions, you can now easily set up more specific functions to manipulate the retention status and period for tasks and events (Listing 17.15).

LISTING 17.15 Functions to change the task and event retention periods

```
function Get-TaskRetention{
  Get-VpxOption -Key "task.maxAgeEnabled","task.maxAge" | `
  Select Key,Value
}

function Set-TaskRetention{
  param(
  [Boolean]$Enabled,
  [int]$Duration = 180)

  Set-VpxOption -Key "task.maxAgeEnabled","task.maxAge" `
    -Value $enabled,$duration
}

function Get-EventRetention{
  Get-VpxOption -Key "event.maxAgeEnabled","event.maxAge" | `
  Select Key,Value
```

```
}

function Set-EventRetention{
  param(
  [Boolean]$Enabled,
  [int]$Duration = 180)

  Set-VpxOption -Key "event.maxAgeEnabled","event.maxAge" `
    -Value $enabled,$duration
}
```

 TIP Notice how the default retention period is hard-coded to be 180 days. This value is the maximum value accepted for these advanced settings.

Now it becomes easy to manipulate the retention settings. Some examples are presented in Listing 17.16.

LISTING 17.16 Changing the task retention period

```
PS C:\Scripts> Get-TaskRetention | ft -AutoSize

Key                 Value
---                 -----
task.maxAge           180
task.maxAgeEnabled False



PS C:\Scripts> Set-TaskRetention $true 120
PS C:\Scripts> Get-TaskRetention | ft -AutoSize

Key                 Value
---                 -----
task.maxAge           120
task.maxAgeEnabled  True



PS C:\Scripts> Set-TaskRetention $false
```

```
PS C:\Scripts> Get-TaskRetention | ft -AutoSize

Key                 Value
---                 -----
task.maxAge           180
task.maxAgeEnabled  False
```

N O T E vSphere Client 4.1.0 has a bug in the Tasks and Events Retention policy form. The fields are not displayed correctly. See Chapter 20 for more information on this bug and how we discovered it.

You might have noticed that most, if not all, vSphere auditing centers around the Get-VIEvent cmdlet. The Get-VIEvent cmdlet is powerful, but use it wisely to avoid long-running scripts.

Scripting Tools and Features

CHAPTER 18

Scheduling Automation Scripts

IN THIS CHAPTER, YOU WILL LEARN TO:

Having invested time and effort in learning PowerCLI and making some great scripts, it is now highly likely that you will want to run these scripts on a regular basis. While some scripts are needed only on an ad hoc basis, others lend themselves to being run at regular intervals. One of the primary goals of this book is to save you time with automation, so with these scripts at your disposal you don't want to be setting an alarm every week to remind yourself you need to run a script. This chapter will examine vCenter Server's scheduling capabilities, help you schedule your own scripts to run when required, and move you closer to running a dynamic datacenter.

Use the vCenter Server Scheduler

vCenter Server has built-in capabilities that allow you to schedule and run tasks. In this section, we will examine the scheduled tasks available and how to create them with PowerCLI.

Creating vCenter Server Scheduled Tasks

From within the vSphere Client, you can create a number of scheduled tasks for common operations such as powering on a virtual machine (VM), taking a snapshot of a VM, or remediating an ESX(i) host against a VMware Update Manager baseline. The full list of available tasks is as follows:

► Change the VM power state

► Clone a VM

► Deploy a VM

► Migrate a VM

► Create a VM

► Create a snapshot of a VM

► Add a host

► Change cluster power settings

► Change resource pool or VM resource settings

► Check compliance for a profile

If vCenter Update Manager has been installed, the following tasks will also be available:

► Scan for updates

► Remediate

These tasks are available via the vSphere Client once you navigate from the home page to the Scheduled Tasks area. From this area, you can manage current scheduled tasks and make new ones. You will notice, if you have vCenter Update Manager installed, that two scheduled tasks exist by default: VMware vCenter Update Manager Update Download and VMware vCenter Update Manager Check Notification. These tasks are used by vCenter Update Manager to keep up-to-date with the various patches available for the different versions of ESX(i) and also to determine whether VM patching is being used (see Chapter 13, "Maintain Security in Your vSphere Environment," for more details about vCenter Update Manager).

Unfortunately, as of PowerCLI version 4.1, there are no built-in cmdlets for managing vCenter Server scheduled tasks directly. However, by using some objects and methods detailed in the SDK, you'll be able to automate the creation of vCenter Server scheduled tasks. In this chapter, we'll show you some fairly simple examples that do not require in-depth knowledge of the SDK. To create more advanced examples you will benefit from reading Chapter 19, "The SDK," which will teach you how to work with the SDK.

In the first example, we will use elements from the SDK to create a vCenter Server scheduled task that powers off all the VMs containing the string `PrintServer` in their name at 8 p.m. (20:00) once every 7 days. Although not the most practical application, it does show the basic techniques you'll use to develop your own automated scheduled tasks (Listing 18.1).

LISTING 18.1 Creating a PowerOff VM scheduled task

```
$VMs = Get-View -ViewType VirtualMachine -Filter `
 @{"Name" = "PrintServer*"}


foreach($vm in $VMs){

 $ma = New-Object VMware.Vim.MethodAction
 $ma.Argument = $null
 $ma.Name = "PowerOffVM_Task"

 $dts = New-Object VMware.Vim.DailyTaskScheduler
```

Scripting Tools and Features

PART V

```
$dts.Hour = 20
$dts.Minute = 0
$dts.Interval = 7

$spec = New-Object VMware.Vim.ScheduledTaskSpec
$spec.Name = "PowerOff " + $VM.name
$spec.Description = "PowerOff " + $VM.name
$spec.Enabled = $true
$spec.Notification = "monitoring@virtu-al.local"
$spec.Action = $ma
$spec.Scheduler = $dts

$si = Get-View ServiceInstance
$stm = Get-View $si.Content.ScheduledTaskManager
$stm.CreateScheduledTask($vm.MoRef,$Spec)
}
```

Given that Listing 18.1 includes using the SDK, let's step through each section to make it clear what we did at each point.

First, we retrieved a vSphere .NET object for every VM with `PrintServer` in the name and stored it in the $VMs variable:

```
$VMs = Get-View -ViewType VirtualMachine -Filter `
 @{"Name" = "PrintServer*"}
```

Then, we cycled through each of those VMs:

```
foreach($vm in $VMs){
```

Now, on to the important parts, which require some familiarity with the SDK. We created a number of new objects; we used quite descriptive names so that part should not be too scary!

To create the scheduled task later in the script, we needed to supply an action, so we created that first and saved it in the $ma variable:

```
$ma = New-Object VMware.Vim.MethodAction
$ma.Argument = $null
$ma.Name = "PowerOffVM_Task"
```

TIP To create other types of vCenter Server scheduled tasks, you will need to check the SDK for the task name (e.g., `PowerOffVM_Task`) and any required parameters. Chapter 19 will help you with this task since its purpose is to show you how to navigate and use the SDK.

We also needed to supply a schedule for how often the task should run. In this example, it will run at 20:00 every 7 days. We created the necessary values and stored them in the $dts variable:

```
$dts = New-Object VMware.Vim.DailyTaskScheduler
$dts.Hour = 20
$dts.Minute = 0
$dts.Interval = 7
```

With those in place, we created the specification for the scheduled task and stored all of the necessary values in the $spec variable. Notice that we supplied the Action and Scheduler properties via the two objects ($ma and $dts) we just created:

```
$spec = New-Object VMware.Vim.ScheduledTaskSpec
$spec.Name = "PowerOff " + $VM.name
$spec.Description = "PowerOff " + $VM.name
$spec.Enabled = $true
$spec.Notification = "monitoring@virtu-al.local"
$spec.Action = $ma
$spec.Scheduler = $dts
```

Finally, we created the vCenter Server scheduled task. Notice how we supplied the $vm and $spec variables to the CreateScheduledTask Method:

```
$si = Get-View ServiceInstance
$stm = Get-View $si.Content.ScheduledTaskManager
$stm.CreateScheduledTask($vm.MoRef,$Spec)
```

When we ran the script in Listing 18.1 in our environment, we generated a scheduled task for each of the VMs with PrintServer in their name. You can see that if you have a lot of scheduled tasks to create, using this method can save you a lot of time. Working through the New Scheduled Task wizard in the vSphere Client would soon become tedious, and the process is prone to errors.

Reporting on vCenter Server Scheduled Tasks

Now that you have started the automation of vCenter Server scheduled task creation, you may quickly get to the point where you need to report on the tasks that have been created. Again, as of PowerCLI 4.1, there is no cmdlet for achieving this. However, it is possible to use elements from the SDK to create this reporting capability. Listing 18.2 is a function that you can use to retrieve vCenter Server scheduled tasks.

LISTING 18.2   Retrieving scheduled tasks

```
function Get-vCenterScheduledTask{
    <#
    .SYNOPSIS
        Retrieve vCenter Scheduled Tasks.
    .DESCRIPTION
        Retrieve vCenter Scheduled Tasks.
    .NOTES
        Source:  Automating vSphere Administration
        Authors: Luc Dekens, Arnim van Lieshout, Jonathan Medd,
                 Alan Renouf, Glenn Sizemore
    .EXAMPLE
        Get-vCenterScheduledTask | Select-Object
         Name,Description,NextRunTime,PrevRunTime,State,
         Notification
    #>

    $si = Get-View ServiceInstance
    $scheduledTaskManager = Get-View
     $si.Content.ScheduledTaskManager
    $tasks =
     $scheduledTaskManager.RetrieveEntityScheduledTask($null)
    $scheduledtasks =
     foreach ($task in $tasks){(Get-View $task).info}
    $scheduledtasks
}
```

By selecting a subset of the available properties from the returned scheduled task objects, we were able to return a quick summary to the console. Notice that, in addition to the scheduled tasks for print servers that we created, the function will also return built-in scheduled tasks from VMware Update Manager if it has been installed into vCenter Server. (For brevity, only the first two results for print servers are shown in the output listing that follows.)

```
Get-vCenterScheduledTask | Select-Object
 Name,Description,NextRunTime,PrevRunTime,State,Notification

Name         : VMware vCenter Update Manager Update Download
Description  : A pre-defined scheduled task to download software
               patch definitions.
```

```
NextRunTime   : 11/17/2010 04:06:00
PrevRunTime   : 11/16/2010 04:06:00
State         : success
Notification  :


Name          : VMware vCenter Update Manager Check Notification
Description   : A pre-defined scheduled task to check update
                notifications
NextRunTime   : 11/16/2010 22:41:00
PrevRunTime   : 11/16/2010 21:41:00
State         : success
Notification  :


Name          : PowerOff PRINTSERVER01
Description   : PowerOff PRINTSERVER01
NextRunTime   : 11/23/2010 20:00:00
PrevRunTime   : 01/01/0001 00:00:00
State         : success
Notification  : monitoring@virtu-al.local


Name          : PowerOff PRINTSERVER02
Description   : PowerOff PRINTSERVER02
NextRunTime   : 11/23/2010 20:00:00
PrevRunTime   : 01/01/0001 00:00:00
State         : success
Notification  : monitoring@virtu-al.local
```

You can generate a more extensive report containing all properties and save it to a
CSV file for further distribution by using the following code:

```
Get-vCenterScheduledTask | Export-CSV
  C:\Scripts\ScheduledTasks.csv -NoTypeInformation -UseCulture
```

Use the Windows Scheduler

So far in this chapter you've seen how to create vCenter Server scheduled tasks.
However, the scope of what can be achieved with these is somewhat limited in that
there are only 12 types of tasks that you are able to schedule. Now, let's examine how

you can schedule PowerCLI scripts to run on a regular basis rather than needing to run them interactively.

Scheduling Scripts on Windows

Since way back in the Windows NT days, it's been possible to schedule commands to run at a particular time in the Windows operating system. Originally, this capability was available with the `at` command, so for instance you would run something like the following to copy files from one location to another at 8 p.m.:

```
at 20:00 cmd /c copy C:\Scripts\*.* \\server01\backup
```

Eventually this capability evolved to appear in the Windows interface via Scheduled Tasks in Control Panel. This feature gave you functionality similar to the `at` command, but through the more familiar Windows interface that was driving the success of that operating system.

At the same time, another command-line option for managing scheduled tasks in Windows operating systems appeared: `schtasks.exe`. It has many more options available, but with those options comes greater complexity in creating a basic scheduled task. Although the `at` command is still available in Windows, even in the latest release of Windows Server 2008 R2, `schtasks.exe` has become Microsoft's recommended command-line method of creating scheduled tasks. Listing 18.3 shows how to create a scheduled task that schedules the Copy Files batch file to run once a day, every day, at 8 p.m. until December 31, 2010. Be sure to adjust the code for the time format used in your location.

LISTING 18.3 Creating a scheduled task with `schtasks.exe`

```
schtasks /create /tn "Copy Files" /tr C:\Scripts\CopyFiles.bat
 /sc daily /st 20:00 /ed 12/31/2010
```

With Windows Server 2008 and Windows Vista, scheduled tasks within the GUI were given an overhaul. Many new features were added, including additional triggers such as At Startup or Workstation Lock; new actions, such as sending an email; and new conditions, such as "don't run this task if the laptop is using battery power." However, even by the release of Windows Server 2008 R2 and Windows 7, there were still no native PowerShell cmdlets to accompany these new features and you were consequently required to use `schtasks.exe` for scheduled task management. All is not lost, though; included in the Windows 7 Resource Kit is a PowerShell module containing advanced functions that can be used for scheduling. We will examine this module in more detail in the section "Working with the Scheduled Tasks Module" later in this chapter.

Dealing with PowerCLI Issues When Scheduling Scripts

Now that you are ready to schedule some of the PowerCLI scripts you have put together, let's look at how you go about doing this. In particular, let's examine some of the potential issues that are worthy of your attention:

► Pathname issues

► Cmdlet availability issues

► -PSConsole parameter issues

► Argument issues

► Server issues

Throughout this section we will use the script ESXiHostReport.ps1 to illustrate the examples. This script is not intended to perform spectacular feats, but rather serves as a means to help demonstrate. For completeness, the contents of ESXiHostReport.ps1 are made available in Listing 18.4. A connection is made to vCenter Server and a CSV report is created based on the number of ESX(i) hosts and VMs.

NOTE   Before you run ESXiHostReport.ps1, be sure to change the name of the vCenter Server to match your own environment. You will also need to change the output location if you do not have a C:\Scripts folder.

LISTING 18.4   ESXiHostReport.ps1

```
# Note: Adjust the name of your vCenter Server here
Connect-VIServer virtuvc

# Note: Change the location of the output from C:\Scripts if
 necessary
$VMCount = @(Get-VM).count
$VMHostCount = @(Get-VMHost).count
$MyObject = New-Object PSObject -Property @{ vCenter =
 "$global:DefaultVIServer"; VMs = $VMCount;
 VMHosts = $vMHostCount}
$MyObject | Export-Csv C:\Scripts\ESXiHostReport.csv'
 -NoTypeInformation -UseCulture

Disconnect-VIServer -Confirm:$false
```

Pathname Issues

Up until now, you most likely executed a PowerShell script from the console by typing in the name of the script, prepended with a `./`, typically while in the directory where the script is located. For instance, to run a script named `ESXiHostReport.ps1`, you would type the following:

```
./ESXiHostReport.ps1
```

To enable this script to run as a scheduled task, you first need to make sure that it can be run from good old `cmd.exe`. You'll find the syntax required for that in Listing 18.5.

LISTING 18.5 Running *ESXiHostReport.ps1* from cmd.exe

```
C:\WINDOWS\system32\windowspowershell\v1.0\powershell.exe
 -Command C:\Scripts\ESXiHostReport.ps1
```

However, you may not always have such an easy path to the location of the script file. A more complicated path, particularly one involving spaces, can cause the first very common issue. As soon as the path involves a space, you must enclose the path in both double and single quotes and prefix it with the ampersand symbol. So, to run the `ESXiHostReport.ps1` script from a folder with a more complex path, take a look at Listing 18.6 for the syntax.

LISTING 18.6 Running ESXiHostReport.ps1 from cmd.exe using spaces

```
C:\WINDOWS\system32\windowspowershell\v1.0\powershell.exe
 -Command "& 'C:\My Scripts\ESXiHostReport.ps1'"
```

Many people have spent a lot of time getting frustrated with this particular issue, particularly when the syntax is so nonintuitive. Thankfully, in PowerShell version 2 Microsoft introduced the `-File` parameter, which makes this task a lot easier. Now, only single or double quotes are required for paths that include spaces (Listing 18.7).

LISTING 18.7 Running ESXiHostReport.ps1 from cmd.exe using -File

```
C:\WINDOWS\system32\windowspowershell\v1.0\powershell.exe
 -File 'C:\My Scripts\ESXiHostReport.ps1'
```

NOTE Don't be confused by the location of `PowerShell.exe` when running version 2. The original design decision from the time of version 1 to place the executable in a folder with the path `C:\WINDOWS\system32\windowspowershell\v1.0` does not look quite so smart in hindsight. Issues such as backward compatibility led to leaving the path, folder, and filename the same, rather than introducing a new folder name that reflects the current version.

Cmdlet Availability Issues

Another issue to be aware of when scheduling PowerCLI scripts is to make sure that the PowerCLI snap-in is loaded so that the PowerCLI cmdlets are available to the script. Typically while creating scripts you will be working from your regular administration workstation or server, so you will have ensured that the PowerCLI snap-in has been added to your session. Usually this is accomplished by placing the command to load the snap-in in your PowerShell profile. However, when it comes time to transfer the script to the management server that you use to run scripts, you need to ensure that the PowerCLI snap-in has been installed on that server and that the snap-in is loaded at the time the script is executed.

The simplest solution is to place the `Add-PSSnapin` cmdlet at the top of your script like so:

```
Add-PSSnapin VMware.VimAutomation.Core
```

However, if you are initially testing your script on your workstation, then it's likely that the PowerCLI snap-in is already loaded. You will see an error every time you test the script on a system that has the snap-in already loaded. A slightly more elegant solution is to use an `If` statement to test whether the PowerCLI snap-in is available and only load it if that is not the case:

```
if ((Get-PSSnapin -Name "VMware.VimAutomation.Core" -ErrorAction
  SilentlyContinue) -eq $null )
{Add-PSSnapin "VMware.VimAutomation.Core"}
```

NOTE If your scripts are using cmdlets from the additional PowerShell snap-in for VMware Update Manager, covered extensively in Chapter 13, then you will need to add that snap-in too. Use this code: `Add-PSSnapin VMware.VumAutomation`.

-PSConsole Parameter Issues

Another approach to ensuring that the cmdlets you plan to use are available is to use a PowerShell console file. A PowerShell console file is an XML-based file that contains details of PowerShell snap-ins and is saved with a `.psc1` file extension. The console file can be used to load required snap-ins when executed from `PowerShell.exe` using the `-PSConsole` file parameter. PowerCLI ships with a console file, `C:\Program Files\VMware\Infrastructure\vSphere PowerCLI\vim.psc1`. The contents of the file by default are the following:

```
<?xml version="1.0" encoding="UTF-8"?>
<PSConsoleFile ConsoleSchemaVersion="1.0">
```

```
    <PSVersion>1.0</PSVersion>
    <PSSnapIns>
        <PSSnapIn Name="VMware.VimAutomation.Core"></PSSnapIn>
    </PSSnapIns>
</PSConsoleFile>
```

So to execute the `ESXiHostReport.ps1` script, you could use the code in Listing 18.8.

LISTING 18.8 Running `ESXiHostReport` from `cmd.exe` using a console file

```
C:\WINDOWS\system32\windowspowershell\v1.0\powershell.exe
 -PSConsoleFile ""C:\Program Files\VMware\Infrastructure\
    vSphere PowerCLI\vim.psc1"
      -File C:\Scripts\ESXiHostReport.ps1
```

Again, if your scripts are using cmdlets from the PowerShell snap-in for VMware Update Manager, you can use the same approach with a console file. The installation of this snap-in adds a line to the `vim.psc1` console file, `<PSSnapIn Name="VMware .VumAutomation"></PSSnapIn>` and, consequently, is available by the previous method.

> **TIP** You can create your own console files using the PowerShell cmdlet `Export -Console`. This cmdlet is useful for creating a custom console containing snap-ins from multiple third-party vendors of PowerShell cmdlets.

Other useful parameters that you may wish to use for running a PowerShell script from the command line are listed in Table 18.1. The full list of parameters can be obtained by typing `powershell.exe /?` either from `cmd.exe` or a PowerShell console.

TABLE 18.1 Useful parameters for running a PowerShell script

Parameter	Description
-NoExit	Does not exit after running startup commands
-NonInteractive	Does not present an interactive prompt to the user
-NoProfile	Does not load the Windows PowerShell profile

Argument Issues

Having familiarized yourself with the various options for running a script with `PowerShell.exe` and decided which parameters meet the requirements for the script you wish to schedule, you now need to create a scheduled task in Windows to run the script. Use the Task Scheduler in Windows Server to create a new basic task. Follow the wizard to do the following:

1. Create a task based on the times and dates for the schedule you require.

2. Choose the Start A Program action.

3. When prompted for a program or script to run, paste in the command you wish to run.

Let's run a script called `ESXiHostReport.ps1` to demonstrate using the same code from Listing 18.8:

```
C:\WINDOWS\system32\windowspowershell\v1.0\powershell.exe
  -PSConsoleFile "C:\Program Files\VMware\Infrastructure\
    vSphere PowerCLI\vim.psc1"
  -File C:\Scripts\ESXiHostReport.ps1
```

When you paste a run command that includes arguments, the Create Basic Task wizard recognizes that the command might include arguments and prompts you to confirm, as shown in Figure 18.1. Choose Yes to see the Add Arguments (Optional) field populated with the correct data automatically.

FIGURE 18.1   The Create Basic Task wizard

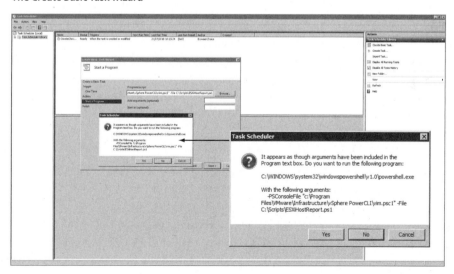

Follow the onscreen instructions to finish creating the task. You have now scheduled one script to run automatically. The section "Working with the Scheduled Tasks Module" later in this chapter covers how to automate the creation of scheduled tasks.

Scripting Tools and Features

PART V

Server Issues

Now that you are aware of these potential issues, a good suggestion for scheduling your scripts is to run them from a dedicated management server. Rather than attempting to schedule your scripts from your own workstation, have a dedicated server for the task and use service accounts with only the required level of permissions to schedule the scripts. Naturally, this approach requires you to transfer your scripts from your test environment (which of course you have been running them in first) to the management server. Ensure that all the system requirements for PowerCLI are met on the management server and that you have amended the PowerShell Execution Policy to permit running scripts. (By default, it doesn't.)

 TIP By default, the PowerShell Execution Policy on a Windows Server installation is set to Restricted. Before running scripts on that server, you will need to change that policy. We recommend changing the policy to AllSigned. The AllSigned policy requires that all executable scripts be signed with a digital certificate. The digital signature reduces the risk of unauthorized or malicious changes to your scheduled scripts—if they are not resigned after a change, they will not run. You can find more details about script signing via `Get-Help about_signing`.

Working with the Scheduled Tasks Module

As of the release of Windows Server 2008 R2, no PowerShell cmdlets allow you to work directly with scheduled tasks. You can use either the Windows built-in command tool `schtasks.exe` or the Scheduled Tasks module. Let's take a look at the Scheduled Tasks module.

Included as part of the Windows 7 Resource Kit is a PowerShell module known as the PowerShell Pack. This module, written by former PowerShell Development Team member James Brundage, contains 10 individual modules. Each module provides advanced functions that extend the automation capabilities of the Windows operating system beyond what ships with out-of-the-box PowerShell cmdlets. In fact, there are around 600 additional functions! One of these modules, TaskScheduler, contains functions specifically for automating scheduled tasks.

The PowerShell Pack module is also available as a separate download from the Microsoft Code Gallery website. The best place to go to download it is `http://code .msdn.microsoft.com/PowerShellPack`.

SNAP-IN OR MODULE

You are already familiar with PowerShell snap-ins, since this is the delivery mechanism for PowerCLI. However, in PowerShell version 2 snap-ins have evolved to a newer concept known as *modules*. Although you can still use snap-ins, modules make it easier for scripters to distribute their code to others. Creating a snap-in involves compiling code into a .NET assembly and then registering that assembly with PowerShell. Creating a module involves using built-in, module-management PowerShell cmdlets to package cmdlets, functions, variables, and other PowerShell commands into a module. Once created, a module can be easily distributed by being copied to the target server or workstation and imported with the `Import-Module` cmdlet. (Some modules, like the PowerShell Pack, are still distributed via an MSI package, which extracts them to the right location for you.) You can find more information about modules by typing `Get-Help about_modules`.

Once you have downloaded `PowerShellPack.msi`, run through the installation accepting all the defaults. To have access to all the functions included in the PowerShell Pack module, you need to use the `Import-Module` cmdlet to add them to your PowerShell session:

```
Import-Module PowerShellPack
```

However, for this example we are only interested in the TaskScheduler module included as part of the PowerShell Pack module, so gain access to that subset of functions via the following:

```
Import-Module TaskScheduler
```

To find out which functions are included in the TaskScheduler module, use this code:

```
Get-Command -Module TaskScheduler

CommandType Name
----------- ----
   Function Add-TaskAction
   Function Add-TaskTrigger
   Function Connect-ToTaskScheduler
   Function Get-RunningTask
   Function Get-ScheduledTask
   Function New-Task
   Function Register-ScheduledTask
   Function Remove-Task
```

```
Function Start-Task
Function Stop-Task
```

To get more information about how an individual function works, you can use
`Get-Help`. For instance, to find out how you can use `New-Task`:

```
Get-Help New-Task
```

Since everything in the TaskScheduler module is a function, it's possible for you to
view exactly how it has been put together. You will observe that they are similar in
structure to those used in this book. So, to find out exactly how `New-Task` works,
use the following:

```
Get-Command New-Task | Select -ExpandProperty ScriptBlock
```

Now that you know how to get the TaskScheduler module and information about
how it works, let's look at some examples. First, we will use functions from the
TaskScheduler module to create the same scheduled task that we created earlier via
the Create Basic Task wizard. We will schedule the `ESXiHostReport.ps1` script
to run automatically. The following functions `New-Task`, `Add-TaskTrigger`,
`Add-TaskAction`, and `Register-ScheduledTask` are required.

As with most commands in PowerShell, it should be fairly obvious (by looking at the
names) what each command is likely to do. In this particular instance, however, you
should be aware that the `New-Task` command does *not* create the scheduled task;
rather it creates a scheduled task definition with some default values. The output from
running `New-Task` shows the default values used to create a base definition:

```
New-Task

RegistrationInfo : System.__ComObject
Triggers         : System.__ComObject
Settings         : System.__ComObject
Data             :
Principal        : System.__ComObject
Actions          : System.__ComObject
XmlText          : <?xml version="1.0" encoding="UTF-16"?>
                   <Task version="1.2" xmlns="http://schemas.
                     microsoft.com/windows/2004/02/mit/task">
                     <RegistrationInfo />
                     <Triggers />
                     <Settings>
                       <MultipleInstancesPolicy>IgnoreNew
```

```
          </MultipleInstancesPolicy>
          <DisallowStartIfOnBatteries>true
           </DisallowStartIfOnBatteries>
          <StopIfGoingOnBatteries>true
           </StopIfGoingOnBatteries>
          <AllowHardTerminate>true
           </AllowHardTerminate>
          <StartWhenAvailable>false
           </StartWhenAvailable>
          <RunOnlyIfNetworkAvailable>false
           </RunOnlyIfNetworkAvailable>
          <IdleSettings>
            <Duration>PT10M</Duration>
            <WaitTimeout>PT1H</WaitTimeout>
            <StopOnIdleEnd>true</StopOnIdleEnd>
            <RestartOnIdle>false</RestartOnIdle>
          </IdleSettings>
          <AllowStartOnDemand>true
           </AllowStartOnDemand>
          <Enabled>true</Enabled>
          <Hidden>false</Hidden>
          <RunOnlyIfIdle>false</RunOnlyIfIdle>
          <WakeToRun>false</WakeToRun>
          <ExecutionTimeLimit>PT72H
           </ExecutionTimeLimit>
          <Priority>6</Priority>
        </Settings>
        <Actions />
      </Task>
```

We then add the trigger and action for the task, before completing it with `Register -ScheduledTask`. That command causes the new task to appear in the list of tasks in the Scheduled Tasks GUI (Listing 18.9).

LISTING 18.9   Creating a scheduled task with the ScheduledTasks module

```
New-Task | Add-TaskTrigger -DayOfWeek Monday, Tuesday, Wednesday,
 Thursday, Friday -WeeksInterval 1 -At "8:00 PM" |
 Add-TaskAction -Path "C:\WINDOWS\system32\windowspowershell\
 v1.0\powershell.exe"
 -Arguments "-PSConsoleFile `"c:\Program Files\VMware\
```

```
Infrastructure\vSphere PowerCLI\vim.psc1`"
-File C:\Scripts\ESXiHostReport.ps1" |
Register-ScheduledTask ESXiHostReport
```

TIP   In Listing 18.8, we needed to use PowerShell's escape character (`, also known as a backtick) to be able to supply the path to the PSConsoleFile. Since the path contained spaces, we had to enclose it within double quotation marks. However, we were already using double quotation marks to supply the long string to the -Arguments parameter of Add-TaskAction. Consequently, if we had not used the escape character only the text -PSConsoleFile would have been used and the command would have failed. By using the escape character, we caused PowerShell to treat the subsequent characters literally. In this case, the double quotation marks (") will be treated as a string character and the correct information can then be passed.

Creating one scheduled task via this method will not save you a lot of time. But what if you had 10 or 50 scheduled tasks to create? Then automation is what you need. Let's look at an example where all the details of the tasks you need to create are stored in a CSV file. Table 18.2 lists the scheduling details. Table 18.3 lists the path and argument details for each task.

TABLE 18.2   Task scheduling details from CSV file

Name	Days	WeeksInterval	Time
Task1	Monday	2	10:00 p.m.
Task2	Tuesday	3	7:00 a.m.
Task3	Wednesday	1	4:00 p.m.

TABLE 18.3   Task paths and arguments from CSV file

Name	Path	Arguments
Task1	C:\WINDOWS\system32\windowspowershell\v1.0\powershell.exe	-PSConsoleFile "c:\Program Files\VMware\Infrastructure\vSphere PowerCLI\vim.psc1" -File c:\Scripts\Task1.ps1
Task2	C:\WINDOWS\system32\windowspowershell\v1.0\powershell.exe	-PSConsoleFile "c:\Program Files\VMware\Infrastructure\vSphere PowerCLI\vim.psc1" -File c:\Scripts\Task2.ps1"
Task3	C:\WINDOWS\system32\windowspowershell\v1.0\powershell.exe	-PSConsoleFile "c:\Program Files\VMware\Infrastructure\vSphere PowerCLI\vim.psc1" -File c:\Scripts\Task3.ps1"

There are only three tasks in this example, but whether you need to create 3, 10, or 50 scheduled tasks, you can use the same code to create them. All you need to do is use the `Import-CSV` cmdlet to import the data from the CSV file and then feed the values into the respective scheduled task functions, as we did in Listing 18.10.

LISTING 18.10 Creating scheduled tasks from a CSV file

```
$tasks = Import-CSV tasks.csv
 foreach ($task in $tasks){
    New-Task | Add-TaskTrigger -DayOfWeek $task.Days
    -WeeksInterval $task.WeeksInterval -At $task.Time |
    Add-TaskAction -Path $task.Path -Arguments $task.Arguments |
    Register-ScheduledTask $task.Name
 }
```

Using the script in Listing 18.10, all three scheduled tasks were created within seconds in our lab environment. You can confirm that they were created successfully with the `Get-ScheduledTask` function:

```
Get-ScheduledTask

Name   Status LastRunTime          NextRunTime
----   ------ -----------          -----------
Task1 Ready  12/30/1899 00:00:00 12/13/2010 22:00:00
Task2 Ready  12/30/1899 00:00:00 11/30/2010 07:00:00
Task3 Ready  12/30/1899 00:00:00 12/01/2010 16:00:00
```

The SDK

IN THIS CHAPTER, YOU WILL LEARN TO:

Although the PowerCLI product has grown over the various releases, there still will come a time when you won't find a cmdlet to do the task you have in mind. That's when you have to start looking at the vSphere API. These API give you full access to all the vSphere management components. Working with the vSphere API might appear to be an obscure black art, but rest assured, once you find your way around, you will find them easy to use.

Now, why would a book on PowerCLI bother with the vSphere API? The answer is simple. With the help of the vSphere API, your scripts can go that extra mile. The PowerCLI cmdlets cover a large part of the functionality that's available in a vSphere environment, but not everything. There are, for example, some properties that you cannot retrieve or change through the PowerCLI cmdlets. And that's where the vSphere API comes in. Luckily, the PowerCLI developers realized from day one that it would be difficult to offer a product that could only do part of the job. That is why they provided access to the vSphere API through specialized cmdlets called `Get-View` and `Get-VIObject`.

This chapter will show you how to use the vSphere API to perform functions that would otherwise not be available to you.

Work with the vSphere SDK

The full name of this beast is the *vSphere Web Services SDK*. But most of the time we will refer to it as the *vSphere SDK* or even just the *SDK*. While the SDK is a collection of documents, Web Service Definition Language (WSDL) files, Java libraries, and sample code, we will most of the time refer to one specific document, the *vSphere API Reference*. This reference document provides all the information concerning the data structures that are available through the vSphere API. This section provides a short summary of how the vSphere Web Services are implemented and how you can use them from within your PowerCLI scripts.

WANT TO KNOW MORE?

This chapter only scratches the surface of what is available in and what you can do with the vSphere Web Services. The summary should be enough to give you a rough idea of how the web services are working. If you want to delve deeper, consult Steve Jin's excellent book *VMware VI and vSphere SDK* (Prentice Hall, 2009).

The vSphere API is exposed as a web service that runs on vSphere servers. These servers can be the vCenter Server, an ESX server, or a VMware vSphere Hypervisor server (formerly known as an ESXi server). In other words, you use the same API for the vCenter Server as for the ESX(i) server. So far, so good as a theory. As you might have guessed, this rule doesn't hold true in some cases. For example, to take a screenshot of a guest's console you need to connect directly to the ESX server. And to retrieve tasks and events information, you have to connect to the vCenter Server.

Because the API is exposed as a web service, it is language independent from a client perspective. The requests and responses that your application sends and receives from the vSphere servers use the XML format. The protocol that is used to send and receive these requests and responses is the Simple Object Access Protocol (SOAP). The underlying network protocol used is HTTPS but can be configured as HTTP. The object model that is used contains the three major types of objects listed in Table 19.1.

TABLE 19.1   vSphere API Object Model

Object type	Description
Managed objects	These are server-side objects and represent a vSphere entity (host, guest, datastore, etc.) or a vSphere service (LicenseManager, PerformanceManager, etc.).
Data objects	These contain information about the managed objects. They can contain:
	Managed object properties (number of vCPUs in a guest, mount information about a NFS datastore, etc.).
	Method parameters (for example, the HostVirtualNicSpec, which is a parameter object to the AddVirtualNic method).
	Return values (for example, the GetAlarm method returns an array of Alarm object references).
Fault objects	These are objects that are returned when a method could not be executed correctly. They contain information about the error that has occurred.

An important concept you should understand at this point is that you do not access these vSphere objects directly. The client, the PowerCLI session in our context, has a copy of these vSphere objects. These copies are called the .NET VIObjects, or .NET objects for short. These .NET objects are asynchronous copies of the vSphere objects. That means that when a property in one of the vSphere objects changes, that change will not appear automatically in the .NET object. It is up to the client to refresh its copy, the .NET object!

Use the vSphere API Reference

The vSphere API Reference can be quite intimidating at first view. But rest assured; it all clicks together nicely once you get the hang of it.

TIP The complete vSphere API Reference is available online, but you can also download it and install a local copy. That is handy when you are writing a script and you do not have Internet access.

You access the vSphere API Reference with a web browser (Figure 19.1).

FIGURE 19.1 The vSphere API Reference layout

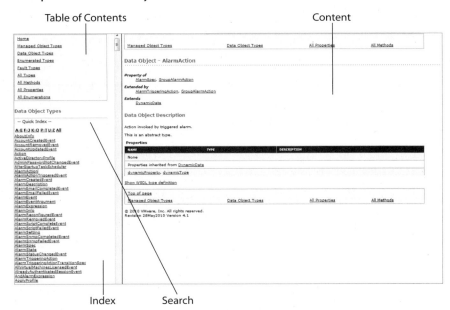

The layout of the vSphere API Reference has four distinct areas, as described in Table 19.2.

TABLE 19.2 vSphere API Reference

Area	Description
Table of Contents	Located in the top-left corner of the screen, the Table of Contents shows the topics that are available in the reference.
Index	The Index provides an alphabetical list of all the elements available under a subject selected in the Table of Contents.

Area	Description
Search	The Search field allows you to specify the full or partial name of the element you are looking for. The results of the search are displayed in a pop-up list below the Search field. When there is more than one hit, you will be able to select a specific element with the help of the cursor keys and the Enter key.
Content	The Content for a specific element is shown in the right-side frame of the browser.

The Table of Contents (ToC) is logic itself if you understand the different object types that live in vSphere. (We described them in the section "Work with the vSphere SDK.") The ToC starts with a list of all the managed objects. As of this writing, there are more than 90 managed objects. The next two entries in the ToC could in fact have been listed together. The enumerated types are just a special type of data object. An enumerated type is a data object with a specific set of predefined values. A good example is the DayOfWeek type, which, as you might have guessed, can only contain the names of the weekdays (Monday, Tuesday, and so on). There are more than 1,420 data objects and more than 190 enumeration types. The next entry in the ToC is the fault type. Fault types are used to pass error information from the server to your application. There are more than 470 fault types.

The following entries in the ToC are there to make your life as an API user a lot easier. Instead of wading through the vSphere objects, these entries (listed in Table 19.3) provide indexes to commonly used concepts in the vSphere objects.

TABLE 19.3   vSphere Object Concepts

Object Concept	Description
All Types	Lists all known object types (managed objects, data objects, enumeration types, and fault objects). There are more than 2,190 entries here.
All Methods	Lists all methods available in the API. There are currently more than 490 available methods for you to call.
All Properties	Lists all the properties and the object(s) where you can find the property. This is the longest list of them all, with more than 4,290 entries.
All Enumerations	Lists all the possible values you can find in the enumerated types. There are more than 910 entries in this list.

There are several ways to use the API Reference, and which you choose depends on what you are trying to find. To be truly proficient, you'll need to acquire a lot of hands-on-experience. The next sections are some use cases to get you started.

Scripting Tools and Features

PART V

Setting a Host in Maintenance Mode

One common task is to set a host into maintenance mode. Let's look to see if there is a method that does this. Enter **maintenance** in the Quick Index field for the All Methods entry. Bingo, you have a winner (Figure 19.2)!

FIGURE 19.2   EnterMaintenanceMode_Task

Just like PowerShell scripts, there is no single correct solution for a problem. You can arrive at the same result via the All Properties entry. Enter **maintenance** in the Quick Index field (Figure 19.3).

FIGURE 19.3   inMaintenanceMode **property**

There is a property called inMaintenanceMode that looks promising. Let's investigate the data object that contains the property (Figure 19.4).

In the description of the property, you can see a link to EnterMaintenance Mode_Task.

FIGURE 19.4   HostRuntimeInfo

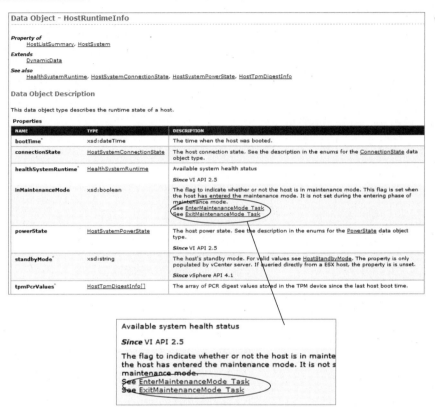

Did the Alarm Fire the SNMP Trap?

As you learned in Chapter 16, "Monitoring the vSphere Environment," you can set up alarms in the vCenter Server that will fire when a specific event occurs in your vSphere environment. As a result, the alarm will execute one or more actions. One type of action that is used often for monitoring is to fire a SNMP trap. This SNMP trap will be transmitted to a monitoring server where you can take appropriate action for the event that occurred.

But what if you're pretty sure the event occurred and you never see the SNMP trap arriving at your monitoring server?

Now this is, perhaps, a question you would not expect to find an answer to in a section on the vSphere API Reference. I include it here to show you that the vSphere API Reference can also be useful even when you do not intend to use the API. All the events that can be created in a vSphere environment are documented under the Data Object Types entry. Let's take a look. Type **snmp** in the Quick Index field (Figure 19.5).

FIGURE 19.5   SNMP events

Two of the entries that appear are obviously related to SNMP traps that are fired by an alarm. Since we want to find out what went wrong, we will have to look for the `AlarmSnmpFailedEvent`. With the techniques you learned in Chapter 17, "Auditing the vSphere Environment," it is quite easy to use `AlarmSnmpFailedEvent` as a filter after the `Get-VIEvent` cmdlet. Doing so lets you investigate whether the problem is due to a failure of the vCenter Server to send out the SNMP trap.

Finding Metrics for Thin Provisioning

When you want to collect statistical data on your thin provisioning, you should know which of many available metrics to use. The vSphere API Reference documents them well. First, select the `PerformanceManager` object in the Managed Objects entry and under the Performance Counters heading you will find the available performance providers (Figure 19.6).

Open the Storage Capacity entry. You can now see all the available metrics (Figure 19.7).

FIGURE 19.6   Performance Counters

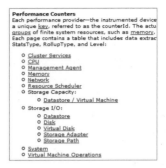

FIGURE 19.7   Storage capacity metrics

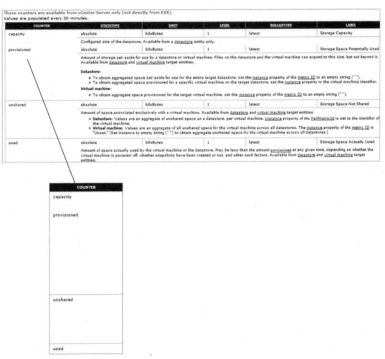

You can compile your report on thin provisioning based on the `provisioned` and `used` metrics. See Chapter 15, "Using Statistical Data," for further details on working with metrics and statistical data.

Scripting Tools and Features

PART V

Can You Migrate This Guest?

In the vSphere client you get a message when a vMotion operation you are trying to do is not possible. The Move-VM cmdlet does not have this functionality. So, how does the vSphere client do this? Type **migrate** in the Quick Index field in the All Methods entry (Figure 19.8).

FIGURE 19.8   Can a vMotion be done?

Notice the CheckMigrate_Task. That looks promising; let's have a look at the method (Figure 19.9).

Let's have a closer look at the parameters this method requires. (On screen, optional parameters have a red asterisk behind their name.) Instead of passing an actual object, you can pass the $null value.

The testType parameter requires an array of strings with the names of the tests that should be executed. But where can you find the test names? For such questions, it's always good to start with the enumeration types. Type **test** in the Quick Index field of the Enumerated Types entry (Figure 19.10).

That enumeration seems to hold the different tests you can use in the testType property (Figure 19.11).

But wait. There was a second entry in the index query result. If you go to the ValidateMigrationTestType enumeration (Figure 19.12), you will see that this is a deprecated type and that in API 4.0 you should use CheckTestType. The small print is important in the vSphere API Reference!

FIGURE 19.9   CheckMigrate_Task

CheckMigrate_Task

Tests the feasibility of a proposed MigrateVM_Task operation.

Required Privileges
System.View

Parameters

NAME	TYPE	DESCRIPTION
_this	ManagedObjectReference	A reference to the VirtualMachineProvisioningChecker used to make the method call.
vm	ManagedObjectReference to a VirtualMachine	The virtual machine we propose to migrate.
host*	ManagedObjectReference to a HostSystem	The target host on which the virtual machines will run. The host parameter may be left unset if the compute resource associated with the target pool represents a stand-alone host or a DRS-enabled cluster. In the former case the stand-alone host is used as the target host. In the latter case, each connected host in the cluster that is not in maintenance mode is tested as a target host. If the virtual machine is a template then either this parameter or the pool parameter must be set.
pool*	ManagedObjectReference to a ResourcePool	The target resource pool for the virtual machines. If the pool parameter is left unset, the target pool for each particular virtual machine's migration will be that virtual machine's current pool. If the virtual machine is a template then either this parameter or the host parameter must be set.
state*	VirtualMachinePowerState	The power state that the virtual machines must have. If this argument is not set, each virtual machine is evaluated according to its current power state.
testType*	xsd:string[]	The set of tests to run. If this argument is not set, all tests will be run.

Parameters

NAME	TYPE
_this	ManagedObjectReference
vm	ManagedObjectReference to a VirtualMachine
host*	ManagedObjectReference to a HostSystem
pool*	ManagedObjectReference to a ResourcePool
state*	VirtualMachinePowerState
testType*	xsd:string[]

FIGURE 19.10   CheckTestType

Home
Managed Object Types
Data Object Types
Enumerated Types
Fault Types
All Types
All Methods
All Properties
All Enumerations

Enumerated Types

test

CheckTestType
ValidateMigrationTestType

FIGURE 19.11 `CheckTestType` **enumeration**

FIGURE 19.12 `ValidateMigrationTestType`

Attentive readers might have noticed that the `CheckMigrate_Task` method apparently only handles vMotion. (We started with `CheckMigrate_Task`; see Figure 19.9.) This seems to be confirmed by the reference to the `MigrateVM_Task` method. But what about SVMotion?

In the first line of the parameters for the `CheckMigrate_Task` method, you notice the `_this` entry, which, in fact, points to the managed object on which the method is called, `VirtualMachineProvisioningChecker`. When you go to the `VirtualMachineProvisioningChecker` object (Figure 19.13), you can see that it provides several other methods. One is the `CheckRelocate_Task` method (Figure 19.14). That method seems to be intended to test the feasibility of the `RelocateVM_Task`—in other words, the SVMotion task.

FIGURE 19.13 VirtualMachineProvisioningChecker

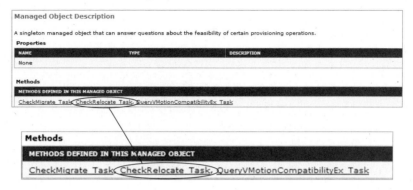

FIGURE 19.14 CheckRelocate_Task

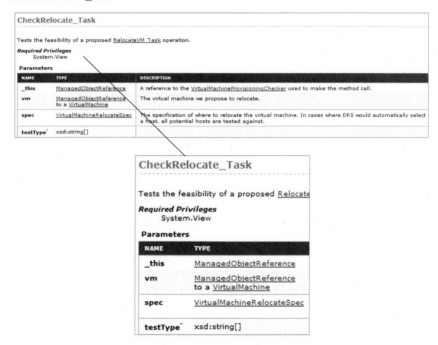

This might seem complex, but rest assured it all links nicely together and, after your first few scripts that use vSphere API, it will become a natural exercise.

Use Managed Objects

As we explained in the beginning of this chapter, a managed object is a server-side object that represents a vSphere object or a vSphere service as they exist inside vSphere. These objects contain all the information vSphere needs to work with these entities. The information present in these objects includes properties (the data objects) or methods (functions you can execute). In your PowerCLI scripts, you cannot access these server-side objects directly. Your scripts will work, as we explained earlier, with an asynchronous copy of the server-side objects. These copies are generally referred to as .NET View objects.

A PowerCLI object, on the other hand, is an object that is returned by a PowerCLI cmdlet. This object is a selection of properties and methods as selected by the PowerCLI Development Team. It is not a 1-to-1 copy of the underlying vSphere object.

NOTE   As a convention, the term managed object in the rest of this chapter will refer to the asynchronous copy, provided by the .NET Framework, of the server-side object. Since a script will have no access to the server-side objects, you shouldn't find it confusing.

The naming convention for these two types of objects in the PowerCLI documentation is as follows:

PowerShell VIObject   A PowerShell VIObject is an object that is returned by a PowerCLI cmdlet. We will use the short name VIObject in the rest of this chapter.

vSphere . NET View Object   A vSphere .NET View object is the client copy of a managed object. We will use the short name View object.

NOTE   Managed objects can link or point to other managed objects. The property that contains such a pointer has the type MoRef (managed object reference). With the Get-View cmdlet you can use a MoRef to retrieve the managed object. There will be a more extensive explanation on MoRefs later in this chapter.

Let's look at some examples so that you can see the difference more clearly.

Managed Object Types

The Get-Datastore cmdlet returns an object for each datastore that is known in the vSphere server your session is connected to. Take a look at the VIObject that the cmdlet returns. The object is a DatastoreImpl type. Most of the VIObjects will have a type name that ends with Impl. That allows a script to recognize where an object comes from. You'll find yourself type-casting parameters on a function, but it also allows you to interpret the results returned by the GetType method (Table 19.4).

```
[vSphere PowerCLI] C:\> $dsImpl = Get-Datastore -Name DS1
[vSphere PowerCLI] C:\> $dsImpl.GetType()
```

TABLE 19.4   Results returned by the GetType method

Characteristic	Return value
IsPublic	True
IsSerial	False
Name	DatastoreImpl
BaseType	VMware.VimAutomation.ViCore.Impl.V1.VIObjectImpl

Now, let's use the Get-View cmdlet to get the vSphere object. Notice that the object returned is a Datastore type. This object is documented in the vSphere API Reference under the Managed Object Types. (You'll remember that a VIObject only contains a subset of all the available properties. The subset is a selection made by the developers.)

```
[vSphere PowerCLI] C:\> $ds = Get-Datastore -Name DS1 | Get-View
[vSphere PowerCLI] C:\> $ds.GetType()


IsPublic IsSerial Name        BaseType
-------- -------- ----        --------
True     False    Datastore   VMware.Vim.ManagedEntity
```

As we said earlier, the VIObjects have a selection (defined by the PowerCLI Development Team) of properties and methods attached. You can use the Get-Member method to view their selection. Let's take a closer look at the properties and methods that are attached to the VIObject that represents a Datastore:

```
[vSphere PowerCLI] C:\> $dsImpl | Get-Member


    TypeName: VMware.VimAutomation.ViCore.Impl.V1.DatastoreMan...
```

```
mpl


Name                    MemberType Definition
----                    ---------- ----------
ConvertToVersion        Method     T ConvertToVersion[T]()
Equals                  Method     bool Equals(System.Object obj)
GetHashCode             Method     int GetHashCode()
GetType                 Method     type GetType()
IsConvertableTo         Method     bool IsConvertableTo(type toT...
ToString                Method     string ToString()
Accessible              Property   System.Boolean Accessible {ge...
CapacityMB              Property   System.Int64 CapacityMB {get;}
Datacenter              Property   VMware.VimAutomation.ViCore.T...
DatacenterId            Property   System.String DatacenterId {g...
DatastoreBrowserPath    Property   System.String DatastoreBrowse...
ExtensionData           Property   System.Object ExtensionData {...
FreeSpaceMB             Property   System.Int64 FreeSpaceMB {get;}
Id                      Property   System.String Id {get;}
Name                    Property   System.String Name {get;}
ParentFolder            Property   VMware.VimAutomation.ViCore.T...
ParentFolderId          Property   System.String ParentFolderId ...
Type                    Property   System.String Type {get;}
Uid                     Property   System.String Uid {get;}
```

EXTENSION DATA

Since PowerCLI 4.1, a new property called `Extensiondata` is present on most of the VIObjects. This property maps to the vSphere object on which the VIObject is based. That means you do not have to use the `Get-View` cmdlet anymore to get at the managed object. Use this new `Extensiondata` property, it will improve the performance of your scripts.

To continue with the previous example, let's investigate the `Extensiondata` property of the `DatastoreImpl` object. As you can see, the `Extensiondata` property is the managed object called `Datastore`.

```
[vSphere PowerCLI] C:\> $dsImpl.ExtensionData.GetType()


IsPublic IsSerial Name      BaseType
-------- -------- ----      --------
True     False    Datastore VMware.Vim.ManagedEntity
```

The vSphere objects typically have a lot more properties and methods attached to them, as the following closer look at a managed object that represents a Datastore reveals:

```
[vSphere PowerCLI] C:\> $ds | Get-Member


    TypeName: VMware.Vim.Datastore

Name                               MemberType  Definition
----                               ----------  ----------
Destroy                            Method      System.Void Destr...
DestroyDatastore                   Method      System.Void Destr...
Destroy_Task                       Method      VMware.Vim.Manage...
Equals                             Method      bool Equals(Syste...
GetAllEventsView                   Method      VMware.Vim.EventH...
GetAllTasksView                    Method      VMware.Vim.TaskHi...
GetEntityOnlyEventsCollectorView   Method      VMware.Vim.EventH...
GetEntityOnlyTasksCollectorView    Method      VMware.Vim.TaskHi...
GetEventCollectorView              Method      VMware.Vim.EventH...
GetHashCode                        Method      int GetHashCode()
GetTaskCollectorView               Method      VMware.Vim.TaskHi...
GetType                            Method      type GetType()
RefreshDatastore                   Method      System.Void Refre...
RefreshDatastoreStorageInfo        Method      System.Void Refre...
Reload                             Method      System.Void Reload()
Rename                             Method      System.Void Renam...
RenameDatastore                    Method      System.Void Renam...
Rename_Task                        Method      VMware.Vim.Manage...
setCustomValue                     Method      System.Void setCu...
SetViewData                        Method      System.Void SetVi...
ToString                           Method      string ToString()
UpdateViewData                     Method      System.Void Updat...
UpdateVirtualMachineFiles          Method      VMware.Vim.Update...
UpdateVirtualMachineFiles_Task     Method      VMware.Vim.Manage...
WaitForTask                        Method      System.Object Wai...
AlarmActionsEnabled                Property    System.Boolean Al...
AvailableField                     Property    VMware.Vim.Custom...
Browser                            Property    VMware.Vim.Manage...
Capability                         Property    VMware.Vim.Datast...
```

Client	Property	VMware.Vim.VimCli...
ConfigIssue	Property	VMware.Vim.Event[...
ConfigStatus	Property	VMware.Vim.Manage...
CustomValue	Property	VMware.Vim.Custom...
DeclaredAlarmState	Property	VMware.Vim.AlarmS...
DisabledMethod	Property	System.String[] D...
EffectiveRole	Property	System.Int32[] Ef...
Host	Property	VMware.Vim.Datast...
Info	Property	VMware.Vim.Datast...
IormConfiguration	Property	VMware.Vim.Storag...
MoRef	Property	VMware.Vim.Manage...
Name	Property	System.String Nam...
OverallStatus	Property	VMware.Vim.Manage...
Parent	Property	VMware.Vim.Manage...
Permission	Property	VMware.Vim.Permis...
RecentTask	Property	VMware.Vim.Manage...
Summary	Property	VMware.Vim.Datast...
Tag	Property	VMware.Vim.Tag[]
TriggeredAlarmState	Property	VMware.Vim.AlarmS...
Value	Property	VMware.Vim.Custom...
Vm	Property	VMware.Vim.Manage...

Data Objects and Their Methods

All the properties in a managed object contain data objects. The data objects can be simple types—for example, the Name property, which is a String type—or they can be other data objects—like the AvailableField property, which is a CustomFieldDef type.

The methods in the managed objects are, simply said, functions you can invoke on these objects. For example, the RenameDatastore method on the Datastore managed object obviously renames a datastore. You can find all the details on this method in the vSphere API Reference if you select the Datastore object in the Managed Object Types entry.

The documentation for each managed object follows a similar layout in the vSphere API Reference. First there is a section that lists:

▶ Where the managed object is used (as a property)

▶ Which methods use the managed object

▶ Which methods return the managed object

► The type on which this managed object is based

► The data objects that are used in the managed object's properties

The next section contains a description of the managed object. This is a must-read section if you are serious about working with managed objects. The description is followed by a tabular list of all the properties of the managed object and a list of all the methods available for the managed object. We also include a detailed description of all the methods.

If you look in the list of methods for the `Datastore` object in the vSphere API Reference, you will notice that there are a number of methods that are marked as being inherited. Let's take the inherited method called `Rename` that exists next to the more specific `RenameDatastore` method. Most managed objects are based on a parent class. Class inheritance ensures that common properties and methods can be defined for a parent class instead of for each of the managed objects.

In the case of the `Datastore` object, you can see (Figure 19.15) that a `Rename_Task` method was inherited from the `ManagedEntity` object, which is itself also a managed object.

FIGURE 19.15   `Rename_Task` **method**

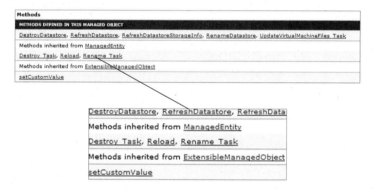

So what's the deal here? We seem to have two different methods—one called `DatastoreRename` and another called `Rename_Task`. And both seem to be doing the same thing: renaming a datastore. The explanation for this can be found in the vSphere API Reference. The `RenameDatastore` method is marked as Deprecated, and it says that you should use the `Rename_Task` method. This is obviously something that the vSphere API developers introduced with version 4.0 of the API. Historically most of the managed objects had their own rename method; in our example, that would be the `RenameDatastore` method.

With API 4.0 it was apparently deemed wiser to use a unified renaming method, and so the developers created a `Rename_Task` method on the `ManagedEntity` object.

Since most of the important managed objects are derived from this ManagedEntity object, they all inherit this unified Rename_Task method.

WHY DO WE HAVE THIS _TASK_ SUFFIX ON THIS METHOD?

To understand this part, you have to know that most of the API methods run asynchronously. When you call the method, your script will continue running immediately after the call of the method. This accommodates long-running tasks that would otherwise block your application or script. To allow you to follow the progress or to wait for the completion of the API method you called, most asynchronous methods return a reference to a Task object. With the help of that Task object, you can check the method call's progress and find out if it completed successfully. In the "Put Some Tips and Tricks to Good Use" section at the end of this chapter, there are two code snippets that show how you can do this in your scripts.

Returning to the unified Rename_Task method from the previous section, the PowerCLI Development Team tried to make life easier for the PowerCLI user. They added synchronous methods in the managed object bindings for all the asynchronous methods that are present in the vSphere API. That's why you see on the Datastore managed object both a Rename and a Rename_Task method. And as you saw earlier, the RenameDatastore method is deprecated but is still available (for now).

```
PS C:\> $ds | gm -MemberType Method | `
  where {$_.Name -like "Rename*"}


   TypeName: VMware.Vim.Datastore


Name                 MemberType Definition
----                 ---------- ----------
Rename               Method     System.Void Rename(string newName)
RenameDatastore      Method     System.Void
RenameDatastore(string...
Rename_Task          Method     VMware.Vim.ManagedObjectReference
...
```

The following code uses the synchronous Rename method from the Datastore managed object. The prompt only comes back when the actual rename is finished. Don't forget that the Rename method is not a method that you will find in the vSphere API Reference. The method was added by the PowerCLI Development Team to the .NET Framework to give you a synchronous version of what is an asynchronous method.

```
[vSphere PowerCLI] C:\> $ds.Rename("DS22")
[vSphere PowerCLI] C:\>
```

Let's verify that the rename was done correctly:

```
[vSphere PowerCLI] C:\> $ds.Name
DS1
```

It looks as if the method call didn't work! Rest assured, the method call did work. You just have to remember that you're using a client-side copy of the actual managed object that exists on the vSphere server.

One method of checking that the name change actually happened would be to get a fresh copy of the `Datastore` managed object like this:

```
[vSphere PowerCLI] C:\> $ds = Get-Datastore -Name DS1 | Get-View
[vSphere PowerCLI] C:\> $ds.Name
DS22
```

Another method to verify that the rename of the datastore was done is to refresh part of the copy that you have. To do that, use the `UpdateViewData` method that the PowerCLI Development Team added to most managed objects. The `UpdateViewData` method allows you to refresh either the complete managed object or specific properties of the object. The ability to specify the properties you wish to refresh can be a significant time-saver if the property itself is a complex data object. It saves even more time if you need to refresh properties on thousands of managed object copies!

```
[vSphere PowerCLI] C:\> $ds.UpdateViewData("Name")
[vSphere PowerCLI] C:\> $ds.Name
DS22
```

Using vSphere Managers

The other major type of managed objects are the service managers. Service managers are special objects that provide services in the virtual environment. Some examples of such services are `EventManager`, `LicenseManager`, and `PerfManager`.

To access the service managers, start from the `ServiceInstance` managed object, which is the root object of the inventory. In the `Content` property, you will find a MoRef for most of the service managers:

```
[vSphere PowerCLI] C:\> Get-View ServiceInstance

ServerClock : 9/11/2010 6:43:13 PM
```

```
Capability   : VMware.Vim.Capability
Content      : VMware.Vim.ServiceContent
MoRef        : ServiceInstance-ServiceInstance
Client       : VMware.Vim.VimClient


[vSphere PowerCLI] C:\> Get-View ServiceInstance | `
  Select -exp Content


RootFolder              : Folder-group-d1
PropertyCollector       : PropertyCollector-propertyCollector
ViewManager             : ViewManager-ViewManager
About                   : VMware.Vim.AboutInfo
Setting                 : OptionManager-VpxSettings
UserDirectory           : UserDirectory-UserDirectory
SessionManager          : SessionManager-SessionManager
AuthorizationManager    : AuthorizationManager-Authorization…
PerfManager             : PerformanceManager-PerfMgr
ScheduledTaskManager    : ScheduledTaskManager-ScheduledTask…
AlarmManager            : AlarmManager-AlarmManager
EventManager            : EventManager-EventManager
TaskManager             : TaskManager-TaskManager
ExtensionManager        : ExtensionManager-ExtensionManager
CustomizationSpecManager : CustomizationSpecManager-Customizat…
CustomFieldsManager     : CustomFieldsManager-CustomFieldsMan…
AccountManager          :
DiagnosticManager       : DiagnosticManager-DiagMgr
LicenseManager          : LicenseManager-LicenseManager
SearchIndex             : SearchIndex-SearchIndex
FileManager             : FileManager-FileManager
VirtualDiskManager      : VirtualDiskManager-VirtualDiskManager
VirtualizationManager   :
SnmpSystem              : HostSnmpSystem-SnmpSystem
VmProvisioningChecker   : VirtualMachineProvisioningChecker-…
VmCompatibilityChecker  : VirtualMachineCompatibilityChecker…
OvfManager              : OvfManager-OvfManager
IpPoolManager           : IpPoolManager-IpPoolManager
```

```
DvSwitchManager             : DistributedVirtualSwitchManager-DV…
HostProfileManager          : HostProfileManager-HostProfileManager
ClusterProfileManager       : ClusterProfileManager-ClusterProfi…
ComplianceManager           : ProfileComplianceManager-MoComplia…
LocalizationManager         : LocalizationManager-LocalizationMa…
StorageResourceManager      : StorageResourceManager-StorageReso…
DynamicType                 :
DynamicProperty             :
```

Managed Object References

Now what is a MoRef? The acronym stands for managed object reference. A MoRef is a data object that is used as a kind of pointer or link to a managed object. You can use the `Get-View` cmdlet to retrieve a copy of the managed object from the MoRef. All managed objects have a property called `MoRef`, which points to the object itself.

The following code shows how to retrieve a service manager through a `MoRef` pointer. First we use the predefined shortcut to get the `ServiceInstance` data object with the `Get-View` cmdlet. And then, as an example, we retrieve the data object that represents the `AlarmManager`. This time we use the `Get-View` cmdlet with the MoRef we retrieved from the `ServiceInstance`, and the `Config.AlarmManager` property.

```
[vSphere PowerCLI] C:\> $si = Get-View ServiceInstance
[vSphere PowerCLI] C:\> $si.Content.AlarmManager


Type                                        Value
----                                        -----
AlarmManager                                AlarmManager



[vSphere PowerCLI] C:\> Get-View $si.Content.AlarmManager


DefaultExpression  Description    MoRef            Client
-----------------  -----------    -----            ------
{VMware.Vim.Stat.. VMware.Vim.Alarm.. AlarmManager-Ala.. VMwa...
```

TIP   A word of warning: Never use hard-coded MoRefs! Always retrieve the MoRef afresh in your session or script.

When you have the service manager's object, you can access all of its properties and call all its methods:

```
[vSphere PowerCLI] C:\> $alarmMgr = `
>> Get-View $si.Content.AlarmManager
[vSphere PowerCLI] C:\> $alarmMgr | Get-Member


    TypeName: VMware.Vim.AlarmManager

Name                     MemberType   Definition
----                     ----------   ----------
AcknowledgeAlarm         Method       System.Void AcknowledgeAlar...
AreAlarmActionsEnabled   Method       bool AreAlarmActionsEnabled...
CreateAlarm              Method       VMware.Vim.ManagedObjectRef...
EnableAlarmActions       Method       System.Void EnableAlarmActi...
Equals                   Method       bool Equals(System.Object obj)
GetAlarm                 Method       VMware.Vim.ManagedObjectRef...
GetAlarmState            Method       VMware.Vim.AlarmState[] Get...
GetHashCode              Method       int GetHashCode()
GetType                  Method       type GetType()
SetViewData              Method       System.Void SetViewData(VMw...
ToString                 Method       string ToString()
UpdateViewData           Method       System.Void UpdateViewData(...
WaitForTask              Method       System.Object WaitForTask(V...
Client                   Property     VMware.Vim.VimClient Client…
DefaultExpression        Property     VMware.Vim.AlarmExpression[...
Description              Property     VMware.Vim.AlarmDescription...
MoRef                    Property     VMware.Vim.ManagedObjectRef...
```

This example with the AlarmManager shows us that there is a method, called GetAlarm. This GetAlarm method will return an array of MoRefs and each MoRef points to an actual Alarm managed object.

The GetAlarm method has one parameter, where you can pass the MoRef of a vSphere entity. A vSphere entity is a managed object, such as a host, a virtual machine, or a folder. When you call GetAlarm this way, the method will return all alarms defined on that specific entity and all the entity's child objects.

```
[vSphere PowerCLI] C:\> $alarmMgr.GetAlarm($null)
```

Type	Value
----	-----
Alarm	alarm-1
Alarm	alarm-10
Alarm	alarm-11
Alarm	alarm-12
Alarm	alarm-15
Alarm	alarm-16
Alarm	alarm-17
Alarm	alarm-18
Alarm	alarm-19
Alarm	alarm-2
Alarm	alarm-20
Alarm	alarm-21
Alarm	alarm-22
Alarm	alarm-23
Alarm	alarm-24
Alarm	alarm-27
Alarm	alarm-28
Alarm	alarm-29
Alarm	alarm-30
Alarm	alarm-31
Alarm	alarm-32
Alarm	alarm-33
Alarm	alarm-34
Alarm	alarm-388
Alarm	alarm-4
Alarm	alarm-481
Alarm	alarm-482
Alarm	alarm-483
Alarm	alarm-5
Alarm	alarm-582
Alarm	alarm-6
Alarm	alarm-681
Alarm	alarm-7
Alarm	alarm-72
Alarm	alarm-73
Alarm	alarm-74
Alarm	alarm-75

Alarm	alarm-76
Alarm	alarm-77
Alarm	alarm-78
Alarm	alarm-8
Alarm	alarm-81
Alarm	alarm-82
Alarm	alarm-83
Alarm	alarm-84
Alarm	alarm-85
Alarm	alarm-9

If you pass $null to an entity instead of a MoRef, the GetAlarm method will return all of the alarms defined in your vSphere environment:

```
C:\> $cluster = Get-Cluster CLUS1
C:\> $alarmMgr.GetAlarm($cluster.ExtensionData.MoRef)


Type                                      Value
----                                      -----
Alarm                                     alarm-681
```

Notice how we used the ExtensionData property to get to the MoRef of the cluster. This avoids the use of the Get-View cmdlet to get to the managed object that represents the cluster—a real time-saver if you need to run this in a somewhat bigger vSphere environment.

As we said earlier, the GetAlarm method returns an array of MoRefs to Alarm objects. That means you have to use the Get-View cmdlet to get a copy of the managed object that represents an Alarm itself. The Get-View cmdlet takes the MoRef and returns the managed object. And again, once you have the managed object, you will have access to all its methods and properties, as shown by the output of the Get-Member cmdlet:

```
[vSphere PowerCLI] C:\> $al = `
>> $alarmMgr.GetAlarm($cluster.ExtensionData.MoRef)
[vSphere PowerCLI] C:\> Get-View $al | Get-Member


      TypeName: VMware.Vim.Alarm


Name          MemberType Definition
----          ---------- ----------
Equals        Method     bool Equals(System.Object obj)
```

```
GetHashCode        Method     int GetHashCode()
GetType            Method     type GetType()
ReconfigureAlarm   Method     System.Void ReconfigureAlarm(VMwa...
RemoveAlarm        Method     System.Void RemoveAlarm()
setCustomValue     Method     System.Void setCustomValue(string...
SetViewData        Method     System.Void SetViewData(VMware.Vi...
ToString           Method     string ToString()
UpdateViewData     Method     System.Void UpdateViewData(Params...
WaitForTask        Method     System.Object WaitForTask(VMware....
AvailableField     Property   VMware.Vim.CustomFieldDef[] Avail…
Client             Property   VMware.Vim.VimClient Client {get;}
Info               Property   VMware.Vim.AlarmInfo Info {get;}
MoRef              Property   VMware.Vim.ManagedObjectReference…
Value              Property   VMware.Vim.CustomFieldValue[] Val…


[vSphere PowerCLI] C:\> Get-View $al



Info          : VMware.Vim.AlarmInfo
Value         : {}
AvailableField : {}
MoRef         : Alarm-alarm-681
Client        : VMware.Vim.VimClient
```

Get to know the available service managers. They will allow you to access the services that are available in the vSphere environment.

Code Parameter Objects

Most of the methods you encounter will need one or more parameters. These parameters are (most of the time) data objects of a specific type themselves. How do you create these data objects? Luckily the PowerCLI Development Team included all the vSphere object types in the PowerCLI binding. This allows you to use the constructor of these data objects, via the New-Object cmdlet, to create an instance of a specific type.

On the New-Object cmdlet, you pass the Typename of the object you want to create. Do so by appending the Typename to the VMware.Vim instance:

```
[vSphere PowerCLI] C:\> $spec = New-Object VMware.Vim.AlarmSpec
```

Scripting Tools
and Features

PART V

```
[vSphere PowerCLI] C:\> $spec | Get-Member
```

```
TypeName: VMware.Vim.AlarmSpec
```

Name	MemberType	Definition
Equals	Method	bool Equals(System.Object obj)
GetHashCode	Method	int GetHashCode()
GetType	Method	type GetType()
ToString	Method	string ToString()
Action	Property	VMware.Vim.AlarmAction Action {get…
ActionFrequency	Property	System.Nullable`1[[System.Int32, m...
Description	Property	System.String Description {get;set;}
DynamicProperty	Property	VMware.Vim.DynamicProperty[] Dynam...
DynamicType	Property	System.String DynamicType {get;set;}
Enabled	Property	System.Boolean Enabled {get;set;}
Expression	Property	VMware.Vim.AlarmExpression Expressi…
Name	Property	System.String Name {get;set;}
Setting	Property	VMware.Vim.AlarmSetting Setting {g…

If a property of the data object is another data object, use the New-Object cmdlet again to create this nested data object. Continue this way until all the required properties of the parameter object are present. (Consult the vSphere SDK Reference or investigate the error that the method will produce when there are properties missing or of the wrong type.)

```
[vSphere PowerCLI] C:\> $spec.Action = `
>> New-Object VMware.Vim.AlarmAction
```

TIP   Always double-check the type of the values you store in the properties. The error messages you get when the type is not correct are rarely easy to decipher.

Find the Method You Need

Just like with a PowerShell script, you will find there is no single correct solution for determining the method you need to use. A lot depends on your experience with the vSphere environment, but an analytical mind and some experience with the vSphere API Reference can help you a lot.

In this section, you'll see examples of using the vSphere API. Each example illustrates a specific aspect of using the vSphere API and shows how you can find the method or property you are looking for to do what you want to accomplish with your script.

Changing the Boot Delay of a Virtual Machine

To change the boot delay of a VM, it is clear you need to look at the VirtualMachine managed object. But the Reference Guide has documented an enormous number of properties. Which one to use? In a case like this, it is easier to go to the All Properties entries and type a word that describes the property you're looking for (for this example, **delay**) in the Quick Index field, as shown in Figure 19.16.

FIGURE 19.16 The bootDelay **property**

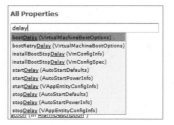

The first entry, bootDelay (VirtualMachineBootOptions), in the returned list looks promising. If you follow the hyperlink, you arrive at the VirtualMachine BootOptions data object. In the Property Of section, you see that the bootDelay data object is referenced in two other data objects: VirtualMachineConfigInfo and VirtualMachineConfigSpec. Now, you have a property that seems to do what you are looking for. If you follow a trail through the vSphere API Reference, you can find the method that will allow you to change that property. But which one to choose? In cases where you want to change something on a vSphere entity, it is always the data object that contains the Spec suffix you need. The Info suffix indicates that this is a data object that can be used to retrieve information from a vSphere entity. That brings you to inspecting the VirtualMachineConfigSpec data object, where you can see that the object is used as a parameter in the ReconfigVM_Task. Bringing everything you've learned thus far all together, you can use this small script to change the boot delay of a virtual machine:

```
$vmName = "PC1"
$delayMS = "5000"    # Boot delay in milliseconds

$vm = Get-VM -Name $vmName
```

```
$spec = New-Object VMware.Vim.VirtualMachineConfigSpec
$spec.bootOptions = `
  New-Object VMware.Vim.VirtualMachineBootOptions
$spec.bootOptions.bootDelay = $delayMS


$vm.Extensiondata.ReconfigVM_Task($spec)
```

Remember that we briefly discussed the New-Object cmdlet and how you can use it to create it objects in the section "Code Parameter Objects." You'll learn more about the creation of data objects and their properties in Appendix A: Basic PowerShell.

Finding the Patches Installed on an ESX Host

To find the patches installed on an ESX host, you can start from the Managed Object Types entry. Enter a common term like the word **patch** in the Quick Index field and you will see only an entry called HostPatchManager in the results.

> **TIP** When you don't know that you need a particular service manager, finding the right search term is a matter of trial and error. In this case, *patch* sounds like something that might get you to the service manager you need. All service managers are located in the Managed Object Types entry.

On the HostPatchManager page, there is a method called QueryHost Patch_Task in the Methods section. This method requires a single parameter, a data object of the HostPatchManagerPatchManagerOperationSpec type. On the reference page for that object, you will find that all the properties are optional. Remember those red asterisks? They mean that no properties are required, which ultimately means that you can pass $null as the parameter to the method, as we did here:

```
[vSphere PowerCLI] C:\> $esx = Get-VMHost esx41.test.local
[vSphere PowerCLI] C:\> $pmMoRef = `
>> $esx.ExtensionData.ConfigManager.PatchManager
[vSphere PowerCLI] C:\> $pm = Get-View $pmMoRef
[vSphere PowerCLI] C:\> $pm.QueryHostPatch()
Cannot find an overload for "QueryHostPatch" and the argument
count: "0".
At line:1 char:19
+ $pm.QueryHostPatch <<<< ()
  + CategoryInfo          : NotSpecified: (:) [], MethodException
  + FullyQualifiedErrorId : MethodCountCouldNotFindBest
```

Notice that the code issued an error. You can't leave out the parameter, even though you don't pass any information. Whenever you want to pass an empty parameter, pass the $null value. Let's try again:

```
[vSphere PowerCLI] C:\> $pm.QueryHostPatch($null)
```

```
Version          : 1.30
Status           :
XmlResult        : <esxupdate-response>
  <version>1.30</version>
  <bulletin>
    <id>ESX400-Update02</id>
    <summary>VMware ESX 4.0 Complete Update 2</summary>
    <releaseDate>2010-06-10T10:00:00+02:00</releaseDate>
    <installDate>2010-07-17T17:06:39.060000+02:00</installDate>
    <matchesPlatform>true</matchesPlatform>
    <newerVibs>false</newerVibs>
  </bulletin>
  <bulletin>
    <id>ESX410-GA</id>
    <summary>ESX upgrade Bulletin</summary>
    <releaseDate>2010-05-18T19:32:18+02:00</releaseDate>
    <installDate>2010-07-18T01:10:08.640000+02:00</installDate>
    <matchesPlatform>true</matchesPlatform>
    <newerVibs>false</newerVibs>
  </bulletin>
                  </esxupdate-response>
```

NOTE The sample used the `QueryHostPatch` method, which is available courtesy of the PowerCLI Development Team, instead of `QueryHostPatch_Task`. Remember that doing so provides a synchronous call to the method.

Finding the Host HWuptime

Suppose you want to know how long the hardware hosting one of your ESX hosts has been powered on. If you enter **uptime** in the All Methods entry, you will find the `RetrieveHardwareUptime` method. From the entry in the SDK Reference, you find out that the method is available on a `HostSystem` managed object, that the method has no required parameters, and that the time is returned as the number of seconds. Using the method, calculating the HWuptime is now rather straightforward:

```
C:\> $esx = Get-VMHost esx41.test.local
C:\> $esx.ExtensionData.RetrieveHardwareUptime()
23522
```

Changing the vCenter Logging Options

By now, you're probably thinking that the SDK Reference is the ultimate resource, but not all information you will ever require while you're working with vSphere is so readily available in the SDK Reference. Let's look at another example.

In the Managed Object Types, you will find the OptionManager, which is obviously what you would look for if you wanted to change vCenter Server options. But if you further investigate the UpdateOptions method, you will find that the OptionValue parameter is required. Now, here's the problem: There seems to be no list of accepted values for the Key and Value fields.

A closer look at the OptionManager object entry provides the solution. The OptionManager object has two properties that hold the answer: the Setting property and the SupportedOption property. When you check those, you'll find that the Setting property holds all the Key-Value pairs for current settings and the SupportedOption property holds the accepted Key-Value pairs. Let's use Get-View to see if you can find the information you need:

```
[vSphere PowerCLI] C:\> $si = Get-View ServiceInstance
[vSphere PowerCLI] C:\> $optMgr = Get-View $si.Content.Setting
[vSphere PowerCLI] C:\> $optMgr.SupportedOption | `
>> where{$_.Key -like "*log*"}


OptionType        : VMware.Vim.ChoiceOption
Key               : log.level
Label             : Logging level
Summary           : Amount of detail collected in the log files
DynamicType       :
DynamicProperty   :

OptionType        : VMware.Vim.IntOption
Key               : TOPN_LOG_BUFFER
Label             :
Summary           :
```

```
DynamicType     :
DynamicProperty :


OptionType      : VMware.Vim.StringOption
Key             : TOPN_LOGING_MODE
Label           :
Summary         :
DynamicType     :
DynamicProperty :
```

The first option returned seems to be the one you are after. Using the following code, you can now obtain the permitted values:

```
[vSphere PowerCLI] C:\> $ll = $optMgr.SupportedOption | `
>> where{$_.Key -like "log.level"}[vSphere PowerCLI] C:\> $ll.
OptionType.ChoiceInfo | ft -AutoSize
```

```
Key      Label        Summary            DynamicType DynamicProperty
---      -----        -------            ----------- ---------------
none     None         Disable logging
error    Error        Errors only
warning  Warning      Errors and warnings
info     Information  Normal logging
verbose  Verbose      Verbose
trivia   Trivia       Trivia
```

After you have retrieved the permitted values, you are ready to call the method. Here's how we did it:

```
[vSphere PowerCLI] C:\> $opt = New-Object VMware.Vim.OptionValue
[vSphere PowerCLI] C:\> $opt.Key = "log.level"
[vSphere PowerCLI] C:\> $opt.Value = "verbose"
[vSphere PowerCLI] C:\> $optMgr.UpdateOptions($opt)
```

Understand Return Values and Faults

Earlier in the chapter, we introduced the Task object. Task managed objects allow you to verify the state of a particular task, check the result of that task, and determine whether any faults occurred. Let's use the PatchManager and see how this works:

```
[vSphere PowerCLI] C:\> $esx = Get-VMHost esx41.test.local
[vSphere PowerCLI] C:\> $pmMoRef = `
```

```
>> $esx.ExtensionData.ConfigManager.PatchManager
[vSphere PowerCLI] C:\> $pm = Get-View $pmMoRef
[vSphere PowerCLI] C:\> $taskMoRef = `
>> $pm.QueryHostPatch_Task($null)
```

Notice in the last code line that the method ends with the _Task suffix; it is an asynchronous task and will return a MoRef to a `Task` object. With the help of the `Get-View` cmdlet, you can get a local copy of the `Task` object. We used the following code:

```
[vSphere PowerCLI] C:\> $task = Get-View $taskMoRef
```

In the `Task` object, you can find the current state of the task. The returned state can be queued, running, success, or error, as shown next:

```
[vSphere PowerCLI] C:\> $task.Info.State
Success
```

In this case, the method call completed successfully. You can find more information about the results of the call to the method in the `Task` object by using `$task .Info.Result`:

```
[vSphere PowerCLI] C:\> $task.Info.Result

Version          : 1.30
Status           :
XmlResult        : <esxupdate-response>
  <version>1.30</version>
  <bulletin>
    <id>ESX400-Update02</id>
    <summary>VMware ESX 4.0 Complete Update 2</summary>
    <releaseDate>2010-06-10T10:00:00+02:00</releaseDate>
    <installDate>2010-07-17T17:06:39.060000+02:00</installDate>
    <matchesPlatform>true</matchesPlatform>
    <newerVibs>false</newerVibs>
  </bulletin>
  <bulletin>
    <id>ESX410-GA</id>
    <summary>ESX upgrade Bulletin</summary>
    <releaseDate>2010-05-18T19:32:18+02:00</releaseDate>
    <installDate>2010-07-18T01:10:08.640000+02:00</installDate>
    <matchesPlatform>true</matchesPlatform>
```

```
        <newerVibs>false</newerVibs>
    </bulletin>
                    </esxupdate-response>
```

Now, let's see what happens when an error occurs. In this example, we used a HostPatchManagerPatchManagerOperationSpec object but we placed a bad value in the cmdOption property. Here's the code we used:

```
[vSphere PowerCLI] C:\> $esx = Get-VMHost esx41.test.local
[vSphere PowerCLI] C:\> $pmMoRef = `
>> $esx.ExtensionData.ConfigManager.PatchManager
[vSphere PowerCLI] C:\> $pm = Get-View $pmMoRef
[vSphere PowerCLI] C:\> $spec = `
>> New-Object VMware.Vim.HostPatchManagerPatchManag
erOperationSpec
[vSphere PowerCLI] C:\> $spec.CmdOption = "wrong_parameter"
[vSphere PowerCLI] C:\> $taskMoRef = `
>> $pm.QueryHostPatch_Task($spec)
```

You can see that we provoked a method failure by passing an incorrect parameter to the esxupdate command.

```
[vSphere PowerCLI] C:\> $task = Get-View $taskMoRef
[vSphere PowerCLI] C:\> $task.Info.State
Error
```

As expected, the method returned an error. Let's see what other information we can get using $task.Info.Error.Fault.GetType():

```
[vSphere PowerCLI] C:\> $task.Info.Error.Fault.GetType()


IsPublic IsSerial Name                        BaseType
-------- -------- ----                        --------
True     False    PlatformConfigFault         VMware.Vim.HostCo...
```

The information returned tells us that fault is a PlatformConfigFault type, which is a kind of catchall fault. You can investigate further through the LocalizedMessage and the Fault properties. Here's how we did that:

```
[vSphere PowerCLI] C:\> $task.Info.Error.LocalizedMessage
An error occurred during host configuration.
[vSphere PowerCLI] C:\> $task.Info.Error.Fault
```

```
Text              : /usr/sbin/esxupdate returned no results, ex…
DynamicType       :
DynamicProperty   :
FaultCause        :
FaultMessage      :
```

As you can see, the faults that are returned are often cryptic. But when you investigate the return code and display some of the `Error` properties, it will become a lot clearer to the script users (yourself included) that something went wrong.

> **TIP**   Whenever you write a script, take a few moments to consider what could cause that script to throw an error. Spend a few minutes writing descriptive, decipherable error messages for each of those faults. You'll thank yourself when one of those faults occurs and you are in a position to rapidly troubleshoot and repair the problem.

Put Some Tips and Tricks to Good Use

The more you work with the vSphere API, the more you'll find the same script elements appearing again and again. It is useful to keep these code snippets for easy reuse in your scripts. This section illustrates some of these general code snippets.

Waiting for an Asynchronous Task

In your scripts you can construct a simple loop to wait for the completion of asynchronous tasks. The following script shows one way of doing this:

```
$taskMoRef = <any_call_to_an_asynchronous_method>
$task = Get-View $taskMoRef
while("running","queued" -contains $task.Info.State){
  $task.UpdateViewData("Info")
}
```

The script loops until the status of the task is no longer `queued` (waiting to run) or `running`. Since the script looks at a copy of the `Task` object, we had to refresh the `Task` object contents periodically. We used the `UpdateViewData` method and specified that only the `Info` property needed to be refreshed.

Better Error Handling after Asynchronous Tasks

The ability of your scripts to intercept errors and produce meaningful error messages will improve their user friendliness. The following code snippet, which you can insert immediately after a wait loop, will check whether a call to an asynchronous method completed successfully. If the call to the method failed, the script displays an error message and then exits.

```
if($task.Info.State -eq "error"){
  $task.UpdateViewData("Info.Error")
  $task.Info.Error.Fault.faultMessage | % {
    $_.Message
  }
  exit
}
```

Finding Service Managers with *Get-View* Shortcuts

As we mentioned earlier, the `Get-View` cmdlet has shortcuts for several of the service managers that you would normally access via the `ServiceInstance` object. But how can you find out which shortcuts are recognized by `Get-View`? The following short function returns a list of the shortcuts you can use with `Get-View`:

```
function Get-GVShortcuts{
  Write-Host "Shortcuts supported by Get-View" `
    -ForegroundColor yellow
  $si = Get-View ServiceInstance
  $si.content | gm -MemberType Property | % {
    if($_.Name -match "Manager"){
      $t = Get-View $_.Name -ErrorAction SilentlyContinue
      if($t -ne $null){
        Write-Host $_.Name
      }
    }
  }
}
```

The Onyx Project

IN THIS CHAPTER, YOU WILL LEARN TO:

Despite what you learned in Chapter 19, "The SDK," working with the vSphere APIs might still seem an obscure black art. To help you on your journey through the SDK, the PowerCLI Development Team created the Onyx Project. This tool shows you how the VMware developers programmed the tasks you use in the vSphere Client. And once you're familiar with Onyx, we'll show you how we used Onyx while developing this book and identified a potentially serious bug in the vSphere Client.

Work with the Onyx Project

Onyx is an application that sits between a vSphere, vCenter, or ESX(i) server, and a vSphere Client or PowerCLI session. Onyx acts as a proxy and intercepts the network traffic between the client and the server. This network traffic uses the Simple Object Access Protocol (SOAP), as we discussed in Chapter 19. To start Onyx, double-click the Onyx.exe file, located in the folder where you extracted the Onyx archive.

Onyx not only intercepts the traffic, but also converts it into script code or displays it as SOAP messages.

The latest Onyx build can produce four types of output:

PowerCLI.NET code

C#.NET 2.0 code

vCO JavaScript code

Raw SOAP messages

Let Onyx Help You

Now, when would you use Onyx?

There are several cases where the help that Onyx offers comes in handy:

- ► You wonder how some of the options in the vSphere Client are configured.
- ► You can't find a cmdlet for what you want to do.
- ► You need to find which SDK method to use.
- ► You are using a SDK method but you can't seem to get the parameters coded correctly.

▶ Your script needs to run in a large vSphere environment and you want to find out if you could optimize the code the PowerCLI cmdlet uses.

▶ You suspect there is a bug in the vSphere environment and you want to investigate.

And there are probably many more circumstances where the Onyx application can come in handy.

Use Onyx

The Onyx application is simplicity itself. You can do any of the following:

1. Connect to a vCenter or an ESX(i) Server.

2. Translate the captured SOAP traffic.

3. Configure the interface, logging, and output.

4. Use the output to find the information you need.

Let's take a closer look at each step.

Connecting to a vCenter or an ESX(i) Server

When you have started the application, you can use the Connect button in the toolbar to connect to a vCenter or an ESX(i) server. (For your convenience, the application also provides a Connection history that remembers the last 10 connections you made.)

When you select the Connect option (the yellow asterisk), you will need to specify the URL of the server you want to connect to, as shown in Figure 20.1.

The other option is the History list box (see Figure 20.2), located to the right of the yellow asterisk. Clicking the drop-down arrow opens the History list box, where you can select one of the 10 connections you made previously.

When you have chosen the Connect option, a new form appears and you can choose to let Onyx start a client for you, as shown in Figure 20.3.

The client can be a vSphere Client or a PowerCLI prompt. In either case, you must provide an account and a password before Onyx can make the connection (Figure 20.4). The application sets itself up as a proxy for the server you specify. When you select the Launch A Client After Connected check box, Onyx automatically starts a client and makes a connection.

Scripting Tools and Features

PART V

FIGURE 20.1 Onyx application

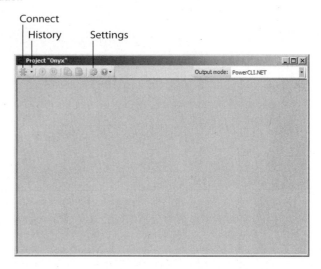

FIGURE 20.2 Onyx History list box

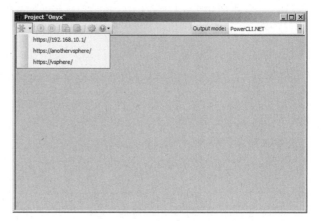

FIGURE 20.3 The Onyx Start A New Connection screen

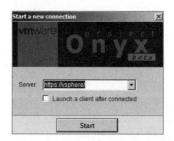

FIGURE 20.4   Client options

If you didn't start a client automatically, you can start the client yourself and make the connection to the Onyx application. To help you set up such a manual connection, the application displays in the title bar the address you can use to connect to the proxy, as shown in Figure 20.5.

FIGURE 20.5   Onyx manual client start

If you want to connect from a PowerCLI prompt, you use the connect cmdlet as follows:

```
Connect-VIServer -Server <IP-address> -Port <portnumber>
-Protocol http
```

The `IP-address` and the `portnumber` are displayed in the title of the Onyx application (as you saw in Figure 20.5). If we take the example from Figure 20.5, this line becomes

```
Connect-VIServer -Server 192.168.111.1 -Port 1545 -Protocol http
```

TIP Note that you have to explicitly specify HTTP on the `-Protocol` parameter with the `Connect-VIServer` cmdlet; the default for this parameter is `https`. Otherwise, you will not be able to make the connection. Onyx needs SOAP to travel over HTTP; without it, the application would not be able to capture and interpret the packets. That is also the reason why the vSphere Client displays the warning "The server you are connecting to is not encrypting its network traffic."

Scripting Tools and Features

PART V

When you want to connect manually with a vSphere Client, you just need to enter the URL from the proxy in the IP Address/Name field. See Figure 20.6.

FIGURE 20.6 Onyx vSphere Client connection

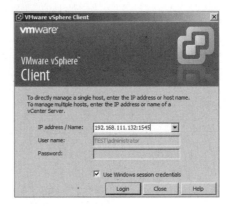

Translating Captured SOAP Traffic

The moment the Onyx application has made the connection to the vSphere server, you can start translating the captured SOAP traffic into code. Click the Start button shown in Figure 20.7.

FIGURE 20.7 Start translating!

Note that you can start capturing the traffic before you make the client connection. To stop the translation process, click the Pause button.

Use the Output mode drop-down list box on the toolbar to select the type of code the application will generate. The capturing process needs to be paused before you change the type of the generated code. On the next startup, the Onyx application will generate code of the newly selected type.

Configuring Onyx

The latest Onyx build comes with a plethora of settings. You access the settings via the Settings button in the toolbar.

Let's do a quick rundown of the available options.

General

The General settings panel, shown in Figure 20.8, has several settings that you normally won't change but that could be interesting in some exceptional cases.

FIGURE 20.8 General settings

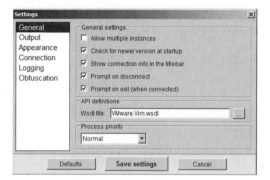

The Check For Newer Version At Startup option is a setting that you will probably have to change, depending where you run the Onyx application. No Internet access or running Onyx on a client behind a proxy are good reasons to deselect this option.

Watch out when changing the process priority. Make sure you don't lock out other applications that you will need.

Output

The Output panel, shown in Figure 20.9, allows you to suppress specific methods from the generated code. This is very useful since some methods are used intensively by the vSphere Client when there is, for example, a screen refresh. And these methods don't contribute to most of the actions you are trying to capture.

FIGURE 20.9 Output settings

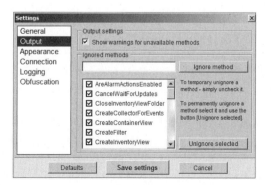

The Show Warnings For Unavailable Methods option informs you when Onyx encounters a nonpublic (or private) API call.

Appearance

If you don't like the font in which the generated code is displayed, the Appearance panel is where you can change that. Simply click the Change button shown in Figure 20.10.

FIGURE 20.10   Appearance settings

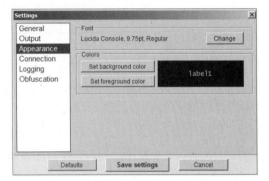

You can also change the background and foreground colors using options on this screen.

Connection

You can change the port numbers used by the Onyx application. Figure 20.11 shows the available settings.

FIGURE 20.11   Connection settings

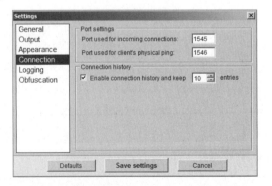

And you can change the number of entries that will be kept in the Connect History.

Logging

By default, the Onyx application does not produce any logging (Figure 20.12). You can use the options in the Logging panel to activate logging and specify the location of the log file. The log level allows you to set the amount of detail that will be logged.

FIGURE 20.12 Logging settings

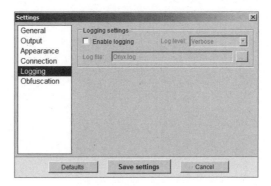

Note that any changes to the Logging settings will require a stop/start of Onyx to become active.

Obfuscation

You can use the Obfuscation panel to ask Onyx to not include sensitive information like accounts and passwords in the generated code and in the log files, as shown in Figure 20.13.

FIGURE 20.13 Obfuscation settings

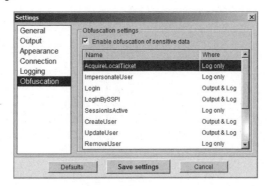

This is a handy feature when you need to send the code or log files to another location for further analysis.

Scripting Tools
and Features

PART V

Using Onyx Output

In this section we are going to change the vCenter Logging level to Verbose, as shown in Figure 20.14, and then take a look at the various types of output code you can get from Onyx.

FIGURE 20.14 vCenter Logging

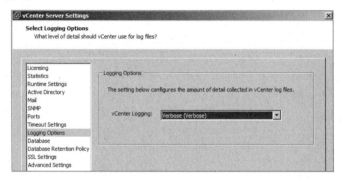

PowerCLI.NET Output

With PowerCLI.NET output selected, the Onyx translator produces this code when you change the vCenter Logging level to Verbose.

```
# ------- UpdateOptions -------

$changedValue = New-Object VMware.Vim.OptionValue[] (1)
$changedValue[0] = New-Object VMware.Vim.OptionValue
$changedValue[0].key = "log.level"
$changedValue[0].value = "verbose"


$_this = Get-View -Id 'OptionManager-VpxSettings'
$_this.UpdateOptions($changedValue)
```

The generated code by the translator is quite straightforward. Onyx always uses the $_this object to represent the managed object, in this case the OptionManager service. As you can probably appreciate, this method of finding out how to change a vCenter Server setting is a bit easier than working your way through the vSphere API Reference.

For completeness, this is the same action for the three other types of code.

C#.NET 2.0 Output

When you select C#.NET 2.0 output mode, Onyx produces the following code:

```
// ------- UpdateOptions -------

VMware.Vim.OptionValue[] changedValue = new VMware.Vim.
OptionValue[1];
changedValue[0] = new VMware.Vim.OptionValue();
changedValue[0].Key = "log.level";
changedValue[0].Value = "verbose";

VMware.Vim.OptionManager _this = new VMware.Vim.OptionManager(_
client, new VMware.Vim.ManagedObjectReference("OptionManager-
VpxSettings"));
_this.UpdateOptions(changedValue);
```

vCO JavaScript Output

For vCO JavaScript output mode, you get the following code:

```
// ------- UpdateOptions -------

var changedValue = System.getModule("com.vmware.onyx").
array(VcOptionValue, 1);
changedValue[0] = new VcOptionValue();
changedValue[0].key = "log.level";
changedValue[0].value = "verbose";

managedObject.updateOptions(changedValue);  // OptionManager
```

Raw SOAP Messages

The Raw SOAP Messages output mode does not produce usable code, but it is very useful for debugging purposes. Take a look:

```
<soap:Envelope xmlns:xsd="http://www.w3.org/2001/XMLSchema"
xmlns:xsi="http://www.w3.org/2001/XMLSchema-instance"
xmlns:soap="http://schemas.xmlsoap.org/soap/envelope/">
  <soap:Header>
    <operationID>A789E270-000000E8</operationID>
```

```
    </soap:Header>
    <soap:Body>
      <UpdateOptions xmlns="urn:internalvim25">
        <_this xsi:type="ManagedObjectReference"
type="OptionManager" serverGuid="99F1DDC6-02B3-4E03-AF1B-
021B2F18075C">VpxSettings</_this>
          <changedValue>
            <key>log.level</key>
            <value xsi:type="string">verbose</value>
          </changedValue>
      </UpdateOptions>
    </soap:Body>
  </soap:Envelope>
```

Note that Onyx only shows you the packet that is sent to the vCenter Server and not the response. If you need to see the response SOAP packet, you must enable logging. With logging enabled, you will find the response packets in the log:

```
<?xml version="1.0" encoding="UTF-8"?>
<soapenv:Envelope xmlns:soapenc="http://schemas.xmlsoap.org/
soap/encoding/"
 xmlns:soapenv="http://schemas.xmlsoap.org/soap/envelope/"
 xmlns:xsd="http://www.w3.org/2001/XMLSchema"
 xmlns:xsi="http://www.w3.org/2001/XMLSchema-instance">
<soapenv:Body>
<UpdateOptionsResponse xmlns="urn:internalvim25"></
UpdateOptionsResponse>
</soapenv:Body>
</soapenv:Envelope>
```

Work with References

Before you can use the code generated by the Onyx application, you'll need to adapt it. Here are a few things to watch out for:

- ▶ Onyx produces hard-coded references for entities.

- ▶ Onyx uses hard-coded MoRefs.

In this section we provide some suggestions for adapting the code.

Hard-Coded References to Entities

Be sure to change hard-coded references to a dynamic method for getting the entity. The following is the way Onyx referenced a cluster:

```
$_this = Get-View -Id 'ClusterComputeResource-domain-c4525'
```

Change the reference to something like this:

```
$_this = (Get-Cluster -Name <clustername>).Extensiondata
```

Hard-Coded MoRefs

When the generated code uses a service manager, the Onyx application gets the managed object by specifying the MoRef directly:

```
$_this = Get-View -Id 'CustomFieldsManager-CustomFieldsManager'
```

This is a valid way of referring to a service manager and you can run the generated script against any vSphere server, but we prefer to show the complete path:

```
$si = Get-View ServiceInstance
$_this = Get-View $si.Content.customFieldsManager
```

Use Onyx in the Real World

As you probably know, you can change the Tasks and Events Retention policy from within the vSphere Client. But as we showed you in Chapter 17, "Auditing the vSphere Environment," you can accomplish the same with a script. As a refresher, the script in Listing 20.1 is the script that we used to call the Set-VpxOption function.

LISTING 20.1 Changing the Events Retention policy

```
function Set-EventRetention{
  param(
  [Boolean]$Enabled,
  [int]$Duration = 180)

  Set-VpxOption -Key "event.maxAgeEnabled","event.maxAge" `
    -Value $enabled,$duration
}


Set-EventRetention $true 120
```

When we tested this script on vSphere Client 4.1.0, we were amazed when we saw the screen shown in Figure 20.15.

FIGURE 20.15 Mixed up Tasks and Events Retention policy

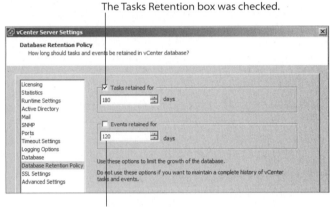

The Events Retention duration was changed correctly, but the script had checked the Tasks Retention box.

Was there a bug in our function?

Onyx to the rescue! When we changed the Tasks Retention policy from the vSphere Client, the code shown in Figure 20.16 was produced by Onyx.

FIGURE 20.16 Onyx output

That looks, indeed, as if the code behind this option in the vSphere Client was mixed up. It confused the Tasks field with the Events field. With the help of Onyx, it was easy to show that there was nothing wrong with our function but that the vSphere Client code had a problem!

PowerGUI and vEcoShell

IN THIS CHAPTER, YOU WILL LEARN TO:

I n every chapter so far, we have used the standard PowerShell console to execute all the sample scripts, which have been stored in text files with `.ps1` extensions. Now, we will examine two GUI automation tools that instead enable scripts to be presented in graphical form for execution.

Understand GUI Environments in Managing Automation

PowerGUI is a graphical user interface and script editor for Microsoft Windows PowerShell. PowerGUI originated in Quest Software in March 2007—initially as a free, community-based tool—right on the heels of the initial release of PowerShell 1.0 in November 2006. Since the original release, many regular updates to the freeware product have shipped and in 2010 a full commercial version, PowerGUI Pro, with additional enterprise style functionality was also made available.

PowerGUI is essentially two tools in one:

► A graphical front-end that bundles a collection of scripts and presents them in GUI form

► A fully featured integrated development environment (IDE) for PowerShell scripts

vEcoShell is freeware tool from Vizioncore. It leverages the technology provided by PowerGUI and ships with functionality specifically included for the virtualization administrator. Like PowerGUI, it features a graphical front-end for scripts as well as an IDE.

These tools can be a good starting point for administrators new to scripting, since it allows them to see the benefits of automation without initially needing to learn a scripting language. Once they become more comfortable and accomplished with automation, the tools are open enough that it is possible to both discover and learn more advanced techniques from within them.

Both PowerGUI and vEcoShell are Microsoft Windows–based tools; both have the common basic requirement of Windows PowerShell. While both will function with PowerShell 1.0, it makes sense to take advantage of the latest features with PowerShell 2.0. PowerShell 2.0 is available by default on Windows 7 and Windows Server 2008 R2; for previous Windows versions, it is available as part of the Windows Management Framework bundle as a separate download from the Microsoft website at `http://support.microsoft.com/kb/968930`.

Since vEcoShell is focused on virtualization, it has an additional system requirement: PowerCLI must be installed. A variety of output formats for vEcoShell are available, including CSV, HTML, and Visio diagrams; if you wish to generate Visio diagrams, Microsoft Visio must be installed on the same machine as vEcoShell.

Use PowerPacks to Manage Automation Scripts

PowerPacks are the focal point of the GUI tool within PowerGUI or vEcoShell. By embedding PowerShell scripts into nodes or actions within a PowerPack, you can create customized management tools based on one or more technologies. Both PowerGUI and vEcoShell ship with default PowerPacks. With these, the functionality you are most likely to need is immediately available. You can import third-party PowerPacks to extend the functionality or create your own PowerPack to meet your specific requirements.

PowerGUI's focus is on the Microsoft Windows system administrator and ships with the following PowerPacks available by default:

- Local System
- Network
- Active Directory
- Exchange 2007

TIP The Active Directory PowerPack requires the Quest Software ActiveRoles Management Shell for Active Directory third-party PowerShell snap-in, and the Exchange 2007 PowerPack requires the Exchange 2007 management tools.

Figure 21.1 shows some of the nodes available in the default PowerGUI PowerPacks.

As previously mentioned, vEcoShell's focus is on the virtualization administrator and ships with the following built-in PowerPacks:

- VMware
- Hyper-V
- Advanced Reporting PowerPack

Scripting Tools and Features

PART V

FIGURE 21.1   Nodes in default PowerGUI PowerPacks

Nodes can be accessed from the Navigation Tree

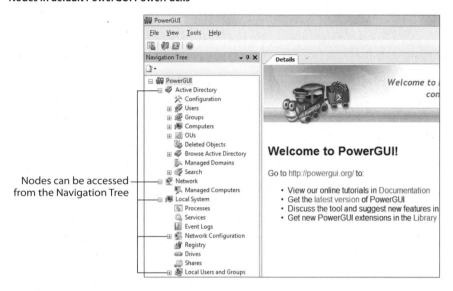

Figure 21.2 shows some of the nodes available in the default vEcoShell PowerPacks.

FIGURE 21.2   Nodes in default vEcoShell PowerPacks

Access built-in PowerPacks from the Navigation Tree

Now that you are aware of what the two tools can do and how they differ, let's examine how either can be used. We will refer to vEcoShell from now on, but remember that you can do exactly the same things with PowerGUI.

POWERGUI VS. VECOSHELL

It is important to mention at this point that, although both of these tools ship with default PowerPacks, it is possible to import any PowerPack into either tool. Free PowerPacks are available for download from the PowerGUI website: `http://powergui` `.org/downloads.jspa`. So, for instance, it would be possible to import the VMware PowerPack into PowerGUI and, conversely, the Active Directory PowerPack into vEcoShell. Fundamentally, they are the same tool—marketed to slightly different audiences—but inevitably with a fair amount of crossover. Since this book is about virtualization, in this chapter we will focus on vEcoShell.

Making a Connection to vCenter Server

Because vEcoShell ships with the VMware PowerPack installed by default, your first task is to make a connection to vCenter Server:

1. From within the VMware PowerPack, locate and highlight the Managed Hosts node.

2. From the right-hand Actions pane, select the Action named Add Managed Host, as shown in Figure 21.3.

FIGURE 21.3   Select Add Managed Host.

3. Enter the login credentials for the vCenter Server or stand-alone host in the same way you would if the standard vSphere Client were being used (Figure 21.4).

The connection details are stored under the Managed Hosts node (Figure 21.5).

FIGURE 21.4   Enter vCenter Server credentials

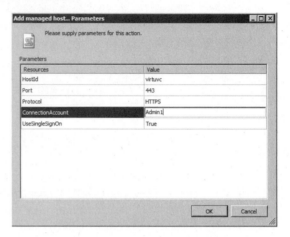

FIGURE 21.5   Managed Hosts connection details

4. Now, from the Actions pane, choose Connect to execute a connection from vEcoShell to that vCenter Server, and after you enter the password at the prompt, the connection will be established.

5. Navigating to the vCenter Server subnode displays a range of nodes that can be explored. Choosing one of these nodes executes the PowerShell code that belongs to that node and displays results in the middle pane. For instance, choosing the Clusters node returns objects for the clusters within the vCenter Server (Figure 21.6).

FIGURE 21.6   Displaying Cluster objects

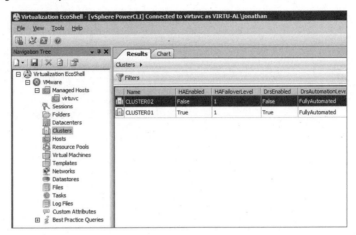

The middle pane, known as the Results pane, is a key area when using vEcoShell. Every time you execute an action to retrieve some information or carry out a system change, the results of that action are displayed there. Let's use the previous example of displaying Cluster objects to demonstrate how you can customize the information displayed in the Results pane.

By default, the Cluster node returns five columns of properties: Name, HAEnabled, HAFailoverLevel, DRSEnabled, and DRSAutomationLevel. You can customize those property columns and do the following:

▶ Sort the objects by a particular column by clicking on the name of the column.

▶ Change the order of the columns by clicking on the name of a column and dragging to an alternate location.

▶ Add property columns to the display or remove existing ones.

▶ Filter the list of objects based on specific criteria.

Figure 21.7 displays the Cluster objects, sorted by the Name column. Notice that you can change the order of columns and are shown other options for adding columns by right-clicking on a column header, such as DRSAutomationLevel.

Nodes within vEcoShell typically return objects in the Results pane. Once the information has been obtained, then most likely you will want to do something with it. This is where the other significant components of vEcoShell—links and actions—come into play. Links are commonly used for retrieving further objects. vEcoShell selects the objects you can choose based on the objects that have already been returned to the Results pane. Actions, on the other hand, perform tasks based on the objects shown in the Results pane.

Scripting Tools and Features

PART V

FIGURE 21.7 Custom Cluster objects

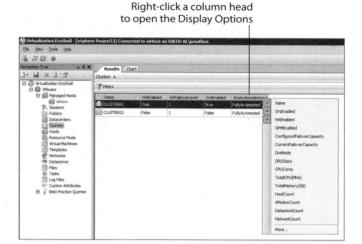

Let's continue with the Cluster example to see how links and actions function.

Working with Links and Actions

You can find the list of objects that can be retrieved through links in the right-hand pane of the vEcoShell console. Figure 21.8 shows the links you can choose from for a cluster.

FIGURE 21.8 Possible Cluster links

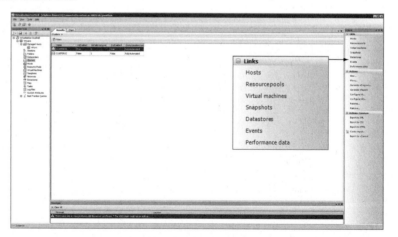

When you highlight single or multiple objects within the Results pane and choose one of the links from the right-hand pane, new objects will be returned to the Results pane. For instance, Figure 21.9 shows results returned after we highlighted Cluster01 in the Results pane and selected the Hosts link. Again, it is possible to sort the results, change the order of the columns, and add or remove columns. Take note of the boxed area; it is a path that allows the user to navigate back to the results previously displayed. Click Clusters.

FIGURE 21.9   Host objects returned from a Cluster link

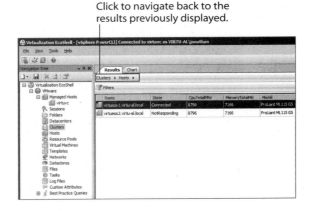

Click to navigate back to the results previously displayed.

Now that the Hosts linked to Cluster01 have been retrieved, new links and actions relevant to those new objects will be available from the right-hand pane (Figure 21.10).

Once the Results pane is populated with all the objects you need, you can begin to look at modifying those objects using actions. The Actions column in the right-hand pane is split between actions specific to the objects in the Results pane and Actions: Common, which are available for any objects in the Results pane. Figure 21.11 shows both specific and common actions available to Cluster objects in the Results pane.

By highlighting single or multiple objects within the Results pane and choosing an action, you execute that action against each object. For instance, let's highlight Cluster 1 in the Results pane, choose the Configure DRS action, and disable DRS for Cluster 1. You'll see a prompt that asks whether you wish to change the DRSEnabled property, the DRSMode property, or both DRS properties. Then, you must supply parameters for the properties you wish to change. Set DRSEnabled to $False, as shown in Figure 21.12.

FIGURE 21.10 New links and actions

FIGURE 21.11 Cluster-specific and common actions

FIGURE 21.12   Setting DRSEnabled to $False

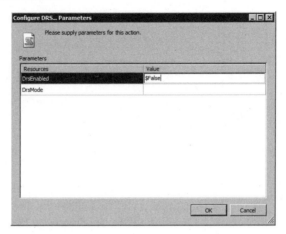

Since this is an action that changes values, you are prompted to confirm the change. Click Yes (Figure 21.13) and click OK to confirm that you want DRS disabled for Cluster 1.

FIGURE 21.13   Confirming that you want DRS disabled

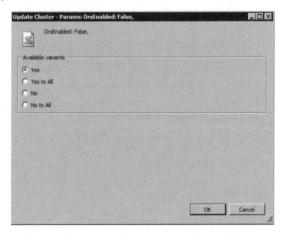

After the action to disable DRS has submitted to the vCenter Server, the Results pane will be updated with the new status of Cluster 1 (Figure 21.14).

By now you may be curious as to how the various nodes, links, and actions are generated. It is possible to examine the PowerShell code for any of these types of items and see for yourself how it works. The code will be exposed in one of two formats: either a single PowerShell cmdlet with specific options (Figure 21.15) or some custom PowerShell code (Figure 21.16). Right-click any node, link, or action and select Properties to view how it was created.

Scripting Tools and Features

PART V

FIGURE 21.14 New status of Cluster 1

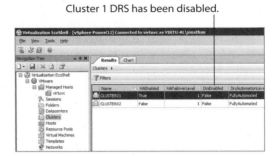

Cluster 1 DRS has been disabled.

For example, by looking at the properties of the Configure DRS action you can see that this action is accomplished simply by using the Set-Cluster cmdlet with a prompt set for both the DRSEnabled or DRSMode parameters and that neither has a default value specified.

Now examine the properties of the Datastores link. Notice that this link uses some of the custom PowerShell code we discussed earlier to retrieve the objects you want to examine in the Results pane.

Using the VMware PowerPack for Reporting

One of the VMware PowerPack's major features is its reporting capabilities. You can easily generate useful reports in common formats such as HTML, CSV, and Visio diagrams for further distribution. The actions used to generate reports are split into the common actions, which create XML, CSV, or HTML output files, and more advanced actions, which create more sophisticated reports known as vReports (HTML) and vDiagrams (Visio).

Say, for example, that you are required to generate a report for all virtual machines that would display the Name, Current PowerState, Number of CPUs, Amount of Memory, and Operating System for each machine in a CSV format. You can generate this report by selecting the Virtual Machines node, highlighting all the VMs returned in the Results pane, and executing the Export To CSV common action. The resulting CSV file contains all properties for each machine. Remove the properties you don't need for your report and the resulting CSV file should resemble the one shown in Figure 21.17.

vReports generate far more sophisticated reports and are available for almost every node in the PowerPack, such as Datacenters, Clusters, Hosts, and Virtual Machines.

The vReports generate different information based on the type of object(s) that are selected. So a vReport for a VM might include information such as Operating System, IP Address, VMware Tools Status, and Disk Size, but for a Host report, it will include items such as Manufacturer, Model, Datastores, and Port Groups.

Within each type of report a wealth of information is presented in a colorful HTML format for each object that has been selected. A section of a typical VM report is shown in Figure 21.18.

FIGURE 21.15 Properties of the Configure DRS action

1. Right-click a node, action, or link.
2. Select Properties to view specific options.

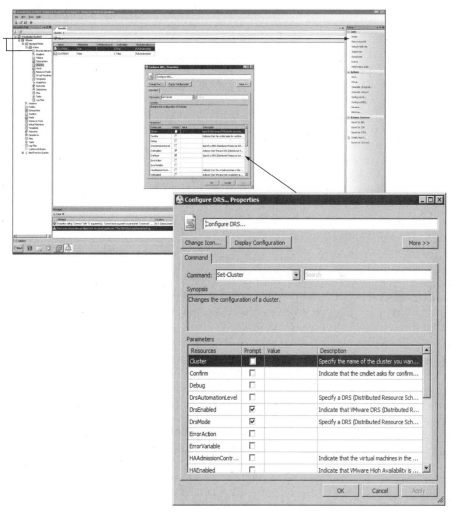

FIGURE 21.16 Properties of the Datastores link

FIGURE 21.17 Example VM CSV report

	A	B	C	D	E
1	Name	PowerState	CPUCount	Memory(MB)	OperatingSystem
2	APP01	PoweredOn	1	3072	Other 2.6x Linux (64-bit)
3	DOMAIN01	PoweredOn	1	2048	Microsoft Windows Server 2008 (64-bit)
4	FILESRV01	PoweredOn	1	512	Microsoft Windows Server 2008 (64-bit)
5	PRINT01	PoweredOff	1	4096	Microsoft Windows Server 2008 (64-bit)
6	TESTVM01	PoweredOn	1	1024	Microsoft Windows Server 2008 (64-bit)
7	VC01	PoweredOn	1	2048	Microsoft Windows Server 2008 (64-bit)
8	VDIMaster	PoweredOff	1	1024	Microsoft Windows 7 (32-bit)

FIGURE 21.18 Example VM vReport

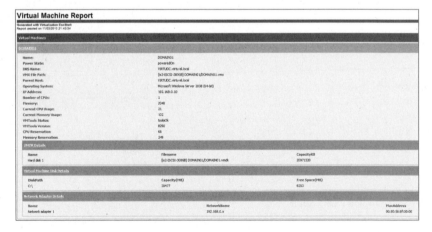

vDiagrams generate Visio diagrams based on the objects selected and are great for quickly and easily producing documentation for a VMware environment. To generate a vDiagram from the VMware PowerPack, it is essential that Microsoft Visio (2003 or later) be installed on the same machine as vEcoShell. To create a vDiagram, select the desired objects and click the Generate vDiagram action. Figure 21.19 shows the parameters available for the Visio diagram.

FIGURE 21.19 Parameters available for the Generate vDiagram action

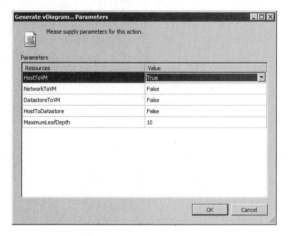

Once you choose the parameters you require, the PowerShell code opens Microsoft Visio and begins to draw the diagram right in front of your eyes! A sample output taken from a vDiagram generated from a Cluster view is shown in Figure 21.20.

FIGURE 21.20 Sample vDiagram

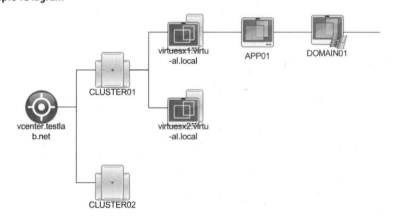

Using the VMware PowerPack for Administration Tasks

The VMware PowerPack is great for producing reports for your VMware environment. However, it is not simply a static reporting tool and can be used for carrying out administration tasks. It is particularly useful for filling a gap for bulk administration tasks that cannot be achieved easily in the standard vSphere Client. Let's look at a very simple but practical example.

Imagine a scenario where you are required to upgrade the number of vCPUs from 1 to 2 in the virtual machines PRINTSERVER01 through 03. (In this example, we will power off the virtual machines to make this change.) Within the vSphere Client when you select multiple virtual machines, the Edit Settings option is grayed out.

Using vEcoShell, however, it is possible to make these bulk changes with ease. Highlight the virtual machines (PRINTSERVER01, PRINTSERVER02, and PRINTSERVER03) and from the Actions pane, choose the Modify action. The dialog box in Figure 21.21 opens, listing the parameters of the virtual machine that can be altered. Enter **2** to upgrade the number of vCPUs from 1 to 2 and the change will be made on each VM. Refreshing the VMs within vEcoShell confirms they have been upgraded to dual vCPU machines (Figure 21.22).

Let's look at another example where the vSphere GUI client doesn't lend itself to automation—networking standard switches. It is highly likely that you will end up with virtual switches that contain multiple port groups. An administration change that involves modifying these port groups—say, setting a VLAN ID on each one—would require a significant amount of repetitive and tedious mouse clicking activity through wizard-based processes. It is almost inevitable that mistakes and inconsistent configurations will result.

You can automate such an activity from the VMware PowerPack. Let's take the example of a standard virtual switch with multiple port groups, currently with no VLAN IDs set, and give them all a VLAN ID of 210. The switch currently is configured with five port groups, as shown in Figure 21.23.

Changing the VLAN ID of each of these port groups with the vSphere Client requires navigating to the properties for each one and manually setting the VLAN ID to 210. However, with the VMware PowerPack you just have to do the following:

1. Select all the port groups in the Results pane.

2. Right-click to open the context menu.

3. Select Actions ➢ Modify VLANID (Figure 21.24).

4. When prompted, specify 210 as the VLAN ID.

FIGURE 21.21   Modify dialog box

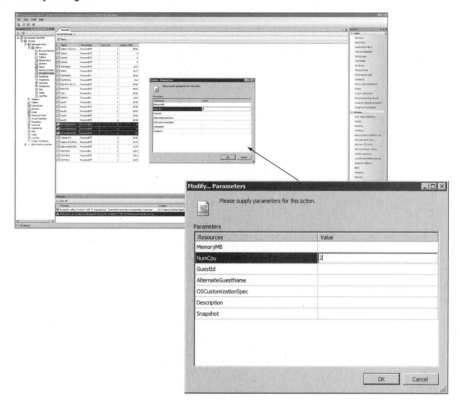

FIGURE 21.22   Print servers with multiple vCPUs

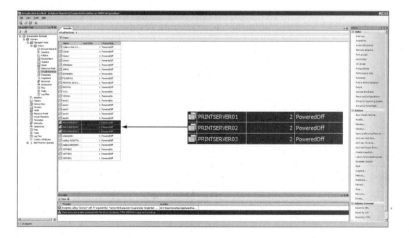

FIGURE 21.23 Standard vSwitch with five port groups

FIGURE 21.24 Modifying the VLAN ID of multiple port groups

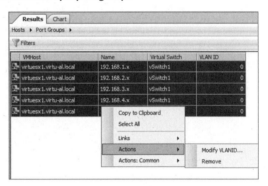

The result is a quick and simple way to set the VLAN ID for multiple port groups. The reconfigured port groups are displayed in Figure 21.25.

These two examples are merely a taste of the administration tasks it is possible to complete with the VMware PowerPack—right out of the box! While using small numbers of multiples, it is not difficult to extend this further and think in terms of tens or hundreds of actions that can be automated, thus saving time, money, and effort. Take the time to explore the other functionality available within the PowerPack and consider how you might extend the PowerPack with your own nodes, links, and actions to automate tasks in your organization.

FIGURE 21.25 Port groups with modified VLAN ID

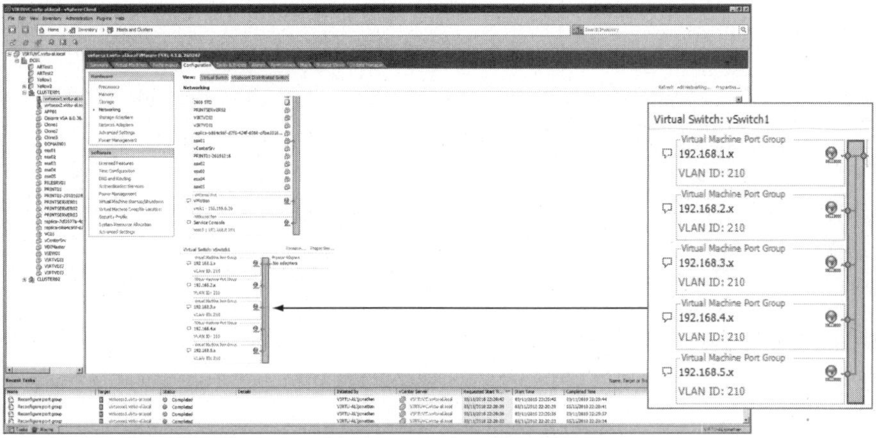

Importing the VMware Community PowerPack

On the PowerGUI.org website, there are nearly 75 third-party PowerPacks. Most were created by community members. They cover a variety of products and technologies. Any of these PowerPacks can be downloaded and imported into either PowerGUI or vEcoShell. The VMware Community PowerPack (formerly known as the Virtu-Al.net PowerPack) started life as a collection of scripts created by Alan Renouf to complement the more formalized and maintained VMware PowerPack.

During 2009, Quest Software ran a PowerPack Challenge competition to find the best PowerPacks created by members of the community during that year. Alan took this opportunity to enhance the Virtu-Al.net PowerPack with many additions in order to enter it into the competition. The sheer scale of scripts within this PowerPack, along with its usefulness and popularity, made it a great choice as the winner of the Best PowerPack in the contest. Since that date, many community members have contributed additional scripts and functionality to the PowerPack. Consequently, Alan made the decision to rename it the VMware Community PowerPack.

To get started with the VMware Community PowerPack, first download from here:

```
http://powergui.org/entry.jspa?externalID=2551&categoryID=290
```

Once the PowerPack is available on a system with vEcoShell, you should navigate to PowerPack Management. PowerPack Management is the place to go to import new PowerPacks, check for updated versions of existing PowerPacks, or remove a

Scripting Tools and Features

PART V

PowerPack when it is no longer required. In this instance, having just downloaded the VMware Community PowerPack, you must import it into vEcoShell and make it available for use.

Click the Import button, browse to the location where the VMware Community PowerPack was downloaded to, and import it. After you complete this task successfully, it will appear along with its current version number in the list of available PowerPacks (Figure 21.26). Once in the list, it can be updated at a later date.

FIGURE 21.26 Importing the VMware Community PowerPack

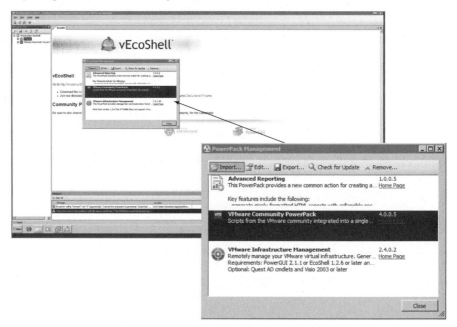

The VMware Community PowerPack requires that a connection to a host or vCenter Server be established using the standard VMware PowerPack. The nodes within the PowerPack subsequently make use of the global variable $global:defaultvi servers to execute PowerShell code against the host or vCenter Server that has been connected to via the VMware PowerPack.

T I P The PowerPack is built with more than 75 nodes of reporting and best practice information put together by many people with significant experience in the field of VMware deployments. This wealth of knowledge is now at your fingertips, and an hour or two spent running and examining the results of each report will lead to the discovery of issues you didn't even know you had.

Let's take a look at five highlights from the PowerPack:

VMs and Templates with Inconsistent Folder Names   This is an issue of untidiness rather than a major problem, but VMs and templates stored in folders on disk with names that do not match the name of the virtual machine or template can lead to confusion. The ability to easily produce a list that identifies these VMs or templates and resolve those inconsistencies via a Storage vMotion is a good thing. Figure 21.27 shows a typical list of inconsistencies.

FIGURE 21.27   VMs and templates that have inconsistent folder names

Host Overcommit   Managers like to know how much money you are saving them. With the Host Overcommit report, it is possible to demonstrate how you are saving them money. By taking advantage of technologies, such as Transparent Page Sharing, to enable the total amount of memory allocated to VMs on a host to exceed the actual physical RAM inside the machine, you may be able to reduce the amount of physical servers you need. Figure 21.28 shows a sample Host Overcommit report.

FIGURE 21.28   Host Overcommit report

Clusters Slot Information   A VMware cluster contains multiple ESX(i) hosts. If the cluster is configured to use High Availability (HA) technology to restart VMs on another host should one host in the cluster fail, then a calculation needs to be made. vCenter Server needs to know how many VMs can be present in the cluster to allow for one (or more) hosts to fail and still have enough resources available to be able to power on all the VMs in the cluster. Enough "slots" need to exist on other ESX(i) hosts for the VMs on the failed host to restart into. The Slot Information node

Scripting Tools and Features

PART V

provides data on the number of remaining slots within the cluster and the CPU and memory figures being used to determine the most expensive VM that the HA calculation is based on. Figure 21.29 shows a typical Cluster Slot Information report.

FIGURE 21.29   Slot Information report

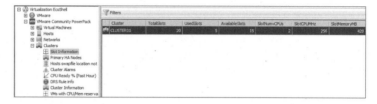

Active Snapshots   Snapshots are a fantastic piece of technology that allow the administrator to revert a VM back to a known state within seconds. Typically, a snapshot is taken before you make significant changes to a VM, such as patching the operating system or installing a new application. They can, however, quickly turn into a large headache if the files a snapshot creates are left to grow for a long period of time and not removed when no longer required. Figure 21.30 shows a report that details current snapshots active in vCenter Server and provides information that helps administrators determine which ones need to be tracked down and removed if possible.

FIGURE 21.30   Active Snapshots report

vCheck   One of the most popular individual script downloads from Alan Renouf's blog, http://www.virtu-al.net/, is the vCheck report. Now incorporated into the VMware Community PowerPack, this report generates an HTML output file containing many of the best practice and common issue nodes from the rest of the PowerPack in summary form. VMware administrators typically have this report emailed to them on a daily basis in order to stay on top of key issues within their organization. Figure 21.31 shows a sampling of the information you can get from a vCheck report.

TIP   Depending on the size of the VMware environment, the vCheck report can take a long time to run. So it is common to schedule vCheck for the early hours of the morning. It can take hours to run, not seconds like pretty much everything else in the PowerPack.

FIGURE 21.31   vCheck report

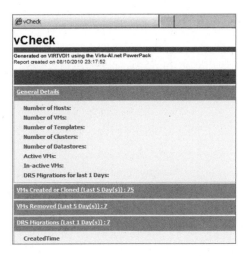

It is also possible, though, to run the vCheck report on an ad hoc basis from the PowerPack. When doing so, you are prompted with the default values for a number of the key checks within the report (Figure 21.32), and you can change them to reflect your environment.

FIGURE 21.32   vCheck report default values

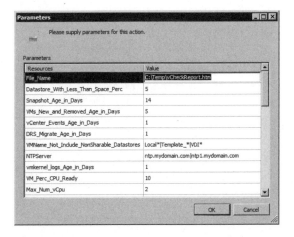

This should give you a taste of the kind of invaluable information that can be obtained via the VMware Community PowerPack. We invite you to further explorer the riches available inside this PowerPack and, if possible, to contribute your own ideas for additional functionality.

Creating a PowerPack

Creating your own PowerPack is a snap; the only limit is your imagination! It's good to organize it within a top-level folder from the start and plan the structure underneath. Use the steps that follow to create a PowerPack:

1. To begin, create a new top-level folder within vEcoShell and name it. For this example, use **vSphere Scripts**; this will be the top-level folder name and will also become the name for the PowerPack.

2. By default, the icon for a folder node looks similar to the one common within the Windows operating system. It is possible to change the icon for the folder node and all the other nodes you will create. A unique icon will give your PowerPack a more professional feel. Your new icon must be in the ICO format.

> **TIP** There is a great, free, online resource at www.convertico.com/. It takes image files in a PNG format and converts them to an ICO file.

3. Once you have an ICO file available, navigate to the properties of the top-level folder you created and use the Change Icon button to select the new icon file. Figure 21.33 shows the Change Icon button.

4. Now, right-click the top-level node and choose Create New PowerPack. When the New PowerPack dialog box opens (Figure 21.34), check the version number. By default, the version number is set to 1.0.0.0; it increments automatically as updates are made to the PowerPack. Next, enter a brief, sensible summary of the PowerPack capabilities in the Description text box.

FIGURE 21.33 Changing the default icon of a PowerPack

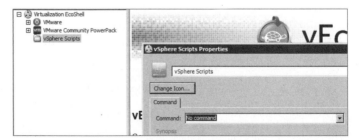

FIGURE 21.34 New PowerPack dialog box

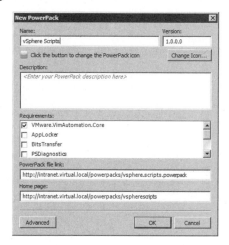

5. The Requirements list box provides a listing of all possible PowerShell snap-ins and modules. To gather the entire list, the cmdlets `Get-PSSnapin` and `Get -Module` are both called twice by vEcoShell, each time with different switches set. Those results are added to the list of PowerShell snap-ins and modules that are currently loaded. Placing a tick in any of the check boxes for the PowerPack will make that snap-in or module a requirement for using your PowerPack. In our example, the PowerCLI snap-in (`VMware.VimAutomation.Core`) is a requirement for using the PowerPack; in case you have not seen them before, `Applocker`, `BitsTransfer`, and `PSDiagnostics` are PowerShell modules available on the current Windows 7 system.

6. The PowerPack file link and Homepage fields should be filled out with the location of where the PowerPack will be stored. This is mainly intended for after the PowerPack has been uploaded to the PowerPack area on the `http://powergui.org` website. However, your PowerPack could be located on a local intranet site, as the PowerPack we created for this exercise was. These links enable users to check for updates to the PowerPack and easily visit the PowerPack home page from the PowerPack Management dialog box within vEcoShell.

7. Click OK to finish. The PowerPack has now been successfully created and can be managed from the PowerPack Management dialog box within vEcoShell.

8. Create a subfolder to store a collection of scripts that go well together—for instance, those you use to interact with virtual machines.

ENFORCING POWERPACK REQUIREMENTS

When you import a PowerPack with requirements, the import dialog box (shown here) provides a list of the required PowerShell snap-ins and modules.

Should a required snap-in or module not be present on the system, an error message appears and you must install the necessary snap-in or module and then try the installation again.

9. To create functionality within the PowerPack, create a new node or script node.

For this example, we created a script node called Get-Stat Yesterday's Average CPU Values. This simple script returns statistical data, the Average CPU values for a VM, from the day before. The user is prompted to enter the name of the VM as part of the script. This example is not intended to be particularly sophisticated, but we want to demonstrate how straightforward it is to begin creating your own PowerPack and make it reusable for others. Figure 21.35 illustrates this script node and shows the code used to generate it. Again, we created a custom icon for the node.

NOTE A node is used when only a single PowerShell cmdlet is required; a script node is used when more advanced functionality via a custom piece of PowerShell code is required.

FIGURE 21.35   Creating a script node

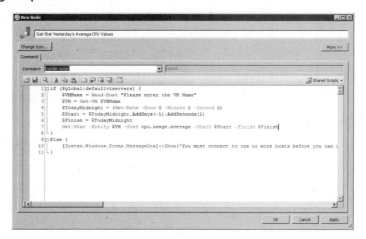

The code is listed here for reference purposes (Listing 21.1).

LISTING 21.1   The Get-Stat Yesterday's Average CPU Values script

```
if ($global:defaultviservers) {
    $VMName = Read-Host "Please enter the VM Name"
    $VM = Get-VM $VMName
    $TodayMidnight = (Get-Date -Hour 0 -Minute 0 -Second 0)
    $Start = $TodayMidnight.AddDays(-1).AddSeconds(1)
    $Finish = $TodayMidnight
    Get-Stat -Entity $VM -Stat cpu.usage.average -Start $Start
    -Finish $Finish
}
Else {
    [System.Windows.Forms.MessageBox]::Show('You must connect to
    one or more hosts before you can use this node. Please click
    on the ''Managed Hosts'' node of the VMware PowerPack,
    connect to one or more of the servers you have configured
    there, and then try again.','Connection not established',
    [System.Windows.Forms.MessageBoxButtons]::OK,
    [System.Windows.Forms.MessageBoxIcon]::Information)
    | Out-Null
}
```

Scripting Tools and Features

PART V

Executing the script node with DOMAIN01 specified as the VM gave us the results in Figure 21.36.

FIGURE 21.36 New script node results

MetricId	Timestamp	Value	Unit
cpu.usage.average	04/11/2010 00:00:00	1.07	%
cpu.usage.average	03/11/2010 22:00:00	1.07	%
cpu.usage.average	03/11/2010 20:00:00	1.06	%
cpu.usage.average	03/11/2010 18:00:00	1.05	%
cpu.usage.average	03/11/2010 16:00:00	1.05	%
cpu.usage.average	03/11/2010 14:00:00	1.09	%
cpu.usage.average	03/11/2010 12:00:00	1.06	%
cpu.usage.average	03/11/2010 10:00:00	1.04	%
cpu.usage.average	03/11/2010 08:00:00	1.05	%
cpu.usage.average	03/11/2010 06:00:00	1.04	%
cpu.usage.average	03/11/2010 04:00:00	1.06	%
cpu.usage.average	03/11/2010 02:00:00	1.1	%

There you go! Your first PowerPack is created (Figure 21.37), and you're now ready to add some more content.

FIGURE 21.37 vSphere Scripts PowerPack

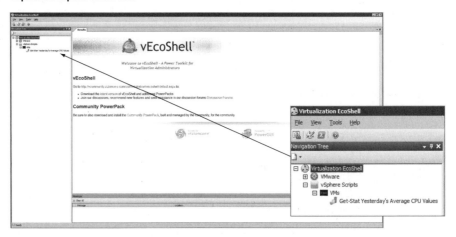

Once you have finished creating your PowerPack, don't forget to share it with the community by uploading it to http://powergui.org.

PowerWF Studio

IN THIS CHAPTER, YOU WILL LEARN TO:

Now that we are nearing the end of the book, we wanted to show you a product that takes an original approach to using PowerShell and PowerCLI. PowerWF Studio is a visual PowerShell development tool that provides an easy way to create powerful automation scripts using a workflow paradigm and a simple drag-and-drop interface instead of a script-only development environment.

Understand PowerWF Studio's Capabilities

Novice users can create workflows by dragging the desired activities from a toolbox. Experienced scripters can create PowerShell scripts that can be automatically converted into visual representations, which can be further extended using the built-in activities. Figure 22.1 shows the PowerWF Studio opening screen.

FIGURE 22.1   PowerWF Studio

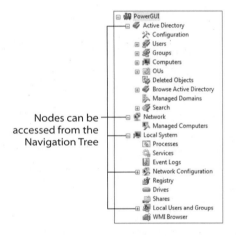

Nodes can be accessed from the Navigation Tree

Simply put, a workflow is a series of steps or activities taken to accomplish a task. Those steps may be sequential or repeated until the desired goal is achieved. For some steps, you may need to make decisions or meet conditions before determining how to proceed.

PowerWF Studio automatically discovers every PowerShell cmdlet in every snap-in and module installed on a computer system and is limited only by the modules that are installed on it. Before you start a project, PowerWF Studio recommends that you perform a quick search of the Internet to find related PowerShell modules from trustworthy sources. These additional cmdlets can greatly simplify your work.

Integrate PowerWF Studio

When PowerWF Studio is installed on a workstation that has PowerCLI installed, it automatically creates a PowerCLI toolbox with activities for each PowerCLI cmdlet, as shown in Figure 22.2.

FIGURE 22.2   PowerCLI toolbox

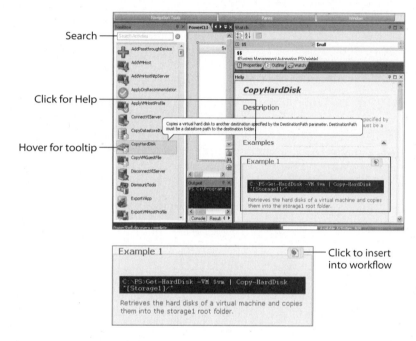

You can use the toolbox to script and get scripting help:

- ▶ Search through the cmdlets by typing in the Search box.

- ▶ Mouse over a cmdlet to see the description extracted from the PowerShell cmdlet help.

- ▶ Click a cmdlet to see the full PowerShell help topic, including sample usage that can be directly imported into PowerWF.

Use PowerCLI in PowerWF Studio

There are two ways to use PowerCLI in PowerWF Studio. You can graphically create a workflow and allow PowerWF Studio to write the script, or you script the workflow yourself using the PowerShell script editor.

Graphical Flow

The easiest way for a novice user to begin scripting with PowerWF Studio is to simply drag and drop cmdlets onto the canvas, but first you'll need to create a new workflow. To do so, you can either select New ➤ New Workflow from PowerShell or click the New Workflow tab shown in Figure 22.3.

FIGURE 22.3   Creating a new workflow

Once you've created a new workflow, you can start scripting by simply clicking any cmdlet and dragging it to the canvas. If you drag a cmdlet group, the entire sequence of activities in the group appears in your workflow, as shown in Figure 22.4.

FIGURE 22.4   Dragging activities onto the canvas

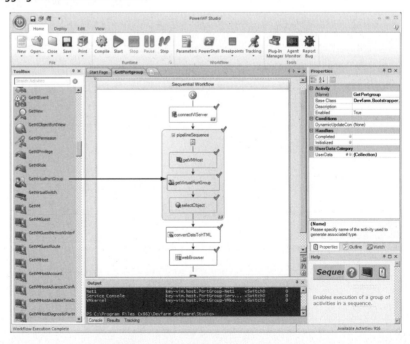

PowerWF Studio uses a number of PowerShell concepts, including the pipeline to connect the output of one PowerShell cmdlet to the input of another PowerShell cmdlet. The output pane shows the script generated behind the graphic representation.

Script Editor

PowerWF Studio includes a PowerShell editor (see Figure 22.5) comparable to the other PowerShell IDEs. To open the script editor, click the PowerShell icon in the ribbon bar.

FIGURE 22.5   **PowerWF PowerShell Editor**

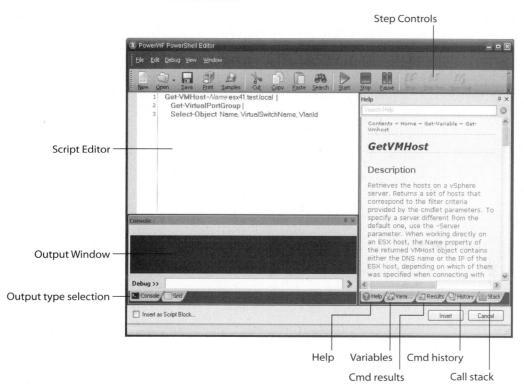

The PowerWF PowerShell Editor provides complete script debugging with the ability to step through a script, view the call stack, and watch variable values. Other features include color syntax highlighting, tab complete, and the display of script results in a data grid and property grid, as well as in the console window.

An interesting feature in PowerWF Studio is that it can automatically create PowerShell scripts based on sorted and selected columns in the data grid or property view. Select Grid from the Output Type tab. Hold down the Ctrl key while selecting columns in the Result Grid to use this feature.

The script editor also lets you import scripts directly from .PS1 files by using the Open dialog box you access from the ribbon bar. Even more interestingly, by selecting the Samples icon from the ribbon bar you open a portal into PoshCode.org and Microsoft TechNet. From there, you can directly import scripts from these top script repositories to help kick-start a project. Figure 22.6 shows just a few of the scripts available for import from PoshCode.org.

FIGURE 22.6 Importing scripts

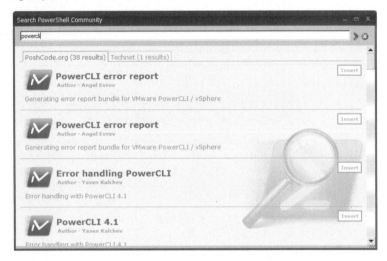

Use a Workflow

One of the features that makes PowerWF Studio so useful is the variety of ways in which you can deploy workflows. Figure 22.7 shows the tools available on the Deploy tab.

FIGURE 22.7 Deploy options

A workflow can be

▶ Deployed as a stand-alone console or Windows application

▶ Packaged as a PowerShell cmdlet, module, or snap-in to be reused within PowerShell

- ▶ Used directly in a development environment
- ▶ Run on a schedule
- ▶ Executed by third-party applications, including integration with Microsoft System Center

Console Applications   One of the easiest ways to use workflows is to deploy them as a stand-alone application. PowerWF compiles the workflow into an executable file that can be run from a command line or shortcut. Workflows deployed as console applications are run from the command prompt (cmd.exe). These workflows interact directly with the console. By using the PowerShell Out-Host cmdlet, the workflow sends data to the cmd.exe StdOut, thereby transforming a PowerShell script into a first-class executable.

Windows Applications   Workflows deployed as Windows applications are executables that are run from Windows Explorer. Windows applications do not interact with the console. Instead, take care to include visualization tools to display data such as the DataGrid or WebBrowser activities found in the Visualization group within the cmdlet toolbox. Remember that these visualizations would be the only means to interact with the workflow.

PowerShell Cmdlets, Snap-ins, and Modules   Workflows can be deployed to PowerShell as cmdlets. Multiple workflows can be bundled together and deployed as a single snap-in or module. The Verb, Noun, Description, Help, and other metadata are specified by you and must be bound to each workflow. Workflows are useful in their own right as PowerShell cmdlets, and there's another advantage to deploying workflows to PowerShell: These cmdlets get rediscovered by PowerWF Studio's PowerShell auto-discovery service. Each cmdlet you deploy comes back into PowerWF Studio as an individual toolbox activity. This means that PowerWF Studio can be used as an authoring tool to extend itself.

WORKFLOW NAMING CONVENTION

When creating a PowerWF Studio workflow, name it using PowerShell's standard verb-noun format. For example, a workflow that deploys a set of VMs for the marketing department should be named something like New-MarketingVM, not deployMarketingVM. That way, the cmdlets will make sense when you deploy the workflows back out to PowerShell. This also allows PowerWF to automatically create meaningful icons when it discovers your cmdlets.

Scripting Tools
and Features

PART V

Cmdlet   If you have a single workflow that you want to make accessible in PowerShell, PowerWF Studio lets you deploy the workflow as a cmdlet. The cmdlet can be executed directly from a PowerShell host or script or can be used as a toolbox item in PowerWF Studio. In this case it's like magic: PowerWF will just find it once it's created.

Snap-In   PowerShell v2–released cmdlets are typically deployed as modules, but PowerWF Studio will continue to let you bundle cmdlets as either snap-ins or modules. Modules require at least PowerShell v2; if you are deploying a workflow for PowerShell v1 you need to create a snap-in. We recommend the use of modules because of their increased portability and the ability to run multiple versions side by side.

Module   If you have a group of workflows that you would like to group together in a convenient, portable package, a PowerShell module is probably the best option. Simply open the workflows you want to include and click the Deploy To Module button. PowerWF Studio will walk you through the steps to create a PowerShell module.

Development   Although this book is about PowerCLI and not about development tools, you should know that PowerWF Studio workflows can be deployed in such a way that they can be used in other development environments. You can create toolbox activities or .NET assemblies. You can also extend or modify a workflow in Visual Studio.

Agent Scheduling   In many cases, you may want the workflow to run on a specific schedule. PowerWF Studio includes an agent that lets you run your workflows hourly, daily, monthly, or on virtually any other schedule you can think of. This feature provides you with another way of scheduling your PowerCLI scripts, and can be accessed by clicking the Agent icon on the Deploy tab.

Operations Manager   Microsoft's System Center Operations Manager provides out-of-the-box monitoring for most of the Microsoft application stack. Typically, deeper monitoring of Microsoft applications or monitoring for third-party or legacy systems requires hiring consultants to build custom management packs or purchasing packs from a variety of vendors. PowerWF Studio provides a third option: Simply create workflows to collect the desired information, add the ToSCOM activity, and walk through a simple wizard to create and deploy a custom management pack.

Service Manager   Service Manager helps automate best practices within an IT organization, especially in cases of incident reporting and problem resolution, change control, and asset life-cycle management. Service Manager is tightly integrated with Operation Manager, Configuration Manager, and Active Directory Domain Services. Service Manager provides a workflow-based authoring tool to handle the logic behind the specific automated actions. PowerWF Studio extends this functionality significantly by allowing users to either create custom toolbox items within the Service Manager authoring tool or directly create Service Manager management packs.

PowerGUI   PowerWF Studio is integrated with PowerGUI using a PowerGUI PowerPack. Once you install the PowerWF PowerPack, you can run workflows in context directly from within PowerGUI, and PowerWF Studio tasks, plug-ins, and activities can be managed from PowerGUI.

PowerScripter   Icomasoft's PowerScripter is a Virtual Infrastructure (VI) Client plug-in that allows user-defined PowerShell scripts to be executed against VMware VI objects. PowerWF Studio workflows can also be directly executed in the VI Client using the integration with PowerScripter.

Create Typical Workflows

The best way to understand how PowerWF Studio is used and what it can offer you is to create a few sample workflows.

Creating New Guests from the DOS Prompt

This section shows you how to create a workflow that creates virtual machines from a DOS prompt by filling in a minimal number of parameters:

1. Launch PowerWF Studio and click the New button on the ribbon bar to create a new workflow named makeVM.

2. Type **NewVM** in the toolbox search bar and drag the newVM activity onto the workflow canvas (Figure 22.8).

FIGURE 22.8   Drag the newVM activity to the canvas.

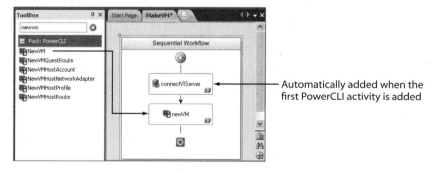

Automatically added when the first PowerCLI activity is added

3. PowerWF Studio automatically adds a connectVIServer activity (Figure 22.9). Click the connectVIServer activity to add the Server, User, and Password parameters. If you will be connecting to multiple servers, you can create input parameters for these values, as discussed in the next steps.

4. Select the newVM activity and create some input parameters for things that will vary between virtual machines you create (Figure 22.10). PowerWF Studio turns each configuration option into an editable property.

5. Double-click the blue arrow next to Name to launch a wizard to create an input parameter (Figure 22.11).

6. Enter **VMName** in the Name field; include a description, if desired; and select the Mandatory Variable check box. Then click Finish (Figure 22.12).

FIGURE 22.9 The connectVIServer activity

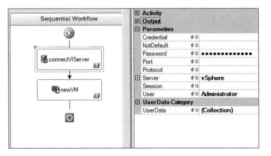

FIGURE 22.10 The newVM parameters

7. Repeat the process of creating input parameters for MemoryMB, CPUs, and DiskMB. You can give these parameters default values so that you do not have to enter them every time you create a new VM. Now when the workflow is run, it will prompt you to enter a name for the new virtual machine as well as the amount of memory and disk space and the number of CPUs to give it (Figure 22.13).

FIGURE 22.11 Define the input parameters.

Double-click the arrow to launch the workflow parameter dialog.

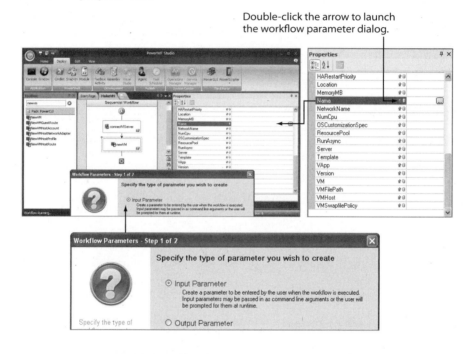

FIGURE 22.12 Select the Mandatory Variable option.

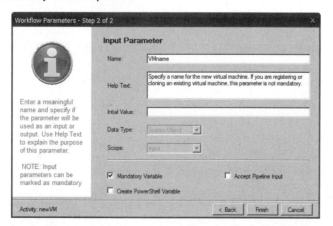

8. You can now deploy this workflow as a command-line executable. Simply click the Deploy tab and click the Console button, as shown in Figure 22.14.

9. This workflow can now be run as a command-line executable on any machine with PowerCLI installed.

FIGURE 22.13   Optional parameters

FIGURE 22.14   Build a console application

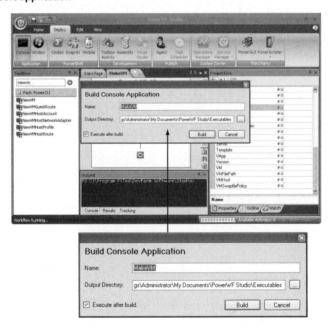

You can use the executable from the command prompt and create a new guest. You will be prompted only for the mandatory parameter, whereas the other parameters are optional and will take the default values you specified in the newVM activity:

```
C:\>newvm
VMName: PC4
```

```
Name                      PowerState Num CPUs Memory (MB)

----                      ---------- -------- -----------

PC4                       PoweredOff 1         512



C:\>newvm /?
Usage: newVM [Parameters]

Parameters:
Name      Required  Description
NumCpu    False     Specify the number of the virtual CPUs of...
MemoryMB  False     Specify the memory size in MB of the new ...
DiskMB    False     Specify the size in MB of the disks that ...
VMName    True      Specify a name for the new virtual machin...
```

Creating a Log Viewer Using PowerWF Studio

You can create an ESX log viewer using only PowerShell and .NET assemblies, but it is easier using PowerWF Studio. The following example shows you how to build a log viewer as a Windows Application using PowerWF Studio and PowerCLI.

1. Launch PowerWF Studio and click the New button on the ribbon. Create a new workflow named **logViewer**.

2. Drop a pipelineSequence on the workflow canvas (Figure 22.15). You will use this activity to connect to the VMHost and pipe data to get the logs.

3. From the PowerCLI toolbox, drop the getVMHost activity into the pipelineSequence. Doing so automatically adds a connectVIServer activity (Figure 22.16).

FIGURE 22.15 pipelineSequence

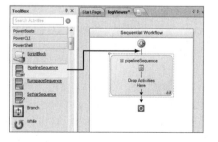

4. As with the previous example, click the connectVIServer activity to add the Server, User, and Password parameters. If you will be connecting to multiple servers, you can create input parameters as discussed in the previous example.

5. From the PowerCLI toolbox, drop a getLogType activity in the pipeline below the getVMHost activity (Figure 22.17). This will find the available log types for the VMHost.

6. We can now assign the output of this pipeline to a PowerShell variable. Click on the pipelineSequence and set the `AssignTo` property to **logs**, as shown in Figure 22.18.

7. Next, loop through the available log types. Do so by dropping in a ForEach activity from the PowerShell toolbox (Figure 22.19).

8. Just like in PowerShell, set the `Condition` property to **$log in $logs** (Figure 22.20).

9. Now that we are looping through the log types, drop in another pipeline Sequence. In that pipeline place a GetLog activity from the PowerCLI toolbox (Figure 22.21). Set the `Key` property to **$log**.

FIGURE 22.16 getVMHost

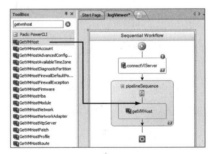

FIGURE 22.17 getLogType

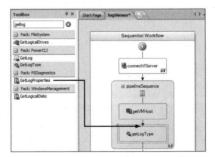

FIGURE 22.18 Assign to a variable

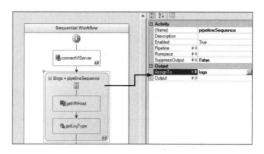

FIGURE 22.19 ForEach

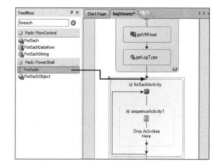

FIGURE 22.20 ForEach condition

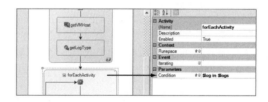

FIGURE 22.21 getLog

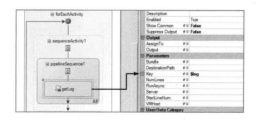

10. Next, add a selectObject activity and set the `ExpandProperty` property to **Entries** (Figure 22.22). This tells PowerShell that what you really want from the selected log are the entries.

11. For performance improvements, set the `SuppressOutput` property for the pipelineSequence to **True** (Figure 22.23). This will allow the pipeline to execute without having to render the results.

12. Ideally, you would like each log to appear as a separate tab in your output. You can do this by renaming tables in the loop using the Log Key and then adding them to a dataset. Drag a RenameDataTable activity from the Mashup toolbox and drop it after the pipelineSequence you just created.

FIGURE 22.22 selectObject

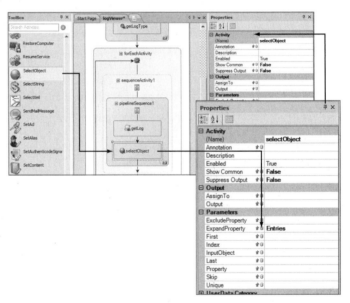

FIGURE 22.23 SuppressOutput

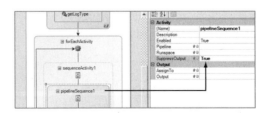

13. If you have run the workflow since adding the last pipeline, you can select Name from the drop-down list. Otherwise, type **pipelineSequence1** for the Name.

14. Type a PowerShell expression for the new name. In this case, type **$log.Key** (Figure 22.24).

15. Now that the table has been properly named, you can add the table to your dataset of results. Drop the addDataSet activity below the renameDataTable activity, as shown in Figure 22.25.

16. Add a DataGrid to the bottom of the workflow to display your results, as shown in Figure 22.26. It is important to change the Data Source property for the DataGrid to **DataSet**. If you don't, PowerWF Studio assumes that you want to bind to the output of the ForEach, which in this case is the output of the last execution of the pipeline.

17. Run the workflow by clicking the Start button on the toolbar. The results should look like Figure 22.27.

FIGURE 22.24 renameDataTable

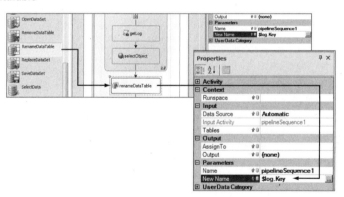

FIGURE 22.25 addDataSet

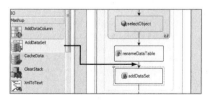

FIGURE 22.26 dataGridView

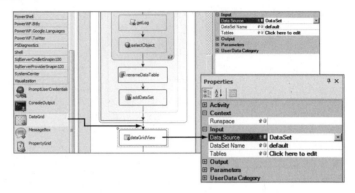

FIGURE 22.27 LogViewer window

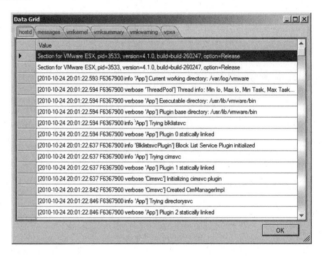

This workflow can now be deployed as a Windows application or even as a PowerShell cmdlet that could be used directly from PowerShell or from PowerWF.

As a point of reference, we've included the PowerShell script had we written this log viewer entirely in PowerShell. Note that you need to know how to present the results in a tabbed dialog box and that you must run the script in STA mode to be able to use Windows Forms. You must either run this script in the Integrated Scripting Environment (ISE) or launch PowerShell with the -STA switch.

LISTING 22.1 LogViewer **script**

```
Add-Type –assemblyName PresentationFramework
Add-Type –assemblyName PresentationCore
Add-Type –assemblyName WindowsBase
```

```
function newTabOfText {
  param(
    [string]$title,
    [string]$text
  );

  $tab = New-Object windows.controls.tabitem
  $tab.Header = $title

  $textbox = new-object windows.controls.textbox
  $textbox.VerticalScrollBarVisibility = "Visible"
  $textbox.TextWrapping = "NoWrap"
  $textbox.FontSize = 14
  $tab.content = $textbox

  $textbox.text = $text

  return $tab
}


$window = New-Object windows.window
$window.Title = "Log Viewer"

$grid = new-object windows.controls.grid
$window.content = $grid

$tabcontrol = New-Object windows.controls.tabcontrol
$grid.Children.Add($tabcontrol)

add-pssnapin *vmware*
Connect-VIServer -Server MyServer -User root -Password insecure
$logs = get-vmhost | get-logtype
$logs | %{
  $lines = (get-log $_ -Numlines 100).Entries
  $content = [string]::join("`r`n", $lines)

  $tab = newTabOfText $_.filename $content
  $tabcontrol.Items.Add($tab)
}
$window.ShowDialog()
```

Register-VMX as a Windows Application

PowerWF Studio allows you to import existing PowerShell scripts, which can then be used as part of a workflow or can be deployed using the various deploy options we discussed earlier.

As an example of such a script import, let's use PowerWF Studio to import the `Register-VMX` script from my "Raiders of the Lost VMX" blog post `http://www.lucd.info/2009/12/02/raiders-of-the-lost-vmx`.

1. Create a new workflow called RegisterVMX.

2. Click the PowerShell icon on the toolbar to launch the PowerShell editor.

3. Paste the script into the script editor.

4. Since you'll want to execute the code whenever the workflow is executed, remove the outermost function. Also, clean up the formatting to take advantage of PowerWF Studio's annotation features. This editor content should look something like Figure 22.28.

FIGURE 22.28 Cleaned up code

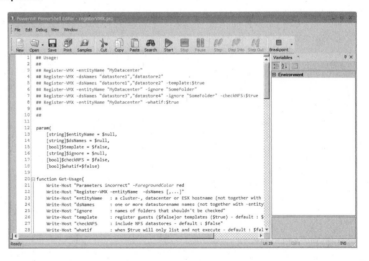

5. When the script block is inserted into PowerWF, you will notice that the script parameters can be set directly using the property viewer. An even better solution is to double-click the blue arrows and create input parameters, like you did in earlier in this chapter when you created a new guest (Figure 22.29).

FIGURE 22.29 Script parameters

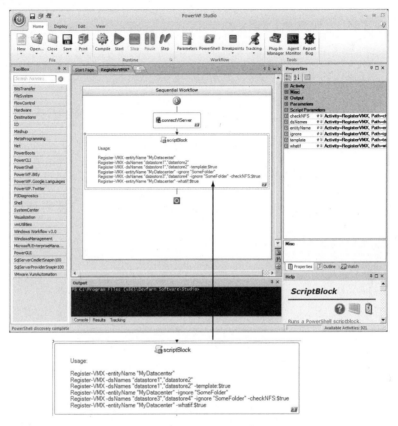

6. The only other change that is necessary is to add a connectVIServer activity to this script. As in the previous samples, set the Server, User, and Password parameters.

7. You can test the workflow directly from PowerWF Studio, or you can deploy it as a console or Windows application.

Bringing It All Together

Now that you have created three useful workflows, let's take advantage of PowerWF Studio's ability to deploy workflows as PowerShell modules:

1. If they are not already open, open the three example workflows you created in the previous sections.

2. Click the Deploy tab and choose the Deploy To PowerShell Module option.

3. Give your PowerShell module a meaningful name like **vmUtilities**; add a description like **Custom VM guest utilities** (Figure 22.30).

4. Customize the verbs and nouns for your PowerShell cmdlets. Double-click `logViewer` and set the verb to **Show** (Figure 22.31).

5. Make sure the Launch PowerShell After Build option is checked and then click the Build button.

6. You can now run these cmdlets directly from PowerShell. Type **show-log Viewer** or one of the other cmdlet names to test it out (Figure 22.32).

FIGURE 22.30 Creating a PowerShell module

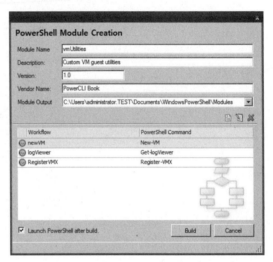

FIGURE 22.31 Renaming cmdlets

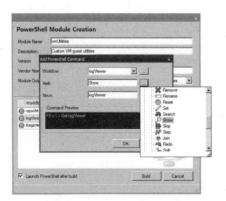

7. The next time you launch PowerWF Studio, it will automatically import this new module and add it to the toolbox. Also, you can force the discovery by launching the Plug-In Manager from the Home tab and selecting Start Discovery Process (Figure 22.33).

8. The vmUtilities module will now be added to the toolbox. You can drag and drop this activity the same as any other PowerWF toolbox activity (Figure 22.34).

FIGURE 22.32 Using the module

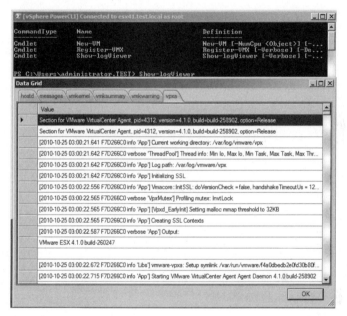

Another feature that will be popular with PowerCLI users is the ability to make PowerWF Studio workflows available in PowerGUI. To accomplish this, simply click the PowerGUI button on the Deploy ribbon. Enter a name for your new PowerPack. Now you can import your new PowerPack using the PowerPack Manager. See Chapter 21, "PowerGUI and vEcoShell," for details on how to import your new PowerPack. Management packs that are created by PowerWF Studio appear in PowerGUI under the entry PowerWF. The PowerPacks themselves are located in the Interop folder in the PowerWF Studio installation folder.

That concludes this chapter, where we briefly looked at PowerWF Studio as an alternative for working with PowerCLI. Keep in mind that there other features of interest in PowerWF Studio that we haven't even touched on. Download a demo version and give PowerWF Studio a spin.

FIGURE 22.33 Plug-In Manager

FIGURE 22.34 vmUtilities in the toolbox

Add a GUI Front-End to Your Automation Scripts

IN THIS CHAPTER, YOU WILL LEARN TO:

Appreciate the Value of a GUI

By now you should have lifted your vSphere automation to a higher level. You have scripts for most, if not all, aspects of the management of your vSphere environment. In Chapter 21, "PowerGUI and vEcoShell," you learned how to incorporate your scripts in these GUI-based working environments. But what if you want to have a free-standing script with a GUI interface without the overhead of running a tool like PowerGUI or vEcoShell? Or what if you can't install any of these tools on the clients where you need to run the script? This could be due to corporate policies, security standards, support requirements, and so on.

Don't despair; using Windows Forms is perfectly possible from within your PowerShell scripts. PowerShell is, as you probably know, closely tied into .NET. And the .NET Framework contains a subset called `WinForms` that lets you integrate Windows Forms into your scripts.

Choose the Correct Tool

The simplest way to use Windows Forms in your PowerShell scripts is to enter the required code from within your favorite PowerShell editor. But you will notice soon enough that this can become quite tedious. Luckily, there are a number of tools available that will allow you to compose your Windows Forms in a GUI environment and the tool will generate the required PowerShell code for you. That code can then be included in your PowerShell script.

Let's start with a free tool. Free is always a good argument to use a tool. But besides its price, *PrimalForms* (Community Edition) from SAPIEN Technologies also delivers. It allows you to design your form in a GUI and with a click of a button it will produce the PowerShell code that creates the form for you. Figure 23.1 shows the Community Edition interface.

SAPIEN also offers a commercial version, *PrimalForms 2009*. The commercial version has several additions. The most interesting ones are a built-in script editor, a packaging tool to create an EXE file, and an integrated run environment. Figure 23.2 shows the commercial version interface.

FIGURE 23.1   **PrimalForms Community Edition**

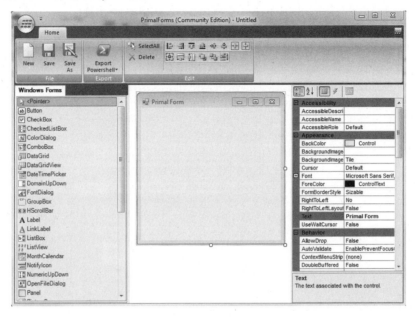

FIGURE 23.2   **PrimalForms 2009**

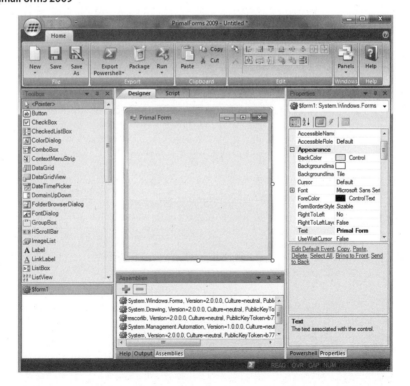

From iTripoli comes another commercial product called *Admin Script Editor,* which is in fact a suite of tools. One of the tools in the Enterprise version of their product is *ScriptForm Designer,* which you can use to create Windows Forms. This tool has an interesting feature that allows you to go back and forth between the script editor and the form designer to make updates to the Windows Form. And you don't need to copy and paste the PowerShell code for the updated form. Figure 23.3 shows the ScriptForm Designer interface.

FIGURE 23.3   **ScriptForm Designer**

Given the complexity of Windows Forms objects, we strongly advise you to select one of these tools to create your Windows Forms.

Create Some Basic WinForms

Windows Forms (WinForms) is a subset of the .NET Framework. You use WinForms to create Windows-based GUIs. You place controls, such as buttons, list boxes, and check boxes, on a form, which is also called a container. User interaction with the Windows Form is managed through events. An event is fired when the user interacts with a control, such as when the user clicks a button. In the code behind the event, you can code what the script should do. Windows Forms are rather complex subjects. In this chapter we will demonstrate some of the basics that you can use to provide a GUI to your PowerShell scripts.

The Form Modes

The basic element when you want to use Windows Forms is the form itself. Let's have a look at the minimal code to display a blank form (see Listing 23.1).

LISTING 23.1 Empty default modal form

```
[reflection.assembly]::loadwithpartialname( `
    "System.Windows.Forms") | Out-Null


$MyForm = New-Object System.Windows.Forms.Form
$MyForm.ShowDialog()| Out-Null
```

The code in Listing 23.1 displays a blank form, with the default size, that waits for the user's interaction. As written, the user can only close the form by clicking the Close icon in the top-right corner of the form. It is called a modal form and is displayed with the ShowDialog method. To return to the script there has to be an action that is triggered by one of the objects on the form, such as an OK button. When the user clicks the button, an event fires and executes code that will close the form.

Another type of form is the modeless form. This kind of form doesn't wait for the user's interaction to return to the script (see Listing 23.2).

LISTING 23.2 Empty default modeless form

```
[reflection.assembly]::loadwithpartialname( `
    "System.Windows.Forms") | Out-Null


$MyForm = New-Object System.Windows.Forms.Form
$MyForm.Show ()| Out-Null
Sleep 5
$MyForm
```

The Show method displays the form and immediately returns to the script. That's why we included a 5-second pause in the script in Listing 23.2. It gives you time to see the form. When the script ends, the form closes as well.

The previous two methods, modal and modeless, have one disadvantage; it's not simple to access values from the form in other parts of the script. For that reason, it's interesting to use the application's Run method to display and interact with a form (see Listing 23.3).

LISTING 23.3 Empty default form run from the application

```
[reflection.assembly]::loadwithpartialname( `
    "System.Windows.Forms") | Out-Null


$MyForm = New-Object System.Windows.Forms.Form
[System.Windows.Forms.Application]::Run($MyForm)
```

We'll come back to accessing values from forms like these later in this chapter.

Adding a Control

Let's start with the simplest form of interaction between the user and your script: a button on a form. There aren't a lot of possibilities with a button on a form. Users can click it or not; those are their only options.

First let's have a look at the PowerShell code to set up a button:

```
$Button = New-Object System.Windows.Forms.Button
$Button.Location = New-Object System.Drawing.Point(41, 41)
$Button.Size = New-Object System.Drawing.Size(82, 33)
$Button.Text = "MyButton"
```

This code creates an object that represents a button. Once you have the button, you have to connect it to the form:

```
$MyForm.Controls.Add($Button)
```

Bringing it all together, we end up with the script in Listing 23.4.

LISTING 23.4 Default form with a button

```
[reflection.assembly]::loadwithpartialname( `
    "System.Windows.Forms") | Out-Null


$MyForm = New-Object System.Windows.Forms.Form


$Button = New-Object System.Windows.Forms.Button
$Button.Text = "MyButton"


$MyForm.Controls.Add($Button)


[System.Windows.Forms.Application]::Run($MyForm)
```

Figure 23.4 shows how the form looks.

FIGURE 23.4   Default form with a button

You will notice that the button is positioned in the top-left corner of the form's canvas—not really what you want to present to your users. To solve this problem, use the Location property that exists on all Windows Forms objects. Similarly, you can use the Size property to specify the dimensions of any of the Windows Forms objects. Our script now becomes the one shown in Listing 23.5.

LISTING 23.5   Sized form with a positioned and sized button

```
[reflection.assembly]::loadwithpartialname( `
    "System.Windows.Forms") | Out-Null

$MyForm = New-Object System.Windows.Forms.Form
$MyForm.ClientSize = New-Object System.Drawing.Size(240, 190)
$MyForm.Text = "My Form"

$Button = New-Object System.Windows.Forms.Button
$Button.Location = New-Object System.Drawing.Point(80, 80)
$Button.Size = New-Object System.Drawing.Size(80, 30)
$Button.Text = "MyButton"

$MyForm.Controls.Add($Button)

[System.Windows.Forms.Application]::Run($MyForm)
```

Take a look at Figure 23.5 to see the end result. Notice how we used the Text property on the form to display text in the form's title bar.

Scripting Tools and Features

PART V

FIGURE 23.5   Sized form with a sized button

Until now, end users had to close the form by clicking the Close icon in the top-right corner of the form. Let's put that functionality behind the button. As mentioned earlier, all user interaction with an object fires one or more events. For this form, you need to capture the event that occurs when the user clicks the button. To capture that event, create an event handler. Then, attach the handler to the Windows Forms object using a special syntax. On the object where you want to define an event handler, for instance, use

```
$object.add_<name-of-the-event> ({script block})
```

Since the code in such a script block can become quite long, it's handier to define a separate function for the event handler and call that function from the script block. With this knowledge, your script now becomes something like the one in Listing 23.6.

LISTING 23.6   Form with event handler

```
[reflection.assembly]::loadwithpartialname(`
    "System.Windows.Forms") | Out-Null


function Button_Clicked($object){
  $MyForm.close()
}


$MyForm = New-Object System.Windows.Forms.Form
$MyForm.ClientSize = New-Object System.Drawing.Size(240, 190)
$MyForm.Text = "My Form"

$Button = New-Object System.Windows.Forms.Button
$Button.Location = New-Object System.Drawing.Point(80, 80)
$Button.Size = New-Object System.Drawing.Size(80, 30)
```

```
$Button.Text = "MyButton"

$Button.add_Click({Button_Clicked($Button)})

$MyForm.Controls.Add($Button)

[System.Windows.Forms.Application]::Run($MyForm)
```

The form and button looks the same as the one shown in Figure 23.5, but this time you can click the button and the form will close.

DISCOVERING EVENTS FOR WINDOWS FORMS OBJECTS

A handy way to discover all the available Events that can be used with a specific Windows Forms object is to employ the Get-Member cmdlet:

```
PS C:\>>> $button = New-Object System.Windows.Forms.Button
PS C:\>>> $button | Get-Member -MemberType Event | Select
Name
Name
----
AutoSizeChanged
BackColorChanged
BackgroundImageChanged
BackgroundImageLayoutChanged
BindingContextChanged
CausesValidationChanged
ChangeUICues
Click
ClientSizeChanged
```

Using a Script Layout Template

When writing a script with a GUI front-end, we normally use the same, standard template. In this template, we create regions for each part in the script. We'll tell you more about those in just a bit. Figure 23.6 gives you an overview of the components we use.

Table 23.1 provides a quick run-through of the different components in the template layout.

FIGURE 23.6   GUI script template

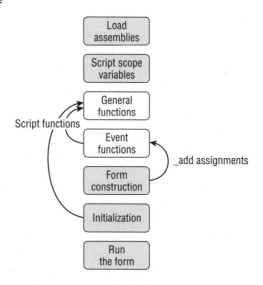

TABLE 23.1   Template layout components

Component	Description
Load assemblies	Load assemblies make sure the different assemblies required for the script are loaded.
Script scope variables	Script scope variables define and (eventually) initialize all variables that are used throughout the script, including inside the functions you use.
General functions	In these (optional) functions, you can store the logic that you use in your script.
Event functions	The functions that handle specific events on controls. These functions are defined with the _add option in the form construction.
Form construction	All the statements used to define the form and the controls it contains. Try to group the statements per control. That makes it easier to find the control's properties you used.
Initialization	All logic that you need to execute to set up the environment for your script. You can call one or more of the general functions from here.
Run the Form	One of the methods to present the form to the user.

You can find an example of a script that uses this layout in the section called "Create a Somewhat Advanced Example" later in this chapter. To give you an idea of what else you can do with Windows Forms objects, we'll expand on some of the other basic controls that are available.

Adding List Boxes

A list box allows users to select one or more entries from a list the script presents to them. As a practical example, Listing 23.7 creates a list box with all the guests that are present in the vSphere environment.

LISTING 23.7 Selecting guests from a list box

```
[reflection.assembly]::loadwithpartialname( `
    "System.Windows.Forms") | Out-Null
[reflection.assembly]::loadwithpartialname("System.Drawing") |
    Out-Null

function Button_Clicked($object){
  $MyForm.close()
}

$MyForm = New-Object System.Windows.Forms.Form
$MyForm.Text = "Guest selection"

$Button = New-Object System.Windows.Forms.Button
$Button.Location = New-Object System.Drawing.Point(107, 205)
$Button.Size = New-Object System.Drawing.Size(78, 22)
$Button.Text = "OK"
$Button.add_Click({Button_Clicked($Button)})

$ListBox = New-Object System.Windows.Forms.ListBox
$ListBox.Location = New-Object System.Drawing.Point(42, 43)
$ListBox.Size = New-Object System.Drawing.Size(198, 17)
$ListBox.SelectionMode = `
    [System.Windows.Forms.SelectionMode]::MultiSimple
$ListBox.Sorted = $true

$MyForm.Controls.Add($Button)
$MyForm.Controls.Add($ListBox)

# Populate the listbox with the names of the guests
Get-VM | %{
  $ListBox.Items.Add($_.Name) | Out-Null
```

```
}

[System.Windows.Forms.Application]::Run($MyForm)

# Display the selected guest(s)
[Windows.Forms.MessageBox]::Show(
   [string]::Join("`n",$ListBox.SelectedItems),
   "You selected",
   [Windows.Forms.MessageBoxButtons]::OK,
   [System.Windows.Forms.MessageBoxIcon]::Information
)
```

Figure 23.7 shows the resulting form with the Guest Selection list box and an OK button.

FIGURE 23.7   A sorted list box

Let's have a closer look at the ListBox object. As you might have noticed, we load a second assembly, called System.Drawing, in the script. This assembly for this script is not absolutely necessary, but it adds other features to all graphics in the form. One of these features is anti-aliasing, which makes the graphical elements look smoother on screen. Notice how the Sorted property allows you to define whether or not the entries in the ListBox object should be sorted.

The SelectionMode property of the ListBox object allows you to specify how values are selected from the list. The available values with the System.Windows .Forms.SelectionMode enumeration are None, One, MultiSimple, and Multi Extended. The script uses the MultiSimple mode, which allows you to click multiple entries without the use of the Ctrl key.

When the user closes the form by clicking the OK button, the selected items are available in the SelectedItems property of the ListBox object. As a confirmation that the script has access to the selected items, a message box will show the selected items.

Adding Check Boxes

The CheckBox control is a handy way of giving the user a yes/no option on the form. Listing 23.8 takes the form you created in Listing 23.7 and adds a CheckBox that allows a user to specify whether to include templates in the list. It gives a yes or no option.

LISTING 23.8 Selecting guests, and optionally templates, from a list box

```
[reflection.assembly]::loadwithpartialname(`
    "System.Windows.Forms") | Out-Null
[reflection.assembly]::loadwithpartialname("System.Drawing") |
    Out-Null


function Button_Clicked($object){
  $MyForm.close()
}


function CheckBox-Changed($object){
  $ListBox.Items.Clear()

  if($CheckBox.Checked){
    Get-VM | %{
      $ListBox.Items.Add($_.Name) | Out-Null
    }
    Get-Template | %{
      $ListBox.Items.Add($_.Name) | Out-Null
    }
  }
  else{
    Get-VM | %{
      $ListBox.Items.Add($_.Name) | Out-Null
    }
  }
}


$MyForm = New-Object System.Windows.Forms.Form
$MyForm.Text = "Guest selection"

$Button = New-Object System.Windows.Forms.Button
$Button.Location = New-Object System.Drawing.Point(107, 205)
$Button.Size = New-Object System.Drawing.Size(78, 22)
```

```
$Button.Text = "OK"
$Button.add_Click({Button_Clicked($Button)})

$ListBox = New-Object System.Windows.Forms.ListBox
$ListBox.Location = New-Object System.Drawing.Point(44, 22)
$ListBox.Size = New-Object System.Drawing.Size(198, 134)
$ListBox.SelectionMode = `
    [System.Windows.Forms.SelectionMode]::MultiSimple
$ListBox.Sorted = $true

$CheckBox = New-Object System.Windows.Forms.CheckBox
$CheckBox.Location = New-Object System.Drawing.Point(44, 162)
$CheckBox.Size = New-Object System.Drawing.Size(141, 24)
$CheckBox.Text = "Include Templates"
$CheckBox.add_CheckedChanged({CheckBox-Changed($CheckBox)})

$MyForm.Controls.Add($Button)
$MyForm.Controls.Add($ListBox)
$MyForm.Controls.Add($CheckBox)

# Populate the listbox with the names of the guests
Get-VM | %{
  $ListBox.Items.Add($_.Name) | Out-Null
}

[System.Windows.Forms.Application]::Run($MyForm)

# Display the selected guest(s)
[Windows.Forms.MessageBox]::Show(
  [string]::Join("`n",$ListBox.SelectedItems),
  "You selected",
  [Windows.Forms.MessageBoxButtons]::OK,
  [System.Windows.Forms.MessageBoxIcon]::Information
)
```

Figure 23.8 shows a check box added to the form.

Notice how the script defines an event on the CheckBox that will fire every time the check box is selected or deselected. In the function for this event, called CheckBox -Changed in the script, we use the $CheckBox.Checked property to interrogate the status of the CheckBox. Depending on the status of the $CheckBox.Checked property, we show only guests or guests and templates.

FIGURE 23.8   Using a check box

Adding Radio Buttons

Now, what if you want the user of your script to be able to select one of a number of exclusive options? You can do that with a number of CheckBox controls and include the logic to make sure that only one of the options is selected at the same time. But there is an easier solution where the Windows Forms will do all the hard work for you. You can use a GroupBox and insert a number of RadioButtons. That way, the Windows Forms will make sure that only one of the options is selected.

Let's change the script in Listing 23.8 and allow the user to select guests or templates, but not both. As you read through the script, see if you can find out how we added the radio buttons to the box, ensured that only one radio button can be selected, and set the form to display Guests as the default.

LISTING 23.9   Selecting guests or templates from a list box

```
[reflection.assembly]::loadwithpartialname(`
    "System.Windows.Forms") | Out-Null
[reflection.assembly]::loadwithpartialname("System.Drawing") |
    Out-Null

function Button_Clicked($object){
  $MyForm.close()
}

function RadioButton-Changed($object){
```

```
    $ListBox.Items.Clear()

    if($GuestsButton.Checked){
      Get-VM | %{
        $ListBox.Items.Add($_.Name) | Out-Null
      }
    }
    else{
      Get-Template | %{
        $_.Name
        $ListBox.Items.Add($_.Name) | Out-Null
      }
    }
  }

$MyForm = New-Object System.Windows.Forms.Form
$MyForm.Text = "Guest selection"

$Button = New-Object System.Windows.Forms.Button
$Button.Location = New-Object System.Drawing.Point(107, 205)
$Button.Size = New-Object System.Drawing.Size(78, 22)
$Button.Text = "OK"
$Button.add_Click({Button_Clicked($Button)})

$ListBox = New-Object System.Windows.Forms.ListBox
$ListBox.Location = New-Object System.Drawing.Point(44, 22)
$ListBox.Size = New-Object System.Drawing.Size(198, 134)
$ListBox.SelectionMode = `
    [System.Windows.Forms.SelectionMode]::MultiSimple
$ListBox.Sorted = $true

$GroupBox = New-Object System.Windows.Forms.GroupBox
$GroupBox.Location = New-Object System.Drawing.Point(42, 163)
$GroupBox.Size = New-Object System.Drawing.Size(201, 36)
$GroupBox.Text = ""

$GuestsButton = New-Object System.Windows.Forms.RadioButton
$GuestsButton.Location = New-Object System.Drawing.Point(7, 11)
$GuestsButton.Size = New-Object System.Drawing.Size(79, 22)
```

```
$GuestsButton.Checked = $true
$GuestsButton.Text = "Guests"
$GuestsButton.add_CheckedChanged( `
    {RadioButton-Changed($GuestsButton)})


$TemplatesButton = New-Object System.Windows.Forms.RadioButton
$TemplatesButton.Location = `
    New-Object System.Drawing.Point(102, 9)
$TemplatesButton.Size = New-Object System.Drawing.Size(94, 26)
$TemplatesButton.Text = "Templates"


$GroupBox.Controls.Add($TemplatesButton)
$GroupBox.Controls.Add($GuestsButton)


$MyForm.Controls.Add($Button)
$MyForm.Controls.Add($ListBox)
$MyForm.Controls.Add($GroupBox)


# Populate the listbox with the names of the guests
Get-VM | %{
  $ListBox.Items.Add($_.Name) | Out-Null
}


[System.Windows.Forms.Application]::Run($MyForm)


# Display the selected guest(s)
[Windows.Forms.MessageBox]::Show(
[string]::Join("`n",$ListBox.SelectedItems),
"You selected",
[Windows.Forms.MessageBoxButtons]::OK,
[System.Windows.Forms.MessageBoxIcon]::Information
)
```

Figure 23.9 shows the resulting form.

Notice how both RadioButtons are added to the GroupBox. This automatically ensures that only one of the RadioButtons can be selected at the same time. During the definition of the GuestsButton object, the script set the Checked property to $true. That means that Guests is the default setting.

FIGURE 23.9   Using `RadioButtons`

Create a Somewhat Advanced Example

In Listing 23.10, we will show how you can combine several controls to create a user-friendly GUI front-end for your script. The script creates an `EventHistory Collector` and will display the captured events in the form. Before starting the collecting of events, the user has the option to define how often the script should look for new events and for how long the script should run. The form also offers the option to save the captured events to an external file.

The script in Listing 23.10 provides a simple interface with a minimal number of controls. Nonetheless, it demonstrates a number of techniques that can be used in GUI front-ends.

As you read through the script, notice that the event logger it creates

- ▶ Only runs on systems with PowerCLI 4.1 installed
- ▶ Prohibits the use of local variables in some functions
- ▶ Removes the event collector when the script finishes
- ▶ Uses a `Timer` control to handle fetching news events
- ▶ Hides the Export button until at least one event is captured
- ▶ Refreshes the `DataGridView` when new events are added
- ▶ Makes use of a `StatusBar` control to display information

#REGION AND #ENDREGION

When you are working with forms that contain a lot of controls, there will be many lines of code for setting up the controls and for defining the events that can occur on some of these controls. To keep a good view on your script, it is important to select an editor that knows how to collapse regions.

Use the #region and #endregion directives to mark individual sections of your script. Use meaningful names in the Identifier string on the #region directive. With an intelligent use of region blocks and an editor that supports these directives, you can have a structured view of your longer scripts. For example, you might have 500 lines of PowerShell code in the general functions region. Once those functions are written, all that code makes it difficult to move around in your script. To overcome this, you simply collapse the regions you're not using to maximize your ability to comprehend the regions you're working with. By compartmentalizing your code into both functions and regions, you will leave yourself with an efficient, maintainable script.

LISTING 23.10 vSphere Event Logger

```
#requires -pssnapin VMware.VimAutomation.Core -version 4.1

#region Load assemblies
$requiredAssemblies = "System.Windows.Forms","System.Drawing"
$requiredAssemblies | %{
  [void][System.Reflection.Assembly]::LoadWithPartialName($_)
}
#endregion

#region Script-scope variables
```

```
$DurationDefault = 5
$PauseDefault = 5
$Finish = $null
$eCollector = $null
$eData = New-Object System.Collections.ArrayList
#endregion

#region General functions
function New-eCollector{
  process{
    $si = Get-View ServiceInstance
    $eventMgr = Get-View $si.Content.EventManager
    $filter = New-Object VMware.Vim.EventFilterSpec

    $filter.disableFullMessage = $false
    $filter.time = New-Object VMware.Vim.EventFilterSpecByTime
    $filter.time.beginTime = Get-Date
    $filter.time.endTime = $Finish

    $script:eCollector = `
        Get-View ($eventMgr.CreateCollectorForEvents($filter))
  }
}

function Invoke-VIEventMonitor{
  process{
    Set-Variable -Name ViewSize -Value 100 -Option ReadOnly

    $events = $script:eCollector.ReadNextEvents($ViewSize)
    while($events){
      $eventInfo = @($events | `
        Select @{N="Time (UTC)"
          E={$_.CreatedTime.ToLongTimeString()}},
          @{N="Type";E={$_.GetType().Name}},
          @{N="Message";E={$_.FullFormattedMessage}})
      $script:eData.AddRange($eventInfo)
      $events = $script:eCollector.ReadNextEvents($ViewSize)
      $ExportButton.Visible = $true
    }
```

```
        $script:EventGrid.DataSource = ""
        $script:EventGrid.DataSource = $script:eData
        $script:EventGrid.Refresh()
        $script:StatusBar.Text = ((Get-Date -Format "HH:MM:ss") +`
            "`tEvents : " + $script:eData.Count)
        $script:EventMonitor.Refresh()
    }
}
#endregion

#region Event functions
function EventMonitor-Load( $object ){
    if($script:eCollector){
        Invoke-VIEventMonitor
    }
}

function Finished-Clicked( $object ){
    $EventMonitor.Close()
    if($eCollector){
        $eCollector.DestroyCollector()
    }
}

function Go-Clicked( $object ){
    $Finish = (Get-Date).AddMinutes($DurationField.Value)
    New-eCollector
    $PauseTimer.Enabled = $true
    $EventGrid.Visible = $true
}

function Export-Clicked ( $object ){
    $SelectExportFile.FileName = `
        "Events" + (Get-Date -Format "yyyyMMdd-HHMMss")
    $SelectExportFile.InitialDirectory = $env:userprofile
    $SelectExportFile.ShowDialog()
    $script:eData | `
        Export-Csv -Path $SelectExportFile.FileName `
            -NoTypeInformation `
```

```
          -UseCulture `
          -Force:$true
}

function Pause-Completed( $object ){
  Invoke-VIEventMonitor
}
#endregion

#region Form construction

#region EventMonitor form
$EventMonitor = New-Object System.Windows.Forms.Form
$EventMonitor.ClientSize = `
    New-Object System.Drawing.Size(401, 338)
$EventMonitor.Text = "Event Monitor"
$EventMonitor.FormBorderStyle = `
  [System.Windows.Forms.FormBorderStyle]::FixedSingle
$EventMonitor.add_Load({EventMonitor-Load($EventMonitor)})
#endregion

#region Duration value
$DurationField = New-Object System.Windows.Forms.NumericUpDown
$DurationField.Location = New-Object System.Drawing.Point(67,18)
$DurationField.Size = New-Object System.Drawing.Size(50, 20)
$DurationField.Value = $DurationDefault
$DurationField.TabIndex = 0
#endregion

#region Pause value
$PauseField = New-Object System.Windows.Forms.NumericUpDown
$PauseField.Location = New-Object System.Drawing.Point(67, 53)
$PauseField.Size = New-Object System.Drawing.Size(50, 20)
$PauseField.Value = $PauseDefault
$PauseField.TabIndex = 1
#endregion

#region Go button
$GoButton = New-Object System.Windows.Forms.Button
$GoButton.Location = New-Object System.Drawing.Point(185, 13)
```

```
$GoButton.Size = New-Object System.Drawing.Size(63, 26)
$GoButton.TabIndex = 2
$GoButton.Text = "Go"
$GoButton.UseVisualStyleBackColor = $true
$GoButton.add_Click({Go-Clicked($GoButton)})
#endregion

#region Export button
$ExportButton = New-Object System.Windows.Forms.Button
$ExportButton.Location = New-Object System.Drawing.Point(185,48)
$ExportButton.Size = New-Object System.Drawing.Size(63, 26)
$ExportButton.TabIndex = 10
$ExportButton.Text = "Export"
$ExportButton.Visible = $false
$ExportButton.UseVisualStyleBackColor = $true
$ExportButton.add_Click({Export-Clicked($ExportButton)})
#endregion

#region Finish button
$FinishButton = New-Object System.Windows.Forms.Button
$FinishButton.Location = New-Object System.Drawing.Point(308,13)
$FinishButton.Size = New-Object System.Drawing.Size(63, 26)
$FinishButton.TabIndex = 3
$FinishButton.Text = "Finished"
$FinishButton.UseVisualStyleBackColor = $true
$FinishButton.add_Click({Finished-Clicked($FinishButton)})
#endregion

#region Datagrid
$EventGrid = New-Object System.Windows.Forms.DataGridView
$EventGrid.Location = New-Object System.Drawing.Point(22, 96)
$EventGrid.Size = New-Object System.Drawing.Size(349, 193)
$EventGrid.Visible = $false
$EventGrid.AutoSizeColumnsMode = `[System.Windows.Forms.DataGridVi
ewAutoSizeColumnsMode]::AllCells
$EventGrid.DataSource = $eBinding
#endregion

#region Statusbar
$StatusBar = New-Object System.Windows.Forms.StatusBar
```

```
$StatusBar.Dock = [System.Windows.Forms.DockStyle]::Bottom
$StatusBar.Location = New-Object System.Drawing.Point(0, 316)
$StatusBar.Size = New-Object System.Drawing.Size(401, 22)
$StatusBar.Text = ""
#endregion

#region SelectExportFile
$SelectExportFile = `
    New-Object System.Windows.Forms.SaveFileDialog
$SelectExportFile.DefaultExt = ".csv"
$SelectExportFile.FileName = ""
$SelectExportFile.Filter = "CSV files|*.csv"
$SelectExportFile.ShowHelp = $true
$SelectExportFile.CheckFileExists = $false
#endregion

#region Various labels
$Label1 = New-Object System.Windows.Forms.Label
$Label1.Location = New-Object System.Drawing.Point(19, 20)
$Label1.Size = New-Object System.Drawing.Size(52, 14)
# $Label1.TabIndex = 0
$Label1.Text = "Duration"

$Label2 = New-Object System.Windows.Forms.Label
$Label2.Location = New-Object System.Drawing.Point(123, 20)
$Label2.Size = New-Object System.Drawing.Size(46, 15)
$Label2.Text = "minutes"

$Label3 = New-Object System.Windows.Forms.Label
$Label3.Location = New-Object System.Drawing.Point(19, 55)
$Label3.Size = New-Object System.Drawing.Size(44, 14)
$Label3.Text = "Pause"

$Label4 = New-Object System.Windows.Forms.Label
$Label4.Location = New-Object System.Drawing.Point(123, 55)
$Label4.Size = New-Object System.Drawing.Size(46, 15)
$Label4.Text = "seconds"
#endregion

#region Add controls to form
$EventMonitor.Controls.Add($DurationField)
```

```
$EventMonitor.Controls.Add($PauseField)
$EventMonitor.Controls.Add($GoButton)
$EventMonitor.Controls.Add($FinishButton)
$EventMonitor.Controls.Add($ExportButton)
$EventMonitor.Controls.Add($EventGrid)
$EventMonitor.Controls.Add($StatusBar)
$EventMonitor.Controls.Add($Label1)
$EventMonitor.Controls.Add($Label2)
$EventMonitor.Controls.Add($Label3)
$EventMonitor.Controls.Add($Label4)
#endregion

#region Timer
$components = New-Object System.ComponentModel.Container
$PauseTimer = New-Object System.Windows.Forms.Timer($components)
$PauseTimer.Interval = $PauseField.Value * 1000
$PauseTimer.add_Tick({Pause-Completed($PauseTimer)})
#endregion
#endregion

#region Initialisation
if(!$defaultVIServer){
  Write-Error "Please connect to a vCenter or ESX(i) server "
  exit
}
#endregion

#region Run the form
[System.Windows.Forms.Application]::EnableVisualStyles()
[System.Windows.Forms.Application]::Run($EventMonitor)
#endregion
```

When you run the script from Listing 23.10, it will produce an event monitor like the one shown in Figure 23.10.

The #requires directive at the start of the script allows you to declare that this script requires PowerCLI 4.1 in order to run. The variables defined in the Script-scope variables region are used in some of the functions. In the functions, the script refers to these variables in this way:

```
$script:eData.AddRange($eventInfo)
```

FIGURE 23.10 Event monitor

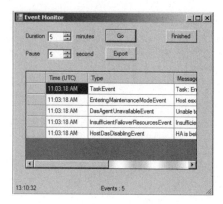

The effect is that the assignments inside the functions will not use any local variables.

Notice how the script removes the event collector when the script finishes. This is required because you are limited to a maximum of 25 open collectors per session.

```
if($eCollector){
  $eCollector.DestroyCollector()
}
```

The script uses a `Timer` control to handle the fetching of new events. A `Timer` is used to raise an event at a user-defined interval. In the control that this script uses, the event calls the `Pause-Completed` function.

```
$components = New-Object System.ComponentModel.Container
$PauseTimer = New-Object System.Windows.Forms.Timer($components)
$PauseTimer.Interval = $PauseField.Value * 1000
$PauseTimer.add_Tick({Pause-Completed($PauseTimer)})
```

Notice how the Export button is not visible when the script starts:

```
#region Export button
…
$ExportButton.Visible = $false
…
#endregion
```

Only when there is at least one event captured will the Export button become visible. This is done in the `Invoke-VIEventMonitor` function:

```
$ExportButton.Visible = $true
```

The DataGridView that displays the captured events needs to be refreshed when new events are added. A simple trick to do this is to change the DataSource property:

```
$script:EventGrid.DataSource = ""
$script:EventGrid.DataSource = $script:eData
```

This is done in the Invoke-VIEventMonitor function. The script then uses a StatusBar control to display information. This control initially starts out with no text. In the Invoke-VIEventMonitor function, the text is updated each time the Timer event fires.

```
$script:StatusBar.Text = ((Get-Date -Format "HH:MM:ss") + `
  "`tEvents : " + $script:eData.Count)
```

As you can see, the possibilities with Windows Forms are huge; we have only scratched the surface here. We recommend you stay in the confines of an editor until you get comfortable with Windows Forms creation. When you're ready to get more in-depth or just want more details on a specific control. visit http://msdn .microsoft.com and search on the type name.

INDEX

Note to the reader: Throughout this index **boldfaced** page numbers indicate primary discussions of a topic. *Italicized* page numbers indicate illustrations.